Degrees
of Latitude

Interior of a shipping merchant's establishment, by A. C. Hauck, probably Rotterdam, 1783, watercolor on paper. 1991-32.

Degrees *of* Latitude

MAPPING COLONIAL AMERICA

By Margaret Beck Pritchard *and* Henry G. Taliaferro

The Colonial Williamsburg Foundation

Williamsburg, Virginia

IN ASSOCIATION WITH

Harry N. Abrams, Inc., Publishers

WILLIAMSBURG DECORATIVE ARTS SERIES

American Coverlets and Their Weavers: Coverlets from the Collection of Foster and Muriel McCarl, including a Dictionary of More Than 700 Weavers
By Clarita S. Anderson

Degrees of Latitude: Mapping Colonial America
By Margaret Beck Pritchard *and* Henry G. Taliaferro

Furnishing Williamsburg's Historic Buildings
By Jan Kirsten Gilliam *and* Betty Crowe Leviner

The Governor's Palace in Williamsburg: A Cultural Study
By Graham Hood

Southern Furniture 1680–1830: The Colonial Williamsburg Collection
By Ronald L. Hurst *and* Jonathan Prown

What Clothes Reveal: The Language of Clothing in Colonial and Federal America, The Colonial Williamsburg Collection
By Linda Baumgarten

Copyright © 2002 The Colonial Williamsburg Foundation

Library of Congress Cataloging-in-Publication Data

Pritchard, Margaret Beck.
  Degrees of latitude : mapping colonial America / by Margaret Beck Pritchard and Henry G. Taliaferro.
     p. cm.
Includes bibliographical references and index.
  ISBN 0-87935-214-0 (CWF : alk. paper)—ISBN 0-8109-3539-2 (H.N. Abrams : alk. paper)
  1. Cartography—United States—History—17th century.
  2. Cartography—Europe—History—17th century. 3. United States—Maps—Early works to 1800. I. Taliaferro, Henry G. (Henry Garland), 1945- II. Title.
  GA405 .P75 2002
  912.755—dc21

                              2002008177

Published in 2002 by The Colonial Williamsburg Foundation in association with Harry N. Abrams, Incorporated, New York.

Front and back covers: Details from *Nova Totius Americæ Tabula,* by Petrus Schenk, Amsterdam, ca. 1680

PRINTED AND BOUND IN SINGAPORE

10 9 8 7 6 5 4 3 2 1

Harry N. Abrams, Inc.
100 Fifth Avenue
New York, N. Y. 10011
www.abramsbooks.com

Abrams is a subsidiary of

For
Anna Glen Butler Vietor

whose encouragement
and support
made this book possible

Degrees *of* Latitude

MAPPING COLONIAL AMERICA

is humbly dedicated & presented

Margaret Beck Pritchard
Henry G. Taliaferro

Canoo, sive Naviculæ
e corticibus arborum.

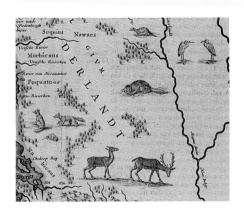

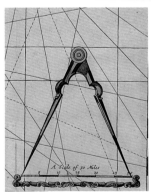

Contents

Foreword

For seventy-five years, the staff of the Colonial Williamsburg Foundation has been blessed with curators, historians, archaeologists, and other researchers who rarely accepted the standard answers to questions about the past. Indeed, they rarely asked the standard *questions*. This book, *Degrees of Latitude: Mapping Colonial America,* is the most recent expression of that approach. Margaret Beck Pritchard, the Foundation's curator of prints, maps, and wallpapers, and independent scholar Henry Taliaferro have used Colonial Williamsburg's splendid and diverse holdings to explore the subject of early maps in a wholly new fashion. No mere review of cartographic documents, *Degrees of Latitude* places maps squarely within their historical and social context in a way other studies have failed to do. Pritchard and Taliaferro treat maps as cultural markers that reveal the interests, wants, and needs of the people who made and used them.

Like most Colonial Williamsburg publications, *Degrees of Latitude* has benefited from the efforts of many at the Foundation. Laura Pass Barry, assistant curator of prints and maps, willingly accepted additional responsibilities while the authors researched and wrote the book. Paper conservator Pamela Young and her team exercised great skill and sensitivity in their treatment of the maps illustrated here. Hans Lorenz and Craig McDougal produced the brilliant photographs, and Jan Kirsten Gilliam indexed the work and crosschecked the obscure inscriptions on the original maps. Donna Sheppard brought her matchless editorial eye to bear on the text, while Joseph Rountree and Helen Olds deftly managed other aspects of the publication process. Independent book designer Greer Allen created the elegant layouts that bring the text to life. To these colleagues and dozens unnamed, we express warmest thanks.

Finally, we wish to convey our deep appreciation to two generous benefactors. Without the encouragement and support of Anna Glen Butler Vietor, this book would never have been published. We also gratefully acknowledge the DeWitt Wallace Fund for Colonial Williamsburg, established by the founders of *Reader's Digest*, for making possible the conservation and cataloging of these objects and for enabling us to exhibit them at Colonial Williamsburg's DeWitt Wallace Decorative Arts Museum.

Ronald L. Hurst
Carlisle Humelsine Chief Curator
Colonial Williamsburg Foundation

Preface

Over the centuries, maps have played a fundamental role in defining the parameters of any culture. They identified routes for explorers and travelers, places that were visited, and parts unknown, and suggest a country's allies and potential enemies. Maps were used to promote settlements, facilitate trade, acquire land, and settle boundary disputes. For America, they tell the story of how Europeans took possession of the land in the New World and fought to substantiate their claims.

Libraries, historical societies, museums, and individuals have collected maps for centuries, generally by gathering material relating to specific geographical areas. Since 1930, Colonial Williamsburg has acquired maps that relate to Virginia during the colonial and post-colonial periods as well as those that illustrate the settlement of the other colonies. By carefully analyzing household inventories, newspaper advertisements, and custom orders that Americans placed with English merchants, curators at Colonial Williamsburg have refined what is known about how maps and charts were utilized. The random, yet conscious, selection of maps owned by our forefathers provides insights into their social and intellectual aspirations. *Degrees of Latitude: Mapping Colonial America* goes beyond a standard cartobibliographical analysis to provide a cultural context for the production and use of these objects that represented, both functionally and symbolically, the expanding world view of enlightened colonial elite. It is this aspect of our collection that sets it apart from most others.

The publication of this volume celebrates the seventy-five years since John D. Rockefeller, Jr., undertook the restoration of Williamsburg to its colonial appearance. He was guided by the vision that future generations would benefit from learning from the past. Perhaps more than any of the other collections amassed by the Foundation, maps reflect the hopes and aspirations of foreign powers competing for control in the New World, define the foundation of a unique American culture, and provide powerful tools for understanding the road to Independence.

Acknowledgments

The publication of this book was made possible through the generous support of The Acorn Foundation, in memory of Alexander Orr Vietor. It was during Mr. Vietor's tenure as curator of maps at Yale University that many of the most important maps in that collection were acquired, establishing it as one of the most outstanding repositories in the country for the study of historical geography. His career is remembered not only for his scholarship, but also for the inspiration he provided to future students. It is our great regret that we never knew him; however, his legacy has been kept alive through his widow, Anna Glen Vietor. We hope that by dedicating this volume to her, she will realize the significant role that she, too, has played in promoting new research into the mapping of colonial America.

Many individuals provided invaluable assistance during the preparation of this book. Several deserve special acknowledgment. Graham Hood and John Sands were instrumental in initiating the project and securing funds. Ron Hurst ensured that time and resources were available and lent moral support. Former curator of maps and prints Joan Downing Dolmetsch conceived the idea of compiling a book on Williamsburg's map collection. Upon her retirement, she generously shared much of her research on numerous maps included in this volume. Laura Pass Barry, associate curator of prints and maps, willingly and graciously assumed additional responsibilities while assisting with research and locating illustrations to accompany the text. Donna Sheppard contributed much more than her thoughtful and meticulous skills as an editor, becoming a close friend throughout the process. We are grateful for the countless hours that she unselfishly gave to guiding us in new directions and critiquing our research and writing. We owe a special word of thanks to Jan Gilliam, who provided valuable comments on the text and prepared the index. Greer Allen's enthusiasm for the subject is evident in his attractive and innovative design. He combined images and text in a way that enables readers to experience a sense of discovery and exploration within the book itself. John J. Moran set the type with the assistance of Jo Ellen Ackerman. Helen Olds shared her remarkable eye for color and monitored the production of this book in Singapore.

Good friends donated objects or funds that have contributed to the success of this project. Marion and Bob Wilson enabled Colonial Williamsburg to acquire one of the most important pieces in the collection, the atlas that belonged to John Custis. Bridget and Al Ritter supported this publication financially and allowed us to photograph and illustrate maps from their collection. Luke Beckerdite and Peggy Scholley, and Sally J. and James A. Thomas also assisted with funding. William C. Wooldridge, Ruth P. and Joseph R. Lasser, Dr. Lee P. Haacker and Glenn Sandison, and Tigger and Irving Jensen, Jr., helped to acquire maps for Colonial Williamsburg that are illustrated in the volume. The exhibition that accompanies this work, "Degrees of Latitude: Maps of America from the Colonial Williamsburg Collection," was partially funded by Gilbert Butler.

Russell Morrison and Owen Henderson gave advice and counsel on ways to shape the map collection. We are particularly indebted to Ashley Bayton-Williams, Philip Burden, Rick Guthrie, and Alice Hudson for their willingness to share research and insights, and for their thoughtful comments on portions of the manuscript. Their scholarly contributions greatly improved the book. Other useful information was provided by dealers in the map trade, especially Richard Arkway, Bob Augustyn, Paul Cohen, Donald Heald, Richard Lan, Ken Nebenzahl, and Bill Reese.

We have incurred an enormous debt of gratitude to individuals and institutions in Britain and the United States, as we often became a challenge to patient and helpful institutional staff members. At the John D. Rockefeller, Jr. Library at Colonial Williamsburg, Susan Shames regularly gave of her time and special talents as both an historian and a librarian. Her sister, Alice Patteson, and Bob Doares in the Department of Historical Training assisted with translating period documents. Former curator of rare books and manuscripts, John Ingram was instrumental in securing John Custis's atlas for the Foundation. His successor, Gail Greve, made that volume accessible on countless occasions. We also offer our sincerest thanks to Juliegh Clark, Del Moore, and Joanne Proper.

Dedicated staff assisted us at the Library of Congress, British Library, Public Record Office, London, and the College of William and Mary. We would like to recognize Gerald R. Wager, head, reference and reader services section, Library of Congress, Kathryn L. Engstrom, Pam van Ee, and, most especially, Ed Redmond in the geography and map division, Library of Congress, Randy Jones Wyatt, Mariners' Museum, Robert S. Cox, American Philosophical Society, and Margaret Cook, special collections, Swem Library, College of William and Mary. Vivian Aldous, archivist, Corporation of London Records Office, Guildhall, and independent scholar Dr. David Mitchell helped decipher seventeenth-century documents.

Most of the maps in this book were carefully conserved under the masterful eye of Pamela Young, who was assisted by Susan Peckham, Valinda Carroll, and Mike Ridgeway. This talented group also oversaw the framing of the collection in preparation for the traveling exhibition. Once conserved, Hans Lorenz and Craig McDougal photographed each object. Others who supplied photographic assistance included Laura Arnette, Tom Austin, Kathy Dunn, Tom Green, Marianne Martin, Mary Norment, Tracey Stecklein, and Barbara Temple.

Joe Rountree managed various aspects of the publication process, including reviewing the printing. John Ogden and Cathy Swormstedt proofread the manuscript in its final stages, spotting mistakes that would have otherwise been missed. The responsibility of ensuring that materials were shipped and received as needed was entrusted to the able hands of Julie Watson.

We are also grateful for the support and assistance given to us by members of the Museums Division at Colonial Williamsburg, most notably Olivia Alison, Trish Bare, Linda Baumgarten, John Davis, Jay Gaynor, Margie Gill, Velva Henegar, Martha Katz-Hyman, John Hyman, Kimberley Smith Ivey, Ginny Lascara, Betty Leviner, Barbara Luck, Jane Mackley, Jonathan Prown, Janine Skerry, Carolyn Weekley, Nancy Ward, Tanya Wilson, and Phil Zea.

Finally, we want to acknowledge the friends and family members whose unwavering support enabled us to endure the difficult periods of writing this book. They provided a constant reminder of what is truly important in life. To Laura Pass Barry, Hope and Bobby Beck, Jane Beck, Luke Beckerdite and Peggy Scholley, Mary Humelsine, Robert Leath, Neal Robinson, Tom Savage, Yelena Shekhovtsova, Eric Spiegel, and Catherine and Rex Swetnam we extend our sincerest thanks and gratitude.

Claiming the Land

Maps and charts of the Americas created in the colonial period provided information beyond the mere dots and lines used to illustrate bodies of water, land configurations, mountain ranges, or even the location of forts and settlements. They recorded more than discoveries, explorations, or specific voyages. Born of scientific calculations made with equipment such as compasses, protractors, surveying chains, quadrants, and pendulum clocks, the empirical nature of maps and charts rendered them authoritative documents that imparted a perception of power and control over the environment. These maps tell the story of how Europeans took possession of land in the New World by royal claims based on discovery and exploration, by companies comprised of private investors who wanted to establish settlements, or by wealthy individuals asserting personal holdings. The obvious way to impose a sense of order over the land was to substantiate ownership by illustrating boundary lines on a chart or map.

Many early maps were produced primarily to set boundaries between lands occupied by separate European powers as well as between individual English colonies. From the first settlements in America, land was regarded as a valuable commodity, and choosing the correct location for settlement was crucial to economic success. By the eighteenth century, conflicts between Great Britain and France for control of North America created a major need for maps with information that enabled the military to prepare for and record battles. Securing their land claims also enabled the two European powers to attain dominance in trade and commerce.

Europeans had become aware of the New World on the other side of the Atlantic Ocean by the sixteenth century. More seaworthy ships and improved navigational instruments made it possible for Portuguese, Spanish, Italian, Dutch, French, and English explorers to cross in ever-larger numbers. Intent on locating a shorter passage to the Orient, they also hoped to find gold in the New World. Although it would be many years before Europeans realized that a Northwest Passage did not exist and gold was not lying about for the taking, they did recognize the potential for substantial profits to be made there. In spite of the strong interest in exploration, it would be the end of the sixteenth century before a concerted effort was made to establish colonies within the present-day United States, save for the Spanish settlement at Saint Augustine in 1565.

In the seventeenth century, the Netherlands' vast wealth from its unparalleled position in world trade enabled the highly sophisticated Dutch map industry to far surpass that of other European powers. Well-funded map publishers employed the most accomplished geographers, designers, engravers, printers, and colorists. *Americae Sive Novi Orbis, Nova Descriptio* by Abraham Ortelius exemplifies the ability of cartographers of the Low Countries to secure and publish the most up-to-date geographic information. In 1587, Ortelius revised an earlier map of North and South America for his atlas *Theatrum Orbis Terrarum*, which included a small finger of water that may well represent the first rendering of the Chesapeake Bay on a printed map.[1] *(fig. 2)* Ortelius's 1587 map seems to have been based on Englishman Arthur Barlowe's narrative of his explorations while accompanying Sir Walter Ralegh in 1584. It is worth noting that Barlowe's information appeared on this map before it did on any English chart.

Significant maps of North America were also created by English explorers in the late sixteenth and seventeenth centuries. Captain John Smith explored the Chesapeake Bay in 1607 and 1608 for the London Company. His map of *Virginia,* the first English colony, published in Oxford in 1612, did much to stimulate the English colonization of North America.[2] *(fig. 3)* However, most Europeans became familiar with the Virginia colony by consulting Dutch copies of Smith's map, again indicative of the Dutch position in the seventeenth-century map trade. As map historian Coolie Verner explained, "The main instrument for the diffusion of Smith data initially was the Hondius-Blaeu copy (1618) which was itself copied by Henricus Hondius. Either of these two folio copies served as the primary source of information about the Chesapeake Bay for all subsequent uses of the data."[3]

The seventeenth century witnessed an increase of wealth in Western Europe that greatly expanded the mar-

2. Detail from *Americae Sive Novi Orbis*, by Abraham Ortelius, Antwerp, 1592, black-and-white line engraving with period color. 1986-81. (Cat. 1) Ortelius engraved an earlier version of this map in 1570. In 1587, he engraved a new plate, revising the geography to reflect more recent discoveries. He continued to publish this version of the map until 1612.

3. Detail from *Virginia,* by Captain John Smith, London, 1624, black-and-white line engraving. G1984-1, gift of Mrs. Anna Glen Vietor in memory of Alexander O. Vietor. (Cat. 5)

ket for imported luxury items, particularly spices from the East Indies. Portugal, Spain, England, and Holland competed for the East Indian trade. By 1700, the Dutch East India Company's monopoly on goods from the Spice Islands virtually excluded other nations from that market, and private investors in Holland were forced to look elsewhere for trade opportunities. North America provided one new resource. In 1614, Dutch explorer and fur trader Adrien Block charted the bays and rivers from present-day Manhattan, past Long Island, and as far as Cape Cod. He produced the first accurate depiction of Manhattan as an island, which was used in part to create a map published by Willem Janszoon Blaeu in 1635.[4] *(fig. 4)* First under the auspices of the New Netherland Company and then under the leadership of the Dutch West India Company, the

Dutch occupied the Hudson River Valley and parts of New Jersey, and controlled the lucrative fur trade in the area until 1664.

Initially, English and Dutch colonies on the North American mainland were owned by jointly held stock companies chartered by European governments. Although subject to royal authority in matters of land distribution and trade, the companies or group of individuals assumed the financial risk. Virginia, Plymouth, and Massachusetts Bay were originally settled by private English companies.[5] Investors in Holland, Sweden, and Finland established settlements in New Netherland, in southeastern Pennsylvania, along the Delaware and Hudson Rivers, and in New Jersey. Maryland and Carolina were formed from large royal grants, called proprietorships, to individuals or

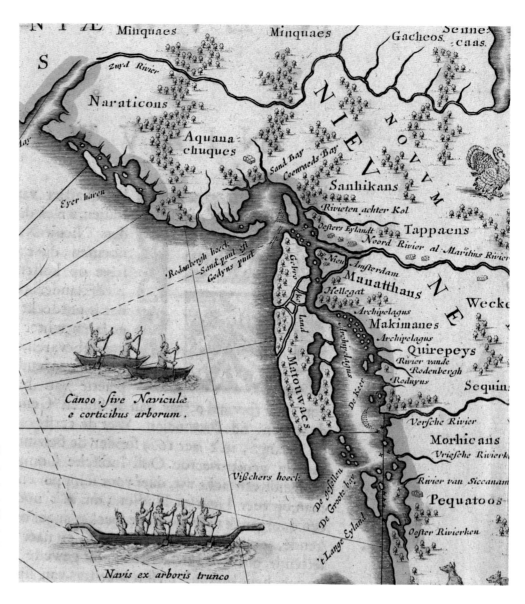

4. Detail
from *Nova Belgica et Anglia Nova*,
by Willem Janszoon Blaeu,
Amsterdam, 1635,
black-and-white line engraving
with period color.
1968-128. (Cat. 8)

groups of individuals.[6] After the English captured the Middle Atlantic colonies from Holland in 1664, these, too, became proprietorships.[7]

Jamestown, the earliest permanent English settlement in North America, was established in 1607 by the Virginia Company, a jointly held stock company. Although its charter was revoked by King James I in 1624 when Virginia became a royal colony, the company's policy of land distribution, set in place under its direction, remained in effect for the rest of the century. The "headright" system allotted fifty acres to each individual who paid his passage to Virginia plus an additional fifty for each person brought over at his expense. Headrights were contingent upon colonists remaining in Virginia for at least three years. The crown stipulated that each landowner pay an annual fee,

known as a "quitrent," of two shillings to the king for every hundred acres he occupied.[8]

Maryland was established in 1632 after Charles I granted a large tract of land to Cecil Calvert, Lord Baltimore. Calvert's success depended on his ability to attract investors with substantial capital who would purchase parcels of his land and supply settlers and tenants to work as laborers. Lord Baltimore was empowered to regulate trade and impose taxes and customs duties. Unlike in the Virginia colony, where all rents and quitrents went to the crown, quitrents and proceeds from sold or rented land in Maryland were claimed by the Calvert family.[9]

In 1635, Lord Baltimore distributed a promotional pamphlet offering land based on the same type of headright system used in Virginia. He proposed grants of two

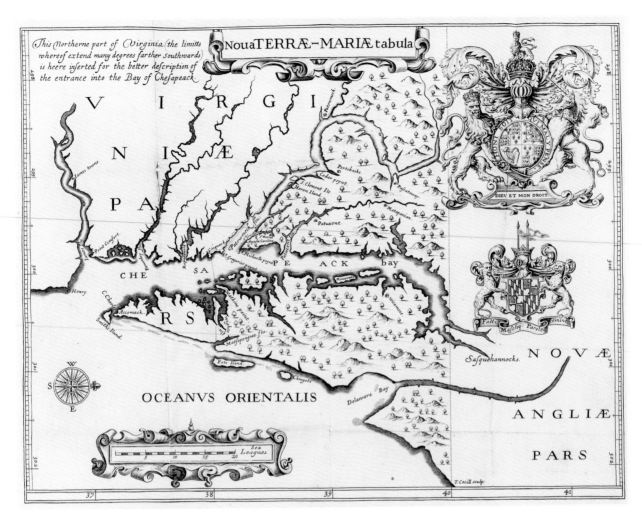

5. *Noua Terræ–Mariæ tabula,* cartographer unknown, London, 1635, black-and white-line engraving.
Courtesy, John Work Garrett Library, Johns Hopkins University, Baltimore, Md.

thousand acres to anyone bringing five men between the ages of sixteen and fifty to Maryland, a greater incentive to potential settlers than Virginia offered. Realizing he had set the laborer to land ratio too high, Lord Baltimore subsequently lowered the acreage from two thousand to one thousand.[10] Those bringing more than five settlers were to receive one hundred acres for each man or woman, fifty for each child, and an additional fifty for each servant. By 1700, it became clear that the headright system had been detrimental to the growth of both Virginia and Maryland. It allowed a few wealthy planters to hoard prime real estate for future speculation, especially along the tributaries of the Chesapeake Bay. Much of this land was ultimately divided among the heirs of the original landholders.[11]

Although the Calverts maintained control of Maryland,

with two brief interruptions, until the Revolution, the geographical description of the grant as outlined in the original charter continued to be a source of dispute. Topographical errors on maps depicting Maryland made it difficult for the Calverts to substantiate their claims. When Lord Baltimore published his first promotional tract, the accompanying map incorrectly illustrated the northern bounds of his grant, the 40° of north latitude, at the head of the Chesapeake Bay rather than at its correct location farther up the Susquehanna River. *(fig. 5)* The mistake had been noticed by 1671, when John Ogilby, royal geographer to Charles II, published a derivative version of Lord Baltimore's map in *America.* Ogilby cleverly extended the northern boundary of Lord Baltimore's tract by adding several extra rows of trees.[12] *(fig. 6)*

The headright system adopted by Virginia and Mary-

6. *Noua Terræ–Mariæ tabula*, by John Ogilby, London, 1671,
black-and-white line engraving. 1984-211. (Cat. 12)

land was also detrimental to the establishment of towns.[13]
From the seventeenth century on, the crown encouraged
urban settlement primarily for regulating trade activities.
Thomas Lord Culpeper, governor of Virginia, received the
following instructions in 1679:

*That there be towns built there one on each great River if
possible, And in order thereunto that after sufficient notice to
provide Warehouses and other conveniences, no ships what-
soever be permitted to load or unload but at the said places
where the towns are designed the chiefest whereof to be near
the above-mentioned fort.*[14]

The Virginia Assembly passed an act in 1691 designed
to ensure effective collection of customs duties by estab-

lishing port towns. The measure specified that all imports
and exports to and from Virginia pass through the designated ports. Founded in 1691, York, today known as Yorktown, was the most significant of these towns.[15]

In *The Present State of Virginia*, 1697, the authors
lamented the lack of towns in the colony. They noted that
the majority of members of the General Assembly, "having
never seen a Town, nor a well improv'd Country in their
Lives, cannot therefore imagine the Benefit of it, and are
afraid of every Innovation that will put them to a present
Charge, whatever may be the future Benefit."[16] Two years
later, Williamsburg, then called Middle Plantation, was
founded as the capital of Virginia ninety-two years after
the colony at Jamestown had been established. *(fig. 7)*

In 1663, Charles II granted the province of Carolina to
eight of his favorites, known as the Lords Proprietors, who

7. A modern strike from the "Bodleian copperplate," engraver unknown, London, ca. 1740, black-and-white line engraving, G1938-196, illustrates the public buildings of Williamsburg. From the top left are The Brafferton, the "Wren Building," and the President's House at the College of William and Mary. Second row from the left are the Capitol, the rear of the "Wren Building," and the only known elevation of the Governor's Palace.

had been helpful to him in regaining the throne lost by his father. They set about promoting Carolina under the headright system just as Lord Baltimore had done in Maryland. *A Brief Description of The Province of Carolina on the Coasts of Floreda* was published in 1666. "All Artificers, as *Carpenters, Wheel-rights, Joyners, Coopers, Bricklayers, Smiths,* or diligent Husbandsmen and Labourers, that are wiling to advance their fortunes" were encouraged to settle there. The Lords Proprietors further emphasized that "if any Maid or single Woman have a desire to go over, they will think themselves in the Golden Age, when Men paid a Dowery for their Wives."[17]

Having had only limited success in recruiting colonists to Carolina, the Lords Proprietors were eager for ways to promote the colony. John Locke, secretary to Lord Ashley,

the Earl of Shaftesbury, one of the most active of the Lords Proprietors, supplied Ogilby with descriptive material and a manuscript map that included many place names along the Carolina coast.[18] He included Locke's promotional material in his book *America,* 1671 along with a printed map entitled *A New Discription of Carolina.*[18] *(fig. 8)* Despite a number of attempts to promote Carolina, the Lords Proprietors failed to achieve an economically viable colony. However, the area remained under their control until 1730 when Carolina was divided into two separate royal colonies.

Unlike the rural land distribution in the southern colonies, New England developed a more urban pattern. The Pilgrims who settled at Plymouth in 1620 were organized under the auspices of the Virginia Company.

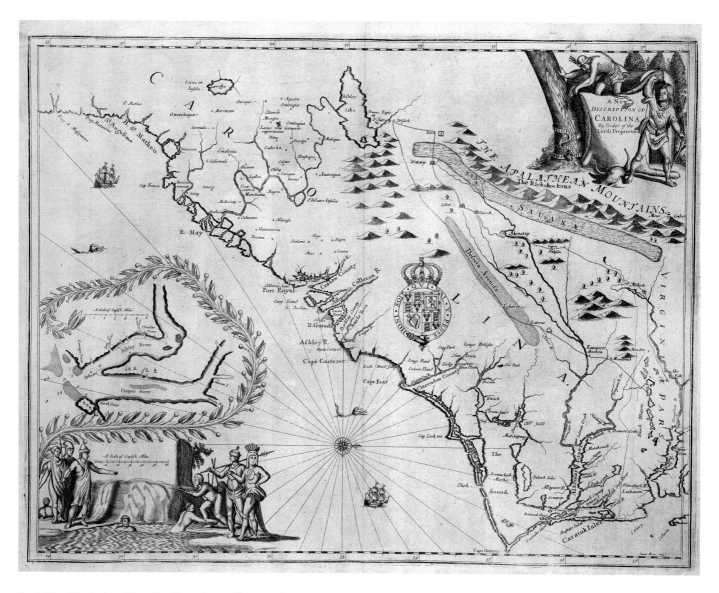

8. *A New Discription of Carolina,* by John Ogilby, London, 1671, black-and-white line engraving. 1989-317. (Cat. 13)

Although the initial plan was similar to that used in Virginia, one-hundred-acre headrights for each person paying his own way, the form it finally took—the township system with the Congregational Church at its center—was entirely different.[19]

Attendance at religious services was mandatory in this New England environment, and the colonists were reluctant to travel far to attend meetings on Thursdays and Sundays. The township, in the words of an anonymous seventeenth-century commentator, allowed for a "comfortable communication" within their towns by forming a plan "square 6 miles eury waye. The houses orderly placed about the midst, especially the meetinghous, the whc we will suppose to be the center of the wholl circumferences."[20] Once a township was granted, sponsors assigned

the land to inhabitants according to need, with the interest of the community taking precedence.

This system was subsequently followed by the Puritans, who arrived in Massachusetts in 1630. Almost immediately, the new settlers dispersed into small towns along the Charles River. Boston, a natural location for a major port, soon became the center for government and trade and the largest town in English-speaking America. Before long, Puritan settlements began to appear in Connecticut, Rhode Island, and New Hampshire. Because the Pilgrims and the Puritans limited the settlers' land allotment to their immediate needs, individual landholdings were distributed much more equitably than in the colonies operating under the headright system, which encouraged self-interest and speculation that occasionally resulted in a single landowner acquiring hundreds of thousands of acres.[21] Within most of the New England townships, families generally owned anywhere between twenty or thirty acres to as many as five hundred.[22]

The Dutch West India Company's approach to land distribution in America initially focused more on trade than on colonization. Financial reverses forced the company to encourage immigration by adopting a charter establishing patroonships, or manorial grants, in 1629. Generous grants of land were offered to any stockholder who planted a colony of at least fifty persons over the age of fifteen. Stockholders received either sixteen miles of navigable waterfront property on one side of a waterway, or eight miles on both sides, which could extend inland for an undetermined distance. Although five patroonships were granted, only Kiliaen van Rensselaer was able to settle his land successfully.[23] Because populating such large tracts was so difficult, land grants had been reduced to a quarter of their original size by 1640. The Dutch West India Company also made a number of small farms available. Those located within the present limits of New York City were reserved for employees of the company.[24]

The fierce trading rivalry between the English and Dutch caused Charles II to decide to take over New Netherland. In March 1664, he conveyed all of the land between the Connecticut colony and the Delaware River to the Duke of York, the future James II, disregarding the fact that this territory continued to be settled by the Dutch, Swedes, and Finns. The Duke of York sent Colonel Richard Nicolls to conquer the Middle Atlantic colonies, and by May, this region was under English rule. Colonists had already developed the landscape to suit their individual needs; consequently, land distribution patterns in this area reflected both English and Continental traditions.

The first governors of New York under the proprietorship of the Duke of York did little but reissue previous grants to the Dutch inhabitants. In 1667, Governor Francis Lovelace established the first English manorial grants, which were comparable to the Dutch model. Since the landlords were given medieval judicial and administrative authority over their holdings, recipients of New York manors exercised virtually complete control over their land.[25]

Governor Edmund Andros offered a more standard headright grant in 1675 that provided sixty acres to any European immigrant, plus fifty acres each for his wife and children. This attempt to promote immigration under the headright system failed miserably, and although Andros also granted larger tracts of land to individuals, he was unwilling to offer the baronial privileges that Lord Balti-more did.[26] It became clear by the 1680s that a major problem facing the New York colony was underpopulation. The constant threat of attacks by the French and French-allied Indians competing with the English for the fur trade discouraged settlement on the frontier, resulting in a severe decline in the pelts available to the English.[27]

A tremendous growth in the demand for grain coincided with the decline in the fur trade. So great was the market, particularly in the West Indies, that merchants began investing in rural tracts of land in New York to grow wheat. Responding to the need for farmland, in 1683, Governor Thomas Dongan reinstated the practice begun by former governor Lovelace of bestowing large manorial grants. The result of the policy was that many New York manor holdings were similar in size to the largest Virginia plantations.

Early maps of the middle colonies played an important role in the seemingly endless controversies over boundary lines occasioned by the large land grants the crown awarded. When the Duke of York granted the New Jersey proprietary to John, Lord Berkeley, and Sir George Carteret, he set the boundaries

on the East part by the maine Sea and part by Hudsons River and hath upon the West Delaware Bay or River and extendeth Southward to the maine Ocean as farre as Cape May at the mouth of Delaware Bay and to the Northward as farre as ye Northermost Branch of the said Bay or River of Delaware which is in fourtie one degrees and fourtie Minutes of Lattitude.[28]

The duke apparently consulted *Novi Belgii* by Nicholas Visscher in determining the boundary, for the map incorrectly depicts the branch of the Delaware mentioned in the grant at 41° 40′ near a settlement called Mecharienkonck.[29] *(fig. 9)* The boundary line was to extend in a straight line between this point to 41° north latitude on the Hudson River.

In subsequent litigation with New York over the location of the line, the residents of New Jersey preferred to abide by the designation of latitude (41° 40′) specified in the grant rather than to the erroneous branch of the Delaware. Because New York colonists had begun to settle along the Delaware River south of the designated latitude, they alleged that the Duke of York had intended the line to be drawn from the head of the Delaware Bay. As a compromise, New York officials proposed running the line from the fork of the Delaware, which they determined was at Easton, Pennsylvania, where the Lehigh River empties into the Delaware. This would have placed almost one-third of the northern portion of present-day New Jersey within the bounds of New York.[30]

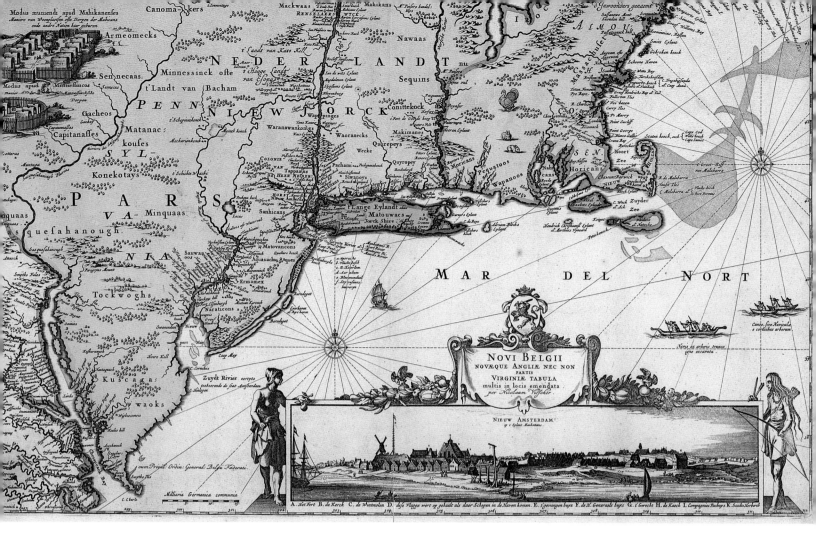

9. Detail from *Novi Belgii Novæque Angliæ Nec Non Partis Virginiæ Tabula,* by Nicholas Visscher, Amsterdam, ca. 1684, black-and-white line engraving with period color. 1968-129. (Cat. 11)
While providing many important place names and serving as a prototype, Visscher's map contained geographical errors that ultimately led to years of litigation among several colonies.

Due to financial difficulties, Lord Berkeley sold his share of New Jersey to John Fenwick, a Quaker, in 1674. That year, the king and the Duke of York were forced to issue new grants since the Dutch had briefly recaptured New York. Displeased that Berkeley had sold the rights to his land to Fenwick, the duke renewed only Carteret's portion. Fenwick subsequently sold his territory to four Quaker proprietors, one of whom was William Penn. In order to clear their title, Carteret and the four entered into a "Quintipartite" deed in 1676 that divided the colony into East Jersey and West Jersey. The duke confirmed the West Jersey grant in 1680.[31] The colony remained divided until 1702 when the proprietors of East and West Jersey surrendered their rights to Queen Anne, thereby establishing New Jersey as a royal colony.

Monarchs sometimes reissued land that had been previously granted by their predecessors. The tract settled as Elizabethtown, New Jersey, was included in the 1664

grant from Charles II to the Duke of York. Colonel Nicolls, who had claimed the duke's property in the region from the Dutch, was subsequently named governor. Prior to being notified that Lord Berkeley and Carteret had been granted New Jersey, Nicolls gave the settlers living in the area of Elizabethtown permission to purchase the title to their lands from the Delaware (Leni-Lenape) Indians. Nicolls's actions led to years of litigation over who actually possessed title because the settlers claimed possession based on their Indian deeds and the colony maintained that the lands belonged to the proprietorship. The dispute led to *A Bill in the Chancery of New-Jersey*. The petition, drafted for the crown against settlers who maintained they had rightfully purchased their land from the Indians, was introduced to the Council of Proprietors in 1745. James Alexander, lawyer, merchant, surveyor general for both East and West Jersey, Council member in New Jersey, and attorney general in both New Jersey and New York, prepared the document. Alexander carefully researched the land conveyance records pertaining to the territory, attempting to show that the land rightfully belonged to the proprietors rather than to the settlers who had purchased it from the Delawares. To reach a wider audience, Alexander arranged through printers James Parker in New York and Benjamin Franklin in Philadelphia to have 250 copies of the bill printed. With the assistance of Lewis Evans, Alexander prepared three maps illustrating the areas in dispute to accompany the bill.[32] The three maps progressed from a map of the East Coast from the Outer Banks of Carolina to Boston, to a map of north and central Jersey, and, finally, to the actual property boundaries in the Elizabethtown tract between Cushetunk Mountain and the Rahway River north of the Raritan. *(fig. 10)*

Considering that 102 subscriptions to the bill were already pledged by 1745, the board agreed to proceed with the project and assume the cost overrun in producing 160 copies. The production costs of £295, however, far exceeded the initial estimates.[33] Although copies were not available until 1746, the Council of Proprietors had filed the bill the previous year. The defendants filed an answer in 1751. In spite of the careful research and preparation on the part of Alexander, the controversy was not resolved until after the Revolution.

William Penn's attempts to achieve religious toleration in England provided the motivating force behind his efforts to establish a colony in America that would attract not only the wealthy, but small landholders, renters, and indentured servants as well. In 1681, Charles II granted Pennsylvania to Penn and gave him the right to determine the form of government, to distribute the land, and to enjoy virtually limitless restrictions on his powers of appointments. Penn began by purchasing five hundred thousand acres from the Delaware Indians to clear the title. Next, he had his surveyor, Thomas Holme, lay out Philadelphia, the main city, where each landholder received ten acres of land for every five hundred he purchased.[34] He immediately published pamphlets to encourage settlement in his new colony, and commissioned Holme to survey and make a map of Pennsylvania. Available in 1687, it provided sponsors and landholders with a comprehensive plan of the various grants.[35] *(fig. 11)*

Penn, too, experienced boundary disputes. He and Lord Baltimore disagreed about the southern boundary of Pennsylvania. Assuming that Lord Baltimore's grant extended to 40° of north latitude as stipulated in the grant, the controversy involved whether it should have been the 40° as accurately surveyed or where it was

thought to be at the time the grant was issued. Penn's grant also called into question the ownership of the three lower counties on the east side of the Delmarva Peninsula that had been settled by Swedes and Dutch. Penn believed that since these lands had been settled before Lord Baltimore's grant, they should not have been included in the latter's claim. Even though his charter specifically excluded previously occupied territory, Lord Baltimore considered them part of his original grant. The boundary line between Pennsylvania and Maryland was not resolved until Charles Mason and Jeremiah Dixon delivered their completed survey in 1768.[36]

In 1660, Charles II created a committee of the Privy Council to advise him on colonial affairs, instructing the group in 1670:

> *You are also by all Wayes and meanes you may to procure exact Mapps, Platts or Charts of all and Every our said Plantations abroad, togeather with the Mapps and Descriptions of their respective Ports, Harbours, Forts, Bayes, Rivers with the Depth of their respective Channells comming in or going up, and the Soundings all along upon the said respective Coasts from place to place, and the same so had, you are carefully to Register and Keepe.*[37]

By 1676, its name having been changed to the Committee of the Lords of Trade and Plantations,[38] the body requested that colonial governors supply them with maps of their holdings in America. The executives were often slow to respond because the individual colonies were expected to absorb the expense. In addition, few men in America were qualified to compile accurate surveys. When the committee asked Lord Baltimore for the best map of Maryland, he replied:

> *The Boundaryes Longitude and Latitude of this Provynce are well described and I sett forth in a Late Mapp or Chart of this Provynce lately made and prepared by one Augustine Herman an Inhabitant of the said Provynce and Printed and Publiquely sold in London by his Majestyes Licence, to which I humbly refferr for greater certaynty and not to give their Lordp's the Trouble of a Large Tedious discreption here.*[39]

Lord Baltimore was fortunate to have someone as capable as Augustine Herrman to create a map of the colony. Herrman immigrated to New Amsterdam before 1633, became a successful merchant-trader of furs and livestock, and relocated to Maryland in 1660. He had been there only a short time before Lord Baltimore commis-

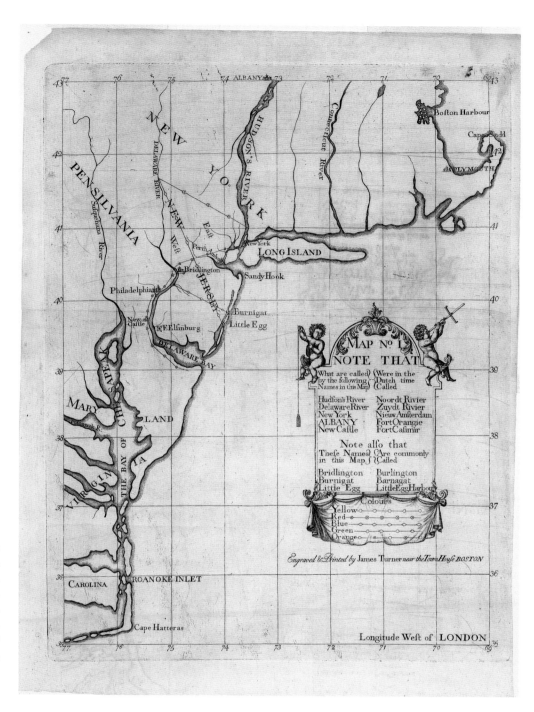

10. New York, Pennsylvania, Maryland,
Virginia, and Carolina,
by James Alexander and Lewis Evans,
Boston, 1747,
black-and-white line engraving.
G1992-29,
gift of Mrs. Anna Glen Vietor
in memory of Alexander O. Vietor.
(Cat. 28)

sioned him to produce the survey. Herrman spent eight years gathering material for the map and another three assembling a final draft. Herrman published the map in 1673, dedicating it to Charles II. Lord Baltimore granted Herrman twenty-five thousand acres of land and the privileges of a manor lord for producing the work, a major source for the geography of the area for the next sixty years. *(fig. 12)* Unfortunately, few maps collected by the Committee of the Lords of Trade and Plantations such as Herrman's survive.

By 1700, England's rapidly increasing wealth and growing influence in world markets had reduced the Dutch domination of foreign trade, and the government began to play a more active role in colonial affairs. In 1696, William III created the Board of Trade and Plantations to replace the Committee of the Lords of Trade and Plantations. The group was composed of eight experts on foreign affairs who advised the Privy Council on imperial matters and trade. They were solely responsible for supervising the government of the colonies, including nominat-

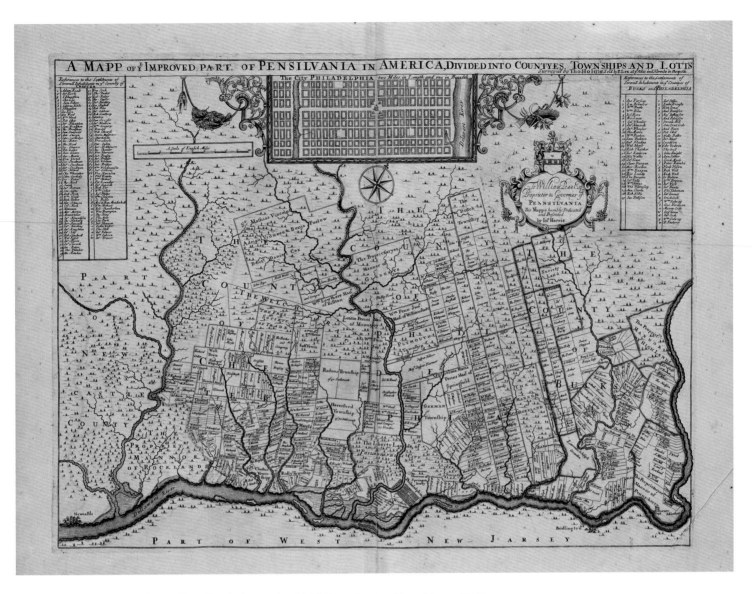

11. *A Mapp of yᵉ Improved Part of Pensilvania in America, Divided into Countyes Townships and Lotts,*
by Thomas Holme, London, ca. 1690, black-and-white line engraving with period color.
(Custis Atlas Cat. 71) This is a reduced version of Robert Greene and John Thornton's seven-sheet
A Map of the Improved Part of Pennsylvania in America, ca. 1687.

ing governors and other high officials, monitoring expenditures of public monies, and reviewing colonial legislation. The board also investigated complaints from colonists, colonial legislatures, and governors and reported their findings to the crown.

Individual colonies often contracted with London merchants to represent their interests to the Board of Trade and Plantations and to act as financial agents. For example, from the 1690s onward, Micajah Perry I provided these services for the Virginia colony, and, briefly, for the colony of Maryland as well, appearing before the board on their behalf no fewer than fifty times between 1704 and 1713.[40]

Perry was the senior partner in the firm of Perry and Lane, the largest London company dealing in the highly profitable tobacco and fur trades during the late seventeenth and early eighteenth centuries.[41] Services included securing credit for clients, arranging shipment of merchandise between England and America, purchasing items for export, and selling tobacco and other goods from the colonies. Perry was also responsible for monitoring duties on tobacco. William Byrd I and II and Byrd II's brother-in-law, John Custis, were among the many planters who transacted business with Perry and Lane.[42]

The firm supplied goods for the Indian trade. William

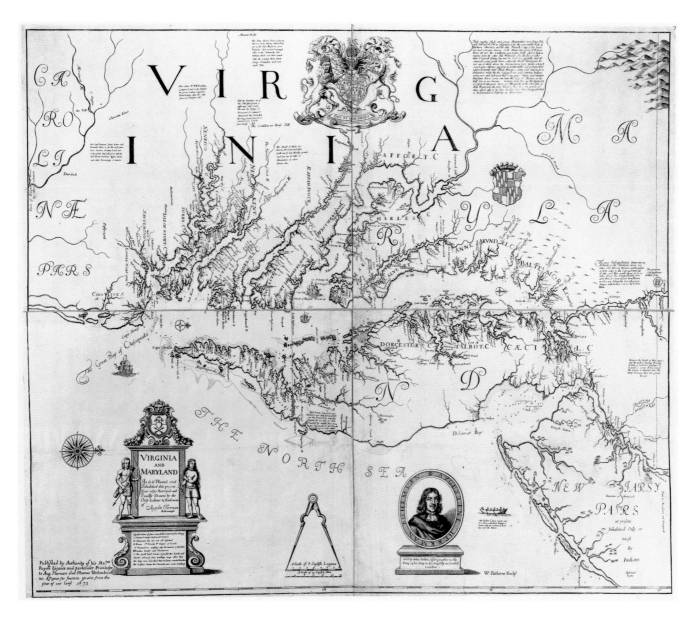

12. *Virginia and Maryland,* by Augustine Herrman, London, 1673, black-and-white line engraving. Courtesy, John Carter Brown Library, Brown University, Providence, R. I.

Byrd I was the largest Indian trader in Virginia in the late seventeenth century, dispatching caravans of about fifteen men and one hundred packhorses several hundred miles south from the trading path that began at the falls of the James River. His activities extended as far as the lands of the Catawbas and Cherokees in what is now South Carolina. In exchange for the skins of beaver, otter, bear, and deer, Byrd supplied Native Americans with pots and pans, cloth, spirits, hatchets, and guns.[43] Byrd I wrote to Perry and Lane in February 1684/85, instructing his merchants about the quality of trade guns: "Pray speake to the gun smith that the dogs [the hammers] of all the gun locks

have good hold otherwise the Indians will not buy them."[44]

To facilitate his affairs in Virginia and Maryland, it is possible that Perry commissioned John Thornton to make *A New Map of Virginia, Maryland, Pensylvania, New Jersey, Part of New York, And Carolina.*[45] *(fig. 13)* The coat of arms of the Perry family and the dedication, *"To M^r. Micajah Perry of London Merchant This Map of Virginia &c.^{a} is humbly Dedicated and Presented* [erasure] *Thornton,"* appear in the left center of the map.

During the War of the League of Augsburg (1689–1697), England and France competed vigorously to establish trade relations with the Indians in the strategically important Ohio Valley. Control of this territory would allow France access to the Ohio River, the only inland passage from Canada to the Lower Mississippi. The crown feared that French domination of lands west of the Appalachian Mountains would prohibit the British from establishing additional settlements in the area while those already living there would be driven out. The government in London further worried that should the English be prohibited from the Ohio Territory, population growth in the colonies along the eastern seaboard would drive down wages to the point where Americans would be less dependent on British wares and more intent on producing their own.[46]

As early as 1698/99, Cadwallader Jones, an Indian trader from Virginia, wrote a proposal to Governor Francis Nicholson recommending that the Virginia government establish trade with Indians at the Great Lakes. Jones was motivated by reading a book by Belgian missionary Father Louis Hennepin, *A new discovery of a vast country in America*, first published in English in 1698, which contained a map of the area. Hennepin had accompanied La Salle on his expedition to Lakes Erie, Huron, and Michigan in 1679 and subsequently descended the Illinois River to the Mississippi. Combining his own explorations of the Blue Ridge Mountains with Hennepin's geography, Jones recommended a route from the falls of the Rappahannock to the lakes. *(fig. 14)* Seventeen cross marks on the map indicated "where the author camped."[47] The Miamis, Illinois, and Hurons were among the tribes Jones located on the map. Jones noted in his proposal, *Lovissiania and Virginia Improved*:

> There is Computed in this Country of Lovissiania two hundred Nations which, by the Conveyance from Lake to lake down to Quebecke, do Yearely Trade through it neare three thousand Miles. I presume Our Desent would be on the Huron Indians which is on the Middle lake. It is presumed all Sotherne Wstern [trade] from thence would be Stopped by us, they having [to go] by the Various meanders of the Lake Erie and Ontario fifteen hundred miles to Quebecke, and Wee Could Afford matters as Easey as the ffrench.
>
> In three yeares Season after the Trade is securely Settled the Vallue of furs Yearely from hence return'd may be with much modesty Computed at one hundred Thousand pounds Sterg.[48]

The Carolinians were also interested in expanding the Indian trade westward. In a 1708 memorial to Charles Spencer, secretary of state for the Southern Department,

Thomas Nairne, Indian agent for South Carolina and author of Carolina's Indian policy, requested that in the next treaty with France, the English claim the area around Mobile. The Carolinians had "setled on the bay of Mowila [Mobile] 150 miles to the East of the Mississipi all the Inhabitants whereof had for 10 years before Submitted themselves and Country to the government of Carolina, and then actually Traded with us."[49] Three years earlier, Nairne had declared: "This Province [Carolina] owed for a long time its Subsistance to ye Indian Trade, wch is now ye main Branch of its Traffick."[50]

The French, in the middle of the War of the League of Augsburg with England, were aware of the British colonists' efforts to expand their Indian trade westward to the Great Lakes. In 1694, French explorer Henri de Tonty expressed the concern that "they [the English] will not fail to subdue all the upper Nations, and consequently will be masters of the trade with our allied Miamis, Illinois, and Outavois, without whom the country cannot survive, and it will be all the easier for them because some of the English in Carolina are [already] settled on a tributary that flows into the river Oyo, which discharges into the Mississippi."[51]

The Native Americans played a critical role between the English and French in their struggle for control of the Ohio territory. In 1677, the Iroquois Confederacy, which claimed the Ohio Country, created the Covenant Chain that allied them commercially and strategically with the crown. Meanwhile, the French maintained close trade ties to the Iroquois' rivals, the Algonquians.[52] Although technically allied with the English, the Iroquois considered them to be incompetent military allies and adopted a more neutral approach in their relationships with both nations. Through careful maneuvering, the Iroquois represented themselves to the English as spokesmen for the Far Indians (Algonquians) who traded with the French. Eager to thwart the English-Iroquois alliance and to maintain their own trade activities with the natives, the French established agreements with the eastern Indians. The result was that neither power was assured of assistance from the Iroquois.[53]

13. *A New Map of Virginia, Maryland, Pensilvania, New Jersey, Part of New York, and Carolina*, by John Thornton, London, ca. 1723–1728 (originally published ca. 1701), black-and-white line engraving with period color. 1940-418. (Cat. 16)

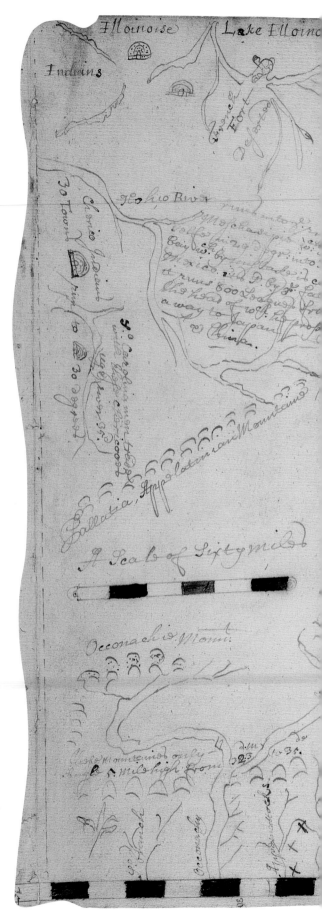

14. *Lovissiana Pars Discovered by Father Louis Hennepin of Hoilnault*
@ Dedicated to W^m y^e 3^d. King of England 1698,"
by Cadwallader Jones, Virginia, 1698/99,
pen and ink. Courtesy, Public Record Office, London,
CO/5/1350, MPG1221.

After leading an unsuccessful expedition against the French in Quebec and Montreal in 1709, Governor Francis Nicholson of Maryland, Colonel Peter Schuyler, mayor of Albany, New York, and Colonel Samuel Vetch, who became governor of Nova Scotia, appealed directly to Queen Anne for support in driving the French from the American frontier. Their first step was to secure the loyalty of the Indians, so they selected four kings from the Five Nations of Iroquois to be presented to the queen at court. *(fig. 15)* The officials hoped that the Indians would be impressed with the splendors of London and the might of the British Empire. By having them meet with ecclesiastical authorities, Nicholson, Schuyler, and Vetch anticipated renewed interest in sending missionaries to America. Accompanied by Nicholson, Schuyler, and others, the four kings sailed from Boston in 1710.[54]

During their audience with Queen Anne, the Iroquois requested greater support from the crown to stop French encroachments. They also met with the Board of Trade, which promised assistance. The visit proved successful as the Indian kings agreed to join with the English to attack Quebec. In 1711, English and Indian troops gathered in Albany to await the British fleet that left Boston at the end of July for Quebec by way of the Saint Lawrence River. Since many British ships ran aground in the unfamiliar river, the commander of the fleet decided to abort the attack and return to England. Although Nicholson was able to convince the Indians to retain their allegiance, the incident did nothing to strengthen their confidence in the British military.

The Yamassee Indians attacked English settlers on the Carolina frontier in 1715, driving them back to within thirty miles of Charleston. Rumors held that the French were behind the attack.[55] By December 1717, the Carolinians were expressing concern over French activities on the Mississippi in a memorial to the Board of Trade. A copy was also sent to Virginia Governor Alexander Spotswood for his verification. In his response to the Lords Commissioners, the governor described the trade route that the French had established from the Saint Lawrence River to the mouth of the Mississippi and warned that the French were gaining favor with the Indians.

In 1720, Spotswood responded to another letter from the Board of Trade regarding the threat of French encroachment. The governor enclosed a map showing that the Indian settlements were closer to the French than to the English, thus posing the threat of a French allegiance with the Native Americans. *(fig. 16)* After several appeals to the crown, Spotswood was allowed to expand

15. *Sa Ga Yeath Qua Pieth Tow King of the Maquas,* by John Simon after a painting by John Verelst, London, 1710, black-and-white mezzotint engraving. 1999-49. Portraits were painted of each of the four Indian sachems while they were in London. A set of the engravings taken from the paintings was sent to the governors of Virginia, Maryland, New York, and Massachusetts to be hung in their Council chambers. Sets were also sent to New Hampshire, Rhode Island, and Pennnsylvania.

Virginia westward by granting large amounts of land in two newly established counties, Spotsylvania to the northwest and Brunswick to the southwest. The governor awarded the tracts under very favorable terms; for instance, he convinced the crown to forego collecting quitrents for a ten-year period.[56] Spotswood himself laid claim to forty thousand acres in Spotsylvania County.

Conflict over control of the Ohio Territory was reflected in a cartographic war between England and France. French mapmaker Guillaume Delisle published *Carte de la Louisiane et du Cours du Mississipi* in 1718.[57] *(fig.*

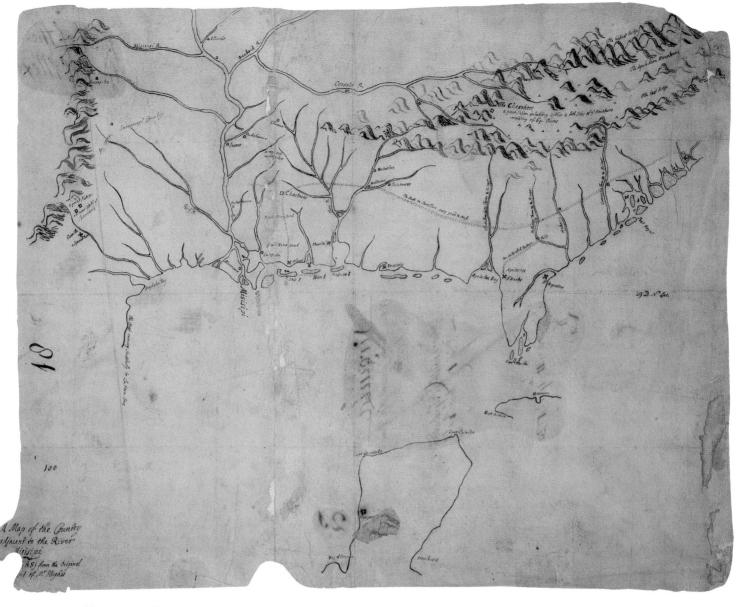

16. *A Map of the Country adjacent to the River Misisipi- copy'd by A*[lexander *S*[potswood] *from the Original Draught of M*ʳ *Hughes*, manuscript map sent by Alexander Spotswood to the Board of Trade, ca. 1720, pen and ink. Unfortunately, Price Hughes's map of the Southeast that Spotswood copied is now lost. Courtesy, Public Records Office, London, CO/700/Virginia 2.

17) The title is somewhat misleading because the area depicted extended from New York west to the Rocky Mountains and from the Great Lakes south to Florida and the Gulf of Mexico. Since the English had not explored much of the territory portrayed on the map, it became a primary source for information. Distributed widely in Europe, inventories reveal that Virginians owned copies of Delisle's map too. For the colonists on the East Coast and the English back home, the disturbing feature of the map was that Delisle reduced the western boundaries of the British colonies, thereby adding territory claimed by the English to French Louisiana.

Two years later, Herman Moll published *A New Map of the North Parts of America claimed by France. (fig. 18)* While Moll borrowed some information from Delisle, he also included new data from surveys by Nathaniel Blackmore, Richard Berisford, and Thomas Nairne that he cited on the map.[58] Moll directly challenged the boundary lines that Delisle included to mark territory claimed by France by explaining in a legend on his map:

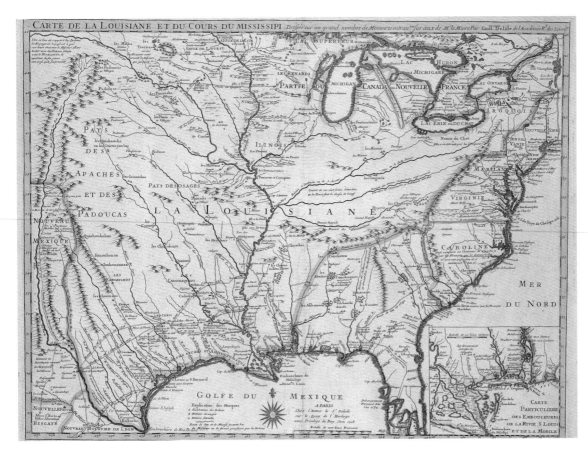

17. *Carte de la Louisiane et du Cours du Mississipi,* by Guillaume Delisle, Paris, 1718, black-and-white line engraving with period outline color. 1953-202. (Cat. 20)

18. *A New Map of the North Parts of America claimed by France,* by Herman Moll, London, 1720, black-and-white line engraving with period outline color. 1967-17. (Cat. 21)

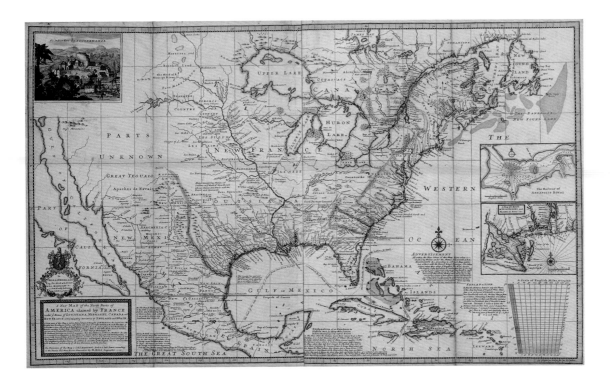

The French Divisions are inserted on purpose, that those Noblemen, Gentlemen, Merchants, &c. who are interested in our Plantations in those Parts, may observe whether they agree with their Proprieties, or do not justly deserve ye name of Incroachments: and this is ye more to be observed because they do thusly Comprehend within their limits ye Cherakeys and Iroquois, by much ye most powerfull of all ye Neighboring Indian Nations, the Old Friends and Allies of the English, who ever esteemed them to be the Bulwark and Security of all their Plantations in North America.[59]

Moll realized the importance of maintaining a peaceful relationship with the Iroquois and Cherokees, tribes with which the English had traded for years. French encroachment in territories these tribes inhabited posed a real threat to the economy and security of the region.[60] The *South Carolina Gazette* reported in 1736:

As the Indian Trade is of the greatest Importance to the Wellfare of this Province, not only as it affords us near one 5th part of the Returns we make to Great-Britain (in Exchange for the woollen and other British Manufactures we yearly receive from thence,) but principally as it is the Means by which we keep and maintain the several Nations of the Indians surrounding this Province in Amity and Friendship with us, and thereby prevent their falling into the Interest of France *or* Spain.[61]

The French had built outposts along the Mississippi River and the Great Lakes by the 1740s. British officials gradually realized they needed to establish their own forts to counteract French activity, which they did in 1749 by erecting Fort Halifax in Acadia (today, Nova Scotia) to rival the French fort at Louisbourg. The following year, the Earl of Halifax, president of the Board of Trade, moved more aggressively to thwart the French by authorizing the Ohio Company to grant two million acres on the upper Ohio. The company planned to attract settlers to the newly opened lands and agreed to construct a fort to protect them.

By the mid-eighteenth century, relations between the French and English had become increasingly strained. In 1750, the Board of Trade once again "Ordered that the draught of a circular letter be prepared to the several Governors upon the continent of America, for a map or chart of their respective provinces, and the best information they can get of the exact boundaries and the settlements or encroachments of any foreign powers."[62] The commissioners soon began to receive the maps. Perhaps the most outstanding was Joshua Fry and Peter Jefferson's draft of

Virginia, sent only one year after the request.[63] Concurrent with the Board of Trade's efforts to gather information, London cartographers and publishers began to produce maps and pamphlets that illustrated British claims in North America. Dr. John Mitchell, formerly of Virginia but now a resident of London, undertook to make a general map illustrating the situation in America from the British point of view. A doctor, botanist, and member of the Royal Society of London, Mitchell was well suited for the task, and the commissioners of the Board of Trade allowed him access to the newest surveys.

Mitchell obtained information from several sources. For the geography of the Ohio River Valley, he consulted a journal compiled by Christopher Gist, who explored the area in 1750 for the Ohio Company. Mitchell relied heavily on Fry and Jefferson's work for Virginia. Peter Collinson, an influential London Quaker, wrote to Benjamin Franklin in 1752:

Docr. Mitchell showed Mee a New Mapp of Pensilvania sent over by your Governor. The Doctor is Makeing a New Mapp of all our Colonies for the Board of Trade, Haveing the Assistance of all these Manuscrip Mapps and which are abundance in particular a Mapp sent by an Officer of the York Forces, which much fuller Discribes the Country and Settlements on Mohawk, Oswego and the fork of Susquehanna then your Governers Mapp.[64]

Published in 1755, John Mitchell's *Map of the British and French Dominions in North America with the Roads, Distances, Limits and Extent of the Settlements* is one of the most important cartographic publications of the eighteenth century.[65] *(fig. 19)* He depicted the boundaries as established by the original charters for each colony, thereby arguing that the English claims overrode current French encroachments beyond the mountains.

The outbreak of war generated the need for other significant works. Emanuel Bowen and John Gibson created an oversize wall map called *An Accurate Map of North America describing and distinguishing the British, Spanish and French Dominions on this great Continent; exhibiting the Present Seat of War and the French Encroachments in 1755.*[66] Since this map was drafted while Bowen was serving as geographer to George II, he probably had access to the same reports and surveys that were available to Mitchell. Bowen and Gibson's geography of the area in dispute with the French is similar—but not identical to—Mitchell's.

In Philadelphia, Lewis Evans made *A general Map of the Middle British Colonies. In America; Viz Virginia, Màriland, Dèlaware, Pensilvania, New-Jersey, New York, Connecticut, and*

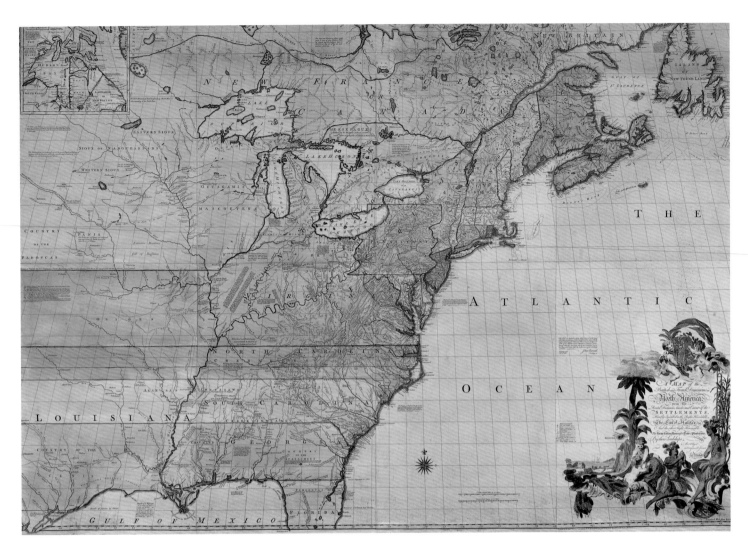

19. *A Map of the British and French Dominions in North America,*
by John Mitchell, London, 1755,
black-and-white line engraving
with period color.
1955-407. (Cat. 33)

Rhode Island, 1755 for the same reasons. *(fig. 20)* Along with his map, Evans published a pamphlet in which he gave credit to the sources he consulted—Fry and Jefferson for Virginia, the Reverend Thomas Clap for Connecticut, and William Douglass and Thomas Pownall for additional information on that colony.[67] However, much of the geography on Evans's map came from his own explorations of Pennsylvania, New Jersey, and New York, which he had begun to survey as early as 1737. He also gleaned substantial information about the frontier from Indian traders whom he met while traveling. Because Evans's work used firsthand knowledge to show the relationship of the Middle Atlantic colonies to the Ohio Valley, it was the most accurate English map of the region.

Thomas Jefferys was the most prolific cartographer and publisher of maps of America at the time of the French

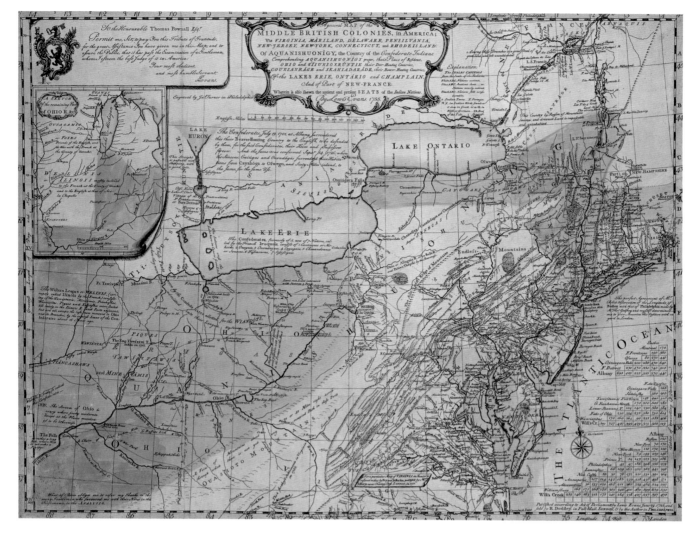

20. *A general Map of the Middle British Colonies in America,* by Lewis Evans, Philadelphia, 1755,
black-and-white line engraving with period color. 1968-122. (Cat. 34)

and Indian War, 1756–1763, the American phase of the global conflict known as the Seven Years' War. In 1754, Jefferys published *The Conduct of the French with Regard to Nova Scotia,* which strongly disputed French claims in North America. Despite his Francophobe leanings, Jefferys also sold maps of America by French cartographers. In the very year that Jefferys published his polemical anti-French views, he imported an assortment of maps, charts, and plans from French geographers.[68]

As noted by historian J. B. Harley, it is evident that American maps dominated Jefferys's interest. In the inventory of the stock advertised in his catalog of 1763, Jefferys listed fifty-five American maps ahead of maps of Europe, Africa, England, Scotland, and Ireland. The Board of Trade paid Jefferys regularly for engraving new maps and purchased many from his inventory.[69] He received

commissions from them to produce Fry and Jefferson's *A Map of the most Inhabited part of Virginia,* William Gerard De Brahm's *A Map of South Carolina and a Part of Georgia* (Cat. 37), and Captain Samuel Holland's *The Provinces of New York and New Jersey; with part of Pensilvania, and the Province of Quebec. (fig. 21)*

The French actively participated in the cartographic struggle to document and claim territory in North America as well. Among the numerous French maps published in 1755 were Jean Nicholas Bellin's *Partie Occidentale de la Nouvelle France ou Canada* and Jean Baptiste D'Anville's large-scale wall map of *Canada Louisiane et Terres Angloises.* Although it is apparent that D'Anville had access to some of the same surveys available to Mitchell, D'Anville added more details to the French areas of the Mississippi Valley and included an inset view of the Saint Lawrence River

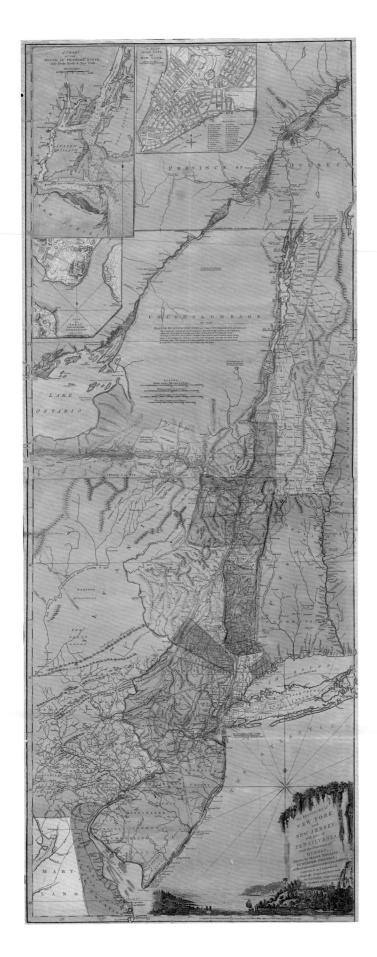

based on the latest French reports. In addition, he located all of the French forts in the Ohio Valley, including Fort Duquesne.[70]

The establishment of the Ohio Company in 1750 had naturally caused the French great concern. In 1752, the Marquis Duquesne arrived in Quebec to assume the position of governor-general of New France with instructions to take possession of the Ohio Valley. The marquis oversaw the construction of Presque Isle and Fort Le Boeuf, the present sites of Erie and Waterford, Pennsylvania, respectively. Upon learning that the French had erected forts within the territorial limits granted in their charter, Governor Robert Dinwiddie of Virginia dispatched twenty-one-year-old Major George Washington to the Ohio to demand the peaceable withdrawal of French troops. When he returned to Williamsburg, Washington reported that the French had no intention of abandoning their positions.[71] *(fig. 22)*

At the request of Governor Dinwiddie, the House of Burgesses quickly enacted legislation appropriating ten thousand pounds for equipment and troops to build a fort at the fork of the Ohio at the Allegheny and Monongahela Rivers (Pittsburgh today) and to advance westward toward the French. In February 1754, Virginians began to build Fort Prince George at the site Washington selected on the Ohio River. Two months later, well-armed French troops arrived at the partially constructed fort and forced

21. *The Provinces of New York and New Jersey; with part of Pensilvania, and the Province of Quebec,* by Captain Samuel Holland, London, August 17, 1776, black-and-white line engraving with period color. 1988-23.

22. Manuscript map drawn by George Washington during the campaign of 1753–1754, which he sent to Governor Dinwiddie, Virginia, pen and ink. Washington noted, "The French are now coming from their Forts on Lake Erie & on the Creek, to Venango to Erect another Fort— And from thence they design to the Fork's of Monongehele and to the Logs Town, and so to continue down the River building at the most convenient places in order to prevent our settlements &c. N. S. A Little below Shanapins Town in the Fork is the place where we are going immediately to Build a Fort as it commands the Ohio and Monongehele." Courtesy, Public Record Office, London, MPG1/118.

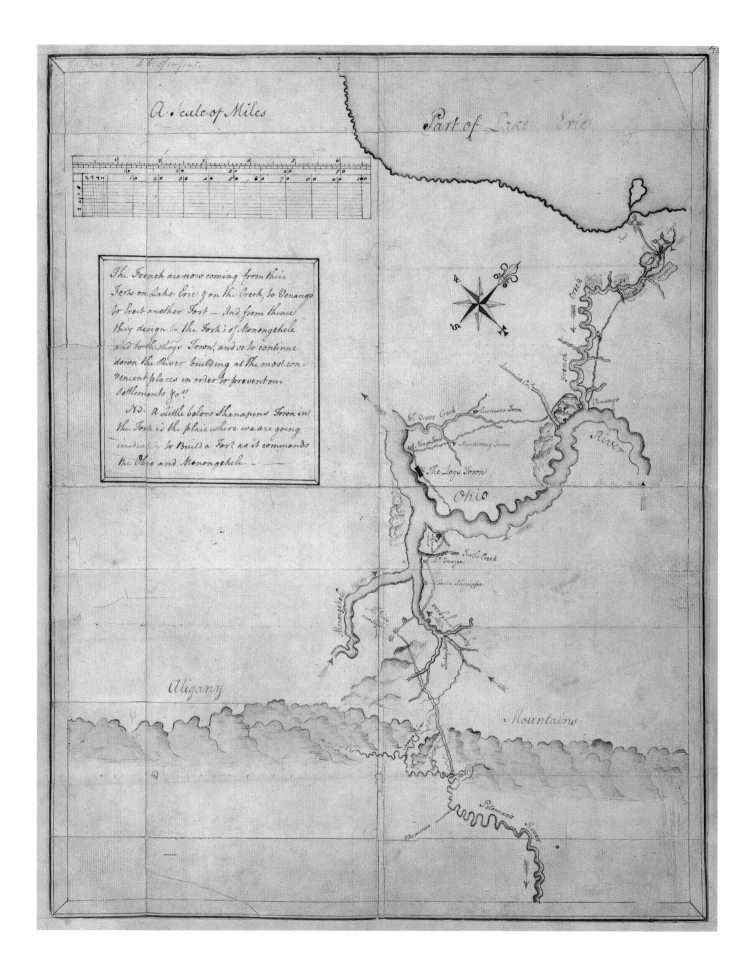

the Virginians to surrender it. The French finished constructing the fort, which they renamed Fort Duquesne. At the time, Washington and his troops were encamped at Great Meadows, about sixty-five miles southwest of the forks of the Ohio. Having received word that French troops in the vicinity of Great Meadows were planning to attack, Washington advanced. After a brief confrontation, several French soldiers, including Commander Joseph Coulon de Villiers de Jumonville, were brutally murdered by Washington's Indian allies under the leadership of Iroquois chief Tanaghrisson.[72]

Anticipating French retaliation, Washington started to erect Fort Necessity at Great Meadows. On July 3, 1754, 700 French soldiers and 350 Indians from Fort Duquesne attacked Fort Necessity. Upon surrendering, Washington was forced to sign articles of capitulation. Article seven stated:

> Since the English have in their power an officer and two cadets, and, in general, all the prisoners whom they took when they assassinated Sieur de Jumonville they now promise to send them with an escort to Fort Duquesne, situated on Belle River, and to secure the safe performance of this treaty article, as well as of the treaty Messrs. Jacob Van Braam and Robert Stobo, both Captains shall be delivered to us as hostages until the arrival of our French and Canadians herein before mentioned.[73]

As a result of this provision, British Captains Jacob Van Braam and Robert Stobo were taken as captives to Fort Duquesne. During his imprisonment, Stobo studied the layout of the fort in minute detail. His notes and a sketch that suggest how the English could attempt to recapture the fort were smuggled to British headquarters by a friendly Indian. Stobo's *Plan of Fort Le Quesne* was engraved and published in London, first by J. Payne in 1755, and again in 1768 by Robert Sayer and Thomas Jefferys.[74] *(fig. 23)*

Shortly after the capture of Fort Necessity and news of the articles of capitulation reached London, Parliament voted to send additional troops to America. In February 1755, Major General Edward Braddock was posted to North America as commander and chief of the British forces there. Not long after he arrived, Braddock met with the colonial governors in Alexandria, Virginia, to announce plans for three major campaigns to capture Forts Duquesne, Niagara, and Frederick. Equipped with intelligence from Stobo, Braddock was to lead the attack on Fort Duquesne himself. Through information from Indian scouts, the French were made aware of Braddock's advance and ambushed his troops ten miles east of Fort Duquesne. The British troops suffered a bitter defeat, and Braddock died from wounds he received in the battle. One month later, the decision was made to postpone the second phase of Braddock's plan, the attack on Fort Niagara, until the following year.

Colonel William Johnston, Indian agent for New York, led the third phase of the campaign, the expedition to Fort Frederick on Lake Champlain. Forewarned, the French attacked the British en route. Johnston rallied and repositioned his men, ultimately forcing the enemy to retreat. *A Prospective Plan of the Battle fought near Lake George on the 8th of September 1755* published in Boston later that year illustrates the unsuccessful tactics of the French military. It is the first print published on these shores depicting a North American battle. *(fig. 24)* Compiled by Samuel Blodget, it was accompanied by an explanatory pamphlet containing "a full, tho' short, History of that Affair. By Samuel Blodget, occasionally at the Camp when the Battle was fought."[75]

The war in America concluded in 1759 with the French defeat at Quebec. By the Treaty of Paris, 1763, Great Britain acquired all of Canada and the lands east of the Mississippi River. Britain also acquired Florida from the Spanish. In 1764, the Privy Council recommended to George III that new surveys be obtained for the recently acquired lands:

> We find ourselves under the greatest difficulties arising from the want of exact Surveys of those Countries, many parts of which have never been surveyed at all, and others so imperfectly that the Charts and Maps thereof are not to be depended upon, and, in this situation, we are reduced to the necessity of making Representations to Your Majesty, founded upon little or no Information.[76]

The Privy Council proposed that North America be divided into two parts, a northern and a southern district, with a surveyor general appointed for each area. Captain Samuel Holland, a Dutch military engineer who had served in a unit of Royal Americans during the French and Indian War, was appointed to the northern post; William Gerard De Brahm, a German military engineer under Emperor Charles VII, to the southern. Their initial task was to supply updated charts of the American coast from Canada to the West Indies. Fortunately, many of the engineers who had come to America during the French and Indian War stayed and continued to produce surveys helpful to Holland and De Brahm. Bernard Romans, De Brahm's deputy surveyor general, produced a chart of the

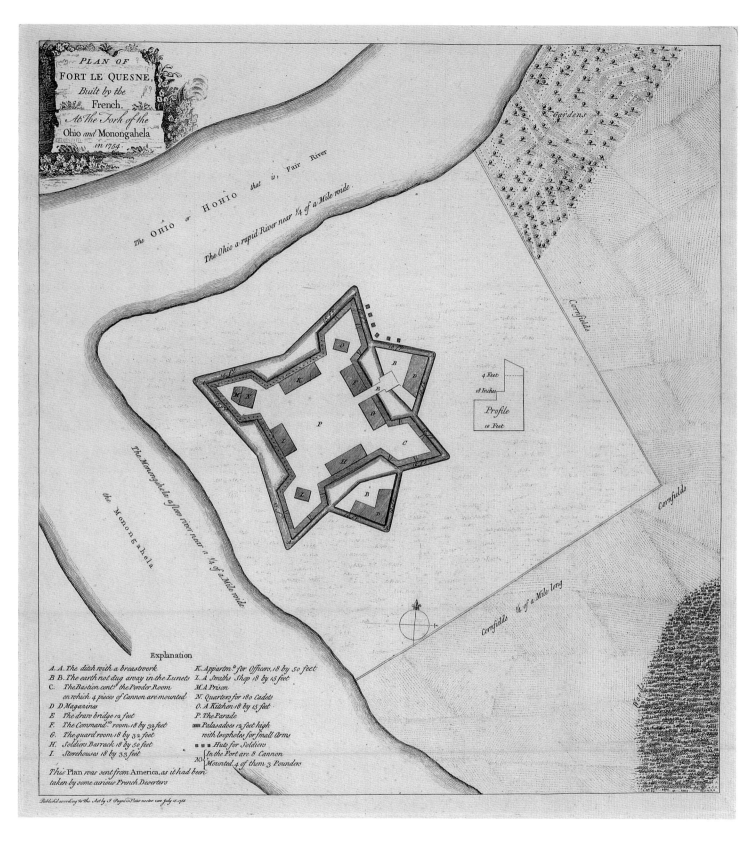

PLAN OF
FORT LE QUESNE,
Built by the
French,
At The Fork of the
Ohio and Monongahela
in 1754.

The OHIO or HOHIO that is Fair River

The Ohio a rapid River near ¼ of a Mile wide

Gardens

Cornfields

The Monongahela a slow river near a ¼ of a Mile wide

the Monongahela

4 Feet
18 Inches
Profile
10 Feet

Cornfields

Cornfields ¼ of a Mile long

Woods

Explanation

A. A. The ditch with a breastwork
B B. The earth not dug away in the Lunets
C.   The Bastion cont.ʳ the Powder Room
     on which 4 pieces of Cannon are mounted
D D Magazines
E   The draw bridge 12 feet
F. The Command.ᵗˢ room 18 by 32 feet
G. The guard room 18 by 32 feet
H. Soldiers Barrack 18 by 50 feet
I.   Storehouses 18 by 33 feet

K. Appartm.ᵗˢ for Officers 18 by 50 feet
L. A Smiths Shop 18 by 15 feet
M. A Prison
N. Quarters for 180 Cadets
O. A Kitchen 18 by 15 feet
P. The Parade
▄▄▄ Palasadoes 12 feet high
     with loopholes for small Arms
▪▪▪ Huts for Soldiers
N³ { In the Fort are 8 Cannon
    { Mounted 4 of them 3 Pounders

This Plan was sent from America, as it had been
taken by some curious French Deserters

Publish'd according to the Act by I. Payne in Pater noster row July 16: 1755.

23. *Plan of Fort Le Quesne, Built by the French, At the Fork of the Ohio and Monongahela in 1754,*
by Captain Robert Stobo, London, 1755, black-and-white line engraving. 1985-74. (Cat. 29)

Florida peninsula. Military engineers John Montresor and Bernard Ratzer, both recruited by the British to serve in America during the French and Indian War, provided useful information for the surveyor generals. In the years between the French and Indian War and the Revolutionary War, substantial topographical improvements were made over earlier surveys, and roads and passages on the frontier were newly illustrated.

An impressive number of maps were issued on the eve of the American Revolution. In 1768, Thomas Jefferys and London print- and mapseller Robert Sayer produced *A General Topography of North America and the West Indies*, a monumental volume containing 100 maps on 109 sheets. Many of the maps were later included in *The American Atlas: or, a Geographical Description of the Whole Continent of America . . . By The Late Mr. Thomas Jefferys, Geographer to the King, and Others*, published by Robert Sayer and John Bennett in 1776, five years after Jefferys's death. *The American Atlas* consisted in large measure of updated states of Jeffreys's important maps. The following year 1777, the partners produced the two-volume *North American Pilot*, once again composed mostly of earlier maps originally produced by Thomas Jefferys. The first volume contained maps of Newfoundland, Labrador, and the Saint Lawrence; the second, charts of the coasts of New York, New England, Pennsylvania, Maryland, Virginia, the two Carolinas, and Florida. Sayer and Bennett also sold the useful *American Military Pocket Atlas; being an approved Collection of Correct Maps, both General and Particular, of the British Colonies; Especially those which now are, or probably may be The Theatre of War*, published in 1776. The maps in this work were folded and bound in an octavo volume so that they could easily be transported in the field. It is commonly referred to as the "holster atlas."

Because the British Admiralty needed reliable navigational charts for the Atlantic Coast, they commissioned Joseph Frederick Wallet Des Barres, who had worked closely with Samuel Holland and Captain James Cook during the French and Indian War, to conduct extensive nautical surveys. From 1763 to 1774, Des Barres surveyed the coasts of Nova Scotia, Sable Island, and New Brunswick. He carefully depicted the beaches, fields, and markers along the shoreline and produced soundings for harbors and channels far superior to those on previous charts. In 1774, Des Barres returned to England and began to compile his work into a marine atlas. To supplement his own charts, he compiled, edited, and adapted the surveys of others such as Holland and Cook. *The Atlantic Neptune* ultimately became a valuable resource for the royal navy during the final months of the Revolution.[77]

To pay the debts incurred by the Seven Years' War, including the cost of commissioning maps of newly acquired territories, the British imposed a stamp act on the thirteen colonies. News of the passage of the Stamp Act reached America by mid-April 1765. As irritating as the tax itself was, Parliament's refusal to hear any of the colonies' petitions against the bill generated tremendous resentment. The colonial legislatures maintained that they alone should have the right to levy their own taxes. Parliament's disregard of the protests prompted a response in the Virginia House of Burgesses. Under the leadership of Patrick Henry, several burgesses drafted a list of resolves reiterating the position they had taken in the petitions. Although the burgesses passed only the mildest four of Henry's seven resolutions, newspapers in other colonies reported that the Virginia Assembly had approved all seven. This led to the belief that Virginians' sentiments against taxation without representation were stronger than those that probably existed.[78]

Equally distasteful was the Quartering Act that forced colonials to house British troops, especially in New York, headquarters of the British army in America. There, the level of indignation toward the troops and the British government was so high that Commander in Chief General Thomas Gage ordered his most experienced engineer, John Montresor, to produce a new map of the city in anticipation of future confrontations. Montresor's map was important because it showed a detailed layout of Manhattan and depicted for the first time the area beyond the city. *A Plan of the City of New-York & its Environs* was published in 1767. *(fig. 25)*

Although Parliament repealed the Stamp Act in 1767, it enacted the Townshend Duties that placed duties on tea, paper, lead, and paint imported into the colonies. This measure caused the New England colonies to draw up nonimportation agreements that were eventually adopted in some of the southern colonies as well. These voluntary

24. Detail from *A Prospective Plan of the Battle fought near Lake George*, by Samuel Blodget, Boston, 1755, black-and-white line engraving. 1984-44. (Cat. 32) The plan illustrated the military strategy of the French troops. They formed into three straight lines. The first row fired and then moved to the rear, followed by the subsequent rows, advancing slowly each time.

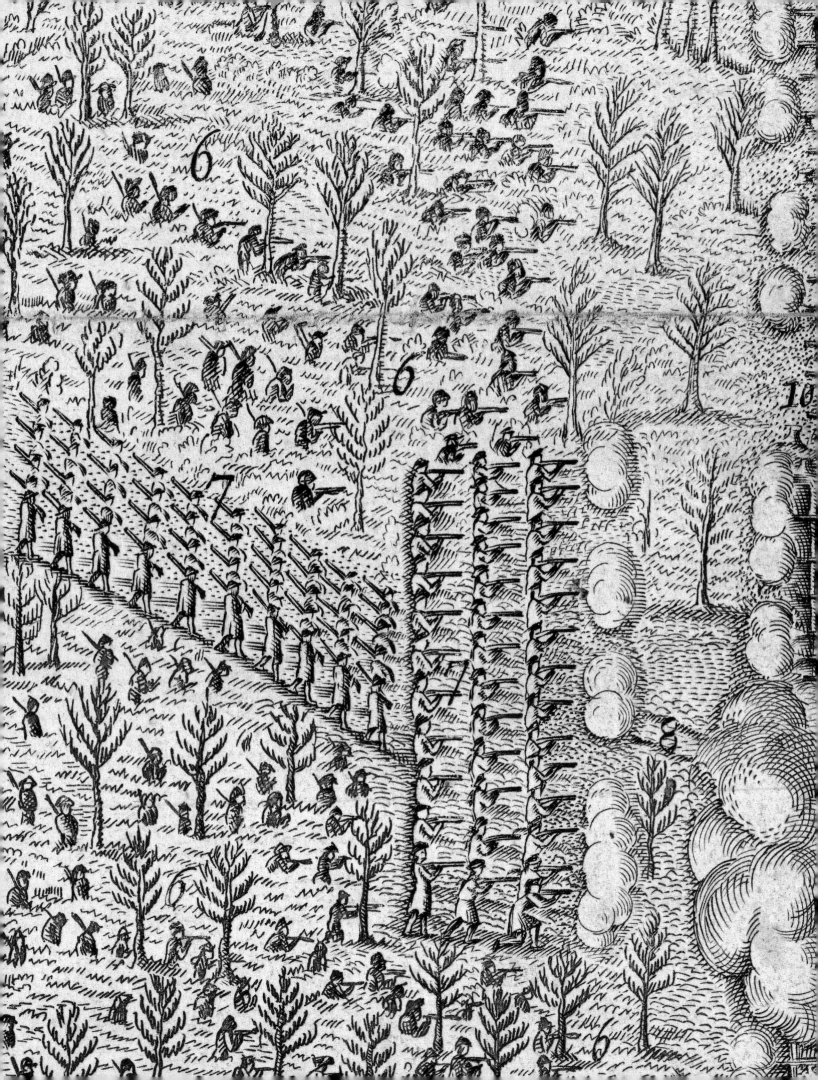

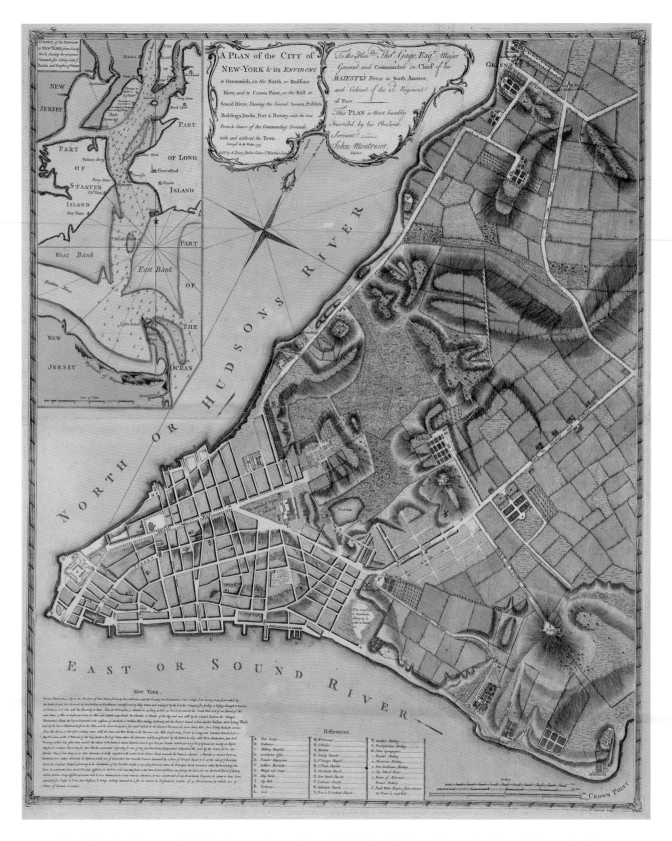

25. *A Plan of the City of New-York & its Environs to Greenwich, on the North or Hudsons River, and to Crown Point, on the East or Sound River, Shewing the Several Streets, Publick Buildings, Docks, Fort & Battery, with the true Form & Course of the Commanding Grounds, with and without the Town,* by John Montresor, London, 1767 (this copy reissued in 1775), black-and-white line engraving with period color. 1974-56.

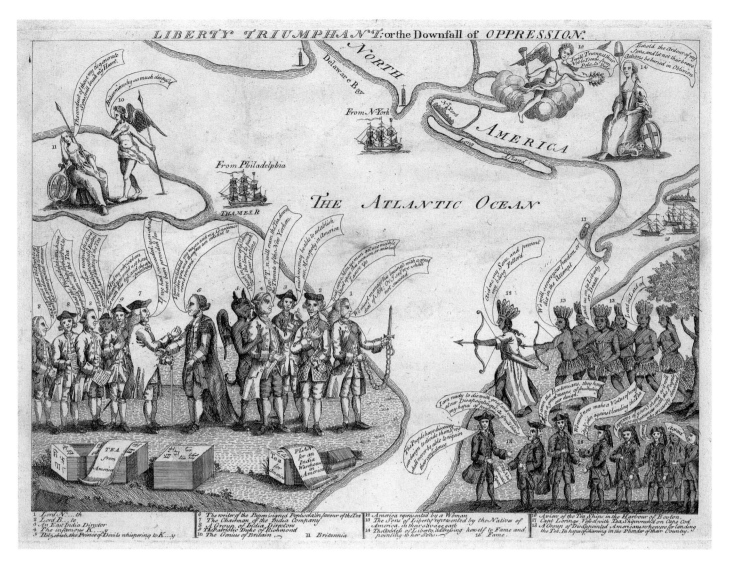

26. *Liberty Triumphant; or the Downfall of Oppression,* London, ca. 1774, black-and-white etching and engraving. 1960-44. The action in this political satire takes place on a map. England is pictured on the left; America on the right. The tories in England are lamenting the loss of income resulting from the American boycott of English goods.

agreements were intended to restrict the importation of English goods, primarily luxury items and those taxed under the Townshend Duties. *(fig. 26)* In 1770, Prime Minister Lord North repealed all of the Townshend Duties except for the one on tea. However, resentment and violence, particularly in New England, had escalated to the point where the British government found it necessary to reinforce the troops stationed there.

Shortly after reinforcements arrived in Boston, an angry mob of colonists gathered outside the customhouse and began to taunt a British sentry on duty. The incident was clearly initiated by the Americans. The situation escalated, and shots rang out. Five colonials were killed. Only twenty-three days after the confrontation, Paul Revere

produced *The Bloody Massacre perpetrated in King Street Boston. (fig. 27)* The print is inaccurate since it shows a line of British soldiers firing on the Americans. However incorrect, Revere's striking image became a strong anti-British propaganda tool.

Parliament passed the Tea Act in 1773 that effectively undercut the price of tea sold in America. The outraged Bostonians threw 342 chests of East India Tea Company tea into the harbor, and the British government responded by closing the port of Boston to all shipping and enacting a series of restrictive measures called the Coercive Acts, or, as the colonists referred to them, the Intolerable Acts. Representatives from each colony met in the first Continental Congress at Philadelphia where they formally

The BLOODY MASSACRE perpetrated in King—Street BOSTON on March 5th 1770 by a party of the 29th REGT.

Engrav'd Printed & Sold by Paul Revere Boston

Unhappy Boston! see thy Sons deplore,
Thy hallow'd Walks besmear'd with guiltless Gore:
While faithless P—n and his savage Bands,
With murd'rous Rancour stretch their bloody Hands;
Like fierce Barbarians grinning o'er their Prey,
Approve the Carnage, and enjoy the Day.

If scalding drops from Rage from Anguish Wrung,
If speechless Sorrows lab'ring for a Tongue,
Or if a weeping World can ought appease
The plaintive Ghosts of Victims such as these;
The Patriot's copious Tears for each are shed,
A glorious Tribute which embalms the Dead.

But know, Fate summons to that awful Goal,
Where Justice strips the Murd'rer of his Soul:
Should venal C—ts the scandal of the Land,
Snatch the relentless Villain from her Hand.
Keen Execrations on this Plate inscrib'd,
Shall reach a Judge who never can be brib'd.

The unhappy Sufferers were Messrs. Saml. Gray, Saml. Maverick, Jams. Caldwell, Crispus Attucks & Patk. Carr
Killed. Six wounded two of them (Christr. Monk & John Clark) Mortally

27. *The Bloody Massacre perpetuated in King Street Boston,* engraved by Paul Revere after a drawing by Henry Pelham, Boston, 1770, black-and-white line engraving with period color. 1966-1.

28. Detail from *A Plan of the Town and Harbour of Boston,* by John De Costa, London, 1775, black-and-white line engraving with period color. 1963-730. (Cat. 51)

resolved not to import or consume goods from Great Britain.

By spring 1775, patriots in Massachusetts had begun to stockpile arms and ammunition. General Gage was ordered to take precautionary measures. On April 19, he dispatched troops to Concord to confiscate powder belonging to the Massachusetts Continental Congress. Aware of the mission, Boston patriots sent Paul Revere and William Dawes to Lexington to alert the militia there. After a confrontation at Lexington during which eight Americans were killed and another ten wounded, the British troops continued to march to Concord. Having been warned, the patriots thwarted British strategy by

hiding most of their arsenal. The Regulars achieved little militarily, but succeeded in further inciting the angry residents of Massachusetts. As the British proceeded back to Boston, the militia, hiding behind trees and fences, attacked from all sides. *A Plan of the Town and Harbour of Boston* was the first printed map to depict the skirmishes at Lexington and Concord. *(fig. 28)* The battle—and thus the map—was more important for its psychological effect than for its military significance.[79]

While the previous map of the engagements at Lexington and Concord was produced for the public, *A Plan of the Action at Bunkers Hill* was published in England in 1775 by William Faden as a formal document of the battle between

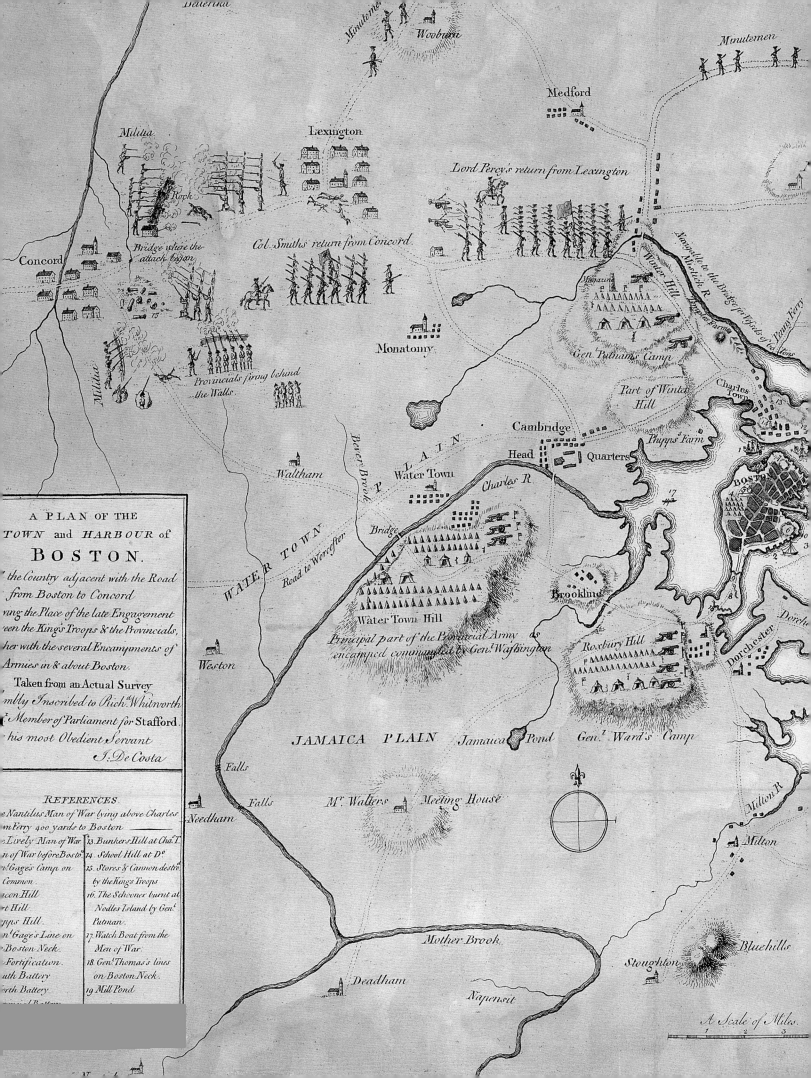

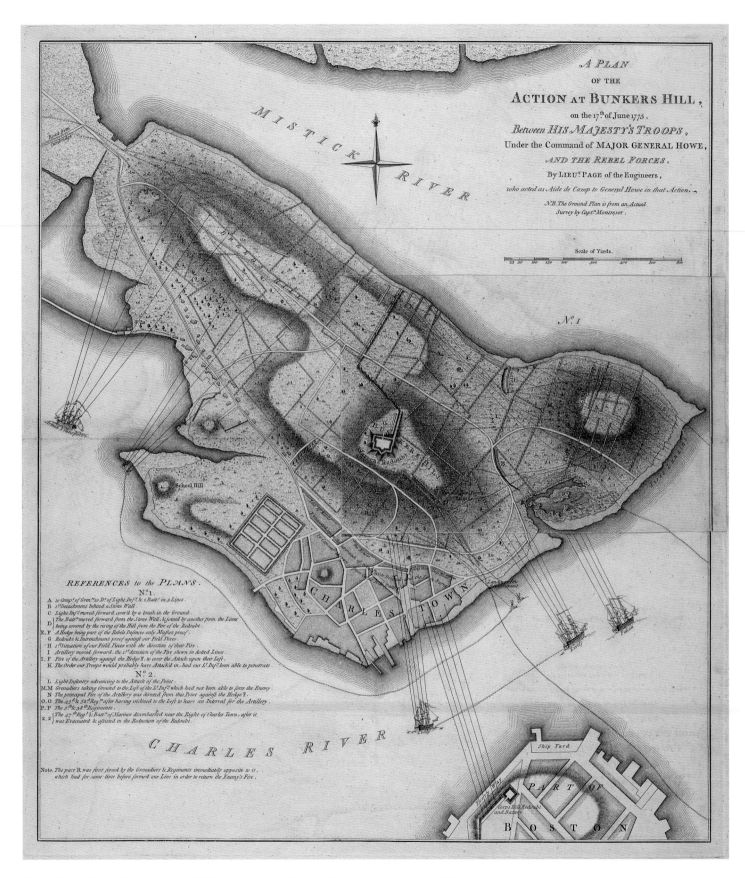

29. *A Plan of the Action at Bunkers Hill,* by Lieutenant. Thomas Hyde Page, London, 1775, black-and-white line engraving with period color. 1989-36. (Cat. 52)

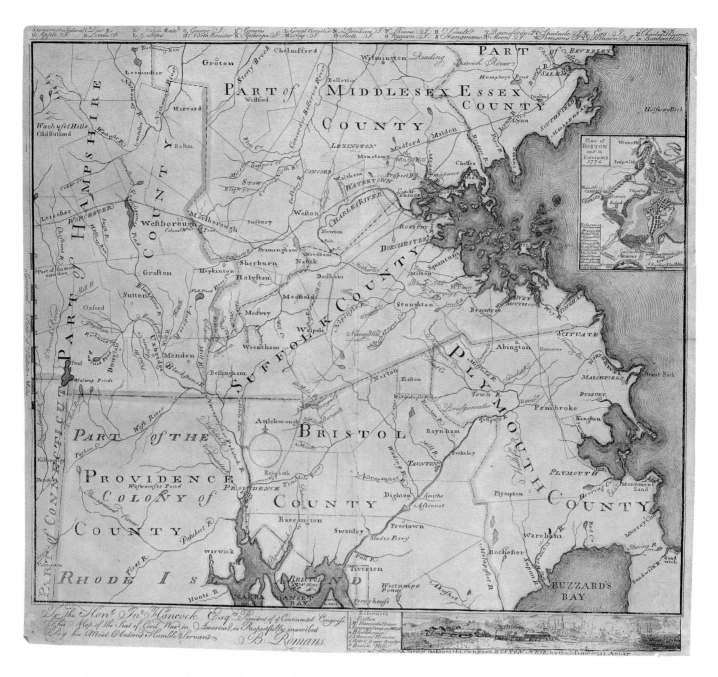

30. *Map of the Seat of Civil War in America*, by Bernard Romans, probably Philadelphia, 1775, black-and-white line engraving with period color. 1996-824. (Cat. 53)

the English and Americans that took place on June 17, 1775.[80] *(fig. 29)* Popularly known as the Battle of Bunker Hill, the conflict actually took place on Breed's Hill, depicted here and on other maps as Bunker Hill. The incorrectly named Breed's Hill is to the northwest of the site also incorrectly identified as Bunker Hill.

Bernard Romans soon published the *Map of the Seat of Civil War in America,* 1775, the first map published in America that related to the Revolutionary War.[81] *(fig. 30)* It, too, illustrated troop movements and positions around Boston and Charlestown. Advertisements and an accompanying view, also by Romans, appeared in the *Virginia* and *Pennsylvania Gazette*s, among other papers. The propaganda overtones are particularly apparent in the September 1775 advertisement from the *New York Gazette*:

> *This map of* Boston, *etc. is one of the most correct that has ever been published. The draught was taken by the most skilful Draughtsman in all America, and who was on the spot at the engagements of Lexington and Bunker's Hill.*

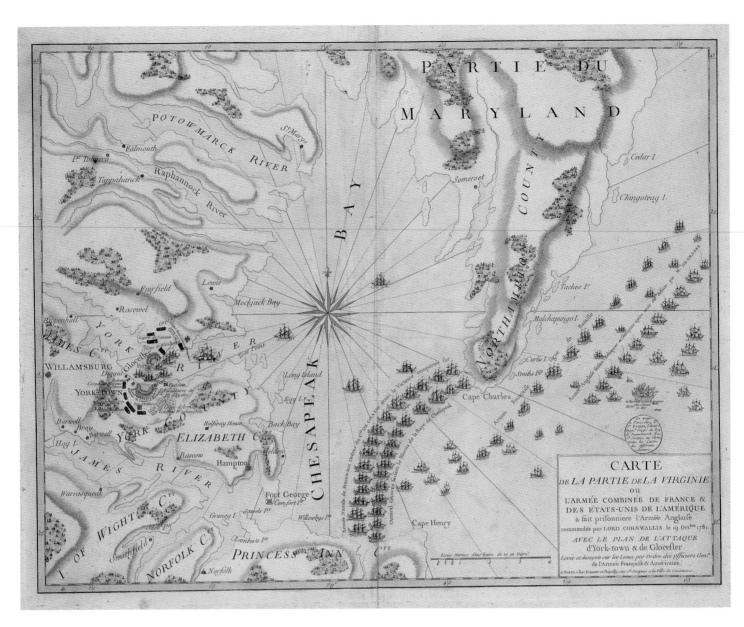

31. *Carte de la Partie de la Virginie ou L'Armée Combinée de France & Des États-Unis de l'Amérique a fait prisonniere l' Armée Anglaise*, by Esnauts and Rapilly Paris, ca. 1782, black-and-white line engraving with period color. 1974-164. (Cat. 65)

Every Well-wisher to this country cannot but delight in see-ing a plan of the ground on which our brave American Army conquered the British ministerial forces. Price plain 5s. Coloured, 6s and 6d.[82]

The French also produced military maps during the war years. In 1778, George Louis Le Rouge published *Atlas Americain septentrional* containing about twenty-five French versions of maps originally published by Thomas Jefferys. Le Rouge also published *Pilote Americain septentrional* in which some of the most interesting maps depict events during the Yorktown campaign.

Carte de la Partie de la Virginie ou L'Armèe Combinèe de France & L'Armée Combinèe de France & Des États-Unis de L'Amérique, ca. 1782 illustrated the land troops under Washington, Lafayette, and Rochambeau and the French blockade at the mouth of the Chesapeake Bay.[83] *(fig. 31)* The British army under General Cornwallis was entrenched at Yorktown. Mean-while, twenty-eight French ships under the command of

32. *Plan of the investment of York and Gloucester*, by Sebastian Bauman, Philadelphia, 1782, black-and-white line engraving. 1950-769. (Cat. 68)

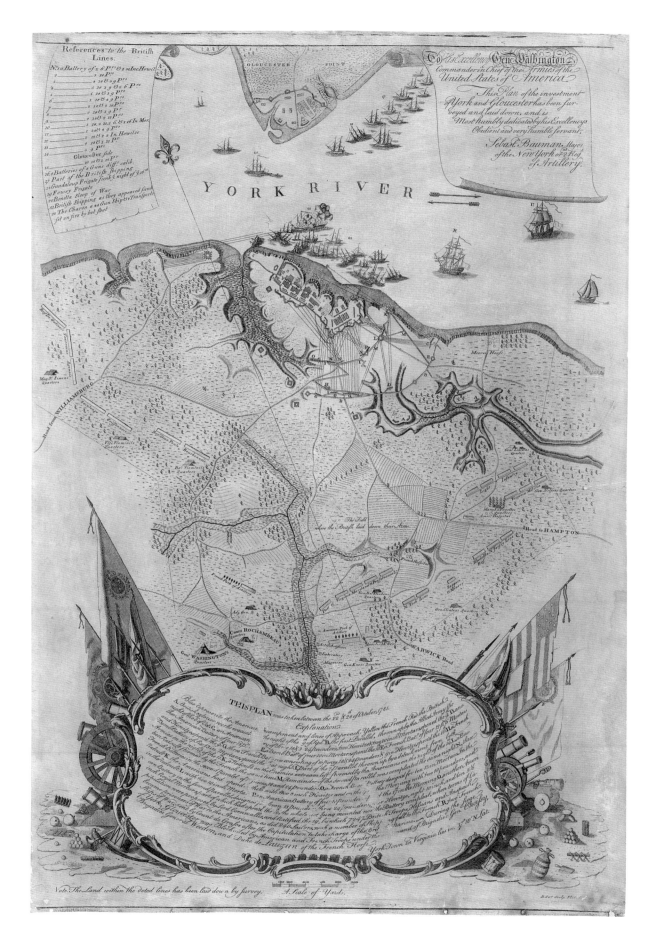

François Joseph Paul, Comte de Grasse, anchored at the entrance to the bay to await the British navy. The French fleet had been positioned for more than a week when the British arrived under the command of Rear Admiral Thomas Graves. While the two forces were skirmishing at sea, a second well-armed French fleet under the command of the Comte de Barras arrived. Suffering heavy losses, the British fleet was forced to withdraw, leaving Cornwallis surrounded on both land and sea.[84]

Compiled by Sebastian Bauman, an American version of the surrender, the *Plan of the investment of York and Gloucester,* was engraved and published in Philadelphia in 1782.[85] *(fig. 32)* A topographical engineer, Bauman fought in the Seven Years' War and served under General Washington during the entire Revolution, fighting in New York, New Jersey, and Pennsylvania before going to Yorktown. Immediately after the battle, Bauman surveyed the positions of the opposing troops and consequently produced the only American survey that illustrated the final battle of the Revolution.

As a result of the Treaty of Paris that ended the Revolutionary War, 1783, the United States acquired all of the land between the Allegheny Mountains and the Mississippi River which resulted in substantial westward migration. Surveys were begun in 1786 in the region west of the Ohio River. The terms of the treaty also established boundary lines between the United States and Canada and set the borders with Spanish holdings in Florida and Louisiana. Three new states were added to the nation in the 1790s: Vermont (1791), Kentucky (1792), and Tennessee (1796). In the Louisiana Purchase of 1803, the United States acquired from France all the land between the Mississippi River and the Rocky Mountains. Five new states were created out of the Northwest Territory: Ohio (1803), Indiana (1816), Illinois (1818), Michigan (1837), and Wisconsin (1848). The need for maps was clear. Initially, however, most new maps of the United States, wherever produced, were revised, updated versions of maps made between 1755 and 1783.

Once the United States gained its independence, a system for mapping the individual states had to be developed. Whereas formerly most maps of America had been engraved, printed, and published in England and France, after 1783, the entire process and expense of creating new maps shifted to this side of the Atlantic.

In 1785, Congress established the General Land Office. All public lands surveyed prior to settlement were to be divided into retangular units one mile square, which in turn were subdivided into sections and quarter-sections. The vast western territories of the United States were laid out under this system in the nineteenth century. At first, few state governments were able to fund the survey and publication of maps of their counties and boundaries, so, with the exception of New York, the first individual state maps were privately compiled and published. By 1840, both government agencies and private companies were establishing ambitious mapping programs. While the accuracy of maps depicting the newly formed United States far exceeded that of the previous century, they lack much of the visual and psychological appeal of the early maps of America. After the European struggle for control of land, trade, and commerce in America ended, the primary motivation for recording territory in North America was eliminated. Once viewed as tangible evidence of the hopes and aspirations of foreign powers in America, today, these maps provide powerful tools for understanding the road to American Independence.

1. For a full description of this map, see Cat. 1.

2. Smith's map of *Virginia* was published in Capt. John Smith, *A Map of Virginia. with a Description of the Countrey, the Commodities, People, Government and Religion* (Oxford, 1612), Capt. John Smith, *The Generall Historie of Virginia, New-England, and the Summer Isles* (London, 1624), and Samuel Purchas, *Purchas his Pilgrimes* (London, 1613). For a full description of Smith's map of *Virginia,* see Cat 5. On a return visit to America in 1614, Smith surveyed the New England coastline. See Cat. 6.

3. Coolie Verner, "Smith's *Virginia* and its Derivatives: A Carto-Bibliographical Study of the Diffusion of Geographical Knowledge," in R. V. Tooley, comp., *The Mapping of America* (London, 1980), p. 171.

4. For a full description of this map, see Cat. 8.

5. Virginia was made a royal colony in 1624. In 1691, William and Mary granted a new charter combining Plymouth and Massachusetts Bay into one colony. Massachusetts continued to have corporate status until the Revolutionary War.

6. Carolina remained a proprietary colony until 1730, Maryland until the Revolution.

7. New Jersey remained a proprietary colony until 1702. New York was made a royal colony when the Duke of York succeeded to the throne as James II. Maryland, Delaware, and Pennsylvania remained proprietary colonies until the Revolution.

8. In colonies governed by the crown, much of this money was used for building and maintaining roads and public buildings. Proprietary colonies also attempted to entice settlers by offering some form of the headright and quitrent systems.

9. Edward T. Price, *Dividing the Land: Early American Beginnings of Our Private Property Mosaic* (Chicago, 1995), p. 99.

10. Russell R. Menard and Lois Green Carr, "The Lords Baltimore and the Colonization of Maryland," in David B. Quinn, ed., *Early Maryland in a Wider World* (Detroit, Mich., 1982), pp. 177, 189.

11. In an unpublished study of colonial patents in Caroline County, Va., Henry Taliaferro shows that the time elapsed between taking up tracts of land along the Rappahannock River and those immediately inland on the ridge that separates the Rappahannock watershed from that of the Mattaponi was as much as 50 years.

12. For a full description of this map, see Cat. 12.

13. Warren M. Billings, John E. Selby, and Thad W. Tate, *Colonial Virginia: A History* (White Plains, N. Y., 1986), pp. 134–135, provides a good description of how headrights gave rise to a plantation system in Virginia and explains the detrimental effects it had on the development of the colony.

14. "Proposals in Regard to Virginia," *Virginia Magazine of History and Biography,* XXV (1917), p. 71. A slightly different version of the proposals is in John W. Reps, *Tidewater Towns: City Planning in Colonial Virginia and Maryland* (Williamsburg, Va., 1972), p. 65.

15. For an excellent account of the town acts of Virginia and Maryland, see Reps, *Tidewater Towns,* chaps. 4 and 5.

16. Henry Hartwell, James Blair, and Edward Chilton, *The Present State of Virginia, and the College,* ed. Hunter Dickinson Farish (Williamsburg, Va., 1940), p. 5.

17. *A Brief Description of The Province of Carolina on the Coasts of Floreda,* 1666, facsimile with an introduction by John Tate Lanning (Charlottesville, Va., 1944), pp. 9–10. Also quoted in Hugh T. Lefler and William S. Powell, *Colonial North Carolina: A History* (New York, 1973), pp. 42–43.

18. William P. Cumming, *The Southeast in Early Maps,* rev. by Louis DeVorsey, Jr. (Chapel Hill, N. C., 1998), pl. 35, illustrates Locke's manuscript map. Locke was the author of the "Fundamental Constitutions," the autocratic legal system adopted by the Proprietors for the colony that created continual dissatisfaction for the Carolinians.

19. Price, *Dividing the Land,* p. 35.

20. Quoted in Peter Benes, *New England Prospect: A Loan Exhibition of Maps at the Currier Gallery of Art, Manchester, New Hampshire* (Boston, 1981), p. xx.

21. Price, *Dividing the Line,* pp. 38–39.

22. *Ibid.,* p. 61. As future generations divided land among themselves, smaller New England parcels became less commercially viable, forcing families to disperse at a more rapid rate than in the southern colonies.

23. Van Rensselaer was an Amsterdam diamond merchant whose grant covered much of present-day Albany, Columbia, and Rensselaer Counties.

24. Price, *Dividing the Land,* p. 217.

25. Sung Bok Kim, *Landlord and Tenant in Colonial New York: Manorial Society, 1664–1775* (Chapel Hill, N. C., 1978), pp. 27–43.

26. *Ibid.,* pp. 18–19.

27. *Ibid.,* p. 27.

28. Release from James, Duke of York, to John, Lord Berkeley, and Sir George Carteret, for New Jersey, in William A. Whitehead, ed., *Documents Relating to the Colonial History of the State of New Jersey.* I: *1631–1687* (Newark, N. J., 1880); John P. Snyder, *The Mapping of New Jersey: The Men and the Art* (New Brunswick, N. J., 1973), p. 14.

29. For a full description of this map, see Cat. 11.

30. Snyder, *Mapping of New Jersey,* pp. 14–15. Although several ways to resolve the dispute had been proposed by the mid-1750s, King George III did not appoint commissioners to settle the line until 1769.

31. *Ibid.,* pp. 22–23. Carteret died in 1682 and East Jersey was sold as well.

32. For a full discussion of this map, see Cat. 28.

33. For an accounting of all the costs involved in printing the bill, see George J. Miller, "The Printing of the Elizabethtown Bill in Chancery," in *Addresses Before the Board of Proprietors of the Eastern Division of New Jersey,* Pamphlet Series No. 1 (Perth Amboy, N. J., 1942), pp. 13–16.

34. Many of the first settlers in Philadelphia were artisans and shopkeepers, which promoted Philadelphia's extraordinary growth as a business and commercial center. John E. Pomfret, "The First Purchasers of Pennsylvania, 1681–1700," *Pennsylvania Magazine of History and Biography,* LXXX (1956), pp. 147, 154.

35. For a full description of the Holme map, see Custis Atlas Cat. 71.

36. For maps regarding the Penn and Lord Baltimore boundary disputes, see Cats. 11 and 23.

37. Charles M. Andrews, *British Committees, Commissions, and Councils of Trade and Plantations, 1622–1675,* reprint (New York, N. Y., 1970), p. 122, quoted in part in Jeannette D. Black, ed., *The Blathwayt Atlas.* II: *Commentary* (Providence, R. I., 1970), p. 9.

38. In 1668, Charles II replaced the Privy Council with the Council of Trade, and two years later also created the Council for Plantations. In 1672, these two groups merged as the Council for Trade and Plantations.

39. William Hand Browne, ed., *Archives of Maryland: Proceedings of the Council of Maryland, 1667–1687/8,* V (Baltimore, Md., 1887), p. 265. Quoted in part in Edward C. Papenfuse and Joseph M. Coale III, *The Hammond-Harwood House Atlas of Historical Maps of Maryland, 1608–1908* (Baltimore, Md., 1982), p. 18.

40. Jacob M. Price, *Perry of London: A Family and a Firm on the Seaborne Frontier, 1615–1753* (Cambridge, Mass., 1972), pp. 56–57, 77. See also Ali-

son G. Olson, "The Virginia Merchants of London: A Study in Eighteenth-Century Interest-Group Politics," *William and Mary Quarterly*, 3rd Ser., XL (1983), pp. 363–388.

41. During the early years of the eighteenth century, Perry's brother, Peter, was a merchant in York County, Va., and his nephew, Micajah Lowe, acted in the same capacity in Charles City Co., Va.

42. Not only were Byrd II and Custis linked with Perry and Lane in business as plantation owners, but as younger men, both worked for the firm, Custis in London and Byrd in Rotterdam.

43. Pierre Marambaud, *William Byrd of Westover, 1674–1744* (Charlottesville, Va., 1971), p. 16.

44. Marion Tinling, ed., *The Correspondence of the Three William Byrds of Westover, Virginia, 1684–1776*, I (Charlottesville, Va., 1977), p. 29. Micajah Perry had interests in the fur trade at several points between South Carolina and New York as well as in Virginia. Price, *Perry of London*, p. 47. See also W. Neil Franklin, "Virginia and the Cherokee Indian Trade, 1673–1752," *East Tennessee Historical Society's Publications* (1932), pp. 3–21.

45. For a full description of this map, see Cat. 16.

46. Fred Anderson, *Crucible of War: The Seven Years' War and the Fate of Empire in British North America, 1754–1766* (New York, 2000), p. 17.

47. Fairfax Harrison argued that Jones explored some of the northern territories. For a discussion of Cadwallader Jones's map, see Fairfax Harrison, *Landmarks of Old Prince William: A study of origins in Northern Virginia* (Berryville, Va., 1964), pp. 607–613.

48. Cadwallader Jones's essay is printed in full in Fairfax Harrison, "Western Explorations in Virginia Between Lederer and Spotswood," *VMHB*, XXX (1922), pp. 329–334, quote on p. 332.

49. Alexander Moore, ed., *Nairne's Muskhogean Journals: The 1708 Expedition to the Mississippi River* (Jackson, Miss., 1988), p. 76.

50. Nairne to Doctor Marston, Society for the Propagation of the Gospel in Foreign Parts, 1705, SPG MSS A, II, no. 156. Also quoted in Verner W. Crane, *The Southern Frontier, 1670–1732*, reprint (Ann Arbor, Mich., 1956), p. 110.

51. Pierre Margry, ed., *Découverte par Mer des Bouches du Mississipi et établissements de Lemoyne D'Iberville sur Le Golfe Du Mexique (1694–1703)* (Paris, 1880), Pt. 4, p. 4, of *Découvertes et établissements des Français dans l'ouest et dans le sud de l'Amérique septentrionale*. I wish to thank Bob Doares for his translation of the French letter.

52. The Iroquois Confederacy, or Five Nations, comprised the Cayuga, Mohawk, Onondaga, Oneida, and Seneca tribes. In 1720, they became the Six Nations when the Tuscaroras joined. They inhabited the North American Northeast. The Algonquian Indians inhabited Canada.

53. Anderson, *Crucible of War*, pp. 13–21.

54. For a full description of the events leading up to this excursion and the actual trip to London, see John G. Garratt, *The Four Indian Kings* (Ottawa, Can., 1985).

55. Billings, Selby, and Tate, *Colonial Virginia*, p. 183.

56. Much of the land in these two counties was taken up by favorites of the governor and other leading men of the colony, one further example of how the ruling Virginia elite dictated land distribution.

57. For a full discussion of this map, see Cat. 20.

58. Moll gave credit on his map to Blackmore, Berisford, and Nairne. For a full description of this map, see Cat. 21.

59. Herman Moll, *A New Map of the North parts of America claimed by France*.

60. Byrd II of Westover wrote to Charles Boyle, fourth Earl of Orrery, in 1719/20 mentioning an English report about the Mississippi. He noted, "The Indians are very numerous on the branches of this river, and if the French find means to gain them, it will render the English plantations very unsafe." ed., *Correspondence of the Three William Byrds*, I, p. 327.

61. *South Carolina Gazette* (Charleston), June 26, 1736.

62. *Journal of the Commissioners for Trade and Plantations from January 1749–1750 to December 1753 Preserved in the Public Record Office* (London, 1932), p. 89.

63. Joshua Fry was former professor of mathematics at the College of William and Mary and then surveyor of Albermarle Co., Va. Peter Jefferson was the father of Thomas Jefferson and a close acquaintance of Fry's. Together, they had previously surveyed the Virginia-North Carolina dividing line and the boundary dispute over a large land grant to Lord Fairfax in the Northern Neck of Virginia. For a full discussion of this map, see Cat. 30.

64. Leonard W. Labaree et al., eds., *The Papers of Benjamin Franklin* (New Haven, Conn., 1959–), IV, pp. 318–319. Peter Collinson, a Quaker naturalist and antiquary residing in London, enjoyed extensive correspondence with many Americans in the colonies. This letter is also cited in Edmund Berkeley and Dorothy Smith Berkeley, *Dr. John Mitchell: The Man Who Made the Map of North America* (Chapel Hill, N. C., 1974), p. 178. The map to which Collinson was referring probably was made by Lewis Evans at the request of the Pennsylvania General Assembly. This draft was sent to the Board of Trade in 1751. Hazel Shields Garrison, "Cartography of Pennyslvania Before 1800," *PMHB*, LIX (1935), p. 269.

65. For a full description of Mitchell's map, see Cat. 33.

66. For a description of a later version of the Bowen and Gibson map, see Cat. 36.

67. Lawrence Henry Gipson, *Lewis Evans* (Philadelphia, Pa., 1939), pp. 148–149. For a full description of this map, see Cat. 34.

68. In her analysis of the correspondence of the firm of Thomas Jefferys and William Faden, Mary Pedley noted that British and French publishers were continually importing each others' maps, both for resale and as a source for engraving new maps, even during the years when the two nations were at war. Mary Pedley, "Maps, War, and Commerce: Business Correspondence with the London Map Firm of Thomas Jefferys and William Faden," *Imago Mundi*, XLVIII (1996), p. 162.

69. J. B. Harley, "The bankruptcy of Thomas Jefferys: an episode in the economic history of eighteenth century map-making," *ibid.*, XX (1966), p. 35. Although Jefferys (engraver and geographer to the Prince of Wales, and, after George III's accession, to the king) was one of the most prominent mapmakers in London in the mid-eighteenth century, he declared bankruptcy in 1766. Harley concluded that the primary reason for Jefferys's financial difficulties was that he became involved in the production of a series of English county maps in 1765 that required original survey work. Jefferys's American maps relied on secondary sources, a much less costly investment.

70. For references to a number of maps of America published in France at this time, see the 1755 entry under George Louis Le Rouge in Woodbury Lowery, *The Lowery Collection: A Descriptive List of Maps of the Spanish Possessions within the Present Limits of the United States, 1502–1820*, ed. Philip Lee Phillips (Washington, D. C., 1912), pp. 310–311.

71. Washington's report on his trip to Ohio, *The Journal of Major George Washington Sent by the Hon. Robert Dinwiddie, Esq; His Majesty's Lieutenant-Governor, and Commander in Chief of Virginia, to the Commandant of the French Forces on Ohio*, was published in Williamsburg in 1754. Jefferys reprinted Washington's *Journal* in London that same year. The London edition contained a *Map of the Western parts of the Colony of Virginia as far as the Mississipi*. The next year, Le Rouge published a French version. For a description of the French version, see Cat. 30.

72. For a moving account of this tragedy, see Anderson, *Crucible of War*, pp. 5–7.

73. Charles H. Ambler, *George Washington and the West* (New York, 1971), p. 217.

74. For a full description of this map, see Cat. 29.

75. *New-York Mercury* (New York, N. Y.), Mar. 8, 1756. For a full description of this plan, see Cat. 32.

76. *Acts of the Privy Council of England,* Colonial Ser., IV, *A.D., 1745–1766,* reprint (Nendeln, Liechtenstein, 1966), pp. 619–620.

77. For a lengthier discussion of Des Barres and the *Atlantic Neptune,* see Cat. 61.

78. Some colonial newspapers printed the first five resolutions, some six, and a few all seven. John Fleming of Cumberland Co. and George Johnston of Fairfax Co. probably drafted the additional resolves. They were the only others with whom Henry shared his draft. Richard R. Beeman, *Patrick Henry: A Biography* (New York, 1974), pp. 39–40.

79. For a full description of this map, see Cat. 51.

80. For a full description of this map, see Cat. 52.

81. For a full description of this map, see Cat. 53.

82. *New-York Gazette and the Weekly Mercury* (New York, N. Y.), Sept. 11, 1775.

83. For a full description of this map, see Cat. 65.

84. Although the French produced maps pertaining to specific battles, apparently they could not find customers for them in France. French map-maker and seller Jean Lattré indicated to William Faden that he did not want battle plans because there was no market for them in France. However, there was a keen French interest in other types of maps of America and the war. In 1780, the firm of Perrier and Verrier placed an order with Faden for all the maps relating to the war in America, except for the battle plans which "we don't make much of here." Pedley, "Maps, War, and Commerce," p. 162. The map trade between Great Britain and France continued to thrive during the Revolution.

85. For a full description of this map, see Cat. 68.

33. Portrait of the Four Bath Worthies (Richard Jones, Ralph Allen, Robert Gay, and John Wood, Sr.),
attributed to William Hoare, Bath, England, ca.1740, oil on canvas.
Courtesy, Bath Preservation Trust, Bath, England.

"Useful & elegant furniture for screens, halls, large rooms, stair cases"

Maps as Symbolic Objects

The seventeenth and eighteenth centuries were a time of great change in both the Old World and the New. Tremendous advances were being made in the exploration and documentation of the known world. The increased demand for natural resources, furs, tobacco, and slaves resulted in vast accumulations of personal wealth in England and western Europe, which, in turn, created a demand for more of the newly available consumer goods. For European, English, and American gentry alike, greater affluence also afforded more time for leisure activities. Intellectual pursuits in art, literature, and natural sciences created an atmosphere of social refinement. Educated men amassed libraries that reflected their worldly interests and decorated their houses with objects indicative of their scholarly attainments.

By 1700, the fruits of the prospering global economy became accessible to the middle class. Consumption expanded to include household items that went beyond basic comforts. Bound to the mother country by trade restrictions, American colonists strongly influenced by English taste ordered household furnishings and clothes in the latest London fashions. Certain aristocratic elements in the colonies began to regard themselves as the cultural peers of the English gentry and sought accoutrements appropriate for their aspirations. Maps, charts, atlases, and globes became important symbols of the enlightened gentleman. *(fig. 33)*

Newspaper advertisements, custom orders affluent colonials placed with merchants they patronized in London, household inventories, and wills provide insight into which geographic materials they preferred, how they chose to display them, and the high regard they had for those objects. The aesthetic beauty of maps was mentioned in a 1769 advertisement in the *Pennsylvania Gazette*. After identifying the maps that he stocked, bookmaker William Woodhouse concluded by noting that "all of them are elegantly engraved, and some of them beautifully coloured."[1] In 1797, Jonathan Sayward of Maine drafted a will in which he made the proper provisions for his widow but left the house and furnishings to his grandson. Sayward must have considered a "clock, a large Map of North America, the Family and other Pictures" among his most important household furnishings since he specified them "as appurtenant to my Mansion House."[2]

Colonial gentlemen took care to secure the most up-to-date globes since the possession of one indicated that the owner was familiar with such intellectual pursuits as geography, mathematics, and physics. Benjamin Franklin wrote to William Strahan in 1752 requesting "a Pair of Mrs. Senex's improv'd Globes, recommended in the Transactions of the Royal Society, (or Neal's improv'd Globes, if thought better than Senex's)."[3] Another Philadelphian, William Logan, owned "a pair of globes" that he kept in the "Best Parlour."[4] The 1773 inventory of the furniture in Governor William Tryon's house in Fort George, New York, included "1 Globe" in the study.[5] In Williamsburg, Virginia, statesman George Wythe ordered a leather cover for a globe, while "a large and very fine Pair of GLOBES" was advertised in the *Virginia Gazette*.[6] According to cartographic historian Robert Baldwin, "globes were used to demonstrate the extent of imperial power by rulers boldly exploiting the likeness of the orb and the globe."[7]

In the watercolor of the Morse family, the famous geographer Jedidiah Morse of Charlestown, Massachusetts, is pictured with the tools of his trade—a globe and an unfolded map from his textbook. *(fig. 34)* Morse's finger on the globe and the looks of concentration on the faces of his wife and three sons indicate that he is explaining a theory of geography. Elizabeth Morse is listening to the discussion, but the position of the sewing basket and related equipment—her domestic tools—is a device the artist used to separate her from the others.[8]

34. The Family of the Reverend Jedidiah Morse, by Samuel F. B. Morse, Charlestown, Mass., ca. 1809–1810, watercolor on paper. Courtesy, National Museum of American History, Smithsonian Institution.

That females were generally excluded from mathematical and geographical studies is implied in the satirical print *A Female Philosopher in Extasy at solving a Problem* in which the woman was enraptured over using a globe to solve a mathematical problem. *(fig. 35)* The open book on the table is *The Elements of Euclid*, a popular publication on geometry from the seventeenth century.

A noteworthy American exception to the typical curriculum for females of the eighteenth and early nineteenth centuries was in place at Westtown School, a Quaker boarding facility near Philadelphia where both male and female students used terrestrial and celestial globes to learn mathematics, geometry, and astronomy. For about forty years, girls were also instructed in how to make silk-embroidered globes. *(fig. 36)* That the globes

were created not merely as exercises in female domesticity but also for instructional purposes was suggested in an 1816 letter by Rachel Cope to her parents:

I hope that they will recompense me for all my trouble, for they will certainly be a curiosity to you and of considerable use in instructing my brothers and sisters, and to strengthen my own memory, respecting the supposed shape of our earth, and the manner in which it moves (or is moved) on its axis, or the line drawn through it, round which it revolves every 24 hours.[9]

Colonial gentlemen began to amass impressive libraries of learned works, including those on natural science and geography.[10] Cotton Mather of Boston, Benjamin Franklin

36. Embroidered globe by Ruth Wright, Westtown, Pennsylvania, 1815, silk embroidery on silk. Courtesy, Henry Francis du Pont, Winterthur Museum, Winterthur, Delaware.

35 *A Female Philosopher in Extasy at solving a Problem,* artist unknown, London, ca. 1770, black-and-white mezzotint engraving with period color. 1973-250.

and James Logan of Philadelphia, and Thomas Jefferson and the three William Byrds of Virginia assembled major library collections during the seventeenth and eighteenth centuries. By 1700, Mather owned the largest library in America, recording in his diary:

> [A widow] had a Parcel of Books, which once belong'd unto the Library of our famous old Mr. CHANCEY; and if I would please to take them, she should count herself highly gratified, in their being so well bestowed. I singled out, about FORTY BOOKS, and some of them large Ones, which were now added unto my Library, that has already between two and three thousand in it.[11]

Similarly, the catalog compiled in 1760 of James Logan's library contained 2,076 titles in 2,547 volumes. At one point, Logan considered adding a library wing to Stenton, his Germantown residence, but later noted, "I have now fully changed that purpose and resolve to bestow all my Latin, Greek, Oriental & Matheml Books on ye City of Philadia to be plac'd in a Room in their fine State house which I suppose may vie with any in America."[12]

When bookbinder and printer John Stretch inventoried the contents of the Byrd library after 1751, it contained 2,345 volumes. By the time the library was put on the market in 1777, 4,000 books were advertised in the *Virginia Gazette*.[13] Three and one-half of the twenty-three bookcases in the library contained the Byrds' collections of "History, Voyages, Travels, &c." Within this section were books on navigation, geography, trade, commerce, and atlases.

37. The Library of Samuel Pepys's house, Buckingham Street, London, attributed to S. Nicholls, London, ca. 1693, watercolor on paper. Courtesy, Pepys Library, Magdalene College, Cambridge.

An important Virginia library belonged to Byrd II's brother-in-law, John Custis. A book bearing the gilded spine title "English Atlas" was included in the 1749 inventory of the collection. Although the atlas was fifty-one years old and many of the maps were outdated by the time Custis's library was inventoried, it was the second item listed; only Mark Catesby's highly regarded two-volume *Natural History of Carolina, Florida, and the Bahama Islands* preceded the "English Atlas."

An indication of his high regard for the atlas was the staggering price Custis paid for it in 1698—six pounds, twelve shillings.[14] A comparison of the cost with items in contemporary household inventories of that date puts its value in perspective. The most expensive entry in the 1700 inventory of John Ferne of Middlesex County, Virginia, included "1 feather bedd rugg 1 pr. blanketts bolster pillows curtaines vallance/head cloth tester and bedstead 7.0.0."[15] Ferne's bed and hangings were worth virtually the same price that Custis paid for his atlas.

A library was a masculine space, a sanctum where gen-tlemen withdrew to pursue their scholarly interests, so maps were appropriate subject matter for the walls. *(figs. 37 and 38)* In his 1701 will, Virginian William Fitzhugh wrote, "I Give my son William my own & wife's pictures & the other 6 Pictures of my Relations together with the Large Mapp in my Study."[16] The 1770 inventory of Virginia Governor Lord Botetourt's estate listed a "Map of N. & S. America" in the library. Since the map was included in the same entry with the hearth equipment, it likely hung over the chimneypiece.[17] By the 1770s, placing maps over mantels had been customary for almost a century. In his 1679 catalog, London mapseller John Garrett had described a map of the world in four sheets on linen and rollers as "a fit ornament for a chimney piece."[18]

The inventory of William Tailer of Dorchester, Massachusetts, included at least a dozen maps and identified the rooms in which he chose to hang them.[19] Regrettably, the record does not identify the titles of the maps. Newspaper advertisements contain additional descriptive information about the preferences of colonial Americans and the vari-

38. *Charles concluding a Treaty of Marriage, with the Daughter of the Nobleman,* published by Carington Bowles, London, August 31, 1787, black-and-white line engraving. 1959-83, 7.

ety of choices available to them. Merchant Gerard Duyck-inck advertised in *The New-York Journal; or, the General Advertizer,* 1768:

> *A New Map of the Province of New-York and New-Jersey, with Part of Pennsylvania, and the Government of Trois Rivieres and Montreal, drawn by Capt Holland, engraved by Thomas Jefferies, Geographer to his Majesty; four and a half Feet high, Breadth 21 Inches: Also the Map of the Globe, . . . and the four Quarters, in four Sheets, two Sheets, and one Sheet—in Sheets or on Canvis and Rollers. Maps and Charts of different Sorts and Sizes.[20]*

The following year, bookseller William Woodhouse announced in the *Pennsylvania Gazette* that he had for sale at his shop in Front Street, Philadelphia:

> *Green's new Chart or Map of North and South-America; Lewis Evans's Map of the Middle British Colonies, with some Improvements by John Gibson; D'Anville's new Map of North-America; Map of Nova-Scotia; Chart of the Great River St. Lawrence; Map of Canada; a new Chart of the Coasts of France, &c. &c. A new Map of England, &c. A new Map of the Kingdom of Ireland; a Map of Hispaniola; of Guadaloupe; of the West-Indies, &c. &c. All of them are ele-gantly engraved, and some of them beautifully coloured.[21]*

Robert Wells imported a large assortment of maps into Charlestown, South Carolina, in 1772:

> *MAPS,* Coloured, with Ledge and Roller, on Canvass. *SCIENTIA Terrarum et Cœlorum; Or, THE HEAVENS and EARTH astronomically and geographically delineated and displayed, containing the most curious and useful particu-lars In the Solar, Starry and Mundane Systems, faithfully enumerated and delineated according to the latest Observa-tions. By S. Dunn.* Four Sheets.
>
> *A new and accurate Map of EUROPE divided into its Empires, Kingdoms, States Republicks, &c. with many Improvements and Illustrations. By T. Kitchin, Geographer.* Four Sheets.
>
> *ASIA, according to an accurate Map of the [Mons]ieur D'anville, divided into its Empires, Kingdoms and States,*

39. John Moubray with Indian Servants,
attributed to Thomas Hickey,
probably India, ca. 1790,
oil on canvas. Courtesy, British Library,
Oriental and India Office.

with the latest Improvements, shewing the European Settlements in the East Indies, &c. Four Sheets.

A new and compleat Map of all AMERICA and of the West India and other Islands depending thereon; with a copious Table fully shewing the several Possessions of each European Prince and State as settled by the last Treaty of Peace, the Clauses whereof relative thereto are all inserted. By John Gibson Geographer. Four Sheets.

An Accurate Map of NORTH-AMERICA and all the West-India Islands belonging to or possessed by the several European Potentates or States. By Emanuel Bowen and John Gibson, Geographers. Four Sheets.

A new and accurate Map of AFRICA, according to the Sieu[r] D'anville, with many Improvements. Illustrated with a summary Description of its Trade, Natural Produce, Manners and Customs of Natives, European Settlement, and other useful Particulars. Four Sheets.

A Map of the most inhabited Parts of NEW-ENGLAND. Containing Massachusetts-Bay, New Hampshire, Connecticut and Rhode Island, divided into Counties and Townships. The whole composed from actual Surveys, and the Situations adjusted by Astronomical Observations. Four Sheets.

A Map of the most inhabited Parts of VIRGINIA, the Province of MARYLAND, with Part of Pennsylvania, New-Jersey and North-Carolina. Drawn by Joshua Fry and Peter Jefferson. Four Sheets.

A Map of the Provinces of NEW-YORK and NEW-JERSEY, with Part of Pennsylvania and the Governments of Trois Rivieres and Montreal. Drawn by Capt Holland and engraved by T. Jefferys, Geographer Royal. Three Sheets.

MAPS of the WORLD, EUROPE, ASIA, AFRICA, NORTH AMERICA, SOUTH-AMERICA From the latest and best Observations. Each o[?] Two Sheets. &c. &c. &c.[22]

40. *M.ʳ Foote in the Character of Major Sturgeon, in the Manor of Garrat,* by John Boydell after a painting by John Zoffany, London, August 14, 1765, black-and-white mezzotint engraving. 1941-218.

Maps were often specified for the hall, which was generally the most important and visible space. In 1720, London printseller Thomas Bowles offered for sale "large Mapps upon Cloath for Halls &c."; later, Peter Griffin advertised that he would furnish "Gent: halls, or Large Rooms wᵗʰ Maps or Prints on Rollers."[23] *(fig. 39)* The term "hall" should not be confused with the narrow passage of today. Until the mid-eighteenth century, the family ate, socialized, and entertained in the hall. Visitors entered the house directly into the hall where the walls displayed objects indicative of the owner's station in society. *(fig. 40)*

The practice of hanging maps in halls was fashionable in the colonies as well as in the mother country. Large maps prominently displayed in halls exhibited their owner's awareness of and interest in an expanded world view. Edward Mosely's map of North Carolina, described as "a very large Map, (being Five Feet long, and Four Feet broad, on Two Sheets of Elephant Paper) it's not only Useful, but Ornamental, for Gentlemens Halls, Parlours, or Stair-cases" was offered for sale in a *Virginia Gazette* in 1737.[24] As the eighteenth century progressed, people experienced greater needs for privacy and formality. To meet these needs, they created a separate entrance by partitioning off a portion of the hall called a passage. As separate dining spaces evolved on the opposite side of the new entrances, the flanking "hall" became known as the parlor. Edward Moseley's map was deemed a suitable accouterment for either the hall or parlor.

Maps were also displayed on dining room walls. Henry Bowcock of York County, Virginia, had four maps in his dining room in 1729–1730.[25] Listed in the dining room in the 1760 inventory for Grace Lloyd of Chester County, Pennsylvania, was "a Map of Jersulem."[26] Finally, Philip Ludwell Lee had "1 Map Carolina" in the dining room of

41. The dining room in the Governor's Palace at Williamsburg.

42. *His Excellency Arthur Dobbs, Esq[r]*,
engraved by James MacArdell
after a painting by William Hoare,
London, ca. 1753–1765,
black-and-white mezzotint engraving.
1995-205.

Stratford Hall, his Westmoreland County, Virginia, home.[27]

In 1766, John Henry, surveyor of Hanover County, Virginia, decided that he wanted to make a more accurate map of Virginia than the one produced a decade earlier by Joshua Fry and Peter Jefferson. Henry petitioned the House of Burgesses several times but was never successful in raising the funds necessary to complete the map since Fry and Jefferson's was very highly regarded. Despite Henry's failure to secure the support of the Burgesses, Governor Botetourt paid ten pounds in November 1769 to subscribe to and help publish the map.[28] Botetourt also attempted to secure a royal warrant for its production. When Henry's map was published in 1770, Virginians considered it inferior to Fry and Jefferson's, and it was poorly reviewed in the *Virginia Gazette*.

Despite the criticisms leveled at Henry and his work, Lord Botetourt chose to hang his map in the most prominent location in the Governor's Palace, over the mantel in the dining room, instead of the more acceptable Fry and Jefferson map, which he hung in the parlor. Botetourt naturally used the dining room for eating, but he also conducted business there since the inventory showed the room contained two desks and a writing table. Graham Hood argued that there was overwhelming evidence to suggest Botetourt's dining room was "the intellectual center of the house and the setting for frequent cultural interaction between governor and gentry."[29] *(fig. 41)* It is likely that the governor may have endorsed Henry's map because he was Patrick Henry's father. Only a few years earlier, the younger Henry had been the moving force behind the resolves against the Stamp Act. That Botetourt helped fund Henry's map and placed it in such a visible and important location in the Palace was probably not for the geography it imparted but to serve as a diplomatic show of support for the Virginians during a time of steadily mounting tension between the royal government and its American colonies.

Finally, while there is little question of the symbolic nature of the selection and placement of maps within a gentleman's personal domestic space, there is another instance where the emblematic nature of maps is even more apparent—in portraiture. In 1753, Irish-born Arthur Dobbs was appointed governor of North Carolina. Prior to his colonial appointment, he had served in the House of Commons in the Irish Parliament, as engineer-in-chief and surveyor general of Ireland, and had been deeply involved in promoting a search for a northwest passage to India. Shortly after being assured of his role as governor of North Carolina, Dobbs spent several weeks in Bath, England. While there, he had his portrait done by the fashionable painter William Hoare. *(fig. 42)* As was often the case, the artist chose to depict his sitter surrounded by artifacts that reflected his station. Portrayed with a globe in the background, Dobbs holds a compass suggestive of his role of surveyor general of Ireland and his interest in locating the passage to India. The most significant feature of the portrait is that Dobbs chose to be illustrated holding a map of North Carolina. At the time the portrait was painted, he had never set foot in America, yet Dobbs perceived his position as governor of North Carolina as a great achievement, one worthy of being committed to canvas. The Carolina map was the visual device that suggested his official position as one of authority, knowledge, and power.

NOTES

1. *Pennsylvania Gazette* (Philadelphia), Jan. 5, 1769.

2. Will of Jonathan Sayward, 1797, York County Probate Court, Alfred, Me., in Jane C. Nylander, *Our Own Snug Fireside: Images of the New England Home, 1760–1860* (New York, 1993), p. 63.

3. Labaree et al., eds., *Papers of Franklin,* III, p. 323. William Strahan was a Scottish-born printer living in London. John Senex, F.R.S., was an English map engraver, cartographer, and globemaker. After his death in 1740, Senex's widow continued to sell maps and globes. The globemaker Franklin referred to as Neal was probably John Neale (fl. 1750).

4. Reed Laurence Engle, Stenton, 18th & Windrim Streets, Philadelphia, Pennsylvania, Historic Structure Report (1982), Appendix A-9.

5. Dartmouth MSS, Box 22, fol. 916, William Salt Library, Stafford, Eng. The complete inventory appears in Appendix 6 in Graham Hood, *The Governor's Palace in Williamsburg: A Cultural Study* (Williamsburg, Va., 1991), pp. 303–306.

6. Alexander Craig Account Books 1749–1756, p. 185, Galt Family Papers, Earl Gregg Swem Library, College of William and Mary, Williamsburg, Va.; *Virginia Gazette* (Williamsburg) (Purdie and Dixon), Sept. 17, 1772.

7. Robert Baldwin, "Globes as symbols of political and navigational authority," *Map Collector,* LXI (1992), p. 4.

8. Richard J. Moss, *The Life of Jedidiah Morse: A Station of Peculiar Exposure* (Knoxville, Tenn., 1995), p. 144.

9. Quoted in Margaret B. Schiffer, *Historical Needlework of Pennsylvania* (New York, 1968), p. 51. For information on the globes made at Westtown School, see Susan Burrows Swan, *Plain & Fancy: American Women and Their Needlework, 1700–1850* (New York, 1977), pp. 60–61, and Judith Tyner, "The world in silk: embroidered globes of Westtown School," *Map Collector,* LXXIV (1996), pp. 11–14.

10. Studies of inventories suggest that books appeared more frequently in New England households of average means than they did in the southern colonies. Gloria L. Main, "Probate Records as a Source for Early American History," *WMQ,* 3rd Ser., XXXII (1975), pp. 89–99.

11. Thomas Goddard Wright, *Literary Culture in Early New England, 1620–1730* (New Haven, Conn., 1920), p. 127.

12. Edwin Wolf 2nd, *The Library of James Logan of Philadelphia 1674–1751* (Philadelphia, Pa., 1974), p. xxxv.

13. Kevin J. Hayes, *The Library of William Byrd of Westover* (Madison, Wis., 1997), pp. 73, 78.

14. Inscribed on the flyleaf of John Custis's "English Atlas" is "6 pounds 15 shill:" Below is his bookplate bearing the printed date "Septemb. 7th 1698:"

15. Inventory of John Ferne, May 6, 1700, Middlesex County, Va., Will Book [A], 1698–1713, in Room-By-Room Inventories: 1649–1729, transcriptions of Virginia inventories (TR 35.1), I, p. 77, John D. Rockefeller, Jr. Library, Colonial Williamsburg Foundation, Williamsburg, Va. I wish to thank Laura Pass Barry for locating references to objects of value comparable to John Custis's Atlas.

16. Stafford County, Va., Will Book, Liber Z, 1699–1709, Wills and Codicils, pp. 92–102, in Richard Beale Davis, ed., *William Fitzhugh and His Chesapeake World, 1676–1701* (Chapel Hill, N. C., 1963), p. 379.

17. Hood, *Governor's Palace,* Appendix 1, p. 289. The original manuscript of the inventory is in the Botetourt Papers, Virginia State Library and Archives, Richmond, Va.

18. Peter Barber, "Necessary and Ornamental: Map Use in England under the Later Stuarts, 1660–1714," *Eighteenth Century Life,* XIV (1990), p. 2.

19. Abbott Lowell Cummings, ed., *Rural Household Inventories: Establishing the Names, Uses and Furnishings of Rooms in the Colonial New England Home, 1675–1775* (Boston, 1964), pp. 114–118.

20. *New-York Journal; or, The General Advertiser* (New York, N. Y.), May 5, 1768.

21. *Pa. Gaz.*, Jan. 5, 1769.

22. *South Carolina and American General Gazette* (Charleston), Mar. 30, 1772.

23. Thomas Bowles, *A Catalogue of some Prints & Maps, Printed for & Sold by Thomas Bowles*, in Timothy Clayton, *The English Print, 1688–1802* (New Haven, Conn. 1997), pp. 23, 108.

24. *Va. Gaz.*, Sept. 9, 1737.

25. Inventory of Henry Bowcock, 1729/30, York County, Va., Orders & Wills, XVII, pp. 53–57.

26. Margaret B. Schiffer, *Chester County, Pennsylvania, Inventories, 1684–1850* (Exton, Pa., 1974), p. 315.

27. Inventory of Philip Ludwell Lee, 1776, Westmoreland County, Va., Inventories and Accounts, VI, p. 173.

28. Botetourt's account books, Badminton House, Gloucestershire, Eng. He sent one of John Henry's petitions to the Earl of Hillsborough on Nov. 24, 1768, Hood, *Governor's Palace*, pp. 159 and 324, n. 59.

29. *Ibid.,* p. 156.

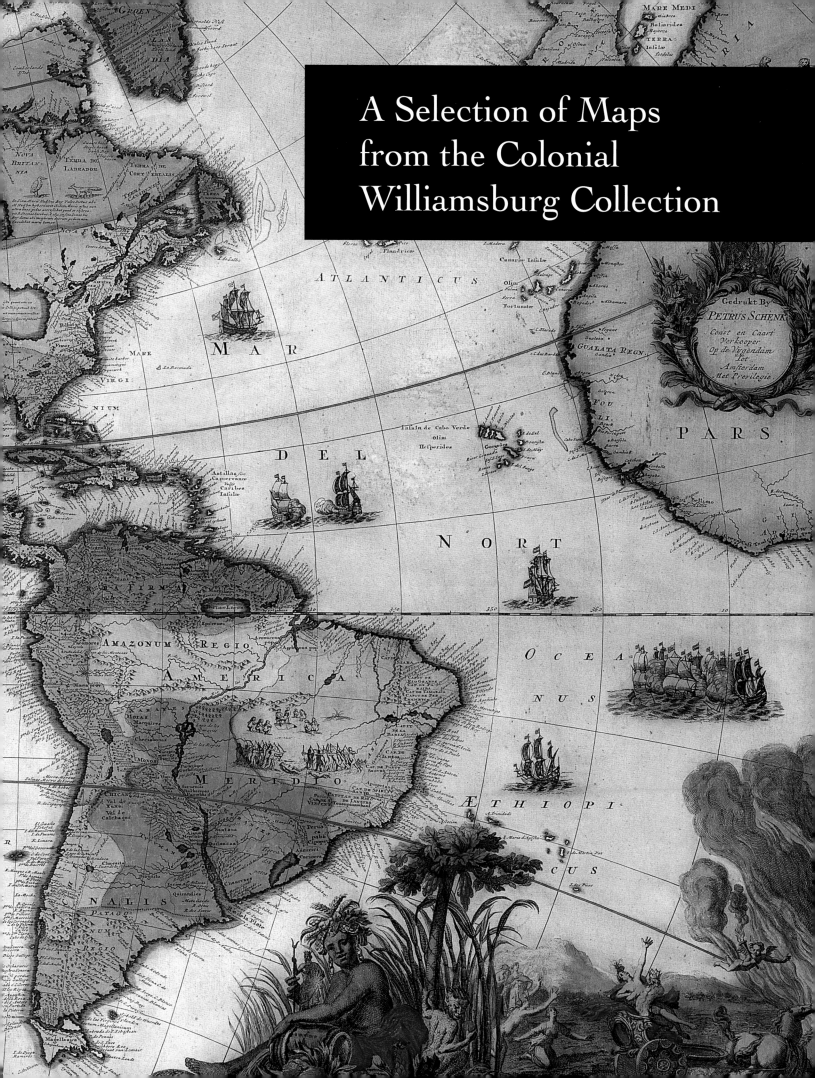

A Selection of Maps
from the Colonial
Williamsburg Collection

43. *Americae Sive Novi Orbis.* (Cat. 1)

1 AMERICAE SIVE / NOVI ORBIS, NO- / VA DESCRIPTIO

Abraham Ortelius (after Gerard Mercator), cartographer and probably engraver; Christopher Plantin, printer; published in *Theatrum Orbis Terrarum* by Abraham Ortelius

Antwerp, 1592 (originally published in 1587). Black-and-white line engraving with period color. H. 13⅞″, W. 9⅛″

Cum Privilegio decennali / Ab. Ortelius delineab. / et excudeb 1587 is in the lower right corner

Two states of the map are known:
State 1: (this copy) As described
State 2: The date in the lower right was removed and *Terra del Fuego* and *Fretum le Maire* were added. Ca. 1628[1]

References: Burden, *Mapping of North America,* entry 64; Deák, *Picturing America,* entry 14; Karrow, *Mapmakers of the Sixteenth Century,* p. 20; Legear and Ristow, "Sixteenth-Century Atlases," pp. 5–54; Moreland and Bannister, *Antique Maps,* pp. 246–248; Tooley, "Identification of the Maps of America," pp. 320–324; Wolff, ed., *America,* p. 90

Abraham Ortelius is considered one of the most influential figures in the history of modern cartography. *Theatrum Orbis Terrarum,* originally published in 1570, is generally regarded as the first modern atlas because Ortelius based his information on contemporary charts and maps. To produce it, he assembled the most accurate works of eighty-seven cartographers, all of whom he acknowledged in the atlas, a rather uncharacteristic gesture for sixteenth-century cartographers. Descriptive text accompanied each map.

Ortelius continually updated the maps and geographical information in subsequent editions of the *Theatrum,* which remained popular throughout the sixteenth century. In fact, the demand was so great that during the forty-two years the atlas remained in print, no fewer than thirty-four Latin editions were published, followed by editions in Dutch, German, French, Spanish, English, and Italian.[2]

Early editions of the *Theatrum* included only one map devoted solely to the Americas, *Americae Sive Novi Orbis.* Largely derived from Gerard Mercator's twenty-one-sheet world map published in 1569, it was reengraved three times during the life of the atlas. The first two maps bearing this title appeared in editions from 1570 to 1587. The most noteworthy feature was the geographical misrepresentation of the west coast of South America, which showed a large bulge protruding into the Pacific Ocean.

44. Detail of South America from *Americae Sive Novi Orbis,* by Abraham Ortelius, Antwerp, 1570, black-and-white line engraving with period color. Courtesy, Hope and Bobby Beck.

45 Detail of South America from *Americae Sive Novi Orbis,* by Abraham Ortelius, Antwerp, 1592, black-and-white line engraving with period color. 1986-81. (Cat. 1)

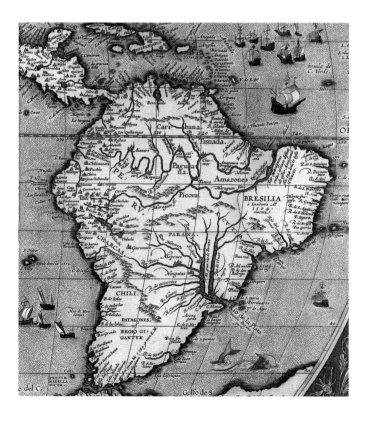

46. Detail of the Chesapeake Bay region from *Americae Sive Novi Orbis*, by Abraham Ortelius, Antwerp, 1570, black-and-white line engraving with period color. Courtesy, Hope and Bobby Beck.

47. Detail of the Chesapeake Bay region from *Americae Sive Novi Orbis*, by Abraham Ortelius, Antwerp, 1592, black-and-white line engraving with period color. 1986-81. (Cat. 1)

(fig. 44) This distortion appeared frequently on maps throughout the sixteenth century.[3] In the new plate Ortelius engraved in 1587 (this copy), he corrected the distortion and illustrated "Chili" not as simply a town but as the entire region encompassing the southwest coastline.

The most important change in the 1587 version was the inclusion of a body of water, or inlet, that may be the first illustration of the Chesapeake Bay on a printed map.[4] *(figs. 46 and 47)* This finger of water, which flows due west, is depicted directly below *Apalchen* and above *Wingan Dekoa*. Arthur Barlowe, who explored the area during Sir Walter Ralegh's 1584 expedition, identified "Wingandacoa" as the land inhabited by Native Americans under the rule of King Wingina. In the narrative of the voyage, Barlowe wrote, "The king is called Wingina, the countrey Wingandacoa, (and nowe by her Majestie, Virginia)."[5]

These first English colonists investigated the area around the mouth of the Chesapeake Bay in 1584 and 1585 where they found more fertile land and deeper harbors and channels around Wingandacoa than at Roanoke Island. Their favorable recommendations influenced Ralegh's decision to locate the Virginia colony on the Chesapeake rather than in North Carolina.

Just how Ortelius acquired knowledge of Wingandacoa is unclear. Richard Hakluyt, one of Ralegh's directors in the Virginia experiment, published Barlowe's account of the 1584 Virginia expedition in 1588, the year after Ortelius's map was engraved with *Wingan Dekoa* and the body of water thought to be the Chesapeake Bay. Perhaps Hakluyt shared Barlowe's manuscript with Ortelius prior to its publication because they had been corresponding since their initial meeting in England in 1577.[6] A 1587 letter from Hakluyt to Ralegh documents that he consulted Ortelius's earlier rendering of Virginia.[7] Given the opportunity, Hakluyt would likely have suggested to Ortelius that he include the Chesapeake Bay on his map.

1986-81

1. Philip Burden, *The Mapping of North America: a list of printed maps 1511–1670* (Rickmansworth, Eng., 1996), pp. 79–81.

2. Upon Ortelius's death in 1598, the map plates were sold to J. B. Vrients, who continued to print from them. By 1612, the year of Vrients's death, competition made Ortelius's atlas unprofitable and publication ceased.

3. For a discussion of the distortions in early representations of South America, see Uta Lindgren, "Trial and Error in the Mapping of America during the Early Modern Period," in Hans Wolff, ed., *America: Early Maps of the New World* (Munich, 1992), pp. 145–160.

4. Bob Augustyn was the first to call my attention to this feature. This theory was subsequently discussed in Burden, *Mapping of North America,* p. 79.

5. David B. Quinn and Alison M. Quinn, eds., *Virginia Voyages from Hakluyt* (London, 1973), p. 4.

6. George Bruner Parks, *Richard Hakluyt and the English Voyages,* ed. James A. Williamson (New York, 1928), p. 62.

7. Quinn and Quinn, eds., *Virginia Voyages,* p. 91.

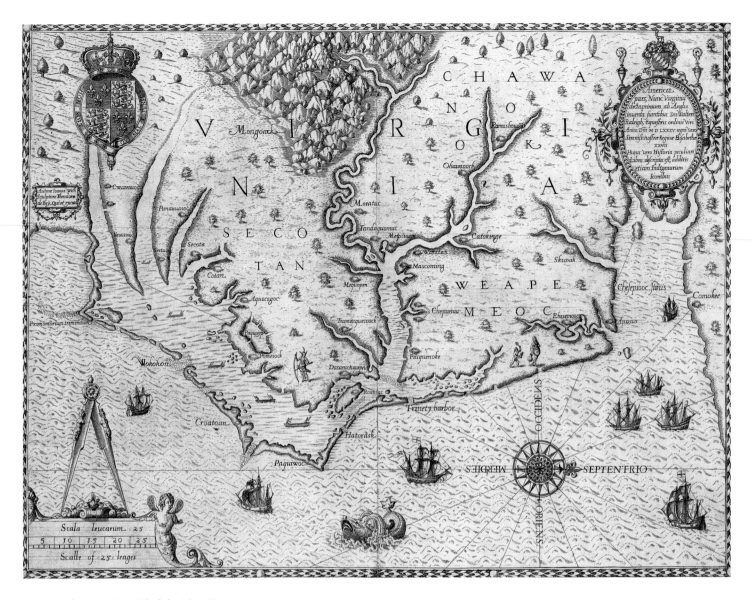

48. *Americæ pars, Nunc Virginia.* (Cat. 2)

2 *Americæ / pars, Nunc Virginia / dicta, primum ab Anglis / inuenta. sumtibus Dn. Walteri / Raleigh, Equestris ordinis viri/ Anno Dñi · M D · LXXXV regni vero / Sereniss: nostræ Reginæ Elizabethæ / XXVII / Hujus vero Historia peculiari / Libro discripta est, additis / etiam Indigenarum / Iconibus*

John White, cartographer; Theodore de Bry, engraver; published in *Grands Voyages*. Part I: *Admiranda Narratio fida tamen, de Commodis et Incolarvm Ritibus Virginæ* by Theodore de Bry

Frankfurt, 1590. Black-and-white line engraving. H. 11⅞″, W. 16½″

Autore Ioanne With/ Sculptore Theodore/ de Brÿ, Qui et excud is in a small cartouche on the left. A scale of leagues is in the lower left corner. The title cartouche is in the upper right corner

Three states of the map are known:
State 1: (this copy) The town of Chesapeake was spelled *Ehesepiooc*
State 2: An attempt was made to correct the spelling of Chesapeake by superimposing a "C" over the "E," but both are visible
State 3: The "E" in *Chesepiooc* was removed. Only traces remain on the corrected plate

References: Burden, *Mapping of North America,* entry 76; Cumming, *Mapping the North Carolina Coast,* pp. 48–57; Cumming, *Southeast in Early Maps,* entry 13; Cumming, Skelton, and Quinn, *Discovery of North America,* pp. 178–180, 185, 193–205; Fite and Freeman, *Book of Old Maps,* entry 26; Hulton, "Images of the New World," pp. 195–214; Morrison et al., *On the Map,* fig. 3; Phillips, *Virginia Cartography,* pp. 3–18; Schwartz and Ehrenberg, *Mapping of America,* p. 77; Suárez, *Shedding the Veil,* entry 39; Wallis, *Raleigh and Roanoke*

In 1584, Queen Elizabeth I granted Sir Walter Ralegh a charter enabling him to settle an English colony in America. Ralegh promptly dispatched two ships under the leadership of Captains Arthur Barlowe and Philip Amadas, who were directed to reconnoiter the area above Spanish Florida. On a second trip to America led by Sir Richard Granville the following year, the colonists established their headquarters on Roanoke Island on the Outer Banks of North Carolina, naming the region Virginia. John White and Thomas Hariot were important members of the group.[1] Although little is known of his background as an artist, White was sent to draw and record the geography, natives, and natural history of the area. Hariot's experience as a surveyor and writer complemented White's artistic renderings. Educated at Oxford University, Hariot was perhaps the most renowned English mathematician of his time. During the year the two spent at Roanoke Island

fort, they gathered a substantial amount of information about the inhabitants, the flora and fauna, and the terrain.

White's map was the first printed English record of Ralegh's attempts to plant a colony in the New World. It delineates the region between the mouth of the Chesapeake Bay and Cape Lookout, North Carolina. The rendering of the Roanoke colony and the Outer Banks were relatively accurate considering the lack of accurate surveying instruments and the changeable nature of the terrain. For example, some of the islands White and Hariot charted have since disappeared.[2] Other important features are the locations and names of various Native American settlements.[3] The map was the first to include the name *Chesepiooc Sinus*. On this rare copy of the first state, the town of Chesapeake was spelled *Ehesepiooc*. (fig. 49)

Theodore de Bry published White's map and engravings with Thomas Hariot's *A briefe and true report of the new found land of Virginia*. Many of White's original drawings are in the British Museum.

G1984-46, anonymous gift

1. White appears to have made five voyages to the New World.
2. The only inlet that has remained open over the 400 years since this map was published is Okracoke, identified as "Wokokon" on White's map.
3. Hariot was to study the Algonquian language and Native American customs in addition to the geography and natural resources of the area. William P. Cumming, *Mapping the North Carolina Coast: Sixteenth-Century Cartography and the Roanoke Voyages* (Raleigh, N. C., 1988), p. 51.

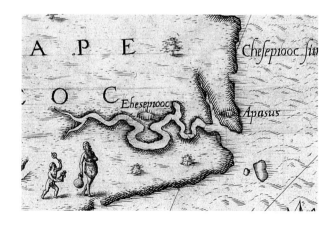

49 Detail of *Ehesepiooc* from, *Americæ pars, Nunc Virginia,* by John White, Frankfurt, 1590, black-and-white line engraving. G1984-46. (Cat. 2)

Montes Apalatci, in quibus aurum argentum & æs inueniuntur.

Apalatci

In hoc lacu Indigenæ
argenti grana inueniunt.

Oustaca

Onatheaqua

Appalou

Potanou

Ebiamana

Anouala

Hicaranaou

F L O R I D A

P R O V I N C I Æ

AB INDIGENIS DICTA IAQVAZA

Astina

Choya

Vtina

Patchica

Eloqualé

Aquouena
Cadica

Edelano
Chilli

Enecaqua
Melona
Omittaqua

Caffi

Hiouacara

Axona
Iracana

Hic defendit
Damphilus Vernaez
Sinus Moguili

Mocoso

Mayarca

Calanay

Onachaquara

Malica

Sequiana

Homoloua

Carolina

Saraualti
Almacani

Maij

F. Garunna

Charenta

F. Iyens

Mathiaca

Mayarca

Maira

Marracou

Laudonnierum ince pit

Patica

Belfinum

Promab consum.

Promi Gallicum

Lacus
aquæ dulcis.

Sorrochos

Ribaldus secunda
nauigatione hic appulit

F. Sorrochos.

Mexicani Sinus pars

Sinus Ioan-
nis Ponce

Adeo magnus est hic lacus
ut ex una ripa conspici altera
non possit. Distat a Charle-
fort 180 leucis.

Oathkaqua

Promi: Cānaueral.

F. Canotes

Lacus &
Insula Sarrope

Mocoffou

F. Pacis

Aquatio

Bimini

Bahara.

Yocajouque siue maior
Lucaya.

Zagareo.

C A L O S

Calos

Prom: Floridæ

Rupes

Hæc maris pars plena est Insulis, scopulis, breuibus et puluuiis valde insidiosis.

Insulæ dictæ
Testudines

Scopuli dicti
Martyres

OCCIDENS

Hauana

Portus
Matanicæ.

Cuba insula.

Mons Christi

Cauana

Guanagnarico

Cuspis S.
Antonij

Xagua

Insula
Pinorü

Portus Patris

Isabella

Portus
Principis

Cubanacan

Iardines scopuli, na-
uigantibus formidabiles

S. Christi.

S.
Trinitatis

Albayhamo

Baracca

Promont.
Crucis

S. de Iulacobi

Portus absconsus.

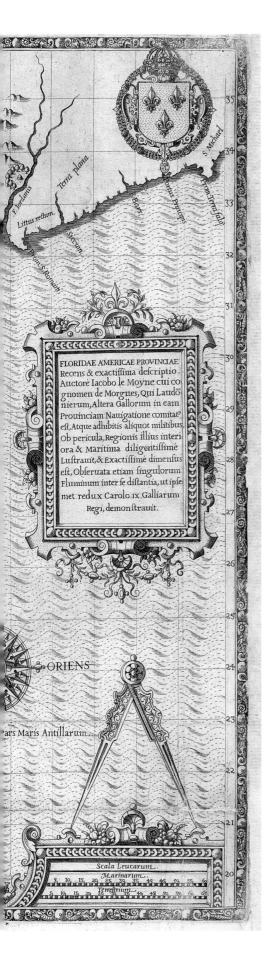

50. *Floridae Americae Provinciae,* 1591. (Cat. 3)

3 *FLORIDAE AMERICAE PROVINCIAE /
Recens & exactissima descriptio/ Auctorè Iacobo le
Moÿne cui co- / gnomen de Morgues, Qui Laudō- /
nierum, Altera Gallorum in eam / Prouinciam
Nauigatione comitat / est, Atque adhibitis aliquot
militibus, / Ob pericula, Regionis illius interi- / ora &
Maritima diligentissimè / Lustrauit, & Exactissimè
dimensus / est, Obseruata etiam singulorum/
Fluminum inter se distantia, ut ipse- / met redux
Carolo. IX. Galliarum / Regi, demonstrauit*

Jacques Le Moyne de Morgues, cartographer; Theodore de Bry,
engraver; published in *Grands Voyages.* Part II: *Brevis Narratio
Eorum Quæ in Floridae Americæ Provicia* by Theodore de Bry

Frankfurt, 1591. Black-and-white line engraving. H. 14½", W. 18"

The coat of arms of Philip II, King of Spain, is in the upper left
corner; that of Charles IX, King of France, is in the upper right
corner. The title is contained in an ornamented frame in the center right. A scale containing both nautical and land leagues is in
the lower right corner

One state of the map is known

References: Burden, *Mapping of North America,* entry 79; Cumming,
Southeast in Early Maps, entry 14; Faupel, "Appraisal of *Floridae
Americae Provinciae,*" pp. 193–206; Faupel, "Le Moyne's map of
Florida," pp. 33–36; Fite and Freeman, *Book of Old Maps,* entry 20;
Hulton, *Work of Jacques Le Moyne De Morgues;* Hulton, "Images of
the New World," pp. 195–214; McCorkle, *America Emergent,* entry
37; Schwartz and Ehrenberg, *Mapping of America,* p. 77

On February 8, 1562, a group of Frenchmen sponsored by Huguenot Admiral Gaspard de Coligny sailed for
America to establish a settlement in Florida. Coligny
wanted to create a French foothold on the southeastern
coast for political, religious, and economic reasons. After
making landfall on April 29, they began the task of surveying most of modern-day Florida, Georgia, and South
Carolina to find a suitable location. Jean Ribault, commander of the expedition, ultimately selected a site off
Port Royal Sound in Florida, today South Carolina, and
began the construction of Charlesfort. By June, the fort
was erected and Ribault returned to France for reinforcements, leaving the colonists under the authority of Albert
de la Pierria. Suffering from harsh leadership and a lack of
adequate provisions, the remaining Frenchmen revolted,
and by early 1563 they abandoned Charlesfort and
returned home.

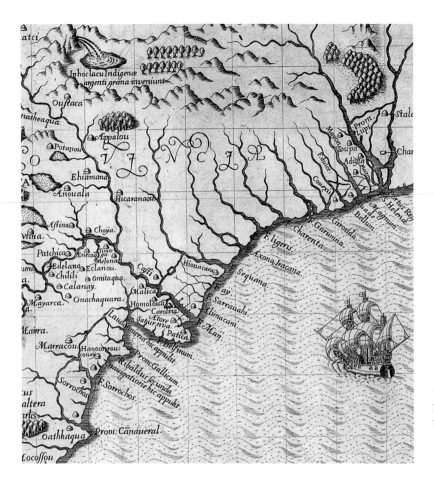

51 Detail from *Floridae Americae Proviniciae*, by Jacques Le Moyne, Frankfurt, 1591, black-and-white line engraving. 1984-58. (Cat. 3)

A second expedition set out on April 22, 1564, under the leadership of René Goulaine de Laudonnière, lieutenant of New France, who had accompanied Ribault on the previous journey. They explorers constructed Fort Caroline six miles from the mouth of the Saint Johns River, from which they explored the coast. The role of artist Jacques Le Moyne was "to chart the sea-coast and to observe the situation of the towns and the depth and course of the rivers, and also the harbours, the houses of the people, and anything new there might be in that province."[1] Le Moyne spent fifteen months in Florida compiling surveys and recording Native American customs.

In September 1565, a Spanish force under the command of Pedro Menéndez de Avilés captured Fort Caroline and massacred most of the French inhabitants. Laudonnière and Le Moyne were among the handful of French who were lucky to escape and return to France. It is not known if Le Moyne managed to gather his sketches before fleeing. If he did not, then the artist must have re-created some observations from memory because Le Moyne shared his findings with King Charles IX after returning to France.[2]

Little is known of Le Moyne's activities until he appeared in London in 1581 where he became acquainted with Sir Walter Ralegh, who commissioned drawings of Florida, perhaps to assist those planning the expeditions to Virginia. Le Moyne also met German publisher Theodore de Bry and discussed publishing an illustrated account of his American experiences. Not until after the artist's death was de Bry able to secure Le Moyne's manuscripts from his widow. Le Moyne's illustrations and the map attributed to him were published in part two of de Bry's *Grand Voyages*, 1591.

In the title of the map, de Bry credited Le Moyne, "who most diligently surveyed the interior and sea coasts of that region with some soldiers, whom he took with him because of the dangers, and very accurately measured the distances between each of the rivers as he himself showed on his return to Charles IX, King of the French dominions."[3] In spite of de Bry's attribution, the absence of a surviving manuscript draft for the map and the inclusion of information about which Le Moyne would not have had firsthand knowledge raise questions about the actual source. Since Le Moyne left no other known cartographic works, his skills as a geographer are difficult to assess. Unlike *Americæ pars, Nunc Virginia* (Cat. 2), published by de Bry after John White, there are many inaccuracies in the de Bry-Le Moyne rendering of the Southeast. Some of the errors can be attributed to the possible loss of Le Moyne's field notes and the consequent need to redraw from memory. To reconstruct the geography on paper, Le Moyne also could have consulted the published reports of Laudonnière, Ribault, and others who left accounts of the 1564 expedition.[4]

Cartographic historians agree that either Le Moyne or de Bry had access to earlier Spanish maps, which would account for the presence of topography unknown to the French in the early 1560s. That more than one source was used is evident in differences between both compass orientation and the variation in the scale of latitude between Spanish and French territories.[5] Some scholars believe that Le Moyne compiled the manuscript draft after he met Ralegh, who could have supplied him with information from the Spanish. Others subscribe to the theory that de Bry himself embellished Le Moyne's geography.[6] Despite de Bry's strong anti-Spanish sentiments, his inclusion of the coat of arms of Philip II of Spain, king when the French were attempting to establish a colony in Florida, acknowledges the Spanish presence.[7]

This map was the first to delineate the area from Cuba northward to North Carolina in any detail. The depiction of the coastline is generally correct with respect to latitude; however, inaccuracies recording longitude resulted in a rendering that extended the land too far east. A large body of water at the top may be Le Moyne's impression of the Sea of Verrazano; just beneath, a large waterfall may represent Native American accounts of either Niagara Falls or the Great Lakes. Although much of the geography is inaccurate, a significant feature is the appearance of French names along the Atlantic seaboard.

1984-58

1. *Narrative of Jacques Le Moyne de Morgues,* translated from the Latin text in de Bry, *Grands Voyages,* Pt. II, in Paul Hulton, *The Work of Jacques Le Moyne de Morgues: A Huguenot Artist in France, Florida, and England,* I (London, 1977), p. 119.

2. Referring to his assignment to chart the coast and observe and record the natives, Le Moyne wrote, "This assignment I carried out as faithfully as I could, as I showed his majesty, when after having escaped the extreme treachery and atrocious cruelty of the Spaniards, I returned to France." *Ibid.* Faupel argues that under the circumstances of the Spanish attack, it would have been impossible for Le Moyne to escape with his drawings. W. John Faupel, "Appraisal of the Illustrations," Appendix I in Sarah Lawson, *A Foothold in Florida: The Eye-Witness Account of Four Voyages made by the French to that Region and their attempt at Colonisation 1562–1568* (East Grinstead, West Sussex, Eng., 1992), p. 153 n. 4. See also W. J. Faupel, "Le Moyne's map of Florida: fantasy and fact," *Map Collector,* MCMXC (1990), p. 34.

3. Faupel, "Appraisal of *Floridae Americae Provinciae,*" in Lawson, *Foothold in Florida,* p. 193.

4. René de Laudonnière, *L'Histoire notable de la Floride, situee es Indes Occidentales,* ed. Martin Basanier, was published in Paris in 1586. It was translated into English and published by Richard Hakluyt in London in 1587. Based on the expedition of 1562, Ribault's report, *The whole and true discouerye of Terra Florida,* was published by Thomas Hacket in 1563. De Bry published Le Moyne's *Brevis Narratio* in Latin and German in 1591. Another Frenchman who escaped the Spanish massacre was a carpenter named Nicolas Le Challeux. His account of the attack, *Discours de l'histoire de la Floride,* was published in Dieppe in 1566.

5. Faupel, "Le Moyne's map," pp. 33–36.

6. For the former argument, see R. A. Skelton, "The Le Moyne-De Bry map," *Map Collector,* MCMXC (1990), pp. 47–53. For the latter, see Faupel, "Appraisal of *Floridae Americae Provinciae,*" pp. 193–206, and Faupel, "Le Moyne's map," pp. 33–36.

7. I would like to thank Laura Pass Barry for her analysis of the two coats of arms on this map. Timothy Duke, Chester Herald, College of Arms, London, confirmed her conclusions regarding their identities. Previously, it had been suggested that they were the arms of Henry IV of France and the French coat of arms.

4 *Occidentalis Americæ partis, / vel, earum Regionum quas Chri- / stophorus Colombus primū detexit / Tabula Chorographicaè multorum/ Auctorum scriptis, præsertim verò ex / Hieronymi Benzoni (qui totis XIIII / annis eas Provinciaˢ diligenter / perlustravit) / Historia, / conflata & in æsmcifa à / Theodoro de Bry Leodˢ. / Anno M D XCIIII*

Theodore de Bry (based on the accounts of Girolamo Benzoni), cartographer and possibly engraver; published in *Grands Voyages.* Part IV: *Americæ Pars Quarta Insignis & Admiranda Historia* by Theodore de Bry

Frankfurt, 1594. Black-and-white line engraving with period color. H. 13″, W. 17⅛″

In the upper left corner are the arms of Philip II, King of Spain. The title is contained in an ornamental frame in the upper right corner.

One state of the map is known

References: Burden, *Mapping of North America,* entry 83

IN 1541, Girolamo Benzoni left his hometown of Milan and set sail for the New World, where he spent fourteen years in the West Indies and Central and South America. Benzoni participated in numerous expeditions in the area and observed the landscape, natives, and, perhaps most significantly, Spanish atrocities against the Indians.

After returning to Milan in 1555, Benzoni began writing about his experiences in the Spanish territories in the New World. Ten years later, Benzoni published *La Historia del mondo nuovo* along with seventeen woodcuts of scenes he had witnessed during his travels.

Theodore de Bry, a Protestant with strongly anti-Spanish sentiments, devoted three of the ten volumes of his *Grands Voyages* to Benzoni's accounts. The first described the journeys of Columbus, the second, Hernando Cortés' campaigns in Mexico, and the third, Francisco Pizarro's conquest of Peru. Increasingly aware of Spanish brutalities in the New World, Europeans welcomed Benzoni's interpretation which reinforced their views.

Engraved to accompany Benzoni's account of Columbus's explorations, this map illustrates the destinations of his four voyages to America. De Bry noted beside one of the islands in the Bahamas, "On the first voyage Columbus landed on this island. He named it Desiderata and set up a cross to the memory of Christ's name."[1] Whether Columbus actually erected a cross is not known, although the flag for the expedition was a green-crowned cross on a white ground.[2] The island probably was San Salvador, thought to be the site of the explorer's first landing.

Alongside Haiti is the notation, "Columbus took possession of this island on the second voyage, and named it Hispaniola." Beside Trinidad, de Bry claimed, "On the third voyage Columbus was carried to this island, which he named from the pearls, of which he yielded a fifth part to the king." Finally, just above Panama, de Bry recorded that "Columbus arrived at this place on the fourth and last voyage." Benzoni's account, published by de Bry, was the means by which most Europeans learned of the voyages of Columbus.

1986-83

1. Bahama Island proper was placed too far north on this map.
2. Samuel Eliot Morison, *The Great Explorers: the European Discovery of America* (New York, 1978), p. 401.

52 Detail of the West Indies from *Occidentalis Americæ partis,* by Theodore de Bry (after the accounts of Girolamo Benzoni), Frankfurt, 1594, black-and-white line engraving with period color. 1986-83. (Cat. 4)

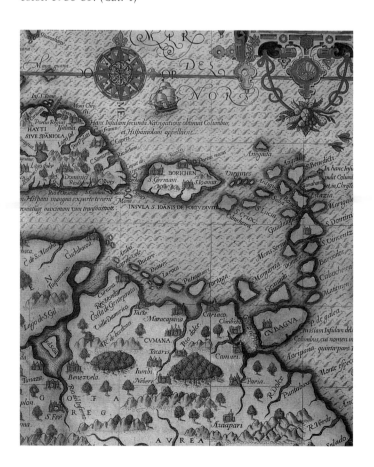

53 *Occidentalis Americæ partis.* (Cat. 4)

5 VIRGINIA

Captain John Smith, cartographer; William Hole, engraver; published in *A Map of Virginia, With a Description of the Country,* in the *Generall Historie of Virginia, New-England, and the Summer Isles* by Captain John Smith, and in *Purchas his Pilgrimes* by Samuel Purchas

London, 1624 (originally published in 1612). Black-and-white line engraving. H. 13⅛", W. 16⅝"

An inset view of Powhatan in a hut surrounded by Native Americans is in the upper left corner. Beneath is the inscription *Powhatan / Held this state & fashion when Capt. Smith / was deliuered to him prisoner / 1607.* A compass rose with north to the right is in the lower left. A banner with the title *VIRGINIA* is in the upper center. Just below is the royal coat of arms. A cartouche consisting of a compass surmounting the scale of leagues and the inscription *Discouered and Discribed by Captayn John Smith/ 1606/ Grauen by William Hole* is in the lower center. A Native American with a bow in his right hand, a club or pipe in his left, and a pig slung at his hip is in the upper right corner. Beneath is the legend *The Sasquesahanougs / are a Gyant like peo-ple & thus / a-tyred.* In the lower right is Smith's coat of arms. In the upper right and left are the numbers *1690* and *1691,* which refer to the page numbers in *Purchas his Pilgrimes.* In the lower right corner is *Page 41 / Smith,* a reference to the page number in *The Generall Historie of Virginia*

Twelve states of the map are known[1]:

State 1: Dates, figures of longitude, and the Smith coat of arms were not included. 1612

State 2: *1606* was added to the scale of leagues and *1607* to the third line of text beneath Powhatan in the upper left corner

State 3: Smith's arms, without the motto, were added in the lower right corner

State 4: Longitude was added, as was the motto beneath Smith's arms

State 5: Three place-names, *Gunters Harbour, Taverners roade,* and *Winstone Iles,* were added

State 6: Three additional place-names, *Sparkes/ Content, Democrites/ tree,* and *Burtons Mount,* were added

State 7: The *Purchas his Pilgrimes* page numbers *1692* and *1693* were added in the upper left and right corners. Ca. 1624–1625

State 8: Three new names, *Featherstones/ Baye, Bollers bush,* and *Sparkes Poynt,* were added. *Page 41/ Smith* was added in the lower right corner. *Sparkes/ Content* added to state 6 was changed to *Sparkes/ Vaylley*

State 9: Three new place-names, *Washeborne/ C:, Blands/ C:,* and *Downes dale,* were added. *Bollers bush* added to state 8 was changed to *Boolers bush*

State 10: (this copy) As described. The page numbers for *Purchas his Pilgrimes* were changed to *1690* and *1691*

State 11: The Indian's hair was reengraved with cross-hatching

State 12: There is a crack in the plate from the 38° latitude in the bottom border through the continuation mark in Chesapeake Bay

References: Arber, ed., *Smith Works;* Barbour, *Three Worlds of Smith;* Burden, *Mapping of North America,* entry 164; Cumming, *Southeast in Early Maps,* entry 32; Cumming, Skelton, and Quinn, *Discovery of North America,* pp. 257–261; De Vorsey, "American Indians and Early Mapping of the Southeast," pp. 72–77; Fite and Freeman, *Book of Old Maps,* entry 32; McCary, *Smith's Map of Virginia;* McCorkle, *America Emergent,* entry 38; Morrison et al., *On the Map,* fig. 7; Phillips, *Virginia Cartography,* pp. 19–24; Ristow, "Smith's Map of Virginia," pp. 135–172; Sanchez-Saavedra, *Description of the Country,* pp. 1–13; Verner, "Smith's *Virginia,*" pp. 13–172

ONE OF THE MOST important printed maps ever produced, Captain John Smith's representation of Virginia based on his explorations of the Chesapeake Bay in 1607 and 1608 is a key object in Colonial Williamsburg's collection. The accuracy and detail far surpassed any other depiction of North America at the time it was made. Smith's *Virginia* served as the prototype for maps of the area for over fifty years.

In December 1606, the London Company sent three vessels to America under the command of Captain Christopher Newport, who was instructed to find a safe port at the entrance of a navigable river in Virginia, "that which bendeth most toward the North-west for that way you shall soonest find the other sea."[2] Finding a passage to Asia and exploring the mineral resources of America were implicit in the company's mission. The ships arrived at Jamestown in May 1607. Shortly afterward, a party of just over twenty men, including Smith and Robert Tindall, under the leadership of Captain Newport set out to explore the James River as far as the falls, the present site of Richmond.[3]

Upon their return, the men found that natives had attacked the Jamestown settlement during their absence, killing one colonist and wounding seventeen. The colonists immediately began to fortify Jamestown and obtain rations for the starving Englishmen. By the end of June, Captain Newport left for England to secure provisions and recruit new settlers. After Newport left, Smith assumed the role of supply officer, bartering with neighboring Indians for food. While exploring the mouth of the Chickahominy River in December 1607, Indians captured Smith and held him prisoner for several weeks. Eventually, Smith negotiated his release with their powerful chief Powhatan.

In June 1608, Smith and fourteen men set out in an open boat to explore the Chesapeake. They covered about three thousand miles between June and September, sailing to the northern tip of the Chesapeake Bay, up the Potomac River as far as present-day Georgetown, and

54 *Virginia.* (Cat. 5)

investigating the Patuxent, Susquehanna, Rappahannock, and Piankatank Rivers before returning to Jamestown.

All along the way, local Indians willing to trade food for trinkets approached them. Smith took advantage of these encounters to ask the Native Americans about the geography. He included many new features they related to him on the map beyond the Maltese crosses, explaining, "As far as you see the little Crosses on riuers, mountaines, or other places, haue beene discovered; the rest was had by information of the *Savages*, and are set downe according to their instructions."[4] The contributions of Native Americans to Smith's understanding of the geography of the region played a significant role in the overall accuracy of his work. Firsthand knowledge of the Chesapeake Indians and the locations of their villages make it invaluable because Smith named ten tribes and located one hundred sixty-six of their villages.

After he was wounded by an accidental gunpowder explosion, Captain Smith returned to England in September 1609. The next year, he began work on *A Map of Virginia, With a Description of the Country*, published in Oxford in 1612 by Joseph Barnes. This map, beautifully engraved by one of England's finest engravers, William Hole, accompanied Smith's written description. Cartographic historians have questioned whether Smith actually drafted the manuscript map used as the source for the printed version.[5] It is possible that he may have consulted sketches by Robert Tindall or Nathaniel Powell. Regardless of who the actual draftsman was, Smith was primarily responsible for charting the vast area. The map was included in two later publications, John Smith's *The Generall Historie of Virginia, New-England, and the Summer Isles*, 1624, and Samuel Purchas's *Purchas His Pilgrimes*, 1625.

Three distinctive geographical features on Smith's map influenced subsequent works: the eastward turn of the head of the Chesapeake Bay, the Delmarva Peninsula, which extends too far to the east, thereby considerably enlarging the area, and the pronounced "Z" shape of the Potomac River. The eastward distortion of the Delmarva Peninsula was probably due to the fact that Smith never explored the Atlantic coast of the Eastern Shore.

Historians have often suggested that the Susquehanna Indian illustrated on Smith's map was borrowed from Theodore de Bry's *A Weroan or great Lorde of Virginia. (fig. 55)* While similarities exist, it is clear that Smith's Indian was based on his written description. The native depicted by de Bry was an Algonquian Indian from North Carolina. Bare-chested and wearing a necklace of pearls or copper beads, the subject's long hair is bound up at the ends in a

55 Detail from *A weroan or great Lorde of Virginia*, by Theodore de Bry, Frankfurt, 1590, black-and-white line engraving. 1983-286, 3.

knot under the ears with three feathers attached at the forehead and above each ear.

The Susquehanna Indian *(fig. 56)* Smith illustrated wears his hair loosely rather than knotted under the ears and adorned with feathers as de Bry's did. Of the Susquehannas' clothing, Smith wrote:

Their attire is the skinnes of Beares and Woolues, some haue Cassacks made of Beares heades and skinnes that a mans necke goes through the skinnes neck, and the eares of the beare fastned to his shoulders behind, the nose and teeth hanging downe his breast, and at the end of the nose hung a Beares Pawe: the halfe sleeues comming to the elbowes were the neckes of Beares and the armes through the mouth, with pawes hanging at their noses. One had the head of a Woolfe hanging in a chaine for a Iewell [jewel].[6]

The object pictured in the Susquehanna's left hand has been identified as a hatchet or cudgel, but close examination reveals that it could not be a hatchet because the end does not have a straight, sharp surface of the type necessary for chopping. Although the implement could be some

56 Detail of the Susquehanna Indian from *Virginia,* by Captain John Smith, London, 1624, black-and-white line engraving.
G1984-1, gift of Mrs. Anna Glen Victor in memory of Alexander O. Vietor. (Cat. 5)

57 Wolf's Head Ornament, maker unknown, America, ca. 1640–1653, wolf skull with buckskin, deer hair, and wool. Courtesy, Skokloster Castle, Uppland, Sweden, photo by Samuel Uhrdin.

form of club, it very closely resembles Smith's description of a Susquehanna tobacco pipe as "3 quarters of a yard long, prettily carued [carved] with a Bird a Beare, a Deare, or some such devise at the great end, sufficient to beat out the braines of a man."[7]

The wolf's-head pendant worn by Smith's Indian, which was not depicted in any of de Bry's illustrations, was a type apparently worn by Leni-Lenape or Susquehanna Indians. The earliest known surviving example of one of these pendants, made from the jaws of a mature eastern wolf, is in a collection at Skokloster Castle, Sweden, one of a number of surviving artifacts from the seventeenth-century collection of Count Carl Gustaf Wrangel, objects presumably presented as ceremonial gifts to Johan Printz, colonial governor of New Sweden from 1642 to 1653.[8] *(fig. 57)* Herbert C. Kraft, of the Seton Hall University Museum, who examined the wolf's head in the Skokloster Castle collection, described the object as follows:

[It was] constructed around portions of the maxilla sawed or broken away from the nasal and cranial portions of a wolf's skull, and a mandible from which parts of the ascending rami have been removed. Beginning with these tooth-bearing elements, seemingly with gum tissue attached, the artisan constructed an artificial head from a buckskin covering stuffed with deer hair. The tooth-bearing elements were meticulously fashioned into the formed "head" by sewing the buckskin "lips" to the gum tissues in a way that left the teeth exposed. An indigo-dyed woolen trade cloth tongue was included for realism.[9]

G1984-1, gift of Mrs. Anna Glen Vietor in memory of Alexander O. Vietor

1. Verner, "Smith's *Virginia,*" pp. 135–172, provided a complete carto-bibliographical analysis of the John Smith map. In 1819, a new plate was engraved from a copy of state 10. It was published in Richmond, Va., to accompany a new edition of Smith's *Generall Historie.*

2. *Instructions by way of advice, for the intended Voyage to Virginia,* Edward Arber, ed., *Capt. John Smith Works 1608–1631* (London, 1895), p. xxxiv.

3. Tindall produced a draft map during this expedition that Capt. Newport took back to London.

4. "Map of Virginia," by Capt. John Smith, Arber, ed., *Smith Works,* p. 55.

5. For a thorough discussion of the arguments for and against attributing the map manuscript to Smith, see Verner, "Smith's *Virginia,*" pp. 139–141.

6. Arber, ed., *Smith Works,* p. 54.

7. *Ibid.*

8. Richard S. Dunn, "Religion, Politics, and Economics: Pennsylvania in the Atlantic World, 1680–1755," in Jack L. Lindsey, *Worldly Goods: The Arts of Early Pennsylvania, 1680–1758* (Philadelphia, Pa., 1999), pp. 18, 228.

9. Herbert C. Kraft, "Lenape and/or Susquehannock Treasures," *Bulletin of the Archaeological Society of New Jersey,* L (1995), p. 6. I want to thank Richard Guthrie for providing this reference and many others.

6 NEW ENGLAND

Captain John Smith, cartographer; Simon Passaeus, engraver; published in *A Description Of New England, New Englands Trails, The Generall Historie of Virginia, New England, and the Summer Isles, Advertisements,* and *Historia Mundi* by Captain John Smith

London, 1624 (originally published in 1616). Black-and-white engraving. H. 11⅞″, W. 14¹⁄₁₆″

An engraved portrait of Smith surrounded by an oval with *THE PORTRAICTUER OF CAPTAYNE IOHN SMITH / ADMIRALL OF NEW ENGLAND* is in the upper left corner. Below the portrait is a poem:

> *These are the Lines that shew thy Face; but those*
> *That shew thy Grace and Glory, brighter bee:*
> *Thy Faire-Discoueries and Fowle-Overthrowes*
> *Of Salvages, much Civilliz'd by thee*
> *Best shew thy Spirit; and to it Glory Wyn:*
> *So, thou art Brasse without, but Golde within.*
> *If so; in Brasse, (too soft Smiths Acts to beare)*
> *I fix thy Fame, to make Brasse Steele out weare.*
> *Thine, as thou art Virtues,*
> *John Davies. Heref:*

The arms of Captain John Smith are in the lower left. The arms of King James I are in the upper right. A scale of leagues appears in the lower right

Nine states of the map are known[1]:

State 1: No date below the scale of leagues

State 2: The date *1614, P Travers,* and *Gerrards Ils* were added

State 3: Smith's arms were added with no motto

State 4: (this copy) As described. Added to this state were the motto *Vincere est Vivere,* the latitude scale in the left margin, and longitude in the top and bottom. This state was published in *The Generall Historie of Virginia, New England, and the Summer Isles*

State 5: *Paynes Ils* was added and *Pasaeus* was changed to *Passæus*

State 6: The printer's name, *Iames Reeue,* was added in place of the name of the former printer *Geor: Low*

State 7: *Prince of great Britaine* under the title was changed to *nowe King* and *Salem* was added

State 8: The arms of the Council of New England were added in the center. *Salem* was erased and placed in its correct position below *Bristow*

State 9: A school of fish was added off Cape Cod. *Boston* and *Charlestowne* were added

References: Arber, *Smith's Works;* Barbour, *Three Worlds of Smith;* Benes, *New England Prospect,* entry 3; Burden, *Mapping of North America,* entry 187; Deák, *Picturing America,* entry 19; Fite and Freeman, *Book of Old Maps,* entry 34; Krieger and Cobb, eds., *Mapping Boston,* pp. 82–83; Suárez, *Shedding the Veil,* entry 42

ON MARCH 3, 1614, Captain John Smith set sail for New England in command of two vessels and a crew of forty-five. The adventurers were sent specifically for whaling and mining gold and copper. Should either venture prove unsuccessful, they were instructed to find another way to cover their expenses, perhaps by bartering for furs and fish. The whales off the coast of Maine, where Smith and his crew landed, were too large and fast for their vessels, and Smith had already experienced difficulties mining in Virginia. Therefore, he left most of his men behind in Maine to fish while he and a crew of eight sailed southward to trade for furs and explore the New England coast.

Smith returned to England after spending only six weeks charting the coastline. While his cargo was not adequate to cover the cost of the trip, he returned with valuable geographic information and great enthusiasm for establishing a colony at Plymouth. By the next summer, Smith had raised enough money to fund two vessels and men for another voyage. Smith and his crew were plagued with difficulties, however. After several encounters with pirate ships, Smith was eventually captured by a French man-of-war. While being held captive, he wrote about his experiences over the past several years. Based on Smith's 1612 explorations, the manuscript was published in 1616 as *A Description of New England* and illustrated the coastline from Penobscot Bay to Cape Cod. Much of the nomenclature was provided by Charles, the fifteen-year-old Prince of Wales, although only a few of those place-names are still used today. The site of "Plimouth" was selected six years before the Pilgrims landed. While the map did not contain the wealth of detail found in *Virginia,* it was nevertheless remarkably accurate and proved to be a valuable resource for subsequent expeditions.

1972-37

1. Burden, *Mapping of North America,* p. 229. Burden also provided a list of publications that contain the various states.

58 *New England*. (Cat. 6)

7 West-Indische / PASKAERT / waer in de graden der breedde over weder- / zÿden vande middellÿn wassende so vergrooten / dat die geproportioneert sÿn tegen bunne / nevenstaende graden der lengde; / Vertonende behalve Europaes zuydelijcste/ alle de Zeekusten van Africa en America, / begrepen in't Octroy bij de H.M H.Staten / Generael der vereenichde Nederl.verleent / aende Generale West Indische Compagnie. / Mitsgaders die van Peru en Chili. / in de groote Zuyd-Zee

Johannes van Keulen (after Willem Janszoon Blaeu and Pieter Goos), cartographer; engraver unknown

Amsterdam, ca. 1680. Black-and-white line engraving with period color. H. 32⅛", W. 39¼"

A cartouche in the upper left corner contains the imprint *Gedruckt / t' AMSTERDAM, / Bij / PIETER GOOS / Op't Water inde Ver- / gulde Zee-Spiegel. / Seyn nu te Bekoomen/ By Iohannus van Kuelen.* The title is enclosed within a decorative cartouche in the center right above the continent of Africa. An inset of the lower third of South America is in the upper portion of the continent of Africa

One state of the map is known[1]

References: Burden, *Mapping of North America*, entry 233; Campbell, "One map, two purposes," pp. 36–38; Deák, *Picturing America,* entry 22

Dᴜᴛᴄʜ publishers dominated the map trade throughout the seventeenth century. During those years, the majority of published maps were produced in Amsterdam or were printed in other countries using Dutch plates. Occasionally, makers simply copied Dutch prototypes directly. This important map was originally published by Willem Janszoon Blaeu and was reissued by Jacobus Robyn and Pieter Goos before being reengraved by Johannes van Keulen.

By 1596, Willem Janszoon Blaeu had established a business for the production of maps, globes, and scientific instruments. After Blaeu practiced his trade for about five years, the States General granted him a stipend to print a seaman's guide with maps and charts.[2] In 1623, he received a ten-year exclusive right from the government to publish *Tables of the declination of the sun and of the most important planets, with the different uses of the North Star calculated anew for the use of all navigators by Willem Jansz. Blaeuw.*[3] Having access to information from the most up-to-date discoveries and explorations and financial support

from the States General played large roles in the tremendous success of the Blaeu firm.

Blaeu published his first *Paskaert,* or passage chart, a monumental work illustrating the Atlantic Ocean, in 1621. It was the first to name the Dutch settlements *Niew Nederlant* and *Fort Nassau* and to illustrate the first printed rendering of Manhattan Island.

Nine years later, Blaeu published a second *West Indische Paskaert.* He added updated information on the Middle Atlantic region and many tributaries of the Chesapeake Bay, corrected the shape of the Delmarva Peninsula to reflect its true configuration more accurately, and improved his earlier geography of New York Harbor. However, Blaeu eliminated Cape May, the Delaware River, and Cape Henlopen, which had been included on the earlier chart. Most important, the second *West Indische Paskaert* was the first sea chart to use Mercator's projection. A major difficulty in sailing was that a straight line on earlier sea charts was not a straight line when sailing. Geographer Gerard Mercator achieved fame for devising a way to draw the world with its north-south dimension stretched to its east-west dimension at the equator, thereby compensating for the way the shape of the earth flattens on paper. He introduced this new method of projection in 1569.

One of the more unusual features retained by van Keulen was Blaeu's rendering of the lower regions of South America. Since the southern third of the continent could not be accommodated within the map as a whole, Blaeu simply included it as an inset, one of the first depictions of the 1616 discovery of the Straits of Le Maire and Cape Horn. Prohibited by the Dutch East India Company's policy of not permitting nonmembers to pass through the Strait of Magellan or the Cape of Good Hope, Amsterdam merchant Isaak Le Maire and Willem Schouten of Hoorn set out, largely at their own expense, to search for an alternate route around South America to the Far East. They named the strait they found for Le Maire and the Cape for Hoorn.

1959-438

1. Burden, *Mapping of North America*, pp. 289, 291, provided information on the various states of Blaeu's map. He concluded that the van Keulen chart was a derivative rather than a separate state and that van Keulen retained the Goos imprint.
2. The States General was the governing authority in the Netherlands.
3. Lloyd A. Brown, *The Story of MAPS*, reprint (New York, 1979), p. 171.

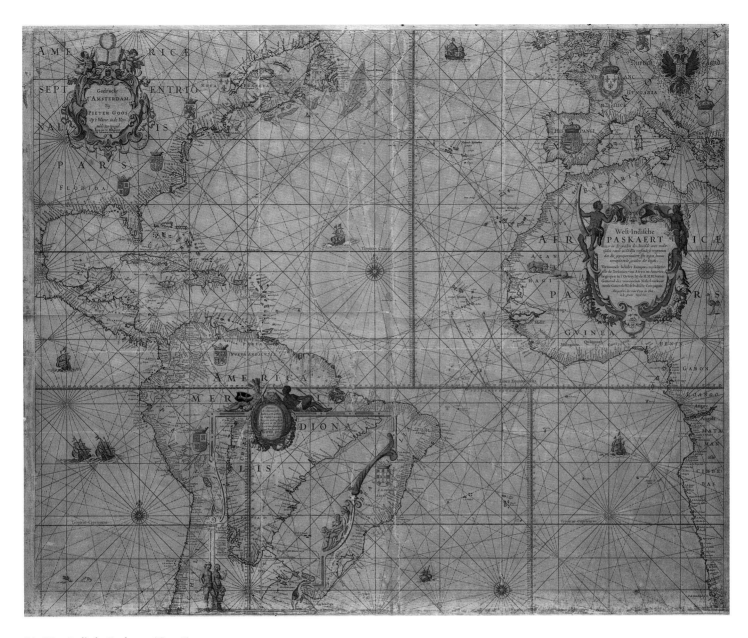

59 *West-Indische Paskaert.* (Cat. 7)

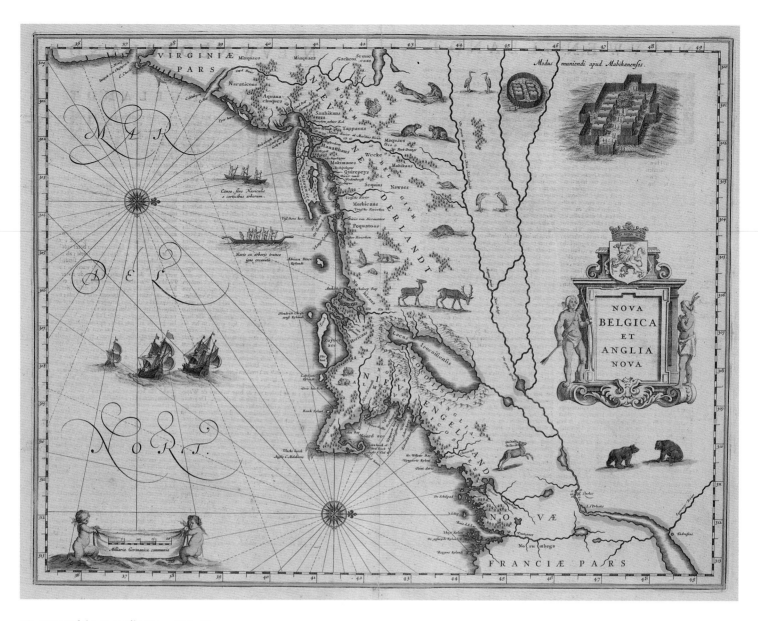

60 *Nova Belgica et Anglia Nova.* (Cat. 8)

8 *NOVA / BELGICA / ET / ANGLIA / NOVA*

Willem Janszoon Blaeu, cartographer; engraver unknown; published in *Nieuwe Atlas* by Willem Janszoon Blaeu and Joan Blaeu[1]

Amsterdam, 1635. Black-and-white line engraving with period color. H. 15¼", W. 19¾"

One of the most noteworthy features is Blaeu's inclusion of the fauna of northeastern North America—turkeys, cranes, egrets, coyotes, deer, rabbits, and bears. Blaeu was also the first to picture beavers, polecats, and otters. Two fortified Indian villages are in the upper right corner

One state of this map is known, although the atlas was published in four editions and in four languages

References: Burden, *Mapping of North America,* entry 241; Cumming, Skelton, and Quinn, *Discovery of North America,* p. 293; Deák, *Picturing America,* entries 18 and 27; Goss, *Blaeu's The Grand Atlas,* pp. 164–165; Koeman, "Life and Works of Blaeu," pp. 9–15; Schwartz and Ehrenberg, *Mapping of America,* p. 103; Stokes, *Iconography of Manhattan Island,* II, pp. 63–75; Suárez, *Shedding the Veil,* entry 46

In 1609, the Dutch became aware of English explorer Henry Hudson's discovery of the area known today as the Hudson River Valley. The following year, Amsterdam investors in the Dutch East India Company hired Hudson to sail westward to America in search of a northwest passage to the Orient. From the investors' perspective, Hudson's failure to locate a passage made the expedition a failure. However, the explorer returned with reports describing the abundance of fur-bearing animals and friendly natives in the region. Moreover, other European powers had not yet established monopolies on the fur trade in the Hudson River Valley. Another incentive for the Dutch to establish a foothold in what became New Netherland was that it enabled them to compete with the French, who controlled the North American fur trade along the Saint Lawrence River and in Canada.

In 1613, independent Dutch merchants sent explorer and fur trader Adriaen Block, who had ventured to North America two years earlier to explore New Netherland to substantiate the commercial possibilities reported by Hudson. The following year, after a great deal of competition, the merchants united and formed the New Netherland Company. They submitted a map, which Block created based on his explorations, to the States General along with a request for permission to establish a fur trade in America between the 40° and the 45° north latitude. *(fig. 61)* After the New Netherland Company received a three-year mon-

opoly, they established a foothold by erecting Fort Nassau on an island in the Hudson River near present-day Albany. Naming the Hudson River Valley "Niev Nederlandt," the Dutch merchants controlled the fur trade until their contract expired.[2]

Block charted the bays and rivers from Manhattan to Cape Cod and recorded the locations of Indian settlements along the coast. Although he surveyed the coastline carefully, it seems unlikely that Block ventured as far inland as Lake Champlain, which is erroneously located on his draft. The most logical explanation for this error is that Block probably consulted a 1612 French map made by Samuel de Champlain on which *Lacus Irocoisiensis* (Lake Champlain) was placed in New England rather than in its correct location above the Hudson River.

Block's chart was the primary source for Willem Janszoon Blaeu's *Nova Belgica.* Blaeu established his business as a globe and instrument maker and cartographer in 1599 and was joined by his son, Jean, around 1631, ultimately creating one of the greatest map publishing firms of all time.[3] The older Blaeu was appointed hydrographer to the Dutch West India Company in 1633. Two years later, he published *Nova Belgica,* which depicts the geography of the area for the period 1614–1623 when the New Netherland Company and the independent Amsterdam merchants controlled the trade.

In his capacity as hydrographer, Blaeu had access to geographical information from the previous twenty years of trading activity along the New England coast and from Block's explorations. Perhaps the Dutch West India Company encouraged Blaeu to create this map, on which he incorporated several features from Block's chart such as the delineation of Manhattan as an island and the names *Manhates* and *Niev Nederlandt.* Blaeu improved Block's configuration of Cape Cod, the course of the Hudson River, and the origins of both the Hudson and Delaware Rivers. For place-names, Blaeu consulted Smith's *New England* (Cat. 6) and a map made by Johannes de Laet in 1630 titled *Nova Anglia, Novvm Belgivm et Virginia. (fig. 62)* Blaeu's reliance on de Laet was logical since the latter was a director of the Dutch West India Company and one of six commissioners for New Netherland when Blaeu was compiling the map.

1968-128

---

1. The title in Latin is *Theatrum Orbis Terrarum;* in German, *Novus Atlas;* in French, *Le Theatre du Monde;* and in Dutch, *Nieuwe Atlas.*

2. After the New Netherland Company's contract expired Jan. 1, 1618, Dutch merchants enjoyed open trade until 1623 when the newly formed

61 Manuscript map
of New Netherland
attributed to
Adriaen Block,
ca. 1630.
Courtesy,
Algemeen Rijksarchief,
The Hague,
Netherlands.

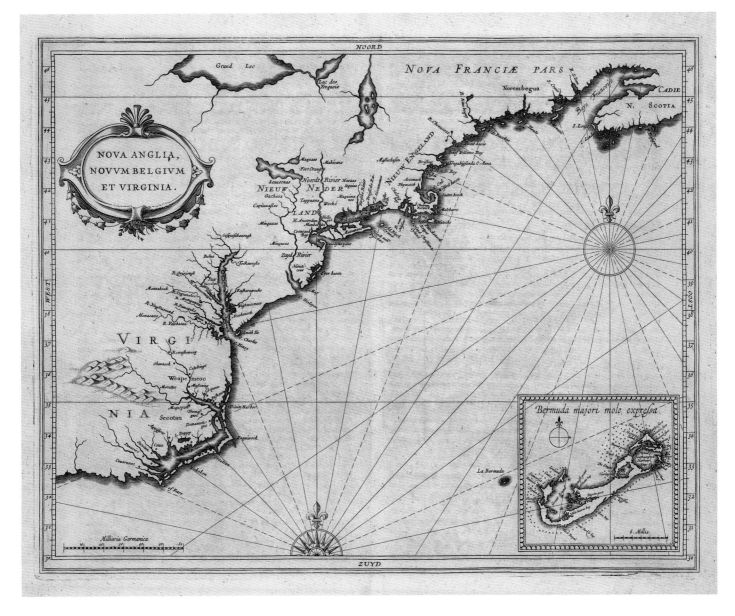

62 *Nova Anglia, Novvm Belgivm et Virginia,* by Johannes de Laet, Leiden, 1630, black-and-white line engraving. Courtesy, Bridget and Al Ritter.

Dutch West India Company was granted the monopoly. Two valuable sources for the history of Dutch settlement in New Netherland are Van Cleaf Bachman, *Peltries or Plantations: The Economic Policies of the Dutch West India Company in New Netherland, 1623–1639* (Baltimore, Md., 1969), and Thomas J. Condon, *New York Beginnings: The Commercial Origins of New Netherland* (New York, 1968).

3. For more information on the Blaeu firm and its role in the cartography of the seventeenth century, see pp. 396–398.

9 *Carta particolare della Virgi / nia Vecchia è Nuoua / La longitu.:ne Comi.:ca da lIsola di Pico di Asores: / D'America Carta. III_*

Sir Robert Dudley, cartographer; Antonio Francesco Lucini, engraver; published in *Dell' Arcano del Mare*. The first edition was published by Dudley, the second (1661) was jointly published by Antonio Lucini and Jacopo Bagnoni

Florence, 1661 (originally published in 1647–1648). Black-and-white line engraving. H. 18⅞", W. 14¹⁵⁄₁₆"

A cartouche containing the title is in the center right of the map

Two states of the map are known:
State 1: Lacking the addition, described below, that appears in the second state
State 2: (this copy) As described. "L.° 6./°" was added in the bottom of the cartouche

References: Burden, *Mapping of North America*, entry 279; Cumming, *Southeast in Early Maps*, entry 44; Cumming, "Early Maps of the Chesapeake Bay Area," pp. 285–286; Dilke and Dilke, "Dudley's Contributions to Cartography," pp. 10–14; Morrison et al., *On the Map*, fig. 14; *The World Encompassed*, entries 190 and 191

S IR R OBERT D UDLEY, an Englishman working in Florence, compiled this chart for his atlas *Dell' Arcano del Mare*, or "Secrets of the Sea."[1] It is significant that Dudley's work was the first atlas to use Mercator's projection for each of the charts. Dudley's atlas also included information about prevailing winds, currents, tides, ship construction, naval warfare, and magnetic deviation.

Sir Robert Dudley, the illegitimate son of the Earl of Leicester, was the brother-in-law of Thomas Cavendish, commander of the third circumnavigation of the world. Dudley studied navigation and shipbuilding at Christ Church, Oxford, where he matriculated in 1588. In 1594, he led an expedition to the Orinoco River and Guiana and attempted an English occupation of Trinidad. Dudley had a command in the Cádiz expedition and was later knighted

for his efforts.[2] His experience and valuable contacts gave him access to the work of other explorers. By the time Dudley began production of this monumental work, he also had collected an impressive library of books on geography and navigation.

In creating *Carta particolare della Virginia Vecchia è Nuoua* (Old and New Virginia), Dudley relied heavily on White's map for the Outer Banks of North Carolina (Cat. 2) and Smith's for the Delmarva Peninsula and much of the Indian nomenclature (Cat. 5). He identified the James River as *R: del Ri*, Newport News as *Forueza Nuoua*, and the Rappahannock River as *R: Toppahanock*. For the Potomac River, Dudley used the same spelling as Smith, *R: Patawomeck*, and included the alternative *Patomock* as well. Importantly, his chart of Virginia and the Outer Banks of North Carolina was the first printed sea chart of that area and the first to name the York River (*R: yorke*).

The distinctive visual quality of the maps in Dudley's atlas is due to the skilled talent of Italian engraver Antonio Francesco Lucini, who claimed he spent twelve years engraving the plates for Dudley's work.
1984-12

1. Although the volume was published in Italy, because its author was English, the work is considered to be the first sea atlas published by an Englishman.

2. For an account of the life of Sir Robert Dudley, see O.A.W. Dilke and Margaret S. Dilke, "Sir Robert Dudley's Contributions to Cartography," *Map Collector,* XIX (1982), pp. 10–14.

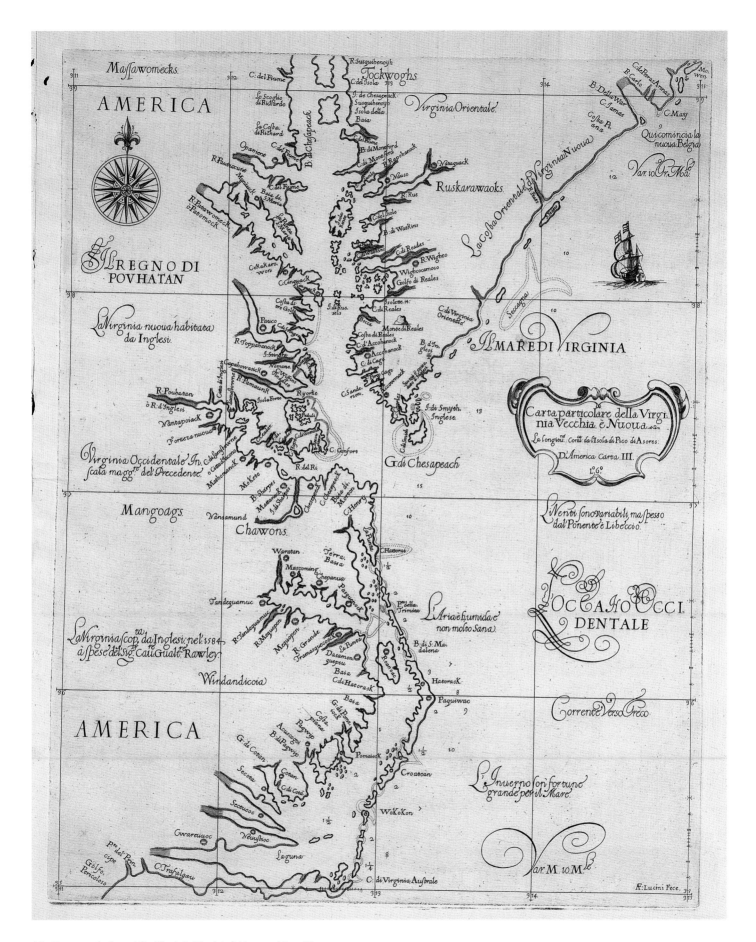

Massawomecks.

AMERICA

IL REGNO DI
POVHATAN

La Virginia nuoua habitata
da Inglesi.

Virginia Occidentale In
scala maggᵉ del Precedente

Mangoags

Chawons.

La Virginia scop. da Inglesi nel. 1584
à spese del sig. Caū. Gualt. Rawley

Windandicoia

AMERICA

R. Susquihenoyh
Tockwoghs
Virginia Orientale

Ruskarawaoks.

Il MARE DI VIRGINIA

G di Chesapeach

La Aria è humida e
non molto Sana.

C. di Virginia Australe

Qui comincia la
nuoua Belgia

Var. 10 Gr. Mai.

Carta particolare della Virgi
nia Vecchia è Nuoua
La longitu Comᵗ da l'Isola di Pico di Asores
D'America Carta III.
No 6º

Li Venti sono variabili, ma spesso
dal Ponente è Libeccio.

L'OCEANO OCCI
DENTALE

Corrente verso Greco

L'Inverno son fortuna
grande per il Mare.

Var. M. 10 M.

F. Lucini Fece.

63 *Carta particolare della Virginia Vecchia è Nuoua.* (Cat. 9)

10 *NOVA TOTIUS AMERICÆ TABULA*

Petrus Schenk (after Jan Mathisz), cartographer; probably engraved by Petrus Schenk (the geographical portion of the map and the view of New York); the two allegorical scenes at the bottom left and right of the map were designed by Philip Tideman and engraved by Willem Van Der Gouwen. The engraver of the remaining four views and the banner at the top is unknown

Amsterdam, ca. 1680. Black-and-white line engraving with period color. H. 23¼", W. 37⅞" trimmed (map only, without attachments)

A decorative border with putti arranging floral swags surrounding a banner containing the title *Nova Totius Americæ Tabula* appears along the top of the map. Within the banner, the word *Americæ* has been pasted over. A circular inset map of the Arctic Circle in the upper left has a small foliage cartouche in which is engraved *Cum Regionum sub Polo Artico aliæ/ ad Europam, aliæ ad Asiam, reliquæ ad/ Americam Spectent. Et singulæ ubi suo/ Toco in tabulis nominatim tradunter a/ se iniricem sint separatæ operæpræ:/ cium putori hic cas conjunctim et ut/ connexæ jacent exhibere, quodgra:/ tum tibisore certo mibi persuadeo.* A scene in the lower left corner depicts America between Indians laden with coins, slaves carrying baskets, and native fauna. The imprint *Gedrukt By/ PETRUS SCHENK/ Const en Caart/ Verkooper/ Op de Vygendam/ Tot/ Amsterdam/ Met Previlegie* is engraved in a cartouche in the right center (in the African continent). A seated Indian with the mythological scene of the rape of Persephone in the background is in the lower right. Five views were attached to the map at the bottom: *Nombred Dios* [a Spanish port and early settlement on the north coast of Panama], *Panama, Nieu Jork, S. Salvador,* and *Caput S. Augustini*

Only one state of the map is known

References: Burden, *Mapping of North America,* entry 313; Deák, *Picturing America,* entries 39 and 55

Around 1655, Jan Mathisz, a relatively obscure Dutch engraver, published a set of four wall maps depicting Europe, Asia, Africa, and America. *(fig. 65)* Mathisz derived the geography of North and South America largely from a 1648 world map by Joan Blaeu.[1] A copy of the first state of the Mathisz map in the British Library has a decorative title banner and five American town views pasted at the top and bottom, respectively. *(fig. 67)* Subsequent editions of Mathisz's map and others copied from it reflect the complex interrelationship between seventeenth-century cartographers and publishers. Mapmakers often purchased old copperplates in order to reissue previously published maps. In other cases, they reengraved earlier maps on new sheets of copper. Mathisz's copperplates appear to have been acquired about 1700 by map publisher Cornelis Danckerts III because one set bearing his imprint is known.

Philip Burden noted that Nicholas Visscher's 1682 sales catalog listed a set of maps of the four continents, thus raising the possibility that, although no copies bearing his imprint are known, the plates for the Mathisz map may have come into the hands of the Visscher family at some point.[2] Regardless of whether Visscher was selling copies of the Mathisz map, he published a reduced version, *Novissima et Accuratissima Totius Americæ Descriptio,* in 1670.[3]

Petrus Schenk engraved his own version of the Mathisz map about 1680, copying the geography directly, but creating his own ornamentation, most notably the two scenes in the lower left and right corners.[4] A decorative banner similar to that attached to the British Library copy of the Mathisz map bearing the title *Nova Totius Americæ Tabula* and a reengraved series of five views were pasted to the top and bottom of Colonial Williamsburg's Schenk map. Although the views on the Colonial Williamsburg map were assembled in a different order from that on the Mathisz, in each case, the central view is of New Amsterdam, the crown jewel of the Dutch American empire. On Schenk's map, this view has been renamed *Nieu Jork.*[5] *(fig. 66)*

Similarities between the period coloring of the map and the attached elements indicate they were done at the same time. In all likelihood, at least twenty-five years passed between the publication of the first issue of the Mathisz map and the Schenk copy. How these two maps came to have similar decorative features attached to them remains a mystery.

The center view illustrating New York is a close copy of the one previously published by Visscher (Cat. 11). That this view was pasted to the only two known copies of Schenk's map is interesting in light of the possibility that the Visscher family may have been in possession of the Mathisz plates.[6]

The depiction of California as an island is a misconception seen on many seventeenth-century maps. It is thought that a Carmelite Friar, Father Antonio Ascension, drew a map based on two Spanish navigators' reports of a large opening in the West Coast and a vast inland sea. Ascension's map was dispatched to Spain, but the ship carrying it was captured by the Dutch and taken to Amsterdam. Curiously, among the most influential supporters of the theory of California as an island was the same Visscher family of mapmakers that may have once owned the Mathisz plates.

Scenes illustrating figures and native flora and fauna frequently ornamented seventeenth-century Dutch maps. Schenk employed Philip Tideman, a German-born painter

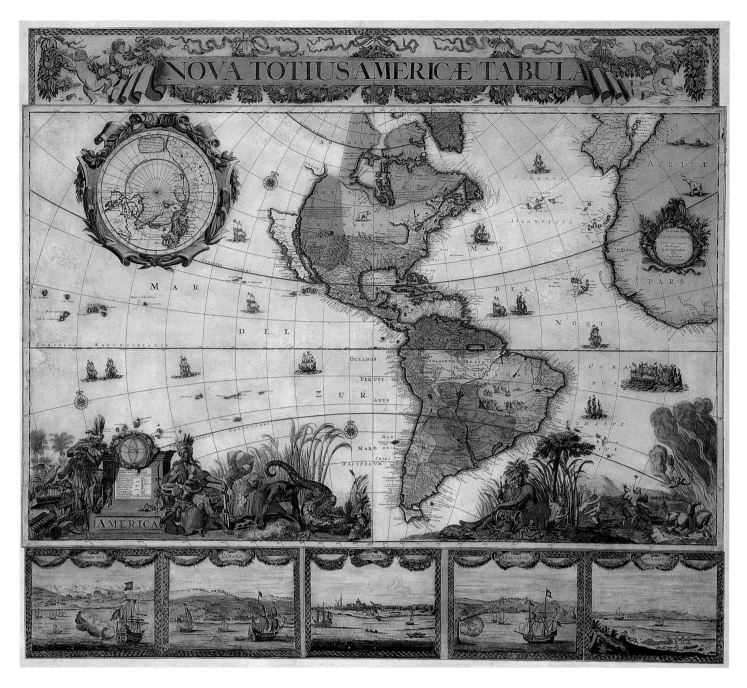

64 *Nova Totius Americæ Tabula.* (Cat. 10)

65 *America*, by Jan Mathisz, Amsterdam, ca. 1650, black-and-white line engraving with period color.
Courtesy, New York Public Library, I. N. Phelps Stokes Collection A-2.

66 Detail of the New York view from *Nova Totius Americæ Tabula,* by Petrus Schenk,
Amsterdam, ca. 1680, black-and-white line engraving with period color. 1961-169. (Cat. 10)

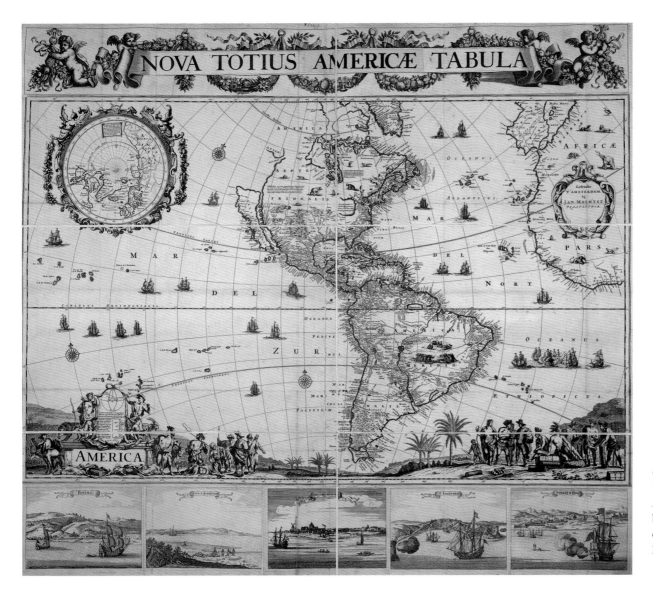

NOVA TOTIUS AMERICÆ TABULA

67 *Nova Totius Americæ Tabula*, by Jan Mathisz, Amsterdam, ca. 1650, black-and-white line engraving. Courtesy, British Library.

working in Amsterdam, to design the decoration for *Nova Totius Americæ Tabula*. Tideman was noted for painting historical and allegorical pictures, primarily for public buildings. In the lower left corner is a scene of Native Americans laden with goods while slaves labor in the background. The Rape of Persephone illustrated in the lower right was a subject suitable for a map depicting continents above and below the equator where the seasons are reversed. Persephone was the daughter of Demeter, the goddess of agriculture. One day while Persephone was gathering flowers, the earth opened up and Pluto emerged in his black chariot, captured her, and took her to the Underworld. Demeter began searching for Persephone rather than tending to her duties, so the crops died. Zeus intervened and ordered Pluto to release Persephone provided she had eaten nothing in the Underworld. Because she had consumed some pomegranate seeds, Persephone

was forced to spend the winter months in the Underworld and the summer on earth. Demeter was happy to have Persephone with her for half the year and made the crops grow again.

1961-169

1. Only three copies of the first issue of the Mathisz map of North and South America are known. The scarcity of copies of the first and subsequent reissues makes it difficult to trace the history of publication.

2. Burden, *Mapping of North America*, p. 405.

3. This map is illustrated in R. V. Tooley, "California as an Island: A Geographical misconception illustrated by 100 examples from 1625 to 1770," in Tooley, comp., *Mapping of America*, plate 41.

4. Ca. 1680 was assigned because Schenk formed a partnership with his brother-in-law, Gerard Valck. After that date, the names of both partners were generally included in the imprint.

5. One other copy of this map with the attached views and title is in a private collection.

6. Tooley, "California as an Island," p. 110.

11 *NOVI BELGII / NOVÆQUE ANGLIÆ NEC NON / PARTIS / VIRGINIÆ TABULA / multis in locis emendata / per Nicolaum Visscher*

Nicholas Joannis Visscher (after Jan Jansson), cartographer; published separately and in *Atlas Contractus* by Nicholas Visscher

Amsterdam, ca. 1684 (originally published ca. 1655). Black-and-white line engraving with period color. H. 18⅚", W. 21½"

In the center left are the same two fortified Indian villages found on Willem Janszoon Blaeu's *Nova Belgica et Anglia Nova* (Cat. 8). An inset view of *Nieuw Amsterdam op t Eylant Manhattans* is in the lower right corner. At the top of the view is a drapery cartouche containing the title surmounted by a coat of arms. To the left is a female Native American wearing an African- or European-style turban. To the right is the figure of a male Native American

Five states of this map are known[1]:

State 1: Lacking Fort Kasimier on the Delaware River. Ca. 1655

State 2: *t' Fort Kasimier* but not Philadelphia was added. Ca. 1656

State 3: *Philadelphia* and nearby place-names such as the Dutch colony of *Niew Amstel* were added. New nomenclature and a key appear around the mouth of the Hudson River. *Penn-syl-va-nia and Niew Jorck* were added. 1684

State 4: (this copy) As described. To the left of the view is *cum Privil. Ordin: General: Belgii Fœderati*

State 5: *Nunc apud Petr: Schenk Iun* was added below Visscher's name. Ca. 1729

References: Burden, *Mapping of North America,* entry 315; Campbell, "Jansson-Visscher Maps," pp. 279–294; Cohen and Augustyn, *Manhattan in Maps,* pp. 32–33; Deák, *Picturing America,* entries 38 and 42; Papenfuse and Coale, *Hammond-Harwood House Atlas,* pp. 38–39; Stokes, *Iconography of Manhattan Island,* I, pp. 119–132, 147–148, 150–152; Suárez, *Shedding the Veil,* entry 50; *The World Encompassed,* entry 250

BY THE TIME Nicholas Visscher published the first state of *Novi Belgii Novæque Angliæ Nec Non Partis Virginiæ Tabula,* the Dutch had occupied New Netherland for about forty years. From 1614 to 1623, Dutch trading activities in the area fell under the leadership of the New Netherland Company and other individual private merchants. Control was granted to the Dutch West India Company in 1623.

Life had become increasingly difficult for the Dutch colonists by the 1640s. Taxes were high, they had suffered through a disastrous Indian war in 1643–1644 that left their defenses weakened, provisions were low, and many were discontent with the West India Company's perceived mismanagement of the colony. In 1649, a group led by Adriaen van der Donck set sail for the Netherlands armed with documents substantiating their complaints.

This *Remonstrance,* formally titled *Vertoogh van Niew-Nederland,* proposed additional colonists for the colony, ways to achieve a more cooperative working relationship between the company and the settlers, and expressed the need to determine the boundaries between New Netherland and the English colonies. Van der Donck and his colleagues' efforts in putting their grievances before the States General, the legislative body governing Holland, led to the government's institution of critical reforms. Perhaps more significantly, Europeans' curiosity about New Netherland stimulated interest in the geography of that colony.

Accompanying the papers delivered to the States General in 1649 was a "perfect map of the country and its situation," drafted in manuscript by an unidentified cartographer.[2] There is little doubt that the map accompanying the *Remonstrance* provided the prototype for subsequent maps, such as this example by Nicholas Visscher and others by Jan Jansson, 1651, Justus Danckers, 1655, Adriaen van der Donck, 1656, and Hugo Allard, 1656.[3] Visscher used a variety of sources to record the geography of the region and included other European and English settlements rather than only Dutch holdings. *Novi Belgii Novæque Angliæ* provided the most detailed rendering of the area, locating many new settlements for the first time. Perhaps the most distinguishing characteristic was the inclusion of the view of *Nieuw Amsterdam* in the lower right corner. *(fig. 69)* The perspective, from Governor's Island, is thought to depict the town as it appeared about 1652. Visscher identified the various structures along the bottom.

Unfortunately, a few geographical errors in this widely distributed map led to boundary disputes that remained unresolved for over a century. A case in point involved the boundary between Pennsylvania and Maryland. The second state contained mistakes that affected the outcome of the controversy, which began when Charles II granted William Penn a charter for Pennsylvania in 1680. Two issues were contested. First, Penn disputed Lord Baltimore's belief that his charter included the Dutch settlements on the east side of the Delmarva Peninsula. Second, the proprietors also questioned whether Baltimore's northern boundary should be at the 40° of north latitude as accurately surveyed or at the latitude where it was thought to have been in 1632 when Lord Baltimore's charter was granted.[4]

Attempting to resolve the issue in 1685, the king decreed that the Delmarva Peninsula should be divided equally from the 40° of latitude as far south as Cape Henlopen. Baltimore lost thousands of acres of land by the

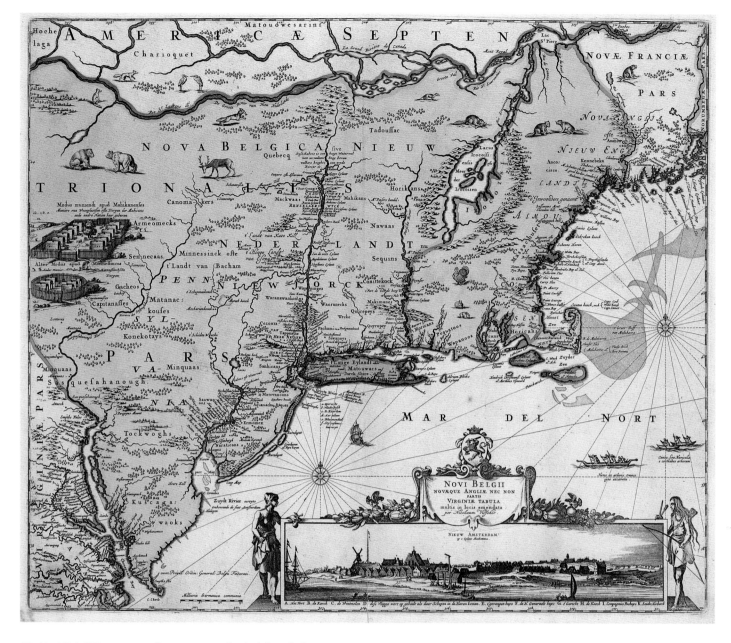

68 *Novi Belgii Novæque Angliæ nec non Partis Virginiæ Tabula.* (Cat. 11)

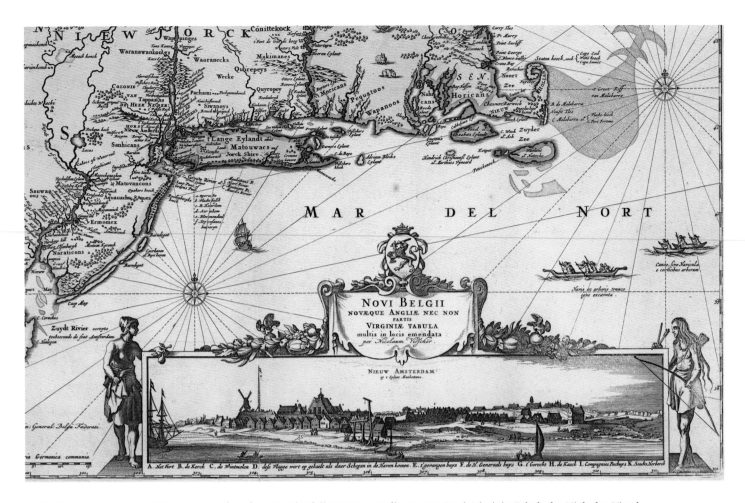

69 Detail of the view of New Amsterdam from *Novi Belgii Novæque Angliæ nec non Partis Virginiæ Tabula,* by Nicholas Visscher, Amsterdam, ca. 1684, black-and-white line engraving with period color. 1968-129. (Cat. 11)

decision because the king consulted Nicholas Visscher's map as a source. Cape Henlopen is actually located at the protrusion of land that the mapmaker referred to as Cape Cornelius; therefore, Visscher's placement of Cape Henlopen was about twenty-five miles farther south than it actually was. *(fig. 70)* Penn's copy of Visscher's map is in the John Work Garrett Library, Johns Hopkins University. On the reverse, in William Penn's hand, is the endorsement "The Map by which the privy Council 1685 settled the Bounds between the Lord Baltimore & I, & Maryland & Pennsylvania & Territories or annexed Countys. WP."[5] This issue was raised again in 1732 when representatives of both sides met, each producing maps to document their positions (Cat. 23).

Another error on Visscher's map led to a boundary disagreement between the colonies of New Jersey and New York. The Duke of York granted the proprietary of New Jersey to his court friends, Sir George Carteret and John, Lord Berkeley, in 1664. He set the boundaries

on the East part by the maine Sea and part by Hudsons River and hath upon the West Delaware Bay or River and extendeth Southward to the maine Ocean as farre as Cape May at the mouth of the Delaware Bay and to the Northward as far as yᵉ Northermost Branch of the said Bay or River of Delaware which is in fourtie one degrees and fourtie Minutes of Latitude.[6]

The duke apparently consulted Visscher's map, which incorrectly depicted the branch of the Delaware mentioned in the grant at 41° 40′ near a settlement called Mecharienkonck. The boundary was to be drawn in a straight line between this point to 41° north latitude on the Hudson River. In subsequent litigation with New York over the location of the boundary line, the residents of New Jersey preferred to abide by the designation of latitude (41° 40′) specified in the grant rather than the erroneous reference to the branch of the Delaware. Because New York colonists had begun to settle in the direction of the disputed boundary, they alleged that the Duke of York

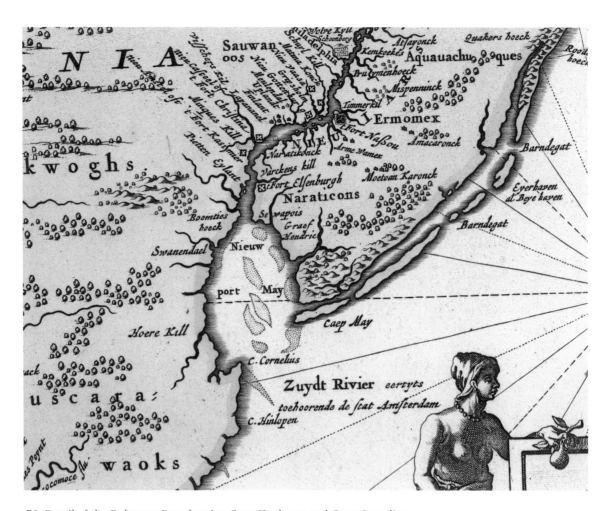

70 Detail of the Delaware Bay showing Cape Henlopen and Cape Cornelius
from *Novi Belgii Novæque Angliæ nec non Partis Virginiæ Tabula*, by Johannis Visscher,
Amsterdam, ca. 1684, black-and-white line engraving with period color. 1968-129. (Cat. 11)

had intended the line to be drawn from the head of the Delaware Bay. As a compromise, they proposed running it from the fork of the Delaware, which they determined was at Easton where the Lehigh River empties into the Delaware. Although a number of resolutions had been proposed by the mid-1750s, King George III did not appoint commissioners to settle the line until 1769.[7]

1968-129

1. Burden, *Mapping of North America*, entry 315. For a more detailed description of the various states, see Tony Campbell, "The Jansson-Visscher Maps of New England," in Tooley, comp., *Mapping of America*, pp. 279–294.

2. Some historians have suggested that the mapmaker may have been Augustine Herrman, who apparently did make a sketch of New York that was not sent to Holland until 1660. I. N. Phelps Stokes, *The Iconography of Manhattan Island, 1498–1909: Compiled from Original Sources and Illustrated by Photo-intaglio Reproductions of Important Maps, Plans, Views and Documents in Public and Private Collections*, I, reprint (New York, 1967), pp. 121, 142. For the Herrman attribution, see Victor Hugo Paltsits, ed., *Minutes of the Executive Council of the Province of New York*, II (Albany, N. Y., 1910), p. xii, and Gunther Schilder and Jan van Bracht, "New light on the mapping of New Netherland," in Joan Vinckeboons, *The Origins of New York* (Zurich, 1988), pp. 14–16.

3. Campbell, "Jansson-Visscher Maps," pp. 279–294.

4. For depictions of Baltimore's representations of the 40° of north latitude, see figs. 4 and 5.

5. Papenfuse and Coale, *Hammond-Harwood House Atlas*, p. 38.

6. Release from the Duke of York to Berkeley and Carteret, in Whitehead, ed., *Documents*, I; Snyder, *Mapping of New Jersey*, p. 14.

7. Snyder, *Mapping of New Jersey*, pp. 14–15.

12 *Noua TERRÆ-MARIÆ tabula*

Cartographer and engraver unknown; published in *America* by John Ogilby

London, 1671. Black-and-white line engraving. H. 11¼", W. 15⅛"

This Northerne part of Virginia (the limitts/ whereof extend farther Southwards,) is heere/ inserted for the better description of the/ entrance into the Bay of Chesapeack is in the upper left corner. A scale of distances is in the lower left. In the upper right is the Calvert coat of arms with attached drapery containing the inscription *The Atchieument of the Right Honourable/ Cæcilius Calvert Baron Baltemore/ de Baltemore Absolute Lord and/ Proprietary of the Provinces of/ Maryland and Avalon*

Only one state of this derivative of "Lord Baltimore's Map" is known

References: Morrison et al., *On the Map,* fig. 13; Papenfuse and Coale, *Hammond-Harwood House Atlas,* pp. 7–11

Published by John Ogilby in 1671, *Noua Terræ-Mariæ tabula* is essentially a second edition of a 1635 map bearing the same title that accompanied a promotional tract for the colony of Maryland.[1] Designed to attract colonists to the New World, such pamphlets generally described the richness of the resources and the potential for economic success there. Lord Baltimore's 1635 tract, *A Relation of Maryland,* also provided an inducement by offering one thousand acres to anyone who would transport laborers to the colony. He offered a further one hundred acres for each additional man or woman, fifty for each child, and fifty for each servant.

The 1635 version that appeared in the promotional tract was designed to illustrate the boundaries outlined in the charter, but it contained errors that later reduced the size of the grant claimed by Baltimore. The 40° of north latitude was incorrectly drawn at the head of the Chesapeake Bay. By 1671, the dotted line marking the northern boundary of the colony had been cleverly altered from the earlier version to include two more rows of trees within Maryland's bounds, extending Lord Baltimore's border farther up the Susquehanna River.[2] The issue in dispute was whether the Maryland border should be at the 40° of latitude as accurately surveyed or at the latitude where it was thought to have been when Lord Baltimore received his grant and published his first map. The Penn family eventually used Lord Baltimore's erroneous map as evidence to illustrate that Pennsylvania's boundary should be farther south. See Cat. 23 for more information about the litigation between the Penns and Calverts.

Ogilby's map was published in a series that included volumes on *Africa, America, Asia, China,* and *Japan.* While not always known for accuracy of description or detail, his books were interesting, well written, and popular with Englishmen proud of their country's expanding trade and exploration.

1984-211

1. For a comparison of these two maps, see figs. 5 and 6.

2. Ogilby probably had assistance from Lord Baltimore in preparing the text and the map, for they both included Cecil Co., which was not created until 1674. Papenfuse and Coale, *Hammond-Harwood House Atlas,* p. 11.

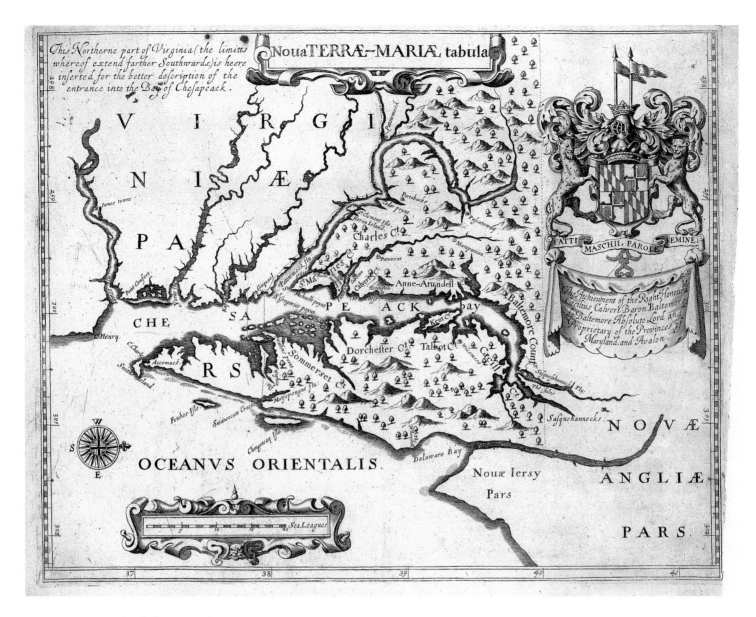

Map text as visible:

This Northerne part of Virginia (the limitts whereof extend farther Southwards) is heere inserted for the better description of the entrance into the Bay of Chesapeack.

Noua TERRÆ-MARIÆ tabula

VIRGINIÆ

PARS

NOVÆ ANGLIÆ PARS

OCEANVS ORIENTALIS

CHESAPEACK bay

Noua Iersy Pars

Delaware Bay

James towne
Point Comfort
C. Henry
C. Charles
Accomack
Smiths Island
Fetches Isle
Swanecutt Creek
Chingoteag Isle
Matapongue flu.
Sommerset Ct.
Dorchester Ct.
Talbot Ct.
Kent Ct.
Cæcill Ct.
Sasquehannocks
The Isles
Sasquehanock Flu.
Baltemore County
Matapanian
Anne-Arundell
Patuxent
Calvert Ct.
St. Maries Ct.
Charles Ct.
Heron Island
St. Clement Isle
Cedar poynt
Portobacke
Piscatoway
Pawtomeck

Sea Leagues

FATTI MASCHII, PAROLE FEMINE

The Achieument of the Right Honourable Cæcilius Calvert Baron Baltemore de Baltemore Absolute Lord and Proprietary of the Provinces of Maryland and Avalon

71 *Noua Terræ-Mariæ tabula.* (Cat. 12)

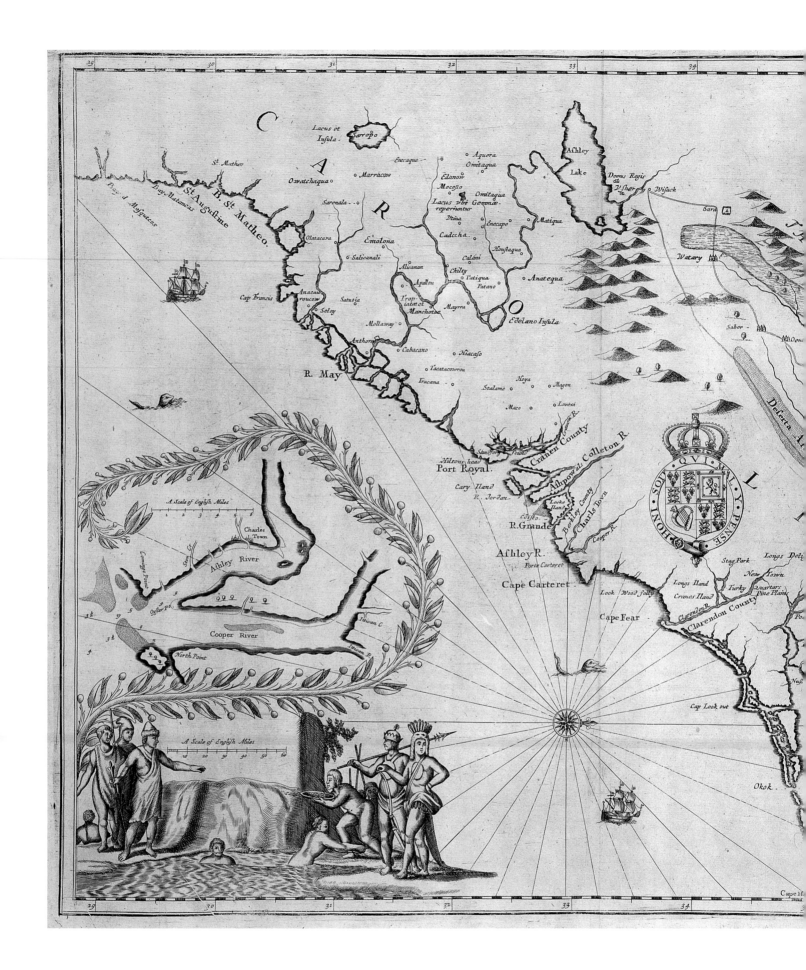

13 *A New / DISCRIPTION OF / CAROLINA / By Order of the / Lords Proprietors*

John Ogilby, cartographer; James Moxon, engraver; published in *America* by John Ogilby

London, 1672. Black-and-white line engraving. H. 16½", W. 21½"

In the lower left corner a scene depicts Native Americans and Europeans beside a pool of water. Just above, within a floral border, is an inset map of the Ashley and Cooper Rivers. In the upper right corner are two Native Americans standing among the trees holding a banner containing the title of the map. In the right center is the royal coat of arms of Charles II

Only one state of the map is known

References: Cumming, *Southeast in Early Maps,* entry 70 and pp. 16–18; Van Eerde, *John Ogilby*

CAROLINA was established in 1663 when Charles II granted the province to eight favorites, known as the Lords Proprietors, who had helped him regain the throne of England. The original grant included the territory between the 31° to the 36½° north latitude, from Jekyll Island, Georgia, to Currituck Inlet, North Carolina. Two years later, the tract was enlarged to include the land between 29° north and 31° latitude, thus adding a large portion of Florida. The grant extended west to the Pacific Ocean.

The Lords Proprietors wanted to attract potential settlers to the area. Just as John Ogilby's map of Maryland (Cat. 12) was a promotional piece for Lord Baltimore, *A New Discription of Carolina* was intended to encourage people to colonize Carolina. Recently established counties in the Carolinas appeared for the first time on Ogilby's map.

John Ogilby advertised in the *London Gazette* in October 1671 that "his second Book of the English Atlas (being America) will be Publisht on Wednesday the 3 of November."[1] In gathering information on Carolina, Ogilby turned to philosopher John Locke, who wrote the "Fundamental Constitutions" for the province. Locke was secretary to Lord Ashley, Earl of Shaftesbury, one of the most influential of the Lords Proprietors. Ogilby's text, taken largely from Locke's information, described Carolina's climate, natural resources, and inhabitants. Ogilby praised the friendliness of the natives and their good relationship with

72 *A New Discription of Carolina by Order of the Lords Proprietors.* (Cat. 13)

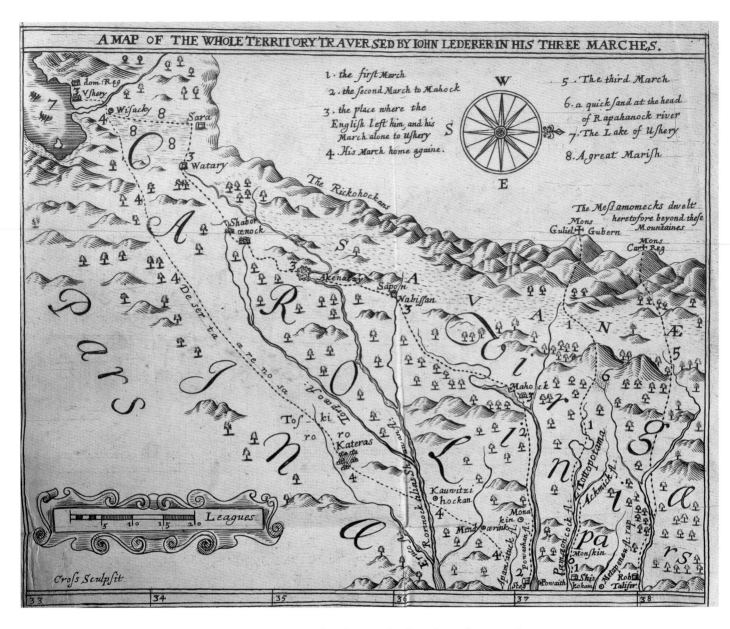

1. the first March
2. the second March to Mahock
3. the place where the English left him, and his March alone to Ushery
4. His March home againe.

5. The third March
6. a quick sand at the head of Rapahanock river
7. The Lake of Ushery
8. A great Marish

Cross Sculpsit

73 *A Map of the Whole Territory Traversed by John Lederer in his Three Marches,* by John Lederer, London, 1672, black-and-white line engraving. Courtesy, Virginia Historical Society, Richmond.

the colonists in great detail. On the map, Englishmen and Indians have gathered congenially in the lower left corner.

For the geography, Ogilby relied heavily on the explorations of John Lederer, a German interested in trade with the Indians, who made three expeditions southwest of Virginia and Carolina in 1669–1670 to locate a route through the Appalachian Mountains. Lederer's explorations ultimately helped open the great Indian path to the Southwest. Accompanied by a printed map illustrating the journeys, his account was published in London in 1672. *(fig. 73)*

Some inaccurate information depicted on Lederer's map unfortunately was borrowed by subsequent mapmakers anxious for new knowledge of England's colonial holdings. Ogilby was among a number of cartographers who included Lederer's imaginary lake of Ushery (renamed Lake Ashley, after the Earl of Shaftsbury, in 1672). Historians have suggested that perhaps Lederer saw the Catawba River during a flood and mistook it for a large lake.[2] Just east of the Appalachians, Lederer recorded a greatly exaggerated *Savanæ* [savanna] that also appeared on Ogilby's map. Lederer helped to establish a route vital to the success of the Virginia Indian trade. Although his accounts provided imporant information, it is regrettable

74 Detail of the cartouche from *A New Discription of Carolina by Order of the Lords Proprietors,* by John Ogilby, London, 1672, black-and-white line engraving. 1989-317. (Cat. 13)

75 Detail from *A New Discription of Carolina by Order of the Lords Proprietors,* by John Ogilby, London, 1672, black-and-white line engraving. 1989-317. (Cat. 13)

that Lederer is commonly remembered for the physical distortions he imposed on the terrain.

1989-317

1. Sarah Tyacke, *London Map-Sellers 1660–1720: A collection of advertisements for maps placed in the* London Gazette *1668–1719 with biographical notes on the map-sellers* (Tring, Herts, Eng., 1978), p. 5.

2. Cumming, *Southeast in Early Maps,* p. 17.

14 *A New Map of the ENGLISH PLANTATIONS in / AMERICA. / both Continent and Ilands, / Shewing their true Situation and distance, from / England or one with another, / By Robert Morden, at the Atlas. in Cornhill/ nere the Royal Exchange, and William Berry / at the Globe. between York House and the New / Exchange in the Strand. LONDON*

Robert Morden and William Berry, cartographers; engraver unknown

London, 1673. Black-and-white line engraving with period color. H. 17½″, W. 21⅛″

The cartouche containing the imprint in the upper left corner illustrates Native Americans. The royal coat of arms of Charles II is located in the upper center. In the upper right corner an inset in the shape of a half circle shows the North Pole and the northern regions of Europe and Canada.[1] A scale of distances in a cartouche flanked by putti is in the lower left

Two states of the map are known:

State 1: Proof state. Only one example is known.[2] (*fig. 78*) The most distinctive feature of this impression is that it lacks the shading along the shorelines indicating water and numerous placenames in Maryland, New Jersey, and in the polar region that were added to the final state. 1673

State 2: (this copy) As described. *Teches I, C Hinlope, Bear hole,* and *Egg Harbor* were added to the Maryland and New Jersey coastline. *The grand Lake* and *Nova Francia,* among other names, were added in the polar region

References: Black, ed., *Blathwayt Atlas,* map 3; Cumming, *Southeast in Early Maps,* entry 73; Deák, *Picturing America,* entry 62

In June 1673, Robert Morden and William Berry advertised in the *London Gazette:*

> A new Sheet Map of all the English Plantations in America, both Continent and Islands: shewing their true scituation, and distance for Trade, either from England, or one with another: as also their chief Towns, Ports, Harbors, Rivers, &c. Also the excellent scituation of the Isthmus of Panama, for Trade to the East-Indies.[3]

Issued as a single sheet rather than as a map intended for inclusion in a published atlas, *A New Map of the English Plantations in America* may represent one of the earliest general maps published to illustrate England's American

76 *A New Map of the English Plantations in America.* (Cat. 14)

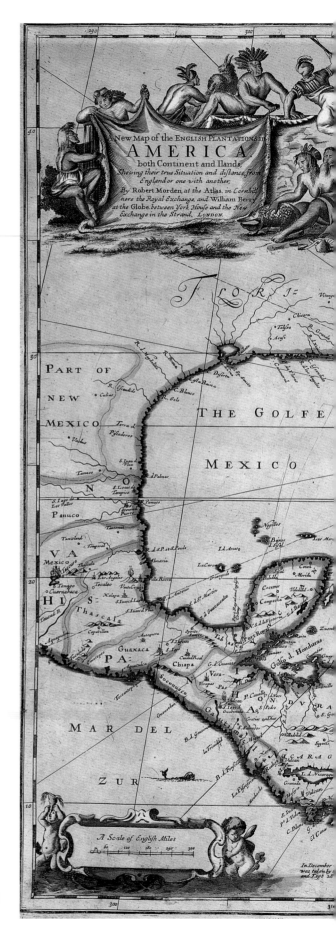

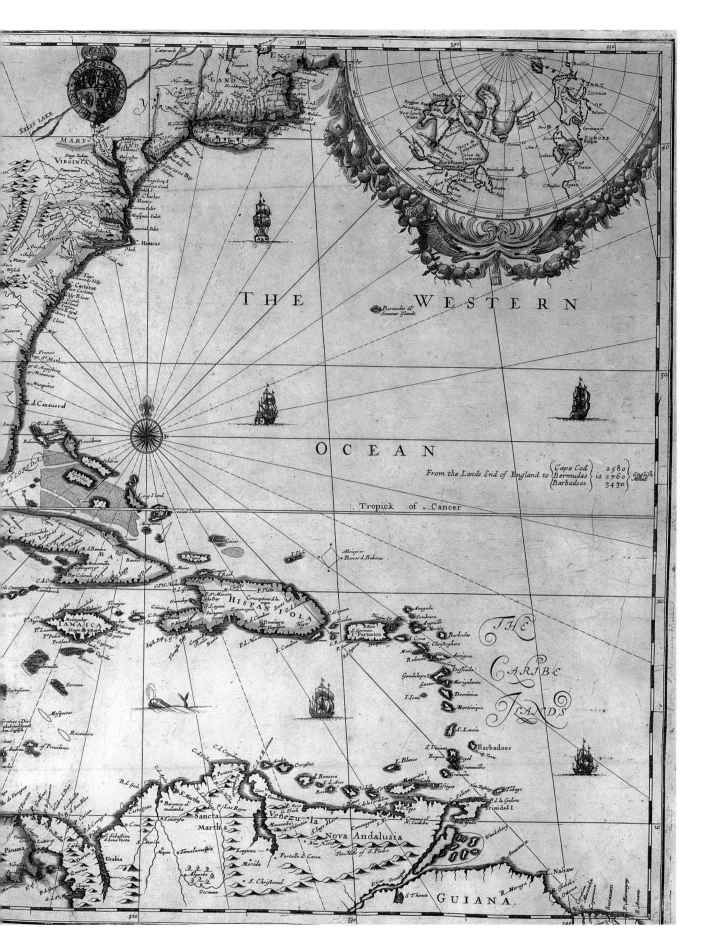

THE WESTERN

OCEAN

From the Lands End of England to { Cape Cod / Bermudas / Barbadoes } is { 2580 / 2760 / 3430 } English Miles

Tropick of Cancer

THE CARIBE ILANDS

77 Detail from *A New Map of the English Plantations in America*, by Robert Morden and William Berry, London, 1673, black-and-white line engraving with period color. 2000-17. (Cat. 14)

78 Proof state of *A New Map of the English Plantations in America*, by Robert Morden and William Berry, London, 1673, black-and-white line engraving. Courtesy, New York Public Library, I. N. Phelps Stokes Collection.

colonies from Hudson Bay to Guiana. Another copy was among the forty-eight assembled in a bound volume of maps and charts owned by William Blathwayt, now in the John Carter Brown Library, Providence, Rhode Island. Blathwayt was a member of the Committee of the Lords of Trade and Plantations, auditor general of plantation revenue, clerk of the Privy Council, and a member of Parliament for many years. Each map in the volume related to the trade and administration of England's American and West Indian colonies in the seventeenth century. That Morden and Berry's *A New Map of the English Plantations in America* is the third in the Blathwayt Atlas suggests that it was intended to provide an overall view of Britain's holdings. The two that preceded it are world maps, while those that follow are more specific.

This map shows the up-to-date, although largely incorrect, discoveries made by John Lederer, the first European to explore and record information about the Piedmont and the Appalachian Mountains. Lederer's map, illustrating each of his journeys, was published in London in 1672, one year before Morden and Berry's. (*fig. 73*) Like the previous map of Carolina by John Ogilby (Cat. 13), *A New Map of the English Plantations* incorporated Lederer's imaginary lake of Ushery and his large savanna.

In 1667, England and Spain signed a non-competing trade agreement that applied to the Americas. Careless wording and a loose interpretation of the territory affected by the document caused both nations to formulate policies relative to the area, creating an environment conducive to privateering, particularly in the Caribbean and Central

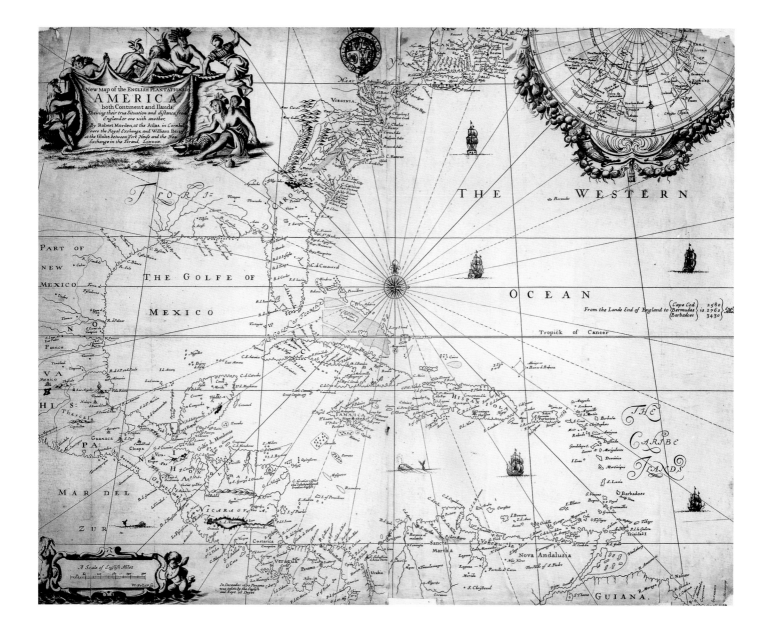

America. After repeated Spanish attacks on the English colony of Jamaica, Governor Thomas Modyford granted the notorious buccaneer, Sir Henry Morgan, permission to retaliate. With a force of nearly two thousand men, Morgan captured, plundered, and burned much of Panama, the richest town in Spanish America. As a result, a new treaty was signed whereby Spain recognized, for the first time, English rights to trade and colonize in the New World.

A notation on Morden and Berry's map by the southwest coast of Central America referred to Morgan's raid: *In December 1670 Panama was taken by the English and Kept 28 Dayes.* The cartographers' advertisement in the 1673 *London Gazette* said that their map illustrated "the excellent scituation of the Isthmus of Panama, for Trade to the East-Indies."[4]

2000-17

1. The polar inset on Morden and Berry's map is identical to that depicted on *A chart of the North Part of America* published by John Seller ca. 1675. Kenneth A. Kershaw, *Early Printed Maps of Canada.* I: *1540–1703* (Ancaster, Ont., Can., 1993), entry 213.

2. I wish to thank Henry Taliaferro and Philip Burden for calling attention to the proof state of this map in the collections of the N. Y. Pub. Lib. See fig. 78.

3. Tyacke, *London Map-Sellers,* p. 9. Morden and Berry collaborated on numerous maps between 1673 and 1677.

4. *Ibid.*

79 *New Map of the Cheif Rivers, Bayes, Creeks, Harbours, and Settlements, in South Carolina.* (Cat. 15)

15 *New Map of the Cheif Rivers, Bayes, Creeks, / Harbours, and Settlements, in / SOUTH CAROLINA. / Actually Surveyed is humbly Dedicated / by / Iohn Thornton. & Rob[t]: Morden*

John Thornton and Robert Morden, cartographers and publishers; engraver unknown

London, ca. 1695. Black-and-white line engraving. H. 19⅜", W. 22½"

Included in the title cartouche in the upper left corner is the dedication *To the Right Honorable/ William Earl of Craven : PALATINE./ Iohn Earl of Bath. George Lord Carteret./ Anthony Lord Ashley. S[r]: Iohn Colleton Barr[t]:/ Thomas Archdale. Thomas Amy. and the Hieres of/ Seth Sothell. Esq.[rs].* In the lower right corner above the scale of distances is *Sold by Iohn Thornton in the Minories and/ Robert Morden in Cornhill: London*

One state of the map is known

Reference: Cumming, *Southeast in Early Maps,* entry 118

J OHN THORNTON and Robert Morden's map of South Carolina provided the names and locations of more than 250 settlers and plantations from the Edisto River northward to the Santee. Maurice Mathews, who immigrated to the colonies as a planter and was surveyor general of Carolina, gathered most of the information, which was incorporated in a manuscript map drawn by Joel Gascoyne about 1685 that now is in the British Library.[1] Mathews illustrated the coastal islands and rivers from Charles Town south to Port Royal in much greater detail than shown on any previous map. He also delineated roads between New London and the Santee Indian fort. Cumming noted, "It was nearly a half a century before any part of North Carolina had a map approaching in quality those based on Mathews's work for the Charles Town settlement."[2]

Thornton and Morden undoubtedly gained access to Mathews's work through Gascoyne, who had earlier apprenticed with Thornton. The wealth of detail made the map a valuable resource for later cartographers such as Nicholas Sanson, Edward Crisp, and Herman Moll. The name *South Carolina* appeared for the first time on this map. 1989-369

1. Cumming, *Southeast in Early Maps,* entry 101.
2. *Ibid.,* p. 19.

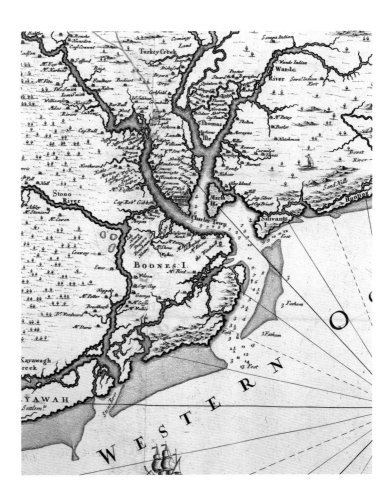

80 Detail from *New Map of the Cheif Rivers, Bayes, Creeks, Harbours, and Settlements, in South Carolina,* by John Thornton and Robert Morden, London, ca. 1695, black-and-white line engraving. 1989-369. (Cat. 15)

16 *A New Map of / VIRGINIA. / MARYLAND, PENSILVANIA, / NEW JERSEY, Part of NEW YORK, / And CAROLINA*

John Thornton, cartographer; engraver unknown; sold by T. Page and W & F Mount

London, ca. 1723–1728 (originally published ca. 1701). Black-and-white line engraving with period color. H. 42⅛", W. 34⅝", in four sheets

The coat of arms of William III is above the cartouche in the upper left corner. The title is followed by the imprint *Sold by T: Page W: & F Mount on Tower Hill.* Below the cartouche is the shield of Cecil Calvert, Lord Baltimore. In the center left are the coat of arms of the Perry family and the dedication *To M^r. Micajah Perry of London Merchant/ This Map of VIRGINIA &c.^{a} / is humbly Dedicated and Presented/* [erasure] *Thornton,/* [erasure]. A scale of distances surmounted by a protractor is in the lower right corner

Two states of the map are known:

State 1: The imprint in the cartouche is *Sold by Reeve Williams, Mathematician/ at the House at the North West Corner of St. Michaels Ally, in Corn-hill./ By John Thornton at the Signe of/ England, Scotland, and Ireland, in the Minories./ And Robt. Morden/ at the Atlas in Corn-hill/ LONDON.* The original inscription (in the Perry dedication cartouche) was *To Mr. Micajah Perry of London Merchant./ This Map of VIRGINIA &c. / is humbly Dedicated and Presented/ By Reeve Williams, John Thornton,/ and Robt. Morden*

State 2: (this copy) As described

In COMPILING *A New Map of Virginia,* John Thornton relied heavily on an earlier chart by Augustine Herrman, who immigrated to New Amsterdam as an agent for the Dutch West India Company prior to 1633. By 1660, Herrman had settled in the Chesapeake. The following year, Lord Baltimore presented him with the first of several land grants that ultimately totaled between twenty and twenty-five thousand acres. In return, Herrman agreed to prepare a map of Maryland. He spent over ten years surveying the Chesapeake and its tributaries, finally sending the completed draft to London where it was engraved in 1673. *(see fig. 12)* Thornton would have been familiar with the work since it was considered the most accurate representation of the Middle Atlantic region at that time.[1]

Thornton made few changes to Herrman's rendering of Virginia and Maryland beyond correcting the geographical orientation from north to right, as drawn by Herrman, and depicting north at the top. Thornton extended the geography to include the northern parts of Maryland, New Jersey, part of New York, and Pennsylvania, located the site of Philadelphia, laid out in 1682 and thus too late to appear on Herrman's map, and included an inset view of part of Carolina in the lower left corner.[2] He kept most of the names of settlements and plantations, although he changed *The North Sea* to *The Virginian Sea.* Thornton copied blocks of explanatory text from the earlier map, putting them in the same places, and kept Herrman's observations on the flow of the rivers. He reproduced notations such as the one that located where *Sr Will Barkley, Conquered and tooke Prisoner the great Indian Emperour Abatschakin, after the Massacre in Virginia.* However, Thornton improved Herrman's soundings in the Delaware and Chesapeake Bays, relying on a map that he published jointly with William Fisher for *The English Pilot The Fourth Book.*[3]

There are also artistic similarities between Herrman's and Thornton's maps. Both contain the coats of arms of King William III and Cecil Calvert, the second proprietor of Maryland. Some of the decorative ships included on Herrman's map appear on Thornton's. Even the protractor surmounting the scale of distances is similar on both.

One curious feature of the Thornton map is the coat of arms of the Perry family with a dedication to Micajah Perry, senior partner in the firm of Perry and Lane, one of the largest tobacco and fur-trading companies in London during the late seventeenth and eighteenth centuries. *(fig. 83)* They had mercantile interests in North Carolina, the West Indies, and Madeira, although their primary trade was with the tobacco colonies of Maryland and Virginia.[4] Among the many planters recorded as doing business with the Perry and Lane firm were the William Byrds of Westover plantation and William Byrd II's brother-in-law, John Custis. Perry and Lane also acted as agents for the College of William and Mary and for Governor Francis Nicholson.

A close examination of the Perry dedication revealed an erasure, suggesting that this version of the map was not the first state published. The only known copy of the first issue is in the collections of the British Public Record Office. Although badly worn, that copy supplied the original imprint of Reeve Williams, John Thornton, and Robert Morden erased from both the cartouche and the Perry coat of arms on state two.

Upon John Thornton's death, the business passed to his son, Samuel, who inherited "all his Mapps, charts, copys, instruments, copper engraved plates and all other things belonging to my calling."[5] According to Alice Hudson, chief of the map division of the New York Public Library, Samuel is known to have erased his father's name from copperplates, often inserting his instead.

It is likely that the first state of the map was published

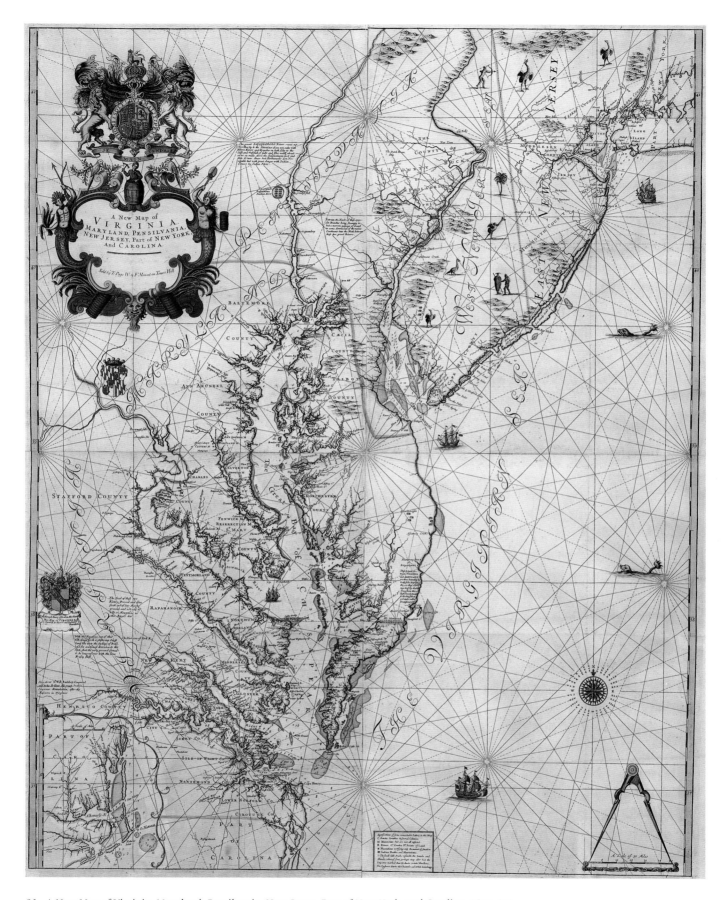

81 *A New Map of Virginia. Maryland, Pensilvania, New Jersey, Part of New York, and Carolina.* (Cat. 16)

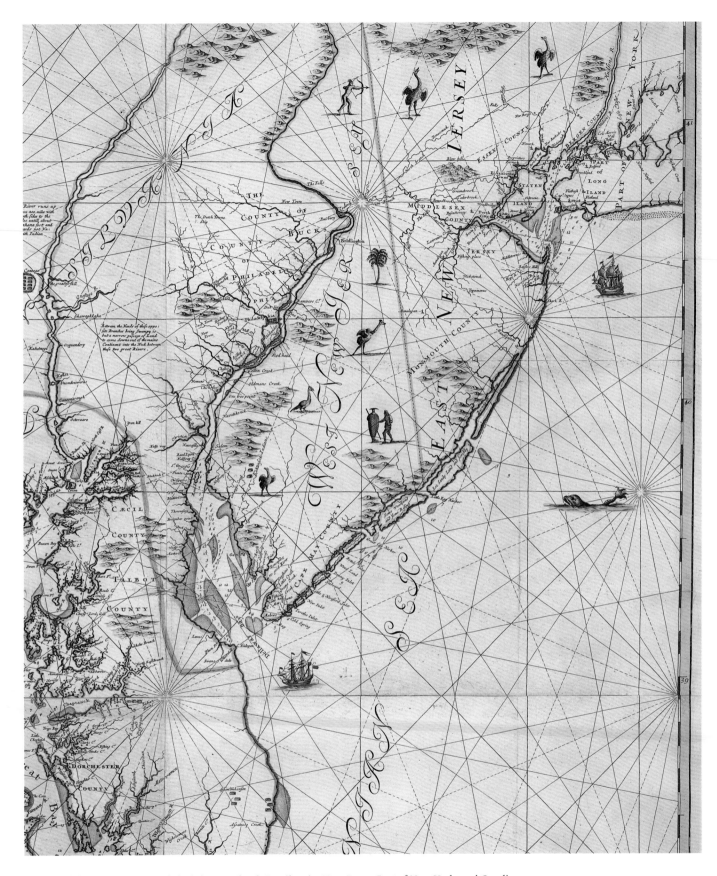

82 Detail from *A New Map of Virginia. Maryland, Pensilvania, New Jersey, Part of New York, and Carolina*,
by John Thornton, London, ca. 1723–1728, originally published ca. 1701,
black-and-white line engraving with period color. 1940-418. (Cat. 16)

no earlier than 1701. It could not predate that year because the Perry family, whose arms appear on the first issue, received their armorial bearings in 1701.[6] The map also bears the arms of William III. When Queen Anne ascended the throne in 1702, she significantly altered the royal arms. The date assigned to the second state, between 1723 and 1728, was based on the publisher's imprint. When Samuel Thornton died in 1715, William Mount and Thomas Page acquired the Thornton plates.[7] Between 1723 and 1728, Mount and Page were also in partnership with Fisher Mount, all of whose names appear on the second state of *A New Map of Virginia. Maryland, Pensilvania, New Jersey, Part of New York, and Carolina.*

1940-418

1. The copy of Herrman's map in the John Carter Brown Library, Providence, R. I., contains a paste-on slip that reads "Sold by John Seller. Hydrographer to the King at his Shop in Exchangᵉ Ally in Cornhill. London." Seller and Thornton frequently worked as partners from about 1677 to 1679. In association with Seller, Thornton published *Atlas Maritimus* and *The English Pilot* between those years. Simultaneously, Thornton became involved with *The English Pilot,* originally begun by Seller about 1671. Following Seller's death in 1701, Thornton formed a partnership with Richard Mount and continued the publication of *The English Pilot.* For other maps by Thornton derived from Herrman, see Custis Atlas Cats. 70 and 73.

2. The inset view of Carolina was copied from Thornton's *A New Map of Carolina.* See Custis Atlas Cat. 72.

3. Coolie Verner, *A Carto-Bibliographical Study of The English Pilot The Fourth Book with Special Reference to the Charts of Virginia* (Charlottesville, Va., 1960), pp. 10–11. Verner's observation that the soundings on the CWF map by Thornton were borrowed from the Thornton and Fisher chart is in his unpublished notes, some of which are in the British Lib.

4. During the early years of the eighteenth century, Micajah Perry's brother, Peter, served as a merchant in York Co., Va., and his nephew, Micajah Lowe, acted in the same capacity in Charles City Co., Va. For a complete discussion of the Perry firm and their activities in America, see Price, *Perry of London.*

5. Tyacke, *London Map-Sellers,* p. 145.

6. Price, *Perry of London,* p. 22.

7. Alice Hudson, "The Grand Samuel Thornton *Sea-Atlas*: a monument to the Thames School of chartmakers," *Map Collector,* LXV (1993), p. 3.

82 Detail of the coat of arms of the Perry family from *A New Map of Virginia. Maryland, Pensilvania, New Jersey, Part of New York, and Carolina* by John Thornton, London, ca. 1723–1728, originally published ca. 1701, black-and-white line engraving with period color. 1940-418. (Cat. 16).

17 *VIRGINIA / MARYLANDIA / et / CAROLINA / IN AMERICA SEPTENTRIONALI / Britannorum industria excultæ / repræsentatæ / â / Ioh. Bapt. Homann S. C. M. Geog. / Norimbergæ*

Johann Baptist Homann, cartographer; engraver unknown; published separately in *Atlas Novus Norimbergæ* by John Baptist Homann[1]

Nuremberg, Germany, ca. 1714. Black-and-white line engraving with period color. H. 19⁷⁄₁₆″, W. 23″

The title and imprint in the lower right corner are contained in a scallop shell surrounded by a planter, Native Americans, and symbolic elements

Two states of the map are known:
State 1: (this copy) As described
State 2: *Cum Privilegio Sac. Cæs. Majest.* was added in the bottom of the cartouche below *Norimbergæ.* 1730

References: Cumming, *Southeast in Early Maps,* entry 156; Morrison et al., *On the Map,* fig. 27

Previous discussions of maps such as John Ogilby's *Noua Terræ-Mariæ tabula* (Cat. 12) and *A New Discription of Carolina* (Cat. 13) have documented that the proprietors of Carolina and Maryland used maps as a way to entice settlers to their lands. Large property owners in royal colonies encouraged immigration in similar fashion. Such was the case with Lieutenant Governor Alexander Spotswood, who arrived in Virginia in 1710. Spotswood quickly became aware that years of tobacco cultivation had depleted the soil in the Tidewater, encouraging men of wealth to look north and west of the colony where vast tracts of uncultivated land could still be obtained at reasonable prices. Spotswood himself acquired thousands of acres on the Rapidan River. He intended to establish a settlement called Germanna and populate it with German colonizers.

The governor also recognized that the security of settlements in eastern Virginia depended on founding outposts in the west. He secured passage of an act that erected and manned Fort Christanna in southwestern Virginia as a buffer against attacks from the Tuscarora Indians.[2] Spotswood planned to build a fortification at Germanna to protect the settlement from Native American incursions from the northwest.

Before Spotswood purchased the Germanna tract, he discovered that the land contained valuable deposits of iron ore. Believing that the colonists' efforts should be

84 *Virginia Marylandia et Carolina in America Septentrionali.* (Cat. 17)

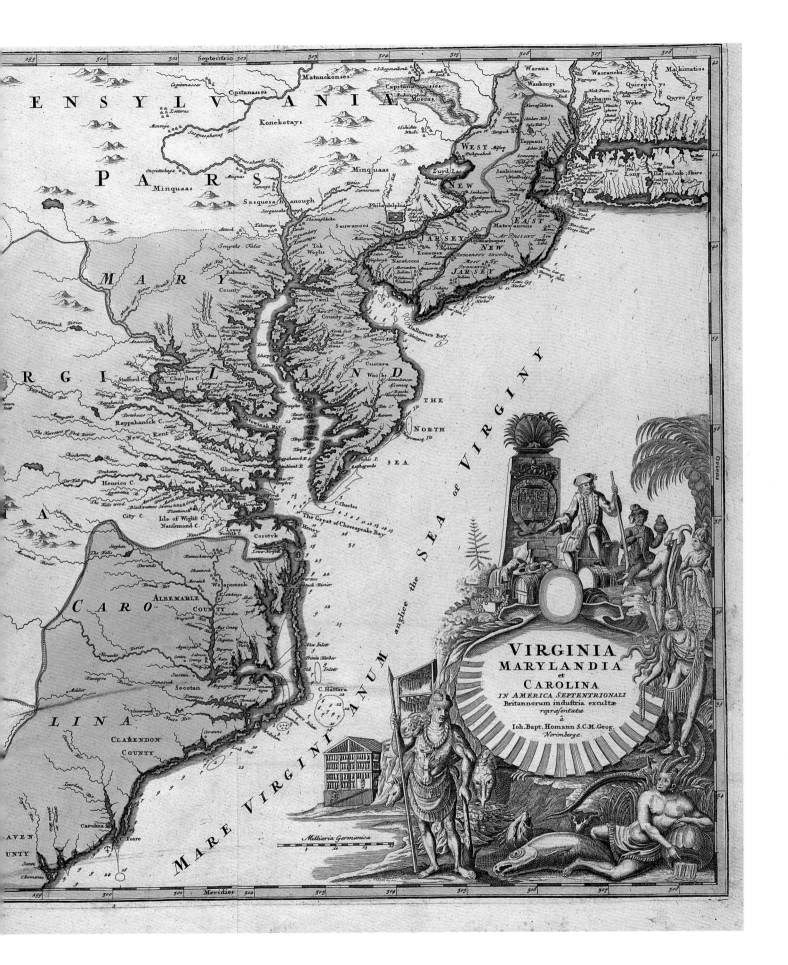

86 (*Above*) Detail of *Germantown Teutsche Statt*
from *Virginia Marylandia et Carolina in America Septentrionali*,
by Johann Baptist Homann, Nuremberg, Germany, ca. 1714,
black-and-white line engraving with period color.
1968-138. (Cat. 17)

85 (*Left*) Fireback excavated at Alexander Spotswood's home
and likely produced at Tubal, one of his three ironworks,
ca. 1720–1730. Courtesy, Virginia Historical Society, Richmond.

focused on exporting raw materials such as timber and tobacco, the Board of Trade disapproved of mining ore. However, Spotswood appreciated that establishing a mining community would further protect the frontier while increasing his personal wealth. He therefore submitted a petition to the Board of Trade for a scheme to mine silver—a more valuable metal—instead of iron ore. He negotiated with a German ore miner, Johan Justus Albrecht, and with promoter Baron Christopf de Gaffenried, to bring some miners to settle Germanna. In April 1714, a group of about forty landed in Virginia. The following year, Spotswood began to construct the furnace for his ironworks. Due to his success in mining ore, Spotswood ultimately built three furnaces in the area. Items such as

kitchen utensils, firebacks, and andirons from his manufactory were offered for sale in Williamsburg.[3] *(fig. 85)*

Probably in 1714, the year Spotswood established the settlement at Germanna, Johann Baptist Homann published *Virginia Marylandia et Carolina* primarily to encourage Germans to come to America, but much of the geography Homann depicted was outdated. Florida extended so far to the north that it formed a western boundary for Virginia, and Lake Erie was delineated far south of its actual geographic location. The cartographic significance of Homann's map was that it was the first to show *Germantown Teutsche Statt*, Spotswood's recent settlement. *(fig. 86)*

That Homann's map was intended to promote German

87 Alexander Spotswood, by Charles Bridges, Virginia, ca. 1735–1736, oil on canvas. 1940-359.

88 Detail of the cartouche from *Virginia Marylandia et Carolina in America Septentrionali,* by Johann Baptist Homann, Nuremberg, Germany, ca. 1714, black-and-white line engraving with period color. 1968-138. (Cat. 17)

immigration to America is reinforced by the cartouche. The well-dressed settler pictured at the top is surrounded by trunks, barrels, gold, exotic fruits, and natives bearing gifts. In the lower background are a tobacco barn indicative of the highly profitable tobacco trade and a shed for drying cod. A dominant feature of the map, this illustration suggested that America was the land of wealth and opportunity.[4] *(fig. 88)*

The Homann family was the most important and prolific supplier of cartographic works in Germany in the eighteenth century. They offered their stock either plain or enhanced with color. While there were certainly variations when color was applied by hand, virtually all of the Homann maps of *Virginia Marylandia et Carolina* were similarly rendered. In most cases, Carolina and East and West

Jersey were colored green, Virginia pink, and Maryland yellow. The cartouche was very rarely, if ever, colored during the period.

1968-138

1. For additional atlases containing Homann's map, see Cumming, *Southeast in Early Maps,* entry 156.

2. Fort Christanna was erected on the south side of the Meherrin River and staffed with rangers who were to assist Indians sympathetic to the English. The rangers were given a salary, supplied with arms, and exempted from paying parish taxes in return for their services.

3. Richard L. Morton, *Colonial Virginia.* II: *Westward Expansion and Prelude to Revolution, 1710–1763* (Chapel Hill, N. C., 1960), p. 483.

4. Sadly, the reality of the German situation in Germanna contrasted quite dramatically with the depiction in the cartouche. In 1715, Huguenot John Fontaine visited Germanna, noting that "the Germans live very miserably." Klaus Wust, *The Virginia Germans* (Charlottesville, Va., 1969), p. 21.

18 *To his Sacred & most Exellent/ Majesty GEORGE by the Grace / of GOD KING of GREAT BRIT- / AIN FRANCE and IRELAND &. / This Map of NORTH AMERICA / (Corrected from the latest Discoveries / and Observations) is most humbly / Dedicated by his Majesty's most Obedient/ Subject & Serv¹. George Willdey*

George Willdey (after John Senex, Charles Price, and John Maxwell), cartographer; H. Terasson, engraver; published in *Atlas of the World* by George Willdey

London, ca. 1717. Black-and-white line engraving with period color. H. 38⅛", W. 25⅞", in two sheets

In the upper left is a portrait miniature of King George I surrounded by an angel with a horn, the figure of Mercury with a caduceus, and a putto. Beneath the portrait miniature is the title within a large stone pedestal. Under the cartouche is an inset illustrating a number of small objects available from his shop with the advertisement *Maps Globes Spectacles Reading Glasses with these and many other usefull Curiosities are made and Sold/ Wholesale and Retail at the Great Toy Shop next yᵉ Dogg Tavern in Ludgate street very Reasonable by G. Willdey.* Various scales are contained within decorative framework in the lower left corner

One state of the map is known

Reference: Alexander, "Willdey's enterprising map," pp. 76–77

Gᴇᴏʀɢᴇ Wɪʟʟᴅᴇʏ's *Map of North America* provides an excellent example of seventeenth- and eighteenth-century cartographers' practice of copying earlier works for their own publications. Except for the omission of a few degrees of longitude on the east side of Willdey's map, the geography was virtually identical to that rendered on an earlier one by John Senex, Charles Price, and John Maxwell published in 1710.[1] *(fig. 90)*

The original cartographers borrowed the geography for their 1710 map, *North America,* from two maps published in 1703 by French cartographers Claude and Guillaume Delisle.[2] By using the Delisles' *Carte du Canada ou de la Nouvelle France* as a source, Senex, Price, and Maxwell were able to provide information on the individual islands in Hudson Bay that previous English maps showed as one large land mass. *Carte du Mexique et de la Floride,* delineating the mouth of the Mississippi River, was copied for the southern portions. Having relied solely on Delisle as a source, however, the three cartographers omitted recent English settlements and place-names such as Williamsburg.

The most interesting feature of Willdey's version of the map is the inset illustrating objects sold by the author at his shop. *(fig. 91)* Among the curiosities he illustrated were a knife box, pocket watch, telescope, combs, razors, shoe buckles, beads, spurs, and eating utensils. The advertisement beneath indicated that Willdey both made and sold these items at his Great Toy Shop.

As a mapmaker, Willdey was known for copying the work of others, often adding decorative elements and his own imprint. He was not known for making significant contributions to the field.

1971-446

1. Although Senex, Price, and Maxwell's *North America* was available as a loose map in 1710, it was also included in their 1714 *English Atlas.* In 1711, Willdey formed a partnership with Price, the latter bringing copperplates for his previously published maps to the new firm. Willdey subsequently reengraved new plates for his *Atlas of the World* based on maps retained by Senex and Maxwell.

2. Evidence suggests that many of the early works attributed to Guillaume Delisle were actually produced by his father, Claude. Guillaume claimed that his father was the first to position the mouth of the Mississippi River correctly. Jean Delanglez, "The Sources of the Delisle Map of America, 1703," *Mid-America,* XXV (1943), p. 279.

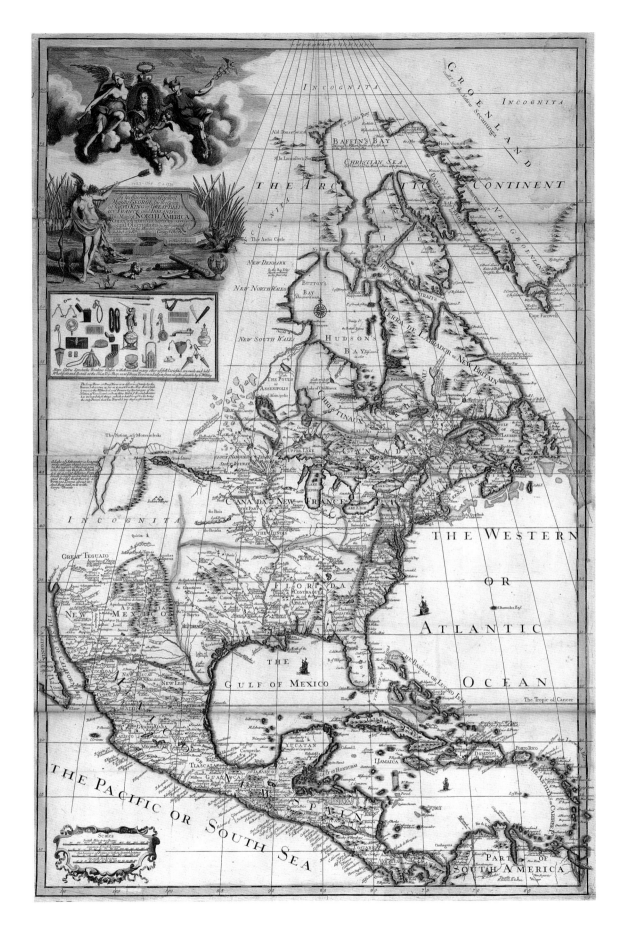

89 *Map of North America.* (Cat. 18)

90 *North America,* by John Senex, Charles Price, and John Maxwell, engraved by John Senex, London, 1710, black-and-white line engraving with period color. 1968-125.

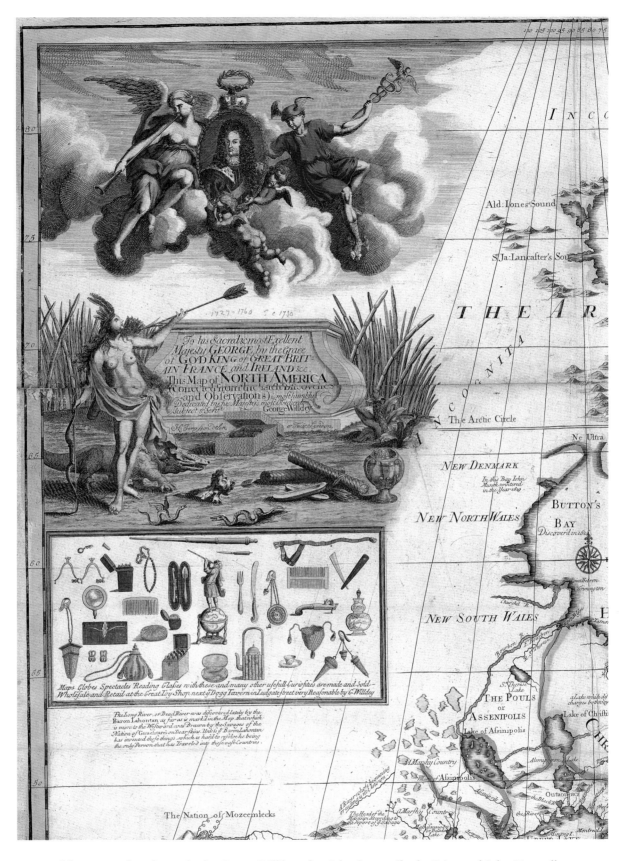

91 Detail from *Map of North America,* by George Willdey, after John Senex, Charles Price, and John Maxwell, London, ca. 1717, black-and-white line engraving with period color. 1971-446. (Cat. 18)

19 *A New and Exact MAP of the DOMINIONS / of the KING of GREAT BRITAIN / on yᵉ Continent of NORTH AMERICA. / Containing/ NEWFOUNDLAND, NEW SCOTLAND, NEW ENG- / LAND, NEW YORK, NEW JERSEY, PENSILVANIA / MARYLAND, VIRGINIA and CAROLINA. / according to the Newest and Most Exact Observations By / HERMAN MOLL Geographer*

Herman Moll, cartographer and engraver; separately issued and published in *The World Described* by Herman Moll

London, post-1735 (originally published in 1715). Black-and-white line engraving. H. 40¼", W. 24¼", in two sheets

The title is contained in a frame in the upper center. In the lower center is a cartouche with the following inscription: *To the Honourable / WALTER DOWGLASS Esqʳ. / Constituted CAPTAIN GENERAL and Chief / Governor of all yᵉ Leeward Islands in America / by her late Majesty Queen Anne in yᵉ Year 1711. / This Map is most Humbly Dedicated by your / most Humble Servant Herman Moll Geogʳ. / 1715.* Surmounting the cartouche is a coat of arms containing various weapons and the inscription *SAPIENTIA ET VIRTUS*
There are five separate insets within the map:

Inset 1: In the lower left corner is southeastern North America, including New France, Louisiana, Florida, and Carolina. Within the inset is the inscription *The Design of this Map is to shew the South Part of / Carolina, and the East Part of Florida, possess'd / since September 1712 by the French and called Loui-/siana; together with some of the principal Indian Set: / tlements and the Number of the Fighting Men Accor: / ding to the account of Capᵗ T. Nearn and others*

Inset 2: In the lower center is *A Map of the Improved Part of / CAROLINA / With the Settlements &c. / By Her. Moll Geographer*

Inset 3: In the lower right corner is *A Map of the / PRINCIPAL PART of NORTH / AMERICA*

Inset 4: Located just above inset three is *A Draught of yᵉ Town and Harbour of / CHARLES-TOWN*

Inset 5: Above inset four and directly to the left of the dedicatory cartouche is a view of Niagara Falls and beavers commonly called "the Beaver Inset"

Five states of the map are known[1]:

State 1: With the imprint *Sold by H. Moll over against Devereux Court without Temple Bar*. The Carolina inset was not yet divided into parishes. *Cherecies 3000 men* was engraved within the Louisiana inset. 1715

State 2: The imprint was changed to *Sold by H. Moll / and by I. King at yᵉ Globe in yᵉ Poultrey near Stock's Market*. 1726

State 3: Moll's name was deleted from the imprint, which retained only *I. King*. *Cherecies 3000 men* within the Louisiana inset was changed to *Cherecies 3000 Men, one of the Kings &c of this Nation was in England 1730*. 1731

State 4: The imprint was changed again to *Printed and Sold by Tho: Bowles next yᵉ Chapter House in Sᵗ Pauls Church-yard, John Bowles at the Black Horse in Cornhill, and by I. King at yᵉ Globe in yᵉ Poultrey near Stocks Market*. The Carolina inset was divided into counties. 1731

State 5: (this copy) As described. This state was taken from the original London plate. The imprint was changed to *Printed and sold by Tho: Bowles next yᵉ Chapter House in Sᵗ Pauls / Church-yard, John Bowles & Son, at the Black Horse in Cornhil. / and by I. King at yᵉ Globe in yᵉ Poultrey near Stocks Market*. Post-1735

Second edition: A new plate was engraved and published in Ireland with *Dedicated to Luke Gardiner, Deputy Vice Treasurer . . . of his Majesties Revenue in Ireland*. The imprint was *Sold by Geo. Grierson, Printer to the King's Most Excellent Majesty, at the King's Arms and Two Bibles in Essex Street*. Possibly 1735

References: Cumming, *British Maps*, pp. 6–12; Cumming, *Southeast in Early Maps*, entry 158 and pp. 21–24; Reinhartz, "Herman Moll Geographer," pp. 18–36; Schwartz and Ehrenberg, *Mapping of America*, pp. 138, 144; Stevens and Tree, "Comparative Cartography," entry 55.

Herman Moll's *A New and Exact Map of the Dominions of the King of Great Britain on yᵉ Continent of North America* is popularly known as the "Beaver Map" in honor of its large inset of Niagara Falls with a colony of beavers at work in the foreground. The Beaver Map, along with the next two maps described in this book, are noted for being among the first and most important cartographic documents relating to the ongoing dispute between France and Great Britain over boundaries separating their respective American colonies. Moll's map focused on English counterclaims to French-occupied territories. The map was the primary cartographic exponent of the British position during the period immediately following the Treaty of Utrecht in 1713. Although France had been forced to cede Nova Scotia, claims to Hudson Bay, and most of Newfoundland to the English, it did retain New France. Off the fishing banks of the Newfoundland coast, Moll noted that under the terms of the treaty, the French were:

> allowed to catch Fish, and to dry them on land, in that Part only, and no other, of the Island of Newfound-Land, which stretches from Cape Bonavista [on the east cost] to the Northern point of the Island, and from thence running down by the Western side, reaches as far as Point Riche: But the Island Cape Briton, as also all others both in ye mouth of the River St. Laurens and the Gulph of the same name, are given by the same Treaty to the French, with all the maner of Liberty, to Fortify any Place, or Places, there.

Moll illustrated the east coast of America from Canada

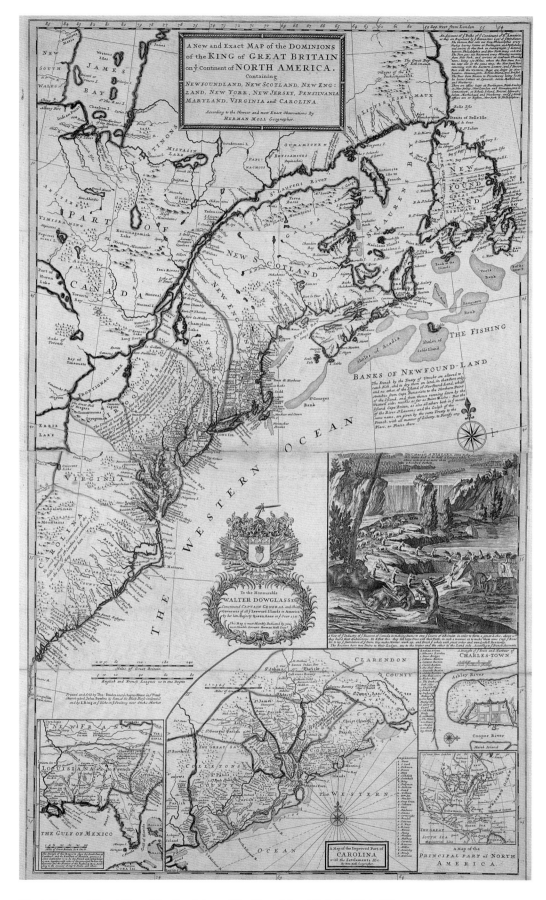

92 *A New and Exact Map of the Dominions of the King of Great Britain.* (Cat. 19)

The Cataract of NIAGARA, some make this Water-Fall to be half a League while others reckon it no more than a hundred Fathom

93 Detail of the beaver inset from *A New and Exact Map of the Dominions of the King of Great Britain*, by Herman Moll, London, post-1735, originally published between 1709 and 1720, black-and-white line engraving. 1968-130. (Cat. 19)

southward to the Gulf of Mexico and the Mississippi River. Along the Appalachian Mountain range, he described the Iroquois, claiming they were *hearty friends to y* *English* and in 1710 had offered their services *ag*[t.] *y* *French in Canada*.[2] The lower left inset of the Gulf of Mexico and the Mississippi River is significant. Moll credited the geography of this area to Thomas Nairne, Indian agent for South Carolina and author of Carolina's Indian policy, who had traveled as far as the Mississippi, dealing with the French and Indians trading in the area.[3]

An Account of y *Posts of y* *Continent of N.*[th] *America as they are Regulated by y* *Postmasters Gen*[l.] *of y* *Post House* is engraved in the upper right corner. This map is generally considered to be the first postal map of the colonies. Cumming noted that the lower center inset depicts a road from *Charles Town* to *Phil, PA*, concluding this was a reference to the post route from Charleston to Philadelphia.[4]

The most striking feature is the inset of Niagara Falls with the beaver scene. *(fig. 93)* The view of Niagara Falls first appeared in Louis Hennepin's *Nouvelle decouverte d'un très grand Pays Situé dans l'Amérique*, published in Utrecht in 1697. The following year, an English version was printed

with newly engraved plates. In 1713, French royal geographer Nicholas de Fer copied Hennepin's view of the falls as a backdrop for a scene of industrious beavers on *Carte de La Mer du Sud & de La Mer du Nord*. De Fer's map provided Moll with the source for his view.

The beaver was an appropriate image for North American maps for two reasons: the animal's importance to the fur trade and its industrious nature. That beaver pelts were a significant part of the lucrative fur trade was also suggested in the cartouche from Pieter Goos's 1666 chart of New Jersey, where the design was centered on the beaver skins. *(fig. 94)* Virginian William Byrd II recorded that

the Fur of these creatures is very valuable, especially in the more Northern Countries, where it is longer and finer. This the Dutch have lately contriv'd to mix with their Wool, and Weave into a Sort of Drugget, that is not only warm, but wonderfully light and Soft. They also make Gloves and Stockings of it, that keep out the Cold almost as well as the fur itself, and do not look quite so Savage.[5]

The beaver symbolized the concept that only the industrious could control the land. Byrd wrote:

Beavers have more of Instinct, that Half-Brother of Reason, than any other Animal, especially in matters of Self-Preservation . . . They perform all their Works in the Dead of Night, to avoid Discovery, and are kept diligently to it by the Master Beaver, which by his age or strength has gain'd to himself an Authority over the rest.[6]

Just as many early map cartouches illustrated America as the land of wealth and opportunity, Moll's depiction of the *Industry of yᵉ Beavers* also related to promoting settlement in America. Since industry was known to produce wealth, the beaver represented what could be achieved with *great order and wonderfull Dexterity*. Adriaen van der Donck published *Beschryvinge Van Nieuvv-Nederlant*, a promotional tract for New Netherland, in 1656. He described the work on the title page as:

Understanding the Nature, Character, situation and fruitfulness of this land; also the profitable and desirable changes falling thereto that may be found for the maintenance of Man. Also the manner and qualities of the Savages or Natives of the land. And the particular story of the wonderful Nature and Character of the BEAVERS.[7]

Hollander Herman Moll came to London during the 1680s and began to work for publishers such as Philip Lea. *The World Described,* the atlas in which this map was published, was the first to illustrate two-sheet maps folded into quarters.[8] Moll's maps were well known in the colonies. The 1741 inventory of the estate of Francis Robinson, "late Usher of the Grammar School of the College of William & Mary," listed "7 Moll's Mapps" valued at £1.6.[9] Philip Fithian, tutor to the children of Robert Carter of Nomini Hall plantation in the Northern Neck of Virginia, recorded in 1774 that George Lee and Mr. Grubb dined there in the afternoon. That evening, "Grubb opened a huge *Molls Atlas* that lay in the room."[10] Carter's copy of Moll's atlas containing this map survives today and bears the label "Case 6, Shelf 7 Robert Carter."[11]

1968-130

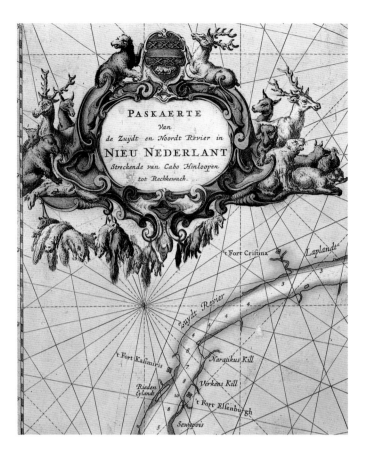

94 Detail of the cartouche from *Paskaerte Van de Zuydt en Noordt Revier in Niew Nederlant,* by Pieter Goos, Amsterdam, 1666, black-and-white line engraving with period color. Courtesy, New York Public Library, Stokes Collection.

1. Cumming, *Southeast in Early Maps,* pp. 207–208; Stevens and Tree, "Comparative Cartography," pp. 87–88.

2. Moll included these comments on the map.

3. The geography Nairne recorded during his journey was published by Edward Crisp in 1711 and represented the first depiction of the Mississippi Valley recorded by a British colonial. Moll claimed on the map that the French had only occupied that region since 1712.

4. William P. Cumming. *British Maps of Colonial America* (Chicago, 1974), p. 10. Moll's information on the postal routes is described on the map.

5. William K. Boyd, ed., *William Byrd's Histories of the Dividing Line Betwixt Virginia and North Carolina,* reprint (New York, 1967), p. 294.

6. *Ibid.,* p. 292.

7. Quoted in Adrian Johnson, *America Explored: A cartographical history of the exploration of North America* (New York, 1974), p. 116.

8. Herman Moll's *The World Described; or A New and Correct Sett of Maps* was first published in 1709. As Moll produced new two-sheet maps, he included them in revised editions of the atlas.

9. *WMQ,* 2nd Ser., I (1921), p. 56.

10. Hunter Dickinson Farish, ed., *Journal & Letters of Philip Vickers Fithian: A Plantation Tutor of the Old Dominion, 1773–1774,* reprint (Charlottesville, Va., 1978), p. 157.

11. John Barden, research report on the Carter library at Oatlands, John D. Rockefeller, Jr. Library, Colonial Williamsburg Foundation, Williamsburg, Va.

20 CARTE DE LA LOUISIANE ET DU COURS DU MISSISSIPI Dressée sur un grand nombre de Memoires entrau.*tres* sur ceux de M.*r* le Maire Par Guill.*aume* Delisle de l' Academie R.*le* des Scien.*ces*

Guillaume Delisle, cartographer; engraver unknown; published separately and in *Atlas François* by C. H. A. Jaillot, 1720, state two, *Atlas Géographique et Universel* by G. Delisle and P. Buache, 1700–1763, state three, and *Atlas Géographique et Universel* by G. Delisle and P. Buache, 1781–1784

Paris, June 1718. Black-and-white line engraving with period outline color. H. 19⅜", W. 25¼"

There is a compass rose in the lower center. Beside it is the imprint *A PARIS/ Chez l'Auteur le S.r Delisle/ sur le Quay de l'Horloge/ avec Privilege du Roy Juin 1718.* An inset of *CARTE/ PARTICULIERE/ DES EMBOUCHURES/ DE LA RIVIE S LOUIS/ ET DE LA MOBILE* is in the lower right

Four states of the map are known[1]:

State 1: (this copy) As described

State 2: New Orleans was added. 1718

State 3: *Ph. Bauche P. G. d. l' A. R. d. S. Gendre de l' Auteur. Avec Privilege du 30 an. 1745* was added in the lower right corner. 1745

State 4: The legend across the top was changed to *Carte de la Louisiane et du Cours du Mississipi Avec Les Colonies Anglaises. Revue, Corigée et considérablem.t / Augumenteé en 1782. Par Guill.aume Delisle de l Academie R.le de Scien.ces* The imprint above the scale of distances was changed to *A Paris /Chez Dezauche successeur des Sieurs/ De l' Isle et Buache, Rue des Noyers près la Rue des Anglis.* Ca. 1782

References: Cumming, *British Maps,* pp. 6–12; Cumming, *Southeast in Early Maps,* entry 170 and pp. 21–24; Cumming et al., *Exploration of North America,* pp. 35–54, 146–157; McCorkle, *America Emergent,* entry 20; Pelletier, "From New France to Louisiana," pp. 85–95; Schwartz and Ehrenberg, *Mapping of America,* p. 146

COVERING the territory between the Hudson River in the east and the Rio Grande in the west, Guillaume Delisle's *Carte de la Louisiane et du Cours du Mississipi* is one of the most significant maps of America ever made. Among its many distinctions, the map provided a relatively accurate depiction of the watershed of the Mississippi, was the first to show New Orleans (second state), and the first to use the name Texas. Because he was mapmaker to the king, Delisle's maps were regarded as quasi-official documents that reflected the opinions and policies of the French government. His expansion of French territorial claims at the expense of the British and Spanish empires caused great alarm in London and Madrid.

Delisle extended Louisiana westward to the Pecos River (*Rio Salado de Apaches*), thereby claiming Texas as a part of that French colony, while restricting the British to the eastern slope of the Appalachian Mountains. He extended Pennsylvania only as far west as the Susquehannah River and asserted that Carolina was originally discovered, named, and settled by the French. However, based on the royal charters of Virginia and North Carolina, Britain claimed all the territory from the Atlantic to the Mississippi.[2] Governor William Burnet of New York was so outraged by Delisle's claims that he wrote to the Board of Trade in 1720:

> *I observe in the last mapps published at Paris with Privilege du Roy par M de Lisle in 1718 of Louisiana and part of Canada that they are making new encroachments on the King's territories from what they pretended to in a former Mapp publishd by the same author in 1703.*[2]

French expansionists at home and English colonists in America were acutely aware of the advantages of gaining control of the American Southwest. The French realized that establishing footholds from the mouth of the Mississippi northward to New France would enable them to dominate the entire interior corridor of North America, thereby securing a monopoly of the fur trade and limiting English colonists to the Eastern Seaboard. The French would also be in a better position to threaten the gold and silver mines in the Southwest that had helped generate great wealth for the Spanish empire.

English colonists were concerned that if the French continued to develop trade relations with tribes in the Mississippi Valley, the safety of English settlements in the area would be endangered. The English, who had traded for years with the Cherokee and Illinois, were also aware that the French could effectively cut into their market.

Delisle understood the strategic importance of the Mississippi Valley and also recognized that little was known of the geography north of the Gulf of Mexico. Therefore, when compiling information on the area, he studied the routes taken by earlier explorers such as Hernando de Soto, René-Robert Cavelier, sieur de La Salle, and Pierre Le Moyne, sieur d'Iberville. Delisle also relied on information gleaned from more recent expeditions such as those of Louis Juchereau de Saint Denis and the reports of missionary François Lemaire.

Delisle was the first "modern" mapmaker to attempt to trace de Soto's route.[3] He recorded where de Soto disembarked south of a slightly erroneously placed *Tampa,* the explorer's path to the Indian town of *Apalaches* (fig. 96), and indicated that de Soto and his men crossed the Santee River, headed northward to the Catawba towns before

95 *Carte de la Louisiane et du Cours du Mississipi.* (Cat. 20)

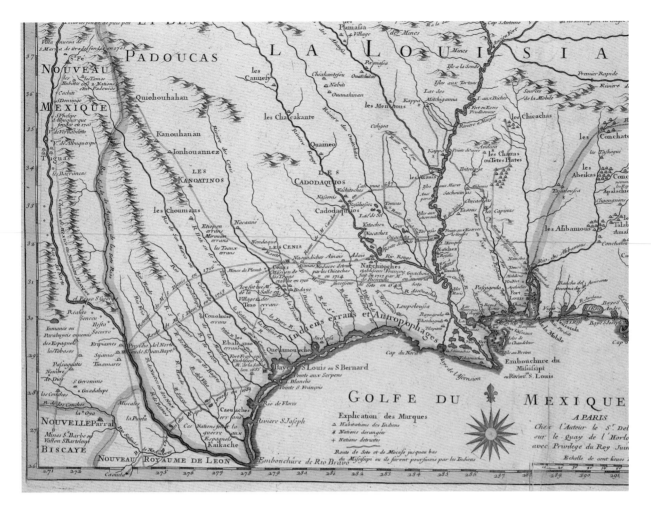

96 Detail of the American Southwest from *Carte de la Louisiane et du Cours du Mississipi,* by Guillaume Delisle,
Paris, 1718, black-and-white line engraving with period outline color. 1953-202. (Cat. 20)

reaching the Appalachians, then took a southwesterly direction into present-day Alabama, passing through *Tascaloussa* en route to the mouth of the Alabama River. Searching for gold, they progressed northwest through the Chickasaw towns, traversing the Mississippi and Alabama Rivers. By 1542, de Soto had advanced southward along the Red River as far as *Guachoia,* where he caught a fever and died. His successor, Luis de Moscoso, led the explorers westward hoping to reach the Gulf of Mexico. Delisle abruptly ended Moscoso's route at *Nacanné* on the Trinity River.

The second exploration recorded on *Carte de la Louisiane et du Cours du Mississipi* was La Salle's of 1684. He intended to establish a fort at the mouth of the Mississippi from which to raid Spanish settlements and silver mines in Mexico.[4] La Salle had previously descended the Mississippi River from the north. Unfamiliar with approaching from the Gulf of Mexico, he was unable to locate it and came ashore at Matagorda Bay, Texas, in 1685. Delisle

noted the location, *Fort Francois Etablissem.ᵗ de M. de la Salle lan 1685,* and La Salle's last attempt to reach Canada in 1687. The most reliable account of these explorations was recorded by Henri Joutel, who accompanied La Salle. Discord among members of the exploration party resulted in La Salle's murder, the location of which was described by Delisle as *Icy fut tué M.ⁱ de la Salle en 1687.* A small group including Joutel and La Salle's brother, Abbé Cavelier, followed the Arkansas River until they reached the Mississippi and from there returned to New France.[5]

La Salle's failure to locate the mouth of the Mississippi was of concern to the French king and made him hesitant to sponsor another expedition. Nevertheless, d'Iberville persuaded Louis XIV to persist. He sailed from France in 1698, successfully located the entrance to the Mississippi, and erected a fort on Biloxi Bay.

In 1714, Louis Juchereau de Saint Denis led the final French expedition illustrated by Delisle. One of the members of Saint Denis's party was a carpenter named Péni-

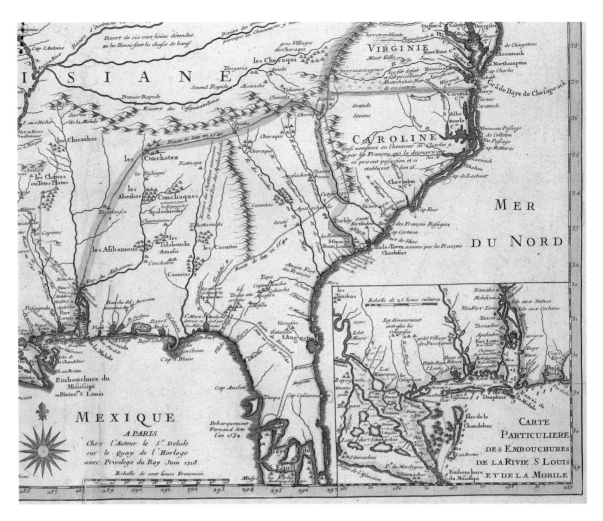

97 Detail from *Carte de la Louisiane et du Cours du Mississippi,* by Guillaume Delisle, Paris, 1718, black-and-white line engraving with period outline color. 1953-202 (Cat. 20)

cault who kept a journal of the expedition. The explorers made their way well into Texas, penetrating the Spanish missions there.[6] Saint Denis made a second journey up the Rio Grande in 1716. He built the important post of Natchitoches in present-day Louisiana, which Delisle included on the map. Delisle also located *Mission de Los Teijas establie in 1716* near the Trinity River in eastern Texas, the first appearance of the name Texas in any form on a printed map.

Despite Delisle's controversial territorial claims on behalf of France, British cartographers recognized the importance of the geography he depicted and were quick to incorporate his work into their own. *Carte de la Louisiane et du Cours du Mississipi* became a primary resource for the American Southwest for many years.

1953-202

1. For information on the states and publication information, see Cumming, *Southeast in Early Maps,* p. 214.

2. Quoted *ibid.,* p. 21.

3. Earlier maps by Ortelius and Blaeu contain place-names in their depictions of the Gulf of Mexico that suggest Europeans possessed some knowledge of de Soto's 1539–1543 explorations.

4. In 1682, La Salle had journeyed from Canada to the mouth of the Mississippi, claiming the Mississippi Valley for France and naming the area Louisiana for King Louis XIV.

5. The Spanish first learned of La Salle's activities in the Mississippi Valley in 1685. French entry into the Gulf Coast area caused great concern to the Spanish whose settlements extended as far up the Rio Grande as New Mexico. Alarmed by the potential threat, Spanish explorer Alonzo de Léon attempted to locate La Salle's colony, illustrated by Delisle as the Spanish road of 1689. Between 1685 and 1699, the Spanish dispatched 11 exploratory expeditions in search of French colonists. W. P. Cumming et al., *The Exploration of North America 1630–1776* (New York, 1974), p. 152.

6. On his map, Delisle erroneously recorded the date of Saint Denis's expedition as 1713.

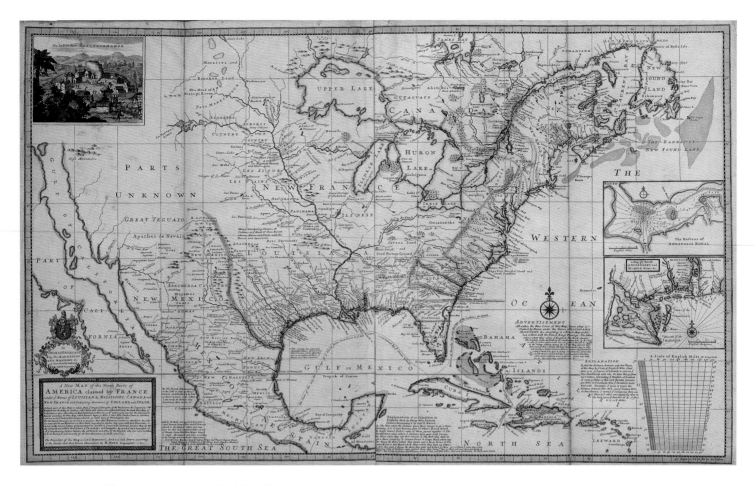

98 *A New Map of the North Parts of America claimed by France.* (Cat. 21)

21 A New MAP of the North Parts of / AMERICA claimed by FRANCE / under yᵉ Names of LOUISIANA, MISSISSIPI, CANADA and / NEW FRANCE with yᵉ Adjoyning Territories of ENGLAND and SPAIN

Herman Moll, cartographer and engraver; published separately and in *The World Described* by Herman Moll[1]

London, 1720. Black-and-white line engraving with period outline color. H. 24⅛″, W. 40½″, in two sheets

In the upper left corner is a scene of *The Indian Fort SASQUESA-HANOK* with Native Americans dancing around a fire. Above the title in the lower left is a dedicatory coat of arms *To / THOMAS BROMSALL / Esq; This MAP of LOUISI / ANA, MISSISSIPPI &c. / is most Humbly Dedicated / By H. Moll Geographer.* A rectangular inset in Nova Scotia map of *The Harbour of / ANNAPOLIS ROYAL* is along the center right side. Beneath is another inset of *A Map of yᵉ Mouth / of MISSISSIPI and MOBILE Rivers &c.* In the lower right corner is *A Scale of English Miles for Longitude.* Throughout the map are areas of text that Moll inserted as explanations or advertisements

Only one state of the map is known

References: Cumming, *British Maps*, pp. 6–12; Cumming, *Southeast in Early Maps*, pp. 21–24; Reinhartz, "Herman Moll Geographer," pp. 18–36

Conflict over control of the Ohio Territory and the Mississippi Valley was reflected in a cartographic war between England and France. In 1718, French mapmaker Guillaume Delisle published *Carte de la Louisiane et du Cours du Mississipi* (Cat. 20). For the British, the disturbing feature of Delisle's map was that he significantly reduced the western boundaries of the British colonies along the East Coast, thereby adding territory claimed by England to French Louisiana.

Two years later, Herman Moll published *A New Map of the North Parts of America claimed by France,* directly challenging Delisle's boundary lines. Moll explained on his map:

The French Divisions are inserted on purpose, that those Noblemen, Gentlemen, Merchants &c. who are interested in our Plantations in those Parts, may observe whether they agree with their Proprieties, or do not justly deserve yᵉ Name of Incroachments; and this is yᵉ more to be observed, because they do thereby Comprehend within their Limits yᵉ Charakeys and Iroquois, by much yᵉ most powerfull of all yᵉ Neighbouring Indian Nations, the old Friends and Allies of the English, who ever esteemed them to be the Bulwark and Security of all their Plantations in North America.

99 Detail of *The Indian Fort Sasquesahanock* from *A New Map of the North Parts of America claimed by France,* by Herman Moll, London, 1720, black-and-white line engraving with period color. 1967-17. (Cat. 21)

French encroachment of territories inhabited by the Iroquois and Cherokees, tribes with which the English had traded for years, posed a real threat to the economy and security of the region. In 1720, William Byrd II of Virginia wrote to Charles Boyle, fourth Earl of Orrery, "The Indians are very numerous on the branches of this river [the Mississippi], and if the French find means to gain them, it will render the English plantations very unsafe."[2] In similar fashion, the *South Carolina Gazette* reported in 1736:

As the Indian Trade is of the greatest Importance to the Wellfare of this Province, not only as it affords us near one 5th part of the Returns we make to Great-Britain (in Exchange for the woollen and other British Manufactures we yearly receive from thence,) but principally as it is the Means by which we keep and maintain the several Nations of the Indians surrounding this Province in Amity and Friendship with us, and thereby prevent their falling into the Interest of France or Spain.[3]

Moll borrowed information from Delisle's map for the location of the mouths of the Mississippi and Mobile Rivers and copied the routes of French explorers René-Robert Cavelier, sieur de La Salle, and Louis Juchereau de Saint Denis. *(fig. 100)* He also included new data from other sources such as Nathaniel Blackmore, Richard Berisford, and Thomas Nairne.[4] Blackmore was surveyor general of Acadia. His major contribution to Moll's map was the inset of *The Harbour of Annapolis Royal* in Nova Scotia. Berisford, a wealthy Charlestown merchant and planter whose father

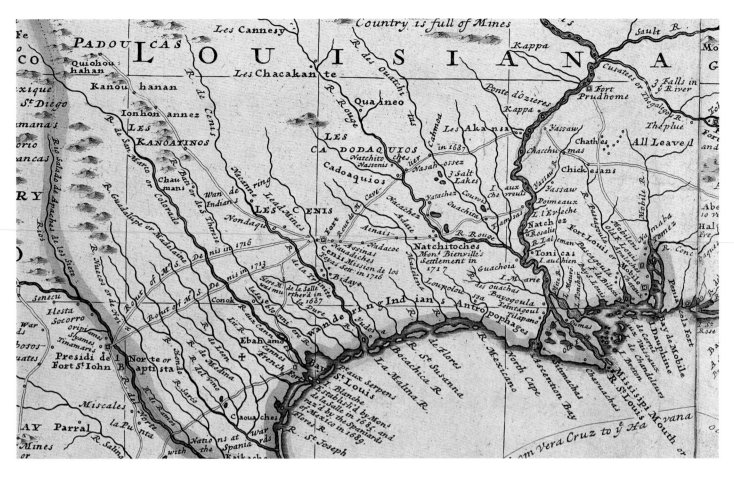

100 Detail of Louisiana from *A New Map of the North Parts of America claimed by France,* by Herman Moll,
London, 1720, black-and-white line engraving with period outline color. 1967-17. (Cat. 21)

had been surveyor general of the province, traveled to England in 1714 and 1715 and probably consulted with Moll.[5] Berisford delivered a memorial to the Board of Trade on "The Designs of the French to Extend their Settlements from Canada to the Mississippi behind the British Plantations" in 1717."[6]

Nairne was Indian agent for South Carolina and author of the colony's Indian policy. Moll incorporated Nairne's surveys of the coasts of Carolina to Florida on both this map and *A New and Exact Map of the Dominions of the King of Great Britain on the Continent of North America* (Cat. 19). One of the most interesting features of Moll's map is his depiction and description of Nairne's journey to Florida in 1702 to capture Spanish-allied Indians. *(figs. 101 and 102)* He and thirty-three Yamassee Indians captured thirty-five Florida Indians and sold them into slavery in Charles Town. Nairne wrote in 1705, "We have these two . . . past years been entirely kniving all the Indian Towns in Florida which were subject to the Spaniards."[7]

Moll improved on Delisle's rendering of the Great Lakes. Lake Huron, for example, was altered in size, shape, and location to represent its true configuration more accurately. A striking feature on Moll's maps is the appearance of California as an island, a misconception seen on seventeenth-century maps. It is thought that a Carmelite friar, Father Antonio Ascension, drew a map based on two Spanish navigators' reports of a large opening in the West Coast and a vast inland sea. Father Eusebio Kino, a Jesuit priest who was the first European to journey overland from California through what is today southern Arizona and into Mexico, drew a map showing California as part of the mainland in 1698. After it was published in 1705, most cartographers abandoned the earlier notion of an insular California.[8]

Moll issued loose copies of *A New Map of the North Parts of America claimed by France,* or, as he mentioned on the map, *you may have his New and Compleat Atlas, or Set of Twenty-Seven Two-Sheet Maps, bound or single, All compos'd and*

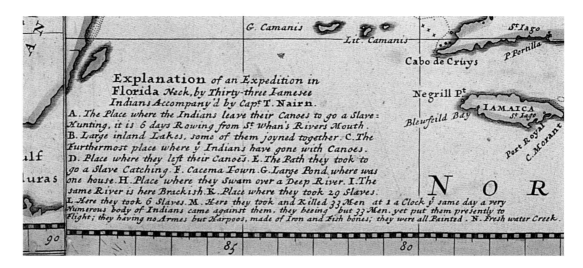

101 Detail of the explanation of Nairne's 1702 journey to Florida from *A New Map of the North Parts of America claimed by France,* by Herman Moll, London, 1720, black-and-white line engraving with period outline color. 1967-17. (Cat. 21)

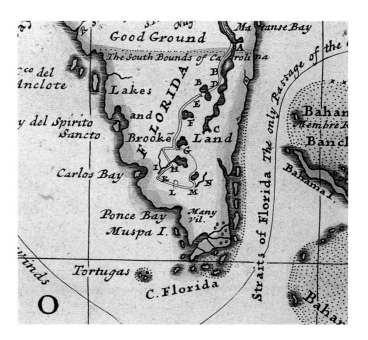

102 Detail of Thomas Nairne's 1702 journey to Florida from *A New Map of the North Parts of America claimed by France,* by Herman Moll, London, 1720, black-and-white line engraving with period outline color. 1967-17. (Cat. 21)

done, according to the Newest and most Exact Observations. The atlas to which Moll referred was *The World Described,* the first to illustrate two-sheet maps folded into quarters. 1967-17

1. Herman Moll's *The World Described; or A New and Correct Sett of Maps* was first published in 1709. As Moll produced new two-sheet maps, he included them in revised editions of the atlas.

2. Tinling, ed., *Correspondence of the Three William Byrds,* I, p. 327.

3. *S. C. Gaz.,* June 26, 1736.

4. Moll credited his sources on the map: *A Great part of this Map is taken from ye Original Draughts of j126 M^r. Blackmore, the Ingenious M^r. Berisford now Residing in Carolina, Capt. Nairn and others never before Published, the South West Part of Louisiana is done after a French Map Published at Paris in 1718.*

5. Cumming, *British Maps,* p. 10.

6. Cumming, *Southeast in Early Maps,* p. 24.

7. Moore, ed., *Nairne's Muskhogean Journals,* p. 8.

8. Crane, *Southern Frontier,* p. 81.

22 *A New & Exact / MAP / OF THE ISLAND OF/ BARBADOES / IN AMERICA / According to an Actual & Accurate Survey/ Made in the Years 1717 to 1721 / Approved by the ROYAL SOCIETY & Authorized / BY HIS MAJESTY'S ROYAL LICENCE*

William Mayo, cartographer; John Senex, engraver

London, 1722. Black-and-white line engraving with period color. H. 37¼", W. 44⅛", in four sheets

In the upper left corner is an inset of *A PLAN / of the / BRIDGE TOWN*. Just beneath is the explanation of the symbols used on the map. To the right of the inset is the cartouche of marine life and flora containing the title imprint. Immediately beneath is a scene of a surveyor at work, presumably in Barbados. In the upper right corner is a dedicatory cartouche to James Bruges (Brydges), Duke of Chandos, containing surveying and mathematical tools on the left side and musical instruments on the right. In the lower right corner is *A PROSPECT OF CODRINGTON COLLEGE &*

Two states of the map are known:

State 1: (this copy) As described

State 2: *Made in the Years 1717 to 1721* was deleted from the title and *Made by William Mayo* was substituted in its place. *Engrav'd by Iohn Senex 1722* was also deleted

References: Campbell, *Early Maps*, pp. 58–60; Campbell, "Printed Maps of Barbados," p. 16

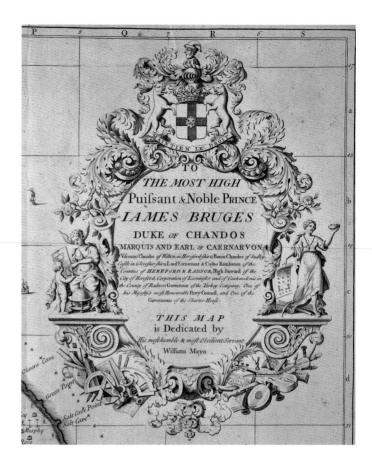

103 Detail of the dedicatory cartouche from *A New & Exact Map of the Island of Barbadoes in America,* by William Mayo, London, 1722, black-and-white line engraving. 1996-7. (Cat. 22)

A WORLD MAP drawn by Columbus's pilot, Juan de la Cosa, in 1500 and subsequently added to over the next eight years indicates that by an early date the Spaniards had explored the Antilles well enough to have acquired a general knowledge of the area. During the sixteenth century, both the Portuguese and Spanish probably visited Barbados en route to Brazil and Hispaniola, although neither country settled there.[1] By the time the English established their colony on Barbados about 1624, the native inhabitants of the island had been captured, enslaved, and transported to the mainland by the Spanish.

The climate and soil of Barbados were well suited for plantations, and the location provided a convenient base from which the English could launch plundering expeditions against the Spanish in the West Indies and South America. Further, coral reefs surrounding the island provided natural protection for the English against Spanish attack. The barrier created by these reefs was so dangerous that only one harbor, Carlisle Bay, proved to be a safe port. When the English arrived, they discovered a bridge that

had been constructed by native inhabitants in the area of Carlisle Bay, so they named the capital Bridgetown. *(fig. 105)*

Landowners initially attempted to grow tobacco and cotton, but by the 1650s, they began to experiment with the production of sugar cane. This crop proved so profitable that within thirty years, Barbados had become the richest of all the English colonies in America, with total exports greater than those from all of the other New World colonies combined.

Individual landholdings in Barbados were small in comparison to those on the North American mainland, however. Few plantations comprised more than two hundred acres.[2] Large tracts in Virginia, Carolina, and Maryland often consisted of thousands of acres of undeveloped land, but in Barbados all arable land was cultivated, and even the smallest planters invested in the equipment and labor force necessary to produce sugar. William Mayo's *A New & Exact Map of the Island of Barbadoes,* published in 1722, identified approximately 986 plantations, designating the

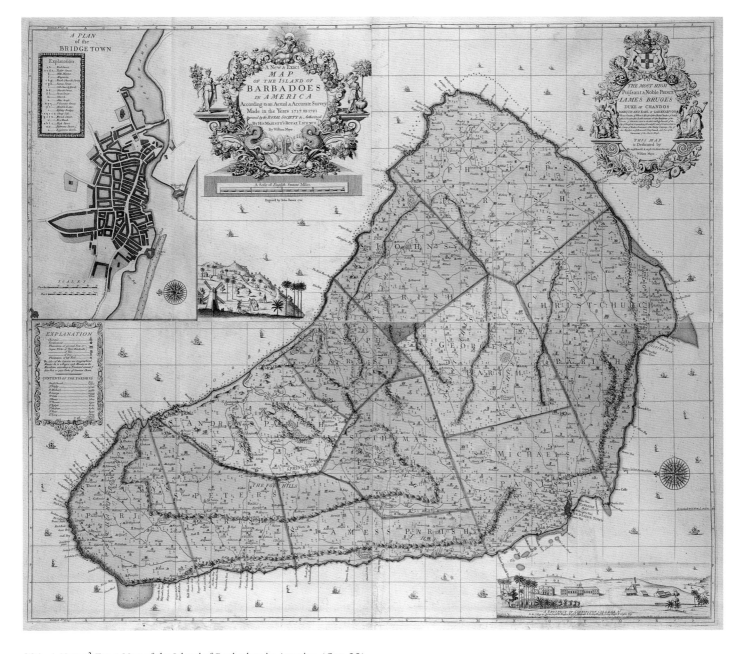

104 *A New & Exact Map of the Island of Barbadoes in America.* (Cat. 22)

A PROSPECT OF CODRINGTON COLLEGE &c.
A the College 300 feet in length. B Manfion Houfe. C Windmill. D Boiling Houfe. E Curing Houfe. F Confets Bay.

105 Detail of *A Plan of the Bridge Town* from *A New & Exact Map of the Island of Barbadoes in America*, by William Mayo, London, 1722, black-and-white line engraving with period color. 1996-7. (Cat. 22)

size of their operation by recording the number of wind-mills each required to process sugar cane. The windmills ranged from one to three, with three symbolizing the largest plantation. Mayo used a representation of a small dwelling to denote the less profitable plantations that produced cotton, ginger, and ground provisions.

In his study of the planter class in the West Indies, Richard S. Dunn classified the size of Barbados plantations according to the number of slaves required to provide an adequate labor force. He identified the largest planters, each of whom possessed substantial land, as owning sixty or more slaves. Middling planters had between twenty and fifty-nine slaves and acreage ranging from thirty to one hundred acres. Small planters were those who owned fewer than twenty slaves but at least ten acres of land.[3]

By 1700, the present eleven parishes had been established on the island. *A New & Exact Map of the Island of Barbadoes* was the first to delineate the individual, legal boundaries between them. As the map illustrates, the

biggest plantations were located in Saint George and Saint John, parishes known for the richest soil and heaviest rainfall. Of the seventy-five plantations Mayo located in Saint George Parish, forty-two were recorded with at least one windmill. In Saint John Parish, thirty-seven of the seventy-five plantations contained sugar works. The northern tip of Barbados where the terrain is rockier and drier was less densely populated. Although Saint Lucy Parish contained seventy-nine plantations, more than Saint George or Saint John, only eighteen were large enough to produce sugar.

Two plantations in Saint John Parish depicted on Mayo's map were owned by "The Society." They originally belonged to Christopher Codrington, former captain general and commander in chief of the Leeward Islands. Upon his death in 1710, Codrington bequeathed the property to the Society for the Propagation of the Gospel in Foreign Parts to endow a college in Barbados. Built between 1714 and 1742, Codrington College, illustrated in the lower

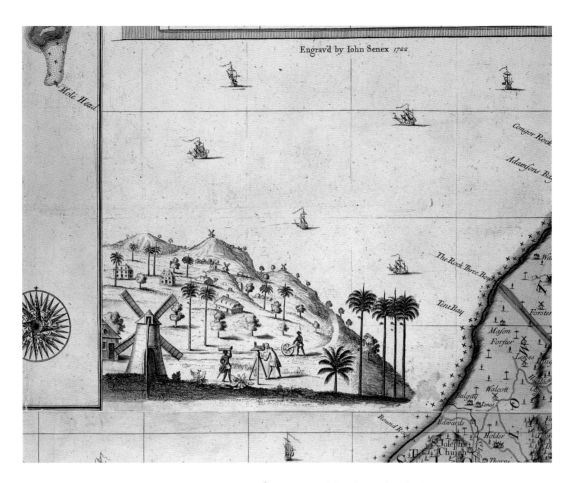

106 Detail of the surveying scene from *A New & Exact Map of the Island of Barbadoes in America*,
by William Mayo, London, 1722, black-and-white line engraving with period color. 1996-7. (Cat. 22)

right of Mayo's map, still exists today.

As Mayo noted in his explanation of the symbols on the map, the mathematical formulas in his survey were based on instructions by Richard Norwood, who published *The Sea-Man's Practice* in 1637. The back described how "to Delineate the Plot of any Forest, Park, Common, or other Piece of Ground."[4] Mayo also noted that he used Gunter's chain for measuring linear distance. Developed in 1620 by Edmund Gunter, this chain consisted of 100 links of 66 feet, with every 10 links marked off with a brass ring. The Barbados landscape depicted on Mayo's map illustrates a surveyor using a compass, which was necessary when employing Norwood's formulas, and a Gunter's chain. *(fig. 106)*

In 1723, Mayo relocated to Virginia where he became one of the most important surveyors of the colony. He accompanied William Byrd II on the 1728 expedition to survey the dividing line between Virginia and North Carolina. Together with the North Carolina contingent, Mayo

prepared a map of the line now in the Public Record Office. Mayo was appointed chief surveyor on behalf of the Virginia colony to settle the boundary dispute regarding the Northern Neck in 1733 (see Cat 27). In 1737, he laid out Byrd's proposed town, which became Richmond, at the falls of the James River.

1996-7

1. Tony Campbell, "The Printed Maps of Barbados from the earliest times to 1873," *Map Collectors' Circle*, XXI (1965), pp. 5–6.

2. Richard S. Dunn, *Sugar and Slaves: The Rise of the Planter Class in the English West Indies, 1624–1713* (New York, 1972), p. 95. The island of Barbados, 21 miles long and 14 miles wide, encompasses only 106,000 acres.

3. A property owner with at least 10 acres was considered by Barbados law to be a freeholder and therefore eligible to vote. Property holders of less than 10 acres were classified as freemen, but they could not vote. *Ibid.,* p. 92.

4. Sarah S. Hughes, *Surveyors and Statesmen: Land Measuring in Colonial Virginia* (Richmond, Va., 1979), p. 34.

23 Pennsylvania, Maryland, and part of Virginia

Cartographer, unknown; Thomas Hutchinson, engraver; John Senex, publisher

London, 1732. Black-and-white line engraving. H. 14¼", W. 9⁷⁄₁₆"

On the reverse, the map is endorsed in manuscript, "Penn & Lord Balt/ The Map which is referr'd to./ Paris"

Two states of the first edition and one state of the second edition are known[1]:

First edition, State 1: Proof state. This state lacked the southern boundary of Maryland but included a scale of distances in the lower left. The dotted circle around Newcastle, Delaware, extended completely from one point on the Delaware River to the other. 1731–1732[2]

State 2: (this copy) The southern boundary of Maryland was illustrated with a dotted line and the words *South Bounds of Maryland*. The northern boundary of Maryland was also illustrated with a dotted line. The southern portion of the dotted line around Newcastle, Delaware, was erased. *Part of Virginia* was added to the lower peninsula of the Eastern Shore, and *PENSILVANIA* and *MARYLAND* were added in the upper left. The scale of distances in the lower left was erased, although traces remain. 1732. This state was reissued in 1735, 1742, and 1760

Second edition: Woodblock copy by Benjamin Franklin. 1733. Reissued in 1736–1737[3]

References: Morrison et al., *On the Map,* fig. 29; Morrison, "Unidentified Manuscript Map," pp. 10–16; Papenfuse and Coale, *Hammond-Harwood House Atlas,* pp. 37–40; Wainwright, "Tale of a Runaway Cape," pp. 251–293; *The World Encompassed,* entry 251

For more than eighty years after William Penn received his grant for Pennsylvania from Charles II on March 4, 1681, the Penn and the Calvert families found themselves embroiled in a bitter dispute over the boundaries between their two colonies. The charter for Maryland granted to Lord Baltimore by Charles I in 1632 gave him the territory from 40° north latitude southward to the south bank of the Potomac River and eastward to the Atlantic Ocean. Since Baltimore's charter specifically excluded land settled prior to his grant, a parallel line was drawn from Watkins Point on the Eastern Shore to the Atlantic Ocean, allowing those already settled south of the line to remain in Virginia.

Penn's charter granted him the territory between 40° and 43° north latitude. His southern border was to extend eastward along the 40° of latitude until it intersected a circle of twelve miles in radius, centered on the settlement of New Castle. Where the arc of the circle intersected the Delaware Bay marked his eastern boundary.[4]

Careless wording in the charters and an inadequate understanding of the region's geography resulted in confusion over the precise limits of each proprietary. Penn and Lord Baltimore disagreed about the location of the southern boundary of Pennsylvania. Assuming that Baltimore's grant extended to the 40° of north latitude as stipulated in the grant, this controversy involved whether his northern boundary should be at that latitude as accurately surveyed or where it was thought to have been in 1632 when his charter was granted.[5]

Penn's grant also called into question the ownership of the three lower counties on the east side of the Delmarva Peninsula that had been settled by Swedes and Dutch. Even though his charter specifically excluded previously occupied territory, Lord Baltimore considered these counties part of his original grant. Penn believed that since they were settled before Baltimore's grant, they should have been excluded from the latter's claim.

In an effort to resolve the dispute over the Delmarva Peninsula, the king ruled in 1685 in favor of Penn, deciding it should be divided equally from 40° north latitude as far south as Cape Henlopen. The western portion was to belong to Baltimore and the eastern to Penn. Baltimore made several unsuccessful attempts to have the ruling set aside, yet despite the definitive decree, the boundary lines were not drawn. This created a financial burden for Penn because colonists residing in the disputed area refused to pay rent for their land until the issue was settled.

The controversy was still unresolved in 1731 when attorney Ferdinando John Paris was solicited to act as mediator between the two parties. In order to determine mutually agreeable boundaries, each side was asked to produce maps to be used in the negotiations that took place in London. At Charles Calvert's insistence, his map was chosen as the one upon which the boundaries were to be negotiated. The map was taken to London cartographer John Senex to be engraved on copper. His journeyman, Thomas Hutchinson, executed the actual engraving.[6] Using the geography depicted on Baltimore's map as a guide, an agreement establishing the borders between the two colonies was drawn up and signed on May 10, 1732.

Three months later, Thomas Penn arrived in Philadelphia armed with documents, instructions, and lists of commissioners each side had selected as preparation for running the line. Lord Baltimore and his commissioners displayed a reluctance to abide by the decisions that had been agreed upon by both parties, so once again the two sides were stalemated.[7] In November 1733, the commissioners were unresolved over the issue of the twelve-mile

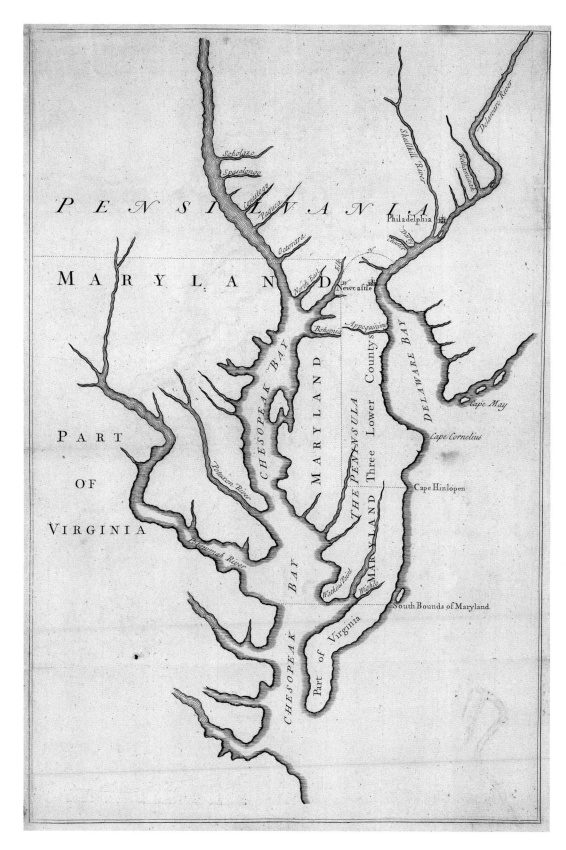

107 Pennsylvania, Maryland, and part of Virginia. (Cat. 23)

radius from New Castle. According to the *Articles of Agreement,* the circle was to be "drawn and marked out at the twelve miles distance from the town of New-Castle."[8] The Pennsylvania representatives maintained that the circle was to be one of a radius of twelve miles starting from New Castle, while those from Maryland held that the twelve miles referred to the circumference of the circle and therefore the radius was only two miles.

It is not known why the Maryland commissioners refused to concede the area around New Castle because the map engraved by Senex, based on Baltimore's own manuscript, shows the twelve-mile radius as described in the *Articles of Agreements. (fig. 108)* Penn's advocates believed that the Maryland representatives were attempting to create an impasse in order to void the contract, which was to run out at the end of the year. Nicholas B. Wainright suggested a plausible explanation for Maryland's position. He speculated that after the two parties reached an agreement in May 1732, Baltimore realized that a serious error on the map he supplied to the negotiating team had cost him thousands of acres because his document placed Cape Henlopen twenty-five miles below its true location. The point of land named Cape Cornelius was actually the true location of Cape Henlopen. *(fig. 109)* James Logan, Penn's advisor, recognized the problem and wrote Ferdinando Paris:

> *I rather think the lower part relating to the Capes has been taken from an old Dutch map amongst our late Proprs papers with the lines run on it in black lead, in the same manner we see them drawn in this, which old map I have heard that gent affirm is ye very same the Committee of the Privy Council had before them & made use of in 1685 upon the hearing between him & Ld Balt.*[9]

The original source for the incorrect location of Cape Henlopen was Nicholas Visscher's *Novi Belgii Novæque Angliæ* (Cat. 11). William Penn's copy is in the John Work Garrett Library at The Johns Hopkins University. On the reverse in William Penn's hand is the endorsement "The Map by which the privy Council 1685 settled the Bounds between the Lord Baltimore & I, & Maryland & Pennsylvania & Territories or annexed Countys. WP."[10]

Upon learning of his mistake, Baltimore went to England to petition the king, claiming that the map used in the negotiations was deliberately forged by Penn in an effort to cheat him out of his rightful territory. Enraged by Baltimore's slanderous accusations against the Penns, particularly in light of the fact that Baltimore had insisted upon using the map in question, Paris enlisted the support of London Quakers to help vindicate his clients and secure

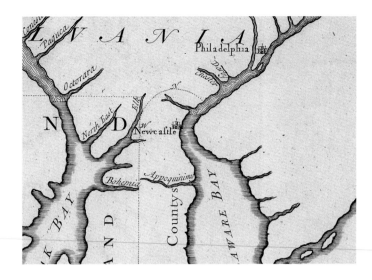

108 Detail of the circumference around New Castle, Delaware from Pennsylvania, Maryland, and part of Virginia, by John Senex, London, 1732, black-and-white line engraving. G1984-43, gift of Mrs. Anna Glen Vietor in memory of Alexander O. Vietor. (Cat. 23)

possession of the three lower counties. One of the tactics Paris used to expose Baltimore's false claim that he had been purposefully deceived was to have new copies printed of the *Articles of Agreement,* accompanied by a new state of the map (state two). Paris personally endorsed most of the several hundred he ordered from Senex with "This is Lord Baltimore's own Plan, Annext to the Arctes of Agreement of 10. May 1732."[11] The copy of Senex's map illustrated in this catalog was endorsed on the reverse by Paris: "Penn & Lord Balt/ The Map which is referr'd to./ Paris." *(fig. 110)*

The boundary line between Pennsylvania and Maryland was not resolved until Charles Mason and Jeremiah Dixon completed their survey in 1768.

G1984-43, gift of Mrs. Anna Glen Vietor in memory of Alexander O. Vietor

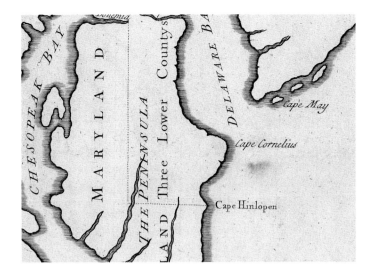

109 Detail of Cape Henlopen and Cape Cornelius from
Pennsylvania, Maryland, and part of Virginia, by John Senex,
London, 1732, black-and-white line engraving. G1984-43,
gift of Mrs. Anna Glen Vietor in memory of Alexander O. Vietor.
(Cat. 23)

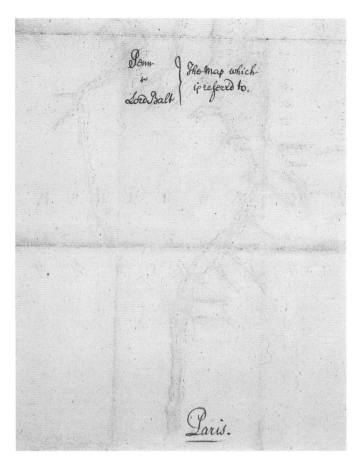

110 Detail of the endorsement on the reverse of Pennsylvania,
Maryland, and part of Virginia, by John Senex, London, 1732,
black-and-white line engraving. G1984-43, gift of Mrs. Anna Glen
Vietor in memory of Alexander O. Vietor. (Cat. 23)

1. For discussions of the various editions and states of the map, see
Morrison et al., *On the Map,* fig. 29, and Nicholas B. Wainwright, "Tale of a
Runaway Cape: The Penn-Baltimore Agreement of 1732," *PMHB* (1963),
pp. 257–273.

2. For an illustration of the proof state, see Wainwright, "Tale of a Runaway Cape," p. 267.

3. For an illustration of Franklin's woodblock engraving of the map,
see *The World Encompassed,* plate LIV.

4. In reality, the 40° of latitude is north of the 12-mile circle around
New Castle, thus leaving a portion of Pennsylvania's boundary open
ended.

5. For depictions of Baltimore's representations of the 40° of north latitude, see figs. 5 and 6.

6. Wainwright, "Tale of a Runaway Cape," p. 257.

7. Frustration over the issue forced Penn to have Franklin print 500
copies of the *Articles of Agreement Made and Concluded Upon Between the Right
Honourable the Lord Proprietary of Maryland, and the Honourable the Propri-
etarys of Pensilvania, &c.* Franklin also produced a woodcut copy of Senex's
map and appended it to his pamphlet, cited as the second edition of the
Senex map. See n. 3.

8. Quoted in Wainwright, "Tale of a Runaway Cape," p. 262.

9. *Ibid.,* p. 264.

10. Papenfuse and Coale, *Hammond-Harwood House Atlas,* p. 38.

11. Morrison et al., *On the Map,* fig. 29.

24 A MAP / of the BRITISH EMPIRE in / AMERICA / with the FRENCH and SPANISH / SETTLEMENTS adjacent thereto

Henry Popple, cartographer; Clement Lempriere, designer; William Henry Toms, engraver of the map portion; Bernard Baron, cartouche engraver; and Richard William Seale, engraver

London, 1733. Black-and-white line engraving with period color. H. 93½″, W. 97″ in twenty sheets, attached and glued to linen

Within a decorative banner along the top is *AMERICA SEPTENTRIONALIS*. In the upper left corner are two engraved views, *FALL of NIAGARA* and *MEXICO*. The title appears in the lower left surrounded by Native Americans, flora, and fauna. In the background, cargo is being unloaded from ships. In the upper right corner are views of the harbors of *QUEBEC* and *NEW YORK*. Along the right side are seventeen separate insets, as follows:

The Harbour of / PLACENTIA.

The Harbour of / ANAPOLIS ROYAL

BOSTON HARBOUR

NEW YORK and PERTH AMBOY HARBOURS

The Town and Harbour of / CHARLES TOWN/ in SOUTH CAROLINA

The BERMUDA or SUMMER ISLANDS

HARBOUR / OF / S.ᵗ AUGUSTINE

The Harbour of Providence

The HAVANA

BAY of S.ᵗ IAGO / in CUBA

KINGSTON HARBOUR in JAMAICA

A Plan of the Harbour of PORT ANTONIO in JAMAICA

FORT ROYAL / in MARTINICA

The Island of / BARBADOES

ANTIGUA

CARTAGENE / on the Coast of NEW SPAIN

HARBOUR / of / PORTO BELLO

In the lower right is a dedicatory strapwork cartouche *To the QUEEN's MOST / EXCELLENT MAJESTY / This MAP is most humbly / Inscribed by / Your MAJESTY's / most Dutiful, most / Obedient, and most / Humble Servant / Henry Popple*. Above the coast of Panama, ships and gunfire represent Sir Charles Wager's engagement with the Spanish fleet in 1707. In the lower right corner is an endorsement of the map by Edmund Halley

Seven states of the map are known[1]:

State 1: No engraved sheet numbers. Sheet ten contained information that was changed within the year of publication. *Ocone River* was shown as the northern fork of the Altamaha River. *GEORGIA* was below and parallel to the name *CAROLINA*. The mouth of the Altamaha River was labeled as *R. Alatamaha or S.ᵗ George's R. now R. May. GLANVILLE COUNTY* was shown south of *COLETON COUNTY. Ogehee or Montgomeries R.* was shown between the Altamaha and Savana Rivers. In the lower right was *London Engrav'd by Will.m Henry Toms & R. W. Seale, 1733*

State 2: (this copy) As described. The colony of Georgia was reengraved and a small section was pasted over the area on sheet ten. The placement of the name *GEORGIA* was no longer beneath and parallel to *CAROLINA* but was angled and intersected *CAROLINA* between the *A* and the *R. GLANVILLE COUNTY* was replaced by *Yamasee Indians. Palachocoola Indians* and *Port Royal* were erased. *Ogehee or Montgomeries R.* was changed to *Ogeeche R.* and its course was altered. *Savannah River* was identified along the coast. Numerous additional place-names were added along the coast, including *Savannah Town*. 1734

State 3: The corrections seen in the overlay were incorporated in sheet ten. Several other changes were made as well. *Ocone River*, which appeared on the previous state as the northern fork of the Altamaha River, was erased and replaced by a mountain range. An engraved annotation along the 29th parallel off the east coast of Florida was added to indicate *The Southern Bounds of CAROLINA, by the last Charter.* Carolina's southern boundary found on the previous states was in manuscript only. 1734

State 4: *R. W. Seale* was removed from the engraver's credit line in the lower right corner. The imprint now was *London Engrav'd by Will.m Henry Toms 1733*. 1734

State 5: Numbers were engraved on the upper right corners of all twenty sheets. 1734

State 6: The imprint in the lower left now was *Sold by S: Harding on the Pavement in S.ᵗ Martins Lane, and by W. H. Toms Engraver in Union Court near Hatton Garden Holborn*. Three lines of pricing followed. Ca. 1734

State 7: The imprint in the lower left was changed to *Sold at Stephen Austen's Bookseller in Newgate Street & by Tho.ˢ Willdey at the great Toy Shop in S.ᵗ Paul's Church Yard London*. Ca. 1740

References: Babinski, *Popple's 1733 Map*; Brown, *Early Maps of the Ohio Valley*, entry 14; Cresswell, "Colony to Commonwealth," pp. 78–80; Cumming, *Southeast in Early Maps*, entry 216; Cumming and Wallis, "Popple's Map, 1733"; De Vorsey, "Maps in Colonial Promotion," pp. 35–45; De Vorsey, "Oglethorpe and the Earliest Maps of Georgia," pp. 22–43; Fowble, *Two Centuries of Prints*, entires 6 and 7; Fowble, "Popple Map," pp. 1–3; McCorkle, *America Emergent*, entry 21; Papenfuse and Coale, *Hammond-Harwood House Atlas*, pp. 32–34; Suárez, *Shedding the Veil*, entry 54; Willingham, "Cartographic Progression of Georgia," pp. 40–41

THE MOST noteworthy feature of Henry Popple's *A Map of the British Empire in America with the French and Spanish Settlements adjacent thereto* is its impressive size, which measures approximately 95 by 100 inches when assembled. Wall-size maps such as Popple's were available in a variety of formats. They could be purchased in loose sheets, bound between boards as an atlas, glued to linen, dissected and folded in marbleized cases, or mounted on linen and attached to rollers for hanging. In the case of the Popple map, the costs of the various formats was noted in the lower left:

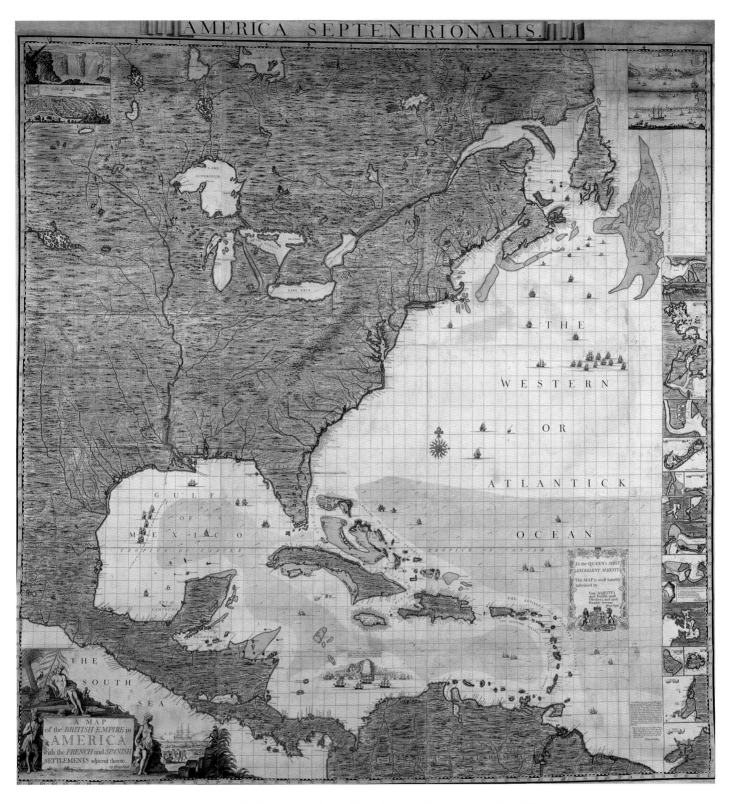

111 *A Map of the British Empire in America with the French and Spanish Settlements adjacent thereto.* (Cat. 24)

VII

FALL of NIAGARA

55
54
53

112 Detail of Niagara Falls from *A Map of the British Empire in America with the French and Spanish Settlements adjacent thereto,* by Henry Popple, London, 1733, black-and-white line engraving with period color. 1955-408. (Cat. 24)

113 Detail of the Great Lakes region from *A Map of the British Empire in America with the French and Spanish Settlements adjacent thereto,* by Henry Popple, London, 1733, black-and-white line engraving with period color. 1955-408. (Cat. 24)

	£	s.	d.
Price in Sheets	1	11	6
Bound	1	16	6
On Rollers & Colour'd	2	12	6

Equally as impressive as the size of the map are its decorative elements. Views of Mexico, Niagara Falls, Quebec, and New York Harbor are in the upper corners. Along the right side are seventeen inset maps. The title cartouche alone occupies an entire sheet.

The struggle between Great Britain and France in North America was reflected in the works of mapmakers in both countries. For example, French cartographer Guillaume Delisle published maps that greatly reduced the western boundaries of the British colonies, thereby adding territory claimed by the English to French Louisiana (Cat. 20).

Delisle's maps enabled the French to claim all of the land drained by the Mississippi River and its tributaries. Had the French been able to gain control of this area, it would have given them access to the Ohio River and an inland passage all the way north from the mouth of the Mississippi to Canada. They would also have gained a monopoly of the Indian fur trade.

The Board of Trade and Plantations had been aware of the threat posed by the increased French presence for several decades. Herman Moll and other English makers published maps as counterclaims to the French assertions (Cat. 21). What was needed, however, was a large-scale English map that delineated the interior of the continent, thereby substantiating their claims to the area. Popple's intention was to illustrate Britain's colonial possessions in America relative to the claims of France and Spain. As noted on the

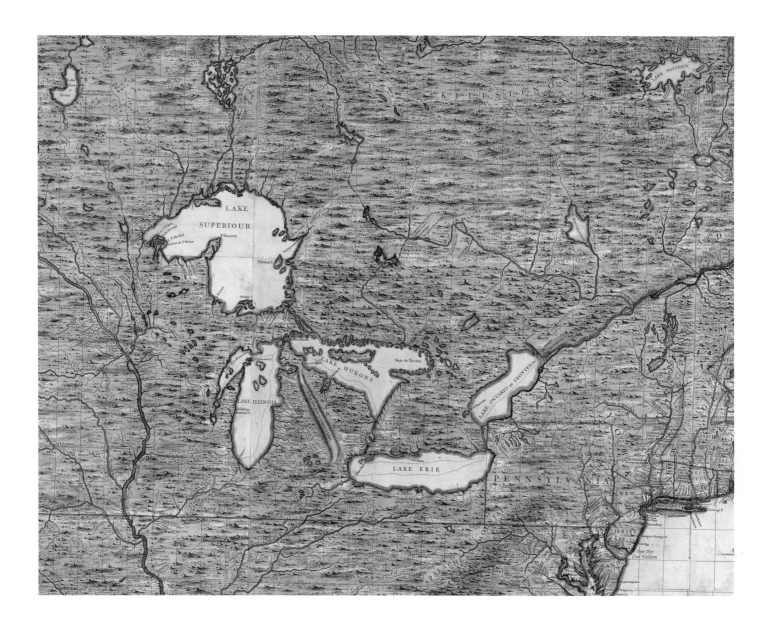

map, he consulted a variety of sources:

> *Mr. POPPLE UNDERTOOK THIS map WITH THE*
> *Approbation of the Right Hounourable the LORDS COM-*
> *MISSIONERS of TRADE and PLANTATIONS; and great*
> *care has been taken by comparing all the Maps, Charts,*
> *and Observations that could be found, especially the*
> *"Authentick Records & Actual Surveys" transmitted to*
> *their LORDSHIPS, by the Governors of the "British Plan-*
> *tations," and Others, to correct the many Errors committed*
> *in former Maps.*

Although the Lords Commissioners approved Popple's undertaking the map, they never sanctioned the execution, so no governing authority sponsored its production.[2]

Since the French had compiled the most accurate and up-to-date information on the Mississippi Valley, Great Lakes, and Spanish settlements in Texas, Popple consulted these sources. For the lower Mississippi and the configuration of the Great Lakes, he used Delisle's 1718 *Carte de la Louisiane et du Cours du Mississipi*. Popple depicted Lake Ontario incorrectly, placing it in a southwest to northeast direction rather than its proper almost due east-west position. He also reverted to the obsolete French name "Illinois" for Lake Michigan. *(fig. 113)* Popple relied on Nicholas de Fer's *La France Occidentale dans L'Amerique Septentrional* for information on the Spanish settlements on the Rio Grande and terrain west of the Mississippi Valley.

For his depiction of the Southeast, Popple had access to a manuscript map by Colonel John Barnwell drawn about 1721.[3] Barnwell's map, on deposit with the Board of Trade and Plantations, contained current information about

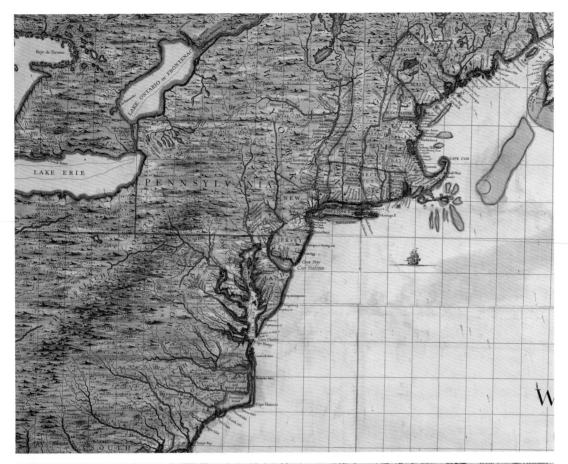

114 Detail from *A Map of the British Empire in America with the French and Spanish Settlements adjacent thereto,* by Henry Popple, London, 1733, black-and-white line engraving with period color. 1955-408. (Cat. 24)

115 Detail of the overlay over Georgia from *A Map of the British Empire in America with the French and Spanish Settlements adjacent thereto,* by Henry Popple, London, 1733, black-and-white line engraving with period color. 1955-408. (Cat. 24)

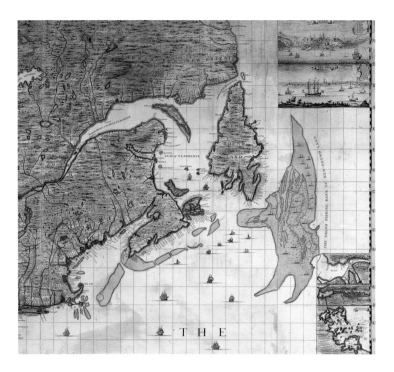

116 Detail from *A Map of the British Empire in America
with the French and Spanish Settlements adjacent thereto*,
by Henry Popple, London, 1733,
black-and-white line engraving with period color.
1955-408. (Cat. 24)

117 Detail of the Charleston, South Carolina, inset
from *A Map of the British Empire in America
with the French and Spanish Settlements adjacent thereto*,
by Henry Popple, London, 1733,
black-and-white line engraving with period color.
1955-408. (Cat. 24)

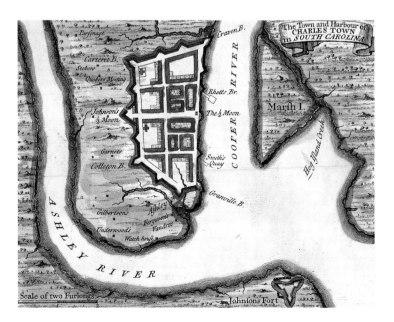

Indian settlements in the interior and located many new sites along the Carolina coast. Unfortunately, Popple chose not to incorporate the most significant features of Barnwell's map—his explanatory notes and legends—but focused instead on features that were less precisely delineated.[4] For New York and the area south of the Great Lakes, Popple borrowed information from explorations shown on Cadwallader Colden's *Map of the Country of the Five Nations*.[5]

As Popple's map neared completion, James Edward Oglethorpe was actively involved in settling the colony of Georgia. Oglethorpe sailed back to England in May 1734 with new information on the geography of the area between South Carolina and Florida.[6] Early states of Popple's map show a very generalized depiction of this region that was altered in subsequent versions. Although it is not known how Popple could have had access to Oglethorpe's maps, shortly after some of the early states of Popple's maps were printed, he updated the geography of the territory between the Altamaha and Saint Johns Rivers. Close examination of sheet ten on Colonial Williamsburg's map reveals a paste-over covering an earlier version that extended the Altamaha River to the Saint Johns River and eliminated an area designated as *Full of Swamps*.[7] *(fig. 115)*

Not only did Popple consult previously published and manuscript sources, he also utilized the skills of mapmaker Clement Lempriere, whom he credited on the map with designing the work. Popple hired Bernard Baron, a French-born engraver who immigrated to England in 1712, to execute the title cartouche.[8] *(fig. 118)* In *The Contents of each Sheet of the Twenty Plates of Mr. Popple's Map of America*, he noted that sheet XVII contained "The *Spanish* Dominions next the *South Sea*, *Guatimala*, &c. with the Title of the Map, encompassed with curious Figures, engraved by Mr. *Baron*."[9] For the remaining sheets, Popple engaged the well-known engraver William Henry Toms, who later collaborated with Lempriere on other projects.

The Commissioners of the Board of Trade and Plantations instructed that Popple's *Map of the British Empire in America* be distributed to each colony in America. Benjamin Franklin ordered two sets, one bound and the other in loose sheets. Franklin added at the bottom of his 1746 order:

I forgot to mention, that there must be some other large Map of the whole World, or of Asia, or Africa, or Europe, of equal Size with Popple's to match it; they being to be hung, one on each side the Door in the Assembly Room; if none can be had of equal Size, send some Prospects of principal Cities, or the like, to be pasted on the Sides, to make up the Bigness.

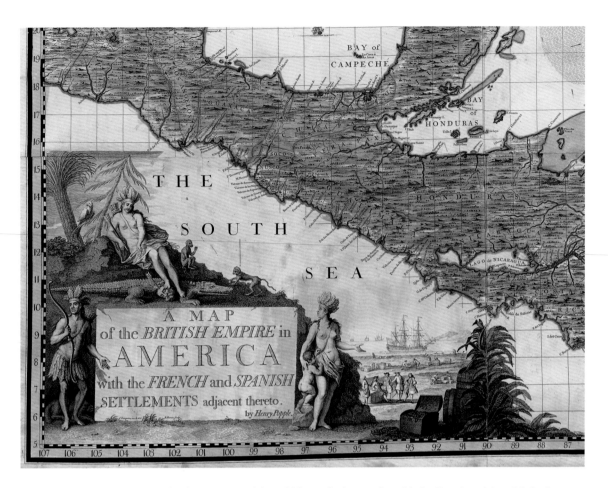

118 Detail of the title cartouche from *A Map of the British Empire in America with the French and Spanish Settlements adjacent thereto,* by Henry Popple, London, 1733, black-and-white line engraving with period color. 1955-408. (Cat. 24)

Five years later, Franklin ordered another on rollers.[10]

Despite the widespread distribution of Popple's map and the fact that it was copied by French and Dutch cartographers, it received some criticism.[11] The geographer's considerable reliance on French sources implied that he supported that nation's territorial claims. Further, some of the boundary lines were viewed as more favorable to the French than to the English. For example, the mapmaker included Fort Niagara in French territory. Although Popple claimed his work had been sanctioned by the Lords Commissioners of Trade and Plantations, it was pointed out in *The Memorials of the English and French Commissaries Concerning the Limits of Nova Scotia or Acadia* that while they may have approved of his intention to produce the map, they "never superintended or approved of Mr. Popple's Manner of executing it." The commissioners added that it "has never in any Negociation between the two Crowns been appealed to by Great Britain, as being correct, or a Map of any Authority."[12]

For three generations, members of the Popple family served in the office of the Board of Trade and Plantations.[13] Henry, however, was offered only a clerkship. Finding that position unprofitable, he resigned to work as a private financial agent for the West Indian governors and some of the British regiments. In that capacity he appeared before the commissioners on numerous occasions.

Popple compiled a manuscript map that lacks much of the detail, but is very similar in appearance to the index, or key map, which accompanied the twenty-sheet map. Prior to this endeavor, Popple had no real experience as a mapmaker. Once he published his monumental *Map of the British Empire in America* in 1733, he never engaged in another cartographic project.

1955-408

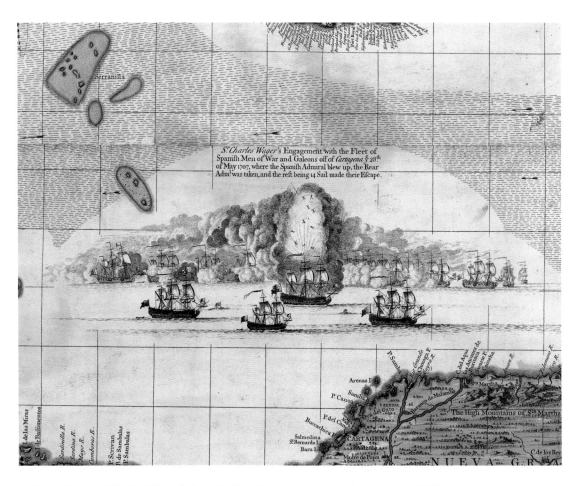

119 Detail of Sir Charles Wager's fleet during the engagement in Cartagena in 1707
from *A Map of the British Empire in America with the French and Spanish Settlements adjacent thereto*,
by Henry Popple, London, 1733, black-and-white line engraving with period color. 1955-408. (Cat. 24)

1. Mark Babinski cited additional states based on manuscript notations that occur on certain copies of the map. It is my opinion that manuscript notations do not constitute separate states unless they can be demonstrated to have been added by the publisher. Mark Babinski, *Henry Popple's 1733 Map of the British Empire in America* (Garwood, N. J., 1998).

2. Cumming, *Southeast in Early Maps*, p. 233.

3. Col. John Barnwell was a colonial agent who immigrated to South Carolina in 1701 where he became involved in Indian affairs. In 1720, he returned to London and urged the Board of Trade and Plantations to protect Carolina from the natives, Spaniards, and pirates.

4. Cumming, *Southeast in Early Maps*, p. 233.

5. Cadwallader Colden was appointed first surveyor general of New York in 1718. In 1724, he published his map in *Papers relating to an Act of the Assembly of New-York for the encouragement of the Indian trade, &c. and for prohibiting the selling of Indian goods to the French, viz of Canada* (printed for and sold by William Bradford in the city of New York, 1724).

6. According to Louis De Vorsey, Jr., Oglethorpe presented a "Map of the Coast of Georgia" that no longer survives to the British War Office. He also distributed maps of the colony to potential settlers from the continent. De Vorsey, "Oglethorpe and the Earliest Maps of Georgia," in Phinzy Spalding and Harvey H. Jackson, eds., *Oglethorpe in Perspective: Georgia's Founder after Two Hundred Years* (Tuscaloosa, Ala., 1989), p. 35.

7. De Vorsey published two essays on Oglethorpe and his use of maps to promote the Georgia colony in which he discussed at great length Pop-

ple's alterations to sheet 10. *Ibid.,* pp. 22–43; Louis De Vorsey, Jr., "Maps in Colonial Promotion: James Edward Oglethorpe's Use of Maps in 'Selling' the Georgia Scheme," *Imago Mundi,* XXXVIII (1986), pp. 35–45.

8. Baron's skill as an engraver was recognized by William Hogarth, who hired Baron to assist with working the copperplates for his well-known series *Marriage-à-la-Mode.*

9. *The Contents of each Sheet of the Twenty Plates of Mr. Popple's Map of America,* Collections of the Eric P. Newman Numismatic Education Society. I wish to thank Mr. Newman for supplying a photocopy.

10. Labaree et al., eds., *Papers of Franklin,* III, p. 77; IV, p. 323.

11. Jean Cóvens and Pierre Mortier published a copy of Popple's map around 1737; George Louis Le Rouge around 1742.

12. Quoted in Donald H. Cresswell, "Colony to Commonwealth: The Eighteenth Century," in Richard W. Stephenson and Marianne M. McKee, eds., *Virginia in Maps: Four Centuries of Settlement, Growth, and Development* (Richmond, Va., 2000), p. 78.

13. Henry Popple's father and grandfather both served as secretary to the board. Upon his father's resignation, Henry's brother Alured inherited the position. Alured later became governor of Bermuda and was succeeded by another brother, William.

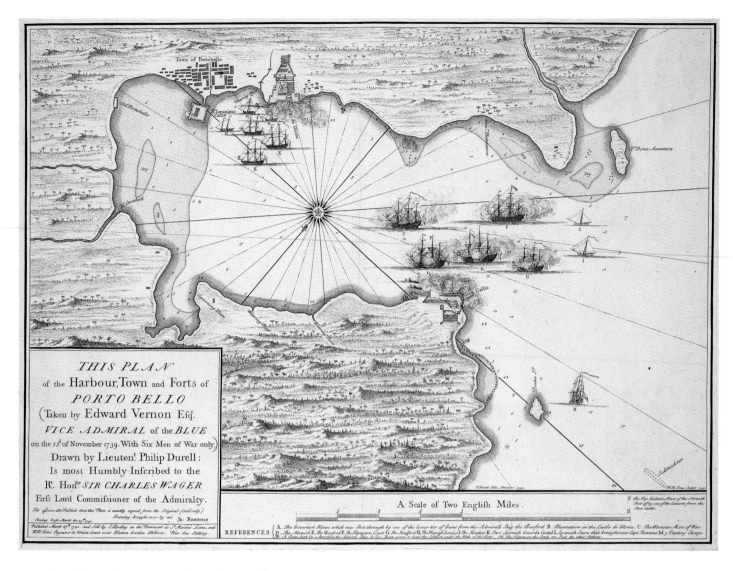

120 *Plan of the Harbour, Town and Forts of Porto Bello.* (Cat. 25)

121 Teapot and cover, Staffordshire, England, ca. 1740–1745, saltglazed stoneware. 1959-419. This teapot and cover was also produced to commemorate Admiral Vernon's success at Portobello. The city is depicted in relief on the other side of the pot, while this side shows Admiral Vernon and Fort Chacre.

25 *PLAN / of the Harbour, Town and Forts of / PORTO BELLO / (Taken by Edward Vernon Esq[r]. / VICE ADMIRAL of the BLUE / on the 22[d]. of November 1739. With Six Men of War only)*

Lieutenant Philip Durell, cartographer; William Henry Toms, engraver; sold by S. Harding and William Henry Toms

London, March 27, 1740. Black-and-white line engraving. H. 17⅜", W. 23⅝"

The title and dedication are engraved within an inset in the lower left corner. Along the bottom are a scale of distances and a key identifying the buildings and ships

Only one state of the map is known

COMMERCIAL and maritime conflicts between England and Spain occurred from the time the two nations founded settlements in the New World. In the second half of the seventeenth century, however, Spain abolished taxes and restrictions on English traders and the two countries established a flourishing, although at times hostile, relationship. With the signing in 1713 of the Treaty of Utrecht, which ended the War of the Spanish Succession, Anglo-Spanish trade was once again restricted, thereby creating friction that increased significantly during the 1720s and 1730s.

Establishing successful commercial relations with Spain was of paramount importance to Sir Robert Walpole's administration and he made several attempts to negotiate economically beneficial trade policies. English merchants, convinced of their country's maritime supremacy and anxious to profit from Spanish riches in the New World, were less interested in reaching a solution through diplomacy and petitioned the government to take military action. To make their case, they cited atrocities such as that incurred

by Captain Robert Jenkins, whose ear was reported to have been cut off by a Spanish officer. This and other incidents caused Parliament to pass legislation forbidding the Spanish from detaining or searching English merchant vessels. Spain refused to abide by the demand and war was declared on October 19, 1739.[1]

Vice Admiral Edward Vernon, among the most vocal advocates of war with Spain, boasted that he could easily capture the Spanish port of Portobello on the coast of Panama. Portobello, an important relay point in transporting Peruvian silver to Spain, was considered the capital of that nation's western empire. In July, three months prior to the declaration of war, Vernon was ordered to "destroy the Spanish settlements in the West Indies and to distress their shipping by any method whatever."[2] Vernon and his fleet of six ships reached Portobello on November 20. The next day, he attacked and captured Iron Castle at the mouth of the harbor, and the Spanish governor surrendered on November 22. Vernon destroyed the Spanish forts with 122 barrels of confiscated gunpowder before he left Portobello with several captured men-of-war and about ten thousand Spanish dollars.

Lieutenant Philip Durell drew the events of the attack, which Captain James Rentone took to London. Rentone was the first to deliver the news of the successful capture of Portobello. Durell illustrated the harbor as the English approached it rather than with the mouth facing west as it actually does. He showed Vernon's assault on Iron Castle, the governor's house, and Gloria Castle. Public acclaim in London over the admiral's success reached unprecedented levels. Numerous medals were struck to commemorate the victory and Vernon became a national hero.[3]

In 1740, the *South Carolina Gazette* offered for sale:

A View of the Town, Castle and Harbour of Porto-Bello, when taken by Admiral Vernon, with the Manner in which it was taken by the said Admiral.[4]

1968-28

1. This war was most commonly known as the War of Jenkins's Ear.
2. Francis L. Berkeley, Jr., "The War of Jenkins' Ear," in Darrett B. Rutman, ed., *The Old Dominion: Essays for Thomas Perkins Abernethy* (Charlottesville, Va., 1964), p. 50.
3. The American Numismatic Society has identified over 160 medals issued to commemorate the event. *Ibid.,* p. 53. Vernon's popularity was so great that his name was memorialized on both sides of the Atlantic, most notably in this country by Mount Vernon, the name Lawrence Washington chose for the plantation that eventually was inherited by his half-brother, George Washington.
4. *S. C. Gaz.,* Oct., 16, 1740.

26 *A / New and Correct Plan of the Harbour / of CARTHAGENA in AMERICA / Seated 10 Degrees 26 Minutes Lat. / North and 75 Degrees 21 Long. / West of London, from a Draught / brought to England by / By Pet. Chassereau Archi: Also a / View of the Fleet as they Anchor'd on yᵉ Coast of Playa / Grande, & as they after moved to yᵉ Forts Sᵗ. Iago Sᵗ. Phi- / lip, & Boccachica & after into yᵉ Harbour in Order to / Besiege yᵉ Town agreeable to yᵉ Accᵗ. brought / over by CAPT: LAWS*

Peter Chassereau, cartographer; Remi Parr, engraver; sold by Thomas Bowles and John Bowles

London, May 25, 1741. Black-and-white line engraving.
H. 21¼", W. 21½"

The cartouche is in the lower left. In the lower right is an inset map showing the transatlantic routes from the English Channel to the West Indies and those used by the Spanish galleons from Old Spain to Cartagena on the coast of Colombia. Printed in letterpress along the lower portion of the map is an explanation of the events that took place in Cartagena from March 9 to April 1, 1741

Only one state of the map is known

FOLLOWING Admiral Edward Vernon's victory at Portobello (Cat. 25), Parliament instructed the Duke of Newcastle, secretary of state for the Southern Department, to send reinforcements to aid in attacks against the Spanish in the Caribbean. Sir Chaloner Ogle was charged with transporting nine thousand men under the command of Major General Charles, Lord Cathcart, to Jamaica. Although not legally obligated to provide military aid beyond the bounds of their own colonies, an American regiment of three thousand men was recruited to join Cathcart. Former Virginia governor Alexander Spotswood was chosen to command the American forces.[1]

Four Virginia companies and several from the Middle Atlantic colonies sailed for Jamaica on October 2 and were later joined by troops from New England. By January 9, 1741, the English and American forces had joined Vernon at Port Royal. Unfortunately, both Cathcart and Spotswood had died so command fell to the less experienced Brigadier General Thomas Wentworth.

The troops arrived at Cartagena on March 4. Chassereau illustrated their movements over the following month on his map and described them at the bottom. The ships first anchored in *Playa Grande* on the windward side of Cartagena, labeled *A* on the map. On March 23, the English finally attacked the forts on the *Boca Chica*, labeled *K*, Boca Chica meaning "little mouth." *(fig. 125)* Although some of the ships were damaged, they were able to penetrate the harbor by the twenty-sixth, leaving only Fort Lazar to capture prior to reaching the Spanish fleet and town of Cartagena. After suffering heavy losses in an unsuccessful assault on Fort Lazar, the commanders decided to return to Jamaica.

From the beginning, Wentworth and Vernon disagreed on military strategy, and, in the end, each blamed the other for the failure of the mission. Vernon favored a quick, decisive action while the more cautious Wentworth preferred to wait until he felt completely prepared. Delays in the Cartagena campaign allowed the Spanish time to prepare and for the rainy, yellow fever season to set in. More English and American troops lost their lives from sickness than from military action.

What little is known of Peter Chassereau is found in an advertisement he placed in the *South Carolina Gazette*:

> Mr. Peter Chassereau, *newly come from* London, *surveys Land, and makes neat Maps thereof, draws Plans and Elevations of all kinds of Buildings whatsoever, both civil and Military, likewise perspective Views or prospects of Towns or Gentlemens Houses or Plantations, he calculates Estimates for Buildings or Repairs, inspects and measures Artificers Works, sets out ground for Gardens or parks, in a grand and rural manner, and takes Levels; Young Gentlemen and Ladys will be attended at their own Houses to be taught Drawing.*[2]

1989-109

---

1. Edward Baradall, attorney general of Virginia, devised a scheme to recruit large numbers of convict laborers that had been transported to the colony. In May 1740, the Assembly enacted a law calling for the service of all persons "who follow no lawful calling or employment." Morton, *Colonial Virginia*, II, p. 527.
2. *S. C. Gaz.*, Dec. 28, 1734.

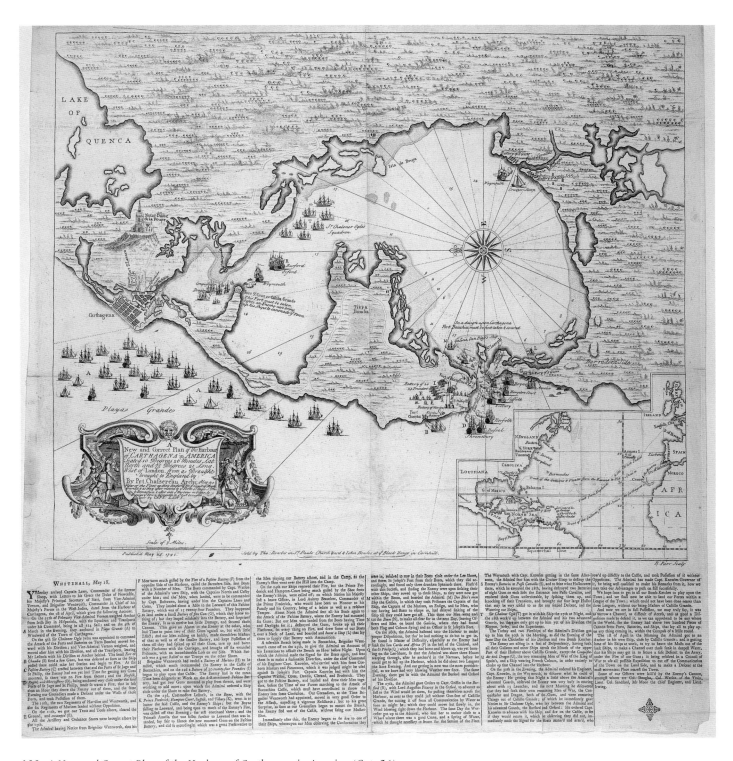

122 *A New and Correct Plan of the Harbour of Carthagena in America.* (Cat. 26)

27 *A SURVEY of the NORTHERN NECK / of VIRGINIA, being / The LANDS belonging to the R^t. Honourable / THOMAS LORD FAIRFAX BARON CAMERON, bounded / by & within the Bay of Chesapoyocke and between / the Rivers Rappahannock and Potowmack: / with / The Courses of the Rivers / RAPPAHANNOCK and POTOWMACK, / in VIRGINIA, / as surveyed according to Order/ in the Years 1736 & 1737*

John Warner (based on surveys by Benjamin Winslow, John Savage, Robert Thomas the elder, and Robert Thomas the younger), cartographer; engraver unknown

London, 1745. Black-and-white line engraving. H. 12″, W. 14″

The Fairfax coat of arms is in the upper left. Beneath is the inscription *The Boundary Line of the Northern Neck in Virginia from the Head Spring of the River Conway/ a Southern Branch of the River Rappahannock, to the Head Spring of the River Potomack/ arising in the Allagany Mountains as Ordered by his Majesty in Council 11.th April 1745./ unto the R.^{t} Hon. Thomas Lord Fairfax the Proprietor thereof.* A scale of distances is in the upper right and a foliate title cartouche surmounted by a scallop shell is in the lower center

Five states of the map are known[1]:

State 1: The title appeared only as *The Courses of the Rivers/ RAPPA-HANNOCK and POTOWMACK,/ in/ VIRGINIA,/ as surveyed according to Order/ in the Years 1736 & 1737.* At the top, the Potomac River was identified as *Potowmack River called Cohongoronta by Coll' Lee since the Date of ye Patent.* The south branch of the Rappahannock was identified as *Rapahannock River S.^{o} Branch lately called Rapidan by Col. Spotswood.* The north branch was *Rapah.^{nk} Riv.^{r} N.^{o} Branch lately called Cannon by Coll. Spotswood.* In Orange County, the Robertson River was noted as *Riv.^{r} called Robertson by Coll. Spotswood. Orange County* was engraved in a single vertical line. 1737

State 2: *by Coll' Lee since the Date of ye Patent* was deleted from the identification of the Potomac River. The three references to Spotswood were deleted and the two branches of the Rappahannock were identified as *Rapahannock River S.^{o} Branch called Rapidan,* and *Rapah.^{nk} Riv.^{r} N.^{o} Branch lately called Cannon,* and the Robertson River, *Riv.^{r} called Robertson. PRINCE WILLIAM COUNTY* extended from *Short Hills* to *Chapawamsick. Orange County* was erased and reengraved in two parallel lines. 1740

State 3: The course of *Thornton's River* in Orange County was corrected and the name was corrected to *Thornton River. PRINCE WILLIAM COUNTY* was erased and repositioned just above Stafford County. *Fairfax County* was added. 1743

State 4: (this copy) As described. The Fairfax coat of arms, augmentation of the title and cartouche, and boundary line with four lines of text were added. Several notations, *Coll. Carter's 50000 Acres, Coll. Page,* above the *Shannondoah River,* and *Cokongoloto,*

were deleted. *The Mannor of Leeds,* in the *Blew* Mountains, *Falmouth, Bristol Furnice,* and *Leet* were added. 1745

State 5: Numerous changes were made including the addition of houses, forts, rivers, and roads such as the *Road from the Ohio* and *Road to Annapolis. Culpeper County* was formed from part of *Orange County. Frederick County* was named. A large tract of land was superimposed over the Fairfax coat of arms. 1749

References: Byrd, "Report of the Commissioners," pp. 401–410; Cresswell, "Colony to Commonwealth," pp. 51–52, 76–77; Foster, "Maps of the First Survey of the Potomac," pp. 149–157; Foster, "Potomac River Maps," pp. 406–418; Harrison, *Landmarks of Old Prince William,* pp. 617–629; Kemper, "Documents Relating to the Boundaries of the Northern Neck," pp. 296–318; Martin, "Warner's Map," pp. 82–83; Ristow, "Early Cartography," pp. 5–7; Stevens and Tree, "Comparative Cartography," entries 83 and 83a; *The World Encompassed,* entry no. 253

ENGLISH monarchs granted numerous tracts of land in America to court favorites in the seventeenth century. Careless wording of the charters and a general lack of knowledge of the geography involved often created disputes over the limits and boundaries of individual grants that lasted for decades. Resolving these disagreements provided motivation for documenting and surveying the land. While in exile in France in 1649, Charles II granted the Northern Neck of Virginia to some of his loyal supporters. After being restored to the throne, Charles reconfirmed the previously granted proprietorship, which eventually was consolidated under a single owner in 1722 when Thomas, sixth Lord Fairfax, inherited it through his mother, Catherine Culpeper Fairfax. According to the charter, Fairfax's tract included the territory between the Rappahannock and Potomac Rivers from the Chesapeake Bay to their headwaters. This sizable grant ultimately amounted to 5,282,000 acres.[2]

On several occasions, the Virginia Assembly questioned both the legality of the grant and the precise boundaries it encompassed. The primary issue was the actual location of the headwaters of the rivers. In the case of the Rappahannock, there was also the question of whether the true head originated at the southern branch, known as the Rapidan, or at the northern branch. Ferdinando John Paris, London counsel to the Penn family, wrote that "Lord Fairfax calls his Territory what every body else calls it, the Northern Neck, but it appears that under pretence of going to the first heads he claims neck and body also, and such a quantity as amounts to 5,200,000 acres."[3]

In 1728, Fairfax's agent, Robert Carter, claimed that the Virginia Council was issuing land patents for tracts in the Shenandoah Valley that fell within the disputed territory.

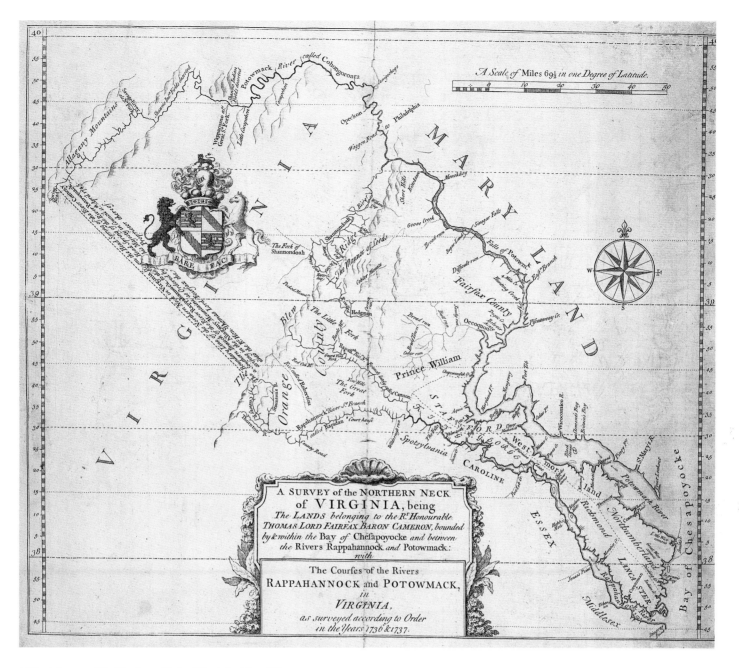

123 *A Survey of the Northern Neck of Virginia.* (Cat. 27)

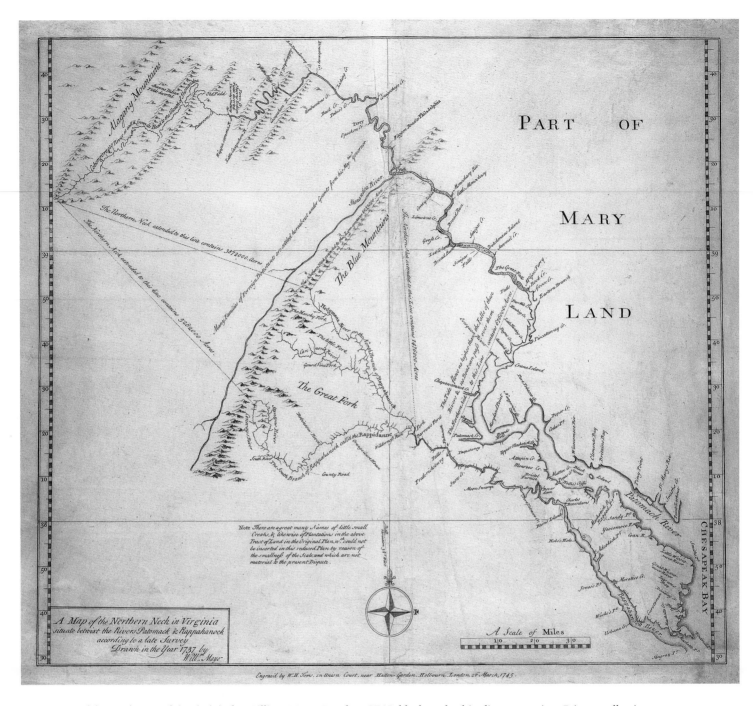

124 *A Map of the Northern Neck in Virginia,* by William Mayo, London, 1745, black-and-white line engraving. Private collection.

The matter came to a head two years later when the House of Burgesses sent a petition to King George II stating that "the head springs of the Rappahannock and Potomac are not yet known to any of your Majesty's subject's; but much inconvenience has resulted to grantees there-from."[4] Fairfax filed a counter petition in 1733 requesting that the Crown appoint a commission to determine and survey the actual bounds of the grant. The Privy Council concurred and requested that the governor and Assembly settle the issue. William Byrd II, John Robinson, and John Grymes were selected to represent the colony's interest, with William Mayo and Robert Brooke as surveyors. Fairfax chose Charles Carter, William Beverley, and William Fairfax as his commissioners. Benjamin Winslow and John Savage were his surveyors.

The officials proposed three separate surveys. The first group was instructed to chart the course and distance of the Potomac River from its confluence with the Sherrando (Shenandoah) River to the head spring. The second team was to survey the south branch of the Rappahannock (Rapidan) River from the fork to the source. The third waterway to be mapped was the north branch of the Rappahannock.[5]

The parties returned with charts of the rivers and field notes describing the terrain and their journeys. Virginia's commissioners instructed Mayo to prepare one map, in duplicate, that integrated the work of each expedition. Since Mayo was one of the surveyors appointed by the opposing side, Fairfax refused to comply with their recommendation and requested that John Warner compile a separate survey. Once the maps had been assembled and all of the commissioners examined the surveyors' findings, they confirmed Lord Fairfax's right to the area between the forks of the Rappahannock, concluding that the actual boundary lay between the head spring of the Rapidan and that of the Potomac.

The commissioners' report and findings and copies of each of the maps were sent to London. Fairfax's London advisors recognized that Mayo's map (fig. 124) was more manageable in size and exhibited a higher quality of draftsmanship than the one prepared by Warner. To ensure that Mayo's map would not provide a strategic advantage to the opposing side, Fairfax authorized a reduced version of Warner's map to present to the Privy Council. (fig. 123) In an attempt to expedite the settlement, Fairfax came to an agreement with the Board of Trade that he would recognize the earlier grants made by the Virginia government and forego collecting rents until the case was resolved.[6]

A resolution was not reached for another eight years. On April 11, 1745, the Privy Council decided that the limits of the Fairfax grant should extend in a straight line from the head spring of the Potomac to that of the Rapidan, as established by the survey of 1736. Accordingly, Governor William Gooch and Fairfax both appointed another commission to run the line. The edition of Warner's map illustrated in this entry was altered to reflect the 1745 ruling.
1961-277

1. Stevens and Tree, "Comparative Cartography," pp. 48, 102–103; unpublished notes by cartographic historian Coolie Verner, made available by Henry Taliaferro. Stevens and Tree and Verner recorded five states of the map, although Verner never personally examined a copy of the fifth state. The Lib. Cong. owns copies of each of the first four states. The dates assigned to the changes follow Verner. See also Walter W. Ristow, "Early Cartography of Virginia's Northern Neck," *The Portolan*, I (1984), pp. 5–7. Ristow identified only four states, dating the fourth 1747. Verner believed that this state reflected the settlement of the Fairfax controversy by the Privy Council on Apr. 11, 1745.

2. Josiah Look Dickinson, *The Fairfax Proprietary: The Northern Neck, The Fairfax Manors and Beginnings of Warren County in Virginia With Maps* (Front Royal, Va., 1959), pp. 1–2.

3. Harrison, *Landmarks of Old Prince William*, p. 622.

4. *Ibid.*, p. 7.

5. The surveyors for the Potomac River were Mayo and Brooke for the Crown and Winslow and Savage for Fairfax. The Rapidan surveyors were Mr. Graeme for the Crown and Mr. Thomas the elder for Fairfax. Mr. Wood for the Crown and Mr. Thomas the younger for Fairfax charted the north branch of the Rappahannock.

6. Dickinson, *The Fairfax Proprietary*, p. 10.

James Alexander and Lewis Evans, cartographers; James Turner, engraver; published in *A Bill in the Chancery of New-Jersey at the Suit of John Earl of Stair, and others, Proprietors of the Eastern-Division of New Jersey; against Benjamin Bond, and some other Persons of Elizabeth-town, distinguished by the Name of the Clinker Lot Right Men*

Boston, 1747. Black-and-white line engraving. H. 15¾", W. 12⅝"

In the center right is a cartouche surmounted by two putti containing the information: *MAP N.º I / NOTE THAT / What are called / by the following / Names in this Map / Were in the / Dutch time / Called / Hudson's River Noordt Rivier / Delaware River Zuydt Rivier / New York / Nieuw Amssterdam / ALBANY Fort Orangie / New Castle Fort Casimir / Note also that / These Names / in this Map / Are commonly Called / Bridlington Burlington / Burnigat Barnagat / Little Egg Little Egg Harbour.* Below is a key indicating how the maps were to be colored

Only one state of the map is known

References: Cumming, *Southeast in Early Maps*, entry 266; Miller, "Printing of the Elizabethtown Bill in Chancery," pp. 1–20; Snyder, *Mapping of New Jersey*, p. 40; Wheat and Brun, *Maps and Charts*, entry 294

T HIS MAP of New York, Pennsylvania, Maryland, Virginia, and Carolina was one of three prepared by the Crown to support its case against settlers who claimed rightful title to land in Newark, Elizabeth, and adjacent territory in New Jersey. The controversy began in March 1664 when Charles II conveyed all of the land between the Connecticut colony and the Delaware River to the Duke of York, the future James II, disregarding the fact that portions of the territory had been settled by Dutch, Swedes, and Finns. The Duke of York sent Colonel Richard Nicolls to capture the Middle Atlantic colonies, and by May this region was under English rule and Nicolls was appointed governor.

The Duke of York subsequently granted the New Jersey proprietary to John, Lord Berkeley, and Sir George Carteret. Before Nicolls learned that New Jersey had been granted to Berkeley and Carteret, he gave the settlers living in the area of Elizabethtown permission to purchase titles to their lands from the Delaware Indians. Nicolls's actions led to years of litigation over who actually possessed title because the settlers claimed possession based on their Indian deeds and the colony maintained that the lands belonged to the proprietorship. The dispute led to *A Bill in the Chancery of New-Jersey*. The petition, drafted for the Crown against settlers who maintained they had rightfully purchased their land from the Delawares, was introduced to the Council of Proprietors in 1745. James Alexander, lawyer, merchant, surveyor general for both East and West Jersey, Council member in New Jersey, and attorney general in both New Jersey and New York, prepared the document. Alexander carefully researched the land conveyance records pertaining to the territory to show that the land rightfully belonged to the proprietors rather than to the settlers.

In 1746, Alexander arranged to have two hundred fifty copies of the bill printed. Alexander prepared three maps illustrating the areas in dispute to be included with the bill as hand-drawn inserts by Lewis Evans. They included a map of the East Coast from the Outer Banks of Carolina to Boston, a map of north and central Jersey, and a depiction of property boundaries between Cushetunk Mountain and the Rahway River north of the Raritan in the Elizabethtown tract. The map illustrated in this entry established the geographic context for the dispute. Noted within the text of *A Bill in the Chancery of New-Jersey* was the fact that it was "copied from part of Popple's large Map of the English Colonies in America, except the red, blue, green, and yellow Colours, and the Notes, which are added."[1]

Despite Alexander's initial conclusion that the maps "could not be had in this country otherwise than by hand," six months later, he commissioned James Turner to engrave them on copper.[2] Ultimately, this proved to be much more costly than Evans's hand-drawn copies would have been. Alexander's accounts for producing the bill indicate that £58.4.7 was spent to procure forty sets of the printed maps. The final cost of £295 for the pamphlet far exceeded the initial estimates. Despite Alexander's careful research and preparation, the controversy was not resolved until after the Revolution.

G1992-29, gift of Mrs. Anna Glen Vietor in memory of Alexander O. Vietor

1. James Clements Wheat and Christian F. Brun, *Maps and Charts Published in America Before 1800: A Bibliography* (New Haven, Conn., 1969), entry 294.
2. Miller, "Printing of the Elizabethtown Bill in Chancery," p. 10.

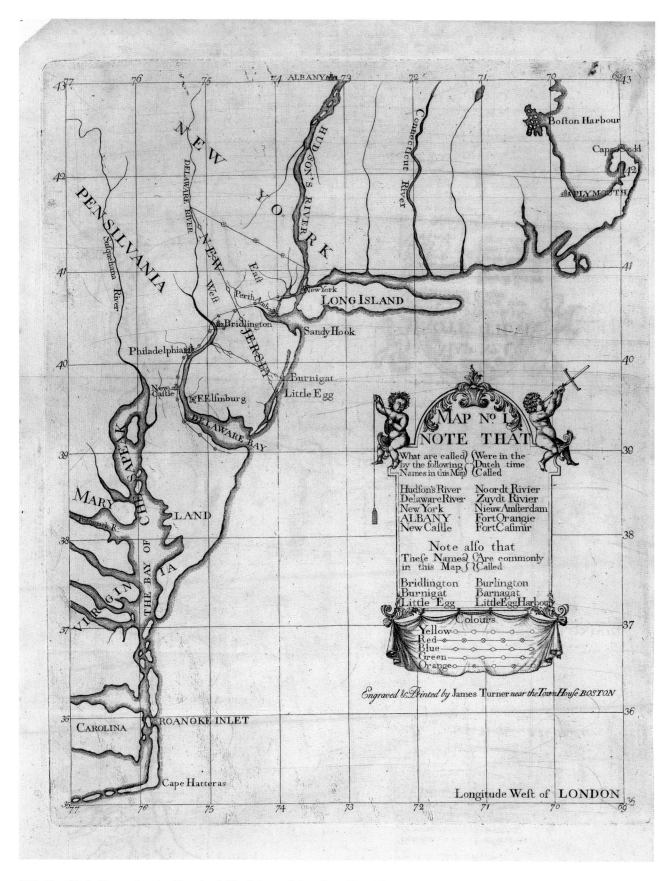

125 New York, Pennsylvania, Maryland, Virginia, and Carolina. (Cat. 28)

29 *PLAN OF / FORT LE QUESNE, / Built by the French. / At the Fork of the / Ohio and Monongahela / in 1754*

Captain Robert Stobo, cartographer; engraver unknown; J. Payne, publisher and printer

London, July 15, 1755. Black-and-white line engraving.
H. 13½", W. 12¾"

The title cartouche is in the upper left corner. In the lower left is the key identifying structures within the fort and the topography

Two states of the map are known:
State 1: (this copy) As described
State 2: In the lower left margin is *Printed for Rob.ᵗ Sayer in Fleet Street and Tho.ˢ Jefferys at the corner of S.ᵗ Martins Lane in the Strand.* 1768

References: Brown, *Early Maps of the Ohio Valley*, entry 26; Kahrl, "Captain Robert Stobo," pp. 141–151, 254–268; Schwartz, *French and Indian War*, pp. 27–29; Schwartz and Ehrenberg, *Mapping of America*, p. 166; Stevens and Tree, "Comparative Cartography," entry 70

IN 1752, the Marquis Duquesne arrived in Quebec to assume the position of governor-general of New France with instructions to take possession of the Ohio Valley. The marquis oversaw the construction of Forts Presque Isle and Le Boeuf, the present sites of Erie and Waterford, Pennsylvania. Since this territory was claimed by Virginia, Governor Robert Dinwiddie dispatched twenty-one-year-old Major George Washington to the Ohio to demand the peaceable withdrawal of French troops. When he returned, Washington reported that the French had no intention of abandoning their positions.[1]

At the request of Dinwiddie, the House of Burgesses quickly enacted legislation appropriating ten thousand pounds for equipment and troops to build a fort at the fork of the Ohio at the Allegheny and Monongahela Rivers (Pittsburgh today) and to advance westward toward the French. In February 1754, Virginians began to build Fort Prince George at the site Washington selected on the Ohio River. Two months later, well-armed French troops arrived at the partially constructed fort and forced the Virginians to surrender it. The French completed the fort, which they renamed Fort Duquesne. By this time, Washington and his troops were encamped at Great Meadows, about sixty-five miles southwest of the forks of the Ohio. Having received word that French troops in the vicinity were planning to attack, Washington advanced. After a brief confrontation, Washington's Indian ally, chief Tanaghrisson, approached the wounded Joseph Coulon de Villiers de Jumonville, the French detachment's commander, cut open his head with a hatchet and reached into the commander's skull, removing the brain tissue with his hands. Almost simultaneously, Tanaghrisson's warriors began to kill other wounded French soldiers.[2]

Anticipating French retaliation, Washington started to erect Fort Necessity at Great Meadows. On July 3, 1754, seven hundred French soldiers and three hundred fifty Indians from Fort Duquesne attacked Fort Necessity. Outnumbered, Washington surrendered and was forced to sign articles of capitulation under which British Captains Jacob Van Braam and Robert Stobo were taken as captives to Fort Duquesne until the previously captured French soldiers were safely returned.

Robert Stobo had arrived in Virginia in 1742 to represent a group of Glasgow merchants. Through his friendship with Dinwiddie, he received a commission as captain in the Virginia regiment and accompanied Washington to Fort Necessity. During his imprisonment, Stobo studied the layout of Fort Duquesne in minute detail. With the help of a friendly Indian, he smuggled out notes and a sketch suggesting how the British could recapture the fort. Stobo's notes were delivered to Washington. When Major General Edward Braddock, commander in chief of the English forces, arrived in Virginia in 1755, he developed a three-pronged strategy to contain the French. Armed with Stobo's notes and map, Braddock led the campaign to force the French to surrender Fort Duquesne. Indian scouts warned the French of the advancing British army, allowing them to set up an ambush. Braddock was mortally wounded during the battle and Stobo's smuggled intelligence fell into French hands. The French realized that Stobo had smuggled the plan and they charged him with spying for the enemy, eventually sentencing him to death. They moved Stobo to Quebec where he ultimately escaped.

Stobo's *Plan of Fort Le Quesne* was engraved and published in London by J. Payne in 1755 and in 1768 by Robert Sayer and Thomas Jefferys in the *General Topography of North America*.

1985-74

1. Washington's report on his trip to Ohio, *The Journal of Major George Washington Sent by the Hon. Robert Dinwiddie, Esq; His Majesty's Lieutenant-Governor, and Commander in Chief of Virginia, to the Commandant of the French Forces on Ohio*, was published in Williamsburg in 1754. Jefferys reprinted Washington's Journal in London that same year. The London edition contained a *Map of the Western parts of the Colony of Virginia as far as the Mississipi*. The next year, Le Rouge published a French version. For a description of the French version, see Cat. 30.

2. For a moving account of this tragedy, see Anderson, *Crucible of War*, pp. 5–7.

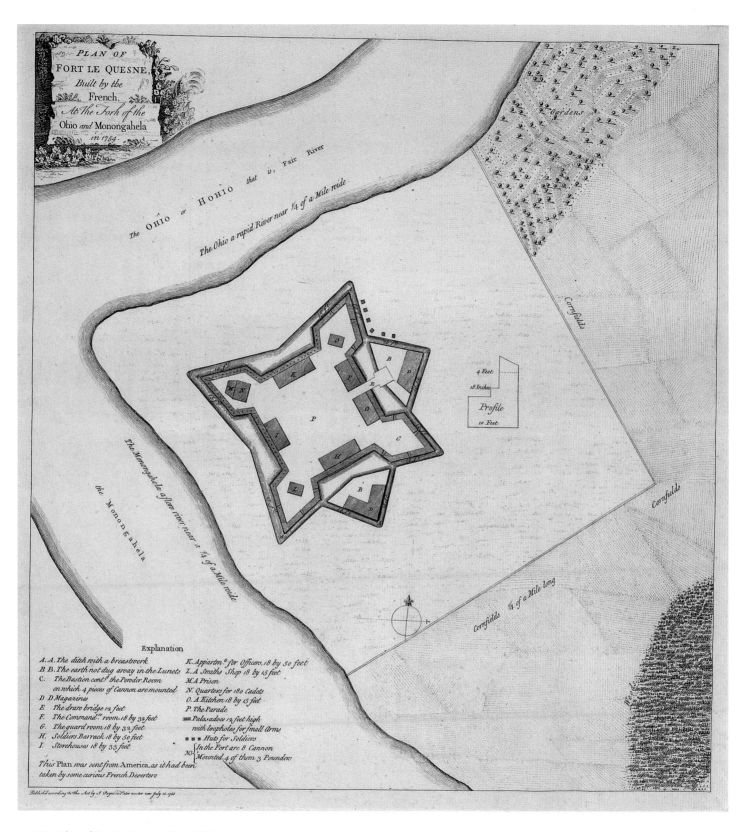

The OHIO or HOHIO that is Fair River

The Ohio a rapid River near ¼ of a Mile wide

Gardens

Cornfields

The Monongahela a flow river near a ¼ of a Mile wide

the Monongahela

4 Feet

18 Inches

Profile

10 Feet

Cornfields

Cornfields ¼ of a Mile long

Woods

Explanation

A. A. The ditch with a breastwork
B B. The earth not dug away in the Lunets
C. The Bastion cont.ᵍ the Powder Room
   on which 4 pieces of Cannon are mounted
D D Magazines
E. The draw bridge 12 feet
F. The Command.ᵗⁿ room 18 by 32 feet
G. The guard room 18 by 32 feet
H. Soldiers Barrack 18 by 50 feet
I. Storehouses 18 by 33 feet

K. Appartm.ᵗˢ for Officers 18 by 50 feet
L. A Smiths Shop 18 by 15 feet
M. A Prison
N. Quarters for 180 Cadets
O. A Kitchen 18 by 15 feet
P. The Parade
▬ Palasadoes 12 feet high
   with loopholes for small Arms
▰▰▰ Huts for Soldiers
N.ᵒ { In the Fort are 8 Cannon
      Mounted 4 of them 3 Pounders

This Plan was sent from America, as it had been
taken by some curious French Deserters

Published according to the Act by J. Payne in Pater noster row July 15. 1755

126 *Plan of Fort Le Quesne.* (Cat. 29)

30 A MAP of / the most INHABITED part of / VIRGINIA / containing the whole PROVINCE of / MARYLAND / with Part of / PENSILVANIA, NEW JERSEY AND NORTH CAROLINA

Joshua Fry and Peter Jefferson, cartographers; Thomas Jefferys, map engraver; cartouche designed by Francis Hayman and engraved by Charles Grignion; published separately and in *A General Topography of North America and the West Indies* by Thomas Jefferys and Robert Sayer, state five, and in *The American Atlas: or, A Geographical Description of the Whole Continent of America* by Robert Sayer and John Bennett, state six

London, 1768 (first published ca. 1753). Black-and-white line engraving with period color. H. 31⅛", W. 49⅛", in four sheets

In the upper left is a chart of distances with the notation beneath: *These Distances with the Course of the Roads on the Map I carefully collected on the Spot and enterd them in my Journal from whence they are now inserted. J. Dalrymple, London Jan.ʸ yᵉ 1.ˢᵗ 1755*. A scale of distances is in the lower left. In the lower right is a cartouche illustrating a wharf scene with a tobacco planter negotiating with a ship captain and laboring slaves. Beneath is the dedication *To the Right Honourable, George Dunk Earl of Halifax First Lord Commissioner,/ and to the Rest of the Right Honourable and Honourable Commissioners, for TRADE and PLANTATIONS. This Map is most humbly Inscribed to their Lordship's,/ By their Lordship's/ Most Obedient & most devoted humble Serv.t Tho.ˢ Jefferys*. Included in the scale of longitude in the lower right is *Printed for Rob.ᵗ Sayer at Nᵒ 53 in Fleet Street, & Tho.ˢ Jefferys at the Corner of S.ᵗ Martins Lane, Charing Cross, London*

Eight states of the map are known[1]:

State 1: The title imprint in the cartouche was *A MAP of the INHABITED part of VIRGINIA . . .* The lower right border contained the imprint *Engrav'd and Publish'd According to Act of Parliament By Tho.ˢ Jefferys Geographer to His Royal Highness The Prince of Wales at the Corner of S.ᵗ Martins Lane, Charing Cross, London*. Ca. 1753

State 2: The word *most* was added to the title imprint, which then was *A MAP of the most INHABITED part of VIRGINIA . . .* The geography in the two western plates was reworked as described below. Ca. 1754

State 3: The figures *65° 19' to 72° 19' Longitude West of London* were added. A note concerning the longitude was added beneath the Dalrymple table. Ca. 1755

State 4: The longitude figures were altered to *75° 19' to 82° 19' Longitude West from London*. 1755

State 5: (this copy) As described. The imprint in the lower right border was altered to *Printed for Rob.ᵗ Sayer at N.ᵒ 53 in Fleet Street, & Tho.ˢ Jefferys at the Corner of S.ᵗ Martins Lane, Charing Cross, London*. 1768

State 6: The date in the title imprint was changed from *1751* to *1775*. 1775

State 7: The imprint was altered to *London, R. Sayer and J. Bennett, 1782*. 1782

State 8: Above the cartouche, a second imprint, *Publish'd 12th May*

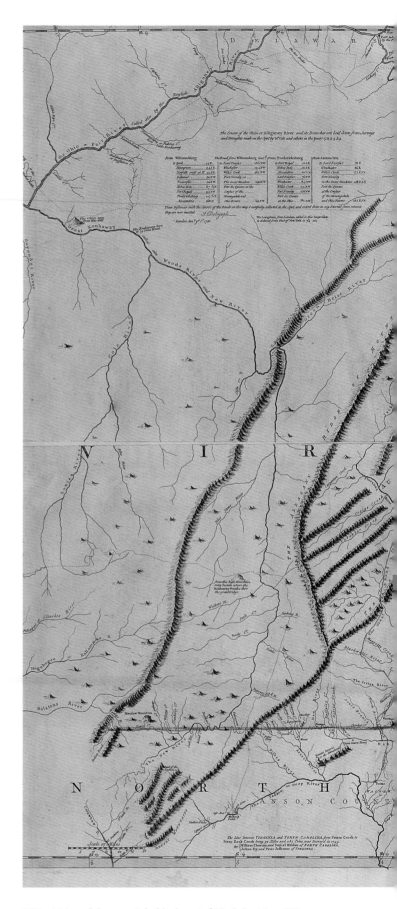

127 *A Map of the most Inhabited part of Virginia.* (Cat. 30)

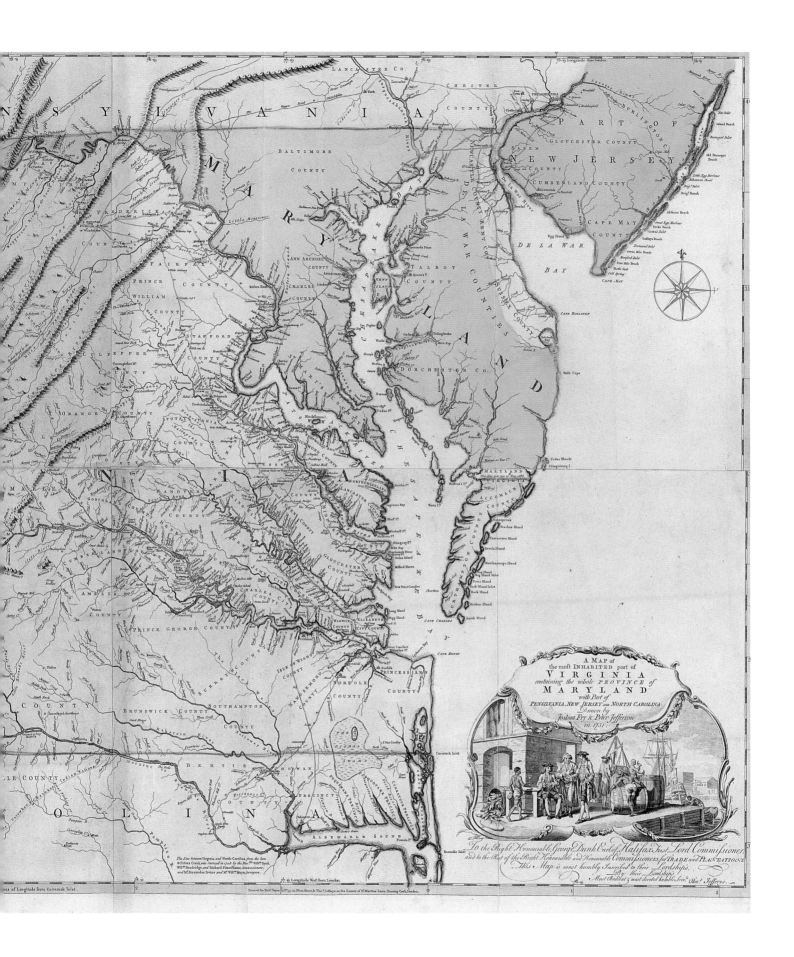

A MAP of
the most INHABITED part of
VIRGINIA
containing the whole PROVINCE of
MARYLAND
with Part of
PENSILVANIA, NEW JERSEY and NORTH CAROLINA
Drawn by
Joshua Fry & Peter Jefferson
in 1751.

To the Right Honourable, George Dunk Earl of Halifax, First Lord Commissioner,
and to the Rest of the Right Honourable and Honourable Commissioners, for TRADE and PLANTATIONS,
This Map is most humbly Inscribed to their Lordships,
By their Lordships,
Most Obedient & most devoted humble Servt. Thos. Jefferys.

1794, by LAURIE & WHITTLE, N.o 53, Fleet Street, London, was added. 1794

References: Cresswell, "Colony to Commonwealth," pp. 54–55, 83–87; Cumming, *Southeast in Early Maps,* entry 281 and pp. 26–29; Elcan, "Peter Jefferson and Joshua Fry—Mapmakers," pp. 13–19; Fite and Freeman, *Book of Old Maps,* entry 61; Fowble, *Two Centuries of Prints,* entry 8; Harrison, "Virginians on the Ohio and the Mississippi," pp. 203–222; Malone, *Fry & Jefferson Map;* McCorkle, *America Emergent,* entry 23; Norona, "Fry's Report," pp. 22–41; Papenfuse and Coale, *Hammond-Harwood House Atlas,* pp. 35–36; Sanchez-Saavedra, *Description of the Country,* pp. 25–34; Schwartz and Ehrenberg, *Mapping of America,* p. 158; Verner, "Fry and Jefferson map," pp. 70–94; *The World Encompassed,* entries 190 and 191.

ONE OF THE FIRST acts of George Montagu Dunk, Earl of Halifax, once he became president of the Board of Trade and Plantations in 1748, was to request information from the colonies concerning activities on the frontiers of English settlements. He was most specifically interested in learning of French encroachments in territories claimed by the British Crown. Since both Virginia and Pennsylvania claimed large areas of the Ohio River Valley, the need for accurate maps became even more pressing as the contest over the area intensified. To fulfill Halifax's request, acting governor of Virginia Colonel Lewis Burwell commissioned Colonel Joshua Fry and Peter Jefferson to prepare a map of the Virginia colony.

Born in England about 1700, Fry was educated at Oxford before immigrating to Virginia in the early eighteenth century. He taught natural philosophy and mathematics at the College of William and Mary prior to moving west. In what would later become Albemarle County, Fry was appointed to a number of official positions, including that of representative in the House of Burgesses and county surveyor. Jefferson had served as surveyor of Goochland County before relocating to Albemarle in 1745, where Fry quickly named him to the position of deputy surveyor. Two years later, they embarked on the first of several monumental mapmaking endeavors. The Governor's Council approved a survey to determine the western limits of Virginia's Northern Neck previously granted to Thomas, Lord Fairfax. Fry was appointed as a commissioner for the Crown and, in turn, secured Jefferson's appointment as one of the surveyors to run the line.[2] *(fig. 128)* Fry and Jefferson also served as joint commissioners to extend the western portion of the boundary line between Virginia and North Carolina in 1749. *(fig. 129)*

Fry and Jefferson's extensive experience prompted acting governor Burwell to select them to supply the neces-

sary information for the new map of Virginia. Not only were the surveyors able to draw upon their previous work, they were also acquainted with men who had explored the western territories. In 1751, only one year after the Board of Trade and Plantations requested a new map of Virginia, Fry and Jefferson delivered a draft to Burwell. It was accompanied by "An Account of the Bounds of the Colony of Virginia & of its back settlements, & of the lands towards the Mountains & Lakes" prepared by Fry.[3] The greatest portion of the report was derived from four published sources, all readily available in England: Louis Hennepin's *A new discovery of a vast country in America,* Henry Joutel's *A journal of the last voyage perform'd by Monsr de la Sale, to the Gulph of Mexico,* Cadwallader Colden's *History of the Five Indian Nations,* and William Stith's *History of Virginia.* In addition, Fry included his own comments and reports from two other Virginia expeditions, one by John Howard and John Peter Salley in 1742, the other by Thomas Walker in 1750.[4]

Burwell transmitted Fry and Jefferson's work to the board in August 1751, and it was presented to the commissioners on March 10 and 11, 1752.[5] Shortly thereafter, the material was given to publisher Thomas Jefferys, geographer to the Prince of Wales, so that it could be engraved and printed. Jefferys engraved the map himself, and commissioned artist Francis Hayman and engraver Charles Grignion to design and execute the cartouche.[6] *(fig. 130)* Hayman's cartouche illustrated the tobacco trade on which Virginia's economy was based. The major rivers and their tributaries in the Chesapeake region were essential to a planter's success because they enabled slaves to load hogsheads of tobacco directly from the wharves onto ships that

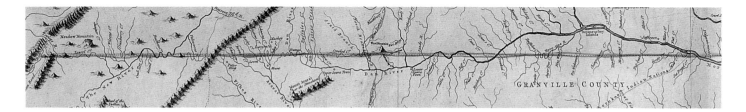

129 Detail of the Virginia-North Carolina dividing line from *A Map of the most Inhabited part of Virginia*,
by Joshua Fry and Peter Jefferson, London, 1768 (first published ca. 1753),
black-and-white line engraving with period color. 1968-11. (Cat. 30)

128 Detail of the Northern Neck from *A Map of the most Inhabited part of Virginia*,
by Joshua Fry and Peter Jefferson, London, 1768 (first published ca. 1753),
black-and-white line engraving with period color. 1968-11. (Cat. 30)

transported the crop across the ocean, eliminating the added expense of land transportation. Shipping the barrels rather than rolling them overland also reduced the chance of damaging the tobacco leaves. In addition, large-scale plantation owners could negotiate directly with ship captains at their own plantations. A contemporary description of Virginia noted:

The chief Rivers are, James, York or Pamunky, Rappahannock, and Patowmack; they not only admit large ships into the very heart of the country, but abound with so many creeks, and receive such a multitude of inferior, yet navigable rivers, that Virginia seems unrivalled throughout the universe for convenience of inland navigation: indeed, it has been observed, and with reason, that every planter here has a river at his door.[7]

Toiling slaves representing the large labor force required for tobacco cultivation were also depicted.

Fry and Jefferson's original manuscript no longer survives and therefore cannot be compared to the printed map, but in all likelihood, Jefferys based his geography directly on their draft. It is known, however, that Jefferys omitted some of the western material that the surveyors supplied from Walker's expeditions.[8] The published work contained Fry and Jefferson's completed border survey for the western bounds of the Northern Neck and for the dividing line between Virginia and North Carolina. The land masses in the Chesapeake region were more accurately rendered than they had been on any previous map. For the first time, the entire Virginia river system was delineated and the correct northeast-southwest parallel

direction of the Appalachian Mountains was portrayed. However, Lake Erie was located several hundred miles too far south and the inaccurately depicted course of the Ohio River was based primarily on hearsay. The compilers must have realized these defects in their draft for they immediately began to revise the information that had been sent to England.

In 1752, Fry was appointed one of three commissioners dispatched to negotiate a treaty with the Six Nations in which the Native Americans agreed not to attack the English living southeast of the Ohio. Accompanying Fry on the expedition across the Appalachians to the forks of the Ohio was Christopher Gist, a surveyor and scout who had previously conducted explorations for the Ohio Company. Gist was the first white American to explore southern Ohio and northeastern Kentucky thoroughly. The following year, George Washington hired Gist to accompany him on his mission to demand that the French retreat from their garrison at Fort Le Boeuf. Gist's knowledge of the topography and his skills as a mapmaker were invaluable to Fry and Washington. He provided the former with updated information to incorporate in the map.

Gist's significant contribution to the revised states of Fry and Jefferson's map was noted in a legend: *The Course of the* Ohio *or* Alliganey River *and its Branches are laid down from Surveys and Draughts made on the Spot by* Mr Gist *and others in the Years 1751.2.3 & 4.* Unfortunately, Fry did not live to see Jefferys' revisions. In February 1754, acting governor Robert Dinwiddie appointed Fry commander in chief of the militia. He was to erect and man a fort at the confluence of the Monongahela and Ohio Rivers for the

130 Detail of the cartouche from
A Map of the most Inhabited part of Virginia,
by Joshua Fry and Peter Jefferson,
London, 1768 (first published ca. 1753),
black-and-white line engraving
with period color. 1968-11. (Cat. 30)

131 Trade card of Thomas Jefferys,
engraved by Anthony Walker, London,
1751, black-and-white line engraving.
Courtesy, British Library.

purpose of driving the French from the area. Fry's second in command was Lieutenant Colonel George Washington. While advancing westward from Winchester, Virginia, on May 25, Colonel Fry fell from his horse and died, leaving Washington in command.

Just how Jefferys received Gist's updated material is unknown. Fry might have added information from Gist's surveys to his own manuscript during the time the two were together in Pennsylvania. Perhaps Jefferys copied directly from Gist's journal and parchment map since they were also sent to London.[9] Materials from Fry and Gist could have been dispatched by way of Captain Dalrymple, who had served as quartermaster under Fry in western Pennsylvania and returned to London in the summer of 1754.[10]

However the revisions made their way to Jefferys, they were substantial enough to require extensive reworking of the two western plates. Lake Erie, previously located too far to the south, was erased from the upper left and replaced with Gist's information about the correct course of the Ohio, Kanawha, and New Rivers and the French settlements along the Pennsylvania border. Dalrymple was credited on the map for providing the table of distances in the upper left corner. State two illustrated the *Great Road from the Yadkin River thro Virginia to Philadelphia* by which many colonists traveled south into western Virginia and North Carolina. It is also interesting to note that Fry and Jefferson computed the longitude by using Philadelphia and Currituck Inlet, North Carolina, as the prime meridians. This map may be the first of any map of North America that used a local point as the prime meridian.

Verner concluded that Jefferys revised the map during the winter of 1754 since the "second edition" was advertised for sale in *The Daily Advertiser* on January 21, 1755.[11] By April, the revised map was available in Williamsburg:

Just PUBLISHED, *and to be sold at the Printing-Office, in Williamsburg, a New and correct* MAP *of the most inhabited Part of* Virginia, *containing also the whole Province of* Maryland, *Part of* Pennsylvania, New-Jersey, *and* North-Carolina, *surveyed in the Year 1751, by* Joshua Fry *and* Peter Jefferson, *and now much corrected and enlarged from several later Observations; taken on the Spot, with the Waggon Roads from* Williamsburg *to* Will's Creek, *both thro' Fredericksburg and Alexandria, including the greatest Part of the River* Ohio, *with the Rivers* Monongahela, Yawyawgany, New-River, Green-Briar, *&c. &c.*[12]

From the time of its first appearance, the Fry and Jeffer-

son map exerted a strong influence on the future cartography of Maryland and Virginia. The English edition was issued in eight states until its final alteration by Laurie and Whittle in 1794. It provided an important resource for both John Mitchell and Lewis Evans, whose own maps of North American appeared in 1755. Also in 1755, French publisher Robert de Vaugondy issued a reduced one-sheet version of the map, *Carte de la Virginie et du Maryland,* that remained in print until 1799. Since it contained little of the revised material, de Vaugondy probably consulted the earlier state of Fry and Jefferson's work. In 1777, George Louis Le Rouge issued *Virginie, Maryland en 2 feuilles par Fry and Jefferson.* Although he reduced the size from four sheets to two, Le Rouge retained the original scale and faithfully copied the updated geography.

1968-11

1. The states listed here are condensed from Coolie Verner, "The Fry and Jefferson map," *Imago Mundi,* XXI (1967), pp. 83–89.

2. For a contemporary description of the journey to survey the line, see John W. Wayland, ed., *The Fairfax Line: Thomas Lewis's Journal of 1746* (New Market, Va., 1925).

3. Fairfax Harrison, "The Virginians on the Ohio and the Mississippi in 1742," *VMHB,* XXX (1922), pp. 205–206; Delf Norona, ed., "Joshua Fry's Report on the Back Settlements of Virginia," *ibid.,* CVI (1948).

4. Salley accompanied Howard on his journey through the Valley of Virginia and across the Allegheny Mountains to the Ohio River. From there, they descended to the Mississippi. According to Norona, Fry's transcript of Salley's journal is the only known contemporary copy. "Fry's Report," p. 27. Dr. Thomas Walker explored southwest Virginia and Kentucky and discovered and named the Cumberland Mountains, Gap, and River.

5. *Ibid.*

6. An advertisement of the map in the *Gentleman's Magazine* documented the assistance of Hayman and Grignion. The map was described as "executed with great accuracy and elegance, and is embellished with a design by *Hayman,* engraved by *Grignion." Gentleman's Magazine,* XV (1755), p. 47.

7. From *"A Compendious Account of the BRITISH COLONIES in NORTH-AMERICA"* on *The Theatre of War in North America* (Cat. 54).

8. For more information on the portions of Fry and Jefferson's draft omitted from the printed map, see Cat. 31.

9. In 1755, Reverend James Maury of Fredericksburg, Va., wrote to his uncle concerning the revisions, noting, "the fuller draughts have been sent over sea by the compilers." Ann Maury, *Memoirs of a Huguenot Family: Translated and Compiled from the Original Autobiography of the Rev. James Fontaine . . .* (Baltimore, Md., 1967), p. 378.

10. Dalrymple has occasionally been credited with supplying all of the revised western material and other revisions to the map; however, with the exception of the table of distances, this is unlikely. Coolie Verner presented five hypotheses for the source of the revisions and concluded that Dalrymple was not the primary one. A comparison of Gist's manuscript with the revised western portions of Fry and Jefferson's map shows that the two coincide precisely. Verner, "Fry and Jefferson map," pp. 76–77.

11. *Ibid.,* pp. 80–81; *Daily Advertiser* (New York, N. Y.), Jan. 21, 1755.

12. *Va. Gaz.,* Apr. 11, 1755.

31 *ESSAY DU COURS DE L' OYO avec les Forts François et Anglois*

Joshua Fry and Peter Jefferson, cartographers; engraver unknown; published in the French edition of *The Journal of Major George Washington* by George Louis Le Rouge

Paris, 1756. Black-and-white line engraving. H. 8″, W. 12⅛″

Only one state of the map, in two editions, is known

References: Brown, *Early Maps of the Ohio Valley*, entry 19; Norona, ed., "Joshua Fry's Report," pp. 22–41; Schwartz, *French and Indian War*, p. 20; Verner, "Fry and Jefferson Map," p. 74

T HE British Ministry, which took the position that the Ohio River and surrounding lands were located within the western bounds of the colony of Virginia, ordered that a message be sent to the French in 1753 demanding that they abandon Fort Le Boeuf and vacate the Ohio region altogether. Upon receiving the order, Lieutenant Governor Robert Dinwiddie dispatched Major George Washington to deliver the message. Washington was unsuccessful in forcing the French to retreat and returned to Williamsburg with the French response that they had every right to establish garrisons in the area since the Ohio River was discovered by La Salle and therefore rightfully belonged to France.

Washington kept a journal of his western mission, which was published in Williamsburg in 1754. *(fig. 133)* Copies were sent to England where Thomas Jefferys reprinted it along with a small *Map of the Western parts of the Colony of Virginia as far as the Mississipi*, not included in the Williamsburg edition. In 1756, George Louis Le Rouge published a French edition of Washington's work, copying the map that Jefferys had included and altering the title to *Essay du Cours de l'Oyo avec les Forts François et Anglois*. The French edition of Jefferys's map is illustrated here. Although Jefferys did not cite his source, evidence suggests that the geography may have come from the western portion of Joshua Fry and Peter Jefferson's draft of Virginia sent in 1751 to Lord Halifax, president of the Board of Trade and Plantations.[1]

Halifax, who had requested that each colony provide information on the western territories, commissioned Thomas Jefferys to engrave, print, and publish the map submitted by the Virginians. Since Fry and Jefferson's manuscript map no longer survives, it is impossible to determine whether Jefferys copied their geography faithfully. The draft was accompanied by "An Account of the Bounds of the Colony of Virginia & of its back settlements,

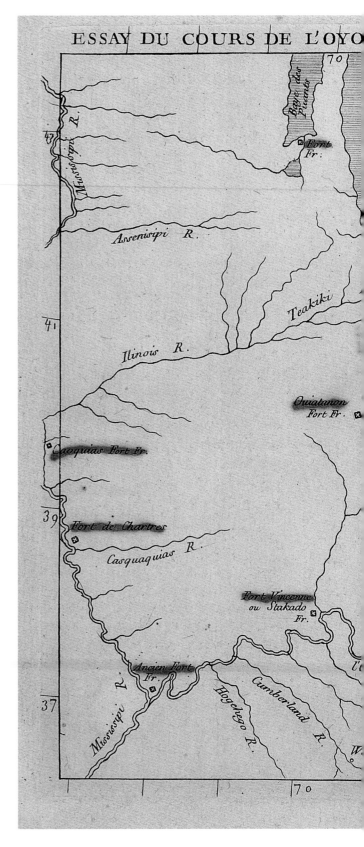

132 *Essay du Cours de L'Oyo avec les Forts François et Anglois.* (Cat. 31)

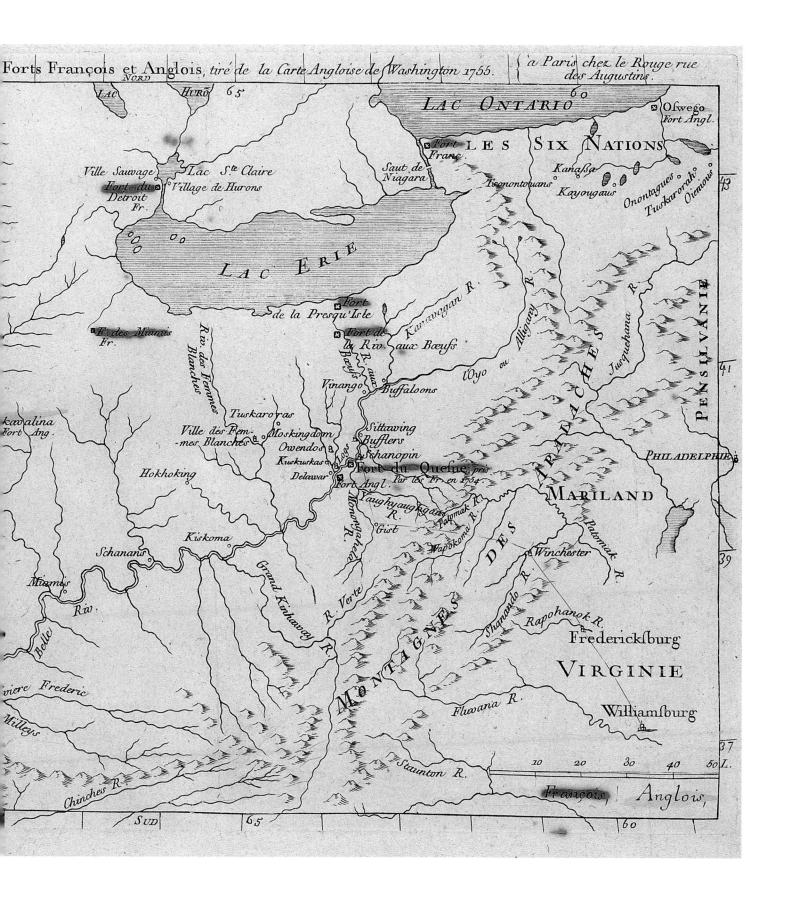

Forts François et Anglois, *tiré de la Carte Angloise de Washington 1755.* *'a Paris chez le Rouge rue des Augustins.*

LAC
NORD
LAC
HURŌ 65
LAC ONTARIO 60
Oswego
Fort Angl.
Fort Franc.
LES SIX NATIONS
Ville Sauvage
Lac Ste Claire
Village de Hurons
Fort du Detroit Fr.
Saut de Niagara
Tsonontouans
Kanassa
Kayougaus
Onontagues
Tuskarorah
Oneious
43
F. des Miamis Fr.
LAC ERIE
Fort de la Presqu'Isle
Kanawagan R.
Penn R.
Jusquehana R.
PENSILVANIE
41
Riv. des Femmes Blanches
Fort de la Riv. aux Bœufs
R. aux Bœufs
l'Oyo ou Alligany R.
Vinango
Buffaloons
Tuskaroras
Ville des Fem- -mes Blanches
Moskingdom
Sittawing
Bufflers
APPALACHES
PHILADELPHIE
Hokhoking
Owendos
Loyo
Shanopin
Kuskuskas
Delawar
Fort-du-Quefne, pris
Fort Angl.
Par les Fr en 1754
MARILAND
kavalina Fort Ang.
Taughyaughqau R.
Patomak R.
Gist
Wapokoma R.
39
Kiskoma
Monongahela R.
Winchester
Patomak R.
Schanans
R. Verte
DES
Miamis Riv.
Grand Kinhaway R.
MONTAGNES
Shanondo R.
Rapohanok R.
Belle
Fredericksburg
riviere Frederic
Fluvana R.
VIRGINIE
Milleys
Williamsburg
37
Staunton R.
10 20 30 40 50 L.
Chinches R.
SUD 65
François, Anglois,
60

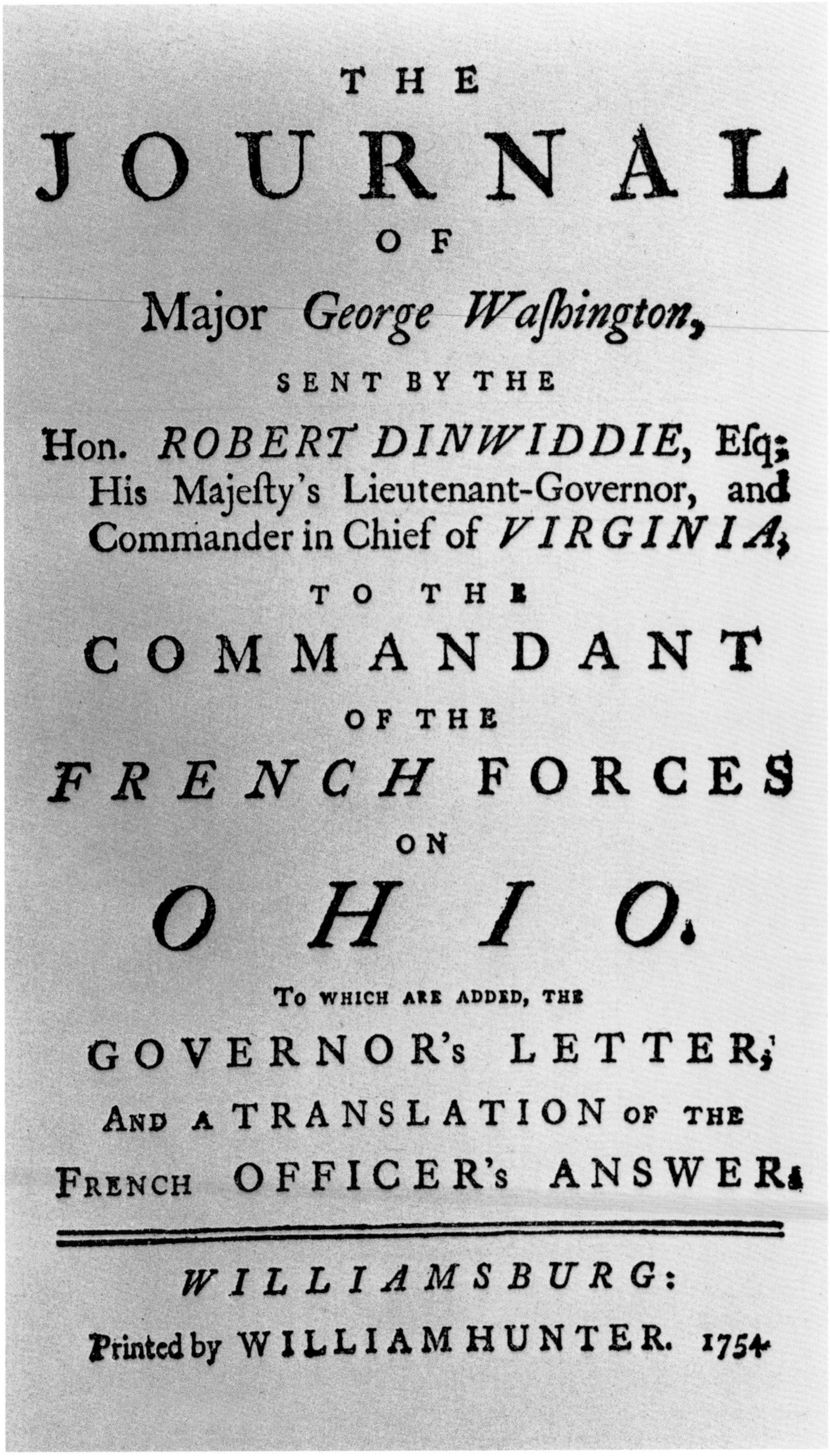

THE
JOURNAL
OF

Major *George Waſhington,*

SENT BY THE

Hon. *ROBERT DINWIDDIE,* Eſq;
His Majeſty's Lieutenant-Governor, and
Commander in Chief of *VIRGINIA;*

TO THE

COMMANDANT

OF THE

FRENCH FORCES

ON

OHIO.

To WHICH ARE ADDED, THE

GOVERNOR's LETTER;

AND A TRANSLATION OF THE

FRENCH OFFICER's ANSWER.

═══════════════════

WILLIAMSBURG:

Printed by WILLIAM HUNTER. 1754.

133 Title page of *The Journal of Major George Washington,*
printed by Wllliam Hunter, Williamsburg, Virginia, 1754.
Colonial Williamsburg Foundation, John D. Rockefeller, Jr. Library.

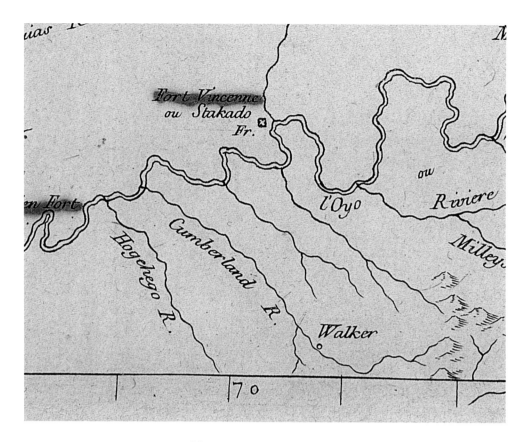

134 Detail from *Essay du Cours de L'Oyo,* by Joshua Fry and Peter Jefferson, published by George Louis Le Rouge, Paris, 1756, black-and-white line engraving. 1988-420. (Cat 31)

& of the lands towards the Mountains & Lakes," prepared by Fry, in which he included reports from two other Virginia expeditions, one by John Howard and John Peter Salley in 1742, and another by Dr. Thomas Walker in 1750.[2] Walker explored southwestern Virginia and Kentucky and named the Cumberland River, Gap, and Mountains.

The surviving report suggests that Fry and Jefferson included information on their original draft that Jefferys chose to eliminate from the printed version. Fry noted in the text that Thomas Walker "built an House on Cumberland River, as is noted in the Map."[3] The printed Fry and Jefferson map did not extend far enough west to include the Cumberland River. Since the river, Walker's house, and other streams mentioned in the report are clearly visible on the map Jefferys published in Washington's *Journal,*

historian Delf Norona concluded that Jefferys used the portion he eliminated from the printed version of Fry and Jefferson's map to create this smaller one. *(fig. 134)* The maps found in the English and French editions of Washington's *Journal* likely provided the only source for information Fry and Jefferson included for the extreme western territory of Virginia.

1988-420

1. Verner, "Fry and Jefferson Map," p. 74. See also Cat. 30.

2. Norona, "Fry's Report." According to Norona, Fry's transcript of Salley's journal is the only known contemporary copy.

3. *Ibid.,* p. 28.

32 *A Prospective Plan of the Battle fought near LAKE GEORGE on the 8th of September 1755, between 2000 English with 250/ Mohawks under the Command of General Johnson and 2500 French and Indians under the Command of General DIESKAU / in which the English were Victorious, captivating the French General with a number of his Men, killing 700 and putting the rest to flight*

Samuel Blodget, cartographer; Thomas Johnston, engraver; published separately and in *A Prospective-Plan of the Battle near Lake George* by Samuel Blodget

Boston, 1755. Black-and-white line engraving. H. 14¼", W. 18¼"

Along the top is a map of the Hudson River from New York to Lake George that includes the layout of Forts William Henry and Edward. A bird's-eye view on the left illustrates troop positions in the early hours of September 8, 1755. Within a scrollwork cartouche in the lower left is the dedication *To His / Excellency William Shirley Esq:ʳ Cap.ᵗ / General & Governour in Chief in & over his Majesty's Province / of yᵉ Massachusetts Bay in New England Major General & Commander in Chief / of all his Majesty's Land Forces in North America. This Plan of yᵉ Battle / fought near Lake George is with all humilily dedicated by your Exxcellencys most / devoted Hum.ᵇˡᵉ Serv.ᵗ: Sam.ˡ Blodget.* Another, illustrating the battle that took place later in the day, is in the right

Two states of the map are known:
State 1: As described but lacking trees surrounding Fort Edward. 1755
State 2: (this copy) As described. Trees were added around Fort Edward

References: Blodget, *Prospective-Plan of the Battle near Lake George;* Cumming, *British Maps*, p. 59; Mugridge and Conover, *Album of American Battle Art*, pp. 1–3; Schwartz, *French and Indian War*, pp. 56–68; Schwartz and Ehrenberg, *Mapping of America*, p. 167; Shadwell, *American Printmaking*, entry 22; Stokes and Haskell, *American Historical Prints*, p. 18; Wheat and Brun, *Maps and Charts*, entry 321

IN FEBRUARY 1755, Major General Edward Braddock arrived in Virginia to command the English forces in America. He immediately developed a three-pronged strategy to contain the French in western Pennsylvania and New York. Braddock himself would lead a campaign to force the French to surrender Fort Duquesne (Cat. 29). The second effort, under the command of Massachusetts governor William Shirley, would be directed at Fort Niagara. The third would be an attack on Crown Point on Lake Champlain. Sir William Johnson, an Indian trader, was promoted to major general in April 1755 and assigned the task of leading the Crown Point campaign. Samuel Blodget's

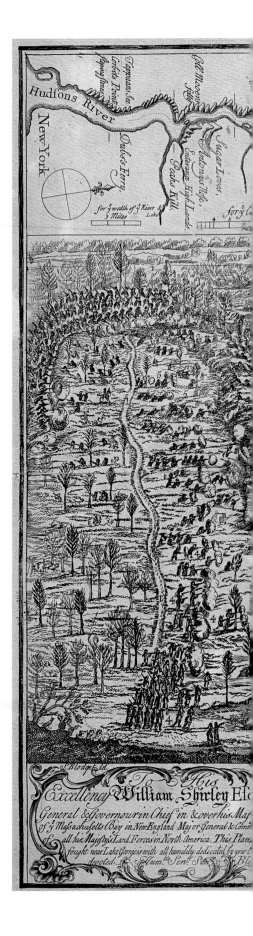

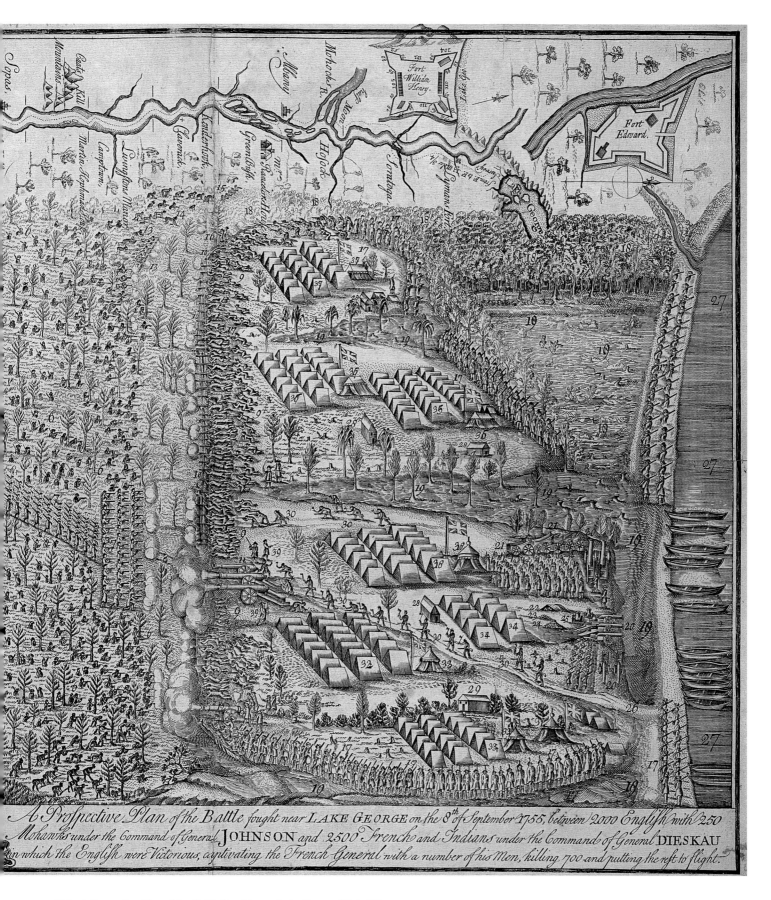

135 *A Prospective Plan of the Battle fought near Lake George.* (Cat. 32)

Prospective Plan of the Battle fought near Lake George depicts Braddock's third initiative.

In the middle of July, Colonel G. Phineas Lyman, Johnson's second in command, began his ascent up the Hudson River. Approximately fourteen miles south of Lake Saint Sacrement, which Johnson renamed Lake George, the troops constructed a fort at the location identified on the map as *Lymans Fort,* which later became Fort Edward. *(fig. 136)* Following Braddock's plan, Johnson intended to sail from Fort Edward to Ticonderoga, where Lake George connects with Lake Champlain, and then head north to attack Crown Point.

French commander in chief Marshal Ludwig August Dieskau was aware of Johnson's movements since Braddock's papers outlining his military strategy had been taken by the French in the battle of Fort Duquesne. Dieskau therefore advanced eastward along Lake Champlain toward the English position. Learning of the French approach, on September 8, Johnson divided his force and dispatched one thousand troops under the command of Colonel Ephraim Williams and about one hundred fifty Indians, including Mohawk sachem Hendrick, to abort their attack. *(fig. 137)* As the English troops marched down the road, the French, who had hidden in ambush, fired on them. Blodget recorded that the enemy "became *invisible* to our Men, by Squatting below the under-growth of *Shrubs,* and *Brakes,* or by concealing themselves behind the *Trees.*"[1] Suffering heavy losses, including Williams and Hendrick, the New England troops retreated to the encampment and barricaded themselves against the advancing French.

Later that day, the French advanced to Lake George. The British military strategists were aware that their regular formations, "drawn up in Order, and beginning their Fire in Platoons," were ineffective on the American frontier, so they "went into the *Indian* Way of Fighting, squatting below the Shrubs, or placing themselves behind the Trees."[2] The French approached the camp and fired from three straight lines as the bird's-eye view in the right depicts. *(fig. 138)* As each line fired, the soldiers moved to the rear, then the second and third rows followed suit. More than 260 French soldiers were killed and the wounded Dieskau was taken prisoner. Clearly, the British regarded this as a great victory. The king made Johnson a baronet and commissioned him a colonel of the Six Nations and "Sole Agent and Superintendent of the said Indians and their Affairs."[3]

Samuel Blodget was born in Woburn, Massachusetts. He kept a trader's shop in Boston and worked as a sutler selling food and supplies to the troops. His print was pub-

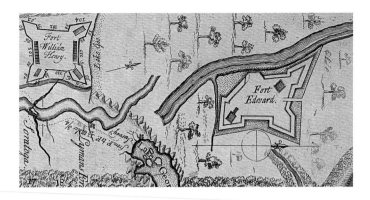

136 Detail of Fort Edward (formerly Fort Lyman) from *A Prospective Plan of the Battle fought near Lake George,* by Samuel Blodget, Boston, 1755, black-and-white line engraving. 1984-11. (Cat. 32) The location of the fort is identified on the Hudson just above Saratoga.

137 *The brave old Hendrick the great Sachem or Chief of the Mowhawk Indians, one of the Six Nations now in Alliance with, & subject to the King of Great Britain,* sold by Elizabeth Bakewell, London, ca. 1740, black-and-white line engraving with etching. 2001-761.

lished in Boston by December 22 accompanied by a pamphlet that explained the progression of the action. As he noted, he was "present in the Camp; and though I could not be in the *Front,* and *Rear,* and on *either Wing,* at the same Time, yet being an independent Person, not belonging to the Army, I had, it may be, as good an Opportunity as any Person whatever, to observe the whole Management on both Sides."[4] Blodget hired Thomas Johnston of Boston, who made heraldic bookplates and maps, to engrave the scene on copper.[5] Johnston's depiction of the battle of Lake George was the first engraving produced in the colonies that illustrated an American battle plan.

By the following January, the view and pamphlet were advertised in the *Boston News-Letter:*

This Day Publish'd, *and Sold by SAMUEL BLODGET, at the South End of BOSTON, near the Sign of the Lamb, and opposite to Capt.* Smith's.

The brave old Hendrick, the great SACHEM or Chief of the Mohawk Indians, one of the Six Nations now in Alliance with, & Subject to the King of Great-Britain.
Sold by Eliz. Bakewell opposite Birchin Lane in Cornhill.

138 Detail from *A Prospective Plan of the Battle fought near Lake George,* by Samuel Blodget, Boston, 1755, black-and-white line engraving. 1984-11. (Cat. 32)

A PROSPECTIVE-PLAN of two of the Engagements the English *had with the* French *at Lake GEORGE, on the 8th of* September, 1755; *exhibiting to the Eye a very lively as well as Just Representation of them; together with Part of the Lake, the Camp, the Situation of each Regiment, with the Disadvantages attending them: The Appearances of the* Canadians, Indians *and Regulars, as they made their Approach to the Breast-work; the Form of the Land and the Enemy; together with the Advantage they had in their Ambuscade against Col.* Williams. *As also a PLAN of* Hudson's River *from* New-York *to* Albany; *with such Marks as will be of great Service to Navigation: Likewise the River and Waggon Road from* Albany *to Lake GEORGE; together with a Plan and Situation of each of the Forts that have been lately built. All which is carefully and neatly struck off from a large Copper Plate.*

There will be Sold with each Plan a printed Pamphlet with Explanatory Notes, containing a full, tho' short His- *tory of that important Affair from the Beginning to the End of it.*[6]

Thomas Jefferys engraved a separate version of the view, also accompanied by explanatory text, in 1756. He later included Blodget's work in his *General Topography of North America* (1768).

1984-44

1. Samuel Blodget, *A Prospective-Plan of the Battle near Lake George, on the Eighth Day of September, 1755. With an Explanation thereof; Containing A full, though short, History of that important Affair* (London, 1756), p. 2.

2. *Ibid.*

3. *Dictionary of American Biography,* s.v. "Johnson, William."

4. Blodget, *Prospective-Plan,* p. 2.

5. Sinclair Hitchings, "Thomas Johnston," in *Boston Prints and Printmakers, 1670–1775* (Boston, 1773).

6. *Boston News-Letter,* Jan. 9, 1756.

33 *A MAP of the / British and French Dominions in / North America. / WITH THE / Roads, Distances, Limits, and Extent of the / SETTLEMENTS, / Humbly Inscribed to the Right Honourable / The Earl of Halifax, / And the other Right Honourable / The Lords Commissioners for Trade & Plantations, / By their Lordships / Most Obliged, / and very humble servant*

John Mitchell, cartographer; Thomas Kitchin, engraver; sold by Millar

London, 1755. Black-and-white line engraving with period color. H. 53¼", W. 76⅝", in 8 sheets, attached and glued to linen

In the upper left is an inset of *A NEW MAP / of / HUDSON'S BAY / and / LABRADOR / from the late / SURVEYS of those COASTS*. In the lower right are the title and dedicatory cartouche decorated with native flora and fauna, native Americans, and putti. To the left of the cartouche in the Atlantic Ocean is the endorsement *This MAP was Undertaken with the Approbation and at the Request / of the Lords Commissioners for Trade and Plantations; and is Chiefly / composed from Draughts, Charts and Actual Surveys of different / parts of His Majesties Colonies & Plantations in America; Great / part of which have been lately taken by their Lordships Orders, / and transmitted to this Office by the Governors of the said Colonies / and others. / John Pownall / Secretary. Plantation Office / Feb.ʸ 13.ᵗʰ 1755*. Below the cartouche is the imprint *Tho: Kitchin Sculp. Clerkenwell Green*. Beneath the lower border is *Publish'd by the Author Feb.ʳʸ 13. 1755 according to Act of Parliament, and Sold by And: Millar opposite Katharine Street in the Strand*. To the left of the island of Bermuda is a list of symbols used on the map

Seven states of the map are known[1]:

State 1: *Miller* and *Katherine* were misspelled in the imprint in the lower border. 1755

State 2: *Miller* and *Katherine* in the imprint in the lower border were corrected to *Millar* and *Katharine*. Ca. 1755

State 3: (this copy) As described. One of the two towns in Massachusetts named *Leicester* in the earlier states was corrected to *Worcester*

State 4: Tables of text were added to the Atlantic Ocean. The scale of distances was moved from the lower right center to above the cartouche. 1755–1757

State 5: Millar's name was deleted from the imprint, which then was *Publish'd by the Author Feb.ʳʸ 13. 1755 according to act of Parliament. Printed by Jefferys and Faden Geographers to the KING at the corner of Sᵗ Martins Lane, Charing Cross, LONDON. Tho: Kitchin, Sculp* was added to the lower right corner. *Clerkenwell Green* was deleted from the engraver's imprint. Numerous place-names were added as well. Ca. 1773

State 6: A dotted boundary line was added dividing Lake Ontario. Ca. 1774

State 7: The title was changed to *A Map of the British Colonies in*

North America. Ca. 1775

References: Berkeley and Berkeley, *Dr. John Mitchell*; Brown, *Early Maps of the Ohio Valley*, entries 24 and 25; Cresswell, "Colony to Commonwealth," pp. 52–53, 81; Cumming, *Southeast in Early Maps*, entry 293 and pp. 25–26; De Vorsey, "Notes on the Maps"; Dorman and Lewis, "Doctor John Mitchell"; Fite and Freeman, *Book of Old Maps*, entry 47; Jones, "Library of Doctor John Mitchell," pp. 441–443; Papenfuse and Coale, *Hammond-Harwood House Atlas*, p. 34; Ristow, "John Mitchell's Map," pp. 102–113; Stevens and Tree, "Comparative Cartography," entry 54; Suárez, *Shedding the Veil*, entry 56; *The World Encompassed*, entry 256

J OHN MITCHELL was not a mapmaker by profession; rather, he was a medical doctor, natural philosopher, and botanist of considerable merit. Yet, his sole cartographic endeavor, *A Map of the British and French Dominions in North America*, was perhaps the greatest produced in the history of America. So highly regarded was his work that it was selected as the document that Great Britain and the United States used to determine the geographic boundaries of the new nation at the Treaty of Paris, 1783, which terminated the Revolutionary War.

Mitchell was born in Lancaster County, Virginia, on April 13, 1711. Little is known of his early education although matriculation records at the University of Edinburgh indicate that one John Mitchell, a "Scotus-Americanus," received a master's degree in 1729 before immediately enrolling in medical school there.[2] After completing his education, Dr. Mitchell returned to Virginia and settled in Urbanna on the Rappahannock River in Middlesex County.

The correspondence of Virginia botanist John Clayton suggests that while in the colony, Mitchell spent considerable time studying native flora and fauna. He was one of many who sent plants, seeds, and specimens to John James Dillenius, professor of botany at Oxford. By 1738, Mitchell began corresponding with Peter Collinson, perhaps the most influential force behind studies of the natural world, who distributed plants and animals gathered by naturalists and collectors across the globe into English gardens and cabinets of curiosity. Collinson encouraged Mitchell to record the anatomy of the male and female American opossum and document his findings in an account presented to the Royal Society of London in 1742. Mitchell wrote scientific reports on other topics as well. His studies on yellow fever led to his being considered the foremost authority on the subject.

By 1745, Mitchell found that the climate in Virginia had become detrimental to his health and he was no longer able to practice medicine. John Bartram of Philadelphia

139 *A Map of the British and French Dominions in North America.* (Cat. 33)

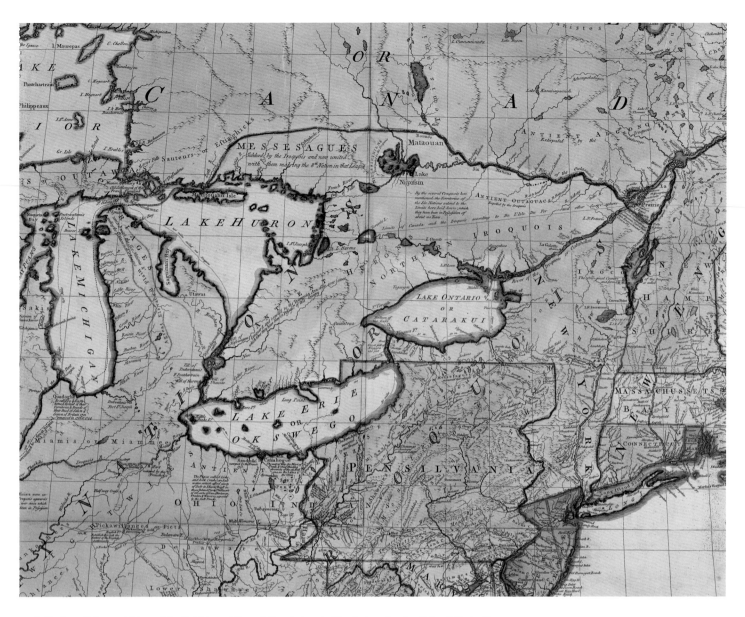

140 Detail from *A Map of the British and French Dominions in North America,* by John Mitchell,
London, 1755, black-and-white line engraving with period color. 1955-407. (Cat. 33)

wrote that if Mitchell "don't remove soon from Virginia, he can't continue long in the land of the living."[3] The following year, Mitchell and his wife settled in London. By 1748, he was proposed for membership in the Royal Society, a group that consisted of doctors, natural philosophers, mathematicians, and curious men with the means to finance the pioneering scientific undertakings of the society. Through this circle of influential friends, Mitchell became known to many of the most powerful nobles and ministers of state, including members of the Board of Trade and Plantations. At the same time the well-respected doctor departed Virginia, the commissioners, under the leadership of George Montagu Dunk, Earl of Halifax, were actively seeking information about the American colonies. They were particularly concerned about French encroachments on the frontiers of territories claimed by the English.

Not only was it critically important to gather updated information from each of the colonies, but Mitchell and the commissioners recognized the need for a comprehensive map that illustrated all of Britain's American holdings and counteracted French claims. Henry Popple had undertaken such a project with his large-scale wall map of 1733, but much of the information was outdated by mid-century and his heavy reliance on French sources for the geography led to the accusation that his work was biased toward the French position (Cat. 24). Mitchell compiled a rough draft of a general map of the American colonies that came to the attention of the board in 1750. After reviewing his work, the commissioners were so impressed with Mitchell's effort, especially by the thorough manner in which he accumulated the data, that they commissioned him to make a second, more complete map. All of the maps, charts, journals, and reports belonging to the Board of Trade as well as the records of the British Admiralty were made available to him.[4]

Mitchell immediately set about the project. For Virginia, he consulted Fry and Jefferson's draft and their accompanying report (Cat. 30).[5] He based his delineation of the Ohio Valley on the journal of Christopher Gist, who had accompanied Fry on an expedition across the Appalachian Mountains to the forks of the Ohio. Gist also went with George Washington on his mission to demand that the French retreat from their garrison at Fort Le Boeuf. While on his assignment to the Ohio, Washington drew a map of the territory that was sent to the commissioners. Mitchell surely consulted it. *(see fig. 22)*

For the Southeast, Mitchell relied heavily on a manuscript map by Colonel John Barnwell, presumed to have been made about 1721. It enabled Mitchell to depict a much more accurate rendering of the area from the Appalachian Mountains to the Mississippi River than had been printed previously. Like Popple, Mitchell consulted French sources, though more judiciously, for the Mississippi Valley and to aid in determining the southern boundary line of Canada. The works of French cartographer and publisher Jacques Nicolas Bellin provided many latitudinal observations.

Mitchell's map was immediately recognized for the political assertions it made on Britain's behalf. Attempting to override French claims, Mitchell had meticulously researched the original charters of each of the colonies and included the findings on the map and in the accompanying pamphlet, *The Contest in America between Great Britain and France, with Its Consequences and Importance,* 1757. The importance of incorporating the history of English colonization was stressed by Governor Robert Dinwiddie in a letter to Mitchell: "I hope every Person will support H. M'y's Rights to the interior Parts of Amer'a, from the No. to the So. Sea, agreeable to former Grants and Patents."[6] The map was an immediate success and was widely distributed in England and America. The Board of Trade issued copies to each of the colonial governors. In April 1755, Collinson wrote to Carl Linnaeus:

Dr. Mitchel has left Botany for some time, and has wholly employed himself in making a map, or chart, of all North

America, which is now published in eight large sheets for a guinea, and coloured for a guinea and a half. It is the most perfect of any before published, and is universally approved.[7]

The high regard for Mitchell's map was underscored twenty-seven years later when it was chosen as the primary cartographic source upon which to base the treaty negotiations in Paris after the Revolutionary War. Benjamin Franklin wrote to Thomas Jefferson in 1790:

I now can assure you that I am perfectly clear in the Remembrance that the Map we used in tracing the Boundary was brought to the Treaty by the Commissioners from England, and that it was the same that was published by Mitchell above 20 years before.[8]

1955-407

1. The various states of Mitchell's maps have been identified in two publications. Both cite changes made to the map as separate editions rather than states, most likely due to the fact that when the text panels were added in the Atlantic Ocean (state 4), Mitchell declared that new information *has given occasion to this Second Edition.* In the interest of uniformity, I have identified each change made to a map as a separate state rather than a separate edition because I believe that separate editions are determined by the creation of new engraved plates. See Stevens and Tree, "Comparative Cartography," pp. 86–87, and Richard W. Stephenson, comp., "Table for Identifying Variant Editions and Impressions of John Mitchell's Map of the British and French Dominions in North America," in Walter W. Ristow, comp., *A La Carte: Selected Papers on Maps and Atlases* (Washington, D. C., 1972), pp. 109–110. Stephenson also identified the various Dutch, French, and Italian copies of Mitchell's map.

2. Berkeley and Berkeley, *Dr. John Mitchell,* p. 7, n. 19, and p. 12. Several of Mitchell's biographers have questioned whether he was born in America or Britain. Substantial proof for his Virginia birth is documented in John Frederick Dorman and James F. Lewis, "Doctor John Mitchell, F.R.S., Native Virginian," *VMHB,* LXXVI (1968).

3. John Bartram to J. F. Gronovius, Dec. 6, 1745, William Darlington, *Memorials of John Bartram and Humphrey Marshall. With Notices of their Botanical Contemporaries* (Philadelphia, Pa., 1849), p. 353.

4. In 1752, Peter Collinson wrote to Benjamin Franklin about Mitchell, "The Doctor is Makeing a New Mapp of all our Colonies for the Board of Trade, Haveing the Assistance of all these Manuscript Mapps and which are abundance." Labaree et al., eds., *Papers of Franklin,* IV, p. 319.

5. Fry's report noted that Thomas Walker "built an House on Cumberland River, as is noted in the Map." Norona, "Fry's Report," p. 28. When Jefferys engraved the printed version of Fry and Jefferson's draft, he did not extend the geography far enough west to include the Cumberland River. Mitchell, however, illustrated both the Cumberland River and Mr. Walker's property.

6. Gov. Robert Dinwiddie to John Mitchell, Feb. 23, 1756, R. A. Brock, ed., *The Official Records of Robert Dinwiddie, Lieutenant-Governor of the Colony of Virginia, 1751–1758,* II (Richmond, Va., 1884), p. 338.

7. James Edward Smith, comp., *A Selection of the Correspondence of Linnaeus and Other Naturalists,* 1821, reprint (New York, 1978).

8. Julian P. Boyd et al., eds., *The Papers of Thomas Jefferson* (Princeton, N. J., 1950–), XVI, p. 326.

34 *A general MAP of the / MIDDLE BRITISH COLONIES, in AMERICA; / Viz VIRGINIA, MARILAND, DELAWARE, PENSILVANIA, / NEW-JERSEY, NEW-YORK, CONNECTICUT, and RHODE ISLAND: / Of AQUANISHUONÎGY, the Country of the Confederate Indians; / Comprehending AQUANISHUONÎGY proper, their Place of Residence, / OHIO and TÏIUXSOXRÚNTIE their Deer-Hunting Countries, / COUXSAXRÁGE and SKANIADARÂDE, their Beaver-Hunting Countries; / Of the LAKES ERIE, ONTÁRIO and CHAMPLAIN, / And of Part of NEW-FRANCE: / Wherein is also shewn the antient and present SEATS of the Indian Nations*

Lewis Evans, cartographer; James Turner, engraver; published separately and in *Geographical, Historical, Political, Philosophical and Mechanical Essays* by Lewis Evans

Philadelphia, Pa., 1755. Black-and-white line engraving with period color. H. 19½", W. 26"

In the upper left corner is a coat of arms with the dedication *To the Honourable Thomas Pownall Esq.ʳ / Permit me, Sir, to pay You this Tribute of Gratitude, / for the great Assistance You have given me in this Map; and to / assure the Public, that it has past the Examination of a Gentleman, / whom I esteem the best Judge of it in America: / Your most obedient, / and most humble Servant, / Evans.* Just below the dedication is an inset map of *A SKETCH / Of the remaining Part / of OHIO R. &c.* The title cartouche is in the top center. Three tables of distances are in the lower right corner, and below the imprint is *Published according to Act of Parliament, by Lewis Evans, June 23. 1755. and / sold by R. Dodsley, in Pall-Mall, LONDON, & by the Author in PHILADELPHIA*

Two states of the map are known[1]:
State 1: (this copy) As described
State 2: *THE LAKES CATARAQUI* was added just north of Lake Ontario. 1756

References: Brown, *Early Maps of the Ohio Valley*, entry 41; Cresswell, "Colony to Commonwealth," pp. 53–54, 82; Garrison, "Cartography of Pennsylvania," pp. 269–274; Gipson, *Lewis Evans*; Klinefelter, *Lewis Evans*; Pownall, *Topographical Description of the Dominions of the United States of America*; Papenfuse and Coale, *Hammond-Harwood House Atlas*, pp. 33–34; *Philadelphia: Three Centuries of American Art*, pp. 64–67; Schwartz and Ehrenberg, *Mapping of America*, p. 165; Suárez, *Shedding the Veil*, entry 57; Wheat and Brun, *Maps and Charts*, entry 298; *The World Encompassed*, entry 255

LEWIS EVANS, the compiler of *A general Map of the Middle British Colonies in America*, was the best geographer working in the English colonies in the mid-eighteenth century. A dedicated scientist, he exchanged scholarly information with Peter Collinson, Benjamin Franklin, colonial administrator Thomas Pownall, New York mathematician and mapmaker Cadwallader Colden, and others. Evans was so knowledgeable on the subject of natural philosophy and properties of electricity that he was invited to give lectures in New York, New Jersey, and South Carolina.[2]

Evans began his cartographic career in 1737 when he was commissioned by James Logan to survey the upper parts of Bucks County, which had recently been released by the Indians to the Pennsylvania proprietors. In 1743, while on a diplomatic mission to Onondaga, seat of the Iroquois confederacy, he mapped the western territories of Pennsylvania and New York. Evans, the first geographer to penetrate those Indian domains, secured official permission to make the trip because he was aware that adequate surveys for the upper Susquehanna regions did not exist. By 1749, Evans had assembled enough information to publish his first major work, *A Map of Pennsylvania, New-Jersey, New-York, and the three Delaware Counties.*

Like John Mitchell in England, Evans became concerned over increased French activity on the frontier. At the same time that Mitchell was compiling a more general *Map of the British and French Dominions in North America* (Cat. 33) from surveys and accounts that had been sent to England, Evans was also gathering new sources to supplement his earlier work in preparation for a new map. He placed his emphasis on the Ohio Valley, the region that was at the center of the friction between England and France. While Evans conceded that the French had rights to certain territory in America, he was convinced that they had severely encroached upon England's holdings. He was troubled by reports that the French had constructed Forts Presque Isle and Le Boeuf in northwestern Pennsylvania, effectively confining the English to their existing coastal settlements.

Evans also feared that the French presence would threaten the southern colonies as well. He warned:

> *The Consequence of the Country between the British Settlements and Missisippi; which must one Day determine, whether the Southern Colonies shall remain the Property of the British Crown; or the Inhabitants, to prevent the entire Defection of their Slaves, which the French will encourage, as the Spaniards now do at St. Augustine, be obliged to fall under the Dominion of France. Let not the Public think this a remote Contingence: If the French settle back of us, the English must either submit to them, or have their Throats cut, and lose all their Slaves.*[3]

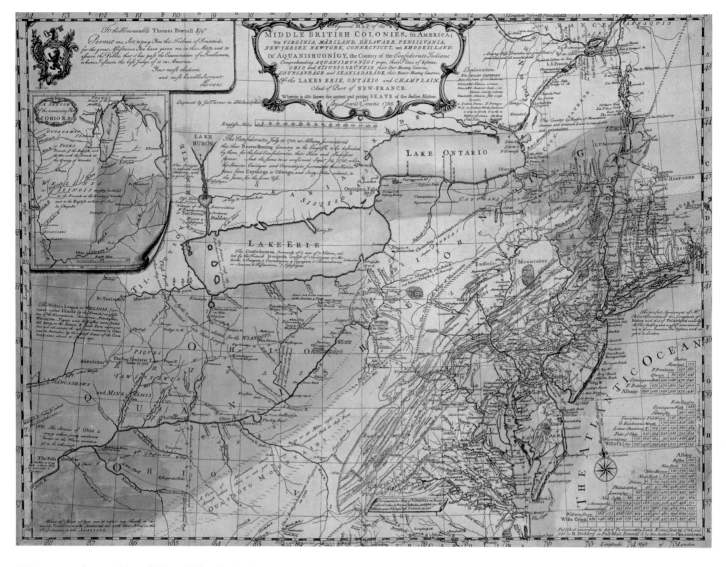

141 *A general Map of the Middle British Colonies, in America.* 1968-122. (Cat. 34)

By mid-1754, Evans incorporated the information from his *Map of Pennsylvania, New-Jersey, New-York, and the three Delaware Counties* into a new map of the middle British colonies, including territories as far west as the Ohio Valley and Great Lakes. In addition to his own geographic observations, Evans gathered the best available material from other surveys to depict areas for which he had no firsthand information. He carefully acknowledged his sources in a pamphlet, referred to as the *Analysis*, which Benjamin Franklin printed to accompany the map.[4]

For Virginia, Evans consulted an early state of Fry and Jefferson's *Map of the most Inhabited part of Virginia* (Cat. 30) and William Mayo's *Map of the Northern Neck of Virginia. (see fig. 124)* From the former, Evans altered the longitudinal position of the Potomac River and added the area claimed by the Ohio Company to Pennsylvania. Mayo's work provided information about the upper courses of the Potomac.

Evans admitted in his *Analysis* that Maryland "is the worst done of all the settlements . . . There is a considerable Error in my General Map, which came Time enough to my Knowledge to be mentioned here, tho' not to be rectified [in the map]."[5] Evans was referring to what he described as the width of the peninsula between Finwick's Island and the south side of Little Choptank River. He noted that he had illustrated the width at sixty-five miles but more recent surveys indicated that this neck of land was five miles wider. Evans consulted Walter Hoxton's *Mapp of the Bay of Chesepeack, with the Rivers, Potomack, Potapsco, North East, and part of Chester* for his rendering of the Chesapeake Bay. *(see fig. 175)*

Evans borrowed from three sources for Connecticut. Thomas Clap, the president of Yale College, provided him with a map of that colony. Evans consulted William Douglass's *A Summary, Historical and Political, of the first Planting, progressive Improvement, and present State of the British Settlements in North America* for the boundary lines for the New England colonies. The most valuable assistance came from his friend Thomas Pownall, who advised Evans in making corrections to his map of 1749 and to Douglass's *Summary*.

Evans's own surveys of Pennsylvania, supplemented by new details of the eastern portions supplied by Pennsylvania deputy surveyor Edward Scull, provided the basis for his rendering of that colony. That Evans had personally journeyed to the western territories gave him a greater perspective for judging the accuracy of reports from others. These expeditions also put him in touch with Indian traders who supplied useful information. He acknowledged a number of them in his *Analysis*, giving special credit to an Indian named "*The Eagle*, who had a good Notion of Dis-

tances, Bearings and delineating."[6] For the territory surrounding the fork of the Ohio and Monongahela Rivers, Evans consulted a manuscript journal by William Franklin, who had accompanied Indian agent Conrad Weiser to the Ohio in August 1748. Dr. Thomas Walker, who led the expedition into Kentucky, assisted Evans with the correct courses and branches of the Ohio River.[7]

Once Evans had prepared the draft, he petitioned the General Assembly of Pennsylvania for funds to help defray the cost of having the map engraved on copper and printed. In October 1754, the House ordered that he be paid fifty pounds for his efforts. Evans's work was anxiously anticipated because many colonists were aware that he had amassed new information on the Ohio Valley. Prior to the publication of Evans's map, Benjamin Franklin wrote:

> We have a new Map going forward in Pensilvania, of the Western Country, or back Parts of our Province, and Virginia, and the Ohio and Lakes, &c. by Lewis Evans, who is for that purpose furnished with all the Materials our Country affords, and the Assembly have to encourage him given £50 towards the Expence. When that is done, Dr. Mitchel's Map may perhaps be something improv'd from it.[8]

Mitchell could have improved his *Map of the British and French Dominions in North America* had he been provided with Evans's data; however, by the time the latter's work was completed, Mitchell's map had been published for five months. Evans believed that Mitchell's geography was not as accurate as his, noting, "Though we have many Copies of Mitchel's Map, nobody pretends to look into them for any Place on our Borders."[9] Nevertheless, many felt that Mitchell's map was superior to Evans's work. The Board of Trade and Plantations had commissioned Mitchell's map, whereas Evans's was compiled without official sanction. Of the two, Mitchell's work depicted more favorable territorial claims for the British. To justify Britain's holdings in America, Mitchell based the boundaries on royal charters for each of the colonies, on patents, and on the right of possession by discovery. Evans based his boundaries on the treaties of Utrecht, Aix-la-Chapelle, and those negotiated with the Iroquois Confederacy. He vehemently disagreed with Mitchell's reasons for establishing Britain's territorial rights, argued against each of Mitchell's points, and concluded, "You lay down Propositions, which, were they admitted, would instead of cutting off the French Rights, [*sic*] only cut off your own."[10]

The small size of Evans's map, which necessitated crowding vast amounts of information into a single-sheet production, diminished its importance in comparison to the monumental scale of Mitchell's. The year following its publication, Virginian James Maury wrote that a new map had appeared, "published by Lewis Evans, Esq., of Philadelphia, and engraven there, and therefore, in that respect clumsily executed . . . The map is but small, not above half as large as Fry and Jefferson's, consequently crowded."[11] Given Evans's limited resources, he could not afford to send his map to London to be engraved. Instead, he commissioned James Turner, a copperplate engraver who had recently moved to Philadelphia from Boston, to execute the work. At the same time, Evans delivered the *Analysis* to Franklin for printing. By July 1755, Evans announced proposals for publishing the map by subscription in the *Pennsylvania Gazette*. The price for the map was advertised in the *New-York Gazette* in November 1755:

> The Price of the colour'd Maps, on superfine Writing-Paper, Two Pieces of Eight; and of the plain Ones, on printing Paper, One Piece of Eight each. With each colour'd Map is given a Pamphlet of four large Sheets and a Half, containing an Analysis of the Map; a Discription of the Face of the Country. the Boundaries of the Confederate Indians, whereon the British Rights are founded, and the Maritime and Inland Navigation of the several Rivers and Lakes contained therein.[12]

Despite the criticisms of Evans's map, it was widely accepted. Copies were quickly pirated in London. In January 1756, Evans asked Pownall to act as his agent to arrange for a London edition of the work. Unfortunately, Robert Dodsley, who handled the London printing, was not able to prevent the unlawful copies even though he had secured a Parliamentary copyright. The first plagiarized version appeared in 1756. In all, sixteen editions derived from Evans's map, all piracies except for one, were published over the next sixty years.[13]

1968-122

1. Lawrence Henry Gipson suggested there may have been an earlier state that omitted the Illinois country. Gipson, *Lewis Evans*, p. 65, n. 25. The map was reengraved in London. For the various states of the English edition, see Walter Klinefelter, *Lewis Evans, Transactions of the American Philosophical Society*, N.S., LXI (Philadelphia, Pa., 1971), pp. 54–56.

2. Klinefelter, "Lewis Evans and his Maps," p. 33.

3. Lewis Evans, *Geographical, Historical, Political, Philosophical and Mechanical Essays. The First, Containing an Analysis of a General Map of the Middle British Colonies in America; And of the Country of the Confederate Indians: A Description of the Face of the Country; The Boundaries of the Confederates; and the Maritime and Inland Navigations of the Several Rivers and Lakes contained therein*, 1755, p. 15, in Gipson, *Lewis Evans, to which is added Evans' A Brief Account of Pennsylvania*, p. 159.

4. Evans, *Geographical, Historical, Political, Philosophical, and Mechanical Essays*, p. 5.

5. *Ibid.*

6. *Ibid.*, p. 10.

7. For more information on Walker, see Cats. 30 and 31.

8. Franklin to Richard Jackson, Dec. 12, 1754, Labaree et al., eds., *Papers of Franklin*, V, pp. 447–448.

9. Evans to Robert Dodsley, Jan. 25, 1756, Klinefelter, *Lewis Evans*, Appendix II, p. 59.

10. *Ibid.*, p. 60.

11. Maury, ed., *Memoirs of a Huguenot Family*, p. 387.

12. *New-York Gazette or the Weekly Post-Boy* (New York, N. Y.), Nov. 23, 1755.

13. Klinefelter, *Lewis Evans*, pp. 54–55. Klinefelter listed the various plagiarized editions of Evans's map.

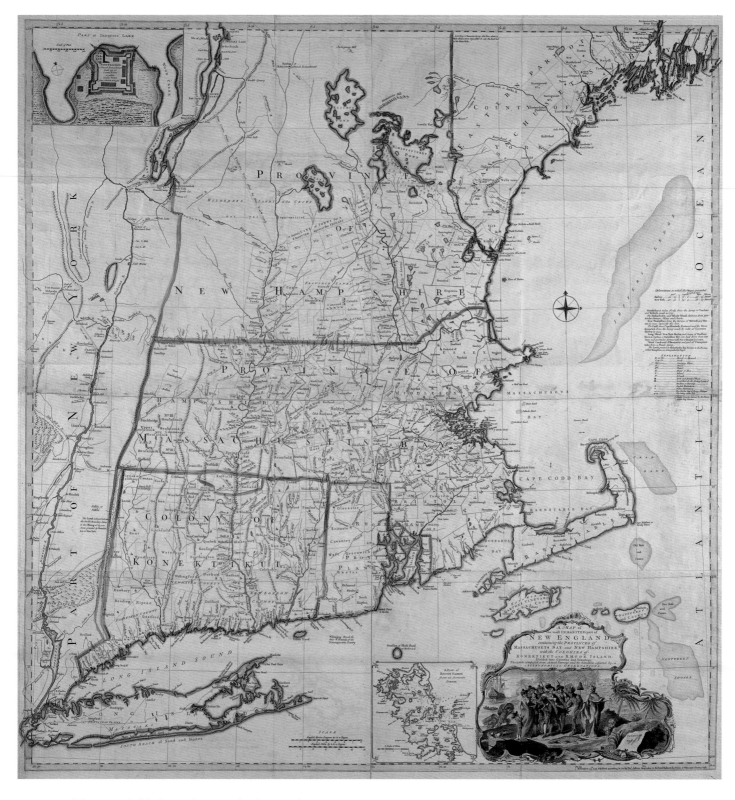

142 *Map of the most Inhabited part of New England.* (Cat. 35)

35 *A MAP of / the most INHABITED part of / NEW ENGLAND, / containing the PROVINCES of / MASSACHUSETS BAY and NEW HAMPSHIRE, / with the COLONIES of / KONEKTIKUT and RHODE ISLAND. / Divided into Counties and Townships: / The whole composed from Actual Surveys and its Situation adjusted by / ASTRONOMICAL OBSERVATIONS*

Braddock Mead (John Green, pseudonym), cartographer; engraver unknown; published separately and in *A General Topography of North America and the West Indies* by Thomas Jefferys and Robert Sayer (state three), and in Jefferys's *The American Atlas: or, A Geographical Description of the Whole Continent of America* by Robert Sayer and John Bennett (state five)

London, 1755. Black-and-white line engraving with modern color. H. 41½″, W. 39″, in four sheets

In the upper left corner is an inset map of *FORT FREDERIK / a French Incroachment / built 1731 at / Crown Point / or rather / Scalp Point / From a French Draught.* Along the right center are *Observations on which this Map is grounded* that includes a list of sources used in compiling the map and an explanation of abbreviations and symbols. *A PLAN of / BOSTON HARBOR / from an Accurate / SURVEY* is in the lower center. The title cartouche includes an imaginary vignette of the landing of the Pilgrims at Plymouth in 1620. In the lower right border is the imprint *November 29.ᵗʰ 1755 Published according to Act by Thoˢ Jefferys Geographer to His Royal Highness the Prince of Wales near Charing Cross*

Six states of the map are known[1]:

State 1: (this copy) As described

State 2: *Konektikut* was corrected to *Connecticut. Providence, Kings, Bristol,* and *Newport* were added to Rhode Island. 1759

State 3: The inset of Fort Frederick was erased and replaced by *A PLAN of the TOWN of BOSTON.* All the country north of *Stephens Fort* (New Hampshire), previously identified as *WILDERNES LANDS of the CROWN not yet appropriated,* was laid out in townships. Ca. 1763–1768

State 4: A note was added above *SARATOGHA LAKE* relating to the boundary between New York and New Hampshire. Ca. 1768

State 5: The imprint was altered to *[London] November 29ᵗʰ 1774 by Thos. Jefferys.* 1774

State 6: The imprint was altered to *Laurie & Whittle . . . 1794.* 1794

References: Crone, "John Green," pp. 85–91; Green, "Further notes on Bradock Mead," pp. 69–70; Cumming, *British Maps*, pp. 45-47; Macklin, "New England Plates," pp. 100–101; Ristow, "Bibliographical Note," pp. vii–ix; Sellers and van Ee, *Maps and Charts*, pp. 172–174; Stevens and Tree, "Comparative Cartography," entry 33

LIKE MANY other maps produced in the early 1750s, *A Map of the Most Inhabited Part of New England* was compiled from a variety of sources, most of which were identified on the map itself. The main prototype was based on a map by Boston physician Dr. William Douglass. Published posthumously in London in 1753, Douglass's map of New England included settlements, rivers, and boundary lines for most of the same areas depicted on Cat. 35.[2] Other sources included a survey of Connecticut made by Gardner and Kellock in 1737. Unknown today, it probably was a manuscript survey that was never printed and published. A draft by Richard Hazzens in 1741 established the boundary between New Hampshire and Massachusetts. Other surveys by Hazzens updated the geography of Long Island, New York Harbor, and the course of the Hudson River. George Mitchell was credited with recording the area around the Merrimack River and the region between New Hampshire and Massachusetts Bay. As noted on the map, *The Coast from Cape Elizabeth Eastward and the River Kennebek* [was taken] *from the Survey made by order of Governor Shirley in 1754.*

It is curious that the cartographer's name did not appear on the title imprint given that most of the sources used to create *A Map of the Most Inhabited Part of New England* were cited. Cartographic historian G. R. Crone identified the maker as John Green based on similarities between this map and others attributed to him. Green was known for providing a list of sources used in compiling his maps, he usually included tables of explanation for geographical terms, and, most important, he distinguished places for which the locations had been determined astronomically.[3] Crone later discovered that John Green was a pseudonym used by Braddock Mead.

Born in Ireland, Mead immigrated to England prior to 1717. In 1728, Mead and an associate, Daniel Kimberley, devised a plot to abduct a twelve-year-old child named Bridget Reading. Kimberley had been hired by the child's father to bring her to London from Dublin, where she had been with a nurse since the death of her mother. Having developed a scheme to procure Bridget's inheritance, Kimberley and Mead took Bridget by force and arranged for a bogus marriage ceremony to be performed between Mead and the child. When they arrived in London, Reading had the two men arrested. Once Kimberley and Mead were released on bail, they again attempted to abduct the child, claiming the marriage was valid. Kimberley was arrested, extradited, and hanged. Mead went into hiding and changed his name to John Green.[4]

Jefferys hired Green to work in his shop around 1750 during the period when Jefferys's primary focus was on publishing maps of America and the West Indies. Much of

143 Detail showing the colony of Connecticut from *A Map of the most Inhabited part of New England*, by John Green, London, 1755, black-and-white line engraving with modern color. 1969-123. (Cat. 35)

what is known about Green's personal life is documented in a 1767 letter from Jefferys to the Earl of Morton. Jefferys confirmed that John Green was indeed Braddock Mead and that he had first made his acquaintance in 1735. Jefferys alluded to the Bridget Reading affair, concluding the letter, "He was a man of warm passions fond of ye Women & Intrigue, having had a correspondence with— Wife for some years before his Death, he afterwards married her, & threw himself out of window 3 story-high in less than 3 months 1757."[5] Despite Green's personal shortcomings, he was a brilliant cartographer who was responsible for some of the best productions from Jefferys's shop.

It has been suggested that Jefferys may have intended Green's map to accompany Fry and Jefferson's *Map of the most Inhabited Parts of Virginia* since both titles include the words *most inhabited part*, share the same format of four folio sheets, and have decorative cartouches depicting scenes relative to their geographic locations. While Fry and Jefferson's map contains a realistic vignette of a planter on his wharf, Jefferys chose an imaginative depiction of the Pilgrims landing at Plymouth in 1620. One of the more curious features is the figure of the Indian holding a pole with a symbolic liberty cap upon it. *(fig. 144)*

Green's *Map of the Most Inhabited Part of New England* was the primary resource for the geography of that area for many years. It was the first large-scale printed map of New England. Jefferys included it in his *General Topography of North America* in 1768, state three. The map also appeared in the *American Atlas* in 1775, state five, and in the atlases of Jefferys's successors. In the upper left corner, the inset

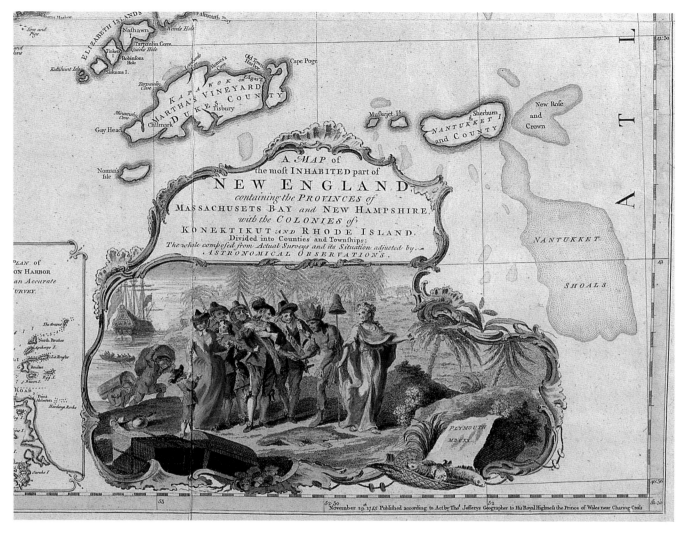

144 Detail of the cartouche from *A Map of the most Inhabited part of New England,* by John Green,
London, 1755, black-and-white line engraving with modern color. 1969-123. (Cat. 35)

of Fort Frederick, built by the French in 1731 at Crown
Point on Lake Champlain, was unique to the first and second states of the map. Since the fort was destroyed during
the French and Indian War, Jefferys replaced it in later
states with a plan of Boston.

1969-123

1. Stevens and Tree, "Comparative Cartography," pp. 70–71; Osher
Map Library web site, "The 'Percy Map': The Cartographic Image of New
England and Strategic Planning during the American Revolution, Cartobib-
liography," pp. 1–8. http://www.usm.maine.edu/~maps/percy/cartobibliog-
raphy.html.

2. Although Douglass's map was not cited as one of the sources on *A
Map of the Most Inhabited Part of New England,* Thomas Jefferys, who pub-
lished the later work, described it in the table of contents of his *General
Topography of North America* as a map based on one by Dr. Douglass. For

information on Douglass's map, see "'Percy Map.'"

3. G. R. Crone, "John Green. Notes on a neglected Eighteenth Century
Geographer and Cartographer," *Imago Mundi,* VI (1950), p. 87.

4. The entire account is given in *Reading. The whole Case and Proceedings
in relation to Bridget Reading, an heiress. Containing an account of Kimberly's
being sent to Ireland to bring over the said Bridget Reading, and of her pretended
marriage to Braddock Mead. . . . to which is added, the tryal of the said Kimberly
with his case, or last dying words, and an original letter sent by him to Mr. Reading,
written some few days before his execution, and Mr. Reading's answer.* London,
Printed by and for R. Phillips; sold by E Nott, H. Dodd, J. Jackson. 1730.
Library of Congress, Law Library, Law Trials (A & E). Shorter summaries of
the affair are in Cumming, *British Maps,* pp. 45–46, and Walter W. Ristow,
"Bibliographical Notes," *Thomas Jefferys, The American Atlas, London, 1776*
(Amsterdam, 1974), p. vii.

5. Jefferys's letter is printed in full in Cumming, *British Maps,* p. 46, and
G. R. Crone, "Further Notes on Braddock Mead, alias John Green, an eighteenth century cartographer," *Imago Mundi,* VIII (1951), p. 69.

36 AN / *Accurate* / MAP / OF / NORTH AMERICA. / *Describing and distinguishing the* / BRITISH and SPANISH / *Dominions on this great Continent;* / *According to the Definitive Treaty* / *Concluded at Paris 10th Feby . 1763 / Also all the* / WEST INDIA ISLANDS / *Belonging to, and possessed by the several* / *European Princes and States.* / *The whole laid down according to the latest and* / *Most authentick Improvements*

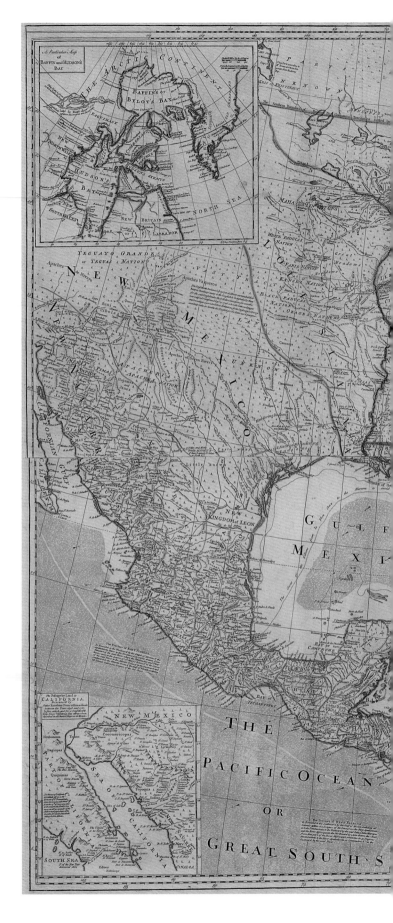

Emanuel Bowen, cartographer; John Gibson, engraver; Robert Sayer, publisher

London, 1775 (originally published in 1755). Black-and-white line engraving. H. 40½", W. 46¼", in four sheets

In the upper left is an inset of *A Particular Map / of / BAFFIN and HUDSON'S / BAY.* An inset of *The Passage by Land to / CALIFORNIA. / Discover'd by / Father Eusebius Francis Kino a Jesuit: / between the Years 1698 and 1701, / before which, and for a Considerable Time Since California has always been / described in all Charts & Maps as an Island* is in the lower left corner. The title cartouche in the upper right corner illustrates representations of a Native American male, female, and child surrounded by fauna. In the lower right corner are a scale of distances and an explanation of symbols used on the map contained in a rococo shell and floral frame

Eleven states of the map are known[1]:

State 1: The title was *An / Accurate / MAP / OF / NORTH AMERICA. / Describing and distinguishing the / BRITISH, SPANISH, and FRENCH / Dominions on this great Continent; / exhibiting the Present Seat of War and the French Encroachments. / Also all the / West India Islands / Belonging to, and possessed by the Several / European Princes and States. / The whole laid down according to the latest and / Most authentick Improvements, By / Eman Bowen Geog.r to His MAJESTY / And John Gibson Engraver.* The imprint in the bottom was *LONDON Printed for ROB.T SAYER opposite Fetter Lane Fleet Street.* Ca. 1755

State 2: The title was changed from *exhibiting the Present Seat of War and the French Encroachments* to *According to the Definitive Treaty / Concluded at Paris 10th Feb.y 1763.* The imprint remained the same. Many of the engraved notes were altered and the XXth Article of the Treaty of 1763 was added in the Atlantic Ocean. Ca. 1763

State 3: The word *FRENCH* was eliminated from the title, which then was *Describing and distinguishing the / BRITISH and SPANISH / Dominions . . .* The imprint was changed to *LONDON, Printed for Robert Sayer No 53 Fleet Street as the Act Directs 2.d July 1772.* Cartographical changes were made in the Hudson Bay area. 1772

State 4: (this copy) As described. The date was changed to *1775*

State 5: The title was altered to *A / NEW / and / CORRECT MAP / OF / NORTH AMERICA, / with the / WEST INDIA ISLANDS. / DIVIDED / According to the last Treaty of Peace, / Concluded at Paris. 10.th Feb.y 1763. / wherein are particularly Distinguished, / THE / SEVERAL PROVINCES AND COLONIES, / which Compose / THE BRITISH EMPIRE, LAID DOWN according to THE LATEST SURVEYS, / and*

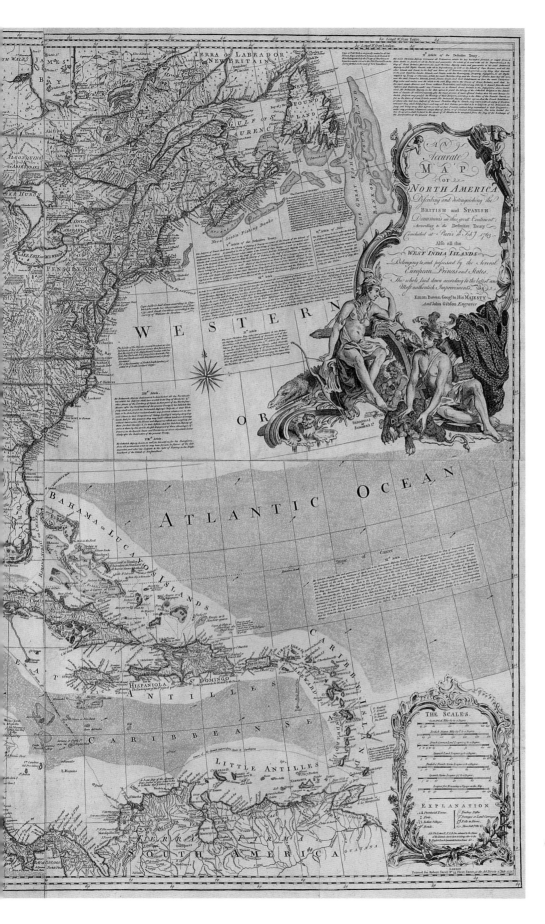

145 *An Accurate Map of North America.* (Cat. 36)

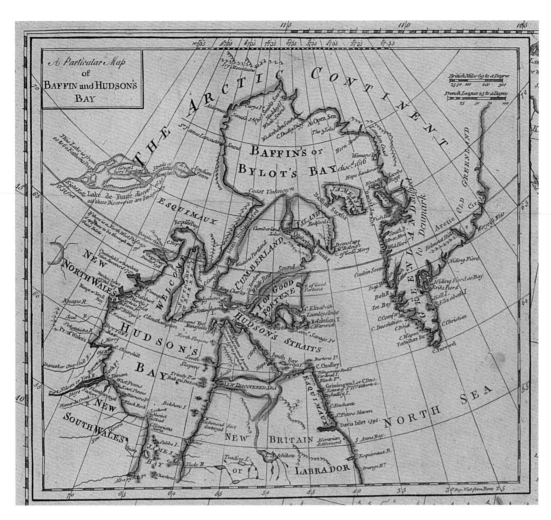

146 Detail of the inset, *A Particular Map of Baffin and Hudson's Bay*, from *An Accurate Map of North America*, by Emanuel Bowen, London, 1775, black-and-whtie line engraving. 1977-3. (Cat. 36)

corrected from THE ORIGINAL MATERIALS, / OF GOVER.*R* POW-NALL, MEM.*BR* OF PARLIA*MT* / 1777. The imprint was changed to *London: Printed for Robert Sayer, No. 53 Fleet Street, as the Act directs. 10th Jan.y 1777.* The only real cartographic changes were in the positions of the boundary lines between the individual colonies. The southern colonies, which previously extended to the Mississippi River, were now bounded by the Appalachian Mountains. The text regarding the Province of Quebec, formerly located south of Newfoundland, was eliminated. 1777

State 6: The imprint was changed to *Printed for Rob.t Sayer and Jn.o Bennett, N.o 53 Fleet Street. As the Act directs. 15.th Feb.y 1777.* 1777

State 7: The date in the title was altered to *1779* and the imprint was altered to *15.th July. 1779.* 1779

State 8: The title was altered to *A / NEW / and / CORRECT MAP / OF / NORTH AMERICA, / with the / WEST INDIA ISLANDS. / DIVIDED / According to the Preliminary Articles of Peace, / Signed at Versailles, 20, Jan. 1783. / wherein are particularly Distinguished, / THE UNITED STATES, / and the SEVERAL COLONIES, / which Compose / THE BRITISH EMPIRE, LAID DOWN according to THE LATEST SUR-*

VEYS, / and Corrected from THE ORIGINAL MATERIALS, / OF GOVER.*R* POWNALL, MEM.*BR* OF PARLIA*MT* / 1777.* A note added in the upper left corner was *The Divisions of this map are coloured according to the Preliminaries signed at Versailles Jan. 20, 1783. The red indicates the British Possessions: The Green those of the United States: The Blue what belongs to the French and the Yellow what belongs to the Spanish.* A dotted boundary line was added between the British and United States possessions. The 1779 imprint and former articles of the Treaty of Paris in 1763 remained unchanged. 1783

State 9: The title was altered to *A NEW MAP / OF / NORTH AMER-ICA, / with the / WEST INDIA ISLANDS. / DIVIDED / according to the Preliminary Articles of Peace, / Signed at Versailles, 20, Jan. 1783. / wherein are particularly Distinguished, / THE UNITED STATES, / and the SEVERAL PROVINCES, GOVERNMENTS &CA / which Compose / THE BRITISH DOMINIONS; / LAID DOWN according to THE LATEST SURVEYS, / and Corrected from THE ORIGINAL MATERIALS, / OF GOVER.*R* POWNALL, MEM.*BR* OF PARLIA.*MT* / 1783.* The imprint was altered to *Printed for Rob.t Sayer and J.no Bennett, No. 53 Fleet Street, as the Act directs, August 15th. 1783.* All information relating to the Peace Treaty of 1763 was deleted and Article III of the 1783 Treaty was added in the upper right corner. *UNITED STATES* was added to the portion of North America designated by the treaty. 1783

State 10: The imprint was changed to *London: Printed for Robt Sayer, Map, Chart & Printseller . . . August 15th 1786.* 1786

State 11: The imprint was erased and *London: Published by Laurie & Whittle, No 53 Fleet Street, 12th May 1794* was added in the bottom of the title cartouche. 1794

References: Cumming and Marshall, introductory notes, *North America at the Time of the Revolution;* Sellers and van Ee, *Maps and Charts,* pp. 8–9; Stevens and Tree, "Comparative Cartography," entry 49

Emanuel bowen and John Gibson's *Accurate Map of North America* appeared simultaneously with John Mitchell's *Map of the British and French Dominions in North America* (Cat. 33) and Lewis Evans's *A general Map of the Middle British Colonies* (Cat. 34). As geographer to George II, Bowen would have had access to the same documents that had been made available to Mitchell, who compiled his map at the request of the commissioners of the Board of Trade and Plantations. However, unlike the other two general maps that made extensive use of recent unpublished surveys and reports, Bowen relied primarily on published sources.

Before he produced this map, Bowen had issued a number of regional maps pertaining to North America in two atlases, *A Complete System of Geography,* 1744–1747, and *A Complete Atlas,* 1752. Those maps were also based largely on earlier works such as Henry Popple's *Map of the British Empire in America* (Cat. 24) and maps by French cartographers J. N. Bellin and J. B. D'Anville. Bowen borrowed from some of his earlier works for *An Accurate Map of North America,* but included new information as well. He relied heavily on the geography Mitchell compiled for areas east of the Mississippi, especially for the course of the Ohio River, and on published French sources for territory west of the Mississippi. Bowen also included Central America and the West Indies, areas not delineated by Mitchell.

At the conclusion of the Seven Years' War, England gained possession of the eastern half of the North American continent with the exception of New Orleans and scattered settlements along the banks of the southern portion of the Mississippi River. Fishing rights off Newfoundland were to be shared by England and France. Bowen was asked to produce a map illustrating the new boundary lines that resulted from the peace treaty. In compiling the data, Bowen elected simply to revise *An Accurate Map of North America . . . exhibiting the Present Seat of War and the French Encroachments,* 1755. He altered the title to *An Accurate Map of North America . . . According to the Definitive Treaty Concluded at Paris 10th Feb.y 1763.* Bowen added the new boundary lines to the original map and placed Treaty Articles IV, V, VI, VII, VIII, IX, and XX, all of which dealt with the geographic terms of the treaty, in the Atlantic Ocean.

Bowen and Gibson's map did not provide vast amounts of new geographic information, yet it was altered and reprinted numerous times between its initial publication in 1755 and the last changes that were made in 1794. Prior to his departure for Virginia to assume the role of governor, Norborne Berkeley, Lord Botetourt, purchased a number of maps to assist with his official duties. He placed three in the front parlor of the Governor's Palace: John Mitchell's *Map of the British and French Dominions in North America,* Fry and Jefferson's *Map of the most Inhabited Part of Virginia,* and Bowen and Gibson's *An Accurate Map of North America . . . According to the Definitive Treaty/ Concluded at Paris 10th Feb.y 1763.*[2]

1977-3

1. The states were taken, with minor corrections, from Stevens and Tree, who originally identified 12 states of this map. "Comparative Cartography," pp. 81–84. Differences in the applied hand coloring of the final issue caused them to designate the changes as separate states. In my opinion, new states were created only when changes were made to the original plate.

2. Hood, *Governor's Palace,* Appendix I, p. 287.

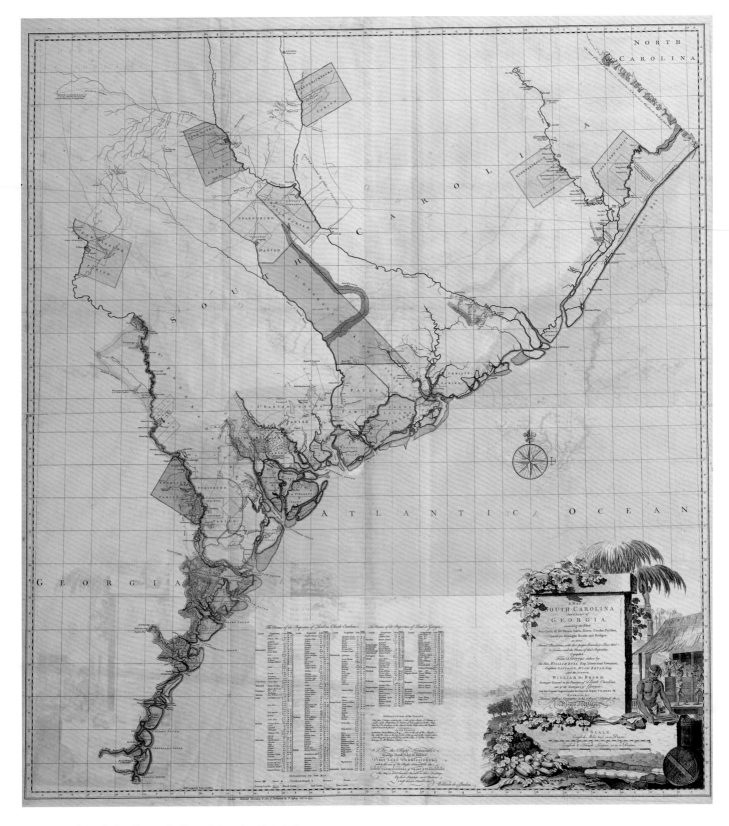

147 *Map of South Carolina and a Part of Georgia.* (Cat. 37)

37 *A Map Of / SOUTH CAROLINA / And a PART of / GEORGIA. / containing the Whole / Sea-Coast; all the Islands, Inlets, Rivers, Creeks, Parishes, / Townships, Boroughs, Roads, and Bridges: / AS ALSO, / Several Plantations, with their proper Boundary-Lines, their / Names, and the Names of their Proprietors. / Composed / From Surveys taken by / The Hon. WILLIAM BULL Esq. Lieutenant Governor, / Captain GASCOIGN, HUGH BRYAN, Esq; / And the AUTHOR / WILLIAM De BRAHM. / Surveyor General to the Province of South Carolina, / one of the Surveyors of Georgia, / And late Captain Engineer under his Imperial Majesty CHARLES VII. / ENGRAV'D BY / Thomas Jefferys, Geographer to his Royal Highness the / Prince of Wales*

William Gerard De Brahm, cartographer; Thomas Jefferys, engraver and publisher

London, October 20, 1757. Black-and-white line engraving with period color. H. 53½", W. 48⅜", in four sheets

In the lower center is a three-column list of *The Names of the Proprietors of Land in South Carolina* and a two-column list of *The Names of the Proprietors of Land in Georgia* accompanied by an explanation of the tables. Beneath the list of the Georgia land-holders is the dedication *To the Right Honourable / George Dunk, Earl of Halifax / FIRST LORD COMMISSIONER; / and to the rest of the Right Honourable the / LORDS COMMISSIONERS, of TRADE & PLANTA-TIONS. / This Map is most humbly Inscrib'd to their Lordships, / By their Lordships most Obedient / & most devoted Humble Serv.t / William de Brahm.* Just below the lower center border is *London Published According to Act of Parliament by T. Jefferys Oct.r 20 1757.* The title cartouche is in the lower right corner

Two states of the map are known:

State 1: (this copy) As described

State 2: The title was altered to *A MAP OF / SOUTH CAROLINA / And a PART of / GEORGIA. / containing the Whole / Sea-Coast; all the Islands, Inlets, Rivers, Creeks, Parishes, / Townships, Boroughs, Roads, and Bridges: / AS ALSO, / Several Plantations, with their proper Boundary-Lines, their / Names, and the Names of their Proprietors. / Composed / From Surveys taken by / The Hon. WILLIAM BULL Esq. Lieutenant Governor, / Captain GASCOIGN. HUGH BRYAN, Esq; / and WILLIAM DE BRAHM Esq.r / Surveyor General of the South.n District of North America, / Republished with considerable Additions, from SURVEYS made & collected by / JOHN STUART Esq.r / His MAJESTY'S Superintendant of Indian Affairs, / By WILLIAM FADEN / Successor to the late T. JEF-FERYS, Geographer to the KING. / Charing Cross 1780.* The imprint below the border was altered to *London. Published as the Act directs, by W.m Faden, Charing Cross, June 1.st 1780.* The dedication to the left of the cartouche was changed to *To the Right Honourable / Lord George Germaine, / FIRST LORD COMMISSIONER; and to the rest of the*

Right Honourable the / LORDS COMMISSIONERS OF TRADE & PLAN-TATIONS. / This Map is most humbly Inscrib'd to their Lordships, / By their Lordships most Obedient / & most devoted Humble Serv.t William Faden

References: Cumming, *British Maps*, p. 15; Cumming, *Southeast in Early Maps*, entry 310 and pp. 27–29; De Vorsey, "De Brahm, Eccentric Genius," pp. 21–29; De Vorsey, "De Brahm, 1718–1799," pp. 41–47; Schwartz and Ehrenberg, *Mapping of America*, p. 167; Sellers and van Ee, *Maps and Charts*, pp. 326–327; Smith, *Georgia's Legacy*, p. 44

WILLIAM Gerard De Brahm, cartographer of *A Map of South Carolina and a Part of Georgia*, was born in southern Germany in 1717. Little is known of his early life. He served in eleven military campaigns in the imperial army of Charles VII of Bavaria before resigning his commission as "Captain Engineer" in 1748. About that time, De Brahm renounced Catholicism in favor of the Protestant faith.[1] He was befriended by Samuel Urlsperger, Bishop of Augsburg, a trustee for establishing the Georgia colony. Urlsperger was active in encouraging displaced Germans to settle in America and sponsored De Brahm's immigration to Georgia in 1751. After he arrived, De Brahm began to explore and record the local terrain. His talents as a military engineer and surveyor were recognized immediately and he was consulted on many projects in South Carolina and Georgia. De Brahm was appointed surveyor general of the latter colony in 1754, a post he shared jointly with Henry Yonge.

De Brahm was selected to oversee plans for fortifying Charleston, and, at the request of Governor John Reynolds, prepared proposals for erecting palisades to shelter the residents of several towns in Georgia in the event of a French attack.[2] Later in his career, the governor of South Carolina commissioned De Brahm to lay out and construct Fort Loudoun, a garrison designed to protect the Carolina-allied Cherokees from frontier attacks by the French and their Indian allies.

All the while he was designing frontier fortifications, De Brahm was also undertaking extensive surveys of coastal Georgia and South Carolina. In the course of his fieldwork De Brahm gathered information on the climate, soil, flora, fauna, and changes in land patterns. In October 1752, he announced his intention to produce a map of the area and solicited information from plantation owners wishing to have their property represented.

> *JOHN WILLIAM DE BRAHM, Captain-Inginier in his late Imperial Majesty* Charles *VIIth's Service, having began a Survey and Collection for a Map of the whole*

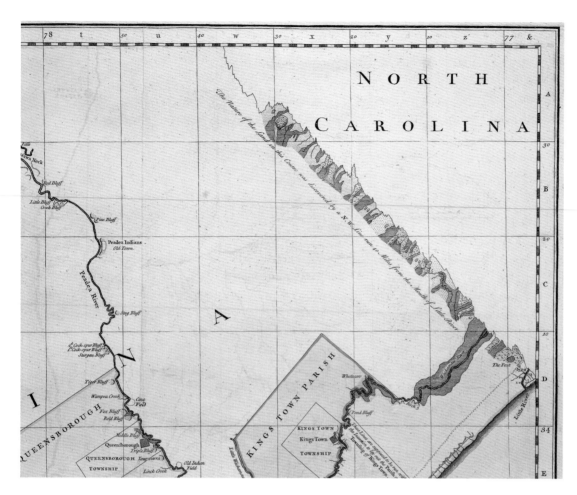

148 Detail of the topography from *A Map of South Carolina and a Part of Georgia*, by William Gerard De Brahm, London, 1757, black-and-white line engraving with period color. 1973-322. (Cat. 37)

Province of South-Carolina, *with part of the Colony of Georgia, and the Sea-Coast as far as the Island of* St. Katharine; *and being desirous to render the same compleat, gives Notice to all Gentlemen, who desire to have their particular Plantations inserted therein, that they will be pleased to send Copies of their respective Plats, for that Purpose, to the Honourable the Lieutenant Governor, or the Honourable* William Bull, *jun. Esq.*[3]

To augment his surveys, De Brahm incorporated earlier works by William Bull, Captain John Gascoigne, and Hugh Bryan.[4] He sent a draft to London where the Board of Trade quickly approved it and commissioned Thomas Jefferys to publish the work. The geography depicted on *A Map of South Carolina and a Part of Georgia* was vastly supe-

rior to any previous map of the area. De Brahm accurately illustrated the positions and courses of the rivers and their tributaries, located the many islands off the coast more correctly, and identified the parish settlements and boundaries on the South Carolina and Georgia coasts.

The engineer included an unusual feature along the border between North and South Carolina. *The Nature of the Land in this Course* was an analysis of the topography De Brahm observed when he ran the forty-mile line from the mouth of the Little River. *(fig. 148)* He meticulously noted marshlands, swamps, oat lands, and pine lands.[5] A list of landowners in the lower right served as an index for locating individual holdings in both colonies.

The decorative cartouche reflects South Carolina's profitable trade in indigo. *(fig. 149)* Designed by an uniden-

149 Detail of the cartouche from
A Map of South Carolina and a Part of Georgia,
by William Gerard De Brahm, London, 1757,
black-and-white line engraving
with period color. 1973-322. (Cat. 37)

tified maker, the scene illustrates slaves processing the indigo into dye cubes and packing them for shipment.
1973-322

1. Louis De Vorsey, Jr., "William Gerard De Brahm: Eccentric Genius of Southeastern Geography," *Southeastern Geographer*, X (1970), p. 23.

2. Louis De Vorsey, Jr., "William Gerard De Brahm, 1718-1799," *Geographers Biobibliographical Studies*, ed. T. W. Freeman (London, 1986), p. 42. For De Brahm's plans for the fortification of towns in Georgia and in Charleston, S. C., see Cumming, *Southeast in Early Maps*, entries 288, 289, and 290.

3. *S. C. Gaz.*, Oct. 30, 1752.

4. Although De Brahm gave credit to these three men in the title of his map, it is not known which surveys were consulted. William Bull was a prominent South Carolinian who served as a commissioner to manage the colony's Indian trade and acted as an advisor to Oglethorpe. Bull was appointed lieutenant governor in 1737. The next year, he prepared a manuscript draft largely copied from a ca. 1731 map by Col. John Barnwell, but with additions. Cumming, *Southeast in Early Maps*, entry 237. Gascoigne compiled two manuscript maps of Port Royal, S. C., one in 1737 and the other in 1748. P. A. Penfold, ed., *Maps and Plans in the Public Record Office: 2. America and West Indies* (London, 1974), nos. 2862 and 2863.

5. This feature was eliminated in the second state of the map.

38 *To the Honourable / Thomas Penn and Richard Penn Esq.ʳˢ / True & absolute Proprietaries & Governours of the Province of / Pennsylvania & Counties of New-Castle Kent & Sussex on Delaware / THIS MAP / Of the improved Part of the Province of / PENNSYLVANIA. / Is humbly dedicated by / Nicholas Scull*

Nicholas Scull, cartographer; James Turner, engraver; John Davis, printer

Philadelphia, Pa., January 1, 1759. Black-and-white line engraving. H. 30¼″, W. 60″, in six sheets

The title and dedication are contained within an elaborate rococo cartouche in the lower left. In the upper right is the explanation of symbols as they appear on the map. *PHILADELPHIA. Engraved by Ja.ˢ Turner, and Printed by John Davis for the Author* is in the lower center. A description of the sources used in creating the map and a scale of distances are in the lower right. Also in the lower right is *Published according to Act of Parliament Jan. 1.ˢᵗ 1759. & Sold by the Author, Nicholas Scull in Second-Street PHILADELPHIA*

Two states of the map are known:
State 1: (this copy) As described
State 2: A road was added from Carlisle eastward to Pine Ford. Four lines of text were added to the right of the Narrows of the Susquehanna at Nelson's Ferry. Ca. 1759[1]

References: Docktor, "Nicholas and William Scull," pp. 11–17; Schwartz and Ehrenberg, *Mapping of America*, p. 169; Sellers and van Ee, *Maps and Charts*, p. 276; Wheat and Brun, *Maps and Charts*, entry 422

Nɪᴄʜᴏʟᴀs Sᴄᴜʟʟ, Jʀ., born in 1687, was raised on his father's estate on the Schuylkill River just north of Philadelphia. Although nothing is known of his early years, he likely acquired surveying skills by working with his father, Nicholas Scull, Sr., who apprenticed to Pennsylvania surveyor general Thomas Holme.[2] The younger Scull apparently was well read because he was a founding member of Junto, Benjamin Franklin's debating club. Describing the club, Franklin wrote, "The first Members [included] Nicholas Scull, a Surveyor, afterwards Surveyor-General, Who lov'd Books, and sometimes made a few Verses."[3]

Nicholas Scull, Jr., was appointed a deputy surveyor for Philadelphia County in 1719. In that capacity, he frequently came into contact with Indian tribes and became proficient in their languages. He also operated a trading post at Great Mountain in partnership with his brother.[4] On numerous occasions, the Provincial Council called on

Scull's experience in matters relating to Indian affairs by relying on him to deliver messages to Indians in remote areas and to serve as an interpreter. On June 10, 1748, the Council appointed Scull surveyor general of Pennsylvania, a position he held until his death in 1761.

A controversial event in Scull's career involved his testimony about events that occurred during the Walking Purchase of 1737. The disagreement involved a tract of land along the Delaware River in Bucks County. When purchasing land from the Indians, the distance a man could walk in a specified period—generally twenty to thirty miles a day—was used to determine the amount of acreage in the transaction.[5] In the 1737 purchase, how much land could be covered in a day and a half of walking at a reasonable pace was to establish the boundaries of the treaty. The walking party consisted of Edward Marshall, James Yates, and Solomon Jennings, acting for the proprietors, and three Delaware Indians. Scull accompanied the group as an official observer. Setting out from the Wrightstown Meetinghouse in Bucks County on the morning of September 19, 1737, the provincial representatives quickly accelerated their leisurely walking pace into a run and were able to cover fifty-five miles in the time allotted, almost doubling the distance that would ordinarily be possible by using Indian methods of measuring land.

Arguments about the events of the purchase between the Indians and the Pennsylvania proprietors went on for twenty years until the king ordered an investigation in 1757. Scull defended the Penns' position by submitting a statement to the Provincial Council. It is highly likely that Scull took a stand in favor of the proprietors because he hoped to receive financial support for his *Map Of the improved Part of the Province of Pennsylvania* from Thomas and Richard Penn, to whom Scull eventually dedicated the work.

As the title suggests, Scull concentrated on the "improved" or settled parts of the province. The far northern and western areas of the present state of Pennsylvania, including Pittsburgh, were omitted. The map located the headwaters of the Juniata River and its tributaries, but not those of the Monongahela and Allegheny.

The map featured details never before rendered on a map of Pennsylvania. Forts, iron forges, mills, meetinghouses, inns, Indian towns, and gentlemen's seats were all depicted. The roads and Indian paths were of particular importance. Scull acknowledged on the map that *the West Branch of the Susquehannah River, & the N. East Branch of the same from Fort-Augusta to Wioming, were taken by Major Shippen.*[6] Joseph Shippen had drawn a map in 1756 that illus-

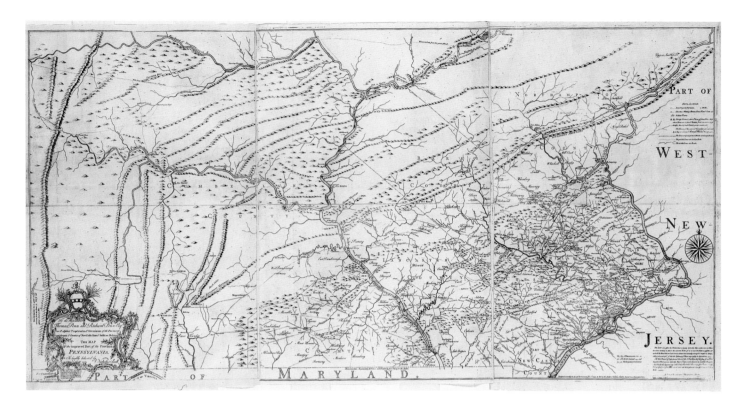

150 *Map Of the improved Part of the Province of Pennsylvania.* (Cat. 38)

trated an Indian path running up the east and west banks of the Susquehanna from Paxtang (Harrisburg) to Shamokin.[7] Although Scull's map did not extend far enough in a westerly direction to include Shamokin, he did illustrate the Indian path from Harris's Ferry at Paxtang to Fort Augusta at the forks of the Susquehanna. Scull also credited Colonel Armstrong, George Stevenson, Benjamin Lightfoot, and John Watson for their assistance, although their specific contributions are unknown. Colonel John Armstrong was both a soldier and a surveyor who laid out the town of Carlisle. Scull probably consulted Armstrong for his knowledge of the Indian paths to Kittanning along the upper course of the Allegheny River. In May 1756, Armstrong led a successful raid on Kittanning, headquarters for the Delaware Indian scalping parties.

Once Scull completed the draft, he commissioned James Turner to prepare it for publication. The map was dated January 1, 1759, although it took six weeks before the announcement appeared in the *Pennsylvania Gazette.*

Scull's was the first large-scale map of Pennsylvania

and the first devoted solely to that colony printed in America.

G1985-73, gift of Mrs. Anna Glen Vietor in memory of Alexander O. Vietor

1. Wheat and Brun, *Maps and Charts,* p. 89.

2. Cartographic historians have mistakenly assumed that the Nicholas Scull who apprenticed with Holme was the author of this map. However, at the time of Holme's death, the younger Scull was only eight years old. Klinefelter, *Lewis Evans,* p. 13, n. 41.

3. Leonard W. Labaree et al., eds., *The Autobiography of Benjamin Franklin* (New Haven, Conn., 1964), p. 117.

4. Kleinfelter, *Lewis Evans,* p. 13. This location is north of what is today Harrisburg, Pa.

5. John W. Docktor, "Nicholas and William Scull of Pennsylvania," *The Portolan,* XXXIII (1995), p. 12.

6. This notation is in the lower right corner of the map.

7. Paul A. W. Wallace, *Indian Paths of Pennsylvania* (Harrisburg, Pa., 1965), p. 158.

39 *A Draught of the / CHEROKEE COUNTRY, / On the West Side of the Twenty four Mountains, / commonly called Over the Hills; / Taken by Henry Timberlake, when he / was in that Country, in March 1762. / Likewise the / Names of the Principal or Head men of each Town, and / what Number of Fighting Men they send to War.*

Henry Timberlake, cartographer; engraver unknown; published in *the Memoirs of Lieut. Henry Timberlake* and in *A General Topography of North America and The West Indies* by Thomas Jefferys and Robert Sayer[1]

London, 1768 (originally published in 1765). Black-and-white line engraving. H. 15⅝", W. 9⅞"

Below the title in the lower left is the list of Cherokee towns with the names of the chiefs and number of warriors residing in each

Only one state of the map is known

References: Cumming, *Southeast in Early Maps*, entry 349; Schwartz, *French and Indian War*, p. 150; Schwartz and Ehrenberg, *Mapping of America*, p. 176; Sellers and van Ee, *Maps and Charts*, p. 298; Williams, ed., *Memoirs of Timberlake*

E NGLAND AND FRANCE officially declared war in May 1756. Only a few months earlier, both countries had appointed a new commander in chief of their forces in America, Louis-Joseph de Montcalm for the French and John Campbell, Earl of Loudoun, for the British. During the first two years of the conflict, the French troops under Montcalm outmaneuvered the British, forcing them to surrender Forts Oswego and William Henry. As a result, Loudoun was recalled and replaced by his second in command, Major General James Abercromby. The tide turned in favor of the British in 1758 when they captured Louisbourg and Forts Frontenac and Duquesne. The following year, the British under the command of Sir Jeffery Amherst took Forts Ticonderoga and Niagara, Crown Point, and Quebec.

Although England claimed victories in the north, conflicts with the Indians forced military strategy to shift to the southern frontier. The Cherokees, one of the most powerful of the eastern Indian nations, inhabited parts of Virginia, western North Carolina, South Carolina, northern Georgia, and what are now Kentucky, Tennessee, and Alabama. For three decades prior to the French and Indian War, they were the largest single Indian nation trading with the British. Like the Iroquois, the Cherokees initially attempted to remain neutral. Ultimately, they agreed to help defend the Virginia frontier, in part because the English promised to construct forts that would protect the Indians as well.

In 1758, as many as seven hundred Cherokee warriors joined the British army in the campaign to capture Fort Duquesne.[2] Having learned of their precarious situation, the French burned and abandoned the fort prior to the attack. The British took possession, renamed the outpost Fort Pitt, and began rebuilding the destroyed structures. Although the mission was a success since England now dominated the Ohio region, the relationship between the Cherokees and the British deteriorated rapidly. According to historian Fred Anderson, British military officers insulted the Indians, already frustrated because they had expected to capture the French and plunder their goods. Disappointed, many of the Cherokees deserted with the ammunition the British had provided. The presence of armed Indians returning home along the Virginia and North Carolina frontiers alarmed many white settlers there. Local militia savagely killed at least thirty Cherokees. Further, when the angry Indians returned home, they discovered that South Carolinians had poached on their hunting grounds, threatening their food supply and diminishing the quantity of skins essential for trade.[3]

Tensions escalated rapidly, and by spring 1759, South Carolina Governor William Henry Lyttelton began preparations for an Indian war. That October, thirty-one Cherokee chiefs journeyed to Charleston in an effort to make peace with the English. Their mission was thwarted when Lyttelton had them arrested and sent as prisoners to Fort Prince George, one of the posts built by the English on the frontier. After negotiations to release the chiefs failed, the Cherokees attacked Fort Prince George on January 19, 1760, and launched raids from Virginia to Georgia, killing over a hundred settlers and traders.

The following June, more than thirteen hundred regulars under Colonel Archibald Montgomery, Carolina rangers, provincial militia, and forty to fifty Catawba warriors attacked the Cherokees at the Lower Towns. Five hundred villages were burned; more than one hundred warriors were captured. Two months later, the Cherokees captured Fort Loudoun, constructed at Winchester in 1756. Fighting resumed in the spring of 1761. Both sides suffered heavy losses. The Cherokees sent a delegation to Fort Prince George in August to begin peace negotiations. The chiefs requested that an officer visit their towns as evidence of the renewed friendship with the Anglo-Americans. Henry Timberlake, an ensign from Virginia who had served under George Washington, volunteered for the mission.

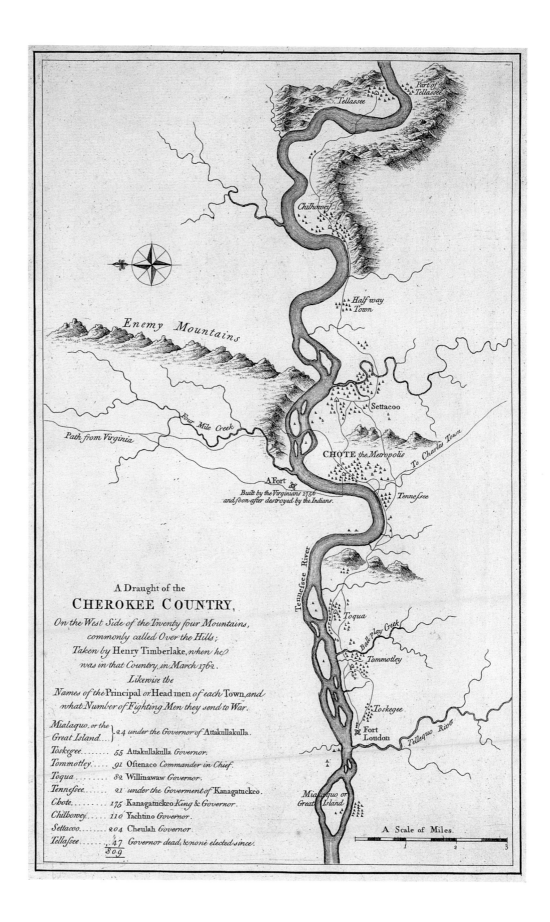

A Draught of the
CHEROKEE COUNTRY,

*On the West Side of the Twenty four Mountains,
commonly called Over the Hills;
Taken by Henry Timberlake, when he
was in that Country, in March 1762.*

*Likewise the
Names of the Principal or Head men of each Town, and
what Number of Fighting Men they send to War.*

Mialaquo, or the Great Island	24	under the Governor of Attakullakulla.
Toskegee	55	Attakullakulla Governor.
Tommotley	91	Ostenaco Commander in Chief.
Toqua	82	Willinawaw Governor.
Tennessee	21	under the Goverment of Kanagatuckco.
Chote	175	Kanagatuckco King & Governor.
Chilhowey	110	Yachtino Governor.
Settacoo	204	Cheulah Governor.
Tellassee	47	Governor dead, & none elected since.
	809	

151 *A Draught
of the Cherokee Country.*
(Cat. 39)

The Three Cherokees, came over from the head of the River Savanna to London 1762.
1 Their Interpreter that was Poisoned.

Oitacite or Man-killer, who Sets up the War Whoop, as, (Woach Woach ha ha hoch Waoch) with his Wampum.

3 Austenaco or King, a great Warrior who has his Calumet or Pipe, by taking a Whiff of which, is their most Sacred emblem of Peace.

4 Uschesees or Great Hunter, or Scalpper, as the Character of a Warrier depends on the Number of Scalps, he has them without Number.

Sold in Mays Buildings Covent Garden, according to Act, by G. Bickham.

152 *The Three Cherokees, came over from the head of the River Savanna to London 1762,*
sold by George Bickham, London, ca. 1765. 1958-484.

In November 1761, Timberlake, Sergeant Thomas Sumter, an interpreter named John McCormack, and a servant set out on a twenty-two-day journey down the Holston and up the Little Tennessee Rivers to the towns of the Overhill Cherokees. Lieutenant Timberlake chose to make the journey by water because he "thought a thorough knowledge of the navigation would be of infinite service, should these people ever give us the trouble of making another campaign against them."[4] The remarkably accurate map Timberlake compiled, oriented with north to the left, depicted the Little Tennessee River from just west of Fort Loudoun into the Great Smokey Mountains, the border country between southwest Tennessee and North Carolina. He located ten Indian villages along the river and, with the exception of *Half way Town,* recorded the number of warriors residing in each. Timberlake's was the first printed map of any part of Tennessee taken from an actual survey.

After spending three months with the Cherokees, Timberlake traveled to Williamsburg, Virginia, accompanied by about seventy-two Indians. He recorded in his *Memoirs,* "On my arrival, I waited on the Governor, who seemed somewhat displeased with the number of Indians that had forced themselves upon me."[5] Ostenaco, one of the chiefs, approached Governor Francis Fauquier about going to London to meet the king. Eventually, it was decided that three of the Cherokees, an interpreter, and Timberlake would make the journey. As had occurred during previous visits by Native Americans to London, the delegation attracted great curiosity. The *St. James Chronicle* reported on July 3, 1762, that "the Cherokee Chiefs are sitting for their pictures to Mr. Reynolds."[6] Although no known painting of the Indian chiefs by Sir Joshua Reynolds survives, he may have provided the source for the print *The Three Cherokees.* (fig. 149)

1990-211

1. *THE MEMOIRS OF Lieut. Henry Timberlake, (Who accompanied the Three Cherokee Indians to England in the Year 1762) Containing Whatever he observed remarkable, or worthy of public Notice, during his Travels to and from that Nation; wherein the Country, Government, Genius, and Customs of the Inhabitants, are authentically described. ALSO The Principal Occurrences during their Residence in London. Illustrated with An ACCURATE MAP of their Over-hill Settlement, and a curious Secret Journal, taken by the Indians out of the Pocket of a Frenchman they had killed,* 1765, reprinted in Samuel Cole Williams, ed., *Lieut. Henry Timberlake's Memoirs, 1756–1765* (Marietta, Ga., 1943).

2. Anderson, *Crucible of War,* p. 458.

3. *Ibid.,* pp. 461–467.

4. Williams, ed., *Memoirs of Timberlake,* p. 41.

5. *Ibid.,* p. 129. Timberlake estimated the number of Indians who went to Williamsburg. Along the way, he encouraged many to return but noted, "We could only reduce our numbers to about seventy-two," p. 128.

6. *Ibid.,* p. 136, n. 77.

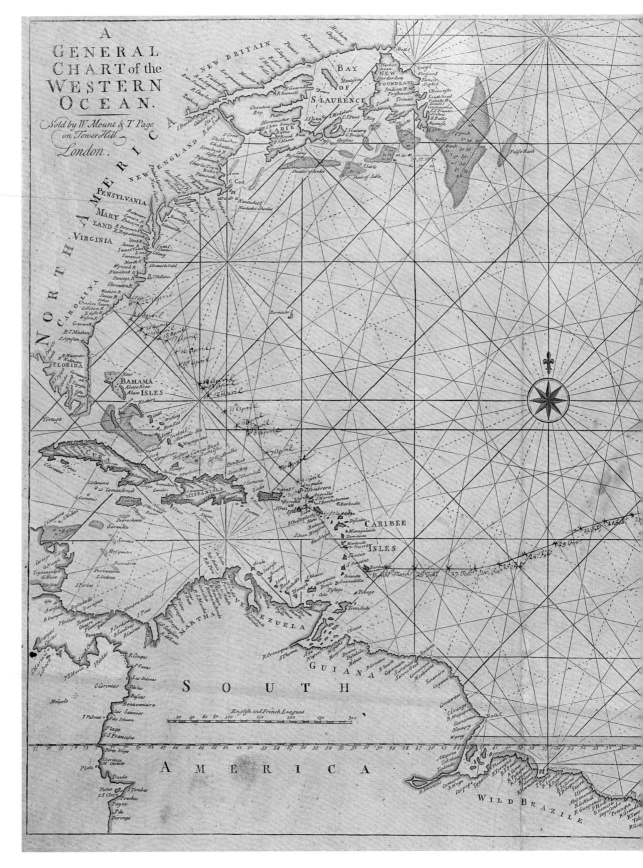

153 *A General Chart of the Western Ocean.* (Cat. 40)

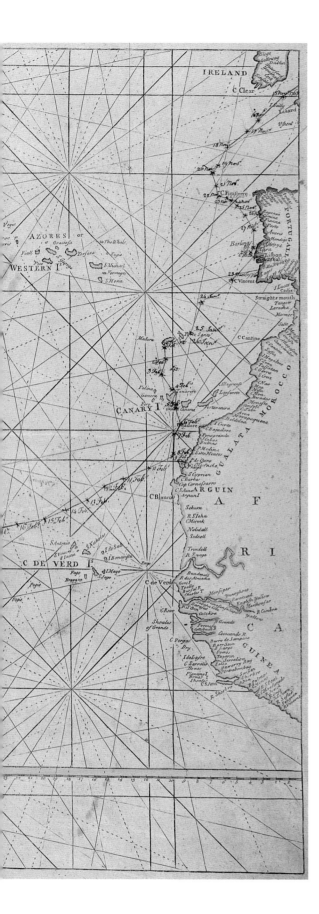

40 A / GENERAL / CHART of the / WESTERN / OCEAN

John Seller, original cartographer; engraver unknown; published in *The English Pilot The Fourth Book,* by William Mount and Thomas Page

London, ca. 1743–1765 (originally published 1721). Black-and-white line engraving with modern outline color. H. 18⅞", W. 23¼"

Two states of the map are known:

State 1: As described before the imprint was reengraved

State 2: (this copy) As described. The original imprint was erased and reengraved in a slightly more florid style

WILLIAM MOUNT and Thomas Page published *A General Chart of the Western Ocean* in numerous editions of *The English Pilot The Fourth Book,* between 1721 and 1773. The geography was copied directly from a chart made by John Seller around 1675.[1] Mount and Page's version depicted no new features and so is of little interest to scholars today as a cartographic document. Of interest, however, are the manuscript notations on this copy, which tracked a voyage that took place in 1765.

The ship set sail around November 15, 1765, the date of the earliest manuscript notation, most likely from a port such as Bristol or Cardiff on the west coast of Britain. Between November 30, 1765, and January 23, 1766, the vessel docked at Lisbon. It then headed south to Madeira, stopped for five days, and continued on a route through the Canary Islands and west to Barbados, where it anchored on March 2. After spending ten days at Barbados, the ship stopped at *Martinito* [Martinique] for five days before reaching Saint Christopher on March 17, where it remained until March 31. From there, the ship went to its final destination, Cape Fear, North Carolina, arriving on April 22, 1766.

The ports of call for this voyage indicate that the ship was transporting trade goods from southern Europe to North Carolina.[2] The vessel would have left England with British products. At Lisbon, it would have taken aboard Portuguese salt, considered to be of better quality than that available in Britain and used extensively in the colonies for preserving meat and fish. Other commodities were Seville oranges and other citrus fruits, port, sherry, and figs. Madeira was a well known source for wine. During the two stops in the West Indies, sugar and rum were likely added to the cargo.

The manuscript notations also indicate the time it took

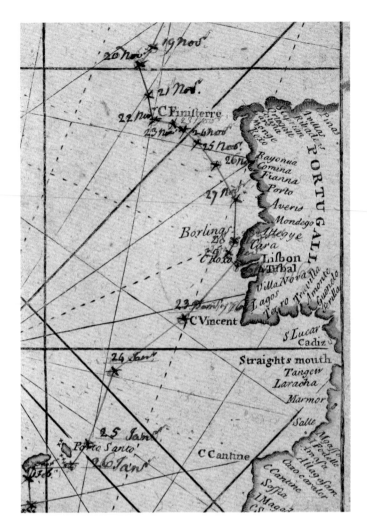

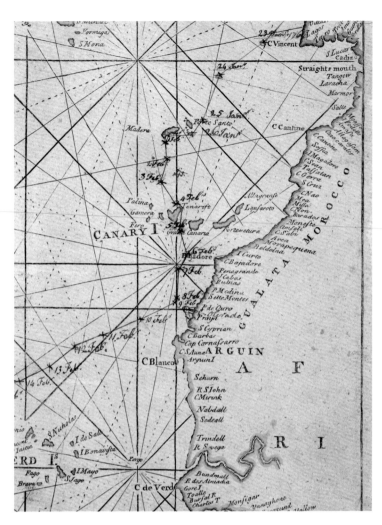

154 Detail of the route off the coast of Portugal
from *A General Chart of the Western Ocean,*
by William Mount and Thomas Page after John Seller,
London, ca. 1743–1765, black-and-white line engraving
with modern outline color. 1989-199. (Cat. 40)

155 Detail of the route through the Canary Islands
from *A General Chart of the Western Ocean,*
by William Mount and Thomas Page after John Seller,
London, ca. 1743–1765, black-and-white line engraving
with modern outline color. 1989-199. (Cat. 40)

156 Detail of the route through the Caribbean Islands
from *A General Chart of the Western Ocean,*
by William Mount and Thomas Page
after John Seller, London, ca. 1743–1765,
black-and-white line engraving with modern outline color.
1989-199. (Cat. 40)

this ship to make its voyage. When sailing in a direct route, a typical transatlantic crossing from east to west lasted six to eight weeks. In this instance, the layovers to acquire cargo extended the journey by about three months. While thus far it has been impossible to pinpoint which ship sailed into Port Brunswick harbor on April 22, 1766, an extant document recorded the names of forty-one vessels containing wine or rum that arrived between October 1765 and October 1766. Unfortunately, the list does not indicate the month or day of entry, so it is not possible to identify the ship that made this voyage.[3]

Landing along the North Carolina coast was dangerous. The colony's transatlantic trade was centered at Port Brunswick at the mouth of the Cape Fear River, which was deeper and safer than other harbors. Consequently, Port Brunswick and Wilmington established closer ties with Great Britain than did other areas of the province. According to Charles Christopher Crittenden, the size of the ships that cleared Port Brunswick during the last three months of 1767 averaged 140 tons (the biggest being 200 tons), considerably larger than the vessels that sailed from smaller North Carolina ports.[4]

1989-199

1. The map was included in copies of *Atlas Maritimus*. Philip Lee Phillips, comp., *A List of Geographical Atlases in the Library of Congress* (Washington, D. C., 1901), IV, entries 4150, map 21, 4151, map 18, 4153, map 45, 4154, map 39.

2. Ships sailing from North Carolina generally carried pitch, tar, turpentine, staves, lumber, and, occasionally, tobacco and deerskins.

3. Dr. Wilson Angley, North Carolina Department of Cultural Resources, brought this document to my attention. It is in the Port Records, Treasurer's and Comptroller's Papers, North Carolina State Archives, Raleigh, N. C. I would like to thank William L. Whitwell for his assistance in locating the port records for North Carolina.

4. Charles Christopher Crittenden, "Ships and Shipping in North Carolina, 1763–1789," *North Carolina Historical Review,* VIII (1931), p. 4.

41 *To the Right Honourable / THE / Earl of Shelburne / His MAJESTY'S Principal / SECRETARY of STATE / for the Southern Department / This PLAN of the COLONY of CONNECTICUT in / NORTH-AMERICA / Is Humbly Dedicated by his Lordship's / Most Obedient Humble / Serv*ᵗ*. / Moses Park*

Moses Park, cartographer (based on surveys by Asa Spaulding, Moses Park, and Samuel Mott); engraver unknown

Possibly New London, Connecticut, November 24, 1766. Black-and-white line engraving with period color. H. 21¾", W. 29⅛"

The title and dedication are in the upper left corner. The explanation of terms and a scale of distances are in the lower right corner within a crudely executed foliate cartouche

Two states of the map are known[1]:

State 1: The Earl of Shelburne's name was spelled without the "e." The Shepoag River was incorrectly located on the west branch of the Ousatonnok River in the town of New Milford. In the *Explanation* in the lower right, the notation *60 to a Degree* appeared under the line *A Scale of English miles. 1766*

State 2: (this copy) As described. An "e" was added to *Shelburne*. The *Shepoag R.* was relocated to its more correct location in the town of Woodbury. *Connecticut R.* was added at the bend in the river above Hadham. *Oyster R.* was added in Milford. *60 to a Degree* was erased. *Lat. 41:10 N./ Lon. 55: 24 W.* was added in Long Island Sound below New Haven. The symbol for county towns was added to mark Windham and New London. The name *Folly* for the Folly River was added just below Hartford

References: Harlow, "Moses Park Map, 1766," pp. 33–37; Schwartz and Ehrenberg, *Mapping of America*, p. 177; Sellers and van Ee, *Maps and Charts of North America*, p. 223; Thompson, *Maps of Connecticut*, pp. 34–35; Wheat and Brun, *Maps and Charts*, entry 58

AFTER England's victory in the Seven Years' War, the Board of Trade initiated plans to improve the postal system in America. George Montagu Dunk, Earl of Halifax, wrote to Connecticut Governor Thomas Fitch on August 11, 1764, suggesting measures to present to the General Assembly regarding the establishment of a ferry system and building suitable structures to ensure the reliable and efficient handling of mail. He further noted:

> *His Majesty's Post Master General having also represented that a Map of the Province under Your Government, with the present Course of the Posts throughout the same clearly markt out, would be of great Use to Him, in the present Undertaking; I am to desire that You will procure and transmit such a Map, together with a State of such alter-*

ations as You apprehend to be wanting for the better Regulation and Improvement of the said Posts.[2]

The following May, the Assembly appointed Asa Spaulding of Norwalk and Moses Park and Samuel Mott of Preston to "survey, measure and make a Plan of this Colony."[3] They were to record county boundaries, towns, post roads, sea-coasts, and navigable rivers and keep a diary of their work.

Spaulding, Park, and Preston apparently completed their map by October. Ezra Stiles noted in his *Itineraries* that "it was presented to the Assembly this October Session and approved. Two Copies were ordered to be transmitted home to the Board of Trade."[4] That same month, Fitch wrote to Henry Seymour Conway, who had replaced Halifax as president of the Board of Trade, that "the Map of the Colony Mentioned in My Letter of the 13th November last I expect will be printed this fall and hope before the end of this year to have the Honor of transmitting it to you."[5] Fitch's letter suggests that the colony intended to have the draft engraved in America prior to sending it to London but subsequent correspondence indicates that it was dispatched on November 13, 1765.[6]

The printed map lacks the imprint of a publisher or engraver. Due to Fitch's indication that the colony intended to have the work published, and because the engraving was more crudely executed than the work of London artisans, it has generally been assumed that the map was engraved in America. One cartographic historian has suggested that it was the work of Connecticut engraver Abel Buell, but no evidence supports this theory.[7] Since the date engraved on the map, November 24, 1766, was one full year after the manuscript draft was sent to London, there was ample time for it to have been engraved and printed in either England or America. However, the first public mention of the map did not occur until January 1, 1768, when it was advertised in the *New-London Gazette*:

> *TO BE SOLD, by Maj.* John Durkee *in* Norwich, *Mr.* Edward Mott *in* Preston, *and at the* Printing-Office *in* New-London, *A neat Copper-Plate Plan of the Colony of* Connecticut, *as taken at the Direction of the General Assembly of this Colony, by* Moses Park. *(Price one Dollar.)*[8]

Over the next two years, the Park map was advertised at least ten times in the *New-London Gazette*. If it actually had been published in 1766, it is curious that no mention was made at that time, especially considering the numerous advertisements that appeared in 1768 and 1769. While the public records for Connecticut clearly document that the

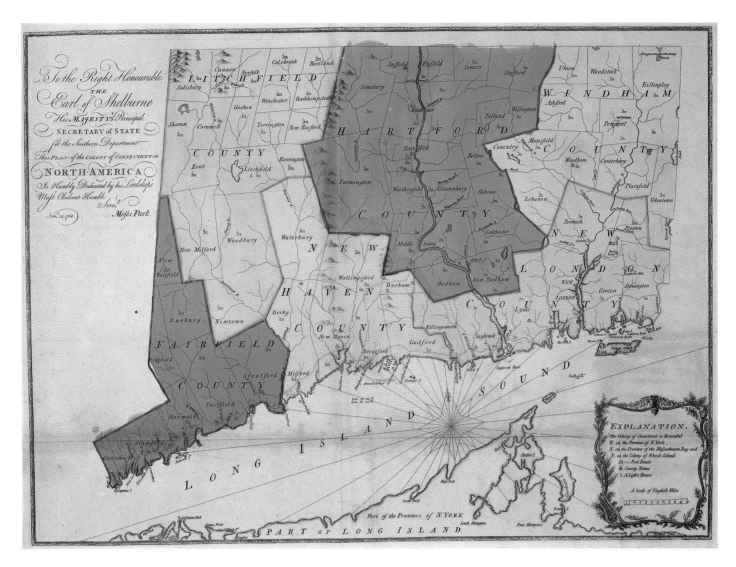

157 *Plan of the Colony of Connecticut in North-America.* (Cat. 41)

task of surveying the colony and compiling the map was given to Spaulding, Park, and Mott, only Park's name appears on the printed map. Why the other two surveyors' names were dropped from the printed work is not known.

The map was dedicated to the Earl of Shelburne, who assumed sole responsibility for administering colonial affairs for the Board of Trade on August 8, 1766. In addition to identifying counties, towns, lakes, rivers, and the coastline, three postal routes from New Haven were shown, a southwest road to Greenwich, another north to Hartford where it forked to follow both sides of the Connecticut River to Suffield and Enfield, and a route eastward to Stonington. A *Plan of the Colony of Connecticut in North America* was the only large-scale map of that colony published during the colonial period.

G1997-40, partially funded by Mr. and Mrs. Joseph R. Lasser, Dr. Lee P. Haacker, Mr. Glenn Sandison, and Mr. and Mrs. Irving F. Jensen, Jr.

1. Edmund Thompson, *Maps of Connecticut Before the Year 1800* (Windham, Conn., 1940), pp. 34–35.

2. Earl of Halifax to Gov. Thomas Fitch, Aug. 11, 1764, "The Fitch Papers: Correspondence and Documents During Thomas Fitch's Governorship of the Colony of Connecticut, 1754–1766," *Collections of the Connecticut Historical Society,* XVIII (1920), pp. 287–288.

3. Charles J. Hoadly, *The Public Records of the Colony of Connecticut, From May, 1762, to October, 1767, Inclusive* (Hartford, Conn., 1881), p. 418.

4. Franklin Bowditch Dexter, ed., *Extracts from the Itineraries and Other Miscellanies of Ezra Stiles, D. D., LL. D., 1755–1794, with a Selection from his Correspondence* (New Haven, Conn., 1916), p. 220.

5. Fitch to Henry Seymour Conway, Oct. 7, 1765, "Fitch Papers," pp. 359–360. Conway replaced Halifax as secretary of state.

6. Fitch to Conway, Nov. 13, 1765; Fitch to Richard Jackson, Nov. 13, 1765, *ibid.,* pp. 370, 373.

7. Schwartz and Ehrenburg, *Mapping of America,* p. 177. Schwartz attributed the Park map to Buell presumably because he was from Connecticut. Although born in Connecticut, as an adult Buell moved to Springfield, Mass., and did not return to New Haven until about 1774–1775. David McNeely Stauffer, *American Engravers Upon Copper and Steel* (New York, 1907), Pt. 1, pp. 34–35.

8. *New-London Gazette* (Conn.), Jan. 1, 1768.

42 *A New and Accurate/ MAP OF / VIRGINIA / Wherein most of the / COUNTIES / are laid down from / ACTUAL SURVEYS. / With/ A Concise Account of the / Number of / Inhabitants, the Trade, Soil, and Produce / of that / PROVINCE*

John Henry, cartographer; Thomas Jefferys, engraver

London, February 1770. Black-and-white line engraving with period outline color. H. 38⅜", W. 52"

The cartouche in the upper right corner contains the title on a stone ornamented with foliate swags. Below is *Engraved by Thomas Jefferys Geographer to the KING.* At the top, a seated woman holds a cornucopia in one hand and a portrait medallion, perhaps suggesting George III, in the other. In the lower left, a slave child carries a tray of fruit. To the right, a seated slave with a hoe in one hand points to a blank tablet with the other. A wooden fence, tropical trees and plants, a ship, and several hogsheads are in the background. Along the entire lower portion of the map is text relating to Virginia

Only one state of the map is known

References: Cresswell, "Colony to Commonwealth," pp. 88–91; Harrison, *Landmarks of Old Prince William*, pp. 634–636; "Henry's Map of Virginia in 1770," pp. 83–85; "John Henry Map of Virginia," pp. 132–133[1]; Sellers and van Ee, *Maps and Charts of North America*, p. 312; Wright, introduction, *John Henry County Map*

ELEVEN YEARS after Fry and Jefferson's highly regarded *Map of the most Inhabited part of Virginia* appeared in the colonies, John Henry[2] announced his plan to make a new map of the province, measuring the roads to provide distances between places and furnishing soundings for the Chesapeake Bay and its tributaries, features lacking on the Fry and Jefferson map. On November 10, 1766, Henry presented the proposal to the House of Burgesses and petitioned for funds to supplement monies he anticipated securing through subscriptions. The House rejected his plea the following month.

Undaunted, Henry advertised his intentions in the *Virginia Gazette,* expressing disappointment that the project "has not got so great a number of subscribers as he expected."[3] Henry again unsuccessfully solicited support from the Burgesses on April 2, 1768. The second petition recorded that "as the Subscription Money is almost exhausted, he will be unable to get the Map thereof Printed."[4] Henry made one final attempt to sway the Burgesses in November 1769 by noting that he had

> intended to have measured the Public Roads, but, for want of proper Encouragement, had not been able to execute it; . . .

and, forasmuch as the Petitioner had been at considerable Expence in forming his Map, and had transmitted it to London, *to be printed, therefore praying the House to grant him such a Consideration as will enable him to measure the Public Roads throughout the Colony.*[4]

The Burgesses refused Henry's request once again.

Although he knew that the work was not as complete as originally hoped, by November 1769, Henry sent a draft to London to be engraved. The lack of financial backing had forced him to rely heavily on previously published maps. Much of the geographic detail was taken from Fry and Jefferson's map published fifteen years earlier (Cat. 30). Henry added soundings in the mouth of the Chesapeake Bay and at the entrances of the James and York Rivers. Where Fry and Jefferson had identified the counties only by name, Henry delineated all of the boundary lines. Curiously, since one of Henry's motives behind producing his map was to encourage settlement on the frontier, the western portion of the map lacks significant detail; much of this area is virtually blank. Perhaps to compensate for some of the map's shortcomings, he included a description of the social and economic situation of the colony at the bottom.

Henry sent his draft to Thomas Jefferys to engrave and print. Unlike his role with the Fry and Jefferson map, Jefferys did not agree to distribute Henry's work, which would have competed with his own productions. The decorative cartouche, designed by an unidentified artisan, suggests that Henry's project was brought to fruition before it was complete. *(fig. 159)* The seated figure in the foreground points to an empty tablet probably designed to contain a dedication.

The printed map was available to the subscribers in February 1770. It was sharply criticized from the beginning. Only seven months after the map appeared, the first negative review was published in the *Virginia Gazette*. Henry responded:

> WHEREAS *some persons, either to colour their parsimony, or from an unacquaintedness with such works, have endeavoured to depreciate my map of* Virginia, *by magnifying some inaccuracies therein, which regard either the situation of some Gentlemens seats or some inconsiderable water courses, I judged it necessary to inform the publick that as the subscriptions could not enable me to be more accurate, not having had any assistance from the legislature, so, in general, the map may be deemed a very good one, when it is considered that the out lines of the colony, as far as the* Allegheny *ridge, together with the rivers and*

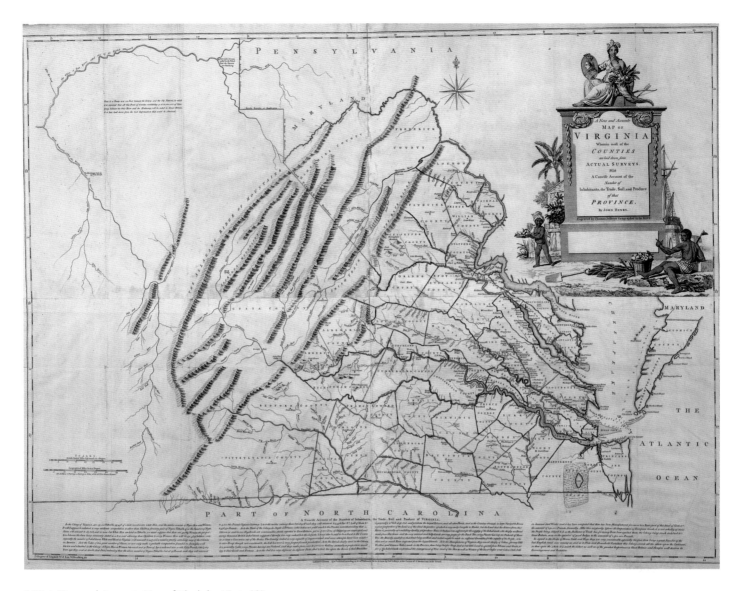

158 *A New and Accurate Map of Virginia.* (Cat. 42)

159 Detail of the cartouche from *A New and Accurate Map of Virginia*, by John Henry, London, 1770, black-and-white line engraving with period outline color. 1955-486. (Cat. 42)

county lines, excepting some of those of Nansemond, Norfolk, *and* Princess Anne, *were either surveyed, at my charge, or draughts of them, furnished me by Gentlemen who informed me they might be depended on; and seeing these are the most essential parts of a map, as all good judges will allow, I hope the impartial world will, upon this information, esteem them as they ought, especially when it is considered that all the most eminent men throughout the colony have encouraged the undertaking, and purchased a great many maps, and that I have been at great expense and pains to execute a work the first of its kind that ever was attempted on the continent of* North America.

JOHN HENRY[6]

Several weeks later, the *Virginia Gazette* printed a witty reply to Henry's outburst, penned under the psudyonom "Geographus."

It must be to colour their parsimony, or out of unknowingness, that any one could attempt to depreciate Mr. Henry's MAP; for the few inaccuracies in it were unavoidable Who would condemn a map in which a few inconsiderable water courses were not exactly laid down? What does it signify if he is mistaken in the breadth and courses of such trifling water courses as Chesapeak, Potowmack, Rappahannock, York and James? Or is it material that none of the roads are laid down; that he has taken notice of but few court houses; that Winchester, Fort Cumberland, and Dumfries, are not in the map; that Norfolk is placed in Princess Anne; that Hog Island is put opposite to James Town; James Town north of Williamsburg, Williamsburg 4 miles from the capitol landing, and a few other such trifling mistakes? I know some of your affected geographical parsimonious ones find fault with Mr. Henry, because he has not given them the longitude of Williamsburg, his first meridian, and because they say there is no great accuracy in the latitudes of some few places in his map. But let them inform Mr. Henry what the longitude and latitude ought to be; let them observe, and send him their observations gratis, or let the legislature take the trouble and expence off his hands. And let every one consider that this is the first map of Virginia, or a work the first of its kind ever attempted in America. I am yours, &c.

GEOGRAPHUS.[7]

Four months later, "C. R." wrote the final discourse published in the *Virginia Gazette* against Henry's map, concluding:

This will convince you that the first Part of C. R. or B. E.'s Accusation was false, and you will clear him of the latter Part when I tell you his Motive for mentioning your Map in the Manner he did. As he is a Man of Genius, he immediately discovered that there were many Errors in your Map. These the Goodness of his Heart would not suffer him to ascribe to your Incapacity, but to your good Taste, which directed you to a better Disposition of Gentlemens Seats, and to assign more beautiful Dimensions and Courses to the Rivers, than those which Nature had allotted them. But though his Opinion was so indulgent, he well knew others might, with a good Deal of Propriety, suggest that Ignorance was the Cause. To be beforehand, therefore, with such ill natured Folks, he allowed your Mistakes (which indeed he could not deny) but at the same Time excused them in the Manner before mentioned. As for my Part, I subscribe to my Friend's Opinion, having often seen your

Maps hung up in Houses, not because they were reckoned useful, but ornamental.

C. R.[8]

Criticism of Henry's map in the *Virginia Gazette* seems to have ended with C.R's comments.

Henry's map was also reviewed by Thomas Pownall, who published *A Topographical Description of Such Parts of North America as are Contained in the (Annexed) Map of the Middle British Colonies, &c., in North America* in 1776. In the preface, Pownall commented on the sources used for his map and noted reservations about the quality of Henry's:

A Map engraved by Jefferys, and called "A New and accurate Map of Virginia," by John Henry, was published in 1770. I was in Hopes to have derived Information from this, but upon Examination of it, it appears to me to be a very inaccurate Compilation; defective in Topography; and not very attentive even to Geography; The Draughtsman or the Engraver has totally omitted the South Branch of the Potômack River: Nor is that curious and interesting Piece of Information, the Communication between the Waters of Virginia and the Waters of the Ohio, which were known when this was published, marked in it. This Map of Mr. Henry has indeed the Division Lines of the Counties of the Province drawn on it, and if they are rightly drawn, it is certainly an Improvement: But while I doubt the Accuracy of the Geography, I cannot be assured of these.[9]

Despite the negative publicity surrounding Henry's work, Governor Botetourt subscribed ten pounds in November 1769 to help publish the map.[10] He also attempted unsuccessfully to secure a royal warrant for its production. Once the map arrived in Virginia, Botetourt hung it in the most prominent location in the Governor's Palace, over the mantel in the dining room. Graham Hood believes there was overwhelming evidence that suggested Botetourt's dining room was "the intellectual center of the house and the setting for frequent cultural interaction between governor and gentry."[11] It seems likely that Botetourt's placement of Henry's controversial map in such a visible location indicated his support for the project and was a diplomatic gesture toward John Henry's son Patrick, one of the moving forces behind the resolves against the Stamp Act.

By December 1770, Henry's map project had virtually ruined him financially and he served notice in the *Virginia Gazette* that he intended to leave the colony. Although Henry never left Virginia, the declaration notified creditors to collect unpaid bills. In April 1771, Henry contacted Thomas Adams requesting his assistance in disposing of copies of his map during an upcoming trip to London. The Virginians' negative response likely forced Henry to consider other markets. He instructed Adams to have as many copies printed as money would allow and then attempt to dispose of them in London and

afterwards in all the Cities & Towns that have any Trade to Virginia in England Scotland & Ireland; & likewise to get a friend to write his correspondt in France to know what number may be Saleable either in Paris, or any other City, or Town in that Kingdom.[12]

Shortly before Henry's death in February 1773, he signed over the rights to the map to Patrick, who had helped support him during his last years. It is doubtful whether Patrick Henry ever realized any monetary gain from his legacy.

1955-486

1. "Henry's Map of Virginia in 1770," *WMQ*, 1st Ser., XIV (1905), pp. 83–85.

2. John Henry was born in Aberdeen, Scotland. Although enrolled in King's College at Aberdeen University for four years, he left before receiving a degree. Henry came to Virginia in Feb. 1727 and immediately began to acquire large tracts of land in Albermarle, Hanover, and Goochland Counties. To supplement a meager income as a farmer, Henry also served as a colonel in the militia and chief justice of Hanover Co. He was also a teacher, proprietor of a country store, and, most important, acted as surveyor of Hanover Co.

3. *Va. Gaz.* (Purdie and Dixon), June 25, 1767.

4. John Pendleton Kennedy, ed., *Journals of the House of Burgesses, 1766–1769* (Richmond, Va., 1906), p. 144.

5. *Ibid.,* p. 266.

6. *Va. Gaz.* (Purdie and Dixon), Sept. 6, 1770.

7. *Ibid.* (Rind), Sept. 27, 1770.

8. *Ibid.* (Purdie and Dixon), Jan. 31, 1771.

9. Lois Mulkearn, ed., *A Topographical Description of the Dominions of the United States of America* by Thomas Pownall (Pittsburgh, Pa., 1949), p. 6.

10. Botetourt's account books, Badminton House, Gloucestershire, Eng. He sent one of John Henry's petitions to the Earl of Hillsborough on Nov. 24, 1768. Hood, *Governor's Palace,* pp. 159 and 324, n. 59.

11. *Ibid.,* p. 156.

12. "The John Henry Map of Virginia—1771: John Henry's Letter to Thomas Adams," Notes and Queries, *VMHB*, LVIII (1950), pp. 132–133.

43 *A Compleat MAP of NORTH-CAROLINA from an actual Survey*

John Abraham Collet, cartographer; I. Bayly, engraver; Samuel Hooper, publisher

London, May 1, 1770. Black-and-white line engraving with period color. H. 30½", W. 43½", in 4 sheets

Along the top after the title is *By Capt.ⁿ Collet. Governor of Fort Johnston. Engraved by I. Bayly.* In the lower right corner is the dedicatory rococo cartouche decorated with a Native American, tiger, and alligator and surmounted with the coat of arms of George III. The dedication is *TO HIS / most Excellent Majesty / GEORGE the III. / King of Great Britain, &c. &c. &c. / This MAP is most humbly dedicated by / His MAJESTY'S / most humble obedient & dutiful Subject / John Collet.* Along the bottom below the border is *Publish'd according to Act of Parliament, May the 1.ˢᵗ 1770, by S. Hooper. N.º 25 Ludgate Hill, London*

Only one state of the map is known

References: Cumming, *North Carolina in Maps*, pp. 18–20; Cumming, *Southeast in Early Maps*, entry 394 and pp. 30–31; Ristow, *American Maps and Mapmakers*, pp. 53, 56; Schwartz and Ehrenberg, *Mapping of America*, p. 181; Sellers and Van Ee, *Maps and Charts of North America*, p. 324

In August 1767, Lord Shelburne, British secretary of state, wrote to General Thomas Gage notifying him of the appointment of John Abraham Collet as commandant of Fort Johnston at the mouth of the Cape Fear River in North Carolina. Shelburne described Collet as an officer and engineer who had formerly been in the French military service before going to England.[1]

Collet arrived in Carolina by December. During that month, he produced a plan of Fort Johnston, a facility he eventually redesigned and rebuilt. The following September, Collet distinguished himself while serving as an aide-de-camp to Governor William Tryon against the Regulators at Hillsborough.[2] Three months later, at Tryon's request, Collet sailed for England to deliver a report on the condition of the colony.[3] Prior to his departure, Tryon loaned Collet a manuscript map of Carolina compiled between 1757 and 1767 by William Churton of Edenton. Churton had served as surveyor for the Granville District just south of the Virginia-North Carolina border and was one of the North Carolina commissioners appointed to extend the boundary line between the two colonies in 1749 with Virginia commissioners Joshua Fry and Peter Jefferson. Collet and an assistant drafted a copy of Churton's map to take with them to England. This map and the accompanying report were delivered to the Earl of Hillsborough along

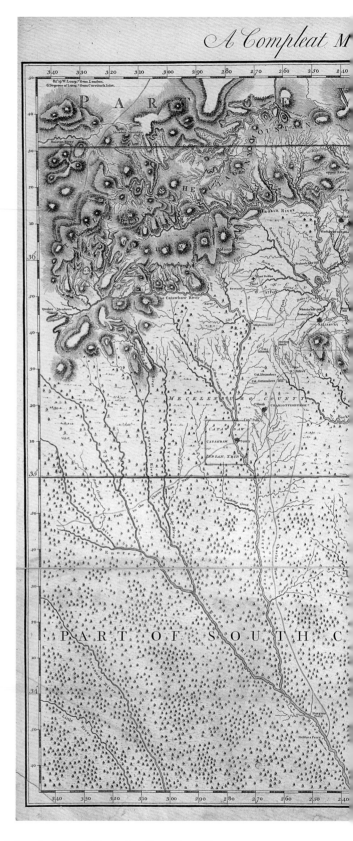

160 *A Compleat Map of North-Carolina.* (Cat. 43)

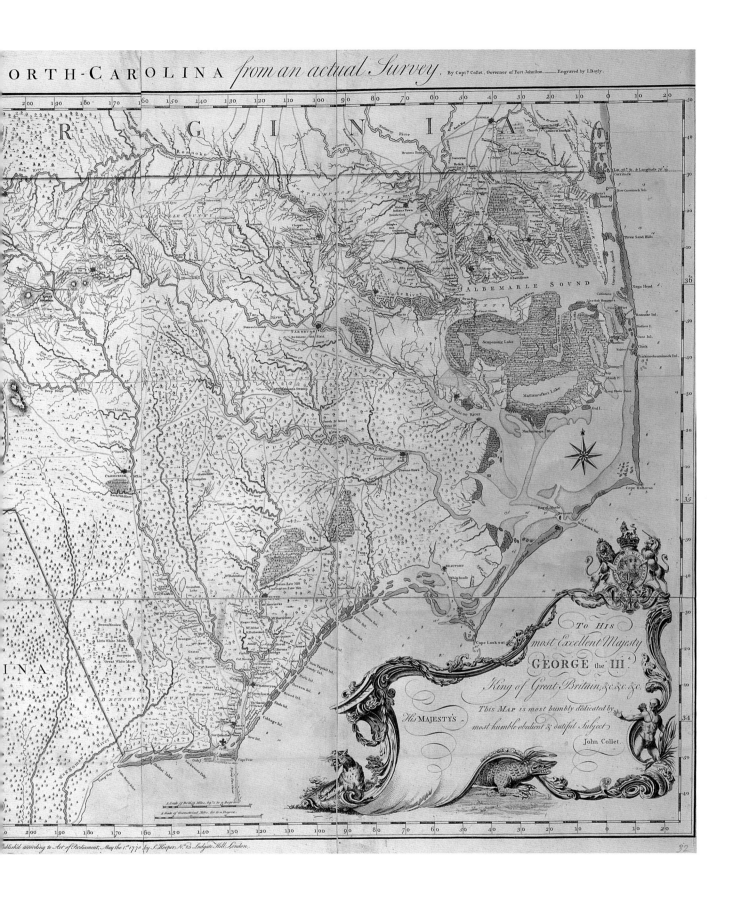

NORTH-CAROLINA *from an actual Survey.* By Captⁿ Collet, Governor of Fort Johnston. Engraved by I.Bayly.

To His
most Excellent Majesty
GEORGE the III.
King of Great Britain, &c.&c.&c.

This Map is most humbly dedicated by
His MAJESTY'S
most humble obedient & dutiful Subject
John Collet.

Publish'd according to Act of Parliament, May the 1ˢᵗ 1770 by S. Hooper N°.25 Ludgate Hill, London.

32

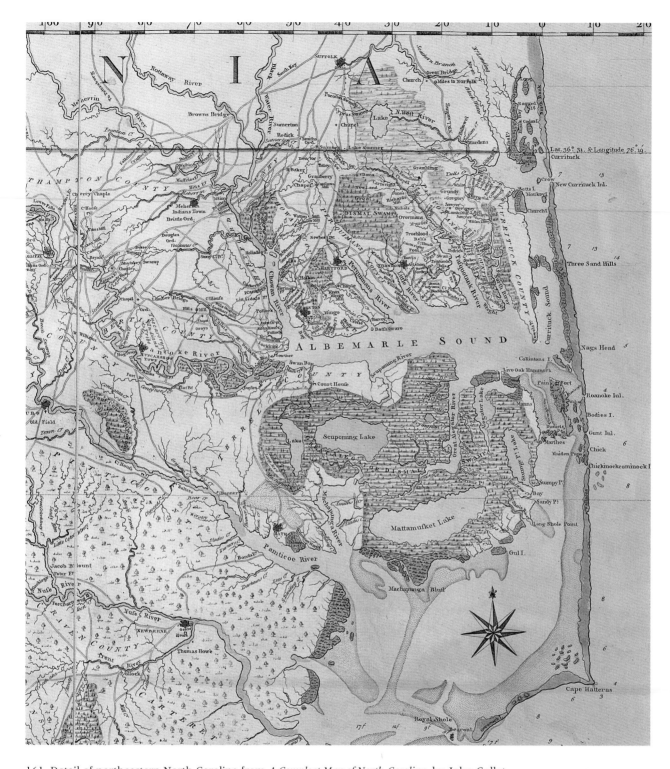

161 Detail of northeastern North Carolina from *A Compleat Map of North-Carolina,* by John Collet,
London, May 1, 1770, black-and-white line engraving with period color.
G1983-300, gift of Mrs. Anna Glen Vietor in memory of Alexander O. Vietor. (Cat. 43)

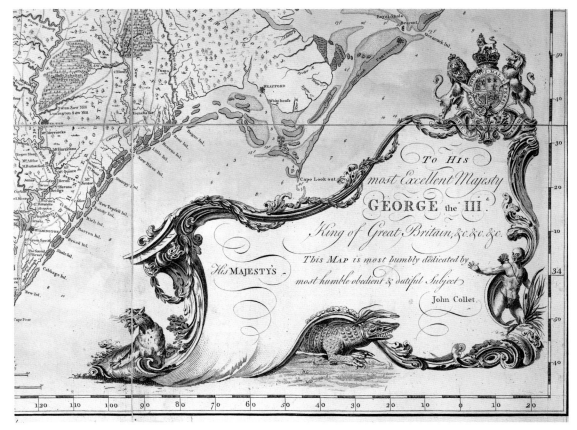

162 Detail of the cartouche from *A Compleat Map of North-Carolina*, by John Collet,
London, May 1, 1770, black-and-white line engraving with period color.
G1983-300, gift of Mrs. Anna Glen Vietor in memory of Alexander O. Vietor. (Cat. 43)

with Tryon's request for funds to conduct new surveys of the colony.[4] The boundary between North and South Carolina needed to be determined in order to resolve disputes over taxation and overlapping land grants.

Collet's rendering of Churton's manuscript was the basis for *A Compleat Map of North-Carolina.* Churton's contribution was not credited either on the draft copy taken to London or on the printed map. Collet added the names of more plantation owners, the locations of several new towns, and soundings at the mouth of the Cape Fear River and Frying Pan Shoals, the latter perhaps taken largely from a map published in 1738 by James Wimple. The most important new information Collet supplied was the delineation of the network of roads in the western part of the colony.[5] Collet's map served as the prototype for subsequent maps of Carolina for several decades.

Collet grew increasingly uncomfortable as hostilities between the colonies and England intensified. To the displeasure of the General Assembly, Collet refortified Fort Johnston in 1774. On June 18, 1775, patriots set fire to the fort. Although Collet escaped, the patriots returned the following day and burned his home and possessions.

G1983-300, gift of Mrs. Anna Glen Vietor in memory of Alexander O. Vietor

1. Shelburne's letter is printed in full in Cumming, *Southeast in Early Maps,* pp. 30–31.

2. The Regulators were a group of North Carolinians whose primary goal was to gain the right to regulate their own local government. Reports of an uprising of a band of Regulators in Hillsborough, N. C., in Sept. 1768 prompted Gov. Tryon to call out the militia.

3. Cumming, *Southeast in Early Maps,* p. 31.

4. *Ibid.*

5. Cumming, *North Carolina in Maps,* p. 19.

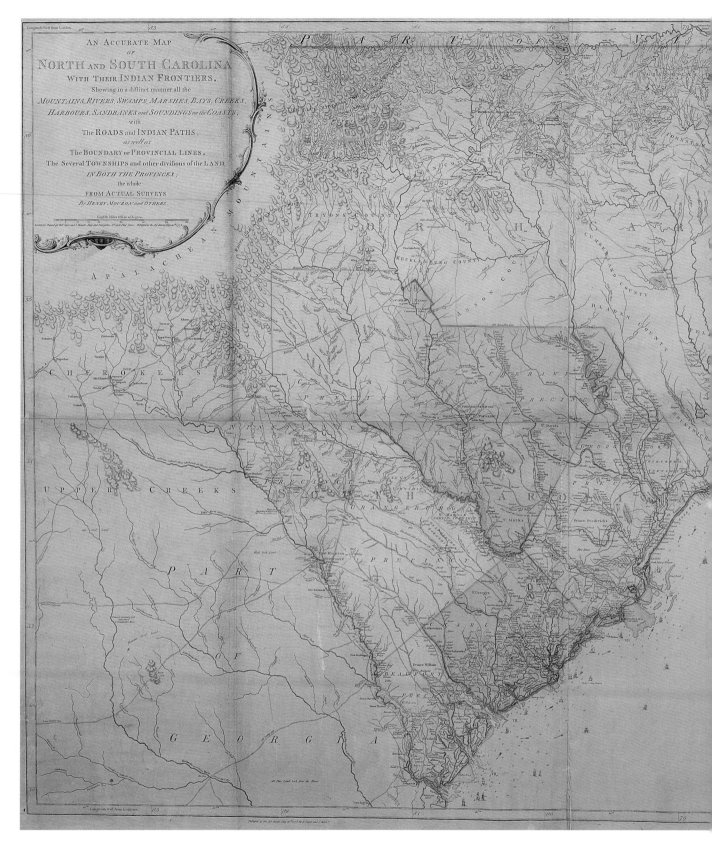

163 *An Accurate Map of North and South Carolina.* (Cat. 44)

44 AN ACCURATE MAP / OF / NORTH AND SOUTH CAROLINA / WITH THEIR INDIAN FRONTIERS, / Shewing in a distinct manner all the / MOUNTAINS, RIVERS, SWAMPS, MARSHES, BAYS, CREEKS, / HARBOURS, SANDBANKS and SOUNDINGS on the COASTS; / with / The ROADS and INDIAN PATHS; / as well as / The BOUNDARY or PROVINCIAL LINES, / The Several TOWNSHIPS and other divisions of the LAND / IN BOTH THE PROVINCES; / the whole / FROM ACTUAL SURVEYS / By HENRY MOUZON and OTHERS

Henry Mouzon, cartographer; Samuel Turner Sparrow, engraver; published in Thomas Jefferys's *The American Atlas: or, A Geographical Description of the Whole Continent of America* by Robert Sayer and John Bennett

London, May 30, 1775. Black-and-white line engraving. H. 40½", W. 56⅞", in four sheets

The title in the upper left corner is bordered on two sides with rococo scrollwork. Below the title is a scale of distances and *LONDON, Printed for Rob.¹ Sayer and J: Bennett, Map and Print-Sellers, Nº 53 in Fleet Street. Published as the Act directs May 30.ᵗʰ 1775*. In the lower right corner are two inset maps, *THE HARBOUR OF PORT ROYAL* and *THE BAR and HARBOUR OF CHARLESTOWN*. Below the lower border on both the left and right is *Publish'd as the Act directs May 30ᵗʰ 1775. by R: Sayer & J: Bennett*

Three states of the map are known[2]:
State 1: (this copy) As described
State 2: A reference to Fort Sullivan was added to the Charlestown inset. The title and imprint were unchanged. 1776
State 3: The Sayer and Bennett imprint was erased and altered to *Published by Laurie & Whittle, 53, Fleet Street. 12ᵗʰ May 1794*. 1794

References: Cumming, *North Carolina in Maps*, pp. 21–22; Cumming, *Southeast in Early Maps*, entry 450; Cumming and Marshall, *North America at the Time of the Revolution*; Guthorn, *British Maps of the American Revolution*, p. 37; Schwartz and Ehrenberg, *Mapping of America*, p. 187; Sellers and van Ee, *Maps and Charts of North America*, p. 298

Henry Mouzon's *An Accurate Map of North and South Carolina* appeared on the eve of the American Revolution, and its up-to-date geography made it the most widely consulted map of the area used in the war effort. According to Cumming, George Washington's cloth-mounted and folded copy is in the collections of the library of the American Geographical Society. The Mouzon map used by the Comte de Rochambeau is in the Library of Congress, and

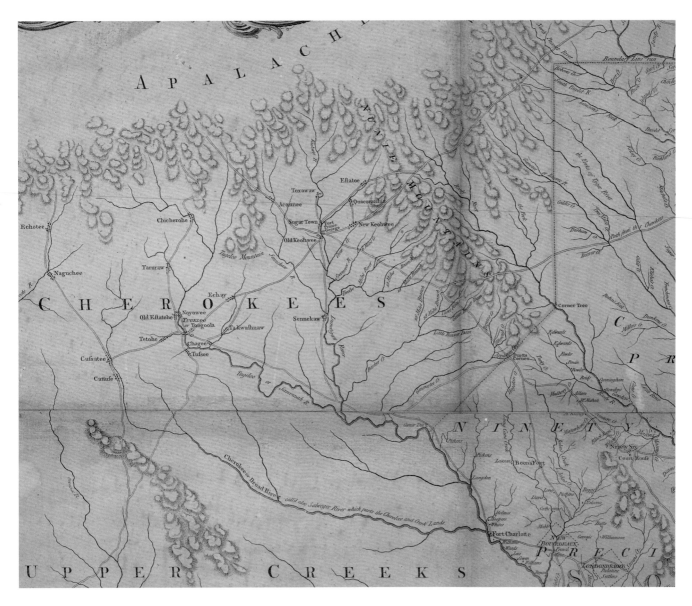

164 Detail of western North Carolina from *An Accurate Map of North and South Carolina,* by Henry Mouzon, London, May 30, 1775, black-and white-line engraving. 1950-396. (Cat. 44)

General Henry Clinton's British Headquarters copy is in the William L. Clements Library, Ann Arbor, Michigan.[3]

Because two cousins, both named Henry Mouzon, were residing in South Carolina when the draft was made, the identity of the one who created *An Accurate Map of North and South Carolina* cannot be determined. The more likely candidate was Henry Mouzon of Craven County, who was a surveyor. An inventory taken at his death in April 1777 recorded "a parcel of surveyors instruments" and "Sundry Maps & 2 copper Plates."[4]

Mouzon announced his intention to publish a new map of the colony of South Carolina by subscription in *The South Carolina and American General Advertiser,* May 6–June 2, 1774. After describing the scale, seven miles to an inch, the landmarks to be included, and the cost to the subscriber, Mouzon added a lengthy explanation about why a new map of South Carolina should be compiled since two already existed.[5] Mouzon was referring to *A Map of South Carolina,* engraved by John Lodge in 1771 and almost certainly compiled by James Cook, and another by Cook published two years later, *A Map of the Province of South Carolina.* Both borrowed heavily from William De Brahm's *Map Of South Carolina and a Part of Georgia* (Cat. 37). Mouzon's most important new contribution was his delineation of the rivers and Indian settlements west of the Cherokee Indian boundary lines.

Mouzon based much of his depiction of North Carolina on John Collet's *A Compleat Map of North-Carolina,* published in 1770 (Cat. 43). To the earlier work, Mouzon added more counties and included information around the Catawba River. Discrepancies between the two maps in the soundings along the coast suggest that Mouzon may have consulted another source as well.

Carolina was separated into two colonies in 1730. *An Accurate Map of North and South Carolina* illustrated the dividing line between the two borders, which had been the subject of dispute. Although the Lords of Trade provided an ambiguous description of the boundaries at the time the colony was divided, the commissioners appointed in 1735 to represent the two provinces agreed to the division at the thirty-fifth parallel of latitude.[6] This resolution also placed the Catawba Indian reservation in South Carolina. Although controversies arose over the years between the two colonies, this agreement essentially fixed the boundary for the rest of the century.

Robert Sayer and John Bennett printed and published Mouzon's map in May 1775. The following year, they included it in *The American Atlas: or, A Geographical Description of the Whole Continent of America,* by "The Late Mr. Thomas Jefferys, Geographer to the King, and Others." That Sayer and Bennett were publishing atlases under Jefferys's name five years after his death indicates the late map publisher's continuing influence in the market. During the Seven Years' War, Jefferys had established himself as the leading authority on the geography of North America. At the close of the conflict, his interests turned toward mapping English counties, a venture that devastated his business and forced him into bankruptcy in 1766.[7] To ease his financial situation, Jefferys entered into a series of partnerships, the most important of which was with London map- and printseller Robert Sayer. In 1768, they published *A General Topography of North America and the West Indies* bearing the imprint of R. Sayer and T. Jefferys. While still engaged in projects with Jeffreys, Sayer also formed a partnership with John Bennett in 1770. When Jefferys died in 1771, his assets were liquidated in accordance with the provisions of his will. Sayer purchased a significant amount of Jefferys's stock. He and Bennett continued to publish Jefferys's maps, compiling many of the titles into various atlases such as *The American Atlas.*

1950-396

1. Sparrow entered into an apprenticeship with the well-known London engraver Thomas Kitchin in 1759. Laurence Worms, "Thomas Kitchin's 'Journey of life': Hydrographer to George III, mapmaker and engraver," Pt. 1, *Map Collector,* LXII (1993), p. 3.

2. Cumming and Marshall, *North America at the time of the Revolution.*

3. Cumming, *North Carolina in Maps,* p. 21.

4. *Ibid.,* p. 22.

5. The entire advertisement is quoted in Cumming, *Southeast in Early Maps,* pp. 333–334.

6. The initial wording of the document produced by the Lords of Trade concerning the boundary was that the line should begin "at the sea thirty miles distant from the mouth of the Cape Fear on the southwest thereof," paralleling the river to its source and then west to the Pacific. They added in June, "but if the Waggamaw River lyes within thirty miles of Cape Fear River, then that river to be the boundary from the sea to the head thereof and from thence to keep the distance of thirty miles parallel from Cape Fear River to the head thereof, and thence a due west course to the South Sea." The agreement reached by the North and South Carolina commissioners was that the line should run northwest from a point on the coast 30 miles southwest of the mouth of the Cape Fear River to the 35° latitude and then due west. David Duncan Wallace, *South Carolina: A Short History, 1520–1948* (Chapel Hill, N. C., 1951), p. 157.

7. J. B. Harley, "The Bankruptcy of Thomas Jefferys: an episode in the economic history of eighteenth century map-making," *Imago Mundi,* XX (1966), pp. 27–48.

45 *A MAP / OF THE / Province OF New York; / with Part of / PENSILVANIA, / AND / NEW ENGLAND, / From an Actual Survey by / Captain Montresor, / ENGINEER, 1775*

John Montresor, cartographer; P. Andrews, engraver; A. Dury, publisher

London, June 10, 1775. Black-and-white line engraving with full period color. H. 57¼", W. 36¼", in four sheets

In the upper left corner is an inset map of the continuation of Lake Champlain. In the upper right corner is an inset of the continuation of the Connecticut River. Beneath the title in the upper right below the inset is the imprint *Publish'd as the Act directs. June 10.ᵗʰ 1775, by A. Dury, Dukes Court S.ᵗ Martins Lane London.* In the right center is the dedication *TO THE RIGHT HONOURABLE/ Sir Jeffery Amherst/ KNIGHT of the BATH, and/ Lieutenant General of his Majesty's Forces &c. &c. &c./ This Map of the Province of/ NEW YORK,/ is humbly Inscribed, by/ His most obliged Humble Servant/ John Montresor/ Engineer.* Below the border in the lower right is *P. Andrews Sculp*

Four states of the map are known[1]:

State 1: Title and imprint as described. Ticonderoga on the southwestern shore of Lake Champlain was marked *Carillon Fort. Tyionderogha or Tienderoga* was located on the east bank. 1775

State 2: *Tyionderogha or Tienderoga,* still located on the east bank, was corrected to *Ticonderoga.* 1775

State 3: (this copy) As described. The location of Fort Ticonderoga was moved to the west bank and was identified as *TICONDEROGA OR/ FORT CARILLON.* Many new place-names were added to the inset map of Lake Champlain

State 4: The imprint was altered to *Republished, with great Improvements, April, 1.ˢᵗ 1777.* 1777

References: Guthorn, *British Maps of the American Revolution,* pp. 34–37; Schwartz and Ehrenberg, *Mapping of America,* p. 186; Sellers and van Ee, *Maps and Charts of North America,* p. 234; Stevens and Tree, "Comparative Cartography," entry 42

Jᴏʜɴ Mᴏɴᴛʀᴇsᴏʀ *(fig. 166)* was trained as a surveyor by his father, James, an engineer in the British royal army. In 1754, the elder Montresor was appointed chief engineer for the British forces under the command of General Braddock. John joined the 48th Regiment, serving alongside his father during several expeditions including Braddock's campaign against Fort Duquesne. The younger Montresor was awarded a commission as practitioner engineer in 1758. During the French and Indian War, he led scouting parties into Canada, earning praise for his valor as an emissary who carried dispatches between Governor William Shirley and General Jeffery Amherst. During his tour of

duty, Montresor surveyed the Saint Lawrence River, Nova Scotia, Canada, and the Middle Atlantic colonies. In 1764, he was assigned the task of constructing a series of redoubts near Niagara and a fort on the shores of Lake Erie. The following year, he was appointed engineer extraordinary and captain lieutenant.

After the French and Indian War, England attempted to institute bills of taxation to help defray the cost of the conflict and fund the future defense of the colonies.[2] The level of indignation toward the British government and their troops quartered in New York was so high that on December 7, 1765, Montresor was summoned by General Thomas Gage to supply him with a map of New York City and its surroundings in anticipation of confrontations. As Montresor's journal reveals, he immediately set about to compile a plan "on a large Scale with its environs and adjacent country together with its harbour, but particularly to shew the ground to the North and North East of the Town."[3] *(see fig. 25)*

Montresor also compiled a map of the whole province of New York and portions of neighboring colonies. In June 1766, he recorded that he was "Employed in shading and putting together the several communications in this Province in order to compile a Draught of it."[4] The following October, Montresor sailed for England for a six-month leave of absence, taking with him several maps that he delivered to the firm of John Rocque for engraving and printing.[5] On May 1, 1767, Montresor noted that he was "Constantly attending at the 2 Engravers to assist them in the Executions of the severnl [*sic*] Draughts I have given them to Engrave for me viz.ᵗ one of Nova Scotia, one of the Province of New York, one of Canada from the first Island to Montreal and one of the City of New York and Environs with the Bosen Harbour and Channel from the Hook."[6] Although *A Plan of the City of New-York & its Environs* was published at that time, this *Map of the Province of New York* did not appear until 1775.

Montresor's general map of New York and the surrounding colonies included important information concerning the boundary between New York and New Jersey. From the time the Duke of York granted the proprietary of New Jersey to Sir George Carteret and John, Lord Berkeley, in 1664, the border between the two colonies had been called into question. It was to have been established

on the East part by the maine Sea and part by Hudsons River and hath upon the West Delaware Bay or River and extendeth Southward to the maine Ocean as farre as Cape May at the mouth of Delaware Bay and to the Northward as farre as ye

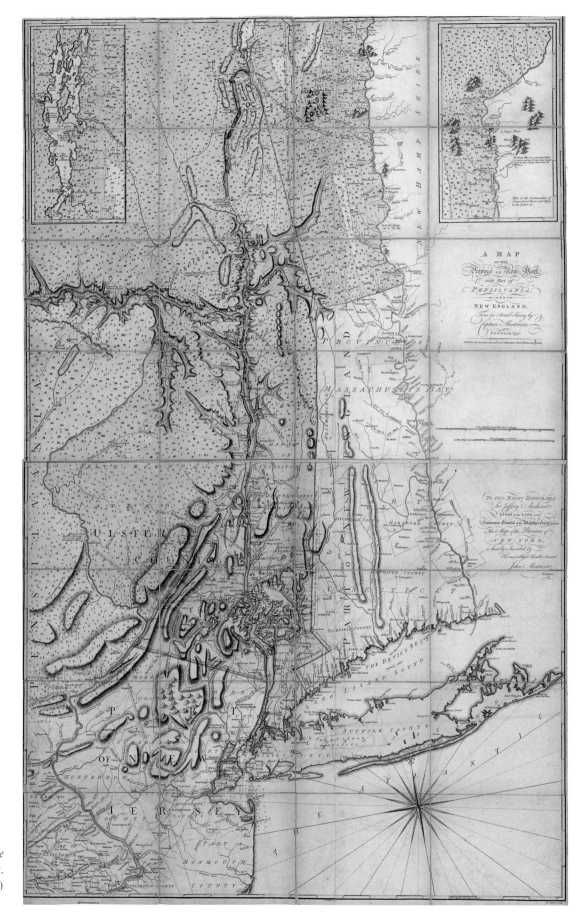

165 *A Map of the Province of New York; with Part of Pensilvania, and New England.* (Cat. 45)

Northermost Branch of the said Bay or River of Delaware
which is in fourtie one degrees and fourtie Minutes of
Latitude.[7]

Apparently, the duke consulted Nicholas Visscher's *Novi Belgii Novæque Angliæ* (Cat. 11), which depicted the branch of the Delaware mentioned in the grant incorrectly at 41° 40' near a settlement called Mecharienkonck. The boundary was to be drawn in a straight line between this point to 41° north latitude on the Hudson River.

Montresor illustrated three locations for the boundary line based on various viewpoints. *(fig. 167)* Residents of New Jersey preferred to abide by the designation of latitude, 41° 40', specified in the grant rather than the erroneous reference to the branch of the Delaware near Mecharienkonck. In 1719, the provincial legislatures of New York and New Jersey appointed a commission to determine the northwesternmost point of the latter colony. They established the location of 41° 40' north latitude at a point on the Fishkill River they named "Station Point." New Jersey maintained that its northern border should extend in a straight line from this point to 40° north latitude on the Hudson. Montresor illustrated this line and designated it as *the division line of 1719 as claimed by the New Jersey as their Northern.*

As the New York colonists began to settle in the direction of the disputed boundary, they took issue with the 1719 agreement, alleging that the Duke of York had intended the line to be drawn from the head of the Delaware Bay. As a compromise, they proposed running it from the fork of the Delaware, which they determined was at Easton where the Lehigh River empties into the Delaware, noted on the map as *the Northern Limit of New Jersey as Contended in Favor of the Crown of the Province of New York.* The third boundary Montresor depicted was *The more modern Reputed Jurisdiction Line between New York and New Jersey for upwards of 50 years past.*

In his 1749 *Map of Pennsylvania, New-Jersey, New-York, and the three Delaware Counties* and his 1755 *A general Map of the Middle British Colonies in America* (Cat. 34), Lewis Evans illustrated the boundary according to the 1719 agreement, using Station Point as the location from which to extend the boundary line. In the *Analysis,* Evans noted "that though the Line between the upper Part of New-Jersey and New-York is not settled, the Station Point in Latitude 41 : 40, on the only Branch of Delaware in that Latitude, was settled by Commissioners and Mathematicians, appointed by Acts of Assembly of both Provinces, and certified under their Hands and Seals, in 1719."[8] Evans

166 Portrait of John Montresor, by John Singleton Copley. Courtesy, Detroit Institute of Arts.

came under sharp criticism from colonists in New York for delineating their southern border at Station Point. In May 1749, the New York *Weekly Post-Boy* published a letter addressed to Mr. Lewis Evans in which the author asserted that "what [information] you received from *James Alexander,* Esq., Surveyor General of *New-Jersey,* with respect to the Northern Bounds of that Province, is little to be depended on, as he is a Proprietor of *Jersey,* and doubtless is for extending that Province as far as he can, and perhaps beyond its true Bounds."[9]

The location of the official boundary was unresolved until 1764 when George III appointed a commission that included experienced surveyors such as Samuel Holland and William De Brahm to settle the line. They decided on a compromise that placed the northwestern point from which to extend the dividing line at the junction of the

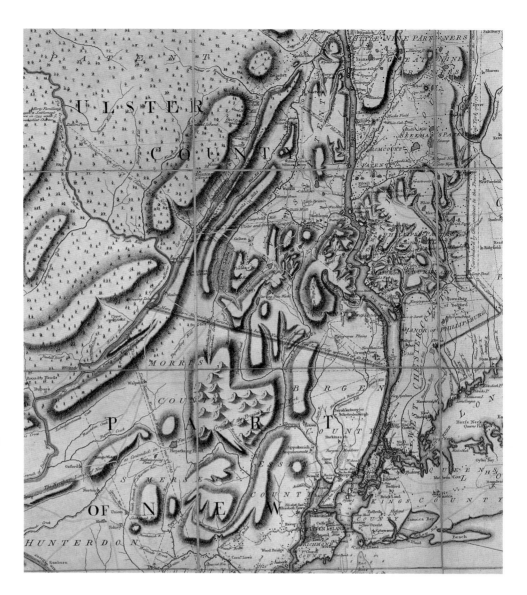

167 Detail of the boundary lines between New York and New Jersey from *A Map of the Province of New York; with Part of Pensilvania, and New England,* by John Montresor, London, June 10, 1775, black-and-white line engraving with period color. 1954-1065. (Cat. 45)

Neversink and Delaware Rivers. Bernard Ratzer ran the line in 1769. His work was subsequently engraved and published by William Faden as *The Province of New Jersey, Divided into East and West commonly called the Jerseys* (Cat. 47). Ratzer was apparently accompanied by Montresor, who recorded in his journal, "In 1769, I divided the Line between the provinces of New York and New Jersey by astronomical observations, so long a bone of contention, and in Chancery so many years."[10] That the line surveyed in 1769 was not illustrated on Montresor's map published in 1775 suggests the geography had not been updated since the original draft was delivered to Rocque's shop in 1766. By 1775, London publisher A. Dury had acquired some of Rocque's plates.

1954-1065

1. Stevens and Tree, "Comparative Cartography," pp. 76–77.

2. The Navigation Acts forced all colonial commerce to be carried on British vessels. The legislation adversely affected many American merchants. The Quartering Act, which compelled colonials to house British troops, was particularly offensive to New York residents since the headquarters of the British army was located there.

3. G. D. Scull, ed., *The Montresor Journals, Collections of the New-York Historical Society for the Year 1881* (New York, 1882), p. 342.

4. *Ibid.,* p. 375.

5. Although John Rocque died in 1762, his wife, Mary Ann Rocque, carried on his business.

6. Scull, ed., *Montresor Journals,* p. 392.

7. Release from the Duke of York to Berkeley and Carteret in Whitehead, ed., *Documents,* I; Snyder, *Mapping of New Jersey,* p. 14.

8. Evans, *Geographical . . . Essays,* in Gipson, *Lewis Evans,* p. 155.

9. *Ibid.,* pp. 21–22.

10. Scull, ed., *Montresor Journals,* p. 119.

46 PLAN / of the / CITY of NEW YORK, in / NORTH AMERICA: / Surveyed in the Years 1766 & 1767

Bernard Ratzer, cartographer; view based on a drawing by Captain-Lieutenant Thomas Davies; Thomas Kitchin, engraver; Thomas Jefferys and William Faden, publishers

London, January 12, 1776. Black-and-white line engraving with period color. H. 47½", W. 38⅝", in two sheets

Within an asymmetrical foliate border in the upper left corner is the inscription *To His Excellency/ Sir Henry Moore, Bar.ᵗ/ Captain General and Governour in Chief, In and Over HIS MAJESTY'S Province of/ NEW YORK/ and the Territories depending thereon in America/ Chancellor and Vice Admiral of the same./ This Plan,/ of the City of New York and its Environs,/ Survey'd and Laid down:/ Is most Humbly Dedicated, by His Excellency's/ Most Obed.ᵗ Humble Servant,/ B. Ratzer/ Lieut.ᵗ in His Majestys 60.ᵗʰ or/ Royal American Reg.ᵗ* Along the edge of the cartouche is engraved *Tho.ˢ Kitchin Sculp.ᵗ Engraver to His Late Royal Highness/ the Duke of York, &c.* The title cartouche in the lower left corner of the map is decorated with a scene suggestive of the fur trade. Beneath the title is a list of references on the map. The imprint, *London, Publishd according to Act of Parliament Jan.ʸ 12. 1776: by Jefferys & Faden. Corner of S.ᵗ Martins Lane. Charing Cross,* is adjacent to the title cartouche. In the lower right corner is a *Scale of 5000 Feet, Scale of One Mile,* and a *Scale of Yards.* Along the bottom is *A South West View of the City of New York, Taken from the Governours Island at ***

Two states of the map are known:
State 1: Lacking the imprint adjacent to the title cartouche. 1770
State 2: (this copy) As described

References: Cohen and Augustyn, *Manhattan in Maps*, pp. 73–77; Cumming, *British Maps*; Cumming, "Montresor-Ratzer-Sauthier Sequence of Maps," pp. 55–65; Deák, *Picturing America*, entry 121; Fowble, *Two Centuries of Prints in America*, entry 17; Guthorn, *British Maps of the American Revolution*, p. 39; Schwartz and Ehrenberg, *Mapping of America*, p. 192; Sellers and van Ee, *Maps and Charts of North America*, p. 242; Wallis, *American War of Independence*, entry 103

Bᴇʀɴᴀʀᴅ Rᴀᴛᴢᴇʀ's *Plan of the City of New York*, first published in October 1770, has been described as perhaps the finest map of an American city produced in the eighteenth century. The British recruited Ratzer, a Swiss-born engineer, to come to America and serve in the French and Indian War. He was commissioned as a lieutenant on February 20, 1756, in the 60th Regiment, the Royal American Regiment of Foot. By 1773, he had reached the rank of captain.[1]

Colonial resistance to the Stamp Act of 1765 led General Thomas Gage, commander in chief of British forces in America, to commission John Montresor to construct a new map of New York. Montresor's *Plan of the City of New York & its Environs* was a hasty and somewhat faulty production. *(see fig. 25)* Ratzer immediately began to compile a new map of the city that expanded and refined Montresor's effort. While Montresor illustrated Manhattan Island north through Greenwich Village, Ratzer extended his draft to cover all of the area to about where 50th Street is today. To the west, Ratzer included a portion of New Jersey; to the east, a large section of Brooklyn where uncultivated land still existed. He identified the streets and the buildings in the Bowery by name and added much more information about the wharves along the East River. Ratzer's precise depiction of a number of large estates showed ornamental plantings, tree-lined roads, and cultivated fields.

The view along the bottom of Ratzer's map, titled *A South West View of the City of New York, Taken from the Governours Island*, was drawn by Captain-Lieutenant Thomas Davies and provided an accurate depiction of the city as it appeared in 1760 from Governor's Island.[2] *(fig. 170)* Davies attended the Royal Military Academy at Woolwich, which was noted for instructing officers in topographical drawing.[3] From 1758 to 1760, he served under Sir Jeffery Amherst in Canada, producing a number of illustrations of the British campaigns against the French. During the course of his assignments in America, Davies painted more than forty topographical illustrations.[4] Several were included in a series of twenty-eight views known as *Sceneographia Americana*, published in London in 1768 from drawings by British military officers to commemorate England's victories in the French and Indian War.

Davies's view extends from the Jerseys on the left, to Manhattan from the Battery to Corlear's Hook (Crown Point on the map) in the center, then to a portion of the Long Island shoreline on the right. At one time, it was suggested that the cloud of smoke visible just above Saint George's Chapel represented the great fire of 1776; however, closer examination revealed that the smoke originated from a point on the shoreline where a ship was undergoing repairs. Further, the fire occurred on the west side of the city, while the smoke Davies illustrated was located on the east side. Finally, the first state of Ratzer's map was advertised for sale in the *New-York Gazette* in October 1770, six years before the fire of 1776.[5]

The title cartouche is composed of hogsheads and trunks that surround a colonist and a Native American. *(fig. 171)* In the center oval are two beavers, two hogsheads, and the blades and sails of a windmill. By depicting elements largely associated with the fur trade, the design

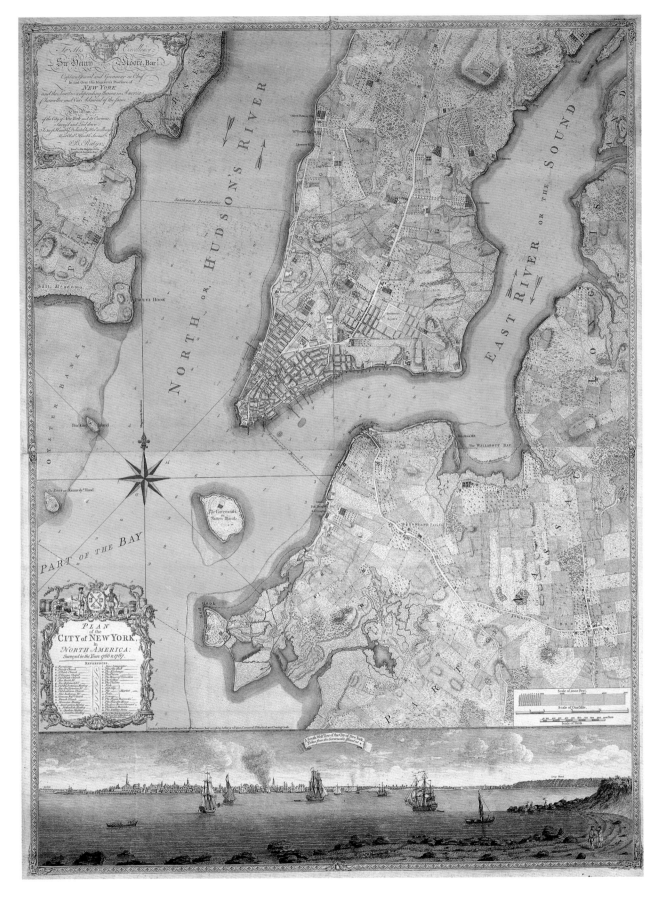

168 *Plan of the City of New York.* (Cat. 46)

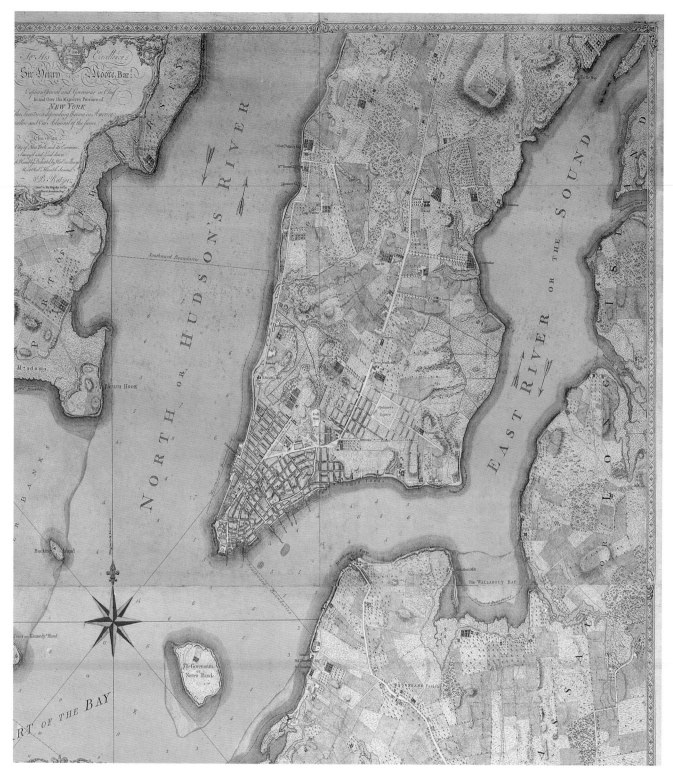

169 Detail from *Plan of the City of New York,* by Bernard Ratzer, London, January 12, 1776, black-and-white line engraving with period color. G1986-52, gift of Mrs. Anna Glen Vietor in memory of Alexander O. Vietor. (Cat. 46)

170 Detail of *A South West View of the City of New York*, by Thomas Davies, from *Plan of the City of New York*,
by Bernard Ratzer, London, January 12, 1776, black-and-white line engraving with period color.
G1986-52, gift of Mrs. Anna Glen Vietor in memory of Alexander O. Vietor. (Cat. 46)

reflects the industrial and commercial features of the colony.

Ratzer's map was first published by Thomas Kitchin, who also engraved and published John Mitchell's *Map of the British and French Dominions in North America* (Cat. 33).[6] In January 1776, Ratzer's map was reissued by the firm of Jefferys and Faden.[7]

G1986-52, gift of Mrs. Anna Glen Vietor in memory of Alexander O. Vietor

1. Cumming, *British Maps*, p. 97, n. 31.

2. Cohen and Augustyn, *Manhattan in Maps*, p. 76. The authors noted that the Davies view, which bears the date of 1760, first surfaced in the market in the mid-1980s and was purchased at auction by a private collector.

3. Stephen W. Sears, "The Lion's-Eye View: A British Officer Portrays Colonial America," *American Heritage Journal*, XXIX (1978), pp. 98–107.

4. *Ibid.*, p. 99.

5. The first issue of Ratzer's map bears no publication date. The date 1770 was assigned based on the *N.-Y. Gaz.* advertisement. Only two copies of the first state are known, Deák, *Picturing America*, entry 121.

6. Kitchin apprenticed to Emanuel Bowen in 1732, and, together with his son, became hydrographers to the king in 1773. As early as 1758, Kitchin had also served as engraver to the Duke of York. Kitchin was a proficient engraver and an artist as well. In addition to engraving maps, he also produced trade cards, decorative prints, portraits, books on drawing and painting, and political cartoons. Worms, "Kitchin's 'Journey of life,'" p. 4.

7. In 1764, Faden apprenticed under James Wigley, a Fleet Street engraver, and became a freeman of the Clothworkers' Company in 1771. Two years later, he became a partner in the firm of Thomas Jefferys, which had been operated by the family since Jefferys's death in 1771. Faden remained in partnership with the Jefferys family until 1776. For additional information on the relationship between the firm of Thomas Jefferys and William Faden, see Pedley, "Maps, War, and Commerce."

171 Detail of the cartouche from *Plan of the City of New York*, by Bernard Ratzer, London,
January 12, 1776, black-and-white line engraving with period color.
G1986-52, gift of Mrs. Anna Glen Vietor in memory of Alexander O. Vietor. (Cat. 46)

47 THE / PROVINCE of NEW JERSEY, / Divided into / EAST and WEST, / commonly called / THE JERSEYS

William Faden (based on surveys by Bernard Ratzer and Gerard Bancker), cartographer and engraver; published in *The North American Atlas, Selected from the Most Authentic Maps, Charts, Plans, etc.* by William Faden

London, December 1, 1777. Black-and-white line engraving with period outline color. H. 31½″, W. 23″, in two sheets

A rural scene with a farmhouse and trees with raccoons in the foreground surrounds the title in the upper left corner. Beneath is *Engraved & Published by W.ᴹ FADEN, Charing Cross,/ December 1.ˢᵗ 1777.* An inscription below the engraver's imprint is *This Map has been drawn from the Survey/ made in 1769 by order of the Commission-ers/ appointed to settle the partition Line between/ the Provinces of New York & New Jersey by/ Bernard Ratzer, Lieut.ᵗ in the 60.ᵗʰ Reg.ᵗ and/ from another large Survey of the Northern/ Parts in the possession of the Earl of Dunmore/ by Gerard Banker. The whole regulated and/ ascertained by Astronomical Observations.* In the lower right corner are *ASTRO-NOMICAL OBSERVATIONS,* longitude and latitude readings for five locations in America

Two states of the map are known:
State 1: (this copy) As described
State 2: The imprint was altered to *SECOND EDITION with consider-able Improvements/ Engraved & Published by W.ᴹ FADEN Charing Cross,/ December 1.ˢᵗ 1778.* Also added was the explanation that *In this Second Edition Great use has been/ made of several Military Surveys generously/ Communicated by Officers of the/ British Troops and of the Regiments/ of Hesse and Anspach*

References: Guthorn, *British Maps of the American Revolution,* p. 39; Lunny, *Early Maps of North America,* p. 28 and pl. XXII; Schwartz and Ehrenberg, *Mapping of America,* p. 193; Snyder, *Mapping of New Jersey,* pp. 57–59

WILLIAM FADEN, who compiled *The Province of New Jersey, Divided into East and West commonly called the Jerseys,* cred-ited the geography to surveys made by Lieutenant Bernard Ratzer and Gerard Bancker.[1] A survey by Bancker enabled Faden to modify the northern part of the colony. Little is known of Bancker's abilities as a mapmaker except that he served as a public surveyor in New York. He produced *A Map of the Province of New York* in 1772, and compiled *A Plan of Fort George in the City of New York* (date unknown).[2] According to Faden's inscription, Bancker gave a draft of his survey of northern New Jersey to John Murray, Earl of Dunmore, who fled Virginia in July 1776. After a brief stop in New York, Dunmore returned to London, apparently with Bancker's manuscript map.

Ratzer, an experienced surveyor and draftsman of the 60th Royal American Regiment of Foot, apparently sup-plied the initial draft of New Jersey. He had laid down the line between that colony and New York for the boundary survey of 1769 and included information regarding neigh-boring borders and rivers.[3] Ratzer's only known work relating specifically to New Jersey is a manuscript "Map of the Road from Trenton to Amboy" that he copied in 1762 from John Dalley's survey of 1745.[4]

Ratzer's 1769 survey was undertaken in an effort to resolve the century-long dispute over the location of the boundary line between the two colonies. The origins of the controversy lay in the casual wording of the 1664 grant from the Duke of York to the New Jersey proprietors and an inadequate understanding of the geography at the time the grant was made.[5] The issue remained unresolved until 1764 when George III appointed a commission to settle the line. Experienced surveyors Samuel Holland and William De Brahm rejected the claims of both colonies and decided on a compromise between the bounds that placed the northwestern point at the junction of the Neversink and Delaware Rivers at 40° 21′ 19″ rather than the former 41° 10′ as specified in the original grant.[6] From there, the line was to extend to the 41° of north latitude on the Hudson River. This ruling cost New Jersey several hundred thou-sand acres. In 1769, Bernard Ratzer was selected by the Boundary Commission to survey the new line. On Faden's map, the line drawn by Ratzer was noted as *Boundary as Settled by the Commissioners in 1769.*

Faden also illustrated a boundary dispute between East and West Jersey. In 1664, the Duke of York granted the New Jersey proprietary to John, Lord Berkeley, and Sir George Carteret. Due to financial difficulties, Lord Berke-ley was forced to sell his share to John Fenwick, a Quaker, the following year. About the same time, the king and the Duke of York were forced to issue new grants since the Dutch had briefly recaptured New York. Displeased that Berkeley had sold his rights to Fenwick, the duke renewed only Carteret's portion. Fenwick subsequently sold his ter-ritory to four Quaker proprietors, one of whom was William Penn. In order to clear their title, the four met with Carteret and executed a "Quintipartite" deed in 1676 that divided the colony into East Jersey and West Jersey. The boundary between the two colonies was to run in a straight line from the east side of Little Egg Harbor to the point on the Delaware at 41° 40′ north latitude.

Rapid growth in both halves of the colony created the need to survey the boundary. In 1687, George Keith, sur-veyor general for East Jersey, ran only a portion of the line, from Little Egg Harbor to the South Branch of the Raritan

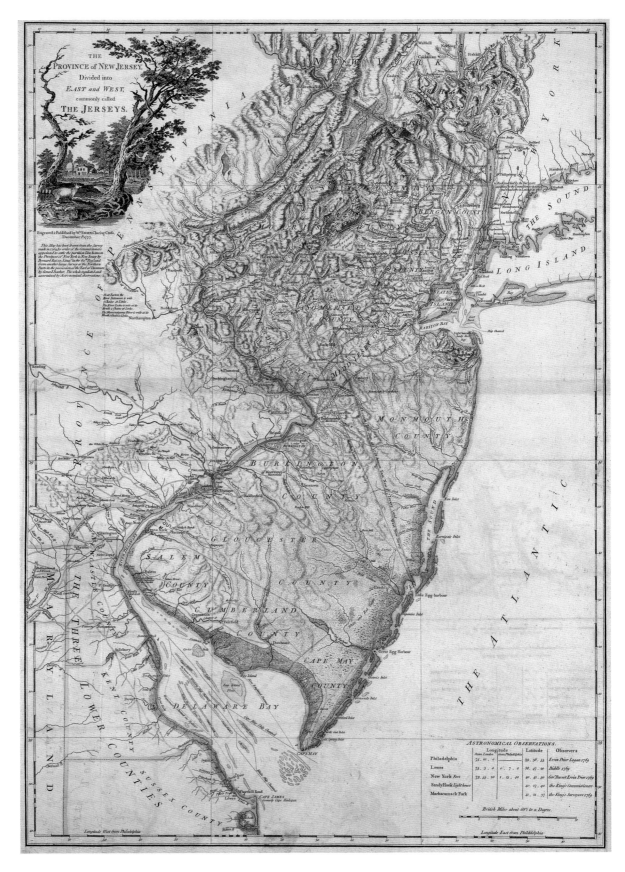

172 *The Province of New Jersey, Divided into East and West, commonly called the Jerseys.* (Cat. 47)

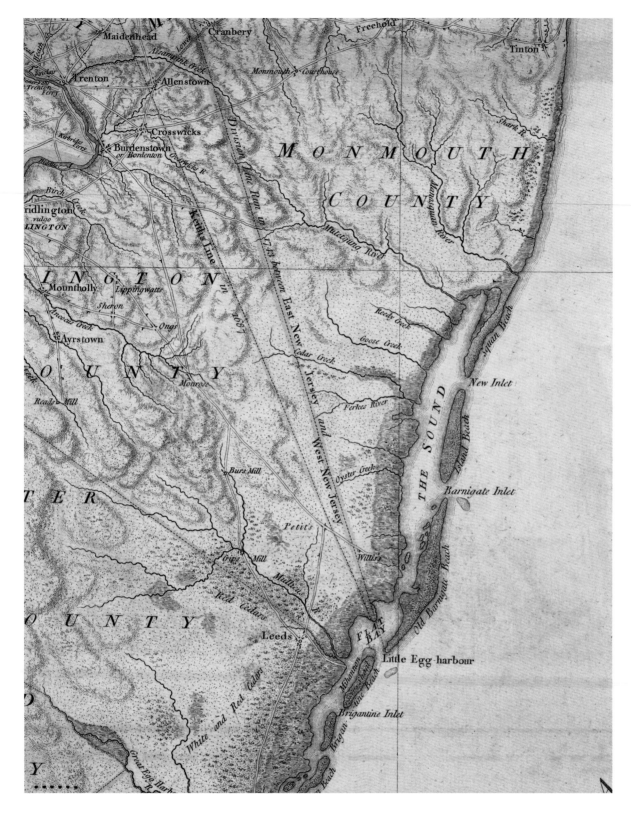

173 Detail from *The Province of New Jersey, Divided into East and West, commonly called the Jerseys,*
by William Faden, London, December 1, 1777, black-and-white line engraving with period
outline color. 1986-121. (Cat. 47)

River near Three Bridges, identified on Faden's map as *Keith's Line in 1687*. For the territory northwest of Three Bridges, the governors of East and West Jersey agreed on an operational boundary based largely on the courses of the rivers. As the population continued to increase, so too did the need to extend the boundary line. In 1719, the provincial legislatures appointed a commission to determine the northwesternmost point of the colony. They established the location of 41° 40' north latitude at a point on the Fishkill River they named Station Point. However, funds were not available to run the line until 1743. The East Jersey commissioners hired John Lawrence to survey the boundary that Faden included as the *Division Line Run in 1743 between East Jersey and West New Jersey*. Although the line was extended to Station Point, West Jersey did not officially recognize the decision and it remained in dispute until 1855.

Faden was apprenticed to a Fleet Street engraver named James Wigley in 1764. From 1773 to 1776, he was a partner in the firm of Thomas Jefferys, which the family had operated since the latter's death in 1771. According to Mary Pedley, the dissolution of Faden's partnership with the Jefferys firm was advertised in the *London Evening Post*, October 29–31, 1776.[7] Thereafter, Faden's maps bore only his name in the publisher's imprint.

1986-121

1. For more information on Bernard Ratzer, see Cat. 45. Faden misspelled Bancker's name as *Banker*.

2. Josephine French, ed., *Tooley's Dictionary of Mapmakers, A–D*, rev. ed. (Tring, Herts, Eng., 1999), p. 79.

3. Snyder, *Mapping of New Jersey*, p. 60.

4. *New Jersey Road Maps of the 18th Century*, 1964, reprint (Princeton, N. J., 1981), entry 1.

5. For a more detailed discussion of the dispute between New Jersey and New York regarding the boundary, see Cat. 44.

6. John E. Pomfret, *Colonial New Jersey: A History* (New York, 1973), p. 160.

7. For information on the relationship between the firm of Thomas Jefferys and William Faden, see Pedley, "Maps, War, and Commerce," p. 171, n. 11.

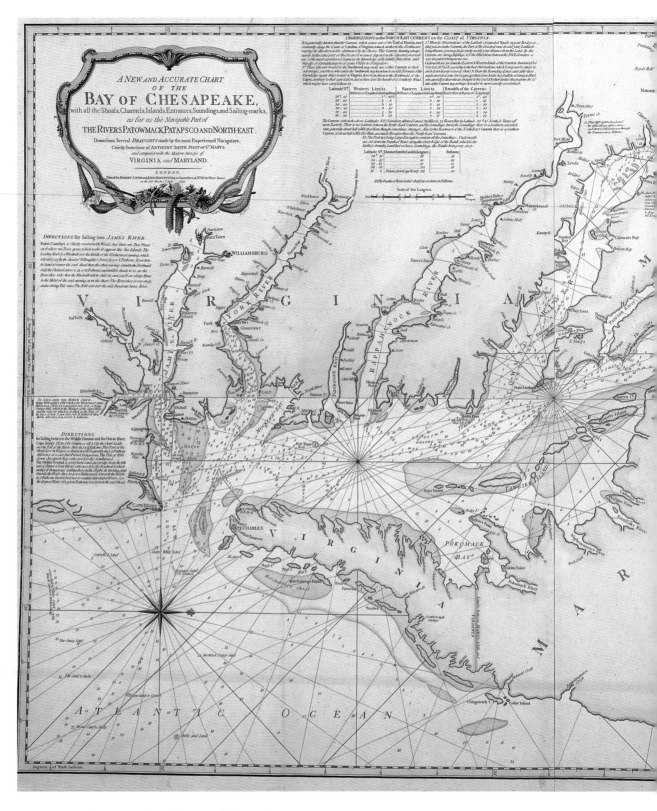

174 *A New and Accurate Chart of the Bay of Chesapeake.* (Cat. 48)

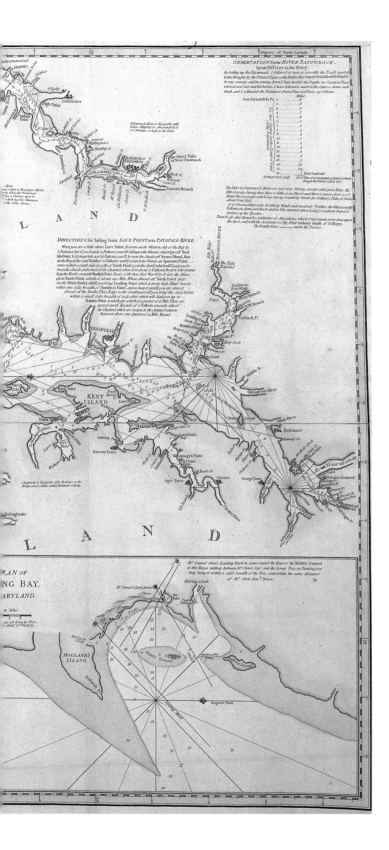

48 A NEW AND ACCURATE CHART / OF THE / BAY OF CHESAPEAKE, / with all the Shoals, Channels, Islands, Entrances, Soundings, and Sailing-marks, / as far as the Navigable Part of / THE RIVERS PATOWMACK, PATAPSCO AND NORTH-EAST. / Drawn from Several DRAUGHTS made by the most Experienced Navigators, / Chiefly from those of ANTHONY SMITH PILOT OF S.T MARYS; / and compared with the Modern Surveys of / VIRGINIA and MARYLAND

Anthony Smith, cartographer; engraver unknown; published in *The North American Pilot for New England, New York, Pensilvania, Maryland, and Virginia; also, the Two Carolinas, and Florida* by Robert Sayer and John Bennett

London, 1777 (originally published July 1, 1776). Black-and-white line engraving with modern color. H. 38½", W. 55⅞", in four sheets

The cartouche is in the upper left. Below the title is *LONDON./ Printed for ROBERT SAYER and JOHN BENNETT, Map & Chartsellers, at N.° 53 in Fleet Street./ as the Act directs. 1.st July 1776.* Various instructions for navigating are included throughout the map

Five states of the map are known:

State 1: The imprint was *London: Sayer & Bennett, 1st July 1776. With a Book of Directions. 1776*[1]

State 2: The title of the map was *A NEW AND ACCURATE CHART/ OF THE/ BAY OF CHESAPEAKE,/ with all the Shoals, Channels, Islands, Entrances, Soundings, and Sailing-marks,/ as far as the Naviga-ble Part of/ THE RIVERS PATOWMACK, PATAPSCO AND NORTH-EAST./ Drawn from several DRAUGHTS made by the most Experienced Navigators,/ and compared with the Modern Surveys of / VIRGINIA and MARYLAND.* The imprint was altered to *LONDON./ Printed for ROBERT SAYER and JOHN BENNETT, Map & Chartsellers, at N.° 53 in Fleet Street./ as the Act directs. 1.st July 1776. 1776*

State 3: (this copy) As described. The title was lengthened to include *Chiefly from those of ANTHONY SMITH PILOT of S*T*. MARYS.* Added to the upper right corner were *OBSERVATIONS in the RIVER PATOWMACK, by an Officer of the Navy* and in the center left directions were added *TO SAIL OVER THE HORSE SHOE. Degrees of North Latitude* was added in the upper right and lower left borders

State 4: John Bennett's name was deleted from the imprint below the title. The imprint now was *LONDON./ Printed for ROBERT SAYER Map, Chart & Printseller N.° 53 Fleet Street. 1783*

State 5: The lower imprint was altered to *London: Laurie & Whittle, 12th May, 1794. 1794*

References: Cresswell, "Colony to Commonwealth," pp. 59, 104–105; Morrison and Hansen, *Charting the Chesapeake,* pp. 32–22; Papenfuse and Coale, *Hammond-Harwood House Atlas,* p. 31; Stevens and Tree, "Comparative Cartography," entry 15; *The World Encompassed,* entry 247

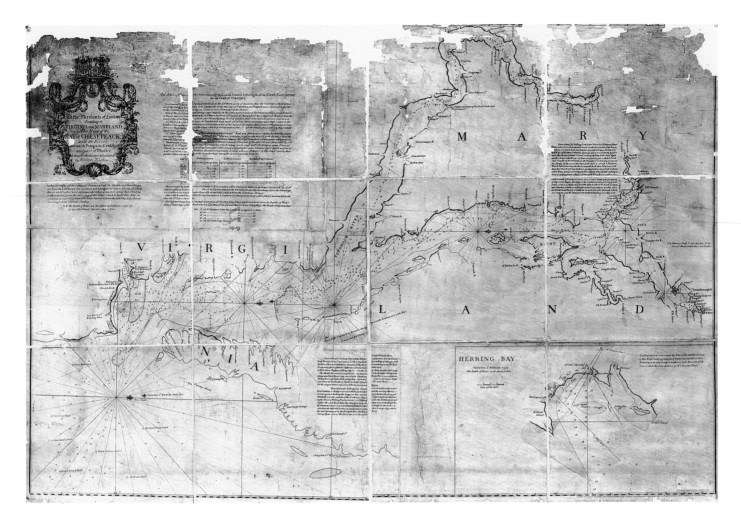

THE Chesapeake Bay and its tributaries shaped the development of Virginia and Maryland in several ways. They provided an internal system of transportation that facilitated settlement and trade since seaworthy ships could sail up the rivers and conduct transactions directly with individual plantation owners. The convenience of inland navigation made seaports unessential. The vast network of waterways allowed for the large-scale production of tobacco that enabled Virginia and Maryland to become the wealthiest English colonies on the North American mainland. The Chesapeake Bay's 48 principal tributaries have 102 branches that provide 1,750 miles of navigable routes.[2] Although the mouths of the major rivers that flow into the bay are broad and free of reefs, they contain numerous shoals and spits of sand that created challenges for colonial navigators. As a result, by the 1640s, men familiar with navigating local waters established themselves as pilots to assist merchant ships entering and exiting the bay. Ship captains who chose to avoid piloting fees or attempted to enter the bay when experienced pilots were unavailable often ran aground.

Although navigators who frequented the area recorded their courses and made observations that would be useful for subsequent voyages, the first large-scale marine chart of the Chesapeake Bay was not published until 1735. The information was compiled by Walter Hoxton, a merchant marine captain involved with the tobacco trade. *(fig. 175)* During his twenty-three voyages to Maryland, Hoxton made copious notes on shoals and currents and took numerous soundings. Instructions for navigating between Middle Ground and Horseshoe Shoals, entering the James River, and sailing from Love Point into the Patapsco River were engraved on his map. He also included a table to assist captains in determining their distance from land by providing soundings taken at various compass variations. One of his most important contributions was the inclusion of an extensive account of the Gulf Stream.

Although it supplied an indispensable tool for mariners navigating the Chesapeake Bay, Hoxton's chart delineated only those waters with which he was most familiar and omitted the important western shore tributaries—the James, York, Rappahannock, and Patuxent Rivers. Never-

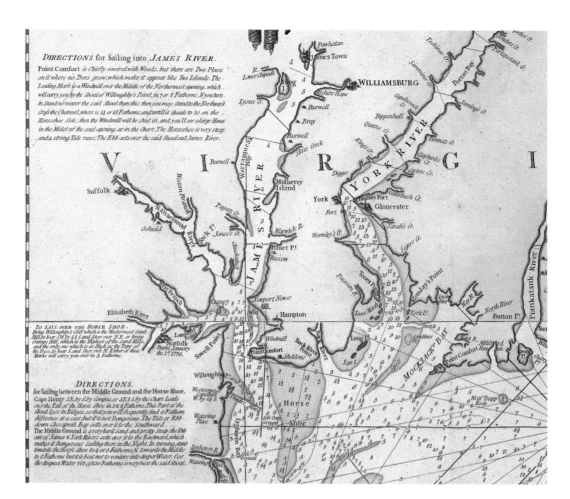

175 *To the Merchants of London Trading to Virginia and Maryland, This Mapp of the Bay of Chesepeack, with the Rivers Potowmack, Potapsco, North East. and part of Chester . . . ,* by Walter Hoxton, London, 1735, black-and-white line engraving. Courtesy, Maryland Historical Society, Baltimore.

176 Detail from *A New and Accurate Chart of the Bay of Chesapeake,* by Anthony Smith, London, 1777, black-and-white line engraving with modern watercolor wash. 1953-573. (Cat. 48)

theless, it remained the most useful work for the area until 1776, when Anthony Smith's *New and Accurate Chart of the Bay of Chesapeake* was published. Smith, a pilot in Saint Mary's County, Maryland, had assisted the royal navy in surveying the Potomac River. A significant portion of his work—format, orientation, and soundings in the bay—was borrowed from Hoxton. Like the earlier chart, Smith provided little information beyond the shoreline. He included the same instructions about how to navigate between Middle Ground and Horseshoe Shoals, enter the James River, and sail from Love Point into the Patapsco River, and Hoxton's observations on the Gulf Stream. Smith also incorporated the same inset map of Herring Bay in the lower right.[3]

Smith added a scale for longitude and latitude and provided many new soundings for Horseshoe Shoals, Middle Ground, and the Hampton Roads. He also included information on the tributaries along the western shore that Hoxton had omitted. Smith benefited from Joshua Fry and Peter Jefferson's *Map of the most Inhabited part of Virginia* from which he located the names of towns, islands, creeks, and plantations along the James, York, Rappahannock,

and Patuxent Rivers. He added other data along the Potomac and provided the soundings absent from the earlier work.

As the Revolutionary War approached, Smith's *New and Accurate Chart of the Bay of Chesapeake* filled an important niche for the British in planning military strategy. Less than two years after his chart was published in London in Sayer and Bennett's *North American Pilot,* it was copied by two French cartographers. George Louis Le Rouge published *Baye de Chesapeake en 4 Feuilles* for his *Pilote American Septentrional.* Later that year, another copy was made at the request of the French minister of the navy, Gabriel de Sartine, for the atlas *Neptune America-Septentrional.*

1953-573

1. Stevens and Tree, "Comparative Cartography," pp. 61–62.

2. Arthur Pierce Middleton, *Tobacco Coast: A Maritime History of Chesapeake Bay in the Colonial Era* (Newport News, Va., 1953), p. 31.

3. Hoxton's motivation for including an inset of Herring Bay may best be explained by the possibility that he was associated with Samuel Chew, whose house and plantation were located there. *Ibid.,* p. 75.

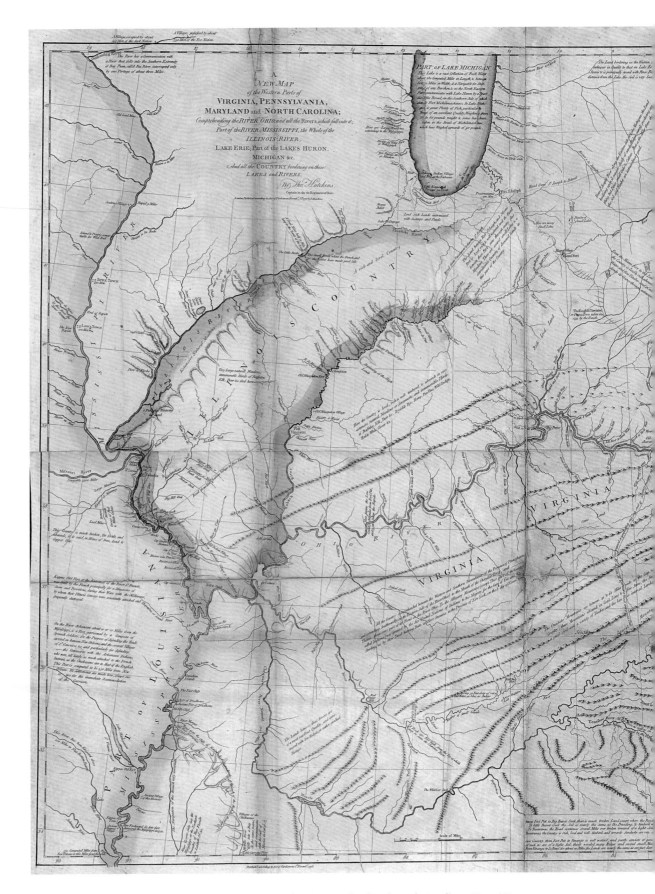

177 *A New Map of the Western Parts of Virginia, Pennsylvania, Maryland and North Carolina.* (Cat. 49)

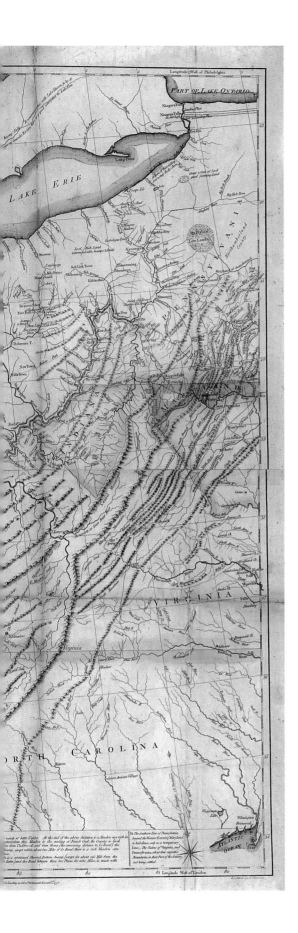

49 *A / NEW MAP / of the Western Parts of / VIRGINIA, PENNSYLVANIA, / MARYLAND and NORTH CAROLINA; / Comprehending the RIVER OHIO, and all the Rivers, which fall into it; / Part of the RIVER MISSISSIPPI, the Whole of the / ILLINOIS RIVER, / LAKE ERIE; Part of the LAKES HURON, / MICHIGAN &c. / And all the COUNTRY bordering on these / LAKES and RIVERS. / By Tho.ˢ Hutchins. / Captain in the 60 Regiment of Foot*

Thomas Hutchins, cartographer; John Cheevers, engraver; published to accompany *A Topographical Description of Virginia, Pennsylvania, Maryland, and North Carolina, Comprehending the Rivers Ohio, Kenhawa, Sioto, Cherokee, Wabash, Illinois, Missisippi, &c.* by Thomas Hutchins

London, November 1, 1778. Black-and-white line engraving with period color. H. 35¼", W. 43½", in four sheets

In the upper left beneath the title is the imprint *London, Published according to Act of Parliament Novemb.ʳ yᵉ 1ˢᵗ 1778 by T. Hutchins.* In the lower right are *Remarks* describing the terrain between certain locations. In the lower right and left, below the border, is another imprint, *Publish'd according to Act of Parliament Novemb.ʳ 1.ˢᵗ 1778.* Also below the border in the lower right is *Engrav'd by J. Cheevers*

One state of the map is known

References: Brown, *Early Maps of the Ohio Valley,* entry 51; Cresswell, "Colony to Commonwealth," pp. 58, 98–101; Guthorn, *British Maps of the American Revolution,* pp. 30–31; Sellers and Van Ee, *Maps and Charts of North America,* p. 169; Tucker, comp., *Indian Villages of the Illinois Country,* pl. XXIX

Lᴵᴛᴛʟᴇ is known about the early life of Thomas Hutchins, born in Monmouth County, New Jersey, in 1730. According to his obituary in the *New-York Daily Gazette,* his parents died when he was young. Rather than asking relatives for assistance, Hutchins "chose to seek some business; and accordingly before he was sixteen, went to the Western Country, where he was soon appointed an ensign, and paymaster-general to the forces there; after some time he became deputy engineer."[1] In 1757, his name was included in a list of officers serving in a Pennsylvania regiment later redesignated as the 60th Royal American Regiment of Foot. Led by General John Forbes, the 60th Regiment captured Fort Duquesne from the French on November 24, 1758. Forbes garrisoned the burned and abandoned fort with troops under the command of Colonel Hugh Mercer. While stationed at the renamed Fort Pitt, Hutchins, who served as lieutenant and quartermaster, laid out plans for new fortifications.[2]

Hutchins's reputation as a talented surveyor and engineer led to posts on the frontier that provided him with the opportunity to conduct new surveys and explore areas not yet adequately mapped by the British. He served as assistant engineer on Colonel Henry Bouquet's expedition north of the Ohio River to subdue and make peace with the Indians in 1764. Hutchins mapped their journey up the Ohio River from Fort Pitt to Big Beaver Creek and across country as far as the Muskingum River. The result of his work was *A Topographical Plan of that part of the Indian-Country through which the Army under the Command of Colonel Bouquet marched in the Year 1764*, published in Philadelphia in 1765. (fig. 178) In 1766, Hutchins investigated the territory acquired from France by the 1763 Treaty of Paris with Captain Harry Gordon, chief engineer in the Western Department of North America, and George Croghan, deputy Indian agent. He kept a journal of their trip from Philadelphia to Pittsburgh, then down the Ohio and the Mississippi Rivers to New Orleans. From there, the group proceeded from Lake Pontchartrain to the Atlantic Ocean, up the coast to Pensacola, Florida, and finally south to Havana, Cuba. During his travels, Hutchins recorded the territory he explored in preparation for his published work.

On December 20, 1771, Hutchins presented a preliminary *Account of the Countery of the Illinois* at a meeting of the American Philosophical Society.[3] The following May, he published his "PROPOSALS *for publishing, by Subscription, a* MAP *of the* INTERIOUR PARTS *of* NORTH AMERICA" in the *Virginia Gazette*:

> THIS MAP *comprehends the whole Country that lies between the thirty sixth and forty seventh Degrees of Latitude, and the seventy ninth and ninety fourth Degrees of Longitude; in which the great Rivers* Mississippi *and* Ohio, *with the numerous smaller Streams which empty into them, as well as the Lakes* Erie, Huron, *and* Michigan, *are accurately delineated; every considerable Town of the various* Indian *Nations which inhabit those Regions, with the Extent of their respective Claims, are also particularly pointed out.*
>
> *This Map contains an Extent of more than eight Hundred Miles in Length, and nearly seven Hundred in Breadth, which is not excelled, and hardly equalled, by any Country on the Face of the Earth, for its Beauty and the Fertility of its Soil, and which must soon become a most important and very interesting Part of the* British *Empire in* America. *The Author assures the Publick that a great*

> *Part of the Country, and most of the Rivers and Lakes, are laid down from Surveys, corrected by the Observations of Latitudes, carefully executed by himself, on the Campaigns he had the Honour of serving during the Whole of the last War, and the Department he has been constantly employed in since the final Treaty with the Western and Northern* Indians, *in 1764.*
>
> *This Map, which is delineated on a Scale of twenty Miles to an Inch, shall be neatly engraved, and accompanied with an Analysis, or a particular Description of the Face of the Country, its Lakes, Rivers, Timbers, Soil, and Climate. The Whole to be ready for Delivery as soon as the Subscribers amount to a Number adequate to defray the unavoidable Expense of the Publication.*
>
> *As the Author has been particularly requested, by a Number of Gentlemen, to undertake and publish this Map, and one Hundred Subscribers are already engaged, he wishes, for more speedily accomplishing the Design (and as the Work is meant and intended for the general Benefit and Information of his Majesty's good Subjects) that those who may think proper to encourage it will, as soon as possible, send their Names to the Post Office in* Williamsburg, Virginia.[4]

Hutchins's appeal to the American Philosophical Society and his advertisement in the *Virginia Gazette* suggest that he had already completed drafts by 1772. He must have made revisions, however, for he mentioned in the preface of *A Topograhical Description of Virginia, Pennsylvania, Maryland, and North Carolina*, printed to accompany the map, that his geography was based on observations made as late as 1775:

> *Those parts of the country lying* westward *of the* Allegheny *mountain, and upon the rivers* Ohio *and* Mississippi, *and upon most of the other rivers; and the lakes (laid down in my Map) were done from my own Surveys, and corrected by my own Observations of latitudes, made at different periods preceding, and during all the campaigns of the* last *war (in several of which I acted as an Engineer) and* since *in many reconnoitring tours, which I made through various parts of the country, between the years 1764 and 1775.*[5]

Hutchins continued his prefatory remarks by acknowledging the contributions of other mapmakers whose work had been helpful. He noted that William Gerard De Brahm had shared his observations and surveys and that he had relied on Lewis Evans for information on the branches of the Ohio and Allegheny Rivers.[6] Hutchins also said he

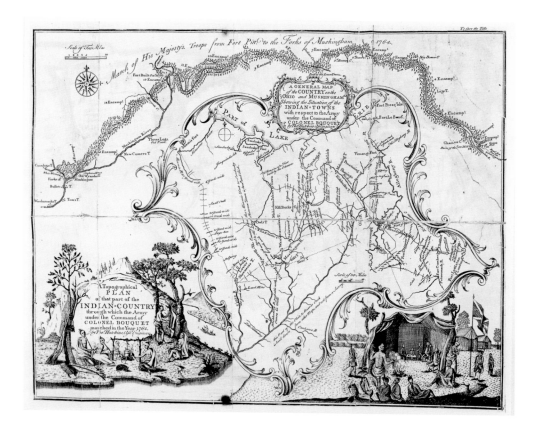

178 *A Topographical Plan of that part of the Indian-Country through which the Army under the Command of Colonel Bouquet marched in the Year 1764,* by Thomas Hutchins, Philadelphia, 1765, black-and-white line engraving. Courtesy, The Library Company of Philadelphia.

included the territory lying to the east of the Allegheny Mountains to illustrate new information on the location of navigable branches of the Ohio and Allegheny Rivers that flowed within close proximity to branches of rivers located in Virginia and Pennsylvania.

In addition to providing the first significant depiction of Trans-Appalachia, Hutchins included descriptions of the characteristics of the soil in various areas, places suitable for farming, the locations of meadowlands, timber, swamps, and deposits of salt, coal, petroleum, and lead. Buffalo hunting grounds were also indicated. Hutchins's map was one of only a few to show Vandalia, here "Indiana," proposed as the fourteenth colony during the late 1760s. Vandalia would have encompassed most of present-day West Virginia and Kentucky.

Hutchins went to London in 1777, and his map was published in November 1778. Still there in August 1779, Hutchins was taken into custody and charged with high treason for refusing to take up arms against his native country. He was accused of communicating information to Benjamin Franklin, then ambassador to the court of France. Hutchins noted that he was kept in Clerkenwell Prison for seven weeks, "loaded with irons, put among felons, and treated with every kind of severity and insult, and forbidden to see or write to his friends."[7] Once

released, Hutchins went to France before sailing to Charleston, South Carolina, where he served in the southern army under General Greene. On July 11, 1781, he was appointed geographer general to the United States, a post he held until his death.

1974-664

1. *New-York Daily Gazette* (New York, N.Y.), May 20, 1789.

2. Hutchins's plan of Fort Pitt and the surrounding country is in the collections of the Historical Society of Pennsylvania, Philadelphia. Frederick Charles Hicks, ed., *Thomas Hutchins, A Topographical Description of Virginia, Pennsylvania, Maryland, and North Carolina, Reprinted from the original edition of 1778* (Cleveland, Ohio, 1904), p. 14.

3. *Ibid.,* p. 19.

4. *Va. Gaz.* (Purdie and Dixon), May 28, 1772.

5. Hutchins, *Topographical Description,* preface.

6. Hutchins noted, "I have compared my own Observations, and Surveys, respecting the lakes, with those made by Captain Brehm, of the 60th Regiment of Foot (who was for many years employed as an Engineer in North America) and I find, that they correspond with more exactness than Surveys usually do, which are made by different persons, at different times;—and I am happy in this opportunity, of expressing my obligations to this Gentleman, for the cheerfulness with which he furnished me with his Surveys and Remarks. It is fit also, that I should take notice that in the account which I have given of several of the *branches* of the Ohio, and Alleghany rivers, I have adopted the words of the late ingenious Mr. Lewis Evans, as I found he had properly described them in the Analysis to his Map of the Middle Colonies." *Ibid.*

7. *Ibid.,* p. 23.

50 *To the American / Philosophical Society, / This. Map of the PENINSULA / Between DELAWARE & / CHESOPEAK BAYS / with the said Bays / and Shores adjacent / drawn from the most / Accurate Surveys is / inscribed by / John Churchman*

John Churchman, cartographer; attributed to Henry Dawkins, engraver[1]

Probably Philadelphia, ca. 1779. Black-and-white line engraving with period outline color. H. 22⅝", W. 17⅜"

In the lower center is a *Scale of British Statute Miles.* The title is contained within the lower right portion of a two-part rococo cartouche, the upper portion of which is blank

Two states of the map are known:
State 1: (this copy) As described
State 2: The word *humbly* was inserted before *inscribed* in the title. The Susquehanna River was extended northward beyond the upper border of the map to Middletown and seven new tributaries were added above the *Canawango* in Pennsylvania. 1786

References: Morrison et al., *On the Map*, fig. 47; Papenfuse and Coale, *Hammond-Harwood House Atlas*, pp. 59–60; Ristow, *American Maps and Mapmakers*, pp. 118–119; Sellers and van Ee, *Maps and Charts*, pp. 295–296; Wheat and Brun, *Maps and Charts*, entry 477

T HE Chesapeake Bay and its tributaries were the most significant factors in defining the economic development of the surrounding colonies. They provided an internal system of transportation that stimulated economic growth and enabled planters to transport goods to market efficiently and conveniently. As the colonies expanded west, they continued to rely on water routes for trade. To avoid the high costs of land transportation over an inadequate road system, farmers in central Maryland and Pennsylvania shipped produce to Baltimore by way of the Susquehanna River, which empties into the Chesapeake Bay. Thus, Baltimore had grown dramatically as a major port by the 1750s and 1760s.

Philadelphia merchants believed that much of the profit from trade passing through Baltimore rightfully belonged to them since significant amounts of that city's commerce, primarily its trade in grain, originated in western Pennsylvania. In an effort to recoup the revenue lost to Baltimore, Thomas Gilpin, a prosperous Quaker merchant, began to study the feasibility of constructing a canal to link the Chesapeake with Delaware Bay, thereby providing an efficient route from western Pennsylvania and Maryland to Philadelphia via the Susquehanna. A canal would also

shorten the voyage between Baltimore and Philadelphia by more than three hundred miles. Gilpin explored the Delmarva Peninsula for potential routes, ultimately proposing five.[2] In February 1769, Gilpin presented his recommendations to a group of Philadelphia merchants. Favorably impressed, they enlisted the assistance of the American Philosophical Society, a group to which Gilpin belonged. On February 17, 1769, his proposals were discussed by the society, which responded by assembling an eight-man committee to survey the lower counties of Delaware to determine the best route.[3] After considering several options, the committee ultimately recommended the construction of both a canal and a road from the Susquehanna to Christiana Bridge in New Castle County, Delaware.[4]

No further mention of the proposed canal appeared in the minutes of the society until ten years later when, on July 23, 1779, "Mr Churchman gave in a memorial relative to a map of the peninsula between Delaware & Chesapeake bays including thirteen counties, asking its examination and recommendation to the public."[5] John Churchman was a surveyor for Delaware, Chester, Bucks, and part of Lancaster Counties, Pennsylvania.

This *Map of the Peninsula between Delaware & Chesopeak Bays*, dedicated to the society, was certainly the one Churchman had presented. One month later, the society responded:

> We are of opinion that he is possessed of sufficient materials, both astronomical observations and actual surveys, to enable him to construct an accurate map, and have no doubt but that he has executed his design with exactness and care, but we can not help expressing our desires of seeing the map laid down on a much larger scale, which would render it more serviceable for promoting the Knowledge of Geography.[6]

Judging from the small scale of the published version and the difficulty in deciphering the locations of his proposed canal routes, it is apparent that Churchman did not take the committee's advice to enlarge the scale.

The only other known published work by Churchman was *An Explanation of the Magnetic Atlas, or Variation Chart, Hereunto annexed; Projected on a Plan Entirely New, By which the Magnetic Variation on any Part of the Globe may be precisely Determined.*[7] Accompanied by a map, the book was published in Philadelphia in 1790. Announcing his proposal to publish this work in the New York *Daily Advertiser*, Churchman substantiated his abilities by citing his previous map:

J. CHURCHMAN returns his cordial thanks to all those who

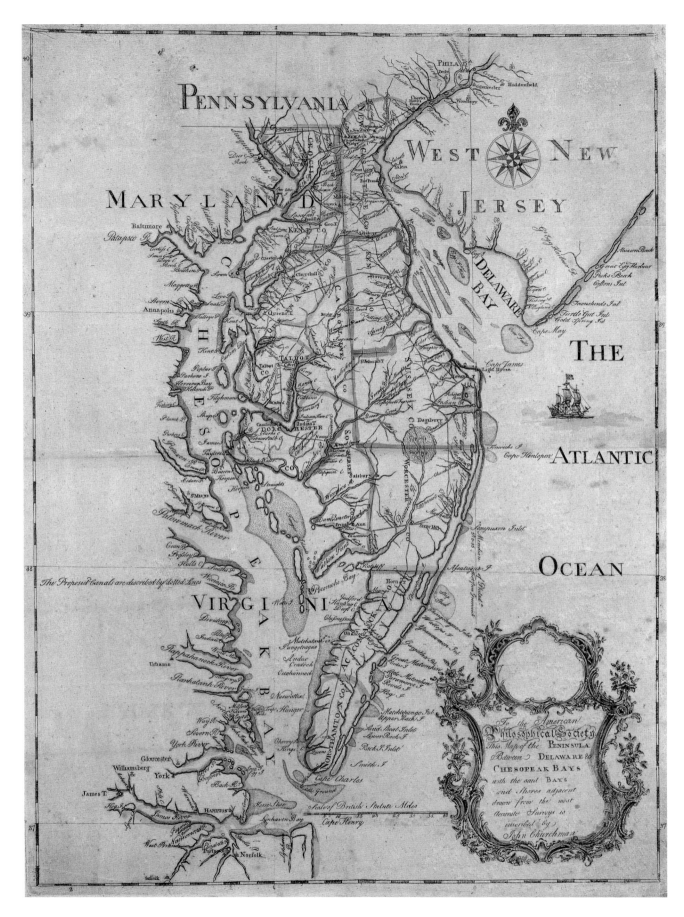

179 *Map of the Peninsula Between Delaware & Chesapeak Bays.* (Cat. 50)

180 Detail from *Map of the Peninsula Between Delaware & Chesopeak Bays,* by John Churchman, probably Philadelphia, ca. 1779, black-and-white line engraving with period outline color. G1995-145, gift of Mrs. Anna Glen Vietor in memory of Alexander O. Vietor. (Cat. 50)

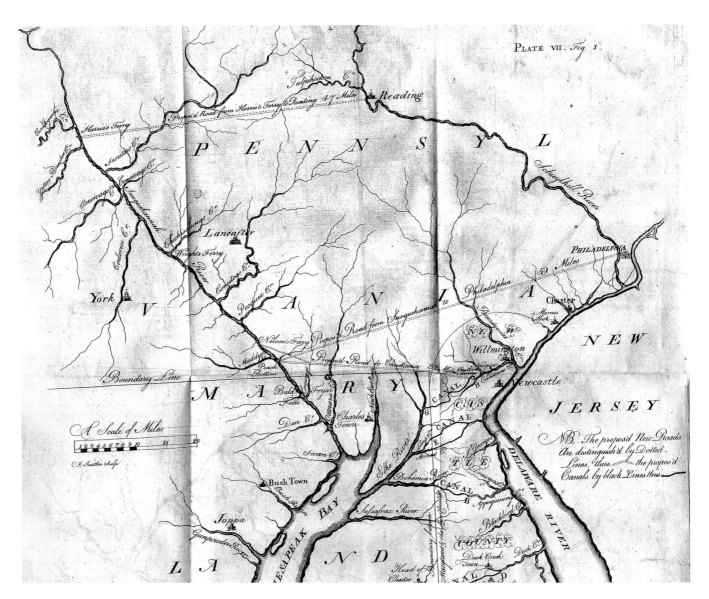

PLATE VII. *Fig. 1*

181 Detail from a map of Pennsylvania, Maryland, and New Jersey showing the roads and canals proposed to link the Delaware and Chesapeake Bays, by W. Thomas Fisher, Philadelphia, 1771, black-and-white line engraving. Courtesy, American Philosophical Society, Philadelphia, Pa.

so liberally furnished him during the late war with materials and other encouragment relating to his map of the peninsula between Chesapeak and Delaware bays including the said bays, the shores adjacent, the maritime parts of West-Jersey, Pennsylvania, Maryland, Virginia and all the Delaware state; and he flatters himself, (although it was performed under many disadvantages) that this small specimen of his first publication in the line of his profession will operate in the public minds, in Favour of the present undertaking.[8]

G1995-145, gift of Mrs. Anna Glen Vietor in memory of Alexander O. Vietor

1. Stauffer noted that the engraving style resembled Dawkins's work and thus ascribed this map to him. *American Engravers*, p. 79.

2. Ralph D. Gray, *The National Waterway: A History of the Chesapeake and Delaware Canal, 1769-1965* (Urbana, Ill., 1967), p. 5.

3. *Ibid.*, pp. 5–6, n. 7.

4. *Ibid.*, p. 6.

5. *Early Proceedings of the American Philosophical Society for the Promotion of Useful Knowledge* (Philadelphia, Pa., 1884), p. 103.

6. *Ibid.*, p. 104.

7. For a discussion of this work, see William Ravenhill, "Churchman's Contours?" *Map Collector*, XXXIV (1986), pp. 22–25.

8. *Daily Advertiser*, May 21, 1789.

Labels on map (as engraved):

7° W. Lon.

Bellerika
Minutemen
Wooburn
Minutemen
Medford
Maldon
Bridges River
Militia
Lexington
Lord Percy's return from Lexington
Chelsea
Rock
Concord
Bridge where the attack began
Col. Smith's return from Concord.
Monatomy
Gen.l Putnam's Camp
Charles Town
Winnsimit
Noddles I.
Provincials firing behind the Walls.
Part of Winter Hill
Ferry Boat
Baker's Brook
P L A I N
Cambridge
Water Hill
Phipp's Farm
BOSTON
Waltham
Water Town
Head Quarters
17
Charles R.
Governor's
Brookline
Dorchester Neck
WATER TOWN
Bridge
Road to Worcester
Castle W.m
King R
Weston
Water Town Hill
Principal part of the Provincial Army as encamped commanded by Gen.l Washington
Roxbury Hill
Dorchester
Thompsons
Speeta
JAMAICA PLAIN
Jamaica Pond
Gen.l Ward's Camp
Mill R.
Moon I.
Falls
Milton
Falls
Mr. Walters
Meeting House
Hangman
Needham
Aleon I.
Mother Brook
Stoughton
Bluehills
Quincey Creek
Deadham
Napensit
A Scale of Miles.
Nantick
7° W. Lon.
Weymouth
Bran

Cartouche:

12.25.

A PLAN OF THE
TOWN and HARBOUR of
BOSTON.

and the Country adjacent with the Road
from Boston to Concord
Shewing the Place of the late Engagement
between the King's Troops & the Provincials,
together with the several Encampments of
both Armies in & about Boston.

Taken from an Actual Survey
Humbly Inscribed to Rich.d Whitworth
Esq.r Member of Parliament for Stafford.
By his most Obedient Servant
I. De Costa

REFERENCES.
1. The Nautilus Man of War lying above Charles
Town Ferry 400 yards to Boston
2. The Lively Man of War
3. Men of War before Boston
4. Gen.l Gage's Camp on
the Common.
5. Bacon Hill
6. Fort Hill
7. Copps Hill.
8. Gen.l Gage's Line on
on Boston Neck.
9. The Fortification.
10. South Battery
11. North Battery
12. Provincial Battery
gained by the Kings Troo
in the Battle 17 of June 1775
13. Bunkers Hill at Cha.T.
14. School Hill at D.o
15. Stores & Cannon destr.
by the Kings Troops
16. The Schooner burnt at
Noddles Island by Gen.l
Putnam.
17. Watch Boat from the
Men of War.
18. Gen.l Thomas's lines
on Boston Neck.
19. Mill Pond

182 *A Plan of the Town and Harbour of Boston.* (Cat. 51)

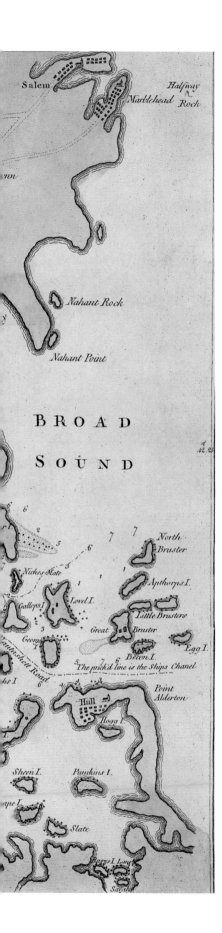

51 *A PLAN OF THE / TOWN and HARBOUR of / BOSTON. / and the County adjacent with the Road / from Boston to Concord / Shewing the Place of the late Engagement / between the King's Troops & the Provincials, / together with the several Encampments of / both Armies in & about Boston. / Taken from an Actual Survey / Humbly Inscribed to Rich^d. Whitworth / Esqr. Member of Parliament for Stafford. / By his most Obedient Servant / J: De Costa*

Jonathan Carver, probable cartographer; C. Hall, engraver; John De Costa, publisher

London, July 29, 1775. Black-and-white line engraving with period color. H. 14½", W. 18¾" (trimmed)

The title and dedication are contained in a rectangular box in the center left. Below, also in a rectangular box, is a list of nineteen *REFERENCES* that refer to locations on the map. Beneath the lower border is the imprint *London Publish'd as the Act directs July 29.th 1775. by J. De Costa Red Cross Street Southwark*

Four states of the map are known:
State 1: One of the islands in Boston Harbor was named *Castle I.* Reference 2 was noted as *The Somers Man of War.* 1775
State 2: *Castle I.* was altered to *Castle W^m* and *Fort* was added. *Wodbourn* was altered to *Woodburn* and the name *Charles Town* was moved from water to land. Reference 2 was changed to *The Lively Man of War.* 1775
State 3: (this copy) As described. A change of command in the camps located just outside Boston was recorded on the map. In the first two states, Water Town Hill was under the command of General Ward and Roxbury Hill was under General Thomas. These were changed to reflect General Washington's command of Water Town and Roxbury under General Ward.[1] 1775
State 4: The imprint was changed to *London. J Hand, Decr 6th 1775.* 1775

References: Cumming, *British Maps*, pp. 65–66, 8–81; Fite and Freeman, *Book of Old Maps*, entry 64; Guthorn, *British Maps of the American Revolution*, p. 19; Nebenzahl, *Atlas of the American Revolution*, pp. 39–41; Nebenzahl, *Bibliography of Printed Battle Plans*, entry 1; Ristow, *American Maps and Mapmakers*, pp. 40–42; Schwartz and Ehrenberg, *Mapping of America*, p. 188; Sellers and van Ee, *Maps and Charts of North America*, p. 196

Following the Seven Years' War, the British government enacted legislation to help defray the costs of the conflict and to fund the deployment of additional troops needed to maintain peace in the newly acquired territories. One of the new revenue-producing measures, the Tea Act offered relief to the financially troubled East India Company, in which many prominent English merchants and aristocrats were investors, by shifting some of the previously paid duties on tea to the American colonies. Parliament granted the company a rebate if the tea was subsequently reexported to America. The revenue lost to the British government was recovered through a three-pence-per-pound tax on the commodity that was to be collected immediately upon its arrival in the colonies. Under the favorable terms of the act, the East India Company dumped large quantities of tea on the America market. The price was kept artificially high by selling through favored American consignors rather than offering it through public auction.

The passage of the Tea Act aroused a great deal of hostility in America. It demonstrated Parliament's willingness to sacrifice the economic interest of the colonies for those of the English merchant class. Furthermore, an important political issue was at stake: denying the English colonists a say in deciding the laws under which they were to be taxed. On November 16, 1773, a crowd of angry Bostonians threw 342 chests of East India Company tea, valued between £11,000 and £18,000, into the harbor.

The Boston Tea Party forced the British government to take a hard line with the Massachusetts provincials. Consequently, Parliament enacted the Coercive Acts—or, as they were often referred to in the colonies, the Intolerable Acts—that effectively abolished the elected upper house of the Massachusetts General Assembly. Equally disturbing was the Boston Port Act, which closed the city's harbor to all shipping unless restitution was made to the East India Company. Attempting to restrain the Boston patriots, George III appointed General Thomas Gage, commander of the British forces in North America, as royal governor of Massachusetts. Gage recognized the need to strengthen the British military presence in Boston and immediately requested additional troops to fortify the city.

Gage became aware that the surrounding towns were gradually withdrawing gunpowder and arms from the Middlesex County Powder House on Quarry Hill near Cambridge, so the British confiscated much of the remaining supply and removed it to Castle William on September 1, 1774. Gage also learned that the Massachusetts Provisional Congress had stored a significant amount of ammunition in the town of Concord. Accordingly, on April 19, 1775, he dispatched a corps of grenadiers and light infantry under the command of Lieutenant Colonel Francis Smith to destroy the military stores there. What ensued was the first battle of the Revolutionary War, which was graphically depicted in De Costa's *Plan of the Town and Harbour of Boston and the County adjacent with the Road from Boston to Concord*.

When the British troops began their march toward Lexington, Smith sent Major John Pitcairn with a detachment ahead to secure the bridge over the Concord River. Forewarned by Paul Revere and William Dawes, about seventy local minutemen under the command of Captain John Parker assembled on Lexington green to await Pitcairn's arrival. Although no one knows who initiated the skirmish in Lexington, British soldiers fired several volleys, killing numerous rebels. Joined by Smith and the remaining troops, Pitcairn's forces returned to their formations and continued toward Concord. Upon their arrival, they discovered that the majority of the military stores had been hidden or removed. The British destroyed what remained of the patriot arsenal on their way to North Bridge, their final destination, where a British soldier fired the first shot followed by a volley from the front rank. *(fig. 183)* Within seconds the provincials advanced, firing. Nearly twenty redcoats were killed. Surprised by the colonists' willingness to fight, the British retreated to Concord.

Realizing that the return to Boston would be more difficult than the march to Lexington and Concord had been, Smith sent a messenger to Gage requesting additional support. In reality, the retreat proved to be even more difficult than Smith had anticipated because the local militia hid in ambush and fired on the British.

The confrontations at Lexington and Concord were of little significance militarily, but they did prove to be of psychological importance. While the British accomplished their mission by destroying what patriot ammunition remained in Concord, the Americans proved to be more competent militarily than expected. On the day after their retreat from Lexington, Lord Hugh Percy wrote:

Whoever looks upon them as an irregular mob, will find himself much mistaken. They have men amongst them who know very well what they are about, having been employed as Rangers agst the Indians & Canadians, & this country being much covd w. wood, and hilly, is very advantageous for their method of fighting.

Nor are several of their men void of a spirit of enthusiasm, as we experienced yesterday, for many of them concealed themselves in houses, & advanced within 10 yds. to fire at me & other officers, tho' they were morally certain of being put to death themselves in an instant . . . . They are determined to go thro' with it, nor will the insurrection here turn out so despicable as it is perhaps imagined at home. For my part, I never believed, I confess, that they wd have atacked the King's troops, or have had the perseverance I found in them yesterday.[2]

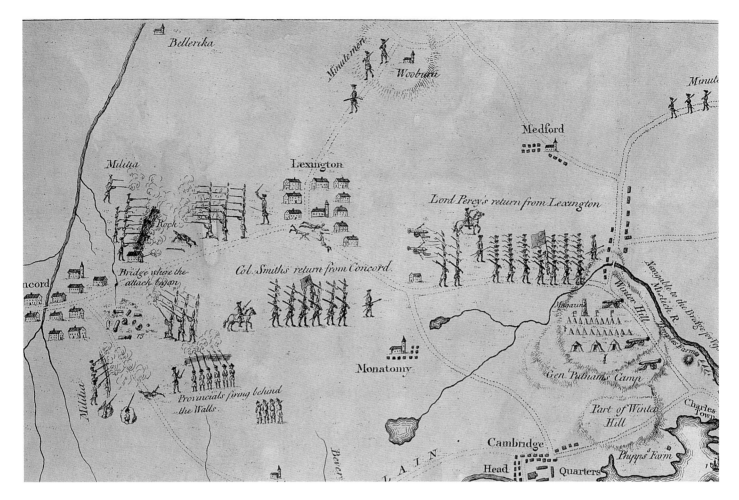

Labels within the map image:

Bellerika

Minutemen

Wooburn

Minut[e]

Medford

Militia

Lexington

Lord Percy's return from Lexington

Naviable to the Bridge for [...]

Rock

Col. Smith's return from Concord

Bridge where the attack began

[n]cord

Mower Hill

Magazine

Gen. Putnam's Camp

75

Monatomy

Provincials firing behind the Walls

Militia

Part of Winter Hill

Charles Town

Phyps's Farm

Beaver

Cambridge

[P]LAIN

Head

Quarters

183 Detail from *A Plan of the Town and Harbour of Boston,* by John De Costa, London, July 29, 1775, black-and-white line engraving with period color. 1963-730. (Cat. 51)

Surviving among the personal papers of General Percy is a manuscript map very similar in content to that published by De Costa. It appears that the surveyor who accompanied Percy's forces made duplicate copies, one of which was sent to London. The supposition that Captain Jonathan Carver was involved in the production of the printed map along with De Costa is supported in a letter of August 8, 1775, from Isaac Foster to Major Robert Rogers in which he wrote, "Carver and Dacosta have finished a new plan of Boston at the request of Whitworth."[3] Richard Whitworth, to whom the De Costa map was dedicated, supported a plan devised by Carver to cross the American continent.[4] Carver appears to have been a surveyor and draftsman with experience in mapmaking because several works by his hand survive in the collections of the British Museum. Born in Massachusetts and educated in America, Carver was wounded at the siege of Fort William Henry in 1757. In 1760, he became a captain in a Massachusetts regiment. Nothing else is known of the career of John De Costa.

1963-730

1. I would like to thank Joan Dolmetsch, whose work with Jeanette Black identified this state and brought it to my attention.

2. William P. and Elizabeth C. Cumming, "The Treasure at Alnwick Castle," *American Heritage,* XX (1969), p. 100.

3. John Thomas Lee, "Captain Jonathan Carver: Additional Data," *Proceedings of the State Historical Society of Wisconsin for 1912* (Madison, Wis., 1913), p. 101.

4. *Ibid.,* p. 102.

52 *A PLAN / OF THE / ACTION AT BUNKERS HILL, / on the 17th. Of June 1775. / Between HIS MAJESTY'S TROOPS, / Under the Command of MAJOR GENERAL HOWE, / AND THE REBEL FORCES. / By LIEUT T. PAGE of the Engineers, / who acted as Aide de Camp to General Howe in that Action. / NB. The Ground Plan is from an Actual / Survey by Capt.n Montresor*

Lieutenant Thomas Hyde Page (after John Montresor), cartographer; engraver unknown; published in *The North American Atlas, Selected from the Most Authentic Maps, Charts, Plans, etc.* by William Faden

London, ca. 1775–1778. Black-and-white line engraving with period color. H. 20", W. 17⅞"

In the lower left are *REFERENCES to the PLANS* that provide a key to the letters on the map and its attachment. The title and *Scale of Yards* are in the upper right. An accompanying overlay was engraved to be attached in the center right portion of the map

Two states of the map are known:
State 1: (this copy) As described
State 2: The title was altered for Charles Stedman's *THE HISTORY OF THE ORIGIN, PROGRESS, AND TERMINATION OF THE AMERICAN WAR*. It then was *A PLAN/ OF THE/ ACTION AT BUNKERS HILL,/ on the 17th. Of June 1775./ Between HIS MAJESTY'S TROOPS,/ Under the Command of MAJOR GENERAL HOWE,/ AND THE AMERICAN FORCES./Engraved for STEDMAN'S HISTORY of the American War./ Published by the Author April 12.th 1793.* An explanation of the symbols for the royal and American armies was added in the lower right. 1793

References: Guthorn, *British Maps of the American Revolution*, pp. 37–38; Macklin, "New England Plates," p. 102; McCorkle, *America Emergent*, entry 65; Nebenzahl, *Atlas of the American Revolution*, pp. 46–47; Nebenzahl, *Bibliography of Printed Battle Plans*, entry 29; Schwartz and Ehrenberg, *Mapping of America*, p. 191; Wallis, *American War of Independence*, entry 53

FOLLOWING the skirmishes at Lexington and Concord, both sides realized that future conflicts were inevitable. While wary of Gage's abilities as a military leader, the British cabinet heeded his request for reinforcements by dispatching additional troops under Generals William Howe, Henry Clinton, and John Burgoyne. Patriot troops added recruits from Connecticut, New Hampshire, and Rhode Island and positioned themselves in an arc around Boston, thereby confining the British troops to the city.

The British generals devised a plan to secure Boston by seizing the highest promontories on the Dorchester and Charlestown peninsulas, which overlooked the city. Fortifications on these two locations would prevent their occupation by the rebels. Having been alerted by patriot sympathizers, the Provincial Congress ordered the assembled militia to seize, establish, and maintain a force on Bunker Hill. Thus, on the evening of June 16, the provincial army moved under cover of darkness to Charlestown Heights and constructed earthworks on Breed's Hill, the smaller of the two promontories. At dawn, the British sloop *Lively* spotted the patriot position and opened fire. After debating their options, the British generals decided on a frontal assault. Howe and his forces moved into position at high tide in the afternoon, landed at Charlestown Point, and marched in columns of four along the shore of the Mystic River. The first two attacks by the Redcoats were met with concentrated musket fire from the Americans that decimated their front lines. Howe's third attempt was more successful. The Americans, suffering from a shortage of ammunition, allowed the British to penetrate the redoubt and were forced to retreat to nearby Bunker Hill.

A Plan of the Action at Bunkers Hill is the most detailed contemporary representation of the battle. It depicts the redoubt constructed by the Americans from a correct geographical perspective; however, like most maps of the battle, the names of Bunker Hill and Breed's Hill were transposed and the battle has been mistakenly known as the battle of Bunker Hill. As stated in the title of the map, the actual survey of Charlestown was made by Captain Lieutenant John Montresor although the detailed delineation of the battle was executed by Lieutenant Thomas Hyde Page, an engineer and aide-de-camp to General Howe.

Page depicted the battle from start to finish beginning with the first landing, the troop positions, and the lines of march. He designed the map using an overlay to provide the information in a logical sequence. Although not a common practice, some military engineers used overlays to illustrate the stages of a particular battle.[1] Prepared using the same scale as the underlying map, the overlay illustrated the events of the initial attack during which the British were repulsed. *(fig. 185)* The information beneath the overlay portrayed the successful penetration by the British troops. *(fig. 186)* Although victorious, the British realized that the Americans were capable of waging a strong campaign against their most experienced soldiers.

William Faden, the publisher, was a partner in the firm of Thomas Jefferys from 1773 until 1776. After that time,

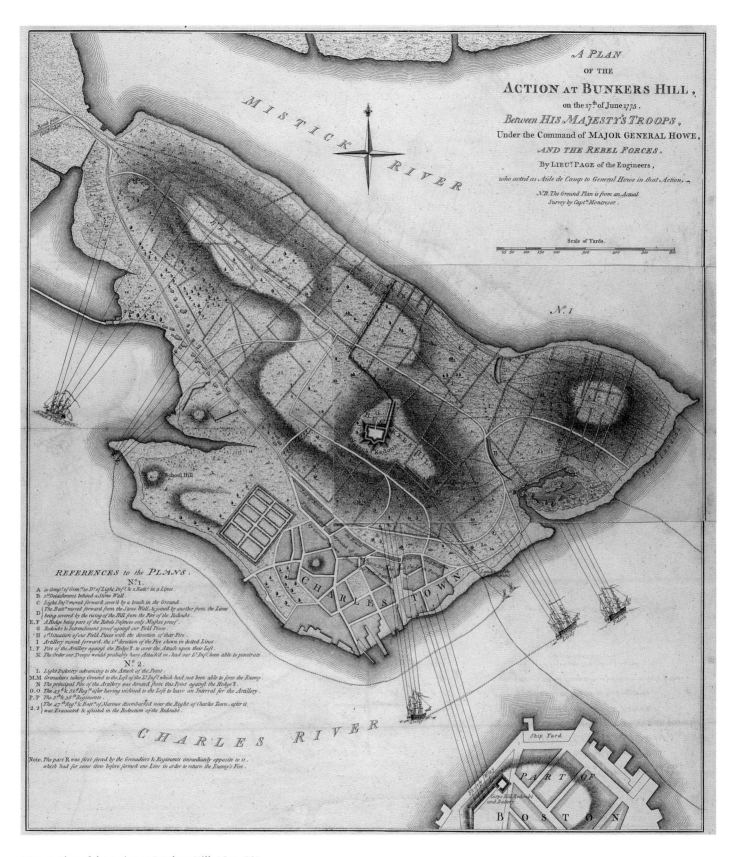

184 *A Plan of the Action at Bunkers Hill.* (Cat. 52)

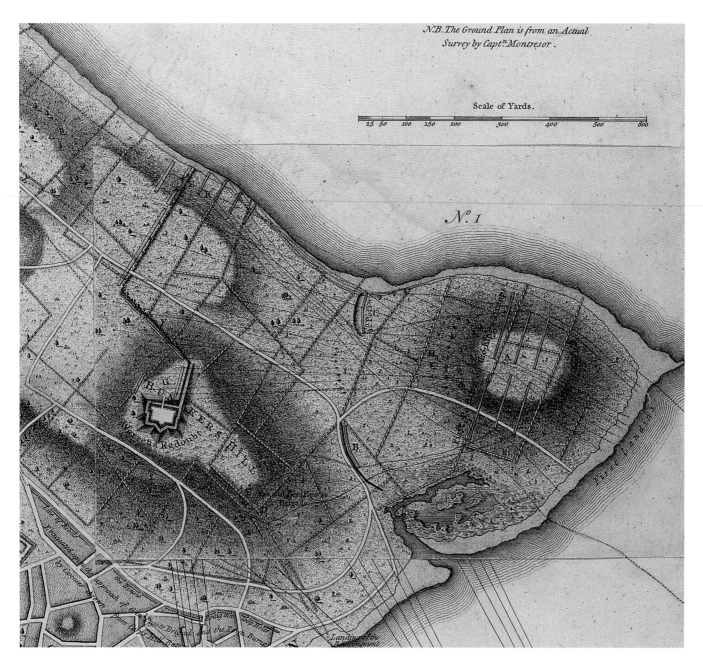

Scale of Yards.

25 50 100 150 200 300 400 500 600

N.o 1

185 Detail of the overlay from *A Plan of the Action at Bunkers Hill*, by Lieutenant Thomas Hyde Page, London, ca. 1775–1778, black-and-white line engraving with period color. 1989-36. (Cat. 52)

he appears to have worked alone.[1] Just as Jefferys's business thrived during the years of the French and Indian War, Faden benefited from the Revolutionary War. Ultimately appointed geographer to the king, Faden seems to have been the publisher of choice for British officers, producing thirty-three maps of American battles between 1776 and 1781.[2]

1989-36

1. The only other map in the Colonial Williamsburg collection that was designed with an overlay, now missing, is *A Plan of the Posts of York and Gloucester in the Province of Virginia*, by Edward Fage (Cat. 66). Since Fage and Page both attended Woolwich Academy, it is likely they learned the technique there.

2. According to Mary Pedley, the dissolution of Faden's partnership with the Jefferys firm was advertised in the *London Evening Post*, Oct. 29–31, 1776. "Maps, War, and Commerce," p. 171, n. 11.

3. Mary Pedley, *The Map trade in the late eighteenth century: Letters to the London map sellers Jefferys and Faden* (Oxford, 2000), p. 10.

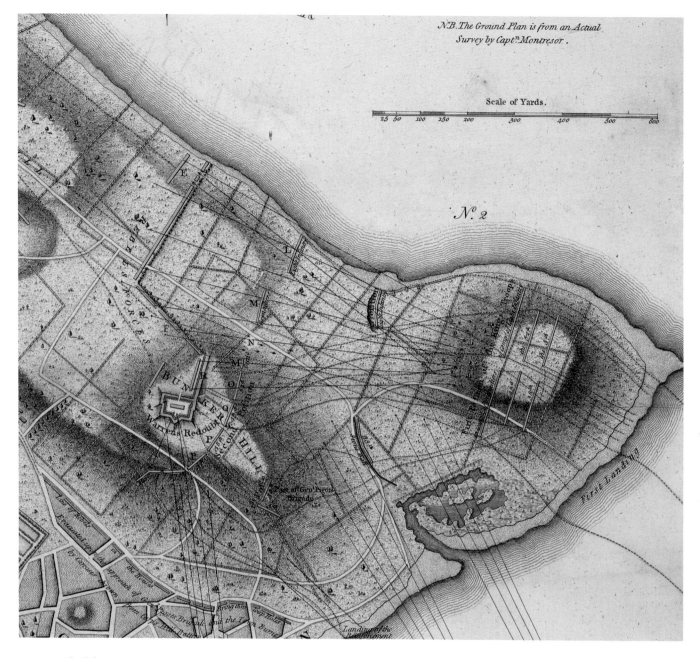

186 Detail of the section under the overlay from *A Plan of the Action at Bunkers Hill,* by Lieutenant Thomas Hyde Page, London, ca. 1775–1778, black-and-white line engraving with period color. 1989-36. (Cat. 52)

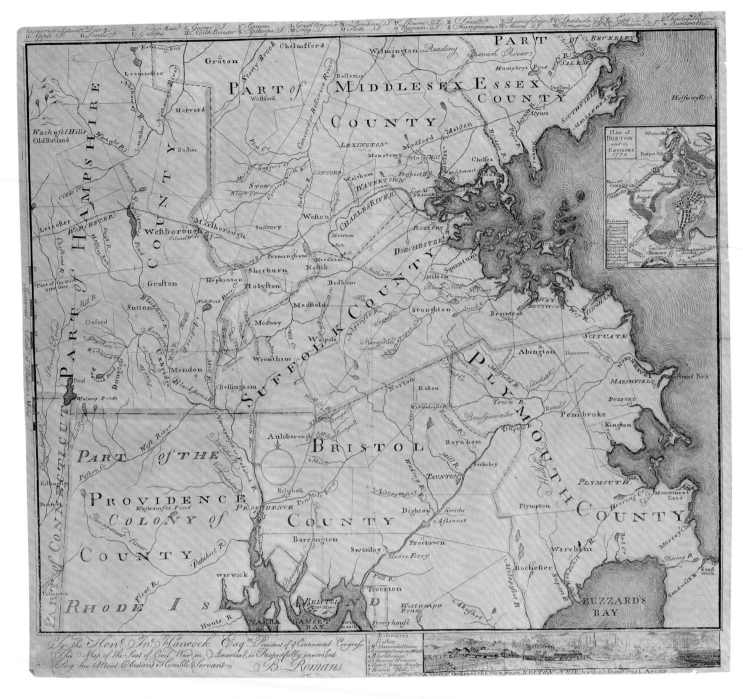

187 *Map of the Seat of Civil War in America.* (Cat. 53)

53 *To the Hon^e. Jno. Hancock Esqre, President of y^e Continental Congress, / This Map of the Seat of Civil War in America, is Respectfully inscribed / By his Most Obedient Humble Servant B: Romans*

Bernard Romans, cartographer; attributed to Abel Buell, engraver[1]

Probably Philadelphia, 1775. Black-and-white line engraving with period color. H. 17⅜", W. 16"

In the upper margin is a key to twenty-six sites located on the map. A *General Scale of Statute Miles* is included in the border along the left side. An inset *Plan of/ BOSTON/ and its/ ENVIRONS/ 1775* with a key identifying twelve sites is along the upper right side. The title is engraved in the lower left underneath the border. In the lower center below the border is a list of *References* identifying seven sites found on *A View of the Lines thrown up on BOSTON NECK: by the Ministerial Army* located in the lower right, also below the border

Three states of the map are known:
State 1: Variations unknown[2]
State 2: (this copy) As described
State 3: A legend was added in the right margin that identified by symbol *Post Roads, Roads not Post Roads, County Lines, Township Lines, Province Lines.* 1775

References: Deák, *Picturing America,* entry 142; Diamant, *Bernard Romans;* Guthorn, *American Maps and Map Makers,* pp. 30–32; Guthorn, *British Maps of the American Revolution,* pp. 40–41; Nebenzahl, *Bibliography of Printed Battle Plans,* entry 12; Sellers and van Ee, *Maps and Charts of North America,* p. 193; Wheat and Brun, *Maps and Charts,* entries 202, 203, 204

BERNARD ROMANS'S *Map of the Seat of Civil War in America* is an important Revolutionary War document, not necessarily for the geography it depicts but because it represents the earliest piece of graphic propaganda relating to the war that was published in America. While the overall map shows boundaries, roads, waterways, and some topographical features, it contains no information about the recent battles in Lexington and Concord and on Breed's Hill. Only the two insets, both small and difficult to read, relate to the recent actions. Were they hastily added at the last minute to a map currently in progress?

The inset *Plan of Boston and its Environs* in the upper right illustrates the major promontories in Boston and Charlestown and extends inward as far as Cambridge. *(fig. 190)* The redoubt constructed by the Americans on Breed's Hill is included; below is the notation *CHARLES Town B^t* [burnt] *June 17.* Romans also located the *Enemy Lines* on the outskirts of Boston and the encampments within. The

provincial lines from Cambridge to Winter Hill were represented. The inset in the lower right corner may be the only contemporary view of the recently constructed British encampments on Boston neck. *(fig. 189)* Romans illustrated the guardhouses in front of John Hancock's house, which was occupied at the time by Major General Henry Clinton.

Romans was born in Holland around 1720, immigrated to England in his youth to study botany and mathematics, and arrived in America in 1756. He spent the next seventeen years working in the southern colonies as a botanist, draftsman, and cartographer. In 1766, he was appointed deputy surveyor for Georgia and was promoted to deputy surveyor for the Southern District of British North America two years later. Romans became one of Florida's greatest promoters. His *Concise Natural History of East and West Florida* was published in New York in 1775.

At the outbreak of hostilities with England, Romans found himself firmly on the side of the patriot cause. Less than a week after the confrontations at Lexington and Concord, Romans presented a plan to the Connecticut Committee of Safety to seize the British fortifications at Fort Ticonderoga. A raid to capture British artillery had been advanced by other daring patriots as well. By the end of April 1775, both the Massachusetts and Connecticut Assemblies had dispatched expeditions to the outpost, one under the command of Colonel Benedict Arnold and the other under Romans. Along the way, Romans was removed from command in favor of Arnold and Colonel Ethan Allen. Romans then adopted an alternative plan to capture the meager British supplies remaining at Fort George. After accomplishing his objective, he rejoined the troops at Fort Ticonderoga.[3]

The rapid acceleration of hostilities in Boston soon offered Romans another avenue for self-promotion. The American victories at Lexington and Concord provided a substantial boost of morale for the rebel militia. Although the Americans technically lost the battle at Breed's Hill, they realized they were capable of waging a strong campaign against Britain's experienced forces. Attempting to capitalize on the wave of enthusiasm, Romans took only five weeks to advertise his map for sale in newspapers. It appeared first in the *Pennsylvania Gazette* for August 23. Romans noted: "This Map of Boston, &c. is one of the most correct that has ever been published. The draught was taken by the most skillful draughtsman in all America, and who was on the spot at the engagements of *Lexington* and *Bunker's Hill.*"[4] While Romans was clearly lacking in modesty, it seems that he was also lacking in honesty since he

188 *An Exact View of the Late Battle at Charlestown June 17th 1775,* by Bernard Romans, probably Philadelphia or Connecticut, 1775, black-and-white line engraving with period color. 1988-234.

189 Detail of the inset *A View of the Lines thrown up on Boston Neck: by the Ministerial Army* from *Map of the Seat of Civil War in America,* by Bernard Romans, probably Philadelphia, 1775, black-and-white line engraving with period color. 1996-824. (Cat. 53)

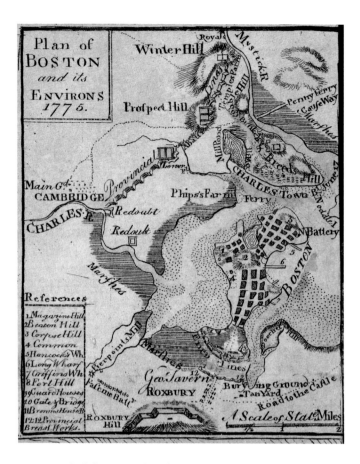

190 Detail of the inset *Plan of Boston and its Environs 1775* from *Map of the Seat of Civil War in America,* by Bernard Romans, probably Philadelphia, 1775, black-and-white line engraving with period color. 1996-824. (Cat. 53)

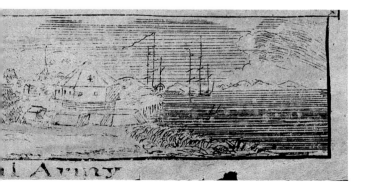

was neither at the Battle of Lexington nor at Bunker Hill.[5] The ad continued with a patriotic appeal: "Every well-wisher to this country cannot but delight in seeing a plan of the ground on which our brave American Army conquered the British Ministerial Forces."[6]

Not satisfied with simply producing a plan of the action at Charlestown, Romans illustrated the town ablaze from the fire set by the British. *(fig. 188)* On the left, the redcoats are firing volleys in the direction of Breed's Hill. According to Romans's biographer, Lincoln Diamant, his previous work as an engraver had been limited to "awkward cartouches, unusual plants and the heads of Florida natives."[7] In December, both the map and view were advertised in the *Virginia Gazette:*

> *Just come to Hand, and to be SOLD at this PRINTING-OFFICE, A large and exact VIEW of the late BATTLE at CHARLESTOWN, Elegantly coloured, Price one Dollar. Also an accurate MAP of The present SEAT of CIVIL WAR, Taken by an able Draughtsman who was on the Spot at the late Engagement. Price one Dollar.[8]*

1996-824

1. The advertisement in the *Pa. Gaz.,* Aug. 23, 1775, credited Nicholas Brooks as the publisher of Romans's map. Rivington's *New York Gazetteer,* Aug. 31, 1775, claimed that the map was published by James Rivington and Messrs. Noel and Hazard. On Sept. 11, 1775, Richard Sause advertised in the *N. Y. Gaz. and Weekly Mercury,* "Roman's MAP OF BOSTON, Is just printed, published, and sold BY RICHARD SAUSE." It is unclear from the wording if Sause was identifying himself as the retailer or whether he claimed to be the printer and publisher as well.

2. Wheat and Brun cited a previously recorded state of this map from the I. N. Phelps Stokes Collection that differed from the one now in the Stokes Collection, New York Pub. Lib. The notes concerning the variations in this state have been lost. Wheat and Brun, *Maps and Charts,* entry 202.

3. For a detailed account of the capture of British artillery at Fort Ticonderoga, see Lincoln Diamant, *Bernard Romans, Forgotten Patriot of the American Revolution* (Harrison, N. Y., 1985), pp. 49–61.

4. *Pa. Gaz.,* Aug. 23, 1775.

5. Diamant, *Bernard Romans,* p. 62.

6. *Pa. Gaz.,* Aug. 23, 1775.

7. Diamant, *Bernard Romans,* p. 62.

8. *Va. Gaz.* (Dixon and Hunter), Dec. 9, 1775.

54 THE THEATRE OF WAR in NORTH AMERICA, with the ROADS and A TABLE OF THE DISTANCES

Cartographer and engraver unknown; Robert Sayer and John Bennett, publishers

London, March 20, 1776. Black-and-white line engraving. H. 16½", W. 21" (map), overall size, including text: H. 29", W.21"

The title appears above the top margin. In the lower right corner is *EVAN'S POLYMETRIC TABLE OF AMERICA./ Shewing the Distances between the Principal Towns, Forts and Other Places in the British Colonies*. In the center, beneath the lower border, is the imprint *London, Printed for R.ᵗ Sayer & Jnᵒ Bennett. N.ᵒ 53 Fleet Street, as the Act directs. 20.ᵗʰ March 1776*. In letterpress below the plate mark are three columns of text titled *A Compendious Account of the BRITISH COLONIES in NORTH-AMERICA*

One state of the map (with three variant texts) is known[1]:

References: Nebenzahl, *Atlas of the American Revolution*, endsheets; Stevens and Tree, "Comparative Cartography," entry 58

AFTER THE skirmishes in the spring and summer of 1775, George III proclaimed that the colonies were in an open state of rebellion. For the English, another war across the Atlantic became inevitable. Map publishers were aware of the interest generated by the conflict and rushed to print works that would inform the public about the territory Britain was endeavoring to retain. One of the earliest maps produced to meet the demand was Robert Sayer and John Bennett's *Theatre of War in North America*.

The map illustrates Canada as far north as James Bay and New Britain, or Labrador, southward through about half of Florida and westward just beyond the Mississippi. Most of the geographical detail was borrowed from another map published by Sayer, Emanuel Bowen's *An Accurate Map of North America* (Cat. 36). Bowen's map was an appropriate choice to copy since it delineated Britain's American holdings as defined by the Paris peace treaty at the end of the Seven Years' War.

No military details were provided: the map was made merely to document the extent and value of Britain's claims in America. In the lower right corner, the polymetric table showing distances between the principal towns, forts, and other places in America was borrowed from Lewis Evans's *A general Map of the Middle British Colonies* (Cat. 34) which, by this time, was being published by Sayer and Bennett as well.

The motive behind the production of this work—to document the importance of retaining the American colonies—was suggested in the text. Written accounts of Newfoundland, Canada, New England, New York, New Jersey, Pennsylvania, Delaware, Maryland, Virginia, the Carolinas, Georgia, and Florida described their advantageous features. Attention was given to the numbers and even to the types of homes occupied by the colonists and to the virtues of areas with pleasant streets or forests. At the lower center of the compendium is *A Table of the Population of the British Colonies in North-America, published in New-Jersey, in November 1765*.

One of the most curious features of this publication is that only eight months after it was produced, Sayer and Bennett reissued it again, but rather than just adding information to the existing copperplate, they had a new plate engraved. The map was pushed farther up on the plate so that James Bay and Labrador extended into and above the longitudinal marking line, thereby including all of Florida rather than the small portion found on the early issue. The only other change in the geography was that slight alterations were made in the rendering of the Mississippi River. *Evan's Polymetric Table of America* was illustrated as *Corrected and Improved* to include distances to more cities—Amboy, Burlington, Charlestown, New Bern, Pensacola, Saint Augustine, and Savannah. Another new feature, a *Survey of the British Colonies, by Thomas Templeman*, provided the square miles, length, breadth, and distance from London for twelve of the capital towns in North America. Sayer and Bennett included a title cartouche on the second map, noting that their new information was *By An American*.
1955-126

1. No changes were made to the map itself. According to Stevens and Tree, the only differences were in the size of the typeset text in the lower half of the map. "Comparative Cartography," entry 58.

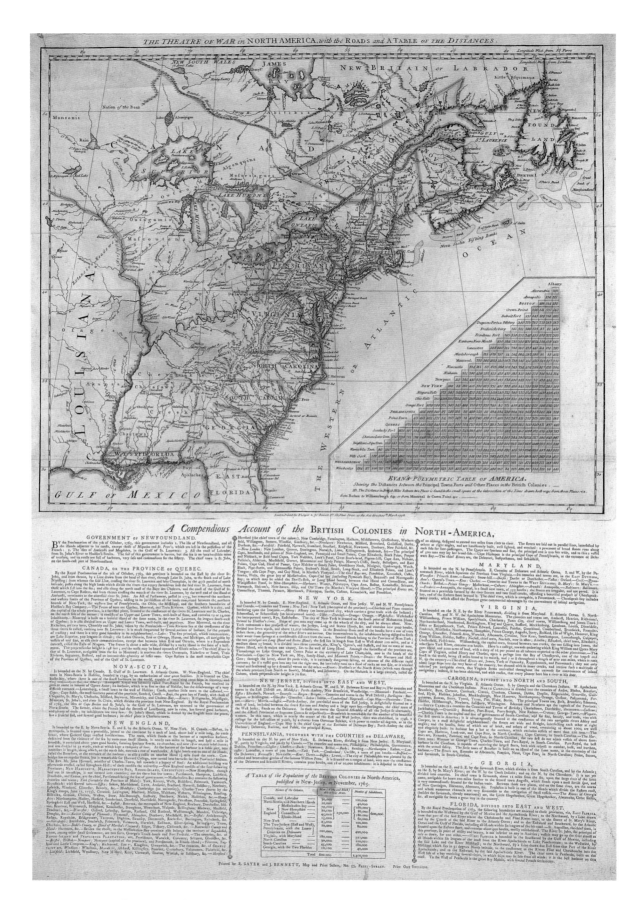

191 *The Theatre of War in North America.* (Cat. 54)

55 *A PLAN OF THE / OPERATIONS of the KING'S ARMY / under the Command of / GENERAL S.^R WILLIAM HOWE, K. B. / IN / NEW YORK / AND / EAST NEW JERSEY, / against the AMERICAN FORCES Commanded / By GENERAL WASHINGTON, / From the 12th. of October, to the 28th. of November 1776. / Wherein is particularly distinguished / THE ENGAGEMENT on the WHITE PLAINS, / the 28th. of October. / By CLAUDE JOSEPH SAUTHIER; Engraved by W.^M FADEN, 1777*

Claude Joseph Sauthier, cartographer; William Faden, engraver; published separately and in *The North American Atlas, Selected from the Most Authentic Maps, Charts, Plans, etc.* by William Faden

London, 1777. Black-and-white line engraving with period color. H. 29¼″, W. 19¼″

The title is in a rectangular box along the left side. Below is a scale of distances and the imprint *Published as the Act directs, Feb·y 25.th 1777, by W. Faden, Corner of St Martins Lane, Charing Cross*

Three states of the map are known:

State 1: (this copy) As described

State 2: Additional fortifications and ships off *Terry Town* (the *Tartar, Phoenix,* and *Roebuck*) were added. *King's Bridge* was corrected to reflect its proper location, but *Dyckman's Bridge* was incorrectly identified as *Philips Bridge.* 1777

State 3: The title was altered for Charles Stedman's *THE HISTORY OF THE ORIGIN, PROGRESS, AND TERMINATION OF THE AMERICAN WAR.* It then was *A PLAN OF THE/ OPERATIONS of the KING'S ARMY/ under the Command of/ GENERAL S.^R WILLIAM HOWE, K. B./ IN/ NEW YORK/ AND/ EAST NEW JERSEY,/ against the AMERICAN FORCES Commanded/ By GENERAL WASHINGTON,/ From the 12th. of October, to the 28th. of November 1776./ Engraved for STEDMAN'S HISTORY of the American War.* A scale of distances and the imprint *Published by the Author April 12.th 1793,* were added beneath the title. 1793

References: Cumming, *British Maps*, pp. 72–74; Guthorn, *British Maps of the American Revolution*, pp. 41–42; Nebenzahl, *Atlas of the American Revolution*, pp. 88–90; Nebenzahl, *Bibliography of Printed Battle Plans*, entry 101; Sellers and van Ee, *Maps and Charts of North America*, p. 320; Stevens and Tree, "Comparative Cartography," entry 45; Wallis, *American War of Independence*, entry 118

The British army's position in Boston was secured after the battle at Breed's Hill because the Americans surrounding the city did not have heavy cannons. However, on March 14, 1776, General Washington installed cannons seized from the British arsenal at Fort Ticonderoga on the hills of Dorchester Heights. General Howe, now in a precarious position, evacuated his troops.

Three months later, Howe was preparing to launch a new campaign against the American forces. The military strategy was planned by Howe and Colonial Secretary George Germain, who believed that New York City was the key to ensuring a decisive British victory because it would enable them to control access to Canada through the Hudson River Valley and separate New England from the other colonies. Howe and his troops sailed for New York on June 11, 1776, and set up camp on Staten Island. Although well situated, Howe waited seven weeks before attacking the Americans encamped on Long Island. The delay allowed British reinforcements, including Admiral Richard Howe, William's brother, Sir Henry Clinton's regiment from Charleston, South Carolina, and Hessian mercenaries to arrive.

The British army attacked the American defenses at Brooklyn Heights on August 27. Overwhelmed, Washington evacuated nearly ten thousand men and supplies across the East River to Manhattan two days later, eventually positioning them at White Plains, New York. Military mapmaker Claude Joseph Sauthier illustrated the British campaign against General Washington in Westchester County from October 12 through November 28, 1776, in *A Plan of the Operations of the King's Army . . . in New York and New Jersey.* The British advanced from Throg's Point [spelled *Frog's Point* on the map] and Pell's Point in the lower right to New Rochelle. They were joined on October 23 by Hessian troops under General Wilhelm Knyphausen. Sauthier plotted Howe's progress toward White Plains, indicating encampments along the way. Troop positions for both armies are shown on October 28, the day of the battle. *(fig. 193)*

Howe directed his assault to Chatterton's Hill, on Washington's right flank, which the British took by about five o'clock in the afternoon. That night, Washington moved his troops five miles back, to North Castle, a position that was easier to defend. Rather than attacking, Howe elected to turn south to capture Fort Washington, the remaining American post on Manhattan. Although the march of the British army southward along the banks of the Hudson and the location of Fort Washington are illustrated on this map, Sauthier showed them in greater detail on *A Topographical Map of the North.^n Part of New York Island* (Cat. 56).

William Faden published this map, which was based on Sauthier's manuscript version, only three months after these operations took place.[1] Sauthier, who was born in

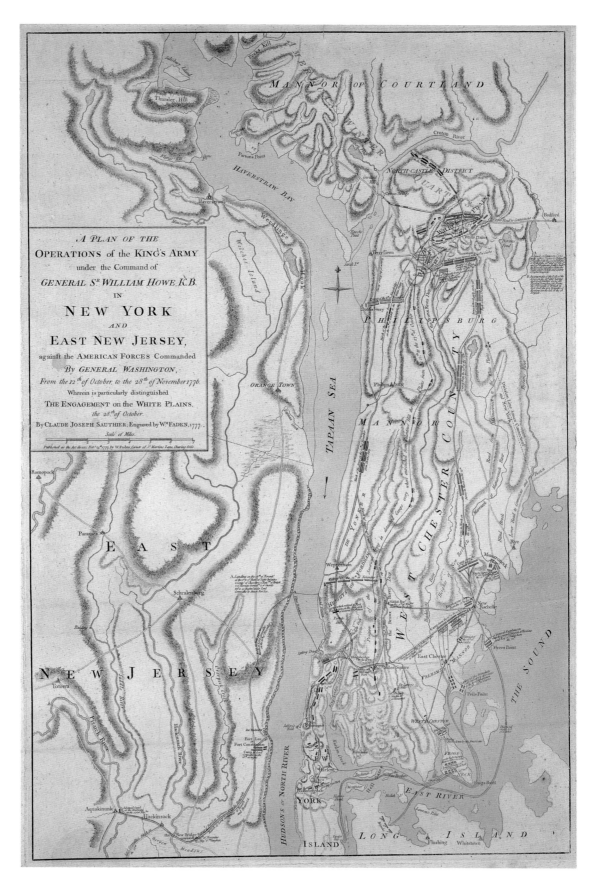

192 *A Plan of the Operations of the King's Army under the Command of General S.ʳ William Howe, K. B. in New York and East New Jersey.* (Cat. 55)

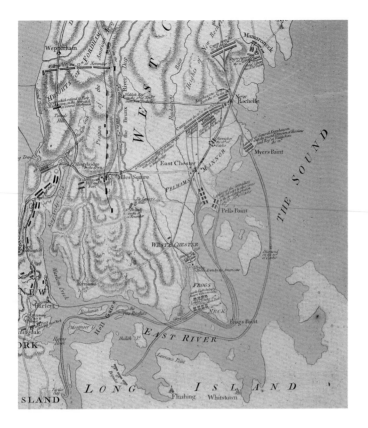

193 Detail of *A Plan of the Operations of the King's Army under the Command of General Sr William Howe, K. B. in New York and East New Jersey* by Claude Joseph Sauthier, London, 1777, black-and-white line engraving with period color. G1971-1278. (Cat. 55)

56 *A Topographical MAP of the North.^n Part / of / NEW YORK ISLAND, / Exhibiting the PLAN of FORT WASHINGTON, / now / FORT KNYPHAUSEN, / with the Rebels Lines to the Southward, / which were Forced by / the Troops under the Command of / THE / R^t. Honble. EARL PERCY, on the 16th. Novr. 1776, / and Survey'd immediately after by Order of his LORDSHIP, / BY CLAUDE JOSEPH SAUTHIER. / To which is added / the Attack made to the North^d. by the Hessians. / Survey'd by Order of Lieut^t. Genl. Knyphausen*

Claude Joseph Sauthier, cartographer; probably William Faden, engraver; published separately and in *The North American Atlas, Selected from the Most Authetic Maps, Charts, Plans, etc.* by William Faden

London, March 1, 1777. Black-and-white line engraving with period color. H. 18⅞", W. 11"

The title is engraved in the upper left corner. Directly beneath is the first of two imprints, *Published by Permission of the R^t Honble the COMMISSIONERS of/ TRADE & PLANTATIONS. by W.^M FADEN, 1777.* Along the right center is a key to identifying the maneuvers. In the center beneath the lower border is *London, Published as the Act directs, March 1.st 1777, by Wm Faden, Corner of St Martins Lane, Charing Cross*

Three states of the map are known:

State 1: (this copy) As described

State 2: Four units were added at the lower center of the map just north of *Snake Hill.* Two columns of troops, *Hessians Column* and *British Column commanded by Earl Percy,* were added. 1777

State 3: The title was altered for Charles Stedman's *THE HISTORY OF THE ORIGIN, PROGRESS, AND TERMINATION OF THE AMERICAN WAR.* It then was *A Topographical MAP of the North.^n Part/ of/ NEW YORK ISLAND,/ Exhibiting the PLAN of FORT WASHINGTON,/ now/ FORT KNYPHAUSEN,/ shewing the several Attacks/ of the/ ROYAL ARMY./ Engraved for Stedmans History of the/ AMERICAN WAR./ Published April 12.th 1793.* 1793

References: Cumming, *British Maps,* pp. 72–74; Guthorn, *British Maps of the American Revolution,* pp. 41–42; Nebenzahl, *Atlas of the American Revolution,* pp. 90–91; Nebenzahl, *Bibliography of Printed Battle Plans,* entry 116; Wallis, *American War of Independence,* entry 116

Strasbourg, France, trained as an architect and surveyor and immigrated to America in 1767. Between 1768 and 1770, he worked closely with Governor William Tryon of North Carolina drafting surveys of towns in that colony. Sauthier accompanied Tryon to New York in 1771 when he became governor there and was appointed surveyor in 1773. Sauthier produced maps for Howe and Lord Percy during the campaigns of 1776 and 1777. He returned to England with Percy in 1777, serving as his personal secretary until 1790.[2]

1971-1278

1. For information about Faden, see Cat. 52.

2. For more information on Sauthier, see Cumming, *British Maps,* pp. 72–74, and Guthorn, *British Maps of the American Revolution,* pp. 41–42.

A̲FTER THE initial battle at White Plains, Howe halted his attack against the main American army and turned south to capture Fort Washington. Sauthier's *A Plan of the Operations of the King's Army under the Command of Generals Sr William Howe, K. B. in New York and East New Jersey* (Cat.

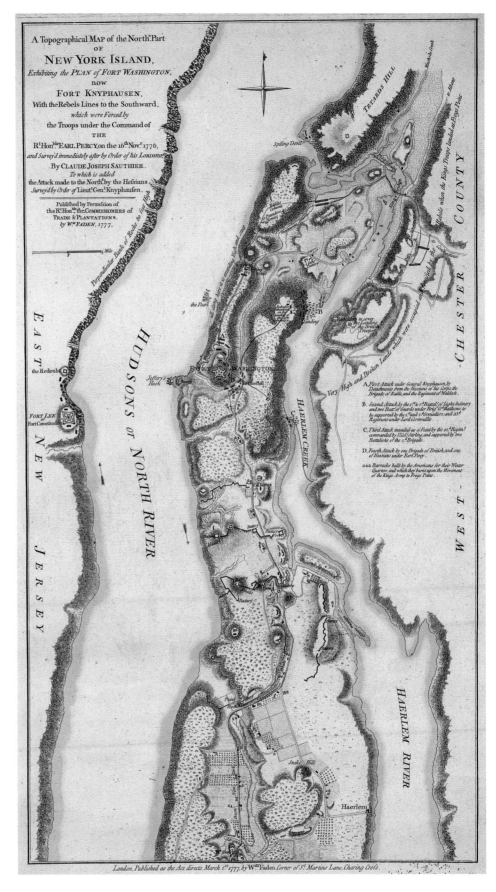

194 *A Topographical Map of the North.ⁿ Part of New York Island.* (Cat. 56)

A View of the Attack against Fort Washington and Rebel Redouts near New York on the 16 of N...

Drawn on the Spot, by Tho. Davies Cap.t R.R. of Artillery.

195 *A View of the Attack against Fort Washington and Rebel Redoubts near New York on the 16 of November 1776 by the British and Hessian Brigades,*
by Thomas Davies, New York, 1776, watercolor. Courtesy, New York Public Library, I. N. Phelps Stokes Collection.

by the British and Hessian Brigades

55) shows the action at White Plains, the descent of Howe's army, and the positions of the American and British troops around Fort Washington. Faden also published a map by Sauthier that depicted, in far greater detail, the British operations to seize the American outpost. *A Topographical Map of the North.ⁿ Part of New York Island* follows every movement of the troops in minute detail.

Washington had to decide whether to defend or abandon Fort Washington on Manhattan across the Hudson from Fort Lee, West 184th Street today. Located on the top of a hill, Fort Washington was thought by the Americans to be impregnable. Washington elected to maintain the fort rather than withdraw. On November 16, Lord Percy and General Knyphausen mounted a six-column attack on the fort that forced the patriots to surrender. Washington's decision not to evacuate Fort Washington was one of his most serious tactical errors. Almost three thousand men were taken prisoner and the British seized large quantities of supplies and weapons. Four days later, General Cornwallis was sent to take Fort Lee although the Americans stationed there had retreated.

Sauthier illustrated the four phases of the attack with the letters A through D. The key at the right identifies the first attack as that by General Knyphausen, the second by General Matthews and Cornwallis, the third was intended as a feint, and the fourth was led by Percy. Sauthier's delineation of upper Manhattan was the most accurate and detailed to date.[1]

1985-167

1. For information about Sauthier, see Cat. 55.

57 *PLAN / of the ATTACK of the FORTS / CLINTON & MONTGOMERY, / upon / HUDSONS RIVER / which were Stormed by HIS MAJESTYS FORCES / under the Command of / SIR HENRY CLINTON, K. B. / on the 6.th of Oct.r 1777. / Drawn from the Surveys of VERPLANK, HOLLAND & METCALFE. / By JOHN HILLS, Lt. 23d. Regt. / and Asst. Engineer*

John Hills, cartographer; engraver unknown; William Faden, publisher

London, June 1, 1784. Black-and-white line engraving with period color. H. 26¼", W. 20¼"

The title is in the upper right corner. Just below is the imprint *London, Published by W.M Faden. Geographer to the King, Charing-Cross, June 1.st 1784.* The scale of distances is in the lower center

Two states of the map are known:
State 1: (this copy) As described
State 2: The title was altered for Charles Stedman's *THE HISTORY OF THE ORIGIN, PROGRESS, AND TERMINATION OF THE AMERICAN WAR.* It then was *PLAN/ of the ATTACK of the FORTS/ CLINTON & MONTGOMERY,/ upon/ HUDSONS RIVER/ which were stormed by HIS MAJESTYS FORCES/ under the Command of/ SIR HENRY CLINTON, K. B./ on the 6.th of Oct.r 1777./ ENGRAVED for STEDMAN'S HISTORY of the AMERICAN WAR./ Published by the Author, April 12.th 1793.* 1793

References: Guthorn, *British Maps of the American Revolution*, pp. 24–27; Nebenzahl, *Atlas of the American Revolution*, pp. 104–106; Sellers and van Ee, *Maps and Charts of North America*, p. 257; Wallis, *American War of Independence*, entry 127

AFTER THE LOSS of Forts Washington and Lee, General Washington made his famous retreat across the Delaware, arriving in Pennsylvania on December 7, 1776. Desperately needing to infuse spirit into his despondent army, Washington made the decision to attack the Hessians encamped at Trenton under Colonel Johann Gottlieb Rall. Catching them off guard and weary from excessive Christmas festivities, Washington scored a remarkable victory. It was followed by another strong show of force against Cornwallis at Princeton on January 3. Washington then withdrew to spend the winter in Morristown.

British strategists planning the campaign of 1777 decided to focus once again on the northern colonies. However, they failed to establish effective communications between their commanders, so General William Howe and Major General John Burgoyne commanded independent operations rather than combining forces. Burgoyne planned to stage an invasion from Quebec using the route from Lake Champlain and the Hudson River, while Howe was determined to take Philadelphia. Apparently, neither general even consulted the other, although Howe left Sir Henry Clinton in New York to defend the city and provide assistance to Burgoyne if needed.

Burgoyne began his descent down Lake Champlain toward Fort Ticonderoga in June. Considered strategically important by both sides, the fort was old and not able to withstand a major attack. The Americans promptly surrendered. Burgoyne decided to proceed soutward by land rather than continuing down Lake George. The delay created by taking the overland route gave the Americans time to make better preparations around Albany. Burgoyne met the American army, led by Horatio Gates, about forty miles from the city. The Americans were ideally situated along the heights of the Hudson. The first battle at Saratoga took place on September 19. Although the British were not defeated, they suffered heavy losses. Two days later, on the verge of pressing on against the patriots, Burgoyne received a communication from Clinton in New York announcing he would provide assistance by creating a diversion near the American-held forts Clinton and Montgomery in the highlands along the Hudson about forty-five miles north of New York City. Burgoyne chose to delay launching another assault immediately, anticipating that significant numbers of Americans would be diverted to thwart Clinton's offensive.

Clinton heard of Burgoyne's difficulties in reaching Albany and decided to send troops up the Hudson by boat. As depicted on *A Plan of the Attack on Forts Clinton and Montgomery*, Verplank's Point, on the east bank of the Hudson a few miles south of the forts, was the site of a small rebel outpost. Clinton predicted correctly that the patriots stationed at Verplank's Point would request reinforcements from Forts Clinton and Montgomery, thereby removing a number of troops from those fortresses. Early on October 6, after investing the point, Clinton crossed the Hudson with most of his forces and marched north, approaching Fort Clinton from the south. From there, the general divided his troops. One division assaulted Fort Clinton while the other advanced on Fort Montgomery. Although many Americans were able to escape from Fort Montgomery, the patriot army suffered heavy losses and both forts were captured. Two American frigates and one galley north of the boom, or *chevaux de frise*, were unable to escape upriver due to high winds and were burned.[1]

Meanwhile, Burgoyne launched a second offensive against the American army at Saratoga. The Americans'

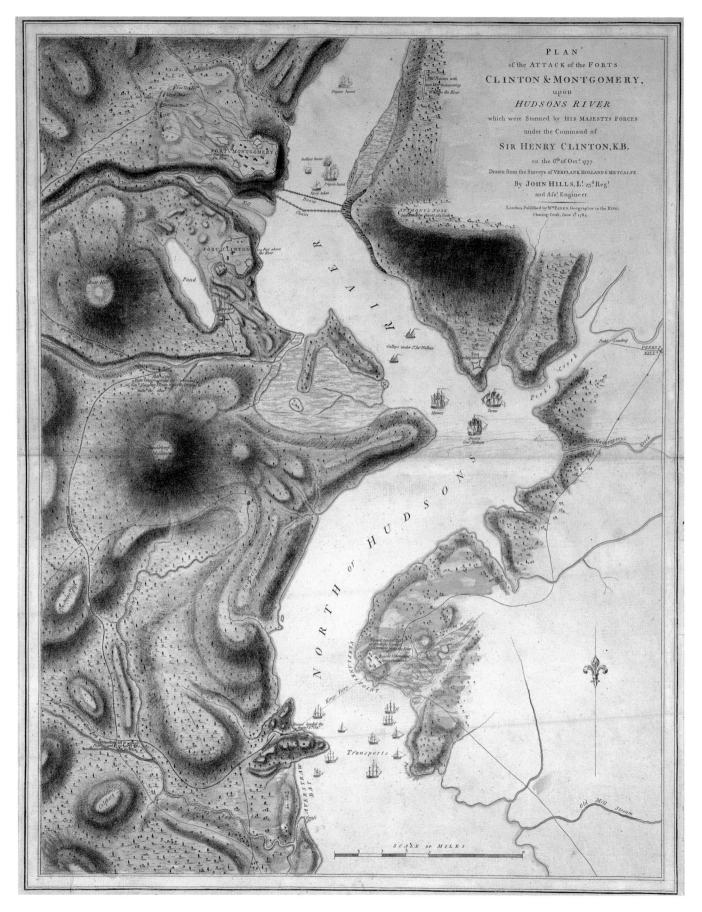

PLAN
of the ATTACK of the FORTS
CLINTON & MONTGOMERY,
upon
HUDSONS RIVER
which were Stormed by HIS MAJESTYS FORCES
under the Command of
SIR HENRY CLINTON, K.B.
on the 6th of Oct.r 1777.
Drawn from the Surveys of VERPLANK, HOLLAND & METCALFE.
By JOHN HILLS, L.t 23.d Reg.t
and Ass.t Engineer.
London, Published by Wm FADEN, Geographer to the KING,
Charing-Cross, June 1.st 1784.

196 *Plan of the Attack of the Forts Clinton & Montgomery.* (Cat. 57)

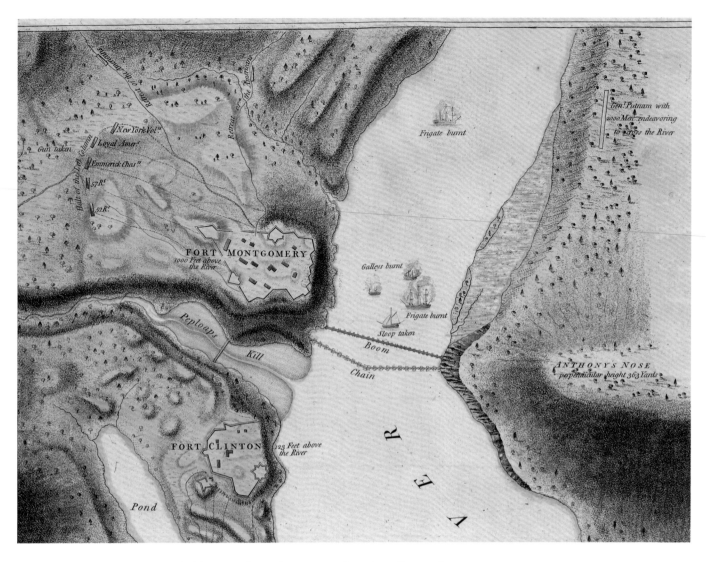

Labels within the map:

New York Vol^{rs}
Loyal Amer^s
Gun taken
Emmerick Chas^{rs}
57 R^t
52 R^t
Retreat of the Portuguan
FORT MONTGOMERY
1000 Feet above
the River
Peploops
Kill
Boom
Chain
FORT CLINTON
123 Feet above
the River
Pond
Frigate burnt
Galleys burnt
Frigate burnt
Sloop taken
ANTHONYS NOSE
perpendicular height 363 Yards
Genl Putnam with
2000 Men endeavoring
to across the River
R
I
V
E
R

197 Detail from *Plan of the Attack of the Forts Clinton & Montgomery,* by John Hills, London, June 1, 1784, black-and-white line engraving with period color. 1985-164. (Cat. 57)

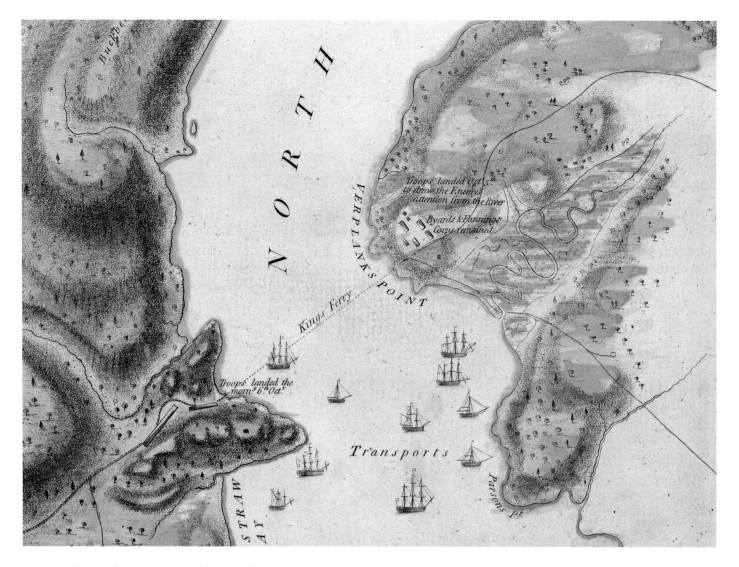

198 Detail from *Plan of the Attack of the Forts Clinton & Montgomery,* by John Hills, London,
June 1, 1784, black-and-white line engraving with period color. 1984-164. (Cat. 57)

position in the strongly fortified terrain gave them a decided advantage and the British were forced to retreat. Burgoyne surrendered on October 17. The American victory signaled a turning point in the Revolution and helped ensure that France would become an ally.

John Hills was a draftsman in the 38th Regiment in New York. During the war, he compiled an impressive number of surveys from Boston to the Chesapeake. Hills produced twenty maps of the province of New Jersey for Clinton, the only Revolutionary War state atlas. This collection is now in the Library of Congress.[2]

1985-164

1. The system of obstructions constructed in the river between Fort Montgomery and Anthony's Nose was called "chevaux de frise." It consisted of a sunken heavy timber frame with iron-tipped spikes that would rip the hull of a vessel sailing above. Mark Mayo Boatner III, *Encyclopedia of the American Revolution* (New York, 1966), pp. 226–227. There was also a chain extending across the river at Fort Montgomery.

2. Guthorn, *British Maps of the American Revolution,* pp. 24–27.

58 *CARTE / DU THÉATRE / DE LA GUERRE / ACTUEL / Entre les Anglais / et les Treize Colonies / Unies de l' Amerique / Septentrionale / DRESSÉE PAR J. B. ELIOT / Ingénieurs des Etats Unis / 1778. / A Paris chez Mondhare / Rue S.ᵗ Jacques / A la Ville de Caen*

J. B. Eliot, cartographer; engraver unknown; Mondhare, publisher

Paris, 1778. Black-and-white line engraving with period color.
H. 28½", W. 21¼"

The title is contained within an oval cartouche surrounded by flags and banners, cannons, cannon balls, and flora and fauna in the lower right half. In the background are regulars attacking a small town or plantation. A scale of distances is in the lower left

Two states of the map are known[1]:

State 1: (this copy) As described

State 2: The title was altered to *CARTE/ DU THÉATRE/ DE LA GUERRE/ ACTUEL/ Entre les Anglais/ et les Treize Colonies/ Unies de l'Amerique/ Septentrionale/ DRESSÉE PAR J. B. ELIOT/ Aide de Camp du Général Washington/ Ou se trouvent les Principaux camps et les Epoques des Combats/ qui se sont donnés/ dans cette partie de l' Amerique/ 1781.* Indexes were also added for *Renvois de Opérations Militaires* and *Suite des Renvois.* 1781

References: McCorkle, comp., *New England in Early Printed Maps,* entry 778.3; Ristow, *American Maps and Mapmakers,* pp. 61–62; Schwartz and Ehrenberg, *Mapping of America,* p. 195; Sellers and van Ee, *Maps and Charts of North America,* pp. 155–156

THE MAP of the theater of war between Great Britain and America by J. B. Eliot is important because its title, *les Treize Colonies Unies de l'Amerique Septentrionale,* may include the first reference on a map to the United States.[2] The cartographer was identified as *Ingénieurs des Etats Unis.* On November 15, 1777, the Continental Congress selected "The United States of America" as the name of the thirteen colonies that formed a government under the of the Articles of Confederation. One month later, French authorities learned of the victory at Saratoga and decided to recognize American independence. By January 8, French foreign minister Charles Gravier, Comte de Vergennes, informed American envoys that France was ready to engage in an alliance. It is not surprising that the name United States was first mentioned on map published in Paris in 1778.

Although the second state of the map referred to Eliot as an aide-de-camp to General Washington, no references to him have been located in the Washington papers. It is also curious that he did not indicate on the map the general's 1777 winter headquarters at Valley Forge, misspelled *Walay Forge.*[3] What Eliot did illustrate were the lines of march taken by the British and American forces during the campaign of 1777, including Lieutenant Colonel Barry St. Leger's unsuccessful diversionary expedition down the Mohawk Valley, Burgoyne's march from Crown Point to Albany, and Howe's campaign to take Philadelphia.

As was usually the case, Eliot appears to have borrowed from several sources in compiling the geography. Some areas were designated by French place-names while others were predominately English, specifically in the northwestern territories that the French knew best. It is clear they were aware of the latest intelligence relating to the Revolutionary War.

Mary Pedley's research on the correspondence of London mapmaker William Faden revealed the remarkable exchange of information between mapmakers of combatant nations during wartime. Between 1776 and 1781, Faden engraved thirty-three maps and plans relating to the conflict in America.[4] Faden had access to intelligence from British officers that would today be regarded as classified. While supplying the British market with the latest information from America, he also participated in an active exchange with French map dealers. In 1777, Faden dispatched four cases of maps to Paris mapseller Jean Nicolas Buache. The value suggests that each case contained hundreds of maps. Buache's shipments to Faden the same year indicate that large inventories of French maps were shipped to England as well.[5] In the same month that France signed the Treaty of Alliance with America, Faden sent maps of Rhode Island, Newport, and New Jersey to Buache.[6] Regular exchanges of maps between French and English mapsellers continued throughout the war.

1958-633

1. Walter Ristow suggested that another state of the map with the same title and date appeared between the first and second states discussed here. He described it as having a "slightly different orientation, extending northward to include a larger segment of Maine and curtailing the southern extremity." I have concluded that the map Ristow described as a second edition is from a different plate. Ristow, *American Maps and Mapmakers,* p. 62.

2. Tim Coss suggested that a map by Didier Robert De Vaugondy, *Carte des Pays connus sous le nom de Canada,* 1753, was altered in 1778 to *Carte du Canada et des Etats-Unis,* thereby becoming the first map to name the United States. The evidence for the changes predating Eliot's map, however, is inconclusive. Tim Coss, "The first unrecorded map mentioning the 'United States,'" *Map Collector,* LXV (1993), pp. 34–35.

3. Ristow speculated that since this and another map by Eliot were published in France, Eliot may have served as a liaison between France and the American general, although the Département des Cartes et Plans, Bibliothèque Nationale, Paris, has no evidence of a such a connection. Ristow, *American Maps and Mapmakers,* p. 62.

4. Pedley, *Map trade in the late eighteenth century,* p. 10.

5. *Ibid.,* pp. 13 and 28, n. 42.

6. *Ibid.,* p. 39.

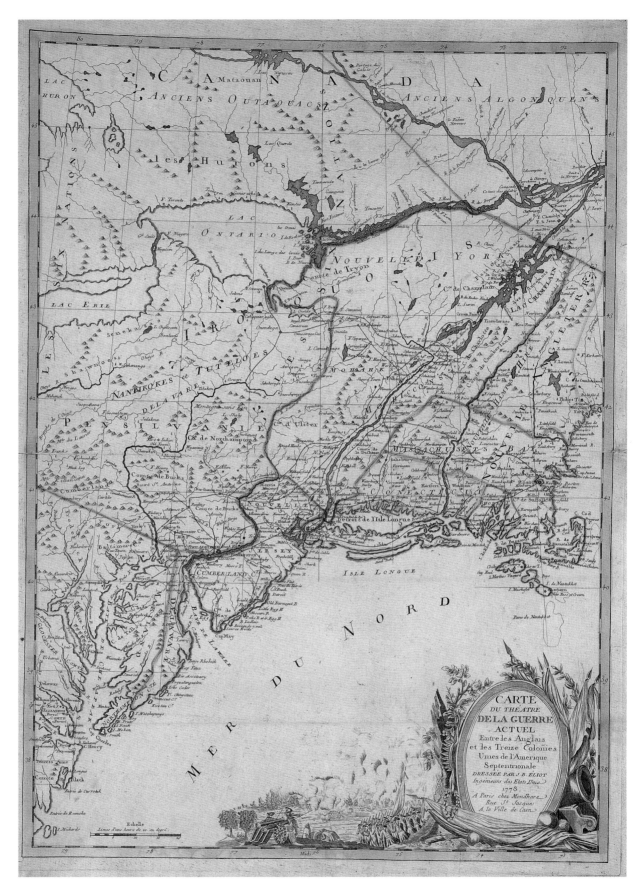

199 *Carte du Théatre de la Guerre Actuel Entre les Anglais et les Treize Colonies Unies de l' Amerique Septentrionale.* (Cat. 58)

59 *SKETCH / of the / NORTHERN FRONTIERS / of / GEORGIA, / extending / from the MOUTH of the RIVER SAVANNAH / to the TOWN of AUGUSTA, / By ARCHIBALD CAMPBELL / Lieut^t. Col^l. 71st. Reg.^t*

Archibald Campbell, cartographer; William Faden, engraver; published by William Faden and in Jeffery's *The American Atlas: or, A Geographical Description of the Whole Continent of America* by Robert Sayer and John Bennett[1]

London, May 1, 1780. Black-and-white line engraving. H. 29", W. 24½"

A two-part inset of the *Continuation of/ SAVANNA RIVER,/ from/ Ebenezer to Augusta* dominates the upper left quarter of the map. The title is contained in a circle below the insets. Below is the imprint *Engraved by Willm Faden Charing Cross./ 1780*. Along the center right are *References to the Attack of/ SAVANNAH/ on the 28.th December 1778*. A scale of distances is in the lower center. In the lower center below the border is the imprint *LONDON, Published as the Act directs May 1.st 1780 by Wm Faden corner of St Martins Lane Charing Cross*

One state of the map is known[2]

References: Cumming, *British Maps*, pp. 71 and 100, n. 62; Fowble, *Two Centuries of Prints in America*, entry 12; Nebenzahl, *Bibliography of Printed Battle Plans*, entry 74; Sellers and van Ee, *Maps and Charts of North America*, p. 340; Wallis, *American War of Independence*, entry 129; Willingham, "Cartographic Progression of Georgia," pp. 45–46

THREE YEARS of intense campaigning in New England and the Middle Atlantic colonies brought the British no closer to crushing the rebel uprising in America than they had been in 1775. Instead, the determination of the thirteen colonies to become independent was gaining strength. In 1778, the war began to take an ominous turn for the British when France allied with America. By summer, Britain had control of only two cities, New York and Newport, Rhode Island. Three years of disappointing results in New England and the middle colonies caused British strategists to recommend to Clinton, the new commander in chief, that he mount a campaign in the South, where a strong contingent of loyalist support was presumed to exist.

Clinton sent Lieutenant Archibald Campbell and thirty-five hundred men to launch an offensive against Savannah and Charleston. Sailing from New York, Campbell landed off Tybee Island at the mouth of the Savannah River on December 23. Although he had intended to wait for rein-forcements from General Augustine Prevost, commander of the British forces in East Florida, recent intelligence convinced Campbell that Savannah was ill equipped to mount a successful defense against an attack.

On December 29, Campbell's troops moved to Girardeau's [*Gerardos* on the map], about two miles east of Savannah.[3] The Americans, under the command of Major General Robert Howe, were positioned to the east of the city. An African-American guided Campbell's men through the swamps to the rear of Howe's troops, enabling them to attack from both the front and rear. The Americans were no match for the British regulars and suffered a quick defeat. Howe retreated to Cherokee Hill, about six miles northwest of the city. Prevost soon arrived to reinforce Campbell and the town of Augusta was taken on January 29, 1779.

Borrowing from *A Map of South Carolina and a Part of Georgia* by William Gerard De Brahm (Cat. 37), Campbell illustrated the water route from Savannah to Augusta. Along the way, he identified the locations of property owners, river crossings, and roads. Little military information was provided, although Campbell pinpointed the initial landing at *Gerardos* with the location of the British ships offshore.

Campbell began his career in the army as a Fraser Highlander and served in America during the French and Indian War, producing at least two maps, *A Map of the Island of Guadeloupe* (1760) and *Sketch of the Coast Round the Island of Dominique* (1761).[4] He was recruited again for service in America in 1775. His ship entered Boston Harbor while the city was in rebel hands and he was imprisoned until the following year when he was exchanged for Ethan Allen. Upon his release, he led the expedition to Georgia. Campbell was appointed governor of Jamaica in 1781 and produced a *Survey of the South Coast of Jamaica* the next year.[5]

1985-285

1. For the relationship between Faden, Jefferys, and Sayer and Bennett, see Cat. 52.

2. Stevens and Tree identified two states but did not indicate any changes to the plate. They appear to have identified a later printing of the map from the unaltered copperplate. "Comparative Cartography," p. 64.

3. It should be noted that the map is oriented with north in a 45° angle toward the upper right.

4. The 71st Regiment was better known during the Revolutionary War as the Fraser Highlanders, named for Simon Fraser, who had been active in the second Jacobite rebellion. Although Fraser commanded his regiment in the French and Indian War, he did not accompany them on their return to America.

5. French, ed., *Tooley's Dictionary*, p. 228

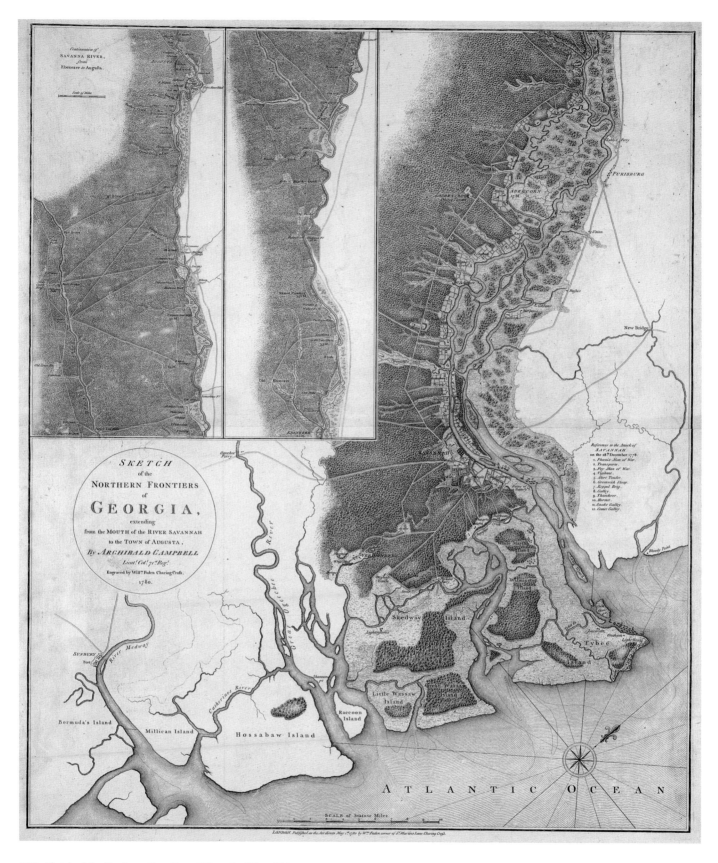

200 *Sketch of the Northern Frontiers of Georgia.* (Cat. 59)

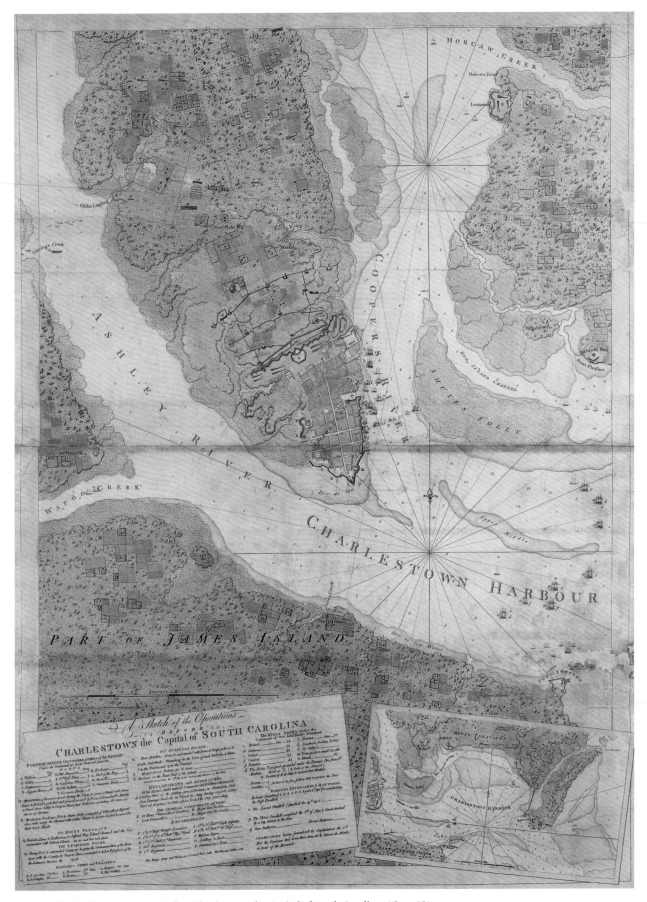

201　*A Sketch of the Operations Before Charlestown the Capital of South Carolina.* (Cat. 60)

60 *A Sketch of the Operations / BEFORE / CHARLESTOWN the Capital of SOUTH CAROLINA*

Joseph Frederick Wallet Des Barres, cartographer; published in *The Atlantic Neptune* by Joseph Frederick Wallet Des Barres

London, June 17, 1780. Black-and-white stipple and line engraving with period color. H. 41½", W. 30¼"

The title, in a rectangular box engraved to look like a sheet of paper torn in the upper right corner, is located in the lower left. Beneath is a key to information depicted on the map. In the lower right is an inset of *CHARLESTOWN HARBOUR*

Two states of the map are known:

State 1: (this copy) As described

State 2: Heavy shading was added to the land. The area around the scale of distances was burnished to resemble a rule with a semicircular protrusion at the right end

References: Cumming, *British Maps*, pp. 51–56, 71; Evans, *Uncommon Obdurate;* Harley, "Map User in the Revolution," pp. 87–91; Nebenzahl, *Bibliography of Printed Battle Plans*, entry 80; Schwartz and Ehrenberg, *Mapping of America*, p. 196; Sellers and van Ee, *Maps and Charts of North America*, pp. 335–336

CONTROL of Charleston Harbor was important to the British because it would provide them with a key base from which to launch operations on the southern front. Sir Henry Clinton departed New York on December 26, 1779,

202 Detail from *A Sketch of the Operations Before Charlestown the Capital of South Carolina*, by Joseph Frederick Wallet Des Barres, London, June 17, 1780, black-and-white line engraving with period color. 1961-217. (Cat. 60)

and, after a difficult thirty-eight-day journey fighting severe storms and strong currents, landed at North Edisto Inlet, about thirty miles southwest of Charleston. He proceeded toward Saint James Island, taking possession of poorly reinforced Fort Johnson, and headed northwest. Anticipating the British would cross the Ashley River at Ashley Ferry, the Americans concentrated their efforts on the opposite bank, unaware that the enemy had positioned themselves at Drayton's plantation, three miles above Ashley's Ferry. The British crossed the Ashley unnoticed on March 29, went down Charleston Neck, and entrenched themselves about eight hundred yards from the American defenses outside the city. Meanwhile, Vice Admiral Marriot Arbuthnot, commander of the royal navy, sealed off the harbor.[1]

Vastly outnumbered, the Americans were surrounded on three sides. General Benjamin Lincoln, commander in charge of the Southern Department, expected reinforcements to arrive from the east, the direction of his only open supply line, but Clinton dispatched Lieutenant Colonels Banastre Tarleton and James Webster to tighten the hold. The Charleston garrison was unable to retreat and Lincoln formally surrendered on May 12. In terms of numbers, the surrender at Charleston was the heaviest loss for the Americans during the war. Once Charleston was secured, Clinton returned to New York, leaving General Cornwallis, his second in command, to manage affairs on the southern front.

Joseph Frederick Wallet Des Barres's *Sketch of the Operations Before Charlestown the Capital of South Carolina* was a detailed record of the campaign that took place in the winter and spring of 1780. It delineated Charleston Harbor north to Hobcaw Creek and south as far as part of James Island. The British approach and final troop positions of both armies were indicated. Des Barres illustrated American and British ships, identifying each in the key and giving the number of guns aboard. The large scale of the map allowed for a detailed plan of the town, wharves, and outlying plantations. *(fig. 193)*

Unlike this map and *A Plan of the Posts of York and Gloucester* (Cat. 66), which were military maps, most of the plates in *The Atlantic Neptune* were coastal charts. The latter were Des Barres's most successful undertakings and formed the greater portion of that publication.[2]

1961-217

1. Boatner, *Encyclopedia of the American Revolution*, pp. 205–214.
2. For a more complete discussion of *The Atlantic Neptune*, see Cat. 61.

61 *A CHART of the COAST / OF / NEW YORK, NEW JERSEY, / PENSILVANIA, / MARYLAND, VIRGINIA, NORTH CAROLINA, &c. / COMPOSED from the deposit of SURVEYS / of the / Right Honourable the Lords of Trade. / with / Soundings & Nautical Remarks from L^t. Jno. Knight of the Navy & others*

Joseph Frederick Wallet Des Barres, cartographer; published in *The Atlantic Neptune* by Joseph Frederick Wallet Des Barres

London, March 1, 1780. Black-and-white stipple and line engraving. H. 62⅜″, W. 29½″, in three sheets

The title is in a square set at a very slight angle in the lower right

Two states of the map are known:
State 1: (this copy) As described
State 2: Information in New York Harbor and Long Island Sound that appeared unfinished on state one has been added here. The Hudson River was extended to the north and the western areas were shaded in. Ca. 1780

References: Cumming, *British Maps*, pp. 51–56, 71; Evans, *Uncommon Obdurate*; Harley, "Map User in the Revolution," pp. 87–91; Morrison et al., *On the Map*, fig. 41; Sellers and van Ee, *Maps and Charts of North America*, pp. 162–163

A Chart of the Coast of New York, New Jersey, Pensilvania, Maryland, Virginia, North Carolina was prepared by Joseph Frederick Wallet Des Barres in early 1780 as the focus of Britain's military campaign shifted to the southern front. Only one month prior to its publication, Sir Henry Clinton sailed from New York to South Carolina when the government recognized the strategic advantage of bringing the southern colonies back into the fold. Although the British occupied Charleston, they ultimately failed to secure the support of loyalists in the Carolinas, so Cornwallis decided to consolidate British control of the South by invading Virginia.

Des Barres's chart provided the royal navy with data essential to maneuvering in the coastal waters of the mid-Atlantic. The most complete information is found in the Chesapeake Bay area where numerous shoals and spits of sand at the mouths of its major tributaries created challenges to navigation. Like most of Des Barres's charts, little topography was illustrated beyond the shoreline; however, close attention was paid to rendering the nature of the coast and to furnishing accurate soundings.[1]

Des Barres was educated in Basle, Switzerland, by two great mathematicians, Daniel and James Bernouilli.[2] He entered the Royal Military Academy at Woolwich near London where his training as a mathematician was enhanced as he learned to solve military problems by applying the principles he had learned from the Bernouillis. Des Barres also studied fortification, artillery, land drainage, surveying, and topographical drawing.[3] Edward Fage, Thomas Page, Thomas Davies, Des Barres, and other officers trained at Woolwich would go on to produce important renderings of eighteenth-century America.[4] *(fig. 204)*

Entering military service in the Royal American Regiment in 1756, Des Barres served in the French and Indian War as an aide-de-camp to General James Wolfe. He surveyed the coasts of Nova Scotia, Sable Island, and New Brunswick from 1763 to 1774, then returned to England to publish his work as the great sea atlas *The Atlantic Neptune*. The outbreak of the Revolution created an urgent need for his coastal charts. In March 1775, the Admiralty approved Des Barres's proposals and allocated additional funds to hasten progress on the project. The following May, he petitioned the Board of Trade for access to surveys housed in their offices.

Des Barres devoted the years from 1774 to 1784 to preparing the plates for his publication, at one point hiring as many as twenty engravers. To supplement the charts he had compiled personally, Des Barres adapted the work of mapmakers Samuel Holland, later appointed surveyor general for the Northern District in America, and Captain James Cook. While taking care to acknowledge the contributions of his colleagues, Des Barres assumed responsibility for compiling, editing, and adapting the existing materials.

The Atlantic Neptune was published piecemeal as portions were completed. Since the charts were issued to British naval officers according to their tours of duty, no two copies are identical. In its most mature form, the work comprised five volumes. The first contained all of Des Barres's own surveys of the coasts and harbors of Nova Scotia. Subsequent volumes included charts of New England largely compiled from Holland's land maps, charts of the Gulf of Saint Lawrence and the islands of Cape Breton and Saint John, charts that extended the coverage of the coast south from New York, and a collection of views of the American coast.

The Atlantic Neptune was a remarkable achievement. Des Barres's extensive training enabled him to produce charts that far surpassed previous works in precision and accuracy. He described how he used a theodolite to measure vertical and horizontal angles that could be calculated trigonometrically. Sightings from previously measured features along the shore could be measured against un-

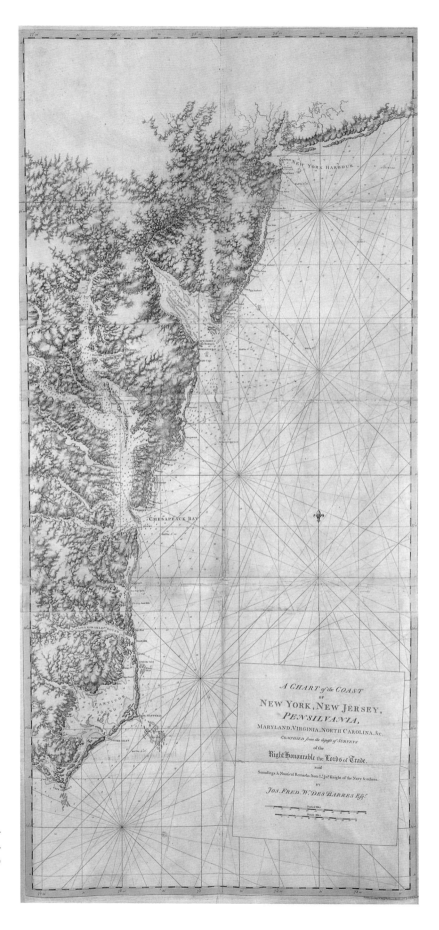

203 *A Chart of the Coast of New York, New Jersey,*
Pensilvania, Maryland, Virginia, North Carolina.
(Cat. 61)

204 *A View of Portsmouth in Piscataqua River,* published by J. F. W. Des Barres in *The Atlantic Neptune,* London, 1781, hand-colored aquatint. Courtesy, Chipstone Foundation, Milwaukee, Wis., photo by Gavin Ashworth.

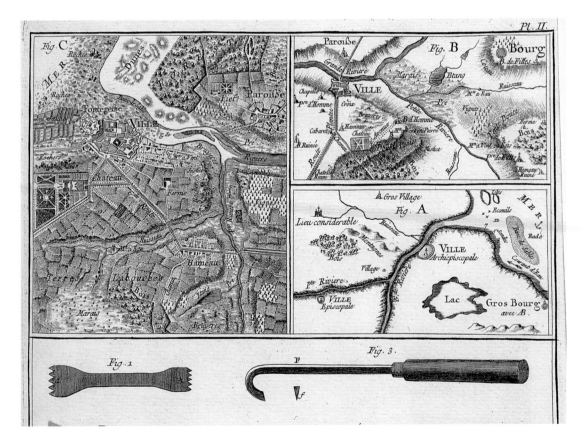

205 Detail from *Gravure* showing various tools used to engrave topographical features on maps, published by Denis Diderot in *Recueil de Planches, sur Les Sciences, Les Arts Libéraux, et Les Arts Méchaniques,* V, Pl. II, Paris, 1767, black-and-white line engraving.

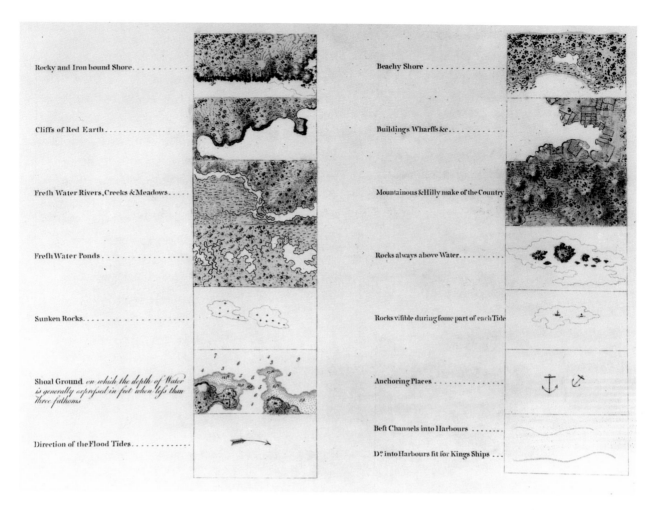

Rocky and Iron bound Shore

Cliffs of Red Earth

Fresh Water Rivers, Creeks & Meadows

Fresh Water Ponds

Sunken Rocks

Shoal Ground *on which the depth of Water is generally expressed in feet when less than three fathoms*

Direction of the Flood Tides

Beachy Shore

Buildings Wharffs &c

Mountainous & Hilly make of the Country

Rocks always above Water

Rocks visible during some part of each Tide

Anchoring Places

Best Channels into Harbours

D.º into Harbours fit for Kings Ships

206 Coastal topography, published by J. F. W. Des Barres in *The Atlantic Neptune,* London, 1774–1782, black-and-white line engraving with stipple. Courtesy, Library of Congress.

recorded points and geometrically triangulated to determine exact locations. Once he charted a coast, Des Barres also noted the topographical features of the shore and took soundings. He included the depths of the water, the nature of the bottom, the location and size of shoals and rocky areas, the best routes to enter and exit channels, information on tides, and places to anchor.[5]

Des Barres took the same comprehensive approach to rendering the nature of the shoreline that he did to the geographical features. His maps show the differences in soil structure, types of beaches and wooded areas, fields, and locations of houses. To portray the topographical information, he devised a system of various types of shading to indicate relief, which he accomplished by using a roulette, or small wheel with embedded spikes, which produced a subtly shaded effect. *(figs. 205 and 206)*

Des Barres's charts provided an indispensable tool for the British navy during the American Revolution, and they remained a significant resource for subsequent United States pilot books well into the next century. Today, they are also revered for their quality and for the highly aesthetic manner in which they were executed.

G1999-242, gift of Mr. William C. Wooldridge

1. Des Barres credited Lt. John Knight with providing the soundings.

2. Daniel Bernouilli has been called the founder of mathematical physics, while James (or John) contributed to the practical application of calculus. Cumming, *British Maps,* p. 56.

3. For information on the curriculum at Woolwich, see Evans, *Uncommon Obdurate,* pp. 4–6, and J. B. Harley, "The Spread of Cartographical Ideas between the Revolutionary Armies," in J. B. Harley, Barbara Bartz Petchenik, and Lawrence W. Towner, *Mapping the American Revolutionary War* (Chicago, 1978), pp. 54–57.

4. Thomas Davies rendered the view of New York at the bottom of Cat. 46. For a map by Edward Fage, see Cat. 66; for Thomas Page, see Cat. 52. Artist Paul Sandby was appointed chief drawing master at Woolwich in 1768.

5. Des Barres to Lord Colville, 1765, in Evans, *Uncommon Obdurate,* pp. 13–14.

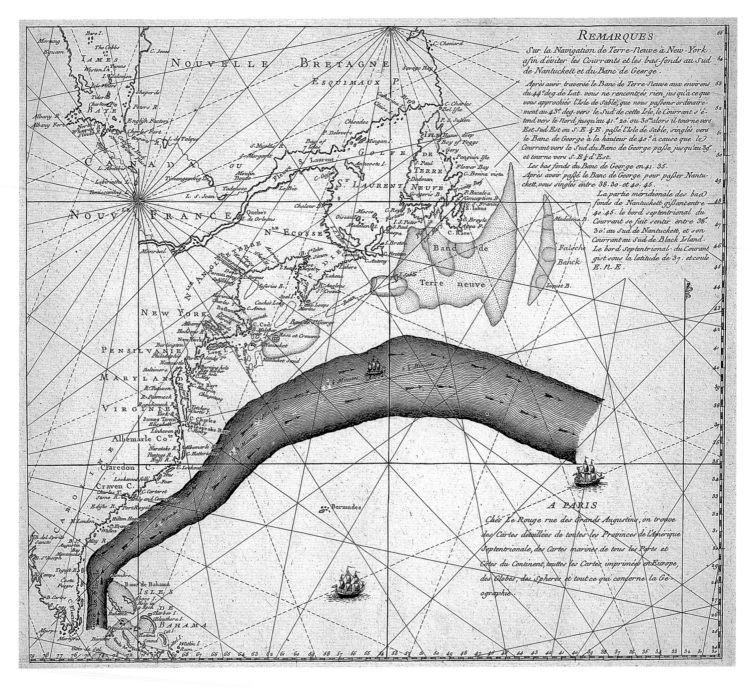

207 The Gulf Stream. (Cat. 62)

62 The Gulf Stream

George Louis Le Rouge (after Timothy Folger), cartographer; engraver unknown

Paris, ca. 1780–1783. Black-and-white line engraving. H. 13¼″, W. 15″

In the upper right corner are *REMARQUES/ Sur la Navigation de Terre-Neuve à New-York/ afin d' éviter les Courrants et les bas-fonds au Sud/ de Nantuckett et du Banc de George.* The flow of the Gulf Stream is clearly delineated in the lower half of the map. In the lower right corner is the imprint *A PARIS/ Chés Le Rouge rue des Grands Augustins, on trouve/ des Cartes détaillées de toutes les Provinces de l' Amérique/ Septentrionale, des Cartes marines de tous les Ports et/ Côtes du Continent, touttes les Cartes imprimées en Europe,/ des Globes, des Spheres et tout ce qui concerne la Gé-/ ographie*

Only one state of the map is known

References: Bache, "Where Is Franklin's First Chart of the Gulf Stream?" pp. 731–741; Carter, *American Traders,* p. 27; Cohn, "Franklin, Le Rouge and the Franklin/Folger Chart," pp. 124–142; De Vorsey, "Gulf Stream," pp. 3–10; De Vorsey, "Pioneer Charting of the Gulf Stream," pp. 105–120; Konvitz, *Cartography in France,* pp. 63–67; McCorkle, *New England in Early Printed Maps,* entry 783.10

208 *Benjamin Franklin,* by John Martin Will after a painting by C. N. Cochin Chevalier, France, 1777, black-and-white mezzotint engraving. 1959-82.

THE Gulf Stream flows northward from the Florida coast to Capes Lookout and Hatteras where those projections force it in an easterly direction. At that point, the Gulf Stream converges with the Labrador Current, a southward flow of cooler waters that push it even farther to the east. Having its source in the Caribbean Sea, the Gulf Stream is characterized by very clear, deep blue water of a higher temperature than that on either side, and strong currents that vary in speed. The strength of the current is such that it frequently took three times as long to travel from New England to South Carolina as it did to return.

While there are earlier references to and descriptions of the Gulf Stream, the first chart to depict the flow is attributed to Benjamin Franklin and Timothy Folger.[1] Franklin first mentioned the Gulf Stream in his journal on a voyage to London in 1726. He wrote, "I cannot help fancying the water is changed a little, as is usual when a ship comes within soundings, but 'tis probable I am mistaken; for there is but one besides myself of my opinion, and we are very apt to believe what we wish to be true."[2] The following day, he recorded, "The water is now very visibly changed to the eyes of all except the Captain and Mate, and they will by no means allow it; I suppose because they did not see it first."[3]

Franklin began to take a serious interest in the Gulf Stream in 1768. As deputy postmaster general for the American colonies, Franklin received a complaint from a Boston customs official that mail packets sailing from Falmouth, England, to New York routinely took longer than merchant ships from London to Rhode Island. This was especially puzzling since packet ships were faster than merchant vessels. Attempting to discover the reason, he consulted his cousin, Timothy Folger, a navigator from Nantucket, who was in London at the time. Folger explained that the slower voyage to New York was due to the Gulf Stream, a current well known to Nantucket whalers. Franklin transmitted Folger's information to Anthony Todd, head of the British Post Office:

> *Whales are found generally near the Edges of the* Gulph Stream, *a strong Current so called which comes out of the Gulph of Florida, passing Northeasterly along the Coast of*

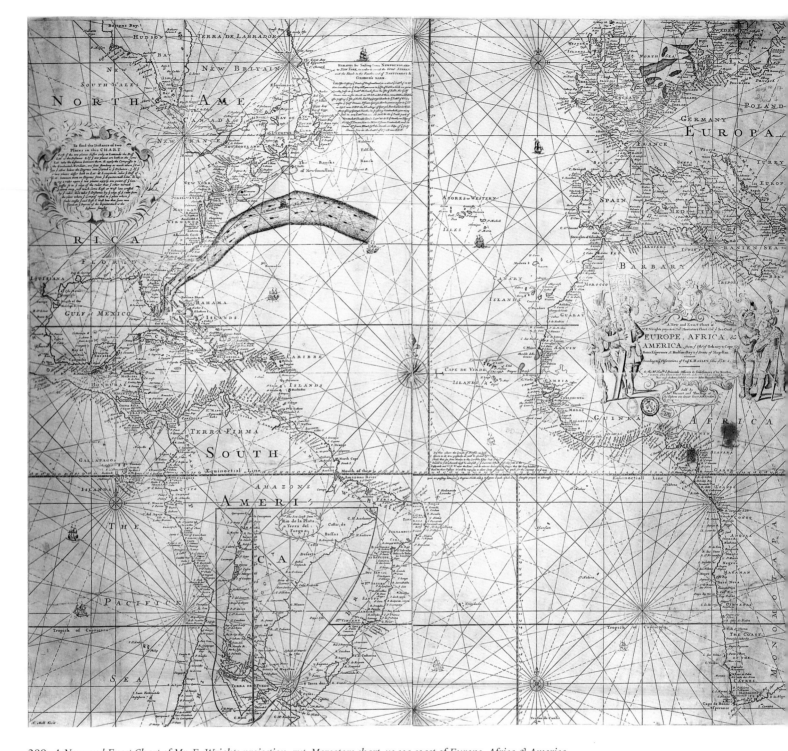

209 *A New and Exact Chart of Mr. E. Wrights projection, rut. Mercators chart, ye sea coast of Europe, Africa & America,*
originally engraved by Herman Moll (the Gulf Stream was added later), published by John Mount and Thomas Page,
London, ca. 1769, black-and-white line engraving. Courtesy, Library of Congress.

America, and the turning off most Easterly running at the rate of 4, 3½, 3 and 2½ Miles an Hour; that the Whaling Business leading these people to Cruise along the Edges of the Stream in quest of Whales, they are become better acquainted with the Course, Breadth, Strength and extent of the same, than those Navigators can well be who only cross it in their Voyages to and from America, . . . Ships bound from England to New York Virginia &ca, who have passages of 8, 9, and 10 weeks, and are still far from Land, and not likely to be in with it for some time, being engaged in that part of the Stream that sets directly against them, and it is supposed that their fear of Cape Sable Shoals, Georges Banks or Nantuckett Shoals, hath induced them to keep so far to the Southward as unavoidably to engage them in the said Gulph Stream, which occasions the length of their Voyage, since in a Calm it carries them directly back, and tho' they may have fair Winds, yet the Current being 60, or 70 Miles a day, is so much Subtracted from the way they make thro' the Water.[4]

Franklin had also requested that Folger draft a chart showing the course and dimensions of the Gulf Stream and provide instructions so that captains bound for Newfoundland and New York could avoid the current. Franklin forwarded Folger's draft and sailing instructions to Todd, suggesting that maps of the Gulf Stream be engraved at the expense of the Post Office and distributed to the captains of the mail packets. Todd received Folger's chart from Franklin on October 29, 1768. By February 17, 1769, the firm of Mount and Page engraved Folger's information on an old plate of an obsolete chart of the Atlantic Ocean.[5] *(fig. 209)* Historian Ellen R. Cohn speculated that, based on the number of packets sailing between England and America in 1768, there would have been little demand for the chart; therefore, few copies of Mount and Page's work were printed, a theory supported because no copy was known to survive until one was discovered in the Bibliothèque Nationale, Paris, in 1978.[6]

In Paris as minister to the French court between 1780 and 1783, Franklin commissioned mapmaker George Louis Le Rouge to publish a new version of the Gulf Stream chart. Cohn argued convincingly that Franklin did not meet Le Rouge until September 1780, thereby suggesting that the map could not predate that time. The map had been engraved by April 1783 when Franklin sent a copy to the French Ministry of the Marine. The same month, Franklin provided a copy to Michel Guillaume de Crèvecoeur, who had been retained by the minister of the Marine to provide information on the geography, population, and manufacturing capabilities of the United States.[7] Franklin's comments on the Gulf Stream were important to Crèvecoeur, who was in the process of preparing a proposal for a packet boat service between France and America. Cohn concluded that, viewed in the context of Franklin's correspondence, the Le Rouge version was intended for French merchant and packet captains.

The Le Rouge chart of the Gulf Stream illustrated in this entry is one of three known copies with a history of having belonged to Franklin.

G1985-1, gift of Mrs. Anna Glen Vietor in memory of Alexander O. Vietor

1. The first reliable information about the Gulf Stream was recorded by Juan Ponce de Leon during his 1513 expedition from Puerto Rico across the Bahama Channel to mainland Florida. In 1590, John White (Cat. 2) described his voyage from the Florida Keys to Virginia by stating," We lost sight of the coast of Florida, and stood to Sea for to gaine the helpe of the current which runneth much swifter a farre off then in sight of the coast. For from the Cape to Virginia all along the shore are none but eddie currents, setting to the South and Southwest." "John White's Narrative of the 1590 Virginia Voyage," in Quinn and Quinn, eds., *Virginia Voyages from Hakluyt,* p. 122. In 1735, Walter Hoxton published a *Mapp of the Bay of Chesepeack (fig. 48a)* that included a written description of the Gulf Stream.

2. Labaree et al., eds., *Papers of Franklin,* I, p. 95.

3. *Ibid.,* pp. 95–96.

4. *Ibid.,* XV, pp. 246–247.

5. The first mention of the printed chart was on Feb. 17, 1769, when Todd sent a copy to John Pownall, secretary of the Board of Trade. Ellen R. Cohn, "Benjamin Franklin, George-Louis Le Rouge and the Franklin/Folger Chart of the Gulf Stream," *Imago Mundi,* LII (2000), p. 132.

6. *Ibid.,* pp. 132, 138.

7. *Ibid.,* p. 135.

63 *SKETCH / of the POSITION of the BRITISH FORCES / at / ELIZABETH TOWN POINT / after their RETURN from CONNECTICUT FARM, / in the PROVINCE of EAST JERSEY: / under the Command of / HIS EXCELL^Y. LEIUT^T. GEN^L. KNYPHAUSEN, / on the 8th. June 1780, / By John Hills, Lieut^t. 23^d. Reg^t. & Ass^t. Eng^r.*

John Hills, cartographer; engraver unknown; published in *Atlas of Battles of the American Revolution* by William Faden

London, April 12, 1784. Black-and-white line engraving with period color. H. 24¼", W. 20⅞"

The title is in the upper right corner. Below is an alphabetical list of references, *A-H*, identifying the positions and works of the British army. In the lower center is the imprint *LONDON./ Published by Willm Faden, Geographer to the KING,/ Charing Cross, April 12.th 1784.* Beneath is a *SCALE of PACES*[1]

One state of the map is known

References: Guthorn, *British Maps of the American Revolution*, pp. 24–27; Nebenzahl, *Atlas of the American Revolution*, pp. 134–135; Nebenzahl, *Bibliography of Printed Battle Plans*, entry 146; Sellers and van Ee, *Maps and Charts of North America*, p. 275

U NLIKE many of the maps published by William Faden that depict important battles of the Revolution, this plan simply documents the positions of the British and Hessians under General Wilhelm von Knyphausen after their unsuccessful raid on Springfield, New Jersey. Although the roads leading from De Hart's Point to the town were drawn, troop movements were not indicated.

While Clinton was in Charleston, General Knyphausen assumed temporary command of the British army in New York. Knyphausen organized a raid on Washington's army at Morristown, New Jersey. Landing at De Hart's Point on June 7, 1780, the forces advanced toward Washington's winter camp. They were met at Springfield Bridge by an American regiment under the command of Colonel Elias Dayton and were forced to retreat. During the night of June 8, Knyphausen removed his troops to the site of the present city of Elizabeth, New Jersey, where they constructed the fortifications recorded on John Hills's plan.

When Clinton returned to New York, he learned of Knyphausen's unsuccessful operation and decided to send reinforcements. It is likely that Hills's draft of the British encampments on June 7 and 8, seen here in printed form, was used to plan the strategy for the subsequent attack. Once again, the British were forced to retreat.

1975-74

1. The *OED* defines a military pace as about 2½ feet.

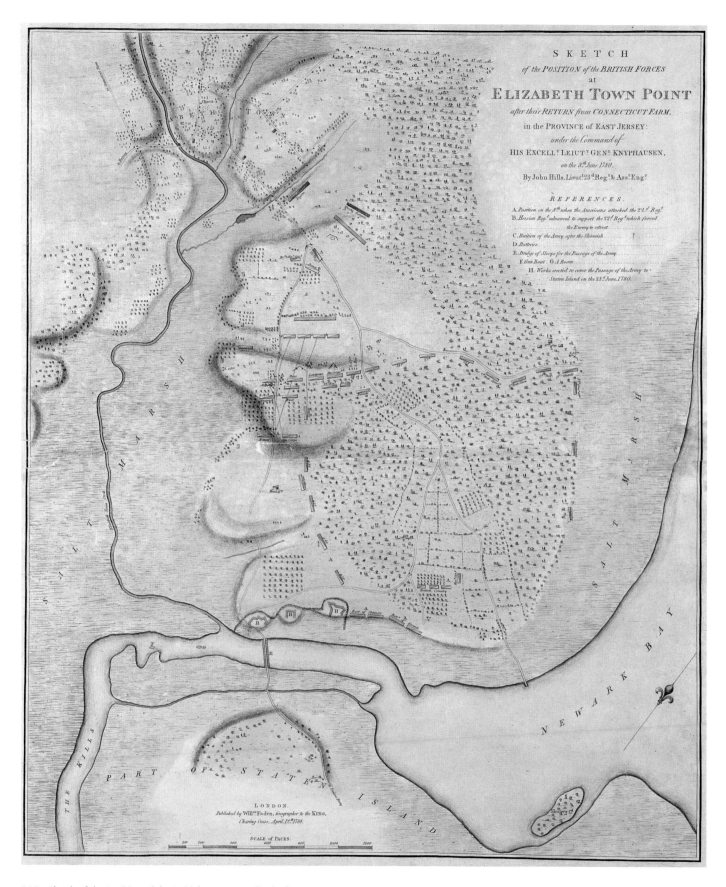

SKETCH
of the POSITION of the BRITISH FORCES
at
ELIZABETH TOWN POINT
after their RETURN from CONNECTICUT FARM.
in the PROVINCE of EAST JERSEY:
under the Command of
HIS EXCELL.Y LEIUT.T GEN.L KNYPHAUSEN,
on the 8.th June 1780.
By John Hills, Lieut.t 23.d Reg.t & Ass.t Eng.r

REFERENCES.
A. Position on the 8.th when the Americans attacked the 22.d Reg.t
B. Hessian Reg.t advanced to support the 22.d Reg.t which forced
  the Enemy to retreat
C. Position of the Army after the Skirmish
D. Batteries
E. Bridge of Sloops for the Passage of the Army.
F. Gun Boat . G. A Boom
  H. Works erected to cover the Passage of the Army to
  Staten Island on the 25.th June. 1780.

LONDON.
Published by Will.m Faden, Geographer to the KING,
Charing Cross, April, 12.th 1784.

SCALE of PACES.

210 *Sketch of the Position of the British Forces at Elizabeth Town Point.* (Cat. 63)

64 *Campagne en Virginie / du Major Général M^{isr}
de La Fayette, / ou Se trouvent les Camps et Marches,
ainsy que ceux / du Lieutenant Général L.^{d}
Cornwallis. / par le Major Capitaine, aide de Camp
du G^{l}. La Fayette*

Michel Capitaine du Chesnoy, cartographer

Probably Virginia, 1781. India ink on paper. H. 35″, W. 44″

The title is in the upper right corner. A scale of distances is in the
lower center

References: Cohen, "Michel Capitaine du Chesnoy," pp. 170–177;
Guthorn, *American Maps and Map Makers*, pp. 9–12; McCorkle,
America Emergent, entry 64; Verner, *Maps of the Yorktown Campaign*,
p. 14

Campagne en Virginie du Major Général M^{isr} de La Fayette was
drawn by the French topographical engineer Michel Capitaine du Chesnoy, one of several aides who accompanied
General Lafayette to America in 1777.[1] At Lafayette's side
for most of his American tour of duty, Capitaine drew
detailed plans of the general's campaigns that are largely
unknown today since only one was ever engraved and published.[2] Manuscript maps such as these were generally
stored among the personal papers of those associated with
the events and thus did not circulate. Even so, they are
vitally important as a primary cartographic record of events.

Capitaine's skills as a draftsman and engineer surpassed
those of his American counterparts. For his *Campagne en
Virginie*, he used Fry and Jefferson's *Map of the most Inhabited part of Virginia* as his source for the geography and place-
names, omitting the Eastern Shore and territory west of
the Appalachian Mountains. He enlarged the scale so that
troop movements could be clearly delineated, chronicling
Lafayette's strategy between April 29 and September 8,
1781, during which time the French general was able to
engage Cornwallis long enough to allow Washington and
Rochambeau to march their armies to Virginia.

After Lord Dunmore's assault that destroyed Norfolk in
January 1776, Virginia was largely spared further military
action until after Charleston fell in 1780. Having defeated
the Americans in both Georgia and South Carolina, the
British significantly strengthened their military position in
the southern colonies, allowing them to turn their attention to Virginia, a primary source for military supplies. In
addition, Virginia tobacco offered the patriots an opportunity to establish credit abroad.

On December 20, 1780, Benedict Arnold, on his first
assignment under Sir Henry Clinton after defecting to the
British, left New York for Virginia with about sixteen hundred troops for the purpose of organizing raids to destroy
military stores. Arnold reached Hampton Roads on December 30 and began his ascent up the James River. He took
the battery at Hoods Point and occupied Richmond for
three days, burning buildings and destroying tobacco,
before withdrawing to Westover plantation.

British General William Phillips sailed from Sandy Hook
in March 1781 to join Arnold and assume command in Virginia. Once Phillips arrived with reinforcements, the two
conducted another raid between April 25 and 27, this time
taking Petersburg and Chesterfield Courthouse. They also
burned a small flotilla of American ships that had assembled in the James River waiting to assist the French navy in
forthcoming operations.

Having been well informed of Arnold's activities, Washington decided to mount an offensive, attacking the traitor
on land and sea. He dispatched twelve hundred light
infantry commanded by Lafayette to Virginia. As Lafayette's Continentals set out, a French force of equal size
from Newport, Rhode Island, was transported to the
Chesapeake in a French fleet commanded by Admiral
Destouches. En route, the French encountered Admiral
Arbuthnot's superior English fleet, also bound for the area.
Aware that the British ships contained more firepower, the
French abandoned the operation and returned to Newport,
leaving Lafayette without adequate reinforcements,
although two thousand Virginia militia had joined him.

The French general's bleak situation was about to take
a turn for the worse. General Clinton returned to New
York after the siege of Charleston, leaving Cornwallis, his
second in command, in charge of the southern campaign.
Prior to his departure, Clinton warned Cornwallis not to
initiate offensive operations if they would jeopardize the
British strongholds in South Carolina and Georgia.
Undaunted by Clinton's instructions and far more ambitious and aggressive than his immediate superior, Cornwallis was determined to launch a campaign in Virginia.
Pressing through North Carolina, Cornwallis arrived in
Petersburg on May 20, 1781, to join forces with the British
raiders. Within a few days, reinforcements from New York
brought the total to about seventy-two hundred men.

Lafayette was well aware that his army was no match
for Cornwallis, so he devised a strategy to engage the
British general in a series of skirmishes:

> *Was I to fight a Battle I'll Be Cut to pieces, the Militia dis-
> persed, and the Arms lost. Was I to decline fighting the*

211 *Campagne en Virginie du Major Général M^{isr} de La Fayette.* (Cat. 64)

Country would think Herself given up. I am therefore determined to Skarmish, But not to engage too far, and particularly to take Care against their Immense and excellent Body of Horse whom the Militia fear like they would So Many wild Beasts.[3]

Holding to his strategy, Lafayette retreated northward as far as Ely's Ford, noted here as *Racoon Ford,* on the Rapidan River as Cornwallis advanced. On June 6, General Anthony Wayne and his corps of about one thousand Regulars from Pennsylvania joined Lafayette.

Cornwallis then moved southeast, entering Richmond on June 16. Four days later, the British began to march toward Williamsburg. Lafayette and his troops shadowed Cornwallis, following at a distance of about twenty miles to the north. In Williamsburg, Cornwallis received instructions from Clinton directing him to send a detachment of three thousand troops to New York and to establish a post at the mouth of the Chesapeake Bay. Clinton suggested that Old Point Comfort, at the end of the peninsula between the York and James Rivers, could serve as a base for naval operations from which to defend and control the Bay.[4] Cornwallis decided to move his troops across the James River to Portsmouth, however. Following closely, Lafayette devised a plan to attack the British rear guard after most of the army had crossed the river. Cornwallis shrewdly realized Lafayette's intentions and, while leading the Frenchman to believe that only his rear guard remained on the peninsula, sent the main army to attack Wayne's detachment at Green Springs late in the afternoon of July 6. Rather than retreating, Wayne counterattacked, bringing the British offensive to a halt. Fortunately for the rebels, Cornwallis attacked so late that the sun set before he could destroy the greatest part of Lafayette's force. Cornwallis crossed the river and his troops made their way to Portsmouth.

By August 22, Cornwallis had moved his command post to Yorktown, with a support site across the York River at Gloucester Point, rather than at Clinton's recommended site of Old Point Comfort. Cornwallis's engineers concluded the position was unsuitable because the channel was too wide to provide adequate land cover for vessels sealing off the entrance to the Hampton Roads.

In addition to the wealth of detail Capitaine's manuscript provides about Lafayette's Virginia campaign, it is also interesting for what it reveals about how military engineers assembled and disseminated information. Although this map was never published, at least two other manuscript copies survive.[5] In 1956, Yale University purchased Lafayette's personal copy, almost certainly made by Capitaine as a presentation piece. *(fig. 212)* This version was enhanced with decorative elements that are lacking on the two other examples. It was mounted on rollers decorated in blue and gold and was housed in a blue box. The Library of Congress recently purchased a set of six of Capitaine's maps from a private American collection that included a third example. *(fig. 213)* It has been suggested that these were Capitaine's personal copies and may have been the prototypes from which duplicates were made as needed for field maps, to plan strategy, or to record battles.[6]

In addition to the many maps Capitaine produced for Lafayette, there is ample evidence that he made copies for others as well. Lafayette wrote on July 23, 1778, that he would employ Capitaine "to make plans of our positions and battle for [General] Washington, for me, and also for the king who will be glad to have an exact draft of [General] Washington's battles."[7] On October 4, at Lafayette's request, Capitaine sent drafts of events in Rhode Island to Washington.[8] Three years later, the general asked Lafayette if he "would permit Mr. Capitaine to furnish me with copies of the drafts, & remarks of the Pilots (taken at Colo. Deys) on the entrence of the Harbour of New York." [9]

Paul Cohen noticed that the Library of Congress copy of Capitaine's Virginia campaign map had a pencil-lined grid with pinholes at various intersecting points, leading him to surmise that it may have been the prototype for the subsequent drafts. Cohen suggested that pins were used to hold tracing paper over the map for copying.[10] The Capitaine map at Colonial Williamsburg appears to be drawn on eighteenth-century tracing paper. Prior to 1853, oil such as walnut, poppy seed, or hazelnut, or varnish was applied to paper to create a transparent effect.[11] It is thus possible that the Williamsburg map was traced from an earlier draft, but there is no evidence that pins ever perforated the surface. Superimposing a modern tracing of one version over the others shows enough variations in the geographical features to conclude that none of these copies was traced directly from another.

Close scrutiny of the Yale version reveals the identical pinhole placement and pencil-lined grid found on the Library of Congress copy; however, the modern tracing once again rules out the possibility that one of the two served as a prototype for tracing. Perhaps the pinhole and pencil-grid suggests another method for transferring the geography other than by direct tracing to reproduce copies. Further, if Lafayette's personal copy had been traced from a master document, there would have been no need for a second pencil-lined grid to accompany the pinholes.

212 *CARTE de la Campagne en VIRGINIE du Major Général Mis de la Fayette on se trouvent les Camps et marches ainsy que ceux du Lieuten.^t Général Lord Cornwallis,* by Michel Capitaine du Chesnoy, probably Virginia, ca. 1781, india ink on paper. Original in Yale University Library, New Haven, Conn., photostat, Colonial Williamsburg Foundation.

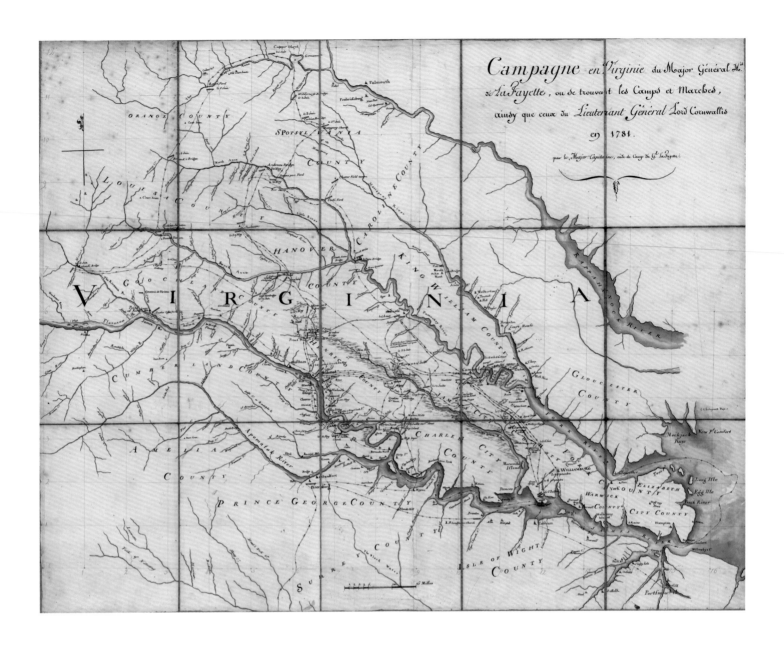

213 *Campagne en Virginie du Major Général M.^{isr} de La Fayette ou Se trouvent les Camps et Marches ainsy que ceux du Lieuten.^t Général Ld Cornwallis en 1781,* by Michel Capitaine du Chesnoy, probably Virginia, ca. 1781, india ink on paper. Courtesy, Library of Congress.

Although it is impossible to determine if more than one engineer was responsible for the geography in these three maps, it is clear that two hands, one French, the other American, were involved in recording the place-names. The Colonial Williamsburg and Yale copies were both rendered by the Frenchman. Not only are some of the names themselves written in French, but the handwriting is in a French style.[12] Although the same French hand is occasionally represented on the Library of Congress version, the majority of place-names appear to have been penned by an American, suggesting that Capitaine may have been assisted by an American engineer.

The Library of Congress and Yale copies were accompanied by a lengthy *Précis de la Campagne 1781, pour Servir à l'intellige.^{ce} de la Carte*, summarizing the Virginia campaign from April through October 19.[13] As far as the Yale copy is concerned, its placement along the left side suggests that the map was prepared after the events had taken place. The Colonial Williamsburg example did not have a *Précis* when it was acquired in 1930. Initially, it was appealing to speculate that this copy, which exhibits signs of heavy use, might have been used by Lafayette in the field. Like the other two, however, the consistency of the ink and lettering clearly indicate that the troop movements and positions were recorded at one time, not as the events occurred.

1930-686

1. Capitaine was commissioned as a captain in the Corps of Engineers in Apr. 1778. Later that year, he was promoted to major.

2. Capitaine's published map was *CARTE DU THÉATRE DE LA GUERRE DANS L'AMÉRIQUE SEPTENTRIONALE.*

3. Stanley J. Idzerda, ed., *Lafayette in the Age of the American Revolution, Selected Letters and Papers, 1776–1790.* IV: *April 1, 1781–December 23, 1781* (Ithaca, N. Y., 1981), p. 131.

4. Cornwallis actually received several messages from Clinton containing conflicting orders about the detachment of troops and establishment of a post. His instructions were further complicated by communications from Lord Germain, British secretary of state for the American colonies, who attempted to control the maneuvers from London. Boatner, *Encyclopedia of the American Revolution,* pp. 1234–1235.

5. According to Cohen, there is a fourth manuscript copy of Capitaine's Virginia campaign map in a French repository.

6. Paul E. Cohen, "Michel Capitaine du Chesnoy, the marquis de Lafayette's cartographer," *The Magazine Antiques,* CLIII (1998), p. 176.

7. Lafayette to Henry Laurens, *ibid.,* p. 175.

8. *Calendar of the Correspondence of Washington.* I: *June 17, 1775–October 14, 1778* (Washington, D. C., 1915), p. 774.

9. Idzerda, ed., *Lafayette in the Age of the American Revolution,* p. 85.

10. Alan Simpson studied the so-called "Frenchman's Map" depicting the city of Williamsburg and discovered pinholes in that map as well. He concluded that a rough draft of the city plan was placed over a blank piece of paper and pins were used to locate landmarks such as the corners of buildings, fences, roads, and trees. These holes were then connected by pencil and, later, by ink. Alan Simpson, *The Mysteries of the "Frenchman's Map" of Williamsburg, Virginia* (Williamsburg, Va., 1984), p. 17.

11. I would like to thank paper conservator Valinda Carroll for her assistance in documenting eighteenth-century tracing paper.

12. I would like to thank Donna Sheppard, who was the first to notice the presence of two hands in the Lib. Cong. map. Simpson consulted eighteenth-century copybooks when attempting to identify the country of origin of the handwriting on the "Frenchman's Map." Capitaine's lettering has a similar feel to that on the "Art d'Ecrire" engravings from Diderot, *Recueil de Planches.*

12. The *Précis* accompanying the map in the Lib. Cong. is on six individual sheets of paper. The text of both is the same.

65 *CARTE / DE LA PARTIE DE LA VIRGINIE / ou / L'ARMÉE COMBINÉE DE FRANCE & / DES ÉTATS-UNIS DE L'AMÉRIQUE / a fait prisonniere l'Armée Anglaise / commandée par LORD CORNWALLIS le 19 Oct.^bre 1781. / AVEC LE PLAN DE L'ATTAQUE / d'York-town & de Glocester / Levée et dessinée les Lieux par Ordre de Officiers Gen^x. / de l'Armée Francaise & Américaine*

Cartographer and engraver unknown; Esnauts and Rapilly and Louis Charles Desnos, publishers

Paris, ca. 1782. Black-and-white line engraving with period color. H. 19", W. 24½"

The title is contained in a square in the lower right corner. The imprint *A PARIS, Chez Esnauts et Rapilly, rue S.t Jacques a la Ville de Coutances* is below. To the lower left of the title is the scale of leagues, *Lieues Marines d'une heure de 20 au Dégré.* A small overlay in the shape of a circle about an inch and one-quarter in diameter was pasted above the title and contained the imprint of another publisher. The second imprint was *On trouve/ à Paris, chez le/ S.r Desnos, Libraire,/ Ingen.r Géogr.e du Roy/ de Dannemarck, Rue/ S.t Jacques, au Globe,/ toutes les Cartes/ des différents/ Auteurs*

One state of the map is known[1]

References: Cresswell, "Colony to Commonwealth," pp. 110–111; Nebenzahl, *Atlas of the American Revolution,* pp. 186–188; Nebenzahl, *Bibliography of Printed Battle Plans,* entry 198; Ristow, *American Maps and Mapmakers,* pp. 44–45; Sellers and van Ee, *Maps and Charts of North America,* p. 316; Verner, *Maps of the Yorktown Campaign,* p. 43

ON August 14, 1781, General Washington received news that would shape his strategy for the remainder of the Revolutionary War. In order to support the American campaign, French Admiral François Joseph Paul, Comte de Grasse, had left the West Indies with a fleet of twenty-eight ships of the line, six frigates, and three thousand troops bound for the Chesapeake Bay. Washington was informed that the admiral planned to return to the West Indies by mid-October. In order to take advantage of de Grasse's support, Washington and Jean-Baptiste-Donatien de Vimeur, Comte de Rochambeau, abandoned their planned assault on Clinton in New York and marched their troops almost five hundred miles to Virginia. They also needed to convince Admiral Jacques-Melchior Saint-Laurent, Comte de Barras, commander of the French fleet at Newport, Rhode Island, to sail to the Chesapeake with French siege artillery and supplies for the army. By August 20, the allied army advanced south and Barras prepared to sail for the Chesapeake.

Clinton was aware that de Grasse's fleet had been dispatched to Virginia but he underestimated its strength. Admiral George Rodney, commander of British naval operations in the West Indies, believed that only a portion of the French fleet would be deployed to the mainland and thus would pose no threat to the superior British naval force. Before poor health forced Rodney to return to England, he instructed his second in command, Admiral Sir Samuel Hood, to take fourteen ships of the line and five frigates and head for the North American coast.

Although de Grasse left the West Indies before Hood, the French took a circuitous route through the Bahama Channel in order to conceal their movements. Hood's direct course and favorable weather conditions caused him to arrive off the Virginia Capes before his adversary. Finding no evidence of the French fleet, Hood sailed up the coast, first to the Delaware Bay and then to New York where he met up with Admiral Thomas Graves. The two British fleets with a combined force of nineteen warships departed New York for Virginia by the first of September.

In the meantime, de Grasse had arrived in the Chesapeake on August 26. Leaving a number of ships at the mouths of the James and York Rivers to stand guard and block supplies intended for Cornwallis, de Grasse disembarked his troops and prepared the transport ships to sail up the bay to Baltimore and Annapolis to relay Washington's army to the Tidewater. When the British navy appeared at the Virginia Capes on September 5, de Grasse dispatched his warships to the mouth of the bay. Although the ensuing battle lasted less than three hours, the British fleet was heavily damaged. Six of Graves's nineteen ships were temporarily taken out of action. The *Terrible,* illustrated in flames on *Carte de la Partie de la Virginie,* was so badly damaged that the British eventually had to destroy the vessel.

During the next two days, the French and British fleets maintained contact but did not engage in combat as they drifted about one hundred miles in the direction of the Carolina Capes, thereby allowing Barras to slip unnoticed into the Chesapeake Bay with the French siege artillery. On September 14, Graves gave up hope of renewing the battle and ordered the British to sail to New York. Surrounded by land and sea, Cornwallis was unable to escape or to receive supplies.

Carte de la Partie de la Virginie depicts a dramatic, somewhat stylized, version of the important role the French navy played in the American victory at Yorktown. Designed for the French market, the map illustrates—and perhaps enhances—the French position at the mouth of

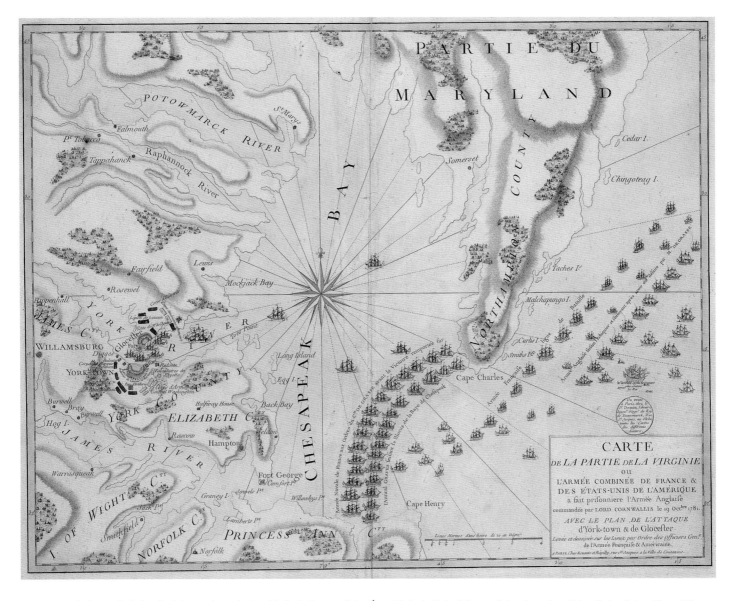

214 *Carte de la Partie de la Virginie ou L'Armée Combinée de France & des États-Unis de L'Amérique a fait prisonniere l'Armée Anglaise.* (Cat. 65)

Reddition de l'Armée Angloises Commandeé par Mylord Comte de Cornwallis aux Armees Combineés des Etats unis de l'Amerique et et Glocester dans la Virginie. le 19 Octobre 1781. Il s'est trouves dans ses deux postes 6000 hommes de troupes regleés Angloises ou Hessoises et 2 40 Batimens dont un Vaisseau de 50 Canons qui a été Brulé 20 Coules Bas ; Ce jour a jamais memorables pour les Etats unis en ce quil assur

A . Yorck Touwn   C . Armeés Angloise sortant de la place .   E Armeé Francoise   G Armeé naval de France
B . Glocester   D . Les Armes des ennemis poseé en Faiseeaux   F Armeé Ameriquaine   H Baye de Chesapeack

215 *Reddition de l' Armée Angloises Commandée par Mylord Comte de Cornwallis aux Armees Combinées des Etats unis de l' Amerique et de France aux ordres des Generaux Washington et de Rochambeau a Yorck touwn et Glocester dans la Virginie. le 19 Octobre 1781,* maker unknown, Paris, ca. 1781, black-and-white line engraving with period color. 1960-879.

ordres des Generaux Washington et de Rochambeau a Yorck town
Matelots 160 Canons de tout Calibre dont 75 de Fonte 3 Mortiers
leurs independances
te de Grace   I Entrée d'Yorck .
                A Paris chez Mondhare rue St Jean de Beauvais près celle des Noyers

the Chesapeake Bay. Admiral Graves's fleet is pictured as they prepared to sail for New York.

1974-164

1. Nebenzahl identified two states, based on the appearance on some copies of an additional pasted-on imprint of publisher Louis Charles Desnos. Nebenzahl, *Bibliography of Printed Battle Plans,* p. 123. As no changes were made to the plate, I believe it does not constitute a change of state. From 1747, Desnos ran his business selling maps and globes from Rue St. Jacques. He published an atlas relating to America in 1795.

2. The exact date of de Grasse's arrival has been questioned. Most recent sources have accepted Aug. 30.

66 *A PLAN of the POSTS / of / YORK AND GLOUCESTER / in the / PROVINCE OF VIRGINIA, / Established by / HIS MAJESTY'S ARMY / under the Command of Lieut.¹ General EARL CORNWALLIS, / together with / The Attacks and Operations of the AMERICAN & FRENCH FORCES / Commanded by / GENERAL WASHINGTON and the COUNT of ROCHAMBEAU, / Which Terminated in the SURRENDER of the said Posts and Army / on the 17ᵗʰ. of October 1781. / SURVEYED by CAPTᴺ. FAGE of the ROYAL ARTILLERY*

Edward Fage, cartographer; published in *The Atlantic Neptune* by Joseph Frederick Wallet Des Barres

London, June 4, 1782. Black-and-white line engraving with period color. H. 40¼", W. 29⅞", in two sheets

In the upper right is an inset map of Gloucester, Northampton, York, Elizabeth, Warwick, Isle of Wight, Nansemond, Norfolk, and Princess Anne Counties. The title and scale of feet are in a rectangle set at an angle in the lower left. Some copies were issued with an overlay showing *The POSITION of the ARMY/ between the Ravines/ on the 18.ᵗʰ and 19.ᵗʰ of Sept. 1781.* This copy lacks the overlay

Two states of the map are known:
State 1: As described, but containing the phrase *chevaux de frise* around redoubt no. 9
State 2: (this copy) As described. The term *chevaux de frise* was erased[1]

References: Guthorn, *British Maps of the American Revolution,* pp. 20–21; Nebenzahl, *Bibliography of Printed Battle Plans,* entry 190; Sellers and van Ee, *Maps and Charts of North America,* p. 318; Verner, *Maps of the Yorktown Campaign,* p. 38

Wᴴɪʟᴇ the French navy under Admiral de Grasse was attempting to block the mouth of the Chesapeake Bay, Washington and Rochambeau were bringing the Franco-American troops to Virginia. Traveling in advance of the main army, the generals arrived at Lafayette's camp in Williamsburg on September 14. They impressed upon Lafayette the necessity of ensuring that Cornwallis remain confined at Yorktown. Surprisingly, Cornwallis took no action. By September 26, the French and American forces had reached the capital. Two days later, the march to Yorktown began.

Yorktown was built on a bluff at a point where the York River is about one-half-mile wide. Although painted almost thirty years earlier, *A View of the Town of York Virginia*

from the River appears to be an accurate depiction of the city's appearance.[2] (*fig. 217*) "Yorktown Creek" to the northwest and "Wormsley Creek" to the southeast created natural ravines. Cornwallis constructed seven inner redoubts and six battery positions joined by a series of entrenchments that together formed a semicircular curve southeast of the city. The primary strongpoint of this inner line of fortifications was known as the "horn work." Beyond the inner line were three more redoubts located in the ravines (Pigeon Quarter), the Fusilier redoubt to the west along the Williamsburg Road, and redoubts 9 and 10 to the southeast. Across the river at Gloucester Point, Cornwallis established a support site with four redoubts and three batteries, also connected by entrenchments. Frigates *Guadeloupe* and *Charon,* each with forty-four guns, and three transports were anchored in the river.

By October 6, the allies were prepared for battle. To divert attention from the Americans constructing the first parallel south of Yorktown, the French positioned themselves west of the Fusilier redoubt. The French were extended the courtesy of firing the first round on October 9. Washington himself fired the first American round from the south. The next day, four more allied batteries joined in the action, causing significant damage to the British army's ability to return fire. The *Charon* and two other vessels were destroyed by French hot shot. On October 14, Washington attacked British redoubts 9 and 10. Both were captured without counterattack, refortified, and tied into the Americans' second parallel.

In desperation, Cornwallis attempted to spike the enemy's guns, which he ordered Lieutenant Colonel Robert Abercromby to do. Abercromby ineffectively spiked six cannon, but the Americans quickly put them back in order. Fage recorded this maneuver as *Sally made by the British against these Batterys Oct.ʳ 16.* The second parallel was complete.

Cornwallis attempted to ferry his army across the York River to Gloucester Point during the night of October 16–17; however, due to severe weather, only one advance force was transported. Cornwallis was stranded in Yorktown. On October 17, the allied forces opened with heavy bombardments. The British were unable to answer. Sometime between nine and ten o'clock that morning, a red-coated drummer and a soldier waving a handkerchief signaled Cornwallis's intention to surrender.

Edward Fage, who had been trained at the Royal Military Academy at Woolwich, illustrated the troop, redoubt, and battery positions of the allied and British armies around Yorktown on the main portion of the map. An

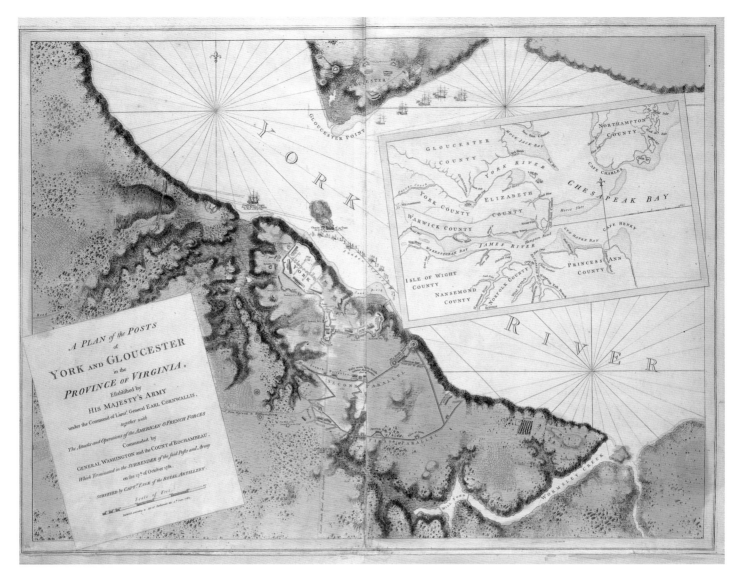

216 *A Plan of the Posts of York and Gloucester.* (Cat. 66)

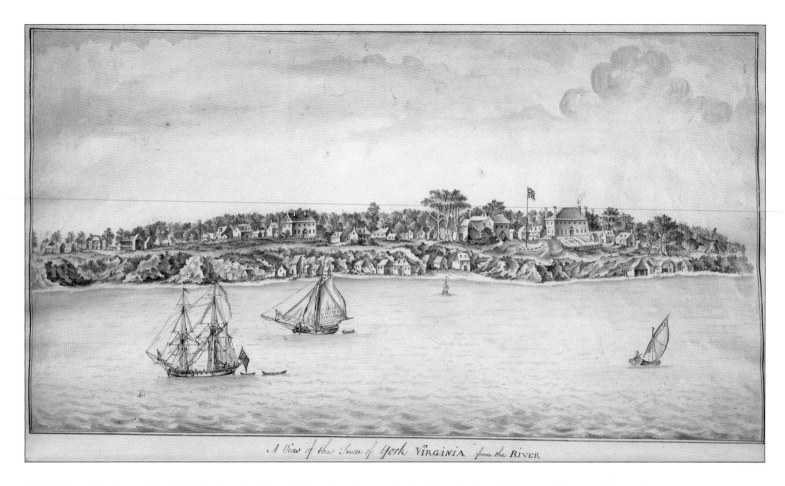

A View of the Town of York Virginia from the River

217 *A View of the Town of York Virginia from the River*, 1755, watercolor wash. Courtesy, Mariners' Museum, Newport News, Va.

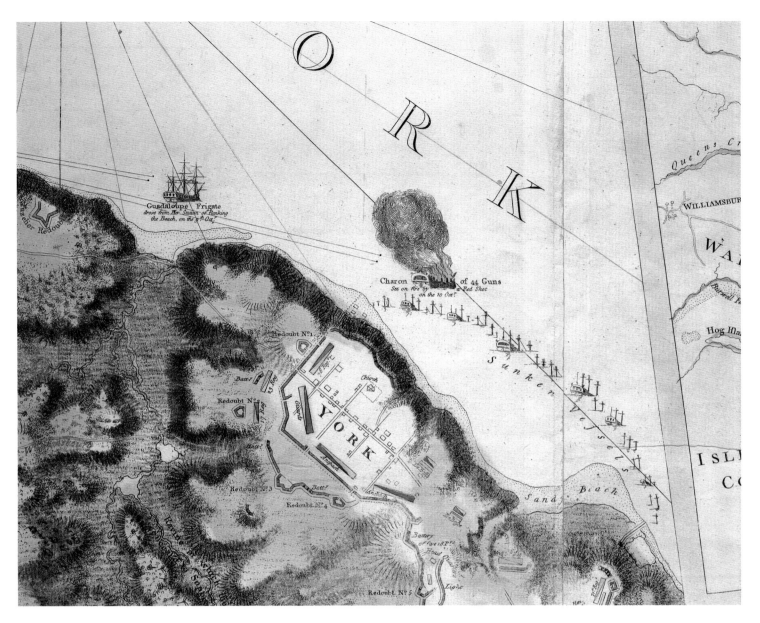

218 Detail from *A Plan of the Posts of York and Gloucester,* by Edward Fage,
published by Joseph Frederick Wallet des Barres, London, 1782,
black-and-white line engraving with period color. 1955-485. (Cat. 66)

accompanying overlay that is missing from this copy pinpointed positions of the British troops in the ravines as the
allies approached the enemy on September 28 and 29. *A
Plan of the Posts of York and Gloucester* is one of a handful of
battle plans that Joseph Frederick Wallet Des Barres published in his *Atlantic Neptune.*

1955-485

1. Nebenzahl, *Bibliography of Printed Battle Plans,* entry 190.

2. Although the artist is unknown, the watercolor was probably
painted by an officer on board the *Success* or the *Norwich.* Both ships were
in the fleet in the York River in 1755. "Observations in several voyages and
travels in America in the year 1736," in E. G. Swem, "Views of Yorktown
and Gloucester Town, 1755," *VMHB,* LIV (1946), p. 102. A traveler
described the city in 1736: "I should just mention the battery, that is the
defense of the town, which at this time was under the direction of an awkward engineer, by trade a barber, and is as despicably contrived for the
safety of the place as it, no doubt, would be conducted in time of danger.
Indeed, Virginia is quite an open country to the incursions of an enemy,
having little to resist an attack by sea." *Ibid.,* p. 101, n. 3.

67 *A PLAN of / YORK TOWN AND GLOUCESTER, / IN THE PROVINCE OF VIRGINIA, / Shewing / the WORKS constructed for the Defence of those Posts / by the BRITISH ARMY, / under the Command of L^t. Genl. EARL CORNWALLIS; / together with / the Attacks and Operations of the American and French Forces, / Commanded by / GEN^L. WASHINGTON and COUNT ROCHAMBEAU, / to whom the said Posts were Surrendered / on the 17.th October 1781. / from an actual SURVEY in the Possession of / JN^O. HILLS, late Lieut^t. in the 23^d. Reg^t. & Ass^t. Eng^r*

John Hills, cartographer; engraver unknown; published in *Atlas of Battles of the American Revolution* by William Faden

London, October 7, 1785. Black-and-white line engraving.
H. 28½", W. 21½", in two sheets

The title is printed in the lower left corner. Below is the imprint *LONDON: Printed for W.^M FADEN, Geographer to the KING, Charing Cross, October 7.th 1785*, and a scale of feet

One state of the map is known

References: Guthorn, *British Maps of the American Revolution*, pp. 24–27; Nebenzahl, *Bibliography of Printed Battle Plans*, entry 195; Sellers and van Ee, *Maps and Charts of North America*, p. 319; Verner, *Maps of the Yorktown Campaign*, pp. 38–39

A Plan of York Town and Gloucester is virtually identical in content to the previous map by Captain Edward Fage.[1] Although the burning of the British ship *Charon* is not depicted here, a reference to it was noted beside the French batteries: *This Battery drove the Guadaloupe* [sic] *from her Station of flanking the Beach & set the Charon on Fire Octr 10.th*

The cartographer was Lieutenant John Hills, an assistant engineer in the 23rd Regiment of Foot.[2] During his career, Hills produced more than fifty maps, some of which depicted battles that he did not witness firsthand. He often borrowed from other reliable surveyors, citing them in his work. It is unclear whether Hills personally compiled *A Plan of York Town and Gloucester* or whether this was the work of another engineer. As Faden indicated in the title, the source was "an actual survey in the possession of John Hills." At the time Faden published this map, Hills was living in Philadelphia.

Hills is most noted for maps depicting New Jersey.[3] William Faden published this map and a *Sketch of the Position of the British Forces at Elizabeth Town Point* (Cat. 63) in his *Atlas of Battles of the American Revolution*.

1975-9

1. For another depiction of the troop positions around Yorktown, see Cat. 66.

2. Most of what is known of Hill's military activities comes from correspondence relating to his contempt of discipline. Guthorn, *British Maps of the American Revolution*, p. 24.

3. Hills produced *A Collection of Plans &c. &c. &c. in the Province of New Jersey*, made for Sir Henry Clinton, which is now in the Lib. Cong. For a complete listing of these 20 maps, see *ibid.*, pp. 25–27.

219 *A Plan of York Town and Gloucester.* (Cat. 67)

68 *To His Excellency Gen.ᶦ Washington /*
Commander in Chief of the Armies of the / United
States of America. / This Plan of the investment /
of York and Gloucester has been sur- / veyed and laid
down, and is / Most humbly dedicated by his
Excellency's / Obedient and very humble servant, /
Sebastⁿ. Bauman, Major / of the New York or 2ⁿᵈ Regᵗ
/ of Artillery

Sebastian Bauman, cartographer; Robert Scot, engraver

Philadelphia, 1782. Black-and-white line engraving. H. 25¼"
(trimmed); W. 17½" (trimmed)

References to the British/Lines in the upper left corner and the dedication and title in the upper right corner are within outlines and
scrollwork intended to represent rolled parchment. Ships are visible in the York River. Throughout the map, letters of the alphabet
identify specific locations. The corresponding explanation in a
scrollwork design is in the lower center. An array of emblems of
war—flags, cannons, cannonballs, swords, drums, and trumpets—
appears on either side. Beneath is a scale of yards. In the lower
right corner is the imprint *R. Scot Sculp. Philad. 1782*

Only one state of the map is known[1]

References: Cresswell, "Colony to Commonwealth," p. 110;
Guthorn, *American Maps and Map Makers*, pp. 8–9; Nebenzahl, *Atlas
of the American Revolution*, pp. 182–184; Nebenzahl, *Bibliography of
Printed Battle Plans*, entry 189; Schwartz and Ehrenberg, *Mapping
of America*, p. 199; Sellers and van Ee, *Maps and Charts of North
America*, p. 318; Verner, *Maps of the Yorktown Campaign*, p. 53;
Vietor, "Bauman Map," pp. 15–17; Wheat and Brun, *Maps and
Charts*, entry 541

Sᴇʙᴀsᴛɪᴀɴ Bᴀᴜᴍᴀɴ's *Plan of the investment of York and
Gloucester* illustrates the same topography and troop positions as the previous two entries. His map, however, is
significant as the first to be published in America that
depicted the allied forces' decisive victory over the British
at Yorktown. Bauman began his survey immediately after
Cornwallis's surrender, completing it in only one week. As
Fage and Hills had done on their maps, Bauman included
the fortifications and troop positions of the British, French,
and Americans.

Born in Frankfurt-am-Main, Germany, in 1739, Bauman was trained in the Austrian army. He immigrated to
the colonies prior to the French and Indian War, during
which he served in the New York Militia Company. On
January 1, 1777, he was assigned to the 2nd Continental
Regiment of Artillery and was promoted to major by September. Bauman became artillery commander at West

Point in 1779.[2] Two years later, he was ordered to Yorktown where he commanded one of the allied batteries.

Bauman forwarded a draft his survey of Yorktown to
Philadelphia where it was engraved by Robert Scot to be
sold by subscription.[3] The following March, the *New York
Packet, and the American Advertiser* announced the forthcoming publication:

Major Bauman, of the New York, or Second Regiment of
Artillery, Has Drawn a Map of the Investment of York and
Gloucester, in Virginia. Shewing how those posts were
besieged in form, by the Allied army of America and
France; the British lines of defence, and the American and
French lines of approach, with part of York River, and the
British ships as they then appeared sunk in it before York-
Town; and the whole encampment in its vicinity.

This Map, by desire of many gentlemen, will shortly be
published in Philadelphia, in order that the public may
form an idea of that memorable siege. Those gentlemen
who incline to become subscribers will apply to the printer
hereof; where the conditions will be shewn, and subscrip-
tion money be received.[4]

In addition to providing substantial detailed military
information, this map is also interesting for its artistic com-
position. Yorktown, Gloucester Point, and troop positions
are confined primarily to the top half of the map. The
lower half is dominated by the explanation that is embellished with ornaments of war. The shape of the scrollwork
cartouche surrounding the explanation, with flags and
banners that thrust upward from both sides, force the eye
to the center of the image. Here, in an open space, is the
very heart of the map, *The Field where the British laid down
their Arms.*

1950-769

---

1. A later version was made using this map as the source. J. F. Renault
made a new drawing that was presented to the Marquis de Lafayette in
1824 during his visit to the United States. This redrawn map was engraved
by Benjamin Tannner and published in 1825. CWF owns the copperplate
engraved by Tanner.

2. Guthorn, *American Maps and Mapmakers*, p. 8.

3. Born in England, Scot came to Virginia and settled in Fredericksburg
before June 1775, working as a watchmaker and engraver. Scot moved to
Philadelphia in 1781. Over the next few years, he conducted a business
from two locations on Front Street. George B. Cutten, *The Silversmiths of
Virginia. Together with Watchmakers and Jewelers, 1694 to 1850* (Richmond, Va.,
1952), p. 41.

4. Rita Susswein Gottesman, *The Arts and Crafts in New York, 1777–1799:
Advertisements and News Items from New York City Newspapers* (New York,
1954), p. 54.

220 *Plan of the investment of York and Gloucester.* (Cat. 68)

69 *THE / UNITED STATES / of / AMERICA / laid down / From the best Authorities, / Agreeable to the Peace of / 1783*

John Wallis (after Jean Baptiste Bourguignon d'Anville), cartographer; engraver unknown; John Wallis, publisher

London, April 3, 1783. Black-and-white line engraving. H. 19″, W. 22⅝″

The title, date, and imprint are contained in an oval cartouche in the lower right corner. Surrounding the oval are an American flag and a trumpeting angel holding a laurel wreath at the top. To the left are the figures of Washington and Liberty; to the right, Franklin, penning an agreement, is flanked by Justice and Minerva

Only one state of the map is known

References: Fowble, *Two Centuries of Prints*, entry 18; McCorkle, *New England in Early Printed Maps*, entry 783.21; Ristow, *American Maps and Mapmakers*, pp. 63–64; Sellers and van Ee, *Maps and Charts of North America*, p. 159

T HE preliminary articles of peace drafted by Benjamin Franklin, John Adams, and Henry Laurens were signed at Versailles on January 20, 1783. Cartographers immediately rushed to issue maps that defined the boundaries of the independent nation. One of the first was John Wallis's *The United States of America laid down From the best Authorities, Agreeable to the Peace of 1783.* As was often the case, this map was borrowed from earlier works, in particular Jean Baptiste Bourguignon d'Anville's *Amérique Septentrionale,* 1746. Based on information gathered by French explorers, d'Anville's map was one of the best of North America available at the time and was copied by many English and continental cartographers. One of the versions most readily available to Wallis was *North America from the French of Mr. D'Anville Improved with The English Surveys made Since the Peace,* published in 1775 by Robert Sayer and John Bennett for Jefferys's *American Atlas. (fig. 223)*

Since the geography shown on Wallis's map had been known for thirty-seven years, it is of little interest cartographically. The noteworthy element is the decorative cartouche, which symbolizes peace in America. The allegorical scene portrays George Washington, alongside Liberty, and Benjamin Franklin, supported by Justice and Minerva, the Roman goddess of wisdom and war, writing the Treaty of Paris. This is the first English map that illustrated the American flag.

1975-128

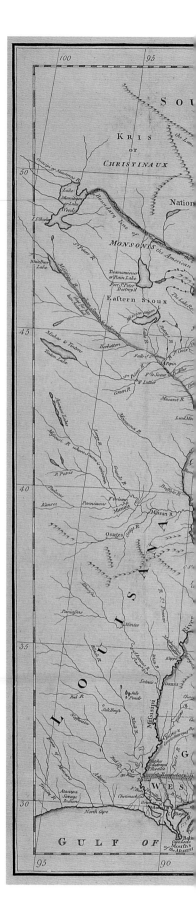

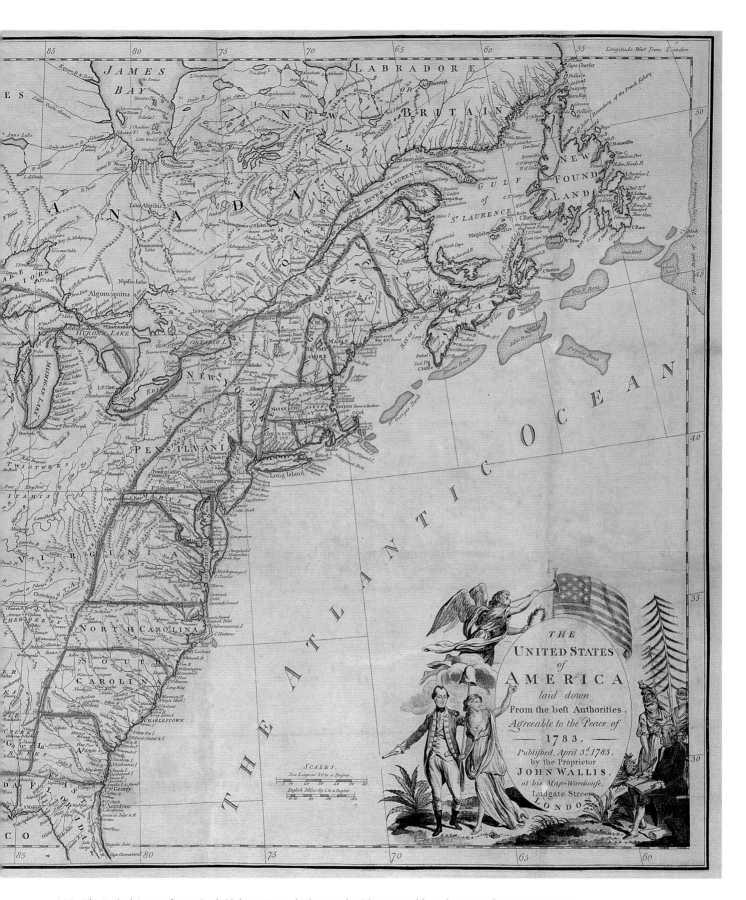

221 *The United States of America laid down From the best Authorities, Agreeable to the Peace of 1783.* (Cat. 69)

222 Detail of the cartouche from *The United States of America laid down From the best Authorities, Agreeable to the Peace of 1783,* by John Wallis, London, April 3, 1783, black-and-white line engraving. 1992-86.

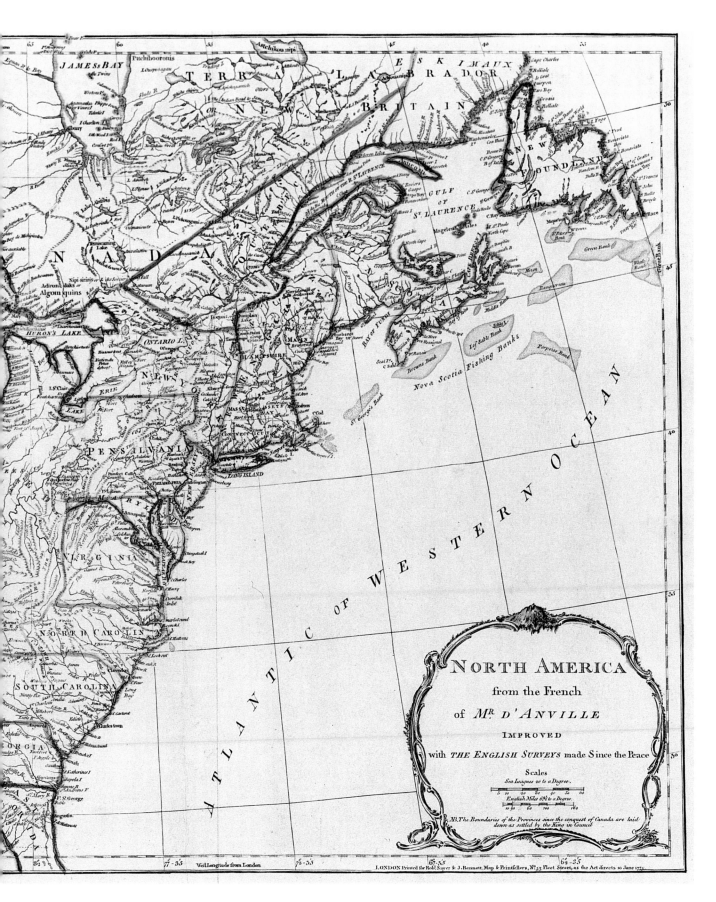

223 *North America from the French of M.ʳ D'Anville Improved with The English Surveys made Since the Peace,*
by Jean Baptiste Bourguignon d'Anville, London, 1775, black-and-white line engraving. 1992-86.

224 *Carte des Etats-Unis de L'Amerique.* (Cat. 70)

70 *CARTE DES ETATS-UNIS / DE L'AMERIQUE / Suivant le Traité de Paix de 1783. / DÉDIEÉ ET PRÉSENTÉE / A S. Excellence M^r. BENJAMIN FRANKLIN / Ministre Plenipotentiaire des Etats-Unis de l' Amérique près la Cour de France, / anc Présid de la conventió de Pensilvanie et de la Societé Philosophique de Philadelphie, &c. &c. / Par son très humble et très obeissan— / Serviteur LATTRÉ*

Jean Lattré, cartographer and probably engraver

Paris, 1784. Black-and-white line engraving. H. 22¼", W. 31" (trimmed)

In the lower center is an inset map titled *SUPLÉMENT/ a/ LA FLORIDE,/ méme Echelle que la Carte.* To the left is a list of the thirteen states and their capitals. In the lower right corner are the title and dedication in the sail of a warship. Immediately above is a shield with the American eagle, thirteen stars, and *E PLURIBUS UNUM*

Only one state of the map is known

References: Cappon, *First French Map;* McCorkle, *New England in Early Printed Maps,* entry 784.10; Ristow, *American Maps and Mapmakers,* pp. 63, 65; Sellers and van Ee, *Maps and Charts of North America,* p. 158

225 Detail of the cartouche from *Carte des Etats-Unis de L' Amerique* by Jean Lattré, Paris, 1784, black-and-white line engraving. G1900-167, gift of Mrs. Anna Glen Vietor in memory of Alexander O. Vietor. (Cat. 70)

Wᴴᴵʟᴇ J. B. Eliot (Cat. 58) was perhaps the first to use the term United States (*Etats-Unis*) on a printed map, and John Wallis (Cat. 69) was the first to illustrate the American flag, Jean Lattré's *Carte des Etats-Unis de L' Amerique* was the first map of the newly created United States published in France after the final treaty was signed on September 3, 1783. As Eliot and Wallis had done, Lattré borrowed the geography from previously published works. His primary source was John Mitchell's *Map of the British and French Dominions in North America* (Cat. 33), the document that Great Britain and the United States used during the treaty negotiations to determine the geographic boundaries of the new nation. Lattré's reliance on the earlier work perpetuated some outdated information. For instance, Lattré identified Williamsburg as the capital of Virginia, when in fact the capital had been relocated to Richmond in 1780. Certain details of the political boundaries were inaccurate as well. Lattré updated the earlier work by adding information on a few battles that took place during the war.

The iconography depicted in the Frenchman's cartouche and his dedication to Benjamin Franklin represent the post-Revolutionary War camaraderie that existed between France and America. Franklin was well known and highly respected in French society. As minister plenipotentiary of the United States to the court of France, he was the most appropriate statesman to honor in such a way.

Although a resident of Bordeaux, Lattré was well known in literary and artistic circles in Paris. His accomplishments extended well beyond those of a cartographer, for he was also an engraver, publisher, editor, and retailer.[1] Lattré's skill as an engraver earned him the appointment as official engraver to Louis XVI and later to the dauphin.

G1990-167, gift of Mrs. Anna Glen Vietor in memory of Alexander O. Vietor

1. Lester J. Cappon, *The First French Map of the United States of America* (Chicago, 1978).

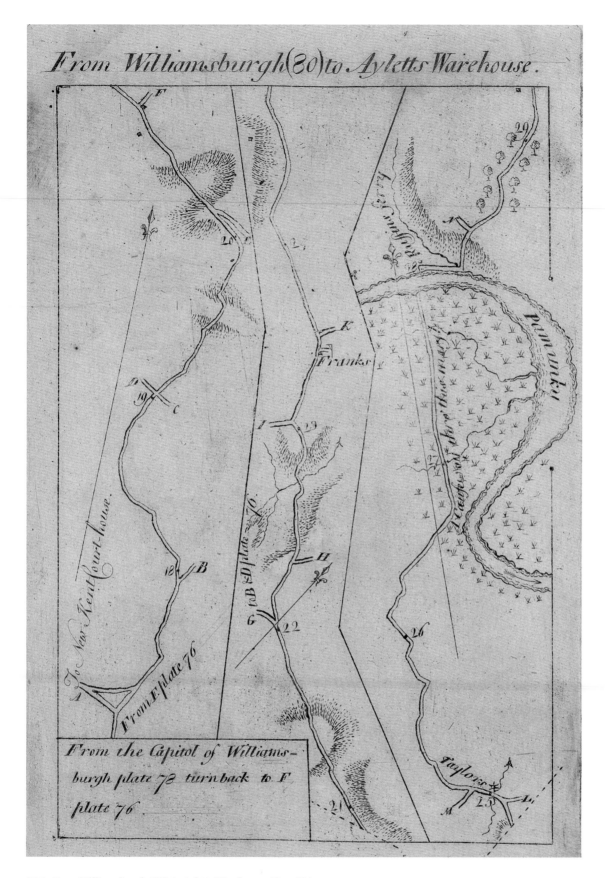

226 *From Williamsburgh (80) to Ayletts Warehouse.* (Cat. 71)

Christopher Colles, cartographer; Cornelius Tiebout, engraver[1]; published in *A Survey of the Roads of the United States of America* by Christopher Colles

New York, 1789. Black-and-white line engraving. H. 7¼", W. 5⅛"

The title is at the top. The map is organized into three strips with mile numbers from 18 to 29

Only one state of the map is known

References: Colles, *Survey of the Roads of the United States of America,* ed. Ristow; Cresswell, "Colony to Commonwealth," pp. 61, 116–117; McCorkle, *America Emergent,* entry 81; Papenfuse and Coale, *Hammond-Harwood House Atlas,* p. 65; Ristow, *American Maps and Mapmakers,* pp. 158–162; Schwartz and Ehrenberg, *Mapping of America,* p. 205; Wheat and Brun, *Maps and Charts Published in America,* entry 560

From Williamsburgh (80) to Ayletts Warehouse was one of a set of eighty-three small strip road maps by Christopher Colles published collectively as *A Survey of the Roads of the United States of America,* the first road atlas of the new nation. Financial constraints forced Colles to reduce the geographic scope of his original intention, thus limiting the final project to the roads from Albany, New York, and Stratford, Connecticut, to Yorktown, Virginia. The overall format was modeled on that introduced by John Ogilby over a century earlier. Each map consisted of two or three separate but contiguous strips that had directional arrows indicating north. Colles best described the project in his "Proposals for Publishing a Survey of the Roads of the United States of America":

> *That the work shall be neatly engraved on copper, each page containing a delineation of near 12 miles of the road upon a scale of about one inch and three quarters to the mile, and particularly specifying all the cross roads and streams of water which intersect it, the names of the most noted inhabitants of the houses contiguous to or in view of the road, the churches and other public buildings; the taverns, blacksmith's shops, mills, and every object which occurs to render it a useful and entertaining work.*[2]

Colles also outlined his procedure for selling the maps by subscription. An individual was to pay a quarter of a dollar at the time of subscribing and then one-eighth of a dollar as each set of six pages was completed and delivered.

Using a perambulator, a large wheel that recorded the distance of each rotation, Colles personally surveyed many of the roads in New York and New Jersey. There is no evi-dence that he ever ventured south of Philadelphia, how-ever. Historians have concluded that the territory from New York to Yorktown, Virginia, was measured during the Revolution by Robert Erskine and Simeon DeWitt, military geographers and successive surveyor generals under George Washington.[3]

The *Survey of the Roads of the United States* was an expensive undertaking for an independent cartographer without a subsidy. There were few advance subscriptions, making it difficult for Colles to finance the project. He appealed for assistance to the New York State Assembly and subsequently to the United States Congress, which forwarded Colles's petition to Postmaster General Samuel Osgood for his recommendation. Despite Osgood's favorable comments, the young Congress had far more pressing matters at hand and Colles's road survey was set aside.

While the work suffered from inadequate funding and was not widely distributed, it is important for the topographical landmarks Colles identified. For the first time, precise routes were illustrated and important locations were pinpointed for the traveler. As Colles explained in his "Proposals," it would be impossible for a traveler to miss his way as "he will have the satisfaction of knowing the names of many of the persons who reside on the road; if his horse should want a shoe, or his carriage be broke, he will by the bare inspection of the draft be able to determine whether he must go backward or forward to a blacksmith's shop."[4] Moreover, Colles's maps suggest aspects of the social and religious framework of America. They provided travelers with destinations for food, shelter, and social interaction by identifying taverns along the routes. He also noted the locations of places of worship, choosing to distinguish Episcopal and Presbyterian churches by separate symbols.

An analysis of landmarks on the maps revealed patterns of settlement that had been in place for well over one hundred years. The urban character of New York and New Jersey contrasted clearly with the rural nature of the South. The extent of the geography Colles included north of Philadelphia was roughly equivalent to what he depicted to the south, but the number of landmarks located there were far fewer. For example, only 4 of the 45 churches or meetinghouses, 15 of the 47 mills, 32 of the 160 taverns, and none of the 23 blacksmith shops identified on Colles's maps were south of Philadelphia.

1983-315, 6

1. Tiebout's name appears on the title page as the engraver, and thus it has been assumed that he engraved all of the 83 plates. None of the indi-

PROPOSALS

FOR PUBLISHING A

SURVEY

OF THE

ROADS

Of the United States of America.

By CHRISTOPHER COLLES. *of New York*

CONDITIONS.

THAT the work fhall be neatly engraved upon copper, each page containing a delineation of near 12 miles of the road upon a fcale of about one inch and three quarters to the mile, and particularly fpecifying all the crofs roads and ftreams of water which interfect it, the names of the inhabitants ... the churches and other public buildings ; the taverns, blackfmith's fhops, mills, and every object which occurs to render it a ufeful and entertaining work, and in every refpect equal to the fpecimen of the three ... annexed.

... That a fet of general maps ... particular page where the defcription of any road is to be found ; thefe maps will then anfwer as an index and will be found more convenient than any other index that can be made.

3. That each fubfcriber fhall pay one quarter dollar at the time of fubfcribing (to defray feveral incidental charges neceffary for the work) and one eighth of a dollar upon the delivery of every fix pages of the work : but fuch gentlemen as are willing to advance one dollar will be confidered as patrons of the work, and will not be entitled to pay any more till the value thereof is delivered in.

4. That fubfcribers fhall pay 20 cents for each of the general maps and three cents for each fheet of letter prefs in the alphabetical lifts or other neceffary explanation of the drafts.

5. That each fubfcriber fhall be confidered as engaging to take 100 pages.

6. That non-fubfcribers fhall pay three cents for each page of the work.

Account of the advantages of thefe Surveys.

A traveller will here find fo plain and circumftantial a defcription of the road, that whilft he has the draft with him it will be impoffible for him to mifs his way : he will have the fatisfaction of knowing the names of many of the perfons who refide on the road ; if his horfe fhould want a fhoe, or his carriage be broke, he will by the bare infpection of the draft be able to determine whether he muft go backward or forward to a blackfmith's fhop : perfons who have houfes or plantations on the road may in cafe they want to let, leafe, or fell the fame, advertife in the public newfpapers that the place is marked on fuch a page of Colles's Survey of the roads ; this will give fo particular a defcription of its fituation that no difficulty or doubt will remain about it. If a foreigner arrives in any part of the Continent and is under the neceffity to travel by land, he applies to a bookfeller, who with the affiftance of the index map choofes out the particular pages which are neceffary for his direction. It is expected many other entertaining and ufeful purpofes will be difcovered when thefe furveys come into general ufe.

Subfcription papers will be fent to moft of the Bookfellers in the Continent

227 Christopher Colles, "Proposals For Publishing a Survey of the Roads of the United States of America," 1789. Courtesy, New-York Historical Society, New York, N. Y.

vidual maps bears an engraver's imprint, however. Discrepancies in the style of engraving have raised the question of who actually executed the plates. Christopher Colles, *A Survey of the Roads of the United States of America, 1789,* ed. Walter W. Ristow (Cambridge, Mass., 1961), pp. 45–48.

2. Christopher Colles, "Proposals for Publishing a Survey of the Roads of the United States of America," 1789, *ibid.,* p. 45.

3. Ristow supplied ample evidence that the surveys used by Colles for the roads between New York and Yorktown were undertaken by Robert Erskine and Simeon DeWitt, surveyors general of the Continental Army. How Colles gained access to the information is unknown since the geographers' field notes were still in the hands of DeWitt. DeWitt probably prepared finished military surveys to be deposited in the War Department. Colles may have had access to them. Colles, *Survey of the Roads,* ed. Ristow, pp. 53–72.

4. Colles, "Proposals," *ibid,.* p. 45.

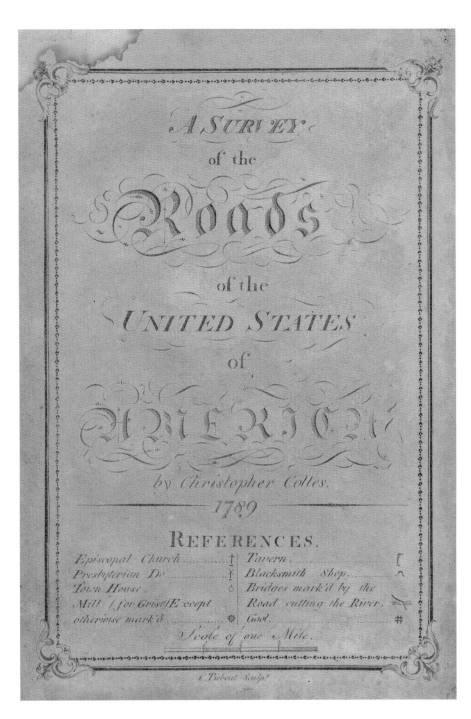

228 Title page from *A Survey of the Roads of the United States of America,*
by Christopher Colles, New York, 1789, black-and-white line engraving. 1983-315, 1.

72 A MAP of the country between ALBEMARLE SOUND, and LAKE ERIE, comprehending/ the whole of VIRGINIA, MARYLAND, DELAWARE and PENSYLVANIA, with parts of/ several other of the United States of America

Thomas Jefferson, cartographer; Samuel Neele, engraver; published in Abbé André Morellet's French translation of *Notes on the State of Virginia* by Thomas Jefferson

Paris (although engraved in London), 1787. Black-and-white line engraving. H. 25", W. 24½"

The title and description of sources used in compiling the map are in a rectangle in the upper right corner. The scale of distances is in the lower right corner

Two states of the map are known:
State 1: (this copy) As described
State 2: The imprint *Published as the Act directs July 13th 1787 by John Stockdale in Piccadilly, London* was added in the lower left. 1787

References: Cresswell, "Colony to Commonwealth," pp. 58, 98–101; Harrison, *Landmarks of Old Prince William*, pp. 636–638; Jefferson, *Notes on the State of Virginia*, ed. Peden; Morrison et al., *On the Map*, fig. 44; Sellers and van Ee, *Maps and Charts of North America*, pp. 161–162; Verner, "Maps and Plates," pp. 21–33; Verner, "Mr. Jefferson Makes a Map," pp. 96–108

FRANÇOIS BARBÉ-MARBOIS, secretary to the French legation at Philadelphia, circulated a questionnaire to several members of the Continental Congress in 1780 requesting information regarding the laws, institutions, and natural features of some of the states. Thomas Jefferson, then governor, was the best qualified to draft a reply for Virginia. He responded to Marbois's queries on December 20, 1781, also circulating his research among friends for their comments. During the winter of 1783–1784, Jefferson began revising his work into what eventually became *Notes on the State of Virginia*. In its final form, the work provided invaluable insights into Virginia's history, natural resources, public institutions, and geographic boundaries.

When Jefferson went to France to serve as United States minister, he took his manuscript with him. In 1785, he made arrangements for French printer Philippe-Denis Pierres to print two hundred copies in English for private distribution.[1] To his dismay, Jefferson learned that a French bookseller had obtained a copy and intended to publish an unauthorized French version, so he arranged for economist, philosopher, and writer Abbé André Morellet to prepare a suitable translation. Morellet encouraged

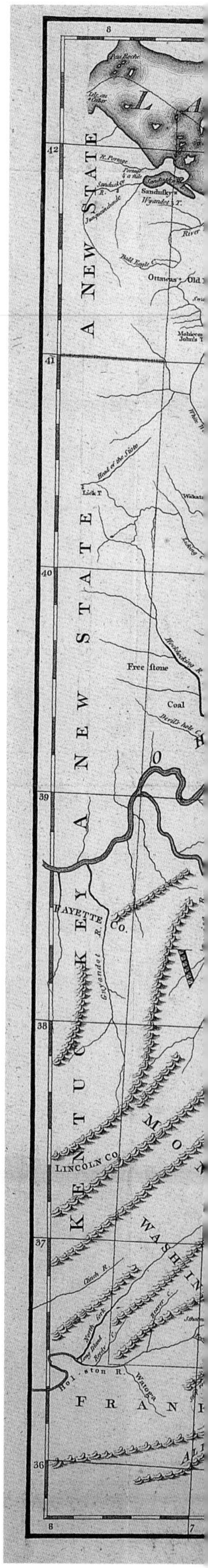

229 *A Map of the country between Albemarle Sound, and Lake Erie, comprehending the whole of Virginia, Maryland, Delaware and Pensylvania.* (Cat. 72)

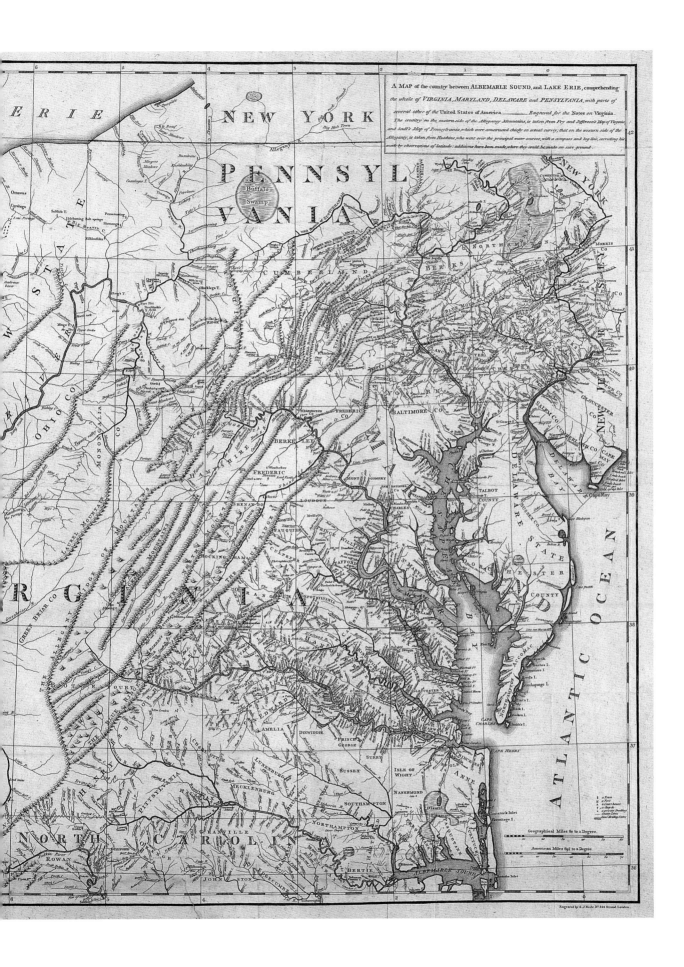

A MAP of the country between ALBEMARLE SOUND, and LAKE ERIE, comprehending the whole of VIRGINIA, MARYLAND, DELAWARE and PENSYLVANIA, with parts of several other of the United States of America. _____ Engraved for the Notes on Virginia. The country on the eastern side of the Allegany Mountains, is taken from Fry and Jefferson's Maps of Virginia, and Scull's Map of Pennsylvania, which were constructed chiefly on actual survey; that on the western side of the Allegany, is taken from Hutchins, who went over the principal water courses, with a compass and log-line, correcting his work by observations of latitude: additions have been made, where they could be made on sure ground.

Engraved by S. J Neele Nº 352 Strand London.

230 Portrait of Thomas Jefferson,
by Gilbert Stuart, 1805–1806,
oil on canvas. 1945-22.

Jefferson to prepare a detailed map of Virginia and neigh-boring states to accompany the work.[2]

As Jefferson's draft neared completion, he asked Edward Bancroft for advice on securing an engraver in London to execute the work:

I wish the favor of you to make two propositions for me, and to inform me of the result. 1. To know from one of the best engravers how much he will ask for the plate and engraving, and in how short a time after he received the original can he furnish the plate, done in the best manner; for the time is material, as the work is in the press. 2. To know of Faden, or any other map merchant, for how much he will undertake to furnish me 1,800 copies, on my send-ing the map to him, and in what time he can furnish them. On this alternative, I am to have nothing to do with the engraver, or any person but the undertaker.[3]

Shortly after Jefferson drafted the letter, he made an unexpected trip to London where he secured the skills of engraver Samuel Neele. Neele sent Jefferson the completed plate, the original drawing, and a proof late in 1786. Jefferson must have been disappointed in the results, for he wrote to William Stephens Smith on January 15, 1787, that he was in the process of correcting the map. "I have got thro about two thirds of the map and have a list of 172 errors, so that we may expect in the whole about 250."[4] Jefferson then proposed that he try to find an engraver in

Paris to make the corrections. Guillaume Delahaye was given the plate on March 5. By March 24, two hundred fifty impressions had been made.

At the same time, Jefferson negotiated with London publisher John Stockdale to produce an English edition of the book. It was decided to include impressions of the map used for the French edition, so the plate was forwarded to Stockdale, who complained to Jefferson that it was "so much worn that the impressions which I want will not be quite legible."[5] Stockdale estimated that about 1,500 pulls had been taken in France. Nevertheless, he added his imprint to the bottom of the plate and printed another 1,025 copies.[6] The plate was once again returned to France where 300 more were printed. Nothing more is known of the use or whereabouts of the plate.[7]

A Map of the country between Albemarle Sound, and Lake Erie, comprehending the whole of Virginia, Maryland, Delaware and Pensylvania was compiled from a variety of published maps, most notably that prepared by Jefferson's father and Joshua Fry between 1750 and 1754 (Cat. 30). In the title, Jefferson gave credit to other sources such as William Scull's map of Pennsylvania published in 1770 and Thomas Hutchins's *A New Map of the Western Parts of Virginia, Pennsylvania, Maryland and North Carolina* (Cat. 49). Jefferson used Lewis Evans's map "to fill intermediate spaces" and John Churchman's *Map of the Peninsula Between Delaware &c Chesopeak Bays* for the Eastern Shore (Cats. 34 and 50).[8] He intended to include the county boundaries as depicted on John Henry's map of Virginia but apparently could not procure a copy in time.[9] Jefferson also relied on assistance from friends who forwarded updated surveys and new information gathered from western explorers.

Given Jefferson's interest in natural phenomena, it is not surprising that he was the first to locate landmarks such as the Natural Bridge and Zane's and Madison's Caves. He referred to the Natural Bridge as "the most Sublime of Nature's works."[10] Jefferson also pinpointed the site of the Indian Grave on the low grounds of the Rivanna River, which he personally excavated.

Jefferson's map depicted *An exact description of the limits and boundaries of the state of Virginia,* and also illustrated his opinion on the future division of the Northwest Territory that Virginia ceded to the nation in 1781. Five new states were shown. *Kentuckey* and *Frankland* (now Tennessee), were named; the remaining three were identified as *A New State.*

1995-13

1. The first edition of Thomas Jefferson, *Notes on the State of Virginia,* was published in France in May 1785. Thomas Jefferson, *Notes on the State of Virginia,* ed. William Peden (Chapel Hill, N. C., 1955), "Introduction," pp. xiv–xvii. For the various editions, see Coolie Verner, *A Further Checklist of the Separate Editions of Jefferson's Notes on the State of Virginia* (Charlottesville, Va., 1950).

2. Jefferson wrote to Edward Bancroft, "The Abbé engaged me to make a map, which I wish to have engraved in London." Andrew A. Lipscomb, ed., *The Writings of Thomas Jefferson,* V (Washington, D. C., 1903), p. 285.

3. *Ibid.* Much of this short summary is based on studies of the history of the production of the map by cartographic historian Coolie Verner. Verner, "The Maps and Plates Appearing with the Several Editions of Mr. Jefferson's 'Notes on the state of Virginia,'" *VMHB,* LIX (1951), pp. 21–33; Verner, "Mr. Jefferson Makes a Map."

4. Julian P. Boyd et al., eds., *The Papers of Thomas Jefferson,* XI (Princeton, N. J., 1955), p. 46.

5. Verner, "Mr. Jefferson Makes a Map," p. 105.

6. *Ibid.*

7. *Ibid.,* p. 106.

8. Jefferson's notations to himself about sources and procedures he should follow when drawing the map are quoted in Coolie Verner, "Mr. Jefferson Makes a Map," *Imago Mundi,* XIV (1959), p. 98.

9. Jefferson wrote to Bancroft, "I shall finish it [the map] in about a fortnight, except the divisions in the counties of Virginia, which I cannot do at all till I can get Henry's map of Virginia." Lipscomb, ed., *Writings of Jefferson,* V, p. 286.

10. Jefferson, *Notes,* ed. Peden, p. 24.

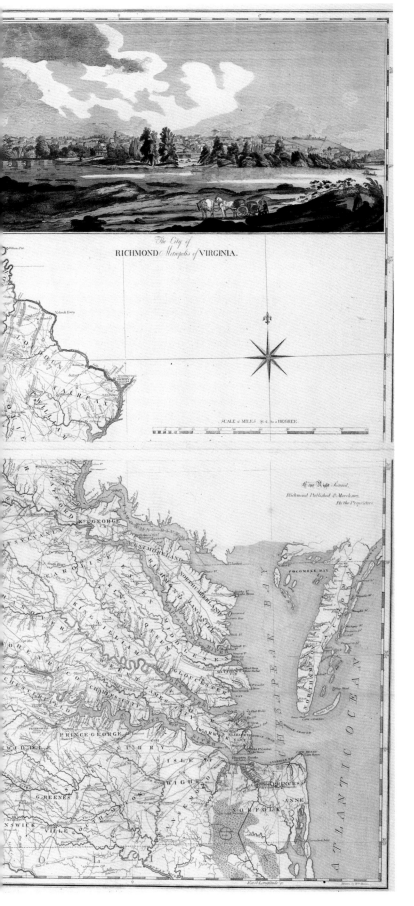

73 *A MAP OF / Virginia / Formed from Actual Surveys, and the / Latest as well as most accurate observations, / BY JAMES MADISON, D. D. / late President of W.ᵐ & Mary College / WITH EXTENSIVE ADDITIONS & / Corrections to the Year 1818*

Bishop James Madison, William Prentis, and William Davis, cartographers; Frederick Bossler, engraver

Richmond, Virginia, 1818. Black-white line engraving with period color (view only). H. 46⅛", W. 70⅞", in six sheets

In the upper left is an inset map of Ohio. Along the lower left side is the dedication *To/ THE GENERAL ASSEMBLY OF/ VIRGINIA/ This Map is Respectfully Inscribed,/ by their Fellow Citizens./ James Madison./ William Prentis./ William Davis./ Proprietors.* Below is an explanation of symbols. The title, in the upper center, is engraved on a representation of a large rock surmounted by a bald eagle with a tree in the background and a tobacco plant in the foreground. In the upper right corner is a view of *The City of/ RICHMOND Metropolis of VIRGINIA.* Below are a compass rose and a scale of miles; below those elements is *Copy Right Secured./ Richmond Published 4.ᵗʰ March 1807./ By the Proprietors*

Two states of the map are known:

State 1: The title is *A MAP OF/ Virginia/ Formed from Actual Surveys, and the/ Latest as well as most accurate observations,/ BY JAMES MADISON, D. D./ late President of W.ᵐ & Mary College.* Beneath the right side of the view of Richmond is the imprint *Engraved by Fred.ᵏ Bossler.* 1807

State 2: (this copy) As described. *WITH EXTENSIVE ADDITIONS &/ Corrections to the year 1818* was added to the title in the upper center. The word *late* was added following James Madison's name. The imprint beneath the right side of the view of Richmond was erased. Two new features, *Salt Works* and *Gypsum Bank,* were added to the list of explanatory notes on the lower left. The many geographic changes, particularly in the inset of Ohio, are too numerous to itemize. 1818

References: Grim, "Building Virginia," pp. 120–121, 139–145; Harrison, *Landmarks of Old Prince William,* pp. 638–639; Ristow, *American Maps and Mapmakers,* pp. 121–122

Aᴌᴛʜᴏᴜɢʜ this volume focuses primarily on the geography of the colonial period in America, it would be remiss not to include Bishop James Madison's *Map of Virginia Formed from Actual Surveys,* the first map of Virginia produced in the Commonwealth and the first comprehensive road map for the state.

Madison, first cousin of President James Madison, graduated from the College of William and Mary in 1771, studied law under George Wythe, and later was ordained in the Church of England. In 1777, Madison became president of

231 *A Map of Virginia Formed from Actual Surveys.* (Cat. 73)

232 Detail of the Ohio inset from *A Map of Virginia Formed from Actual Surveys* by Bishop James Madison, William Prentis, and William Davis, Richmond, Va., 1818, black-and-white-line engraving. 1990-166. (Cat. 73)

233 Detail of the view of Richmond from *A Map of Virginia Formed from Actual Surveys,* by Bishop James Madison, William Prentis, and William Davis, Richmond, Va., 1818, black-and-white line engraving with period color. 1990-166. (Cat. 73)

the college, a position he held for thirty-five years. By the terms of the 1693 charter of the college, the trustees were given the responsibility of designating the surveyor general of Virginia. That duty shifted to the governor in 1779, although the surveyor general was "to be nominated, examined, and certified able by the president and professors of William and Mary college, and if of good character, commissioned by the governour."[1]

Madison's official role as president of William and Mary in selecting the surveyor general undoubtedly interested him. In 1779, he served on the commission that defined the boundary between Virginia and Pennsylvania. Madison's curiosity about the natural world was of long standing. He had been elected professor of natural philosophy and mathematics at the college in 1773. He corresponded with Jefferson on topics such as climate, astronomy, marine life, skin pigmentation, and geography.

Aware of the need for a new scientific map of Virginia, Madison assumed the task of gathering data for the project. His goal was to improve earlier observations of latitude and longitude, to ensure the correctness of newly formed county boundaries, to gather the most up-to-date information on the courses of rivers and bearings on mountains from regional surveys, and to depict the state's boundaries accurately.[2] He sought the assistance of William Prentis of Petersburg to assemble and compile the information. Prentis's initial manuscript was passed to William Davis, who Madison described as "a neat, correct and intelligent draughtsman," so it could be rendered in a form from which the engraver, Frederick Bossler, could produce plates.[3]

Madison did not receive financial assistance from the Virginia Assembly as he may have hoped:

The proprietors finding that most of the other states had recently given encouragement to similar productions and entertaining a high sense of the real dignity and importance of Virginia, embarked in the business, from a well-grounded belief that the magnitude and utility of the work, would insure, if accomplished, a remuneration.[4]

As John Henry had done almost four decades earlier, Madison decided to finance the project through subscription. The cost was to be eight dollars, one to be paid upon subscribing. The price for non-subscribers would be two dollars.

The map, which included extensive topographical features that reflected Madison's interest in natural history, was published on March 4, 1807. The depiction of new roads provided a wealth of detail for travelers and the work became known as the first true road map of Virginia. Numerous errors caused Davis to revise it and a second state was published in 1818, six years after Madison's death. The result was a virtually new map. For instance, more than forty new counties were added to the Ohio inset alone. Even the boundaries of some long-established counties such as Princess Anne were altered.

One of the most striking features is the view of Richmond in the upper right corner. The design, executed around 1805, was taken from a drawing by Charles-Balthazar-Julien Févret de Saint-Mémin. Given Madison's friendship with Jefferson, it is understandable that the state capitol was chosen to embellish the map since Jefferson was responsible for the design of the building. Saint-Mémin's drawing also reflected something of the character of the state. He juxtaposed the tranquil rural terrain with the James River in the foreground against the flourishing city of Richmond, which was described on the map as the *Metropolis of Virginia.*

1990-266

1. William Waller Hening, ed., *The Statutes at Large; Being a Collection of All the Laws of Virginia, from the First Session of the Legislature in the Year 1619* (New York, Philadelphia, and Richmond, Va., 1819–1823), X, p. 53.

2. *Ibid.,* XI, p. 352.

3. Bishop James Madison to William Prentis, Feb. 1, 1805, Earl G. Swem, comp., *Maps Relating to Virginia in the Virginia State Library and other Departments of the Commonwealth* (Richmond, Va., 1914), p. 85.

4. *Ibid.*

5. *Richmond Enquirer* (Va.), Feb. 15, 1805, *ibid.*

5   10   15   20   25   30

part M of
part of

S I L V A

part of PEN

part of N

Onestego R.

Sesquahana or
Indian fort

Skawoghkaha

Oequandary

Cescoe

Vuondonreras

Kahetnage

Oanoonaweng

Oktoraaro

Vandriekge P.

Martius P.

Geys I.

Cronhil
Red Lion
Red Lion

Plum P.

BALTE-

Bush R.

Stone
Balteore M.
Palmers shore

Baker
Hope   Opaquch
Mill   Bohemia M.

Bumbae

Casson

Hunting
Baltimore

Palmeck
Smiths Cr.
Browning

Collets
neck

Turkey Hole

Ports Marsh Sassend Cr.
Chester   Tockler

Duck Cr.

Deep Collet
Creeke

Gunpowder River

Winbos

Sassafrax

Turkeys Cr.

Wolfs Cr.

Howel

Bennits Cr.

-MORE. C.

Woorten

Steele Bone Cr.

Saisbury Or. C   Æ
Beacon Cr.

Murther Cr.

Darrington

Boals

Dee

Poolt I.

Earlo Cr.

CILC.

Alexaning

Patapsko River

Huppers I.

ANNE ARUN-

Swan Cr.

Swan P.

Godling

Creekin   Lang
ford

Bare P.

N. East Branch

Loue P.

Hansford Cr.

Reads Cr.
Causfy
Roads Cr.

Annie Arundel
al Seavorn R.

DEL. C.

Chester R.

Tully
Cousfy   Lords gift.

Broad Cr.

Wrise R.

Lords Man

Arundelton

White hall
South I.

KENT

Resting place   Loyes Cr.

Wootmans

TALBOT. C.

Wighteuxeus

Kent P.

Swland I.

Patowmeck Falls
Antecostin I.

Mattapient

Goppahang

Namesacaut

Popler al
Bemelas ma

Kennis

St. Mihalis R.
Wasse
S.E. inious
Oxford

Sullinbrook

Turkkohs Branch

North Branch

Hering Cr.

Chaptanck   Ile

Chaptnyek

Indian townes

M. Calvert

I. Honk R.

Tyre P.

Le Comps

VIR

Mattapan

Herington

Sharps Isl.   4

Tryps P.

Trips B.

Jerden
Richard Podcysth
Smart Gernis Cr.

Sharpe Cr.

Tisikamkant

Casfambant
als Iands C.

DORCHESTER

Ashquin

Aquasquil

Vasterkont

Plum P.

CALV.

Huntyg Cr.
Chists

Hudsons

Clarkes Cr.
Fishing Cr.

Chico coan

Mattowanon

Pascattaway

Patuxen Um.

War
rington

Oester Cr.

Stephen
Slougter   als

Thomas Cathar

Hallis P. Beni tr. Cr.

STAFFORD
CO.

Pamunk

CHARLES.
CO.

Truman   Halling P.

Oester Cr.

Trasquaqin

Nanticoke R.

Chnumoeren
Nanjinve
Deynton

Portobaco

Polekat P.
Calverton

Coare
Elkenb
ad

Quantico

Ochquavo

Patomock Cr.

Marela
Point

Zachiasswamp

Westwood

Resu
Rection

Cedar

Philps

Wicomoco Cr.

234 Portrait of John Custis IV, by Charles Bridges, Virginia, 1725, oil on canvas. Courtesy, Washington and Lee University, Lexington, Va. The tulip Custis holds symbolized his lifelong interest in natural history.
Custis became a dedicated gardener, corresponding regularly and exchanging rare specimens with Peter Collinson, one of the most famous naturalists in eighteenth-century England.

The Atlas of John Custis, 1698

One of the finest treasures in the John D. Rockefeller, Jr. Library at the Colonial Williamsburg Foundation is a late seventeenth-century English folio composite world atlas, or "atlas factice," with a distinguished Virginia provenance. Unlike a typical atlas published with standardized contents, an atlas factice was usually a unique collection of maps selected and bound to meet the taste or needs of a particular individual. London map publisher Philip Lea assembled this composite atlas for John Custis IV, 1678–1749, scion of one of the most distinguished colonial Virginia families.[1] *(fig. 234)*

The book has a remarkable provenance. Custis appears to have purchased the atlas in 1698. When his estate was divided sixty years later, the volume was assigned to his grandson, John Parke Custis, whose mother had married George Washington. During the years of John Parke Custis's minority, it may have been kept at Mount Vernon. Upon his death, the book was inherited by George Washington Parke Custis, who lived at Arlington House, now the site of Arlington National Cemetery. His daughter, Mary Randolph Custis, married General Robert E. Lee. Endorsed on the reverse of Custis Atlas Cat. 93 is "Presented to/ S. A. Green/ By/ Mrs. M[ary] C[ustis] Lee/ 1872." The Colonial Williamsburg Foundation acquired the atlas in the spring of 1986 thanks to the generosity of Mr. and Mrs. Robert S. Wilson.

As a youth, Custis spent several years in England in the employ of the firm of Perry and Lane, the largest tobacco merchants in London, developing his skills as a businessman. Little is known of Custis's time abroad aside from his association with the Perry firm. However, in anticipation of his return to Virginia, Custis appears to have visited the shop of Philip Lea in 1698 where he purchased maps to sustain his interest in geography once he was back in America. The inventory of Lea's shop, the "Atlas and Hercules," prepared in May 1700 after the mapseller's death, gives an impression of its appearance and contents at the time Custis would have visited. The shop, located in a brick building erected after the Great Fire of 1666, was four or five stories high with living quarters for the family on the upper floors. It was furnished with "press Counters and drawers val at £2.10s.0d." Stock on hand included unbound "Bookes in Quires in the Garrett and Bookes Bound in the Shopp" £40.8s.0d, "Mathematicall Instruments of Brass and wood of all Sorts" £22.10s.6d, "Mapp, Sea Card [charts] prints" £35.15s.0d, and a parcel of "Mapps made upon Cloth" £8.0s.0d. In addition, there were "Globeplates" valued at £10.0s.0d owned jointly with other map publishers and "Sixteene Hundred weight of Copper at 18.d p[er] pound val at £132.08.0," presumably in the form of engraved plates for maps and prints. A separate "printeing Roome" was equipped with a rolling press for printing copperplates, an old chest of drawers, and a table, all valued at £1.2s.6d.[2]

A member of the Virginia gentry, Custis's experiences abroad shaped his desire to acquire the accoutrements symbolic of the learned and elevated status that set him apart from those less fortunate. His estate, valued in 1706 at £8,889, was one of the largest in Virginia.[3] Through his marriage to Frances Parke, Custis was connected to several of the colony's most powerful families: the Parkes, Burwells, Ludwells, and Byrds. Custis made good use of these connections and eventually was appointed to the governor's Council. Well trained in business, he was known to have managed his affairs with acumen showed by few planters of his generation.[4]

Like other prominent Virginians, Custis regarded himself as a cultural peer of the English gentry and amassed an impressive library reflective of his worldly interests. He exhibited discriminating taste in books, maps, paintings, and prints. William Byrd wrote to Custis from London in 1716, "The master [of the ship bringing this letter] has . . . your prints & maps, of which Mr. Perry promised to send you a bill of loading. I hope they will please you, because they are good and not dear."[5] Orders placed with English merchants suggest that Custis surrounded himself with fashionable furniture, silver, glassware, stylish clothes, books, prints, and the like. In 1721, he asked his London agent to lay out forty to fifty shillings in "good comicall diverting prints to hang in the passage of my house; lett them bee good of the sort, or send none. Painting and poetry admit of no medium [quality]."[6]

Custis no doubt took great pride in building his library collections. By 1759, when the library was inventoried, it contained over 450 volumes specializing in medicine, history, belles lettres, and classics, making it one of the largest collections of books in colonial Virginia.[7] The second title in the inventory was "English Atlas." Although the book was sixty-one years old when the inventory was compiled and many of the maps it contained had become outdated, the inventory takers recognized the importance of this atlas by placing it at the top of their list. Such atlases "would have been left 'casually' scattered next to other learned works, in mute tribute to their possessor's learning and wealth."[8]

The inventory of the library amassed by the three William Byrds indicates that three and one-half bookcases were devoted to "History, Voyages, Travels, &c."[9] Among the many folio volumes were "Two large Books of Maps," quite possibly bound copies of loose sheet maps such as those in the composite atlas Custis purchased from Lea. Since Byrd was also residing in London in 1698, he too might have visited Lea's shop around the time Custis acquired his volume. During another stay in London, Byrd recorded in his diary that he was visited by Richard Glynne, Lea's son-in-law and successor, who tried "to persuade me to subscribe to his great pair of globes."[10]

The prominent listing of the atlas in the inventory is underscored by the staggering price Custis paid for the maps. A comparison of the value of the atlas with household furnishings of the period indicates that Custis paid the equivalent of a fine bedstead complete with hangings or a set of twenty mahogany chairs.[11] Loose single sheet maps, charts, and prints in the inventory of Lea's estate accounted for slightly over £35, so Custis's acquisition of the atlas for £6.15s in 1698 represented a significant purchase. That figure amounted to one-fifth to one-sixth of the printed maps Lea kept on hand, less the cost of the binding.

Custis inscribed "Pretium/ 6 pounds 15 shill," the price he paid for the atlas, on the front flyleaf. Below is a printed letterpress book label surrounded by a stamped border of fleurs-de-lis and acorns with the words "Mr. John Custis/ Septemb. 7th. 1698." (fig. 235) No other copies of this book label have been found in volumes from the Custis library, although a loose example has been located in the collection of the American Antiquarian Society.[12]

Although the volume was rebound in the twentieth century, it still retains the original goathide spine label with the title "English Atlas," a name frequently used by

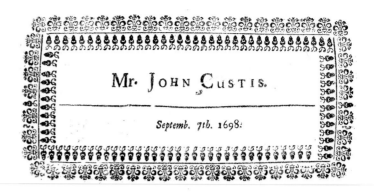

235 This book label of John Custis was pasted to the front flyleaf of his atlas.

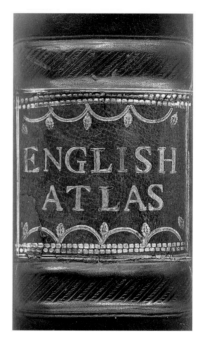

236 The spine label of the English Atlas owned by John Custis, London, 1698.

late seventeenth-century London map publishers to distinguish their works from the popular Dutch works of the period. (fig. 236) Lea advertised that he could supply "The English Atlas, or a Book of Maps of the Empires, Kingdoms and countreys, in the World, containing 20, 40, 50, or 150 Maps."[13] The Custis Atlas contains a manuscript index listing by short title 103 maps, charts, and text sheets.[14] The first 84 essentially form a terrestrial view of the world, mostly English in origin, but with a few maps published in Amsterdam. Maps 85 through 103 are sea charts that make up a complementary marine atlas of the

237 *A New Groundplot of the Citty of Hamburg,* engraved by Herman Moll, published by Philip Lea, London, 1686, Courtesy, Library of Congress. "A Map of Hamburg" was listed in the index to Custis's atlas as map 34, but it was subsequently removed.

world. The 18 maps and charts devoted to England's colonial possessions on this continent document that Custis, a Virginia gentleman of intelligence and means, elected to include the most up-to-date maps of America.

Each of the maps, some of which are now missing, is numbered in the upper right corner. Since the manuscript index is in the same hand as the page notations, it is unlikely that the compiler would have included maps not bound with the collection or skipped numbers in the pagination. In the instance of now-missing map 17, the paper guard to which the map would have been affixed appears

to have been cut, suggesting that it was removed from the binding.[15] In other cases, the acidic copper pigment used to outline boundaries has migrated to adjoining maps. The absence of discoloration from the missing maps suggests that if they were examples, bound into the volume, they were removed at an early date.[16] *(fig. 237)*

Several maps in the atlas show signs of having been bound in earlier volumes. These examples, all of America and by publishers other than Lea, were trimmed to the neat line and mounted by the binder on sheets of paper of uniform size. Many have a second manuscript number

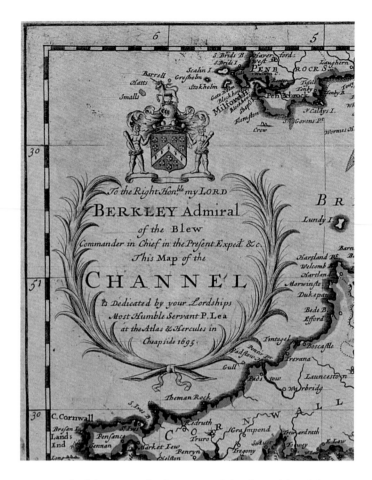

238 *William King of England Scotland France and Ireland,* sold by Robert Morden and Philip Lea, London, ca. 1690, black-and-white line engraving. This print was originally folded into the front of the Custis Atlas as the frontispiece.

239 Detail of the cartouche from *Map of the Channel,* by Philip Lea, London, 1695, black-and-white line engraving with period outline color. (Custis Atlas Cat. 97)

that does not agree with the one assigned in the index or in the upper right corner. Others have pinholes in their corners that predate their inclusion in the Custis Atlas, indicating they may previously have been tacked to walls. Perhaps Custis acquired them earlier and took them to Lea's shop to be bound with his new purchases. Maps of America would have been of special interest to him.

Custis's selection of a martial portrait of William III on horseback during the Battle of the Boyne as the frontispiece suggests that the Virginian was a supporter of the monarch, a logical assumption given the family's close ties to the merchant community in Rotterdam.[17] *(fig. 238)* When William III replaced James II as a result of the Glorious Revolution of 1688, England abandoned its lengthy political rivalry with the Netherlands. Many earlier maps with dedications to former patrons and great men became obsolete, so a flurry of reengraving occurred around 1689–1691. For example, the dedicatory address on

Canaan, or the Land of Promise (Custis Atlas Cat. 52), which had been in print since 1671, was changed in favor of Gilbert Burnet, a confidant of the new king, who appointed him bishop of Salisbury in 1689.[18]

For many maps, it has been difficult to establish the initial publication date and subsequent alterations to the printing plates, or states. Philip Lea apparently published only one map with a date, *Map of the Channel,* 1695.[19] *(fig. 239)* London mapsellers of the period commonly omitted publication dates and kept obsolete maps on the market for many years, fearing that clients regarded previously issued maps as outdated. Five works printed in the late seventeenth century have been helpful in identifying the publication history of many of the sheets in the atlas. The *Term Catalogues* and the *London Gazette* both carried dated advertisements.[20] Lea's sales catalogs of 1685, 1687, and ca. 1698 further verify when maps appeared. Unfortunately, many maps were never advertised. In some cases, a characteristic shared with another map for which the date could be determined supplied an approximate date of publication.[21]

Since composite atlases were not standard publications with a title page, extant copies of those compiled by Lea have been difficult to find. Three other Lea composite atlases have been located: one at the British Library with thirty-one maps; a second at the Library of Congress with twenty-eight; and a third in the Burden collection with thirty-one. Comparing them with the Custis Atlas helped identify the various states of maps that Lea sold. An examination of the contents of the other three atlases underscores the significance of Custis's volume, in which about one-fifth of the maps were of America. The smaller atlases, virtually devoid of American maps, suggest they were compiled to cater to English taste.

The analysis of John Custis's atlas that follows is based on the ninety-four maps and charts and several leaves of text that comprise the book today. For identification purposes, each entry here was assigned the number used in the index. Since the first map was not listed in the index and has no corresponding number, it is identified as "Custis A."

NOTES

1. The life and career of John Custis IV, also known as John Custis of Williamsburg, has been recounted often. See James B. Lynch, Jr., *The Custis Chronicles.* I: *The Years of Migration* (Camden, Me., 1993); James B. Lynch, Jr., *The Custis Chronicles.* II: *The Virginia Generations* (Camden, Me., 1997); E. G. Swem, ed., *Brothers of the Spade: Correspondence of Peter Collinson of London, and of John Custis, of Williamsburg, Virginia 1734–1746* (Barre, Mass., 1957); Jo Zuppan, "John Custis of Williamsburg, 1678–1749," *VMHB,* XC (1982), pp. 177–197; and the letterbook of John Custis, Lib. Cong.

2. Inventory of the estate of Philip Lea, taken May 1, 1700, and exhibited Apr. 30, 1702, Court of Orphans, Common Serjeants Book 5, Box 36, fol. 84b, Corporation of London Records Office.

3. Lynch, *Years of Migration,* p. 172.

4. Price, *Perry of London,* pp. 39–40.

5. Tinling, ed., *Correspondence of the Three William Byrds,* p. 290.

6. Custis letterbook.

7. The inventory in the Custis family papers, Virginia Historical Society, Richmond, Va., was published in full in the *VMHB,* XVII (1909), pp. 404–412.

8. Barber, "Necessary and Ornamental," p. 2.

9. Hayes, *Library of William Byrd,* pp. 107–174.

10. Louis B. Wright and Marion Tinling, eds., *The London Diary (1717–1721) and Other Writings* (New York, 1958), p. 146. Byrd's diaries were written in shorthand. Most often he abbreviated proper names by using only the primary consonants. In this case, he referred to Glynne as "Mr. G-l-n." In Dec. 1712, Glynne and Anne Lea advertised globes of 12 inches in diameter and proposed to publish globes 36 inches in diameter from the Atlas and Hercules in Cheapside. Tyacke, *London Map-sellers,* pp. 116–117.

11. Margaret Beck Pritchard, "Maps as objects of material culture," *The Magazine Antiques,* CLIX (2001), p. 213.

12. R. W. G. Vail, "Seventeenth Century American Book Labels," *American Book Collector* (1933), p. 176.

13. A CATALOGUE of *Globes Spheres, Maps, Mathematical Projections, Books and Instruments,* Made and Sold by *Philip Lea,* at the Sign of the *Atlas* and *Hercules* in *Cheapside, near the corner of* Friday-street, *London,* ca. 1698, p. 2. A copy is in the British Lib.

14. Few of Lea's composites included a title page. When one did, the title was *An Atlas containing ye Best Maps of the severall parts of the World collected by Phil: Lea who selleth all sorts of Mathematicall Books and Instruments.*

15. "Condition Description: The Custis Atlas," Northeast Document Conservation Center, 1998, p. 1, archives, CWF.

16. John Ingram, "The English Atlas of John Custis," *Colonial Williamsburg Journal* (1988), p. 13.

17. The family descended from Edmund Custis (b. 1568), "clothier," of Arlington, Gloucestershire. Edmund's sons John I and Henry immigrated to Rotterdam. The former engaged in the cloth trade. Before his death in the 1660s, John I founded an international trading company in which the sons of Henry were active. Lynch, *Years of Migration,* pp. 18, 35–59.

18. See Custis Atlas Cat. 53.

19. See Custis Atlas Cat. 97.

20. The *Term Catalogues* was a trade journal published quarterly between 1668 and 1711 by John Starkey and Robert Clavell that purported to be a relatively complete index to all printed works in London during those years. Edward Arber, ed., *The Term Catalogues, 1668–1709 A. D.* (London, 1903–1906).

21. *A Map of the Principall Part of Europe* (Custis Atlas Cat. 11), which was advertised in 1693, can be shown to be a companion map to the unadvertised *Turky in Europe and in the Lesser Asia* (Custis Atlas Cat. 46), which could therefore be assigned the same date. The latter has a lengthy dedication to Sir John Lowther, commissioner of the Admiralty from 1689 to 1696, that is repeated on *The Natural Shape of England* (Custis Atlas Cat. 15), also assigned a publication date of 1693.

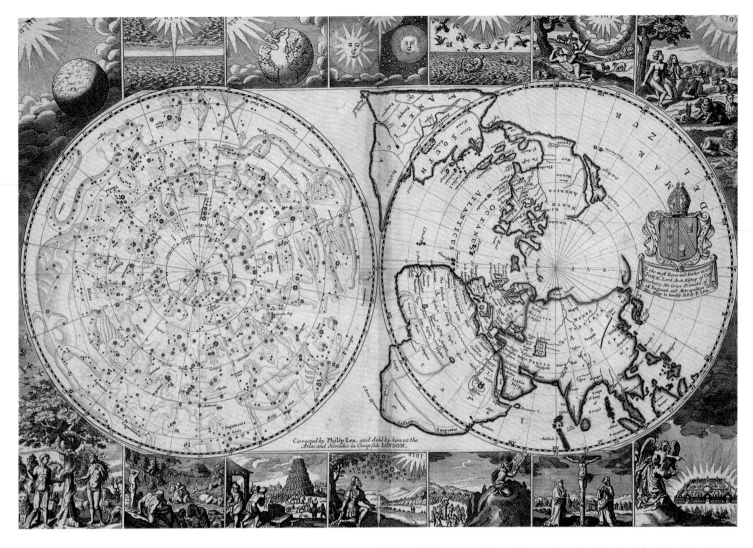

240 Untitled map in two hemispheres: celestial chart of the heavens and the world projected from the north pole. (Custis Atlas Cat. Map A)

MAP A CUSTIS ATLAS

Untitled map in 2 hemispheres: celestial chart of the heavens and the world projected from the north pole[1]

Joseph Moxon or Philip Lea, cartographer; engraver unknown; published separately and in a later edition of the *Sacred Geographie, or Scriptural Mapps* by Philip Lea

London, ca. 1691 (originally published by 1685). Black-and-white line engraving with period outline color to the right hemisphere only. H. 13", W. 21½"

The imprint in the lower center of the sheet is *Corrected by Philip Lea, and Sold by him at the/ Atlas and Hercules in Cheap side LONDON*. A dedicatory cartouche in the right center is *To the most Reverend Father in God/ JOHN Lord Arch Bishop of Can/-terbury. His Grace Primate of/ all England and Metropolitan &c/ This Mapp is humbly D. D. by P. Lea*. The two hemispheres are surrounded by fourteen vignettes with biblical scenes

Four states of the map, with uncertain precedence, are known:
State 1: Advertised in Lea's 1685 sales catalog as "A Celestial and Terrestrial Planisphere in two small sheets," probably with Lea's Poultry address. Dedication unknown. No copy located
Another state: No imprint. The dedicatory cartouche is blank. This may be a proof state. One copy is in the British Library
Another state: *London Printed by J. Moxon. And are to be sold at The signe of Atlas. In Warwick Lane*. The dedication is to John Tillotson, who was appointed archbishop of Canterbury in 1691. Copies accompanied Moxon's *Sacred Geographie*, 1691.
Another state: (this copy) As described

Reference: Shirley, *Mapping of the World*, entry 549

THE TERRESTRIAL map on the right was depicted on a polar projection, resulting in considerable distortion south of the Equator. It was probably based on Jean Dominique Cassini's great circular map of the world, eight meters in diameter, that was laid out on the floor of the Royal Observatory in Paris. The cartographer may have been inspired by an intermediary source such as Jacob Harrewyn's four-sheet world map published in Amsterdam.[2] However, the geography of North America is more advanced on this map than on Harrewyn's, particularly in the configuration of the Great Lakes. New Jersey, Maryland, Virginia, and Carolina were named but Pennsylvania is missing, which suggests that the sheet may have been published before 1681.

This map was formerly attributed to Joseph or James Moxon and thought to date from 1691 based on its appearance in J. Moxon's edition of the *Sacred Geographie* published that year.[3] Six years earlier, however, Lea advertised the map as "A Celestial and Terrestrial Plani-

sphere on two small sheets, projected on the Poles of the world" in his 1685 sales catalog. That the map was included among Lea's stock in 1685 but was not listed in Joseph Moxon's catalog the following year indicates that the map may have originated with Lea. If that were the case, he may have sold the rights to the plate or copies of the map with the Moxons' imprint to be included in their 1691 publication. Lea published the present state between 1691 and 1694 on which the imprint was altered to his Cheapside address and the dedication was to Archbishop Tillotson, who died in 1694.

Lea listed this map in his 1685 and ca. 1698 catalogs but not in that for 1687. It does not appear in any of the other Lea composite atlases examined.

1. This map was identified as Map A because it was not included in the manuscript index.
2. Cassini's map is no longer extant, but J. B. Nolin published a one-sheet reduction in 1696. Shirley, *Mapping of the World*, entry 579. Shirley dated Harrewyn's map ca. 1687. *Ibid.*, entry 534.
3. Joseph Moxon published the *Sacred Geographie, or Scriptural Mapps* in 1671. Another edition with new states of the maps and bearing the imprint of Joseph's son, James, was issued in 1691. The original attribution to the Moxons was made because a copy of this map with the imprint *J. Moxon* appeared in that edition. The map was not included in the 1671 publication. Shirley, *Mapping of the World*, entry 549. See Custis Atlas Cat. 51 for more information on the *Sacred Geographie*.

TEXT B CUSTIS ATLAS
An APOLOGIE / To the Spectator[1]

Possibly Henry Clark, printer

London, ca. 1688. Two leaves of letterpress text, printed on both sides and ruled in red paint or ink that has oxidized to brown.[2] *The DESCRIPTION and USE / Of this MAPP* begins in the center of the left text column

One state of the text is known

An Apologie To the Spectator was designed to accompany *A New Mapp of the World* (Custis Atlas Cat. 1). The introductory *Apologie* consists of a short condemnation of the Dutch dominance of the map trade. Lea attacked the uniform use on Dutch maps of the name "New Netherland" for New England and New York, which by his time was more than twenty years out of date. Lea's moderate approach to French territorial claims suggests a date of publication prior to the outbreak of war with Louis XIV in 1689. The second part, *The Description and Use*, provides a primer on the principles of geography.

Lea listed this text in his ca. 1698 catalog but not in those for 1685 or 1687. It does not appear in any of the other Lea composite atlases examined.

1. This text sheet was identified as Text B because it was not included in the manuscript index.

2. Ruling, or red ruling, by which a margin was painted or inked, usually in red, around a page of text, map, or print, was practiced in England in the seventeenth century. It was considered a luxurious touch that enhanced the beauty and value of the object. In 1663, Samuel Pepys "ruled with red Inke my English *Mare clausum;* which with the new Orthodox title, makes it now very handsome." Robert Latham and William Matthews, eds., *The Diary of Samuel Pepys: A New and Complete Transcription* (London, 1970–1983), IV, p. 107.

1 CUSTIS ATLAS
A NEW MAPP OF THE WORLD BY PHIL, LEA

Philip Lea, cartographer; engraver unknown

London, ca. 1686. Black-and-white line engraving with period outline color. H. 17½″, W. 21″

The title is in a panel at the top. The world is divided into two hemispheres surrounded by ten smaller celestial hemispheres.[1] *The Face of the Sun* is in the top center and *The Face of the Moon* is in the lower center

One state of the map is known

Reference: Shirley, *Mapping of the World,* entry 535

THE GEOGRAPHY of *A New Mapp of the World* is similar to an earlier English hemispheric world map by John Seller. Both were derived from Dutch prototypes.[2] Lea made additions and corrections, particularly in North America, where the newly chartered colony of Pennsylvania was added. Shirley noted that the large italic typeface Lea used to denote more recently discovered areas was different from the block lettering used elsewhere, suggesting that he updated an earlier plate.[3] It should be noted, however, that italics were used throughout the map for some local place-names.

The map was difficult to date because Lea did not include a date or imprint and it was not in his 1685 catalog. He listed a "new seat of Hemispheres, in two sheets," which must be this map, in his 1687 catalog. It appears in Lea's composite atlas in the British Library but not in the other copies examined.

1. Lea's celestial insets were based on the telescopic observations of Cassini and Robert Hooke. Depicting the heavens in this way became an important innovation of English world maps of this period. Shirley, *Mapping of the World*, p. xxxviii.

2. *Ibid.,* entry 460.

3. *Ibid.,* entry 535.

TEXT 2 CUSTIS ATLAS
An Alphabet of EUROPE, and the Parts Adjacent. / By which, with much ease and readiness may be found any Kingdom, Province, City, Town, &c. in the Map

Henry Clark, printer

London, 1687. One leaf of letterpress text, printed on both sides. The imprint at the end is *London, Printed/ by H. Clark / for Philip Lea / Globemaker /at the Atlas and/ Hercules in the/ Poultrey against / the Old-Jury / where you may / have the other / three Quarters / 1687*

Two states of the map are known:
State 1: Advertised in 1683 but no copy located
State 2: (this copy) As described. Probably there were other alterations to the text

An Alphabet of Europe, the explanatory text and index for Overton and Lea's *A New Mapp of Europe* (Custis Atlas Cat. 3), along with advertisements in the *Term Catalogues*, pinpoint the date when Lea relocated his shop to Cheapside. The map and text sheet were first advertised in the *Term Catalogues* in November 1683 with Lea's Poultry address. They were advertised again in the *Term Catalogues* in June 1687 as being sold from Lea's new address at "The Atlas and Hercules in Cheapside." Although the date on the *Alphabet of Europe* was changed to 1687, the Poultry address was not updated to Cheapside, indicating that Lea was working at the Poultry location earlier that year.

Lea listed this text and accompanying map in his 1685, 1687, and ca. 1698 catalogs. State two appears in all of Lea's composite atlases examined.

3 CUSTIS ATLAS
A New Mapp / of / EUROPE. / Divided into it's Principall / KINGDOMS, And Provinces

Philip Lea, cartographer; engraver unknown

London, ca. 1688 (originally published in 1683). Black-and-white line engraving, H. 19″, W. 22¼″

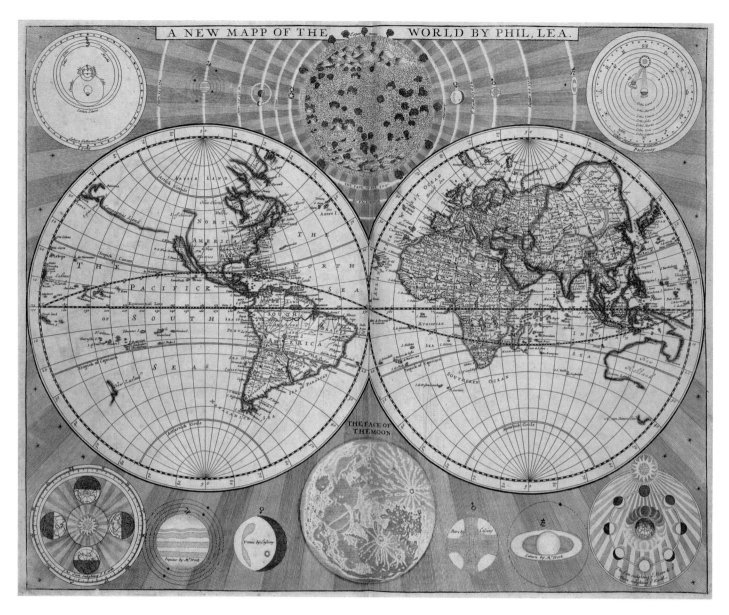

241 *A New Mapp of the World by Phil, Lea.* (Custis Atlas Cat. 1)

The title cartouche in the upper left is followed by the imprint *By Phillip Lea at yᵉ / Atlas and Hercules/ in Cheapside at the Corner of / Fryday Street LONDON. / and by I Overton at/ the white horse without / New gate.* The title cartouche is flanked by putti and is surmounted by an oval portrait of Charles II. Below is a depiction of Europa on a bull. The dedicatory cartouche to the right of Iceland is *To the Right Worshipful/ Sʳ IOHN. LEIGH of / Addington in SURREY / KNIGHT this Mapp is/ Humbley Dedᵗ by PLea.* In the lower center is *Phillip Lea Excudit*

Two states of the map are known:
 State 1: *By Phillip Lea at yᵉ / Atlas and Hercules / in the Poultrey against/ the old Jury LONDON. / and by I Overton at the white horse without / New gate* with the words *Phillip Lea Excudit.* 1683
 State 2: (this copy) As described

First advertised in November 1683, this general map of Europe may be the earliest map published by Lea.[1] *Philip Lea Excudit* and his name in the imprint before that of the more established John Overton show that Lea was the driving force behind the publication, partnering with Overton largely for marketing purposes.

A New Mapp of Europe was one of a set of four maps of the continents that were published separately but advertised together in the *Term Catalogues* in February 1686.[2] Lea listed this map in his 1685, 1687, and ca. 1698 catalogs. State one appears in Lea's composite atlas in the British Library. State two appears in Lea's composite atlases in the Library of Congress and Burden collection.

1. "Price 1 s. on cloth; with Description and colored 5s." Arber, ed., *Term Catalogues*, II, p. 45.

2. For the other three maps of the continents, see Custis Atlas Cats. 6, 8, and 10.

4 CUSTIS ATLAS
EVROPAM / sive / CELTICAM / VETEREM / Sic describere conabar Abrahamus Ortelius

Abraham Ortelius, cartographer; engraver unknown

London, 1684. Black-and-white line engraving with period outline color. H. 15¼", W. 18½"

The title is in a cartouche that features two cornucopias in the upper left corner and a scale of distances is in the lower left. No imprint

*E*vropam sive Celticam Veterem is a reengraving of a map with the same title by Abraham Ortelius.[1] It was advertised as a "new map of Ancient Europe" to be sold by "P. Lea, Globe-maker," in the *Term Catalogues* in November 1684. Lea listed this map in his 1685 catalog but not in those for 1687 or ca. 1698. It does not appear in any of the other Lea composite atlases examined.

1. Abraham Ortelius, *Parergon,* Antwerp, 1595.

TEXT 5 CUSTIS ATLAS
An Alphabet of ASIA, and the Parts Adjacent: / By which, with much ease and readiness may be found any Kingdom, Country, City, Town, &c. / in the Map

Henry Clark, printer

London, 1688 (originally published in 1687)

Two leaves of letterpress text, printed on the front only. The imprint at the end is *LONDON, / Printed by H.C. / for John Overton, / at the White-Horse/ without Newgate, / and collected by / Phillip Lea Globe- / maker, at the At- / las and Hercules in / Cheap-side, next to / the Corner of Fri- / day-Streee* [sic]

Three states of the text are known:
State 1: Advertised in 1687 but no copy located
State 2: (this copy) As described
State 3: *Streee* was corrected to *Street.* 1687–1688

*A*n Alphabet of Asia is the index for Overton and Lea's *A New Mapp of Asia* (Custis Atlas Cat. 6). Lea listed this text

---

in his 1687 and ca. 1698 catalogs but not in that for 1685. State two appears in Lea's composite atlases in the British Library and Library of Congress. State three appears in Lea's composite atlas in the Burden collection.

6 CUSTIS ATLAS
A New Mapp of / ASIA / Divided into Kingdoms & Provinces

Possibly Philip Lea (after Frederick de Wit), cartographer; engraver unknown

London, ca. 1688 (originally published in 1686). Black-and-white line engraving with period outline color. H. 19¼", W. 22½"

A stone tablet with the title and the imprint *Sold by John Overton at the / White Horse with out Newgate and / by Philip Lea at the Atlas and / Hercules in Cheapside LONDON* is in the lower left corner. To the right is a scene of a merchant caravan

Two states of the map are known:
State 1: *Sold by John Overton at the / White Horse with out New gate and/ by Philip Lea. at the Atlas and / Hercules in the Poultry near / Cheapside London.* 1686
State 2: (this copy) As described. The title and imprint in state one were erased. A separate copperplate cut to fit the space contains the same title and a new imprint

*T*HIS is an exact copy, with an English title, of *Accuratissima totius Asiæ Tabula Recens Emendata* published by Frederick de Wit ca. 1680.[1] *A New Mapp of Asia* was one in a set of the four continents.[2] It was advertised in the *Term Catalogues* in February 1686 and November 1690. Lea listed this map in his 1687 and ca. 1698 catalogs but not in that for 1685. It appears in all of Lea's composite atlases examined.

1. Dr. Ir. C. Koeman. comp. and ed., *Atlantes Neerlandici: Bibliography of terrestrial, maritime and celestial atlases and pilot books published in the Netherlands up to 1880* (Amsterdam, 1967–1985), III, p. 212, map 19.

2. For the other three maps of the continents, see Custis Atlas Cats. 3, 8, and 10.

TEXT 7 CUSTIS ATLAS
AN/ ALPHABET / OF / AFRICA / AND THE / Parts Adjacent: / BY WHICH, / With much Ease and Readiness may be found and Kingdom, / Country, City, Town, &c. in the Map

Henry Clark, printer

London, ca. 1688 (originally published in 1687). Two leaves of

242 *A New Mapp of Africa Divided into Kingdoms and Provinces.* (Custis Atlas Cat. 8)

letterpress text, printed on the front only. The imprint at the end is *LONDON, / Printed by H. C. for John Overton at the White-Horse with- / out Newgate. / Collected by Philip Lea, Globe-maker, at the Atlas and / Hercules, near the Corner of Fryday-street, in Cheap-side*

Two states of the map are known:
State 1: Advertised in 1687, probably with the Poultry address, but no copy located
State 2: (this copy) As described

*A*n *Alphabet of Africa* is the index for Overton and Lea's *A New Mapp of Africa* (Custis Atlas Cat. 8). Lea listed this map in his 1687 and ca. 1698 catalogs but not in that for 1685. State two appears in Lea's composite atlases in the Library of Congress and Burden collection but not in the British Library copy.

8 CUSTIS ATLAS
A New Mapp of / AFRICA / Divided into Kingdoms and / Provinces

Possibly Philip Lea (after Frederick de Wit), cartographer; engraver unknown

London, ca. 1688 (originally published in 1686). Black-and-white line engraving with period outline color. H. 19¾", W. 23"

The title cartouche in the lower left consists of a tablet surmounted by two lions. A scene of Europeans and African natives flanks the title, which is followed by the imprint *Sold by J. Overton / at ye White Horse with out New: / gate and by Philip Lea at yᵉ / Atlas and Hercules in / Cheapside / LONDON*

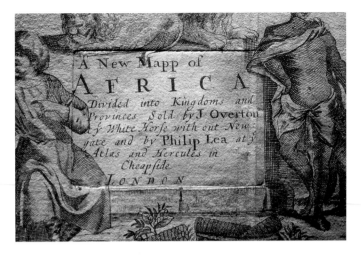

243 Detail of the cartouche showing the imprint of the small plate used for the new title from *A New Mapp of Africa Divided into Kingdoms and Provinces,* possibly by Philip Lea, London, ca. 1688, black-and-white line engraving with period outline color. (Custis Atlas Cat. 8)

Two states of the map are known:

State 1: Advertised in 1686, probably with Lea's Poultry address, but no copy located

State 2: (this copy) As described. The title and imprint in state one were erased. A separate copperplate cut to fit the space contains the same title and a new imprint

Reference: Tooley, "Maps of Africa, Part II," p. 107

Aside from the English title, this is an exact copy of *Totius Africæ Accuratissima Tabula* published by Frederick de Wit ca. 1680.[1] *(fig. 292) A New Mapp of Africa* was one in a set of the four continents.[2] It was advertised in the *Term Catalogues* in February 1686 and November 1690. Lea listed this map in his 1687 and ca. 1698 catalogs but not in that for 1685. State two appears in all of Lea's composite atlases examined.

    1. Koeman, comp. and ed., *Atlantes Neerlandici,* III, p. 212, map 7.

    2. For the other three maps of the continents, see Custis Atlas Cats. 3, 6, and 10.

TEXT 9 CUSTIS ATLAS
An Alphabet of AMERICA, and parts Adjacent: / By which, with much ease and readiness may be found any Country, City, Town, &c. in the Map

Henry Clark, printer

London, 1687

One leaf of letterpress text with no imprint. A short sales catalog is at the foot of the second panel. Ink manuscript notations in a contemporary hand were added to the text

Three states of the text are thought to exist:

State 1: Advertised in 1687 but no copy located. It probably did not contain an imprint

State 1a: (this copy) As described with the manuscript notations

State 2: Two sheets with the imprint *London Printed by HC for John Overton at the White-Horse with- / out Newgate. / Collected by Philip Lea, Globe-maker, at the Atlas and / Hercules, near the corner of Friday-Street, in Cheapside.* Ca. 1690

244 Lea's sales catalog appeared in the lower right corner of *An Alphabet of America,* printed by Henry Clark, London, 1687. (Custis Atlas Cat. Text 9)

A New size of Globes 15 Inches Diamiter, made according to Modern Aſtronomy and Geography, the Southern Conſtellations according to Mr. *Haly's* Obſervation.
A ſize of Globe 10 inches diameter, much corrected.
A Terreſtial Globe 25 inches diameter.
A little pocket Globe, 3 inches diameter.
A TerreſtialDiallingGlobe, 3 inches and a half diameter.
All ſorts of Copernican and Ptolomean Spheres.
A new ſeat of Hemiſpheres, in two ſheets.
A Cœleſtial and Terreſtial Planiſphere.
Euclid's Elements, with the uſes, by *Dechales* a Jeſuit.
Aſtronomys Advancement, illuſtrated with 12 Copper Cuts.
The uſes of a moſt accurate Planiſphere, performing in Aſtronomy the propoſitions of the Globe. The Planiſphere is univerſal and in Paper 17 inches diameter.
Spidell's Arithmetick, price 1 ſhilling.
Ludes Mathematicus: or the Mathemat. Recr. by *Wingates.*

Five new large ſheet Maps of *Europe, Aſia, Africa, America* and *Great Britain* and *Ireland,* with Alphabet. Tables.
A new large four ſheet Map of the Engliſh Empire on the Continent of *America, &c.*
Three new large ſheet Maps *Barbadoes, St. Chriſtophers* and *Jamaica,* wherein is every Plantation, &c. with the names of the poſſeſſors.
11 New large ſheet Maps, *France* with Roads, *United Provinces, Carolina, New-England, Hambourg, Old Europe, Lunem Hiſtoricum per Occidentum.* A Sea-plat of all the *Streights,* part of *Africa,* part of *America,* and part of *Aſia.*
A large Map of *England,* with the reputed diſtances on the Roads, the Arms of the Nobility on each ſide it, 7. foot long, 5 foot 6.inches deep, &c. it may be made up into a book without ill conveniencies to role in a little room, and not fold nor be difficult to find how one part joyns to another, as in other Maps.

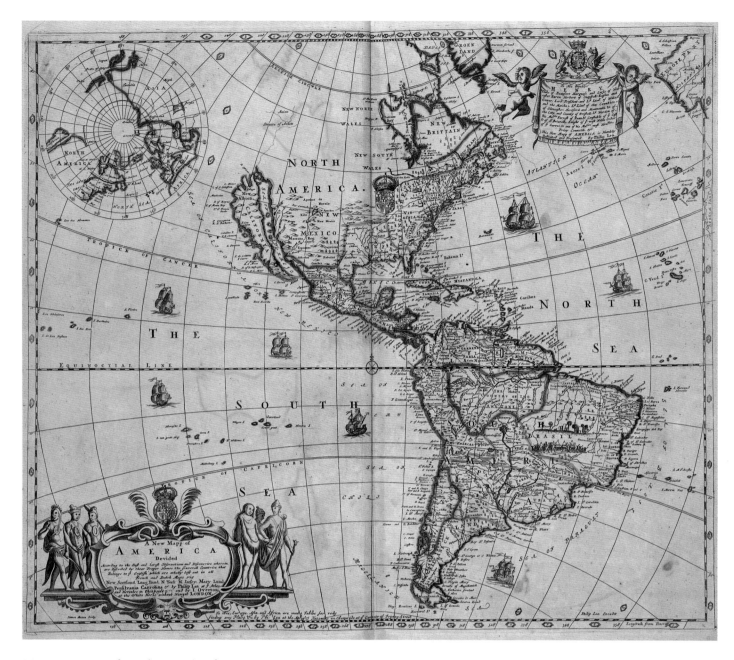

245 *A New Mapp of America.* (Custis Atlas Cat. 10)

*A*n *Alphabet of America* is the index for Overton and Lea's *A New Mapp of America* (Custis Atlas Cat. 10). At some point, the publisher realized that "New York," "Pensilvania," and "Virginia" had been omitted and added them in ink. The same state appears in the copies in the Library of Congress and in the Burden collection. No copy of the one-sheet version without the manuscript notations has been located. The names were inserted when the *Alphabet* was expanded to two sheets and reprinted about 1690. This corrected state appears in Lea's composite atlas in the British Library.

The small sales catalog printed in the lower right was a key to dating the *Alphabet* because the inventory offered for sale could be compared with the maps mentioned in the *Term Catalogues* and the *London Gazette,* the most recent of which were advertised in November 1686. Dating the *Alphabet* also enabled the dating of some of Lea's maps that appeared in the catalog.

Lea listed the *Alphabet of America* in his 1687 and ca. 1698 catalogs but not in that for 1685.

10 CUSTIS ATLAS

A New Mapp of / AMERICA / Devided / According to the Best and latest Observations and Discoveries wherein / are discribed by thear Proper Names the seaverall Countries that / Belonge to yᵉ English which are wholly left out in all / French and Dutch Maps viz / New Scotland. Long Iland. N. York N. Jarsey. Mary Land. / Pensilvania Carrolina &c

Philip Lea, cartographer; James Moxon, engraver

London, ca. 1688 (originally published in 1684). Black-and-white line engraving with period outline color. H. 19¼″, W. 22½″

A hemispheric inset of the north polar region is in the upper left corner. The scrollwork cartouche in the lower left is surmounted by the royal coat of arms and is flanked by six Native Americans. The imprint is *by Philip Lea at yᵉ Atlas/ and Hercules in Cheapside— and by I. Overton/ at the White Horse without Newgat LONDON.* Below and to the left under the cartouche is *James Moxon Sculp;* to the right is *To this, Europe. Asia. and Africa. are made Tables for redy/ finding any Place &c: by Phi: Lea at the Atlas & Hercules in Cheapside at yᵉ Corner of Fryday Street.* In the upper right, within a banner flanked by putti, is the dedication *To His Grace/ HENRY./ Duke of Beaufort . . . one of his ma.ᵗⁱᵉˢ most Hon.ᵇˡᵉ/ Privy Councill. &c. This New Mapp of AMERICA is Humbly/ Dedicated and Presented by Philip Lea. Philip Lea Excudit* is in the lower right corner

Two states of the map are known:

State 1: Advertised in 1684 but no copy located. This state could not have included the reference to the maps of Asia and Africa in the notice beneath the cartouche on state two because they were not published until 1686

State 2: (this copy) As described

References: English Mapping of America, entry 1; McLaughlin, *Mapping of California as an Island,* entry 106; Tooley, "California as an Island," entry 54

A New Mapp of America may be the first general English map of America that shows Pennsylvania, chartered in 1681, and Philadelphia, surveyed two years later. The configuration of the Great Lakes is primitive, and there is no indication of the discoveries of Joliet and Marquette in the upper Mississippi Valley. The Gulf Coast is dominated by a large *B Sp. Of Santo* (Bay of Spiritu Santo), into which flow many small rivers. The Canadian Arctic resembles that depicted on Thornton's *A New Mapp of the World According to Mr. Edward Wright* (Custis Atlas Cat. 85). California is shown as an island.

After the accession of William and Mary to the throne, many favorites of James II fell from favor and dedications to them were removed when maps were reissued. Lea's retention on this map of the dedication to the Duke of Beaufort suggests that state two was issued before 1689.

A New Mapp of America was one in a set of maps of the four continents.[1] It was advertised separately in the *Term Catalogues* for November 1684 and as part of the set in November 1690. Lea listed this map in his catalogs of 1685, 1687, and ca. 1698. It appears in Lea's composite atlas in the Burden collection but not in the other copies examined.

---

1. For the other three maps of the continents, see Custis Atlas Cats. 3, 6, and 8.

---

11 CUSTIS ATLAS
A MAP OF THE PRINCIPALL PART OF EUROPE

Cartographer and engraver unknown

London, 1693 (originally published ca. 1680). Black-and-white line engraving with period outline color. H. 20¼″, W. 22½″

The title along the top of the map is followed by the imprint *By PHIL: LEA Globemaker at yᵉ Atlas & Hercules in Cheap-side London.* A key is in the upper left corner

Two states of the map are known:

State 1: One sheet of a multisheet map with no title or imprint. No copy located. Ca. 1680

State 2: (this copy) As described. Alterations included a title, key, imprint, and new place-names

THE COPPERPLATE for this map was salvaged from an unidentified multisheet hemispheric map of the world. *Turky in Europe* (Custis Atlas Cat. 46) from the same set adjoined this sheet on the right. The two sheets were designed to overlap. A faint engraved score line running a couple of inches in from the left margin of the map of Turky indicates where it was to be trimmed when attached to the right margin of *A Map of the Principall Part of Europe.*

Some place-names such as "North Cap." in northwestern Spain and the key in the upper left apparently were later additions. Lea probably made them after he bought the plates. Lea advertised this map in the *London Gazette* in June 1693 as "A New Map of the Principal part of Europe, very useful to see the Seat of War . . . containing England, Germany, France, Spain, Italy, and Hungary."[1]

Lea listed this map in his ca. 1698 catalog but not in those for 1685 or 1687. State two appears in Lea's composite atlas in the British Library. No states appear in the other copies examined.

1. Tyacke, *London Map-Sellers,* entry 245.

12 CUSTIS ATLAS
A New Mapp / of / ENGLAND SCOTLAND / and IRELAND

Possibly Robert Morden, cartographer; possibly Francis Lamb, engraver

London, ca. 1690 (originally published in 1678). Black-and-white line engraving with period outline color. H. 20½", W. 24"

The title cartouche in the upper left corner is surmounted by the royal arms that rest on two dolphins, each spewing a stream of water. The downward flowing streams frame the title. Below, two warships are engaged in a sea battle.[1] The title is followed by the imprint *By Philip Lea/ At the Atlas & Hercules in Cheap-side/ neere Fryday Street end/ LONDON.* A scale of distances is in the lower left corner. The right side is largely taken up by a genealogical tree of English monarchs

Four states of the map are known:

State 1: The imprint was *Sold by Robert Morden at the Atlas in Cornhill By John Overton at the White Horse without Newgate London.* The genealogical table includes Charles II. 1678

State 2: The imprint was *Sold by Robert Morden at the Atlas in Cornhill and By Phillip Lea at the Atlas and Hercules in Poultrey and by John Seller at the West side of ye Royall Exchange London.* The genealogical table includes Charles II. Ca. 1684

State 3: The imprint was *Sold by Robert Morden at the Atlas in Cornhill and By Phillip Lea at the Atlas and Hercules in Cheapside and by John Seller at the West End of St. Pauls at ye Signe of the Mapp of the World London.* The genealogical table was extended to James II. Ca. 1686

State 4: (this copy) As described. The genealogical table was extended to William and Mary[2]

Reference: Shirley, *Early Printed Maps of the British Isles,* Morden 4, state 4

THIS MAP of the British Isles is a simplified one-sheet copy of Morden and Greene's 1674 multisheet map with the same title engraved by Walter Binneman and Francis Lamb.[3] The genealogical table, which was modified in almost every state, is modeled after a similar chart on Jodocus Hondius's map of England and Ireland.[4]

A New Mapp of England Scotland and Ireland is significant because at the time of its initial publication, it was the first general map to include information from important recent surveys by John Ogilby and William Petty.[5] The map was originally published with alphabetical tables that were not included in the Custis Atlas.

Lea listed the map in his 1685, 1687, and ca. 1698 catalogs. State three appears in Lea's composite atlas in the Library of Congress. No states appear in the other copies examined.

1. The cartouche design was modeled on one that Morden and Berry used on a world map ca. 1676. Shirley, *Mapping of the World,* entry 475.

2. This fourth state was apparently unrecorded until 1977, when a copy was described by Campbell in Weinreb & Douwma, Catalog 17: *The British Isles Part I,* sale catalog, London, 1977, no. 84.

3. Shirley, *Early Printed Maps of the British Isles,* Morden 2. Shirley suggested that Lamb also engraved this version but the quality of the engraving and ornamentation is noticeably inferior.

4. *Angliae Et Hiberniae Nova Descriptio,* 1592, survives in a single copy in the National Library of Wales, Aberystwyth.

5. In 1675, John Ogilby delineated the roads of Great Britain and William Petty published a wall map of Ireland. See Custis Atlas Cat. 21.

13 CUSTIS ATLAS
THE NATURAL SHAPE OF / ENGLAND / With the Names of the / RIVERS, SEAPORTS, / Sand, Hills, Moors, Forrests, and Many other / Remarkes which the Curious will Observe

Philip Lea, cartographer; Herman Moll, engraver

London, ca. 1693. Black-and-white line engraving with period outline color. H. 20", W. 22"

A dedicatory cartouche in the lower left is *To the Right Honourable/ S.ʳ IOHN LOWTHER Baronet,/ One of the Commissioners for the Executing the Office/ of LORD HIGH ADMIRAL of ENGLAND/ A Member of Parliament &c./ This Mapp is Humbly Dedicated by P. Lea.* A scale of distances appears below the dedication. The title cartouche in the upper right, flanked by Neptune and Britannia, is surmounted by the royal arms of William and Mary. The title is followed by the imprint *By Philip Lea at the Atlas & Hercules in Cheapside/ London*

Two states of the map are known:

State 1: Proof state bearing the same title, imprint, and dedication

State 2: (this copy) As described. Many interior place-names were added

References: Shirley, *Early Printed Maps of the British Isles,* Lea 2, state 2; Weinreb & Douwma, Catalog 17, no. 82

For FURTHER information about this map, see Custis Atlas Cat. 15, the first state of *The Natural Shape of England.* Lea listed the map in his ca. 1698 catalog but not in those for 1685 and 1687. State two appears in Lea's composite atlases in the British Library and Burden collection. No state appears in the Library of Congress copy.

14 CUSTIS ATLAS
A NEW MAP / OF ENGLAND / And WALES With / The Direct and CrosRoads / Also the number of Miles between the / Townes on the Roads by inspection in / figures

Philip Lea, cartographer; Sutton Nicholls, engraver; published separately and in some copies of *The Shires of England and Wales* from 1693 by Philip Lea[1]

London, ca. 1690 (originally published ca. 1687). Black-and-white line engraving with period outline color. H. 20¼", W. 19"

The title cartouche in the lower left corner is decorated with military paraphernalia and rests on two dolphins. It is followed by *Sold by Phillip Lea Globemaker/ at the Atlas and Hercules in Cheap/ side near Fryday/ Street.* A table of cities, towns, and shires is in the upper right. A scale of distances is in the lower right corner

Three states of the map are known:
State 1: Same imprint as above. Sutton Nicholls's name appears as the engraver. The map was engraved on four small copperplates. Ca. 1688
State 2: (this copy) As described. Nicholls's name was removed and *Raz Cherbourg* and *C: de Vick* were added. A legend added off Torbay noted the landing there of William III in 1688
State 3: The plates were cut to within the outer margins. Ca. 1695

Reference: Shirley, *Early Printed Maps of the British Isles,* Lea 1, state 2

THIS IS A reduction of Christopher Saxton's 1583 wall map of England and Wales.[2] Lea bought the plates around 1685, made extensive revisions, including the addition of information from Ogilby's road book, and reissued the wall map in several formats. The reduction was engraved on four small copperplates so it could be printed on separate strips of paper. These were gathered and stitched together along the left side so they could be rolled for easy carrying or storage. In this format, the map was known as "The Traveller's Guide."[3] The margins of the four strips in the Custis Atlas copy were overlapped and pasted together to form one contiguous map.

Lea listed the map in his ca. 1698 catalog but not in

those for 1685 or 1687. State three appears in Lea's composite atlas in the Library of Congress. No state appears in any of the other Lea composite atlases examined.

1. See p. 412, n. 47.
2. *Britannia Insularum in Oceano Maxima a Caio,* London, 1683, engraved on 20 plates to a scale of about seven miles to an inch. For a discussion of Lea's revisions and formats for the wall map, see R. A. Skelton, *Saxton's Survey of England and Wales with a facsimile of Saxton's wall-map of 1583* (Amsterdam, 1974), pp. 20–21.
3. The wall map in the same format was also called "The Traveller's Guide." Lea advertised it as such in the *Term Catalogues* for June 1687 and in his ca. 1698 catalog. The term was not used in the 1687 catalog, where Saxton's wall map was simply called "A large Map of England," but the description conforms to that of "The Traveller's Guide."

15 CUSTIS ATLAS
THE NATURAL SHAPE OF / ENGLAND / With the Names of the / RIVERS, SEAPORTS, / Sand, Hills, Moors, Forrests, and Many other / Remarkes which the Curious will Observe

Philip Lea, cartographer; Herman Moll, engraver

London, ca. 1693.[1] Black-and-white line engraving with period outline color. H. 20", W. 22"

A dedicatory cartouche in the lower left is *To the Right Honourable/ S.ʳ IOHN LOWTHER Baronet,/ One of the Commissioners for the Executing the Office/ of LORD HIGH ADMIRAL of ENGLAND/ A Member of Parliament &c./ This Mapp is Humbly Dedicated by P. Lea.* A scale of distances appears below the dedication. The title cartouche in the upper right, flanked by Neptune and Britannia, is surmounted by the royal arms of William and Mary followed by the imprint *By Philip Lea at the Atlas & Hercules in Cheapside/ London*

Two states of the map are known:
State 1: (this copy) As described. This is the proof state
State 2: This state has the same title, imprint, and dedication as the proof state. Many interior place-names were added.[2] Ca. 1693

Reference: Shirley, *Early Printed Maps of the British Isles,* Lea 2, state 1

IN THIS proof copy, the majority of lesser inland towns lack their names and were located only by small circles. Although Herman Moll's name does not appear on the map, the ornamentation surrounding the dedication and scale of distances is identical to that on Custis Atlas Cats. 92 and 97, which he is believed to have engraved. This is one of three maps in the Custis Atlas dedicated to Sir John Lowther, commissioner of the Admiralty from 1689 to 1696.

Lea did not list the proof state in any of his catalogs. It

246 *The Natural Shape of England.* (Custis Atlas Cat. 15)

does not appear in any of the other Lea composite atlases examined.

1. There has been some confusion about the date of this map. Shirley ascribed it to ca. 1690 in *Early Printed Maps of the British Isles,* Lea 2. Campbell dated it to ca. 1695 in Weinreb & Douwma, Catalog 17, no. 83. The correct date is probably 1693. Examples of this proof state were located in copies of the second edition of Lea's *Shires of England and Wales,* which Skelton argued was published in 1693. R. A. Skelton, comp., *County Atlases of the British Isles 1579–1850* (London, 1970), p. 177.

2. See Custis Atlas Cat. 13 for state 2.

16 CUSTIS ATLAS

A MAPP / Containing the / Townes Villages / Gentle-mens Houses / Roads Rivers Woods / and other Remarks / for 20 Miles Round / LONDON

Philip Lea (after Robert Morden), cartographer; engraver unknown; published separately and in some copies of *The Shires of England and Wales* from 1693 by Philip Lea

London, ca. 1690. Black-and-white line engraving with period outline color. H. 20½ ", W. 22"

The small title cartouche in the lower center of the map is followed by the imprint *Sold by Phil. Lea at yᵉ Atlas & Hercules in Cheapside London.* In the lower left is an *Explanation of yᵉ Map. . . Each Square Containing three Statute Miles*

Three states of the map are known[1]:
State 1: (this copy) As described
State 2: *Sold by Tho. Bowles Print Seller in St. Paul's Church Yard & I Bowles at ye Black Horse in Corn Hill . . . 1730.* Putney Bridge was added
State 3: *John Bowles, Print-seller in Mercers Hall, Cheapside . . . 1730.* Printed on silk

Reference: Howgego, *Printed Maps of London*, entry 41

Pʜɪʟɪᴘ Lᴇᴀ's *A Mapp Containing the Townes Villages Gentlemens Houses Roads Rivers Woods and other Remarks for 20 Miles Round London* was essentially a plagiarism of Robert Morden's map of the same title. Lea also published a wall map and a two-sheet version of *20 Miles Round London*, both with accompanying text. Wencelas Hollar's *The Country About 15 Miles any Way from London*, 1670, was the earliest known map to show the environs of the city and introduce the format used by Morden and Lea.[2]

Lea listed a one-sheet map, "London 20 miles round," in his ca. 1698 catalog but not in those for 1685 or 1687. It does not appear in any of the other Lea composite atlases examined.

1. States are given according to James L. Howgego, *Printed Maps of London circa 1553–1850*, 2nd ed. (Folkestone, Eng., 1978), entry 41.
2. For information about Hollar's map, see *ibid.*, entry 34.

17 CUSTIS ATLAS
"A Map of London." Listed in the index but now removed

Iᴛ ɪs ɪᴍᴘᴏssɪʙʟᴇ to determine the identity of this map since Lea published several maps of London during the 1690s. A likely candidate is *This Actuall Survey of London, Westminster & Southwark is Humbly Dedicated to ye Ld Mayor & Court of Aldermen*, published in conjunction with Robert Morden, a reduction of Ogilby and Morgan's great wall map of London, 1682.[1] Another is *A Mapp of the Cityes of London & Westminster & Burrough of Southwark with their Suburbs As it is now Rebuilt since the late dreadfull Fire* by John Oliver, originally published by John Seller and John Hill in 1676, with a second state by Lea about 1693.[2]

Lea listed a one-sheet map of "London and Westminster" in his ca. 1698 catalog but not in those for 1685 or 1687. No map of London appears in any of Lea's composite atlases examined.

1. Howgego, *Printed Maps of London*, entry 42, dated the first state of the reduction to ca. 1690.
2. *Ibid.*, entry 31, dated the first state to ca. 1680, but according to Tyacke, Seller published jointly with Hill in 1676. Tyacke, *London Map-Sellers*, p. 139.

18 CUSTIS ATLAS
The East Part of the RIVER THAMES &c., and *The West Part of the RIVER THAMES* with three small maps of *DOVER and the DOWNES, LONDON, and HARWICH*

Philip Lea, cartographer; possibly Herman Moll, engraver; published separately and in some copies of *The Shires of England and Wales* from 1693 by Philip Lea

London, ca. 1695. Black-and-white line engravings with period outline color. H. 5¼", W. 6¼"; H. 3½", W. 6¼"; H. 5⅜", W. 6¼"; H. 11⅜", W. 18½"

Five individually titled maps taken from four separate plates were printed on one sheet. Along the top of the sheet from left to right are three small maps of *DOVER and the DOWNES, LONDON*, and *HARWICH.* Below are two strip maps of the Thames printed from one copperplate, *The East Part of the RIVER THAMES &c.* (center) and *The West Part of the RIVER THAMES* (below). In the lower right corner is the imprint *Sold by P. Lea at the Atlas & Hercules in Cheapside.* Each map has a scale of distances

Two states of the map, with uncertain precedence, are known:
One state: (this copy) As described
Another state: The inset maps along the top are *Plymouth Sound, Dunkerke,* and *Isle of Wight*

Reference: Weinreb & Douwma, Catalog 17, no. 81, state 1

Tʜᴇ miniature maps at the top were published in Lea's *Hydrographia Universalis*, ca. 1695–1698. The National Maritime Museum's copy of that work contains the map of the Thames with both parts printed on separate sheets. Lea also published multisheet and two-sheet versions of the map of the Thames. The untitled plan of London in the center probably was printed from Wenceslas Hollar's ca. 1675 plate.[1]

Lea listed the map in his ca. 1698 catalog but not in those for 1685 and 1687. State two appears in Lea's composite atlas in the Burden collection. No state appears in any of the other Lea composite atlases examined.

1. Howgego, *Printed Maps of London,* entry 27. The plate evidently was owned by Ogilby and Morgan at one time and probably was purchased by Lea or Morden and Lea from Morgan's estate after 1690.

19 CUSTIS ATLAS
SCOTIA / REGNVM / cum insulis adjacentibus / Robertus Godronius a Straloch descripsit

Cartographer unknown (after Robert Gordon); engraver unknown; published separately and in some copies of *The Shires of England and Wales* from 1693 by Philip Lea

London, ca. 1693. Black-and-white line engraving with period outline color. H. 17″, W. 22¼″

The title cartouche of the main map is in the upper left. No imprint. A scale of distances is in the upper center. A map of the *ORCADES et SHETLANDICÆ INSVLÆ* occupies the right third of the sheet. The title cartouche is at the top and the dedication to *JACOBO DVCI HAMILTONII* is in the lower right corner

One state of the map is known

THIS IS AN English re-engraving of Robert Gordon's map of Scotland that first appeared in Joan Blaeu's *Theatrum* in 1654[1] Several plagiarisms of Gordon's map were published in England during the period, including "A New Map of Scotland by R. Gordon; but corrected and improved by R. Morden," and "The Kingdom of Scotland, with the adjacent islands, described by Robert Gordon of Starloch . . . sold by J. Moxon at the Sign of the Atlas in Warwick-Lane, London."[2]

Lea listed this map in his ca. 1698 catalog but not in those for 1685 or 1687. It appears in Lea's composite atlas in the Burden collection but not in the other copies examined.

1. Peter van der Krogt, *Koeman's Atlantes Neerlandici* ('t Goy-Houten, Netherlands, 1997) 5800:2B.

2. Arber, ed., *Term Catalogues,* II, June 1687, p. 200; *London Gazette,* Feb. 1692, in Tyacke, *London Map-Sellers,* entry 218.

20 CUSTIS ATLAS
The Turnings of the River / FORTH / with ye adjacent County of / CLACKMANAN &c. / part of Stirling shire. / 1688

John Adair, cartographer; Herman Moll, engraver

London, 1688. Black-and-white line engraving with period outline color. H. 15¾″, W. 22″

The dedicatory catouche to *Nobilissimo Domino D. IACOBO Domino de Drummond . . . Ioannes Adair author* is in the lower left. Beneath is a scale of distances. Along the lower center is *Each Squair is a Countey Mille or 1500 Passus.* A key is in the upper right corner. The title cartouche in the lower right corner contains no imprint. *H. Moll Sculp.* is in the lower right

One state of the map is known

References: Simpson, "John Adair," pp. 32–36; Moore, "'Mapp of the Parioch of Tranent,'" p. 75

The Turnings of the River Forth had its origins in a survey of Scotland begun in 1681 by Edinburgh mathematician John Adair. The surveys were to be used to construct a series of county maps for Moses Pitt's twelve-volume *English Atlas,* but Pitt's bankruptcy and other difficulties caused the project to be abandoned. Herman Moll, one of the former engravers for the *English Atlas,* evidently obtained a copy of Adair's survey of Clackmanan and the River Forth, which he published independently in 1688. The plate must subsequently have come into the possession of Lea.

Lea listed the map in his ca. 1698 catalog but not in those for 1685 or 1687. It does not appear in any of the other Lea composite atlases examined.

21 CUSTIS ATLAS
AN EPITOME OF / S^R WILLIAM PETTY'S / LARGE SURVEY OF IRELAND / Divided into its 4 Provinces. 532 Counties. and the Counties into / Their Several Barronies. wherein are Distinguished ye Archbishopricks. / Bishopricks. Citty's. Places that Return Parliament Men. also the / Roads. Bogs. and Bridges

Philip Lea (after William Petty), cartographer; Sutton Nicholls, engraver; published separately and in *Hibernia Anglicana* by Richard Cox, 1689, and in some copies of *The Shires of England and Wales* from 1693 by Philip Lea

London, 1689. Black-and-white line engraving with period outline color. H. 19″, W. 22¼″

The title cartouche in the upper left corner consists of a draped banner surmounted by flora and flags. It is followed by the imprint *By Phillip Lea At the Atlas and Her-/ -cules in Cheapside near Fryday Street LONDON/ And in Westminster Hall near y^e Court of Com-*

247 *A New Map of Ireland.*
(Custis Atlas Cat. 22)

248 *A New Map of Ireland.*
(Custis Atlas Cat. 23)

mon Plea's. A key to the map is in the left center. There is a scale of distances in the lower left with *Sutton Nicholls Sculp* below and *The History of Ireland From/ The Conquest Thereof By the English/ to this Time By Richard Cox. Esqr./ Printed For Joseph Watts at ye/ Angell in St. Pauls Church Yard* to the right. An inset of *BRITTAIN AND IRELAND* framed in scrollwork is in the lower center

One state of the map is known

References: Weinreb & Douwma, Catalog 19, no. 31, state 1; Bonar Law, *Printed Maps of Ireland,* entry 27

In March 1689, James II landed in Ireland with the objective of retaking the throne occupied by William III and Mary. London publishers quickly issued a flurry of maps to satisfy public curiosity, of which Philip Lea's *Epitome of S[R] William Petty's Large Survey of Ireland,* offered for sale in the *London Gazette* in May 1689, was among the earliest.[1] Lea's map was a one-sheet abridgment of Sir William Petty's "Down Survey," the first attempt to record the topography of Ireland on a large scale and in a scientific manner. He published his survey in two forms, as a wall map around 1675 and as an atlas in 1685.[2]

Lea listed the map in his ca. 1698 catalog but not in those for 1685 or 1687. It appears in Lea's composite atlases in the Library of Congress and Burden collection but not in the British Library copy.

1. Tyacke, *London Map-Sellers,* entry 165.
2. For the 15-sheet wall map, see Andrew Bonar Law, *The Printed Maps of Ireland 1612–1850* (Dublin, 1997), entry 13. The atlas *Hiberniæ Delineatio* consisted of four general and 32 county maps. Skelton, *County Atlases,* entry 106. Tyacke described Custis Atlas Cat. 22–23 as based on "Sir William Petty's thirty-two county maps," so it is equally likely that Cat. 21 was also based on the atlas. Tyacke, *London Map-Sellers,* entry 180.

22–23 CUSTIS ATLAS

A New Map of / IRELAND / According to S.[r] W. Petty (But Supplied wth Many Additions / which are not in his Survey nor in any other [map]) Divided into / its Provinces, Counties & Barronies, where in are / Distinguished not only the Bishopricks & Borough[s] but also / all the Bogs, Passes, Bridges, &c: y[t] are in S.[r] W: P. 32 County Maps

Possibly Philip Lea (after William Petty), cartographer; Herman Moll, engraver; published separately and in some copies of *The Shires of England and Wales* from 1693 by Philip Lea

London, ca. 1695 (originally published in 1690). Black-and-white line engraving with period outline color. H. 24", W. 36¼"

Two separate sheets. The top sheet in the upper right corner is numbered "22" and the lower is numbered "23." The main title cartouche in the upper left corner of the top sheet consists of two columns surmounted by the royal arms and military equipment. To the right, Andromeda is chained to a rock; nearby, Perseus fights a dragon. Below the title is a dedication *To their Most Excellent Majesties,/ WILLIAM and MARY/ KING and QUEEN/ of GREAT BRITAIN, FRANCE and IRELAND &c./ And to their Most Hono.[ble] Privy Councill./ This Map is humbly Dedicated by Your Majesties/ Most Dutiful & Loyal Subjects. P. Lea and H. Moll.* In the top center of the upper sheet is a small cartouche with the secondary title *The NORTH Part of/ IRELAND.* To the left is the imprint *London Sold by/ Phillip Lea at the Atlas and Hercules in Cheapside.* In the lower center of the lower sheet is the secondary title *The SOUTH Part of/ IRELAND.* To the left is *H. Moll Fecit,* and to the right is a scale of distances. A key to both maps is in the center left of the lower sheet. An inset of *The Sea-Coast of ENGLAND,/ SCOTLAND and IRELAND also/ HOLLAND part of France &c* is in the lower right corner

Two states of the map are known:

State 1: *London Sold by Phillip Lea at the Atlas and Hercules in Cheapside and in Westminster Hall. Herman Moll in Vanley's Court in Blackfryers.* This state lacks numerous sailing ships and the secondary titles *The NORTH Part of IRELAND* and *The SOUTH Part of IRELAND.* 1690

State 2: (this copy) As described

References: Bonar Law, *Printed Maps of Ireland,* entry 32ii; Weinreb & Douwma, Catalog 19, no. 32, state 2

Like the previous map, this two-sheet map of Ireland was based on Sir William Petty's "Down Survey." It is a reduced version of a wall map of Ireland advertised by Lea and Moll in April 1690.[1] The removal of Lea's Westminster address suggests that state two of the reduction was published after 1694.

The British Library has a separate, beautifully colored, joined copy of state one. Two additional unfinished sheets pasted to the right side show an engraved coastline and rivers for Wales and a part of Scotland.[2] All other details are lacking except for a few names that were added in manuscript. This must have been the engraver's working copy for a version of the map that was never completed.

Lea listed the individual sheets of "Ireland's North Part" and "Ireland's South Part" in his ca. 1698 catalog but not in those for 1685 or 1687. State two appears in Lea's composite atlas in the British Library. No state appears in any of the other Lea composite atlases examined.

1. The wall map agrees in all particulars with Custis Atlas Cat. 22–23 except that it was described in the *London Gaz.* as "3 foot and a half square." Tyacke, *London Map-Sellers,* entry 180.
2. British Lib., K.51.10.2.Tab.

24 CUSTIS ATLAS

A TRUE SURVEY OF / THE EARL OF DONAGALS / BARRONIE OF ENISH-OWEN / Containing the two Adjacent Harbours of Lough- / Foile and Lough Suillie yᵉ Isle of Inche Culmore / and Londonderry By Cap.ᵗ T. Phillips Enginere

Capt. Thomas Phillips, cartographer; Sutton Nicholls, engraver

London, 1689. Black-and-white line engraving with period outline color. H. 18", W. 22¼"

The title cartouche in the upper left corner is surmounted by the royal arms flanked by flags and three gentlemen in seventeenth-century English dress. The title is followed by the dedication *P. Lea To yᵉ Honourable/ Major Generall KIRK & To the Reverend Divine Mʳ-/ GEORGE WALKER Governour of LONDONDERRY./ yᵉ one for yᵉ Releif & yᵉ other for the Defence of/ which Deserving A Perpetuall Comme-/ moration.* Below is *Sutton Nicholls Sculp-* followed by a scale of distances. The imprint *Sold by Phillip Lea Globemaker at yᵉ Atlas & Her-cules in Cheapside London* is in the lower right above an inset. The three insets are *Londonderry; IRELAND;* and *The true Groundplat of the Citty of/ LONDONDERRY*

One state of the map is known

After James II landed in Ireland, he immediately laid siege to Londonderry, the center of Protestant resistance in the north. When it became apparent in July 1689 that the town could not be taken, the siege was lifted. The publication of this survey of the barony of Enishowen with an inset view and map of Londonderry commemorated the failure of the seige.[1] It was based on manuscripts by Captain Thomas Phillips, a military engineer who had been sent to Ireland to make maps and designs for fortifications. Peter Barber speculated that the English government, conscious of the way in which maps could be used for propaganda purposes, dispatched a copy of Phillips's surveys to Philip Lea for publication.[2]

Lea listed the map in his ca. 1698 catalog but not in those of 1685 or 1687. It does not appear in any of the other Lea composite atlases examined.

1. The map was advertised in the *London Gaz.* in Aug. 1689. Tyacke, *London Map-Sellers,* entry 174.

2. The original manuscript plat of *Londonderry* and Lea's printed inset adaptation were reproduced in Barber, "Necessary and Ornamental," figs. 103 and 104.

25 CUSTIS ATLAS

A New Map of / SCANDINAVIA. / or the / NORTHERN KINGDOMS OF / SWEDLAND, DENMARK, / and NORWAY, &c. divided / into their General & Perticular Parts

Philip Lea, cartographer; engraver unknown

London, ca. 1690. Black-and-white line engraving with period outline color. H. 19", W. 23"

The title cartouche in the lower left corner is followed by the imprint *By Philip Lea at the Atlas and/ Hercules in Cheapside London*

Two states of the map are known:

State 1: The imprint is the same as state two but numerous place-names added to the subsequent state are lacking

State 2: (this copy) As described. Numerous place-names along the east coast of Scotland and in the Orkneys were added. An east-west dotted line that intersects the Norwegian coast near *Norre Udden* is labeled *The North Bounds of ye Brittish Sea.* A second, more finely drawn, dotted line labeled *Iuts Riff* runs from the Shetland Islands across the North Sea and ends on the west coast of Denmark at *Hanklit* and *Fermag.* A ship was added in the Baltic Sea

Lea listed the map in his ca. 1698 catalog but not in those for 1685 or 1687. State one appears in Lea's composite atlas in the Library of Congress. State two appears in Lea's composite atlases in the British Library and Burden collection.

26 CUSTIS ATLAS

DANIA REGNUM / In quo sunt / DUCATUS HOLSATIA et SLESVICUM / et / PROVINCIÆ JUTIA, SCANIA, / BLEKINGIA et HALLANDIA /

Frederick de Wit, cartographer; possibly Frederick de Wit, engraver

Amsterdam, ca. 1690 (originally published ca.1680). Black-and-white line engraving with period outline color. H. 20¼", W. 24"

The title cartouche is in the upper right corner. The title is followed by the imprint *Per F. de Wit Amstelodami/ cum Privilegio Poten-tiss. D. D. Ordi-/ num Hollandiæ West frisiæqz.* A scale of distances is in the lower right

Two states of the map are known:

State 1: Lacks the privilege. Ca. 1680

State 2: (this copy) As described. Grid lines, two compass roses in the *Mare Germanicum,* and other minor changes were added

Reference: Koeman, *Atlantes Neerlandici*, III, p. 213

ONLY ONE London publisher, William Berry, advertised an English map of Denmark in the late seventeenth century.[1] Since the demand for maps of this region was not great, Lea and other London publishers relied on Dutch imports such as this example by Frederick de Wit.[2] Once de Wit's black-and-white map was in Lea's hands, it was colored to conform with others in the atlas.

Lea listed an unidentified one-sheet map as "Denmark" in his ca. 1698 catalog but not in those for 1685 or 1687. State two appears in Lea's composite atlas in the Burden collection. No state appears in any of the other Lea composite atlases examined.

1. Tyacke, *London Map-Sellers,* entry 110.
2. De Wit's second state dates after 1689 when he received a privilege from the States General for the rights to publish certain maps. The map was probably intended to replace his *Regni Daniae*, 1660.

27 CUSTIS ATLAS
A NEW MAP OF / RUSSIA or / MUSCOVIE / Divided into its King / doms, Dukedoms, Prin/ cipalities, Provinces, &c

Possibly Robert Morden, cartographer; engraver unknown

London, ca. 1690. Black-and-white line engraving with period outline color. H. 16½", W. 22"

The title cartouche in the upper left corner is followed by the imprint *Sold by Rob.¹ Morden at/ the Atlas in Cornhil./ And by Philip Lee at the/ Atlas and Hercules/ in Cheepside/ London*

One state of the map is known

LEA listed a one-sheet map of "Muscovia" in his ca. 1698 catalog but not in those for 1685 or 1687. This map appears in Lea's composite atlas in the British Library but not in the other copies examined.

28 CUSTIS ATLAS
THE KINGDOME OF / POLAND / With its Several DUKEDOMS & PROVINCES viz yᵉ GREAT / DUKEDOM OF LITHUANIA, & D.ᴰᴹ OF PRUSSIAN, SAMOGITIA, / MAZOVIA, CUJAVIA, BLACK RUSSIA, POLAQUIE, VOLHYNIA / & PODOLIA, in which is UKRAIN or the Country of COSAQUES, / Subdivided into their Palatinates. &c

Philip Lea (after Frederick de Wit), cartographer; engraver unknown

London, ca. 1690. Black-and-white line engraving with period outline color. H. 16½", W. 21"

A scale of distances is in the upper left. The title, in the upper right corner, is contained within a drapery cartouche held by three cherubs and is followed by the imprint *By P. Lea at yᵉ Atlas/ and Hercules in Cheapside LONDON*. Below the title cartouche, other cherubs hold a blank scroll and shield, presumably for a dedication

One state of the map is known

Reference: Malinowski, "Malinowski Collection," Part II, entry 212

THIS MAP of the kingdom of Poland includes much of present-day Ukraine, Belorus, and the Baltic States. It is a close copy of Frederick de Wit's *Regni Poloniae et Ducatus Lithuaniæ Voliniæ, Podoliæ, Ukraniæ Prussiæ et Curlandiæ*, ca. 1680, which is in Lea's composite atlas in the Library of Congress.[1]

Lea listed this map in his ca. 1698 catalog but not in those for 1685 or 1687. It appears in Lea's composite atlases in the British Library and Burden collection but not in the Library of Congress copy.

1. Koeman, comp. and ed., *Atlantes Neerlandici*, III, p. 215, map 98.

29 CUSTIS ATLAS
Novissima et accuratissima / XVII / PROVINCIARUM / GERMANIÆ INFERIORIS / Tabula

Frederick de Wit, cartographer and engraver

Amsterdam, ca. 1680. Black-and-white line engraving with period outline color. H. 18¾", W. 21"

A secondary scrollwork cartouche in the upper left corner has a table and dedication *Spectatissimo Consultissimoqz. Viro/ D.O*

IOHANNI MUNTER/ Consuli Urbis Amstelædamensis,/ nee non/ in Consessu Societatis Indicæ Orientalis/ Assessori gravissimo,/ Tabulam hane D. D. D./ Fredericus de Wit. A scale of distances is in the lower left corner. The title cartouche is in the upper right corner. The title is followed by the imprint *Ex Officina/ FREDERICI DE WIT.* The map was trimmed to the neat line and laid down on a second sheet

Two states of the map are known:
State 1: (this copy) As described
State 2: *Cum Privilegio D. D. Ordinium Hollandiae et Westfrisiæ* was added after de Wit's name. Ca. 1690

Reference: Koeman, comp. and ed., *Atlantes Neerlandici,* III, p. 214, map 65

THE TERM "Seventeen Provinces" was commonly used for the Low Countries (Belgium, Luxembourg, and the Netherlands) in the seventeenth century. In June 1690, Lea advertised "Three new Maps of the Seat of War," which included one of "the 17 Provinces" engraved for him by Herman Moll.[1] For some reason, Lea's map was not available when he assembled the Custis Atlas in 1698, so he substituted de Wit's.

1. Tyacke, *London Map-Sellers,* entry 185.

30 CUSTIS ATLAS
The Seven UNITED PROVINCES / of NETHERLAND. / With its Circumjacent Borders

Philip Lea, cartographer; James Moxon, engraver

London, ca. 1690 (originally published in 1686). Black-and-white line engraving with period outline color. H. 17¼", W. 21"

A secondary or dedicatory cartouche in the upper left center was left blank. The scrollwork title cartouche is in the upper right corner. The title is followed by a blank space where there has been an erasure to the plate and then by the imprint *London Printed for Phillip Lea and Sold at his Shop/ in Cheapside at the Signe of Atlas & Hercules/ Globes, Spheres Mapps Sea-platts and/ other Mathematical Projections./ Are made And Sould.* In the lower right corner a scale of distances is followed by *James Moxon Sculp*

Two states of the map are known:
State 1: No copy located. It had Lea's Poultry address and perhaps that of a second mapseller.[1] 1686
State 2: (this copy) As described

EXCEPT for the English title, this map is a close copy of a Dutch model, probably by Frederick de Wit.

Lea listed a one-sheet map of the "United Provinces" in his 1687 and ca. 1698 catalogs but not in that for 1685. State two of this map appears in all of Lea's composite atlases examined.

1. The map, "sold by P. Lea at the Atlas and Hercules in the Poultry," was originally advertised in Dec. 1686. Arber, ed., *Term Catalogues,* II, p. 190.

31 CUSTIS ATLAS
The SPAINISH NETHERLANDS, / Vulgarly called FLANDERS, Divided / into its X Provinces, wherein are / Delineated the Fortified Towns Roads &c

Philip Lea, cartographer; Herman Moll, engraver

London, ca. 1694 (originally published in 1691). Black-and-white line engraving with full original color. H. 19½", w. 21½"

The title cartouche in the upper left consists of two columns surmounted by the royal arms and military equipment.[1] The title is followed by the dedication *To His Royal Highness/ GEORGE Prince of DENMARK &c./ This Mapp is most Humbly Dedicated and/ Presented by P: Lea* [erasure]. Below and to the left of the cartouche is a key that identifies territories by color: *The staniᵉd Couler Scheweth what is Taken by the Frontier [&c.].* A scale of distances is in the lower left. The imprints, *Sold by P. Lea at the Atlas and Hercules in Cheapside and/* [line erased], and *Herman Moll Fecit,* are in the lower left corner below the scale. The lower right corner of the map has been torn away

Two states of the map are known:
State 1: Herman Moll's name appeared as the engraver, codistributor, and in the dedication.[2] 1691
State 2: (this copy) As described. Moll's name was removed as codistributor and from the dedication but remained as the engraver

THE *Spanish Netherlands* was one of a series of propaganda maps published by Philip Lea during the War of the League of Augsburg. It shows the frontier between France and the Spanish Netherlands (Belgium and Luxembourg) roughly as it existed before the Treaty of the Pyrenees in 1659. Subsequent French territorial gains were located in red.

The coloring was updated periodically to reflect the latest reports from the continent. Although state two is in both the Library of Congress and Custis atlases, the maps were colored differently.[3] The Library of Congress copy shows the fortress of Namur as French, while the Custis

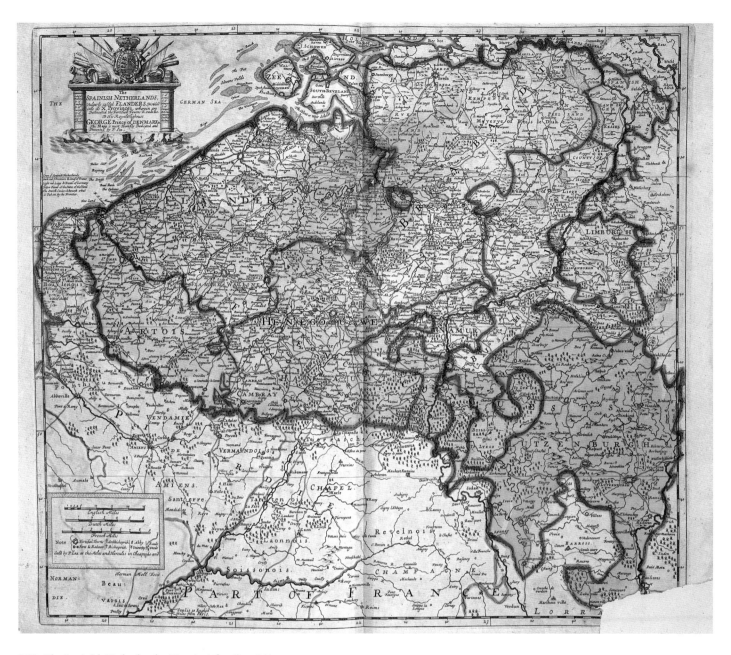

249 *The Spainish Netherlands.* (Custis Atlas Cat. 31)

copy shows it in allied hands. The French held Namur from 1692 to 1695, so the Custis Atlas example was probably colored later.

Lea listed the map in his 1698 catalog but not in those for 1685 or 1687. State two appears in all of Lea's composite atlases examined.

1. The title cartouche is a simplified version of that on Custis Atlas Cat. 22–23, engraved by Moll and originally bearing the joint imprint of Lea and Moll. See also Custis Atlas Cat. 33.

2. The map of the Spanish Netherlands, "Sold by Phil. Lea Globemaker at the Atlas and Hercules in Cheapside, and H. Moll in Vanleys Court in Blackfryers, London," was originally advertised in the *London Gaz.* in Apr. 1691. Tyacke, *London Map-Sellers,* entry 195.

3. The publisher did not follow the color key to the left of the title cartouche in any of the copies examined. The British Lib. copy has no special color at all; only the borders were outlined.

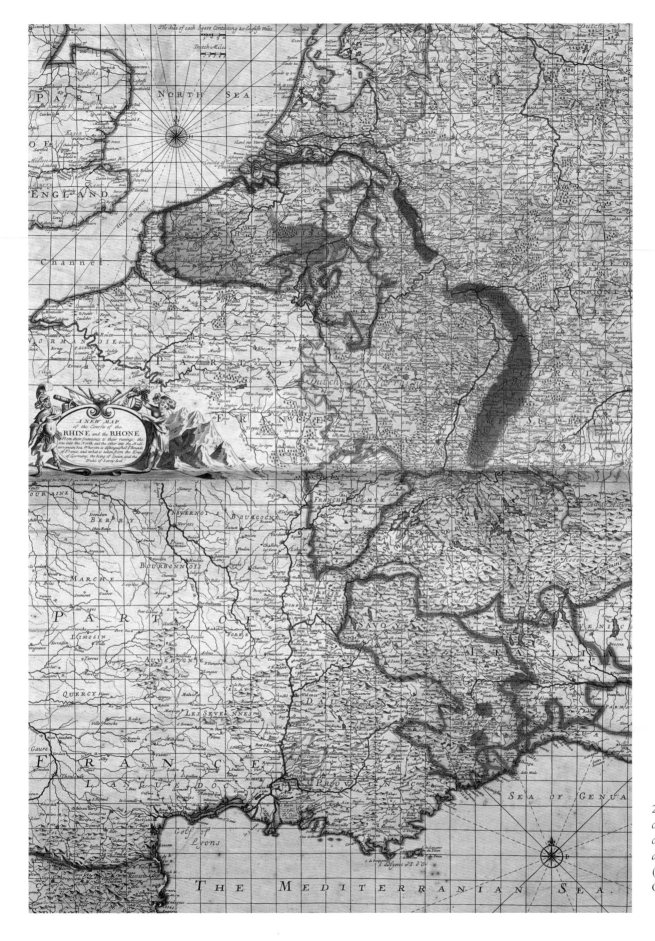

250 *A New Map
of the Courses
of the Rhine
and the Rhone.*
(Custis Atlas
Cat. 32)

32 CUSTIS ATLAS
A NEW MAP / of the Courses of the / RHINE and the RHONE / From their fountaines to their runings; the / one into the North, and the other into the Medi- / terranean Sea. Wherein is distinguished ye Bounds / of France, and what is taken from the Emp: / of Germany, the King of Spain, and the / Duke of Savoy &c

Philip Lea, cartographer; possibly Herman Moll, engraver

London, 1691.[1] Black-and-white line engraving with period color. H. 24½″, W. 17″

This map is vertical in format. A scale of distances is in the upper left corner. The title, in a scrollwork cartouche in the center left, is flanked by allegorical representations of the Rhine and the Rhone. Below is the imprint *Sold by Phill: Lea at the Atlas and Hercules in Cheapside London*. The map was printed in two sheets joined horizontally in the center and slightly cropped at the upper and lower margins

One state of the map is known[2]

*T*he *Courses of the Rhine and the Rhone* illustrates the fluctuating political boundaries created by the conquests of Louis XIV that ultimately culminated in the Treaty of Ryswick in 1697. Like Custis Atlas Cat. 31, the color was probably updated periodically to reflect the latest reports from the continent. Namur is shown in French hands (green), which suggests that this copy was colored between 1692 and 1695. It may be an earlier state of "Frontiers of France, Flanders, Germany, Italy and Spain, stained with several Colours, shewing what is surrendered by the Peace of Riswick, and the bounds of each frontier," advertised in Lea's ca. 1698 catalog. It did not appear in those for 1685 and 1687.

This map, with the imprint trimmed off, appears in Lea's composite atlases in the British Library and Library of Congress. It does not appear in the Burden collection copy.

1. This map was advertised in the *London Gaz.* in Aug. 1691. Tyacke, *London Map-Sellers,* entry 213.
2. In June 1690, Lea advertised "Three new Maps of the Seat of War." One was described as "part of Germany and France . . . Sold by Philip Lea in Westminster Hall, and at the Atlas and Hercules near Friday Street in Cheapside, and by Herman Moll in Yanley's *[sic]*-Court in Black–Fryers." This may be a reference to an earlier state with Moll's imprint as copublisher. *Ibid.,* entry 185.

33 CUSTIS ATLAS
A New Map of / GERMANY / Divided into its / General and Perticular Parts

Herman Moll (after Frederick de Wit), cartographer; Herman Moll, engraver

London, ca. 1694 (originally published in 1689). Black-and-white line engraving with period outline color. H. 19″, W. 21½″

The title in a scrollwork cartouche in the upper left corner is surmounted by an eagle surrounded by military equipment. A cherub is to the right. The title is followed *By P. Lea at the Atlas &/ Hercules in Cheap side near/ Friday Street.* A scale of distances is in the lower right corner

Two states of the map are thought to exist:
State 1: No copy located. Probably with the joint imprint of Herman Moll and Philip Lea. 1689[1]
State 2: (this copy) As described. An old latitude and longitude grid was partially erased

A New Map of Germany was plagiarized from Dutch cartographer Frederick de Wit's *Nova et prae caeteris aliss Correcta Germaniae Tabula,* ca. 1680.[2] Lea listed a one-sheet map of "Germany" in his ca. 1698 catalog but not in those for 1685 or 1687. State two appears in Lea's composite atlases in the British Library and Burden collection. No state appears in the Library of Congress copy.

1. The map was advertised in the *London Gaz.,* Aug. 1689, as a "true Description of Germany . . . By Herman Moll . . Sold at the Author's house in Vanley's Court in Black-Fryers, and by Philip Lea at the Atlas and Hercules in Cheapside, and in Westminster Hall." Tyacke, *London Map-Sellers,* entry 175.
2. Koeman, comp. and ed., *Atlantes Neerlandici,* III, p. 214, map 63.

34 CUSTIS ATLAS
Listed in the index as "A Map of Hamburg" but now missing

Two states of the map are known

References: Reinhartz, "Herman Moll Geographer," pp. 22–23, n. 38

*T*HE COPY of Lea's composite atlas in the Library of Congress contains the second state of *A New Groundplot of the Citty of Hamburg,* engraved by Herman Moll, which must be this map. *(fig. 237)* Lea advertised the first state in 1686 with his Poultry address.[1] It is likely that the dedication was to Laurence Hyde, Earl of Rochester, Lord High Treasurer of England. State two contains the dedication to Hyde even though he had been dismissed from office less than one month after the first state was issued. It is unlikely that Lea altered the dedication although he did change the imprint to *Printed for Philip Lea at the Atlas and Hercules in Cheapside near Friday Street.*

Lea listed this map in his 1687 and ca. 1698 catalogs, which included "Hambourg" and "Hamburgh," respectively, but not in that for 1685. It does not appear in the British Library and Burden collection copies. The Library of Congress copy is illustrated as fig. 237.

1. Arber, ed., *Term Catalogues,* II, p. 190.

35 CUSTIS ATLAS

No map 35 was listed in the index or was present in the atlas

36 CUSTIS ATLAS

Listed in the index as "A New Map of Hungary with its principall Citys" but now missing

"A NEW MAP of Hungary with its principall Citys" probably was a second state of *A New Mapp of the kingdom of Hungary and the States that have been subject to it, with insets of ten cities,* originally published by Richard Palmer and Thomas Terrey.[1] Lea acquired the plate at some point, altering the imprint to *Sold by Phil: Lea at ye Atlas and Hercules in Cheapside London* (state two).

Lea did not include this map in any of his catalogs. State two appears in Lea's composite atlases in the Library of Congress and Burden collection. No state appears in the British Library copy.[2]

1. A first state was originally advertised by Richard Palmer in the *London Gaz.* in Nov. 1686. Tyacke, *London Map-Sellers,* entries 126 and 129. The imprint was *Printed for Tho: Terrey at ye Red Lyon without Newgate, and Ric. Palmer in Fullwood Rents. Near Grayes Inn Stationer.*
2. Both states have a dedication to *His Royall Highness George Prince of Denmark & Norway.*

37–37a–37b CUSTIS ATLAS
A New Mapp of the KINGDOM o / f HUNGARY and the Adjace / nt Countreys

Possibly John Seller, cartographer; engraver unknown

London, ca. 1690 (originally published ca. 1687). Black-and-white line engraving with period outline color. H. 22″, W. 51¼″

The title, in a panel that stretches along the top of all three sheets, is followed by the imprint *By Rob: Morden & Phil: Lea.* The map is in three sheets, only the first of which was numbered

One state of the map is known

IN 1686, Emperor Leopold of Austria, at war with the Ottoman Empire, took the offensive by invading Hungary, which became the focus of the campaign. From 1689, Leopold was allied with Great Britain and the Netherlands against France.

The following year, John Seller and his son gave notice in the *London Gazette* that "the large Maps of Hungary, and the adjacent Countries (drawn from the Original Map sent from Vienna) is now finished."[1] The similarities between this description and *A New Mapp of the Kingdom of Hungary,* also multisheet and including the "adjacent countries," suggest that Morden and Lea's may be a late state of the Sellers' map.

Lea advertised this map as three individual sheets, "Hungary Transilvania. &c.," "Hungary West Part," and "Hungary Middle Part" in his ca. 1698 catalog but not in those for 1685 or 1687. It does not appear in any of the other Lea composite atlases examined.

1. Tyacke, *London Map-Sellers,* entries 141 and 142.

38 CUSTIS ATLAS
PONTI EUXINI / CUM REGIONIBUS VERSUS / SEPTENTRIONEM ET ORIENTEM / ADJACENTIBUS NOVA TABULA an:⁰ 1672. / A JOAN: CHARDIN MIL: AD LOCA INSITUTA

PONTI EUXINI / CUM REGIONIBUS VERSUS / SEPTENTRIONEM ET ORIENTEM / ADJACENTIBUS NOVA TABULA an:º 1672. / A JOAN: CHARDIN MIL: AD LOCA INSITUTA

Herman Moll, cartographer and engraver

London, ca. 1695 (originally published in 1686). Black-and-white line engraving with period outline color. H. 5½″, W. 6⅜″; H. 5⅜″, W. 6¼″; H. 5⅛″, W. 6½″; H. 10⅞″, W. 20⅛″

Above the main map are three subsidiary insets printed from individual copperplates. Two panels with costumed Turkish figures flank a central inset of *The GOLF of CONSTANTINOPLE*.[1] The title cartouche is in the upper center of the map of the Black Sea *(Ponti Euxini)*. No imprint. A scale of distances is in the lower left

Two states of the map are known:
State 1: Lacks the three insets at the top. No imprint. Published in Moses Pitt's English and French language editions of *Travels into Persia and the East-Indies* by Sir John Chardin.[2] 1686
State 2: (this copy) As described

SIR John Chardin, a wealthy Parisian jeweler, traveled and traded in Asia from 1664 to 1677. Chardin, a Huguenot, settled in London in 1681, was appointed court jeweler to Charles II, and was knighted shortly afterward. In 1682, he was chosen a fellow of the Royal Society and published an account of his travels in 1686.

Lea listed this map in his ca. 1698 catalog but not in those for 1685 or 1687. It does not appear in any of the other Lea composite atlases examined.

1. The map of the "Golf of Constantinople" (Sea of Marmara) was originally prepared for Lea's miniature sea atlas, *Hydrographia Universalis*. Both the Lib. Cong. and National Maritime Mus. date the *Hydrographia Universalis* ca. 1700, but a more likely date for first publication is 1695. Phillips, comp., *List of Geographical Atlases*, entry 527; National Maritime Museum, Greenwich, Eng., *Catalogue of the Library*. III: *Atlases & Cartography* (London, 1971), entry 448.

2. Edward Godfrey Cox, *A Reference Guide to the Literature of Travel*, I, 1935, reprint (New York, 1969), pp. 249–250.

39 CUSTIS ATLAS
PORTVGALLIA / et / ALGARBIA / quæ olim / LVSITANIA. / Auctore / Vernando Alvero Secco

Willem and Joan Blaeu, cartographers; engraver unknown

Amsterdam, 1635. Black-and-white line engraving with period outline color. H. 15", W. 19"

The title, contained within a scrollwork cartouche flanked by geographers taking measurements, is in the lower left. A scale of distances is in the lower center. In the lower right is *Amsterdami/ Apud Guiljelmum et Joannem Blaeuw*. This map shows signs of having been bound in an earlier volume. The sheet was trimmed to the neat line and mounted by the binder on a sheet of paper conforming to the size of the other maps in the Custis Atlas. An earlier manuscript notation of "33" is in the upper left corner

One state of the map is known

References: Goss, *Blaeu's Grand Atlas*, pp. 136–137; Resende, *Cartographia impressa dos seculos XVI e XVII*, entry 29; van der Krogt, *Koeman's Atlantes Neerlandici*, entry 6300:2

BECAUSE no London publisher produced a map of Portugal in the late seventeenth century, Lea imported *Portvgallia et Algarbia* from Amsterdam. Originally issued by Willem and Joan Blaeu in 1635, the map was based on one by Fernando Alvares Seco published in Rome around 1561.[1]

1. The map originally appeared in the Blaeus' German language edition of the *Novus Atlas*, 1635. Koeman, comp. and ed., *Atlantes Neerlandici*, I, BL 5. Seco's map was also copied by De Jode, 1565, Ortelius, 1570, Quad, 1594, Hondius, 1600, and others.

40 CUSTIS ATLAS
SPAIN / AND PORTUGAL / BY PHILIP LEA LONDON

Philip Lea (after Frederick de Wit), cartographer; engraver unknown

London, ca. 1690. Black-and-white line engraving with period outline color. H. 19½", W. 22¼"

A scale of distances and a key are in the lower left corner with the imprint *Made & Sold by Philip Lea at yᵉ Atlas and Hercules in Cheapside and in Westminster Hall*. A title cartouche in the lower right is surmounted by the arms of Spain and Portugal and a lion brandishing a sword. It is flanked by Atlas and Hercules, respectively, supporting celestial and terrestrial globes, an allegorical representation of the name of Lea's shop

One state of the map is known

LEA'S MAP of Spain and Portugal was copied from Frederick de Wit's *Accurratissima Totius Hispaniae Portugalliaeq* published in Amsterdam around 1680.[1] Lea advertised a one-sheet map of Spain in his ca. 1698 catalog but not in those for 1685 or 1687. This map appears in all of Lea's composite atlases examined.

1. Koeman, comp. and ed., *Atlantes Neerlandici*, III, p. 214, map 71.

41 CUSTIS ATLAS

THIS NEW / AND ACCURATE / MAPP OF FRANCE / According to the Modern Geography / Devided in its General and Perticular / Parts Governments & Provences / &c. is humbly Dedicated and / Presented by Philip Lea

Philip Lea (after Frederick de Wit), cartographer; Richard Palmer, engraver

London, ca. 1690 (originally published in 1684). Black-and-white line engraving with period outline color. H. 19½", W. 22"

A decorative banner in the upper left corner contains a key. The title cartouche in the lower left corner is surmounted by a second, smaller circle containing the dedication *To the/ Right Honourable IOHN EARLE of/ BRIDGEWATER,/ Viscount Brachley, Baron/ of Elsmeere, Lord Leivtenant/ of the two Countys of/ Buckingham and/ Hertford./ and one of the Lords/ of his Majesties/ most Honourable/ Privy/ Councell.* The whole is surrounded by martial motifs. Below the cartouche is the imprint *Sold by Philip Lea Globe maker at the Atlas/ and Hercules in Cheapside at the Corner of Fryday Street London.* *R Palmer Sculp.* is in the lower right corner

Two states of the map are known:
State 1: No copy located. With Lea's Poultry address. 1684
State 2: (this copy) As described

ONE OF Lea's earliest sheet maps, *This New and Accurate Mapp of France*, engraved by Richard Palmer, was advertised in the *Term Catalogues* in November 1684 "by P. Lea, Globemaker at the Atlas and Hercules in the Poultry." It was based on *Accuratissima Galliae Tabula* by Frederick de Wit, ca. 1680.[1]

Lea listed this map in his 1685, 1687, and ca. 1698 catalogs. It appears in all of Lea's composite atlases examined.

1. Koeman, comp. and ed., *Atlantes Neerlandici,* III, p. 213, map 57.

42 CUSTIS ATLAS

ITALY / Divided into its Several STATES viz the / STATE of yᵉ CHURCH, the K. of SPAIN, / the DUKES of SAVOY, TUSCANY, / MANTUA, MODENA, PARMA, MASSA, / MIRANDOLA, the REPUBLICKS of / VENICE, GENOA, LUCCA, GENEVA, / S.ᵗ MARINO, the PRINCES OF MONA– / CO, PIOMBINA, MASSERAN, / the Bishop of / TRENT &c

Philip Lea, cartographer; engraver unknown

London, ca. 1690. Black-and-white line engraving with period outline color. H. 20", W. 21½"

The title cartouche surmounted by coats of arms is in the upper right corner. A scale of distances and the imprint are in a plinth surmounted by two cherubs brandishing swords with erupting volcanos in the background. The imprint is *Sold by Phillip Lea Globe Maker at the Atlas/ and Hercules in Cheap-Side London*

One state of the map is known

LEA probably published this map about 1690, the year Spain entered the War of the League of Augsburg on the side of the Grand Alliance. The English realized that Spanish possessions in Italy had become vulnerable to attack by France.

Lea listed this map in his ca. 1698 catalog but not in those for 1685 or 1687. It appears in all of Lea's composite atlases examined.

43 CUSTIS ATLAS

A New Map of yᵉ / DUKEDOME of SAVOY. / PRINCIPALITY of PIEDMONT / COUNTY of NICE / DUKEDOME of MONFERRET, / and yᵉ / Adjacent Countries of / MILAN DAUPHINE PROVENCE &c. / With yᵉ Roads & Passages over the / Alpes into FRANCE &c

Philip Lea, cartographer; engraver unknown

London, 1692. Black-and-white line engraving with period outline color. H. 19", W. 22"

The title in the lower right corner is in a large panel flanked by attached columns and surmounted by cherubs and the arms of Savoy. The imprint, in the same panel below, is *Sold by Philip Lea Globemaker/ in Cheapside LONDON/ and in Westminster Hall.* To the left are seven small insets of fortified towns and a scale of distances and key

One state of the map is known

THE independent duchy of Savoy joined the grand coalition against Louis XIV in 1690. It was a great coup for the allies, for Savoy posed a serious threat to the southeastern flank of France and was a protective buffer for Spain's possessions in northern Italy. Savoy made a separate peace with France in 1696 on very favorable terms.

A New Map of yᵉ Dukedome of Savoy was advertised in the London Gazette in August 1692.[1] Lea listed this map in his ca. 1698 catalog but not in those for 1685 or 1687. Lea's composite atlas in the Library of Congress contains a different map titled *A new map of Savoy, Piedmont, and Switzerland, also part of France, Germany and Spain, by P. Lea & H. Moll*. The atlas in the Burden collection contains Robert Morden and Christopher Browne's *H. Jaillot's Map of the Seat of War in Italy cont: ye Duchyes of Milan, Mantua, Parma &c*. No map of Savoy appears in the British Library copy.

1. Tyacke, *London Map-Sellers*, entry 226.

THIS MAP is a close copy of Gerard Mercator's map with the same title, which was originally published in *Italiæ, Sclavoniæ, et Graeciæ tabula Geographicæ*, 1589, the fourth part of his atlas.[1]

Lea listed this map in his ca. 1698 catalog but not in those for 1685 or 1687. It does not appear in any of the other Lea composite atlases examined.

1. van der Krogt, *Koeman's Atlantes Neerlandici*, p. 49, entries 1:002 and 7820:1A.1; Christos G. Zacharakis, *A Catalogue of Printed Maps of Greece and Greek Regions, 1477–1800* (Nicosia, Cyprus, 1982), entry 1325.

44 CUSTIS ATLAS

Listed in the table of contents as "A new generall Map of yᵉ seat of War from yᵉ upper hungary" but now missing

THIS WAS *A New Generall Map of the Seat of War from Upper Hungary to the Isle of Candia* that Lea advertised from his Cheapside and Westminster Hall addresses. Engraved by John Oliver ca. 1691, it was dedicated to the Marquess of Worcester.

Lea did not list this map in any of his catalogs. It appears in all of the other Lea composite atlases examined with the above imprint but with signs of an erasure, indicating there must have been an earlier state.

45 CUSTIS ATLAS
MOREA / olim / PELOPONNESUS

Possibly Robert Morden, cartographer; engraver unknown

London, ca. 1690. Black-and-white line engraving with period outline color. H. 18½", W. 21¼"

The title cartouche is in the lower left corner with a scale of distances below. In the lower center is the imprint *Sold By Robert Morden at the Atlas in Cornhill/ and By Phil: Lea at yᵉ Atlas & Hirculus in Cheapside London*

One state of the map is known

Reference: Zacharakis, *Catalogue of Printed Maps of Greece*, entry 1551, plate 312

46 CUSTIS ATLAS
TURKY IN EUROPE / AND IN THE / LESSER ASIA. &cc

Cartographer and engraver unknown

London, ca. 1693 (originally published ca. 1680). Black-and-white line engraving with period outline color. H. 22½", W. 20¼"

The imprint *Sold by P. L. in Cheapside and at his Shop in WESTMINSTER HALL, near the Court of Common Pleas. also all sorts of Globes Maps &c.* is between the inner and outer boundary of the upper margin. The title cartouche is in a small unornamented rectangle in the upper right corner with a scale of distances below. In the lower right is a dedicatory cartouche *To the Right/ HONOURABLE/ S.ʳ IOHN LOWTHER/ Baronet, one of the Com/ missioners for the Exe-/ cuting the Office of Lord/ High Admirall of Eng-/ land, and a member/ of Parliament &c./ This Mapp is most Humbly Dedi-/ cated by your Honouʳˢ/ most Obedient Servant/ Phillip Lea*

Two states of the map are thought to exist:
State 1: No copy located. Lacking title, imprint, and dedication. Ca. 1680
State 2: (this copy) As described. Other minor details were added

THE COPPERPLATE for this map, which shows the Balkans, Asia Minor, Black Sea, and southern Russia, was salvaged from an unidentified hemispheric wall map of the world. *A Map of the Principall Part of Europe* (Custis Atlas Cat. 11), from the same source, adjoined this plate on the left. The crowded imprint, title, and dedicatory cartouche seem to be afterthoughts to the original design. "Part of Asia" in large letters across the face of the map was probably added as well. Since the map of Europe was first advertised in 1693, it is likely that *Turky in Europe* was revised and published separately the same year.

251 *Turky in Europe and in the Lesser Asia* (Custis Atlas Cat. 46)

Lea listed this map in his ca. 1698 catalog but not in those for 1685 or 1687. It appears in all of Lea's composite atlases examined.

47 CUSTIS ATLAS
THE DOMINIONS OF EMPIRE OF Y^e GRAND SIGNOR / OF THE TURKES / IN EUROPE IN ASIA & AFRICA. / Divided into all it's / BEGLERBEGLIC'S or GOVERMENTS / together wth those other Territories that are Tributarie to it

Philip Lea (after Hubert Alexis Jaillot), cartographer; engraver unknown

London, ca. 1690. Black-and-white line engraving with period outline color. H. 22½", W. 34"

Across the top is a lengthy title in French *LES ETATS DE EMPIRE DU GRAND SEIGNEUR DES TURCS EN EUROPE, EN ASIE, ET EN AFRIQUE, DISTINGUE SUIVANT L'ESTENDUEDE SES BEGLER-BEGLICZ ou GOUVERNMENTS . . . Dresse sur les Relations les plus Nouelles Par le Sr SANSON, Nouvellement Corrige par* [erased]. In the lower left corner is an inset map of Algeria [partially torn]. The scrollwork title cartouche in the lower left center, surmounted by martial objects and flanked by a European and a Turk, is followed by the dedication *TO HIS GRACE/ IAMES DUKE of ORMOND &c.* [the rest of the dedication has been torn away]. In the right center is a large scale of distances with the imprint *London Sold by Phillip Lea at the Atlas and Hercules in/ Cheapside and in Westminster hall* below. The large format necessitated joining two sheets and folding them into the atlas

Two states of the map are known:
State 1: No copy located. The state contained a name, erased in state two, after *Nouvellement corrige par*
State 2: (this copy) As described

THIS MAP is a close copy of one published in Hubert Alexis Jaillot's *Atlas Nouveau*, 1681.[1] Jaillot's maps were newly ornamented, enlarged copies of the maps of Nicholas Sanson. Lea preserved Jaillot's decorative elements and translated the title in the cartouche into English and shortened it. He retained the original title in French above the map. The Westminster Hall address dates the map to the years 1689–1695.

Lea may have intended to publish a series of English editions of Jaillot's maps as William Berry did from 1680 to 1689.[2] Although Berry's maps were issued separately, a small number of bound sets are known.[3]

Lea listed this map in his ca. 1698 catalog but not in those for 1685 or 1687. It does not appear in any of the other Lea composite atlases examined.

1. Mireille Pastoureau, *Les Atlas Français XVIe–XVIIe Siècles Repertoire bibliographique et étude* (Paris, 1984), Jaillot I Aa 1681, no. 43.
2. The British Lib. has a copy of *A New Mapp of ye World Geograficall & Hydrograficall . . . By ye Sieur Sanson, newly Corrected & Amended by Phillip Lea.* Like Custis Atlas Cat. 47, it was copied from Jaillot, with the titles in French and English.
3. Philips, comp., *List of Geographical Atlases,* entry 3442.

48 CUSTIS ATLAS
NATOLIA, quæ olim ASIA MINOR

Jan Jansson, cartographer; engraver unknown

Amsterdam, 1636. Black-and-white line engraving with period outline color. H. 15", W. 19¼"

The title contained in a banner is in the upper center. A scale of distances is in the lower right corner. No imprint

One state of the map is known

Reference: van der Krogt, *Koeman's Atlantes Neerlandici,* entry 8110:1B

49 CUSTIS ATLAS
To the/ Great Czar of / MOSCOVIE / This Map of / TARTARY / Is humbly dedicated / by Robert Morden and / Philip Lea

Possibly Robert Morden (after Nicholas de Wit), cartographer; engraver unknown

London, ca. 1690. Black-and-white line engraving with period outline color. H. 16¾", W. 21¼"

The title cartouche in the form of a seashell held by the figure of Neptune is in the upper right corner

Two states of the map are known:
State 1: Title and dedication as above
State 2: (this copy) As described. Numerous place-names were added in northwestern Siberia and east of the Caspian Sea. The coastline of the *Mare Cang* was extended eastward in the lower right corner. There were other minor changes and additions

MORDEN AND LEA'S *Map of Tartary* is a one-sheet copy of Nicolas Witsen's 1687 multisheet map of Siberia, which at the time was one of the least known parts of the globe.[1]

Witsen's map was the most accurate for the region yet published. Sir Robert Southwell, president of the Royal Society, pronounced it "Columbus like, the discovery of a New World."[2]

The great interest that Witsen's map aroused in English scientific circles was due largely to an innovation in the depiction of Novaya Zembla, an island off the Arctic coast of Russia. Since the sixteenth century, English merchants had sought an Arctic passage to the Far East. The dream seemed to be dashed by a map published in London in 1674 by Stanislav Loputsky that incorrectly showed Novaya Zembla as a peninsula barring the sea route to the east.[3] Witsen corrected Loputsky's error on his 1687 map, depicting Novaya Zembla as an island. Morden and Lea acknowledged that discovery on their reduced and simplified *Map of Tartary* with the notation *Witsen I. Det A. 1688.*

Lea listed the map in his ca. 1698 catalog but not in those for 1685 or 1687. State two appears in Lea's composite atlas in the Burden collection. No state appears in the British Library and Library of Congress copies.

1. In 1664, Witsen traveled with a Dutch legation to Moscow where he collected data on Asiatic Russia. For his 1687 map, *Nieuwe Lantkaarte Van het Noorder en Ooster deel van Asia en Europa*, see Leo Bagrow, *A History of Russian Cartography up to 1800*, ed. Henry W. Castner (Wolfe Island, Ont., Can., 1975), pp. 73–76. See also Johannes Keuning, "Nicolaas Witsen as a cartographer," *Imago Mundi*, XI (1954), pp. 95–110.

2. Dirk de Vries, "Dutch Cartography," in Robert P. Maccubbin and Martha Hamilton-Phillips, *The Age of William III & Mary II: Power, Politics, and Patronage, 1688–1702: A reference encyclopedia and exhibition catalogue* (Williamsburg, Va., 1989), p. 110.

3. Loputsky's map appeared in the *Philosophical Transactions of the Royal Society* (1674). This small map was reproduced in Bagrow, *History of Russian Cartography*, fig. 38. See also Black, ed., *Blathwayt Atlas*, pp. 38–40.

50 CUSTIS ATLAS
A MAP of CANAAN / With the Adjacent COUNTRIES / Very Usefull for the Understanding / of the Old Testament

Philip Lea, cartographer; engraver unknown

London, ca. 1692. Black-and-white line engraving with period outline color. H. 19¾", W. 23½"

The title cartouche is in the left center. The title is followed by the imprint *Sold by P: Lea at the Atlas and Hercules in Cheap-Side; and in Westminster-hall*

One state of the map is known

THIS MAY be a simplified one-sheet reduction of a 5½-foot by 4-foot wall map that Lea listed in his ca. 1698 catalog as "The Land of Canaan, with Historical Ornaments and the Cities of Jerusalem, Babylon, and Nineveh."

Lea did not list the one-sheet version in any of his catalogs. It appears in Lea's composite atlases in the British Library and Library of Congress but not in the Burden collection copy.

51 CUSTIS ATLAS
PARADISE, OR THE GARDEN OF EDEN. / With the Countries circumjacent Inhabited by the PATRIARCHS

Joseph Moxon, cartographer; engraver unknown; published separately but intended to accompany editions of the *Sacred Geographie* by the Moxons and a later edition by Philip Lea

London, ca. 1691 (originally published in 1671). Black-and-white line engraving with period outline color. H. 12½", W. 18½"

In the upper left is a dedicatory cartouche *To the Reverend Father in God–/ HENRY/ Lord Bishop of London. This Mapp/ Is humbly Dedica^ted by P. Lea.* The title, contained in a long scrollwork panel, is in the upper center. In the upper right is a vignette of the expulsion from Paradise. In the lower right, a scale of distances is followed by the imprint *Corrected & Sold by P. Lea, at ye Atlas & Her–/ cules in Cheap side LONDON*

Three states of the map are thought to exist:

State 1: Same title as above but with no imprint. The dedication is *To his Grace George. Duke of Buckingham &c. And Chancelor of Cambridge. This mapp is humbly Dedicated. By Joseph Moxon.* 1671

State 2: No copy located. The dedication was probably altered to read *To the Reverend Father in God–/ HENRY/ Lord Bishop of London. This Mapp/ Is humbly Dedicated by Joseph Moxon.* Ca. 1691[1]

State 3: (this copy) As described

THIS IS ONE of a set of maps that accompanied the text for Joseph Moxon's *Sacred Geographie*, 1671. The maps were ornamented with engraved scenes of biblical events and some included notations specifying where they could be inserted into Bibles.[2]

In 1691, Joseph Moxon's son, James, published a new edition of the *Sacred Geographie* accompanied by new states of the maps. Shortly thereafter, the Moxons sold the plates and publication rights to Lea, who added his imprint.[3]

Lea listed this map in his ca. 1698 catalog but not in those for 1685 or 1687. State three appears in Lea's composite atlas in the British Library. No state appears in the Library of Congress and Burden collection copies.

1. Because similar states that fit this description exist for the other Bible maps, it may be assumed that one existed for *Paradise, or the Garden of Eden,* as well.

2. Maps of this type were introduced in the Lowlands in the sixteenth century. Moxon stated in his introduction that the prototypes for these maps were selected by Dutch ministers. Shirley, *Mapping of the World,* p. 474.

3. For other maps in the series, see Custis Atlas Cats. Map A and 52–55.

52 CUSTIS ATLAS
ISRAELS PERIGRINATION. / or the / FORTY YEARS TRAVELS / of the CHILDREN of ISRAEL / out of EGYPT, through the Red Sea, / and the Wildernesse, into CANAAN / Or the Land of PROMISE

Joseph Moxon, cartographer; engraver unknown; published separately but intended to accompany editions of the *Sacred Geographie* by the Moxons and a later edition by Philip Lea

London, ca. 1691 (originally published in 1671). Black-and-white line engraving with period outline color. H. 12½", W. 18½"

Vignettes running across the lower portion of the map depict (left to right) two sides of a shekel, Jewish religious symbols, Moses, a plan of the camp of the Israelites in the wilderness, Aaron, and the Ark of the Covenant with *Place this Mappe at the/ 33 Chapter of Numbers* above. In the upper left center is a dedicatory cartouche *To his Grace JAMES Duke of/ Ormond &c And Chancelour/ of Oxford. This Mapp is/ humbly Dedicated By P. Lea.* The scrollwork title cartouche in the upper right corner, flanked by two cherubs, is followed by the imprint *Newly Corrected by P. Lea./ And Sold by him at yͤ Atlas and/ Hercules in Cheap–Side LONDON* and a scale of distances

Two states of the map are known[1]:
State 1: Same title as above followed by the imprint *Newly corrected by Joseph Moxon./ Hydrographer to the Kings Most Excellent Majesty./ London. Printed and Sold by Joseph Moxon.* Same dedication as above but followed *By Joseph Moxon.* 1671
State 2: (this copy) As described

LEA listed this map in his ca. 1698 catalog but not in those for 1685 or 1687. State two appears in Lea's composite atlas in the British Library. No state appears in the Library of Congress and Burden collection copies.

1. There appear to be three states of the other Bible maps with the second state retaining Moxon's imprint and with a new dedication. *Israels Perigrination* seems to have only two states, both with the same dedication. For other maps in the series, see Custis Atlas Cats. Map A, 51, and 53–55.

53 CUSTIS ATLAS
CANAAN, / or / THE LAND OF PROMISE. / Possessed by the CHILDREN of ISRAEL: / and Travelled through by our Saviour / JESUS CHRIST; / and His / APOSTLES

Joseph Moxon, cartographer; engraver unknown; published separately but intended to accompany editions of the *Sacred Geographie* by the Moxons and a later edition by Philip Lea

London, ca. 1691 (originally published in 1671). Black-and-white line engraving with period outline color. H. 12½", W. 18½"

The title cartouche in the lower center of the map is followed by the imprint *Corrected by P. Lea./ And Sold by him at yͤ Atlas and Hercules in Cheap-Side LONDON.* It is flanked by (left to right) Atlas, a nativity scene, Christ risen from the tomb, Christ ascending to heaven, the Apostles filled with the Holy Spirit, and Britannia with *Place this Mapp before the/ Gospel of St. Matthew* above. In the upper left is a key printed on a banner held aloft by three cherubs. A cartouche in the upper center is dedicated *To the Right Reverend Father in God/ GILBERT/ Lord Bishop of Salisbury &ct./ This Mapp is humbly Dedicated/ By P. Lea.* In the upper right is a scale of distances held aloft by three cherubs

Three states of the map are known[1]:
State 1: Following the title is *Newly Corrected by Joseph Moxon.* The dedication is *To the Right Reverend Father in God Seth Lord Bishop of Salisbury. This Mapp is humbly Dedicated by Joseph Moxon.* 1671
State 2: Same title and imprint as state one but the dedicatory cartouche was redrawn and the dedication is *To the Right Honourable and Right Reverend Father in God PETER. Lord Bishop of Winchester Prelet of ye Most Nobel-Order of ye Grter &c.*
State 3: (this copy) As described

LEA listed this map in his ca. 1698 catalog but not in those for 1685 or 1687. State three appears in Lea's composite atlas in the British Library. No state appears in the Library of Congress and Burden collection copies.

1. For other maps in the series, see Custis Atlas Cats. Map A, 51–52, and 54–55.

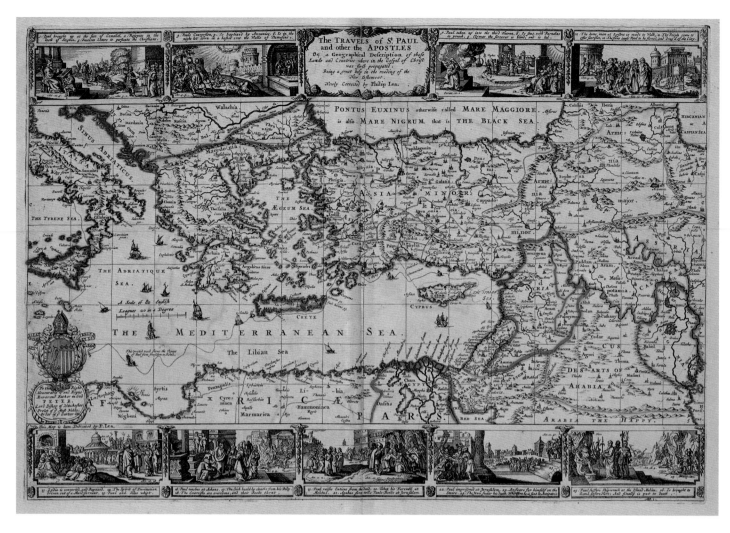

252 *The Travels of S.ᵗ Paul and other the Apostles.* (Custis Atlas Cat. 54)

54 CUSTIS ATLAS

The TRAVELS of S.ᵗ PAUL / and other the APOSTLES / Or, a Geographical Description of those / Lands and Countries where in the Gospel of Christ / was first propagated. / Being a great help in the reading of the / New Testament. / Newly Corrected by Philip Lea

Joseph Moxon, cartographer; engraver unknown; published separately but intended to accompany editions of the *Sacred Geographie* by the Moxons and a later edition by Philip Lea

London, ca. 1691 (originally published in 1671). Black-and-white line engraving with period outline color. H. 12½", W. 18½"

The title cartouche in the upper center of the map is flanked by four vignettes from the life of Saint Paul. The dedicatory cartouche in the lower left is *To the Right/ Honourable and Right/ Rev-* *erend Father in God/ PETER./ Lord Bishop of Winchester/ Prelet of yᵉ Most Nobel-/ Order of yᵉ Garter &c.* Below is *This Mapp is hum. Dedicated by P. Lea.* Across the lower portion of the map are five more scenes from the life of Saint Paul

Three states of the map are known[1]:

State 1: Following the title is *Newly Corrected by Joseph Moxon.* The dedication is *To the Right Reverend Father in God Seth Lord Bishop of Salisbury. This Mapp is humbly Dedicated by Joseph Moxon.* 1671

State 2: Same title and imprint as state one but the dedicatory cartouche was redrawn and the dedication is *To the Right Honourable and Right Reverend Father in God PETER. Lord Bishop of Winchester Prelet of ye Most Nobel-Order of ye Garter &c.* Below the dedicatory cartouche is *This Map is hum. Dedicated by J. Moxon.* 1691

State 3: (this copy) As described

LEA listed this map in his ca. 1698 catalog but not in those for 1685 or 1687. State three appears in Lea's composite atlas in the British Library. No state appears in the Library of Congress and Burden collection copies.

1. For other maps in the series, see Custis Atlas Cats. Map A, 51–53, and 55.

55 CUSTIS ATLAS
A MAPP of JERUSALEM

Joseph Moxon, cartographer; engraver unknown; published separately but intended to accompany editions of the *Sacred Geographie* by the Moxons and a later edition by Philip Lea

London, ca. 1691 (originally published in 1671). Black-and-white line engraving with period outline color. H. 12½", W. 18½"

The title is in a banner along the top of the map. The imprint *Corrected and Sold by P. Lea. at ye Atlas/ and Hercules in Cheap side LONDON* follows. The dedication in the left center is *To the Right Reverend Father in God/ JOHN/ Lord Arch Bishop of York. Pri-/ mat and Metropolitan of England–/ This Mapp is humbly Dedicated/ By P. Lea.* Along the bottom margin are two vignettes. On the left is the Crucifixion; on the right is Solomon being anointed king. Below the lower right margin is *Nehem. 3.* A key locating forty sites is in the right center

Three states of the map are known[1]:
State 1: The title in the banner along the top of the map is *Jerusalem*. No imprint. The dedication is *To the Right Reverend Father in God, John Lord Bishop of Chester. This Mapp is humbly Dedicated By Joseph Moxon.* 1671
State 2: Same title as state one but without an imprint. The dedicatory cartouche was redrawn and is *To the Right Reverend Father in God John Lord Arch Bishop of York. Pri-mat and Metropolitan of England This Mapp is humbly Dedicated By J. Moxon.* 1691
State 3: (this copy) As described

Reference: Rubin, *Image and Reality,* p. 139, fig. 91, state 1

LEA listed this map in his ca. 1698 catalog but not in those for 1685 or 1687. State three appears in Lea's composite atlas in the British Library. No state appears in the Library of Congress and Burden collection copies.

1. For other maps in the series, see Custis Atlas Cats. Map A and 51–54.

56 CUSTIS ATLAS
Nova / PERSIÆ / ARMENIÆ / NATOLIÆ / et ARABIÆ / Descriptio per F. de Wit

Frederick de Wit, cartographer and engraver

Amsterdam, ca. 1680. Black-and-white line engraving with period outline color. H. 18½", W. 21½"

A figure using a protractor, a scale of distances, and the imprint *Amsterdam by Frederick de Wit inde Kalverstraet inde Witte Pascaert* are in the lower left. In the lower right corner is the title on a plinth surrounded by Persians trading with Europeans.

One state of the map is known

Reference: Koeman, comp. and ed., *Atlantes Neerlandici,* III, p. 215, map 97

57 CUSTIS ATLAS
MAGNI / MOGOLIS / IMPERIUM

Henricus Hondius, cartographer; engraver unknown

Amsterdam, 1641 (originally published ca. 1638). Black-and-white line engraving with period outline color. H. 14½", W. 19½"

The title cartouche in the upper left is in the form of a plinth flanked by two costumed figures. The imprint *Amstelodami Apud Ioannem Ianssonium* is in the lower left. A scale of distances is in the upper right

Two states of the map are known:
State 1: The imprint is *Amstelodami Apud Henricum Hondium.* 1638
State 2: (this copy) As described

Reference: van der Krogt, *Koeman's Atlantes Neerlandici,* entry 8300:1:2

58 CUSTIS ATLAS
INDIA / quæ / ORIENTALIS / dicitur, et / INSVLÆ / Adiacentes

Henricus Hondius, cartographer; engraver unknown

Amsterdam, 1644 (originally published ca. 1636). Black-and-white line engraving with period outline color. H. 15½", W. 19"

A large dedicatory cartouche to *Doctrina et virtute præstanti,/ D. CHRISTOPHORE THISIO,/ Mercatori fidelissimo, atq ex/ participantum) SOCIETATS/ INDIÆ ORIENTALIS [&c.] . . . Henricus Hondius* surmounted by a coat of arms is in the lower left. The title cartouche is in the upper center. A scale of distances is in the lower right; to the left is the imprint *Amstelodami. apud Ioannem Ianssonium*

Two states of the map are known:
State 1: Same title and dedication as above but without the Jansson imprint. 1636

State 2: (this copy) As described

References: van der Krogt, *Keoman's Atlantes Neerlandici*, entry 8400:1B:2; Tooley, "Early Maps of Australia, the Dutch period," entry 6

59 CUSTIS ATLAS
IMPERII / SINARVM / NOVA / DESCRIPTIO

Johannes van Loon, cartographer; engraver unknown; published in *Novus Atlas* by Jan Jansson

Amsterdam, 1658. Black-and-white line engraving with period outline color. H. 18½", W. 20½"

The title cartouche flanked by four figures in the lower left corner is followed by *Auctore./ Joh van Loon*. A scale of distances surrounded by cherubs is in the lower right corner

One state of the map is known

Reference: Koeman, comp. and ed., *Atlantes Neerlandici,* II, ME 90B.

60 CUSTIS ATLAS
A MAPP OF THE ISLES OF / IAPON

Cartographer and engraver unknown

London, 1680. Black-and-white line engraving with period out-line color. H. 14½", W. 21"

The inset of A *MAPP/ of/ TUNQUIN* in the upper left corner con-tains a scale of distances. The title cartouche in a rectangular box is in the upper center. A scale of distances is in the lower right corner. No imprint

One state of the map is known

References: Campbell, "Japan: European printed maps to 1800"; Walter, ed., *Japan, A Cartographic Vision,* p. 216

A Mapp of the Isles of Iapon was originally prepared for the English edition of John Baptiste Tavernier's travels to Asia, *Collection of Several Relations,* published by Moses Pitt in 1680.[1] The map is a close copy of one that appeared in the 1679 French and Dutch editions of Tavernier's work. The small inset map of Tunquin, which appeared as a separate map in those editions, was inset in the upper left corner. It is not known when the plate came into Lea's hands.

Lea listed this map in his ca. 1698 catalog but not in

those for 1685 or 1687. It appears in Lea's composite atlas in the British Library but not in the Library of Congress and Burden collection copies.

1. The map may have been engraved by Herman Moll, who produced a number of maps for Pitt during the period 1678–1686. See also Custis Atlas Cat. 38.

61 CUSTIS ATLAS

Listed in the index as "generall Map of yᵉ Coast of Barbary &c." but now missing

This was probably a Dutch map of the period, most likely by Blaeu or Jansson.

62 CUSTIS ATLAS
A / NEW MAP / Containing Barbaria Ægypt / Biledulgerid Sarra Nigr- / itarum Guinea Biafara / Nubia Abissina and / Congo

Joseph Moxon, cartographer; engraver unknown

London, ca. 1686 (originally published in 1670). Black-and-white line engraving with period outline color. H. 22", W. 17"

The title, with no border or cartouche but flanked by three sailing ships, is in the lower center of the map. It is followed by the imprint *Sold by Phillip Lea/ in the Poultrey*

Two states of the map are known:

State 1: Published as one sheet of a twenty-one-sheet hemispheric world map by Joseph Moxon. No copy located. This was a single sheet from the map and thus would have lacked the title and imprint. 1670

State 2: (this copy) As described

In 1670, Joseph Moxon advertised "A large Map of the World . . . 10 feet by 7 feet newly corrected."[1] No copies of the map or loose sheets from it were known until Rodney Shirley located two of Asia bound in a composite atlas compiled by Lea. Philip Burden subsequently identified a third, of America, altered so that it could be sold as a sepa-rate map. An individual title and Lea's imprint, without an address, were added to this sheet.[2]

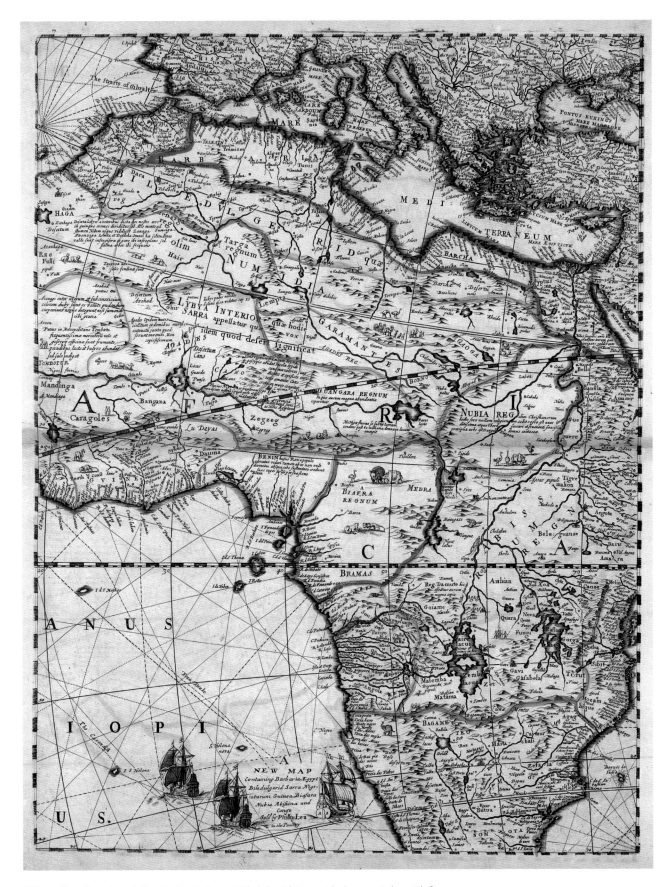

253 *A New Map Containing Barbaria Ægypt Biledulgerid Sarra Nigritarum Guinea Biafara Nubia Abissina and Congo.* (Custis Atlas Cat. 62)

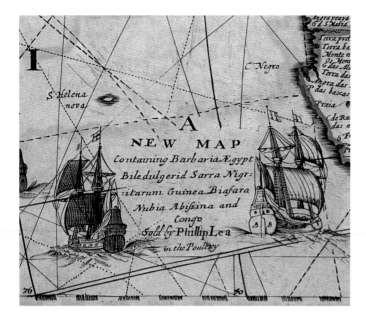

254 Detail of the imprint from *A New Map Containing Barbaria Ægypt Biledulgerid Sarra Nigritarum Guinea Biafar Nubia Abissina and Congo*, London, ca. 1686, black-and-white line engraving with period outline color. (Custis Atlas Cat. 62)

This fourth sheet, *A New Map Containing Barbaria*, was recently discovered in the Custis Atlas. Shirley and Burden were aware that Lea had purchased the plates for the world map at some point. Shirley concluded that the sale occurred after the Moxons last advertised the map in October 1692.[3] Like the third sheet, this newly identified fourth example in its second state has an individual title and imprint. It also has Lea's Poultry address, from which he moved in 1687. He listed it in his catalog for that year but not in that for 1685, so state two must date about 1686.

Although the plates for the twenty-one-sheet wall map had been altered by 1687, Lea advertised the complete map as late as 1699.[4] A large number of complete copies must have been printed before changes were made to the plates.

Lea also listed this map in his ca. 1698 catalog. It does not appear in any of the other Lea composite atlases examined.

1. Shirley, *Mapping of the World*, entry 450, cited an advertisement in the *Term Catalogues*, June 1670.
2. *Ibid.*; Burden, *Mapping of North America*, entry 409. A second copy of this sheet is Custis Atlas Cat. 67.
3. Tyacke, *London Map-Sellers*, entry 230.
4. Arber, ed., *Term Catalogues*, III, p. 290.

63 CUSTIS ATLAS
GVINEA

Jan Jansson, cartographer; engraver unknown

Amsterdam, 1636. Black-and-white line engraving with period outline color. H. 15¼″, W. 20¼″

In the lower left two male merchildren hold a large tusk. The title cartouche in the lower center is flanked by two native figures with a scale of distances below. In the lower right is the imprint *Amstelodami, Sumptibus Joannis Janssonii*

One state of the map is known

Reference: van der Krogt, *Koeman's Atlantes Neerlandici*, entry 8700:2A

64 CUSTIS ATLAS
ÆTHIOPIA / SVPERIOR vel INTERIOR; / vulgo / ABISSINORVM / sive / PRESBITERI IOANNIS / IMPERIVM

Jan Jansson, cartographer; engraver unknown

Amsterdam, 1636. Black-and-white line engraving with period outline color. H. 15¼″, W. 19¼″

A scale of distances is in the lower left. The cartouche in the lower right is in the form of a draped plinth flanked by several native figures. No imprint

One state of the map is known

Reference: van der Krogt, *Koeman's Atlantes Neerlandici*, entry 8720:1B

65 CUSTIS ATLAS
ÆTHOPIA / INFERIOR, / vel / EXTERIOR. / Partes magis Septentrionales, quæ / hic desiderantur, vide in tabula / Ethiopiæ Superioris

Cartographer and engraver unknown

Possibly London, ca. 1690. Black-and-white line engraving with period outline color. H. 15¼″, W. 19½″

The title appears on a lion skin held by two natives in a cartouche in the lower right. No imprint. A scale of distances is below

One state of the map is known

THE quality of the engraving, particularly in the title cartouche, suggests that this is an English copy of a Dutch map. It may have been taken from a map with the same title by Jan Jansson published in Amsterdam in 1636.[1]

1. van der Krogt, *Koeman's Atlantes Neerlandici*, entry 8800:1.

255 *North America Divided into its III Principall Parts.* (Custis Atlas Cat. 66)

66 CUSTIS ATLAS

NORTH AMERICA Divided into its III PRINCIPALL PARTS 1ˢᵗ ENGLISH Part Viz ENGLISH EMPIRE containing yᵉ Articklands near Hudsons Bay New North & South Wales New Britain/ N Foundland N Scotland N England N York N Jarsey Pensylvania Maryland Virginia Carolina Carolania or Florida California Sommer Iˢ Bahama Iˢ Jamaica &c yᵉ CARIBY Iˢ II SPANISH Pᵗ viz N Spain pᵗ of Antilles III FRENCH pᵗ viz N France & pt of yᵉ Cariby Iˢ

Cartographer and engraver unknown

London, ca. 1690 (originally published ca. 1684). Black-and-white line engraving with period outline color. H. 20¼", W. 22¼"

The title is along the top of the map. No imprint

Three states of the map are thought to exist:

State 1: Published as one sheet of an unidentified multisheet hemispheric world map. Ca. 1684

State 2: (this copy) As described. The title may have been added above the upper margin

State 3: Four sailing ships were added[1]

References: McCorkle, *New England in Early Printed Maps,* entry 690.3; McLaughlin, *Mapping of California,* entry 107; Tooley, "California as an Island," entry 55, plate 49, state 3

THIS general map of North America and its companion, *South America,* Custis Atlas Cat. 77, were salvaged from an unidentified hemispheric multisheet map of the world. Because this sheet includes the names Pennsylvania, founded in 1681, and Philadelphia, laid out by 1683, the world map was probably offered by the unknown publisher around 1684. Lea must have bought the plates and issued this sheet separately about 1690 without alteration except for the addition of the title above the upper border.[2]

The map shows the *Savanæ* in the Southeast that was introduced by Lederer in 1672, yet the maker was unaware of the innovations of the 1682 Gascoyne map of Carolina. *(fig. 282).* The depiction of the upper Mississippi was similar to those on maps by Thevenot and Coronelli that were derived from the expeditions of Joliet and Marquette.[3] An *English Empire* extends from the southern shores of the Great Lakes all the way to the lower Mississippi, which flows due south into the head of an unnamed bay on the central Gulf Coast. A great *R. Spirito Santo* is shown flowing into the Florida panhandle. The Rio Grande, called the *R. Escondido,* includes *S Fe* on its upper reaches. Curiously, the course of the river in west Texas is overlaid by a mountain chain with the notation *the River Runs Under.* California is an island, emulating Sanson.[4]

Lea listed a one-sheet "America North" in his ca. 1698 catalog but not in those for 1685 or 1687. State two appears in Lea's composite atlas in the Library of Congress. No state appears in the British Library and Burden collection copies.

1. Tooley, "California as an Island," entry 55, plate 49.

2. It is possible that the title above the map was present from the beginning so that the sheet could be sold separately. It would have been trimmed off or pasted over when the sheets were joined to form the multi-sheet wall map. See Custis Atlas Cat. 70 for a precedent for such a format.

3. Melchisédech Thevenot's map, *Carte de la decouverte faite l' an 1663* [sic 1673] *dans l' Amerique Septentrionale,* was published in Paris in 1681. Conrad E. Heidenreich and Edward H. Dahl, "The French Mapping of North America in the Seventeenth Century," *Map Collector,* XIII (1980), p. 7; Vincenzo Coronelli's map, *Partie Occidentale du Canada,* was published in Paris ca. 1685. *Ibid.,* pp. 8–9.

4. Tooley, "California as an Island," entry 55.

67 CUSTIS ATLAS

A / NEW MAP / Containing the English / Empire Golf of / Mexico Caribes Islands / Granada Guiana / Amazone / and Peru

Joseph Moxon, cartographer; engraver unknown

London, ca. 1686 (originally published in 1670). Black-and-white line engraving with period outline color. H. 22¼", W. 17"

The title in the right center is framed by a merman, a small boat being rowed, a mermaid, a sea monster, and a sailing ship. The title is followed by the imprint *Sold by Phillip Lea*

Three states of the map are thought to exist:

State 1: Published as one sheet of a twenty-one-sheet hemispheric world map by Joseph Moxon. No copy located. This was a single sheet from the map and thus would have lacked the title and imprint. 1670

State 2: Published as one sheet of Moxon's twenty-one-sheet map without an individual title or imprint. Revisions were made to the geography of North America. Ca. 1684

State 3: (this copy) As described

Reference: Burden, *Mapping of North America,* entry 409

JOSEPH MOXON advertised a twenty-one-sheet hemispheric map of the world in the *Term Catalogues* for June 1670.[1] No complete copy has been located, but one or two examples of each of four known sheets survive.[2] Two are in the Custis Atlas (Custis Atlas Cats. 62 and 67). In both instances, the plates were altered so that the sheets could be sold individually. Lea added titles, perhaps outer borders, and his imprint.

Dating the various states and establishing the publication history of these maps is complicated.[3] As discussed in Custis Atlas Cat. 62, Lea purchased the plates from the Moxons about 1686 and altered them. Features such as Pennsylvania, chartered in 1681, may have been added to the plate before Lea bought it. The Moxons must have retained copies of the wall map because in 1692 they advertised "A New Map of the World, 10 Foot 3 Inches long, and 7 Foot deep . . . describing the English Empire in America by their Right Names," which implies that the change had been made by 1686.[4]

Lea listed the map in his 1687 and ca. 1698 catalogs but not in that for 1685.[5] It does not appear in any of the other Lea composite atlases examined.

1. Shirley, *Mapping of the World,* entry 450.

2. *Ibid.;* Burden, *Mapping of North America,* entry 409.

3. When Burden cataloged this map, he recognized that the unlocated first state was one sheet of Moxon's 21-sheet wall map, ca. 1670. Based on

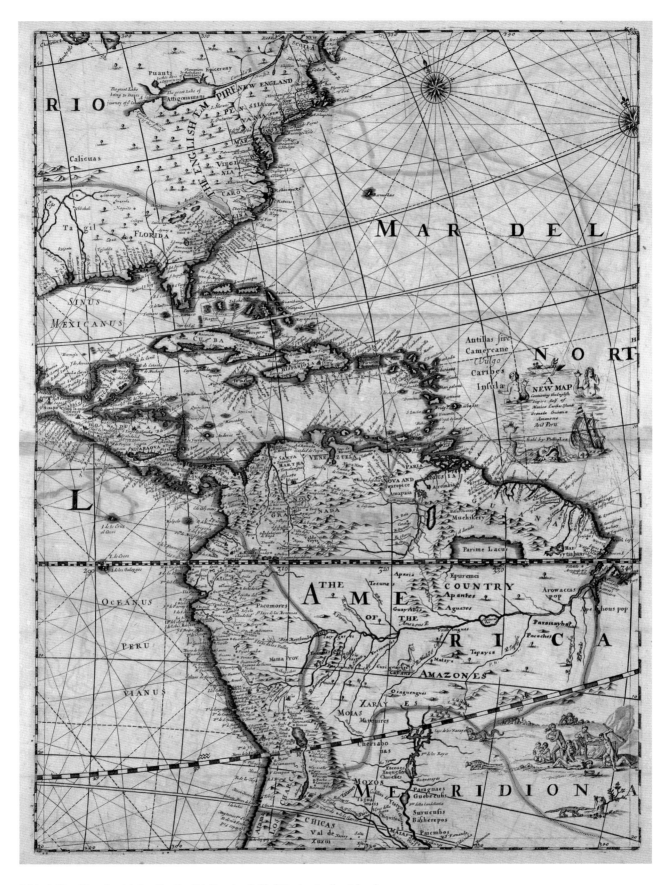

256 *A New Map Containing the English Empire Golf of Mexico Caribes Islands*
Granada Guiana Amazone and Peru. (Custis Atlas Cat. 67)

the presence of "Baltemore," he believed that the later copy he examined was a third state dating about 1730 when the city was established. Burden hypothesized the existence of a ca. 1700 intermediary state with Lea's imprint but lacking the reference to "Baltemore." He was not aware that "Baltemore" appeared on the map in a much earlier context; however, Custis Atlas Cat. 67 is the same state of the map that Burden dated to 1730. That Custis Atlas Cat. 62, a companion sheet from the same wall map, includes Lea's imprint with the Poultry address shows that the changes in this state date to 1686 or earlier.

4. Tyacke, *London Map-Sellers,* entry 230.

5. Lea's 1687 catalog listed separate sheets of "part of America, part of Africa, part of Asia." The first two are Custis Atlas Cats. 62 and 67. The third, of Asia, is likely a later state of one of the two maps identified by Shirley, *Mapping of the World,* entry 450.

68 CUSTIS ATLAS
A NEW MAP / OF THE / ENGLISH EMPIRE IN / AMERICA / VIZ / VIRGINIA NEW YORK / MARYLAND NEW IARSEY / CAROLINA NEW ENGLAND / PENNSYLVANIA NEWFOUNDLAND / NEW FRANCE &c / By Rob: Morden

Robert Morden, cartographer; John Harris, engraver

London, ca. 1695. Black-and-white line engraving with period outline color. H. 19¾", W. 23"

The title cartouche in the right center is surmounted by the royal arms of William III. Below is a scale of distances. To the left is an inset of *the Harbour of/ BOSTON/ or/ Mattathusetts Bay.* A second inset in the lower right corner is *A Generall Map/ of the Coasts & Isles of/ EUROPE, AFRICA/ and AMERICA.* In the upper right of the second inset is the imprint *Sold by Rob.¹ Morden at the Atlas in Cornhill./ And by Christopher Brown at yᵉ Globe/ near the West end of S.ᵗ Pauls/ Churcʜ. London.*[1] In the lower right is *I. Harris scupl.* The map was trimmed to the outer neat line and mounted on a second sheet for inclusion in the atlas

Two states of the map are known:

State 1: (this copy) As described

State 2: In the title, *Revised by Iᵒⁿ Senex 1719* was substituted for *Rob. Morden.* The royal arms were replaced by a dedicatory cartouche to Hewer, Edgly Hewer of Clapham. The imprint was removed. 1719

References: Cumming, *Southeast in Early Maps,* entry 119; McCorkle, *New England in Early Printed Maps,* entry 695.3; Phillips, comp., *List of Maps of America,* p. 564; Stevens and Tree, "Comparative Cartography," entry 20a

257 *A New Map of the English Empire in America.* (Custis Atlas Cat. 68)

WITH King William's War in mind, Robert Morden compiled this map illustrating the relative positions of the English and French territories in North America. The depictions of Canada, the Mississippi Valley, and the Great Lakes were based on important French sources, including maps by Dablon and Thevenot.[2] Morden included outdated information on the Carolinas from *A Map of the Whole Territory Traversed by John Lederer. (fig. 73)* The inset map of Boston was derived from Thomas Pound's *A New Mapp of New England from Cape Codd to Cape Sables*, published in 1691.[3] The coastal outline of the second inset may have been borrowed from a similar one on Thornton, Morden, and Lea's *A New Map of the English Empire*.[4]

Lea listed a one-sheet map titled "English Empire" in his ca. 1698 catalog which could refer to this map or to Custis Atlas Cat. 69. No such title was listed in the catalogs for 1685 and 1687. This map does not appear in any of the other Lea composite atlases examined.

1. Christopher Browne took over Robert Walton's shop, "The Globe," in 1688.

2. Claude Dablon's map, *Lac Superieur et autres Lieux ou sont Les Missions des Peres de la Compagnie de Jesus*, was published in Paris in 1672. Heidenreich and Dahl, "French Mapping of North America," p. 7. For Thevenot, see Custis Atlas Cat. 66, n. 3.

3. McCorkle, *New England in Early Printed Maps*, entry 692.3.

4. *A New Map of the English Empire* was published in four sheets. For more information, see Custis Atlas Cat. 70.

69 CUSTIS ATLAS
A Map of y^e / English Empire in ye Continent of / AMERICA / Viz / VIRGINIA NEW YORK / MARYLAND NEW IARSEY / CAROLINA NEW ENGLAND / PENNSILVANIA

Richard Daniel, cartographer; Walter Binneman, engraver

London, ca. 1684 (originally published ca. 1679). Black-and-white line engraving with period outline color. H. 19½", W. 23½"

A small title cartouche surmounted by the arms of England is in the lower center. A smaller secondary cartouche to the left contains the imprint *Sold by/ R. Morden at ye Atlas/ in Cornhill neer ye Royal/ Exchange/ LONDON.* Between the two is *W. Binneman sculpsit.* A scale of distances is to the right of the title cartouche. An untitled inset of Carolina is in the lower right corner. The map was trimmed to the outer neat line and mounted on a sheet for inclusion in the atlas. The number "63" appears in ink within the neat line in the upper left corner

Three states of the map are known:

State 1: With the title *A Map of ye/ English Empire in ye Continent of/ AMERICA/ Viz/ Virginia New York/ Maryland New Jarsey/ Carolina New England/ By/ R. Daniel Esqr.* Sold by *R. Morden at ye Atlas in Cornhill neer ye Royal Exchange & by W. Berry at ye Globe neer Charing Cross London*, and *Licensed by R. L'Estrange Esqr.* Ca. 1679[1]

State 2: (this copy) As described[2]

State 3: The title was altered to *A New Mapp Of New England and Annapolis with the Country's adjacent.* The imprint is *Sold by C. Browne at the North Gate of the Royal Exchange & by him at the Globe by the West-end of S^t. Pauls Church London.* The inset of Carolina was replaced by a larger one of Boston Harbor, which resulted in the scale of distances shifting to the left of the imprint cartouche. 1712[3]

References: Cumming, *Southeast in Early Maps*, entry 103; Deák, *Picturing America*, entry 63, state 1; McCorkle, *New England in Early Printed Maps*, entry 679.1, state 1; Phillips, comp., *List of Maps of America*, p. 563; Stevens and Tree, "Comparative Cartography," entry 19b

RICHARD DANIEL's map shows the Atlantic coast from the Saint Lawrence River south to the Chesapeake Bay with the Carolinas in an inset.[4] The depiction of the Chesapeake, unchanged in all states, was based on Herrman's 1673 map. *(fig. 12)* In the first state, the watersheds of the Delaware and Susquehanna Rivers resembled those on Morden and Berry's *A Map of New England New Yorke New Jersey Maryland & Virginia*, 1676. State two was revised to include Pennsylvania, chartered in 1681. New England was taken from William Reed's 1665 map. The inset of Carolina was based on Ogilby and Moxon's *A New Discription of Carolina. (fig. 72)*

This map was listed in the index as "A Particular Map of New England." Because Lea was not the publisher, he did not list this map in his catalogs for 1685 or 1687. In his ca. 1698 catalog, he listed "English Empire," which could refer to this map. It does not appear in any of Lea's composite atlases examined. That Lea was not involved in the production or distribution of this map and the presence of manuscript number "63" in the upper left corner suggest it may have been in a previous atlas. Custis may have had it in his possession and asked that it be bound with the others.

1. Sir Roger l'Estrange was the official government censor. The first state has traditionally been dated ca. 1679 because a map with virtually the same title was listed in Arber, ed., *Term Catalogues*, I, 1679.

2. Although Stevens and Tree and McCorkle dated the second state ca. 1684, the erasure of l'Estrange's name suggests that the plate may have been altered after Dec. 1688 when he was removed from office. Stevens and Tree, "Comparative Cartography," entry 19b; McCorkle, *New England in Early Printed Maps*, entry 679.1, state 1.

3. The third state was advertised in the *Daily Courant* (London), Aug. 2, 1712. I wish to thank Ashley Baynton-Williams for this information. Port

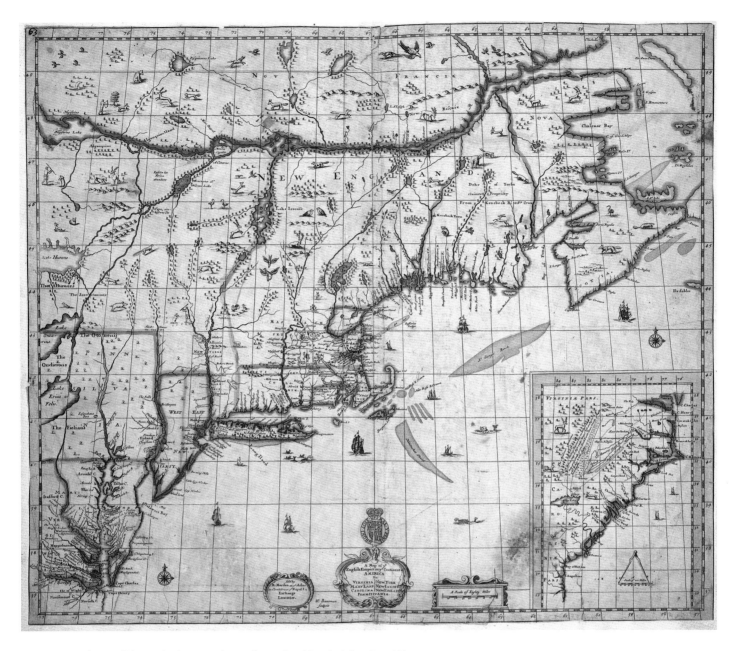

258 *A Map of yᵉ English Empire in yᵉ Continent of America.* (Custis Atlas Cat. 69)

Royal, Nova Scotia, occupied by the English the previous year, was renamed Annapolis Royal in honor of Queen Anne. This revised state may be the first major map to show the Maritime Provinces as English possessions. The inset of Boston Harbor was copied from Thomas Pound's *A New Mapp of New England from Cape Codd to Cape Sables.* McCorkle, *New England in Early Printed Maps,* entry 692.3.

4. Little is known about Richard Daniel. *A Map of yᵉ English Empire* seems to be his only published map. French, ed., *Tooley's Dictionary of Map-makers,* p. 332.

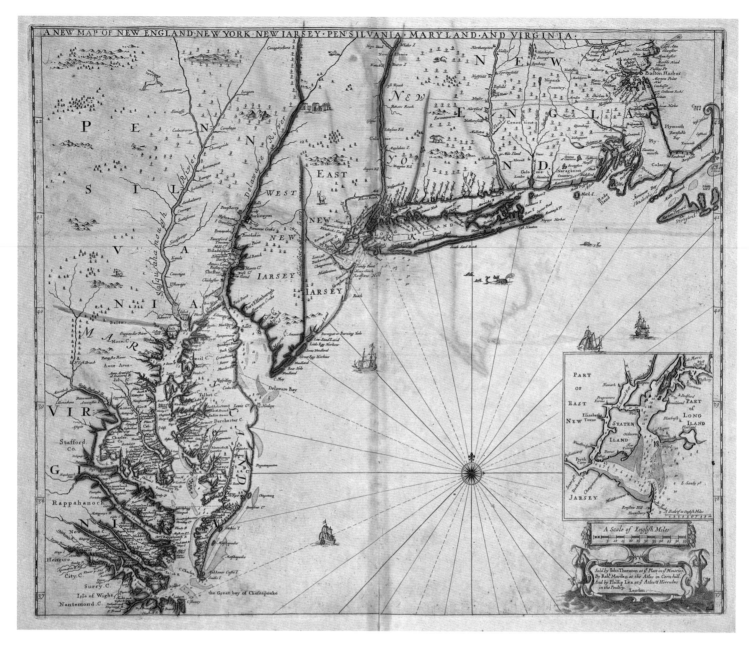

259　*A New Map of New England New York New Iarsey Pensilvania Maryland and Virginia.* (Custis Atlas Cat. 70)

70 CUSTIS ATLAS

A NEW MAP OF NEW ENGLAND NEW YORK NEW IARSEY PENSILVANIA MARYLAND AND VIRGINIA

Possibly John Thornton, cartographer; engraver unknown

London, 1685. Black-and-white line engraving with period outline color. H. 17½″, W. 21¼″

The title is in a border above the map. In the lower right is an inset of New York Harbor. Beneath the inset, a scale of distances surmounts the imprint *Sold by Iohn Thornton at yᵉ Platt in yᵉ Minories./ By Rob.ᵗ Morden at the Atlas in Corn-hill/ And by Phillip Lea at yᵉ Atlas & Hercules/ in the Poultry./ London*

Five states of the map are known:

State 1: No copy located. It lacked the inset chart of New York Harbor and possibly the separate title and imprint

State 2: (this copy) As described. There are alterations on the primary map to the environs of New York

State 3: *By Philip Lea in Cheap-side London* was added to the title. The imprint was altered to *By Philip Lea at the Atlas and Hercules in Cheap-side London*

State 4: Same title and imprint as state three. Numerous alterations were made to the body of the map. The Schuylkill River was redrawn and extended, five counties were shown in East and West Jersey, three lower Delaware counties were shown as part of Pennsylvania, and the boundary between Maryland and Pennsylvania was added in a dotted line

State 5: The words *in Cheap-side London* following Lea's name in the title were erased. The imprint is *Sold by George Willdey at the Great Toy, Spectacle, Chinaware and Print Shop at ye corner of Ludgate Street near St. Paul's, London.* Ca. 1730

References: Cohen and Augustyn, *Manhattan in Maps,* pp. 48–49; Cumming, *British Maps,* p. 31; Deák, *Picturing America,* entry 71; McCorkle, *New England in Early Printed Maps,* entries 680.4 and 685.3; Morrison et al., *On the Map,* fig. 20; Stevens and Tree, "Comparative Cartography," entry 35a

IN MAY 1685, John Thornton, Robert Morden, and Philip Lea advertised a four-sheet "New Map of the English Empire in America viz. New England, New York, New Jersey, Pensilvania, Maryland, Virginia and Caroline" in the *Term Catalogues.*[1] To maximize their profit, they designed it so that the upper right sheet contained the bulk of the geographical information. This section, engraved with its own title, *A New Map of New England New York New Jarsey Pensilvania Maryland and Virginia,* could also be marketed separately. When it was used for the wall map, the title was trimmed off or pasted over.

An example of the separately designed single sheet is in the Custis Atlas. It was based on Thornton and Green's *A*

260 The sheet containing the title cartouche from *A New Map of the English Empire in the Continent of America,* by John Thornton, Robert Morden, and Philip Lea, London, 1685, black-and-white line engraving. Courtesy, Library of Congress.

Mapp of Virginia Maryland, New Jarsey New-York, & New England but was altered to account for the establishment of Pennsylvania in 1681.[2] Close examination revealed that the area around New York was reengraved and that the map originally lacked the inset of New York Harbor. These alterations were taken from a ca. 1683 manuscript map made by Philip Wells for William Penn and the proprietors of East Jersey. *(fig. 261)* Cohen and Augustyn described the

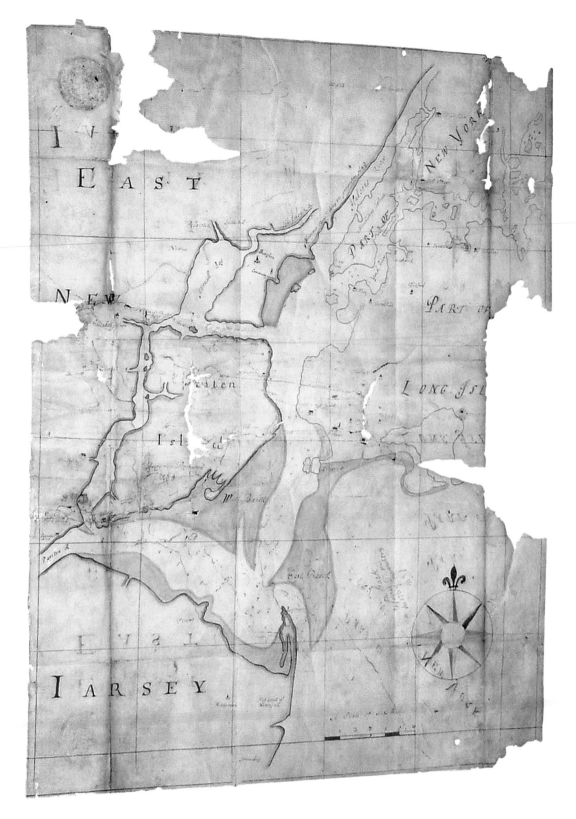

261 Manuscript map of New York Harbor, by Philip Wells, ca. 1683. Courtesy, Collection of Jay Snider, Philadelphia, Pa. In February 1683,
East New Jersey was sold at auction to William Penn and eleven others. Wells was commissioned by the new proprietors to construct a map of
the area around New York Harbor to illustrate their territorial dispute with New York over Staten Island.

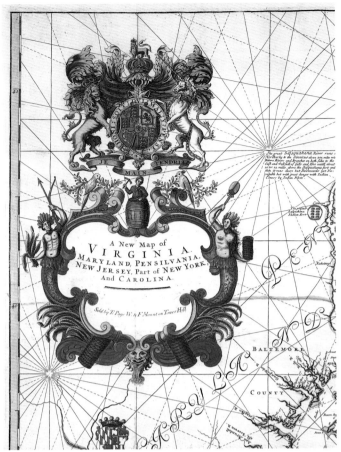

262 Detail of the title cartouche from *A New Map of Virginia, Maryland, Pennsylvania, New Jersey, Part of New York, and Carolina,* by John Thornton, London, ca. 1723–1728, originally published ca. 1701, black-and-white line engraving with period color. 1940-418 (Cat. 16). Thornton altered the design for the cartouche used on *A New Map of the English Empire in the Continent of America* to reflect Virginia's tobacco economy by adding a planter closing a hogshead that presumably contained tobacco leaves.

inset as the first separate printed chart of New York Harbor.[3]

Lea listed this map in his catalogs for 1685, 1687, and ca. 1698. State two appears in Lea's composite atlas in the Library of Congress. State three appears in Lea's composite atlas in the Burden collection. It does not appear in the British Library copy.

1. Only one unassembled, incomplete set survives, in the Bibliothèque Nationale, Paris. McCorkle suggested that the four sheets were an unfinished proof set and were never published. *New England in Early Printed Maps,* entry 685.3. However, the consistent listing of the four-sheet map in Lea's catalogs and the *Term Catalogues* refutes this idea. The map was based on several sources. The title sheet contained a partial depiction of the eastern Great Lakes copied from Morden and Berry's *A Map of New England New Yorke New Jersey &c. Ibid.,* entry 676.3. The lower left sheet, which is missing, was probably based on Gascoyne's *A New Map of the Country of Carolina.* (fig. 282).

2. See Custis Atlas Cat. 73.

3. Cohen and Augustyn, *Manhattan in Maps,* pp. 48–49.

71 CUSTIS ATLAS
A MAPP OF Yᴱ IMPROVED PART OF PENSILVANIA IN AMERICA, DIVIDED INTO COUNTYES TOWNSHIPS AND LOTTS

Thomas Holme, cartographer; John Harris, engraver

London, ca. 1690. Black-and-white line engraving with period outline color. H. 15½", w. 20¾"

The title is in the border along the top of the map. Below the right side of the title is *Surveyed by Tho:Holme. Sold by P. Lea at yᵉ Atlas and Hercules in Cheapside.* A table in the upper left provides *References to the Settlements of/ Severall Inhabitants in yᵉ County of/ CHESTER* with a scale of distances to the right. In the upper center is an inset plan of *The City PHILADELPHIA two Miles in Length and one in Breadth.* A dedicatory cartouche in the upper right is *To William Penn Esq./ Proprietor & Governor of PENNSYLVANIA/ This Mapp is humbly Dedicated/ and Presented./ by Inº Harris.* A table in the upper right provides *References to the Settlements of/ Severall Inhabitants in yᵉ Countyes of/ BUCKS and PHILADELPHIA*

Five states of the map are known[1]:

State 1: Perhaps a proof state. Same imprint as above but lacking the numbered lists of landowners in the upper left and right corners and their corresponding property holdings. Ca. 1690

State 2: (this copy) As described. The numbered lists of landowners in the upper left and right corners and their corresponding property holdings were added

State 3: Lea's imprint was removed from the upper border. The imprint *Sold by Geo: Willdey at the Great Toy, Spectacle, China-ware and Print Shop, at the corner of Ludgate Street, near St. Paul's, London* was added in a rectangle in the lower left corner. Ca. 1730

State 4: The imprint and rectangle were erased from the lower left corner. The map was published by Thomas Jefferys without an imprint. Ca. 1750.

State 5: The imprint *R. Marshall no. 4 Aldermary Churchyard* was added. Ca. 1765

References: Corcoran, *Thomas Holme;* Deák, *Picturing America,* entry 72; Klinefelter, "Holme's Map," pp. 41–74; Penfold, ed., *Maps and Plans,* entry 2790; Phillips, comp., *List of Maps of America,* p. 670; Schwartz and Ehrenberg, *Mapping of America,* plate 70; Snyder, *City of Independence,* fig. 6; Stevens and Tree, "Comparative Cartography," entry 68

In 1681, William Penn was granted sole proprietorship of more than forty-five thousand square miles in a region that he named Pennsylvania. Through vigorous promotion, more than a half-million acres were sold in the first year alone.[2] Because each tract had to be laid out before it could be developed, Penn appointed Thomas Holme surveyor general of the colony in April 1682.[3] Holme had arrived by August and immediately began to survey the

A MAPP OF Yᵉ IMPROVED PART OF PENSILVANIA IN AMERICA, DIVI

The City PHILADELPHIA *two Miles in Length and one in Breadth*

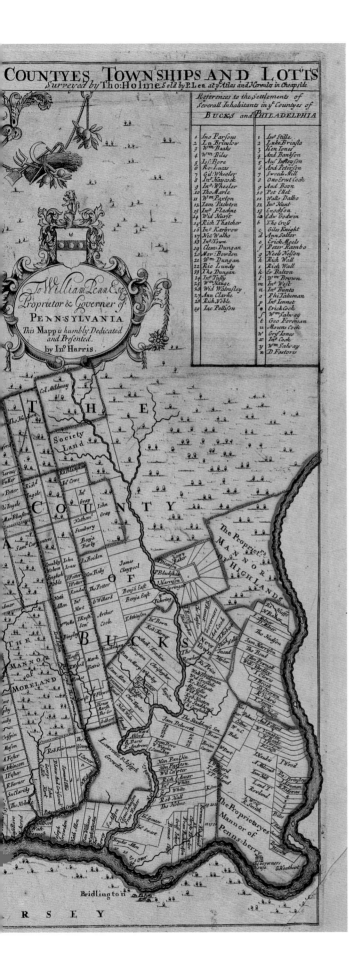

land that had already been purchased and to lay out the future city of Philadelphia. A plan titled *A Portraiture of the City of Philadelphia* was published in London in 1683.[4] Penn then pressured Holme to produce a general map of the seated parts of the colony, complaining from London that "we want a map to the degree that I am ashamed here; . . . all cry out, where is your map, what no map of your settlements."[5]

Penn probably received the finished manuscript by May 1687 and arranged for it to be engraved and printed in London. Originally published by Robert Greene and John Thornton on seven sheets, the map illustrated the "improved," or settled, area of the province along the west bank of the Delaware River, a tract of approximately fifty-five miles in length and thirty-three miles in width.[6] On a scale of one mile to one inch, it located the holdings of 670 settlers. Holme's 1683 *Portraiture of the City of Philadelphia* was included in reduced form as an inset in the upper right corner. The multisheet map, which attempted to name all landowners in an entire province and delineate their holdings, was the most detailed and impressive for any English colony yet published.

A Mapp of y[e] Improved Part of Pensilvania in America, published about 1690, is a reduction of the seven-sheet map described above with a number of alterations. The plan of Philadelphia was moved to the upper center. The names of property owners were updated. To compensate for the reduced format, many of the names that appeared in smaller tracts were removed and placed in the *References to the Settlements* in the right and left corners in state two.

Lea listed this map in his ca. 1698 catalog but not in those for 1685 or 1687. It was listed in the index of the Burden collection copy but at some point the map was removed. No state appears in the Library of Congress and British Library copies.

---

1. The information about the states was largely supplied by Ashley Baynton-Williams.

2. Walter Klinefelter, "Surveyor General Thomas Holme's Map of the Improved Part of the Province of Pennsylvania," *Winterthur Portfolio,* VI (1970), p. 41.

3. Holme had learned his profession under Sir William Petty during the Down Survey of Ireland. See Custis Atlas Cat. 21.

4. Martin P. Snyder, *City of Independence: Views of Philadelphia Before 1800* (New York, 1975), fig. 1.

5. Penn to Thomas Lloyd, Sept. 21, 1686, in Klinefelter, "Holme's Map," p. 42.

6. Snyder, *City of Independence,* fig. 6; Klinefelter, "Holme's Map," fig. 1.

263 *A Mapp of y[e] Improved Part of Pensilvania in America,*
Divided into Countyes Townships and Lotts. (Custis Atlas Cat. 71)

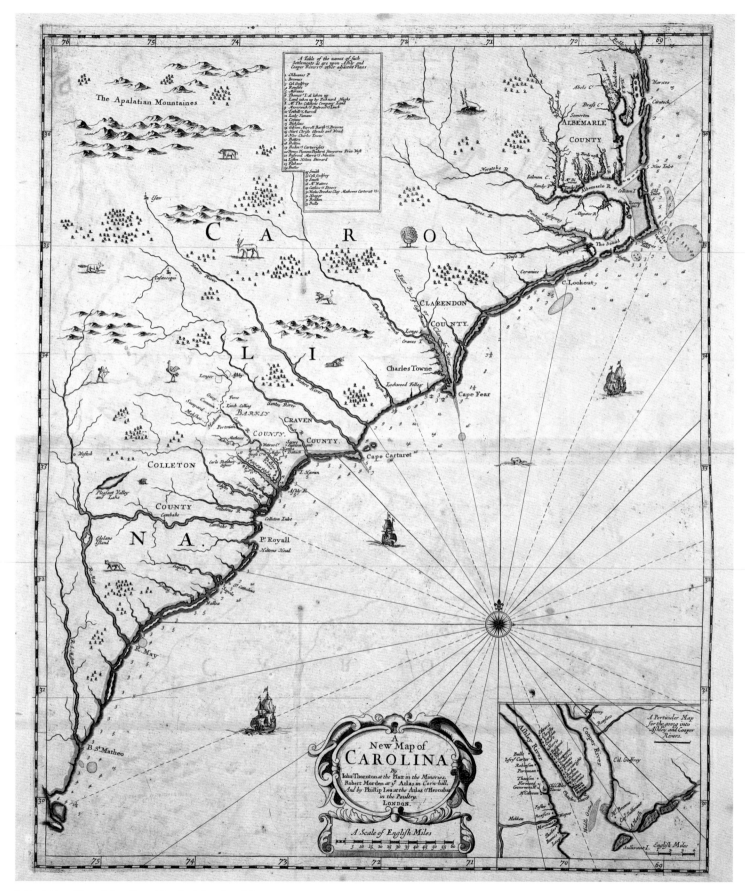

264 *A New Map of Carolina.* (Custis Atlas Cat. 72)

72 CUSTIS ATLAS
A / New Map of / CAROLINA

Possibly John Thornton, cartographer; engraver unknown

London, ca. 1686. Black-and-white line engraving with period outline color. H. 21", W. 18"

In the upper center is *A table of the names of such/ Settlements as are upon Ashly and/ Cooper Rivers & other adjacent Places.* The scrollwork title cartouche in the lower center also contains the imprint *By/ Iohn Thornton at the Platt in the Minories,/ Robert Morden at ye Atlas in Cornhill,/ And by Phillip Lea at the Atlas & Hercules/ in the Poultry,/ LONDON.* Beneath is a scale of distances. An inset in the lower right corner is titled *A Perticuler Map/ for the going into/ Ashley and Cooper/ Rivers*

Three states of the map are known:
State 1: (this copy) As described
State 2: Thornton and Morden's imprints were removed, leaving only Lea's *at the Atlas and Hercules in Cheapside London.* A secondary title, *Ashley and Cooper Rivers,* was added above the inset map. Ca. 1695[1]
State 3: *Sold by Geo: Willdey at the Great Toy, Spectacle, Chinaware and Print Shop, ye Corner of Ludgate Street near St. Pauls London.* Ca. 1730

References: Cumming, *Southeast in Early Maps,* entry 104; Phillips, comp., *List of Maps of America,* p. 818, state 1; Stevens and Tree, "Comparative Cartography," entry 10

T HIS general map of the Carolinas has traditionally been dated about 1685, but as it was not listed in Lea's 1685 sales catalog, that seems unlikely.[2] In May of that year, Thornton, Morden, and Lea advertised a four-sheet wall map titled *A New Map of the English Empire in the Continent of America, viz: New England, New York, New Jarsey, Pensilvania, Maryland, Virginia, and Carolina* that included a sheet devoted to Carolina.[3] This separately issued *New Map of Carolina* advertised in the 1687 catalog is probably a slightly enlarged version of the Carolina sheet from the wall map, so a publication date of 1686 seems reasonable.

A New Map of Carolina is a curious amalgamation of states two and three of Gasgoyne's 1682 map.[4] *(fig. 282)* Some of the improvements along the coast indicate that the cartographer, probably John Thornton, was aware of a manuscript map of Carolina made by James Lancaster in 1679.[5]

Lea listed this map in his 1687 and ca. 1698 catalogs but not in that for 1685. State one appears in Lea's composite atlas in the Library of Congress. State two appears in Lea's composite atlas in the Burden collection. No state appears in the British Library copy.

1. This state has traditionally been dated ca. 1690, but the plate was probably revised and published between 1695 and 1698 when Lea issued the inset of the Ashley and Cooper Rivers separately as a miniature map in his *Hydrographia Universalis.* A secondary title added to the inset at that time also appears in state 2.
2. Cumming, *Southeast in Early Maps,* entry 104; Stevens and Tree, "Comparative Cartography," entry 10.
3. Arber, ed., *Term Catalogues,* II, p. 126. See Custis Atlas Cat. 70. The wall map was listed in Lea's 1685 catalog.
4. The configuration of *Pleasant Valley and Lake* in Colleton Co. is from state 2. The inset, *A Perticuler Map for the going into Ashley and Cooper Rivers,* is from state 3. Cumming reproduced state 3 in *Southeast in Early Maps,* 1962 ed., entry 92, plate 39; state 2 was reproduced in the 1998 ed. State 3 is illustrated as fig. 282 in this book.
5. Cumming, *Southeast in Early Maps,* entry 81.

73 CUSTIS ATLAS
A Mapp of VIRGINIA / MARYLAND, NEW JARSEY, / NEW YORK, & NEW ENGLAND

John Thornton, cartographer; engraver unknown

London, 1679 (originally published ca. 1678). Black-and-white line engraving with period outline color and manuscript additions in red ink. H. 20¾", W. 17¼"

The title cartouche in the upper left corner also includes the imprint *By John Thornton at the Sundy=/ =all [Sundial] in the Minories and by/ Robert Greene at y^e Rose and/ Crowne in Budgrowe./ London.* It consists of a scrollwork frame that rests on a plinth containing a scale of distances. The whole is flanked by two figures of Native Americans, the one on the right holding a bow. An inset of *A Mapp/ of/ NEW ENGLAND,* with a separate scale, is in the lower right corner. The map was trimmed to the outer neat line and mounted on a sheet for inclusion in the atlas. The number "67" appears in ink within the neat line in the upper left corner. Holes in three of the corners suggest that the map may have been tacked to a wall before mounting

Three states of the map are known[1]:
State 1: Same imprint as above. Ca. 1678–1679
State 2: (this copy) As described. The name of the Schuylkill River, *Hore kill or Dillewar R,* was changed to *Skoole kill or Dillewar R, Shakamaxon* and *George Heathnut's Land* were added on the west bank of the Delaware, and *Cohansey* was added in southwestern New Jersey. 1678–1679
State 3: Same imprint as above. Extensive alterations in the vicinity of the Delaware River were added to account for the founding of Pennsylvania. *Philadelphia, Chester,* and *Chichester* were added. *Wicoco* was moved to the east bank of the Delaware, the phrase *Part of Pensilvania* replaced the *Mary* of *Maryland,* and other minor alterations occurred. 1683 or later[2]

References: Black, ed., *Blathwayt Atlas,* map 10, state 1; Fowble, *Two Centuries of Prints,* entry 3; McCorkle, *New England in Early Printed*

265 *A Mapp of Virginia Maryland, New Jarsey, New York, & New England* (Custis Atlas Cat. 73)

Maps, entry 673.3; Morrison et al., *On the Map,* entry 5; Papenfuse and Coale, *Hammond-Harwood House Atlas,* fig. 19, state 1; Stevens and Tree, "Comparative Cartography," entry 88b; Stokes, *Iconography of Manhattan Island,* II, p. 158

This is a general map of the English American colonies from Albemarle Sound in the south to New York Harbor in the north. New England is shown in a separate inset. The lower two-thirds of the map was copied from Augustine Herrman's 1673 *Virginia and Maryland. (fig. 12)* The depiction of the Delaware River was advanced for the period, with extensive information derived from James Wasse's 1676–1677 expedition.[3] The map shows the 1676 division line between East and West Jersey but Pennsylvania does not appear on this state. The cartographer's understanding of the northeast coast of New Jersey and Staten Island was poor but typical for the period. An enclosed Newark Bay lies due west of Staten Island. The Passaic River runs north, then east, and connects with the Hudson.[4] The inset of New England was derived from a manuscript map prepared by William Reed in 1665.[5]

A Mapp of Virginia, Maryland, New Jarsey, New York, and New England provided the prototype for Thornton and Seller's 1681 *A Map of Some of the South and eastbounds of Pennsylvania,* and Thornton, Morden, and Lea's ca. 1685 *A New Map of New England New York New Iarsey Pensilvania Maryland and Virginia.* See Custis Atlas Cat. 70.

This second state is exceptionally rare.[6] The extensive manuscript additions in red ink are virtually identical to the engraved alterations that were made for the third state. Added no earlier than 1683, they probably were made in the publisher's shop before the map was sold, in anticipation of the publication of the third state.[7]

Because Lea was not the publisher, he did not include this map in any of his catalogs. It does not appear in any of the other Lea composite atlases examined.

1. The states are given according to Black, ed., *Blathwayt Atlas,* pp. 80–81.

2. Fowble, *Two Centuries of Prints in America,* entry 3, incorrectly identified state 3 as a "second impression." McCorkle, *New England in Early Prints,* entry 673.3.

3. Black saw some affinity between Thornton's depiction of the Delaware River and that on Seller and Fisher's 1677 *A Mapp of New Jersey in America.* Black, ed., *Blathwayt Atlas,* map 13, pp. 75–76. For an account of Wasse's expedition, see *ibid.,* pp. 76–79.

4. The northeast coast of New Jersey and Staten Island resembles that on states 2 through 4 of John Seller's *A Mapp of New Jarsey.* On state 2, Newark Bay was correctly shown flowing north-south above the northwestern coast of Staten Island. The unnamed Passaic River runs northwest, then east, and connects with the Hudson. States 3 and 4 were revised to show an open-ended Newark Bay due west of Staten Island. The Passaic

was absent altogether. Staten Island was less accurately drawn than on state 2. *Ibid.,* map 13, pp. 75–76.

5. Black called Reed's manuscript "the first official map of Massachusetts and the first locally made map of New England." *Ibid.,* map 8, p. 71.

6. Black located one copy, in the New York Public Library.

7. Because Thornton was probably the cartographer, the revisions must have been made in his shop. The *Alphabet of America,* Custis Atlas Text 9, was revised in a similar manner.

74 CUSTIS ATLAS

Two maps on one sheet: *A / Generall Mapp / Of the Continent and / Islands which bee Adjacent / to / JAMAICA* and *A NEW MAPP of the ISLAND of / JAMAICA / Wherin Every / Towne–| Cotton Workes / Church | Cacao Walke / Sugar Workes | Craules and Pens for / Hoggs and Cattel / Indico Worke / is Described w.th the Names of the Present Proprietors / According to a late Survay thear of / P.Lea*

Philip Lea, cartographer; engraver unknown

London, 1685. Black-and-white line engraving with period outline color, H. 19¼", W. 22½"

The title of the top map, in a large compass rose, is followed by the imprint *By Philip Lea Globe maker/ at the Atlas & Hercules/ in Cheapside at the Corner/ of Fryday Street/ LONDON.* An inset of *THE/ ENGLISH/ EMPIRE* is in the upper right corner. In the lower left corner of the lower map is an inset of *A New/ Draught of/ PORT ROYAL/ by/ Anthony Williams.* The title cartouche in the upper right corner of the lower map is followed by a key identifying important sites

Three states of the map are known:

State 1: No copy located. With Lea's Poultry address. 1685[1]

State 2: (this copy) As described

State 3: No copy examined. With the imprint of George Willdey.[2] Ca. 1730

Reference: Kapp, "Printed Maps of Jamaica," entry 31

Lea listed this map in his 1687 and ca. 1698 catalogs but not in that for 1685. It appears in Lea's composite atlas in the Library of Congress but not in the British Library and Burden collection copies.

1. Arber, ed., *Term Catalogues,* II, p. 137.

2. *Atlases, Maps, Travel and Topography,* Sotheby's sale catalog, London, May 8, 1986 (London, 1986), lot 224.

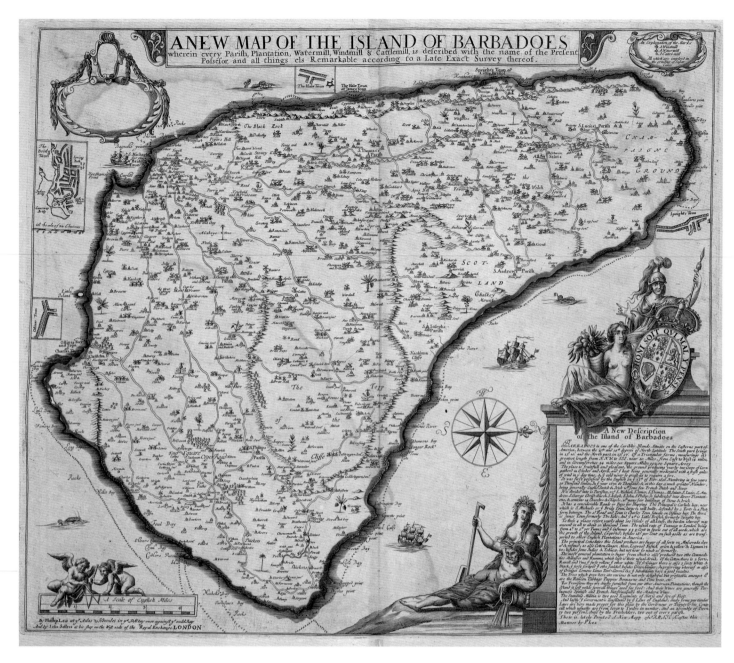

266 *A New Map of the Island of Barbadoes.* (Custis Atlas Cat. 75)

75 CUSTIS ATLAS

A NEW MAP OF THE ISLAND OF BARBADOES / wherein every Parish, Plantation, Watermill, Windmill & Cattlemill, is described with the name of the Present / Possesor, and all things els Remarkable according to a Late Exact Survey thereof

Richard Forde, cartographer; engraver unknown

London, 1685 (originally published ca. 1676). Black-and-white line engraving with period outline color. H. 19¼", W. 21¾"

A blank cartouche is in the upper left corner. A small inset map of Bridgetown is below. In the lower left is a scale of distances surmounted by cherubs with the imprint *By Phillip Lea at yᵉ Atlas & Hercules in yᵉ Poᵘltry ouer against yᵉ ould Jury/ And by Iohn Sellers at his shop on the West side of the Royal Exchange LONDON* below. The title is in a panel along the upper center. In the upper right corner is an explanation of symbols. In the lower right is a tablet that contains *A New Description/ of the Island of Barbadoes* on which two allegorical figures rest. Two seated figures are on the left

Three states of the map are known[1]:

State 1: The imprint in the cartouche in the upper left corner is *This map to be Sold by Mr. Overton at the White Horse without Newgate Mr. Morden at the Atlas in Cornhill Mr. Berry at the Globe in Charing-Cross And Mr. Pask at ye Stationers Arms & Inkbottle on the North Side the Royal Exchange.* Ca. 1676

State 2: (this copy) As described. *Their is lately Printed a New Mapp of Jamaica after this manner by P. Lea,* a reference to Custis Atlas Cat. 74, was added at the end of the *New Description*[2]

State 3: The imprint in the cartouche in the upper left is *Sold by George Willdey at the Great Toy Spectacle, Chinaware and Print Shop, ye corner of Ludgate Street near St. Pauls.* Ca. 1730

References: Black, ed., *Blathwayt Atlas,* map 32; Campbell, "Printed Maps of Barbados," entry 9; Stevens and Tree, "Comparative Cartography," entry 6 and Addenda 6

B Y THE 1650s, landowners on Barbados had begun to experiment with sugar cane production. Based on a first-hand survey by Richard Forde, *A New Map of the Island of Barbadoes* shows the island's prospering sugar plantations shortly before the hurricane of 1675 devastated most of the leeward coast. Forde identified 844 plantations by the owners' names and indicated with symbols the number of windmills, cattle mills, and water mills for each.[3]

Lea listed this map in his catalogs for 1685, 1687, and ca. 1689. It was listed in the index of the Library of Congress copy but at some point it was removed. State two appears in Lea's composite atlas in the Burden collection. No state appears in the British Library copy.

1. The states were taken from Black, ed., *Blathwayt Atlas,* map 32, who surmised that there was an earlier unidentified state. Stevens and Tree listed a state with Lea and Seller's imprints and the printed date 1685. "Comparative Cartography," p. 6.

2. Advertised for sale in Feb. 1685. Arber, ed., *Term Catalogues,* I, p. 115.

3. Dunn, *Sugar and Slaves,* p. 93.

76 CUSTIS ATLAS

Listed in the index as "A Map of ye English Islands" but now missing

This was *The Principall Islands in America belonging to the English Empire* that consisted of five separate maps on one sheet—Jamaica, Barbados, Antigua, Saint Christopher, and Bermuda.[1]

Lea listed this map in his ca. 1698 catalog but not in those for 1685 or 1687. It appears in Lea's composite atlas in the Burden collection but not in the British Library and Library of Congress copies.

1. Campbell, *Printed Maps of Barbados,* entry 14; *Atlases, Maps, Travel and Topography,* Sotheby's sale catalog, lot 224.

77 CUSTIS ATLAS

SOUTH AMERICA Divided into its IIII PRINCIPALL PARTS. I SPANISH PART: vizt Firmland, Guiana, Peru, Chili, p^t of the Country/ of Amazones, & Paraguay II PORTUGALLS P.^t viz: Brazel, & p^t of Paraguay: III ENGLISH p^t vizt Magellanick-land & p^t of Firmland: IIII DUTCH p^t viz p^t of Firmland & ye Isles

Cartographer and engraver unknown

London, ca. 1690 (originally published ca. 1684). Black-and-white line engraving with period outline color. H. 21½", W. 22¼"

The title is along the upper margin. No imprint. The map was trimmed to within the plate mark along the lower edge

Two states of the map are thought to exist:

State 1: No copy located. Published as one sheet of an unidentified multisheet hemispheric world map. The title may have been lacking above the upper margin.[1] Ca. 1684

State 2: (this copy) As described

This map and its companion, Custis Atlas Cat. 66, were salvaged from an unidentified hemispheric multisheet map of the world. *South America* has printed score lines to indicate where the lower edge of Cat. 66 was to be positioned when the sheets were joined. Although the original publisher and date of the wall map are uncertain, the geography on Cat. 66 suggests this state was published ca. 1690.

Lea listed a map of South America in his ca. 1698 catalog but not in those for 1685 or 1687. This map did not appear in any of the other Lea composite atlases examined.

1. It is possible that the title above the map was present from the beginning so that the sheet could be sold separately. It would have been trimmed off or pasted over when the sheets were joined to form the multisheet wall map. For a precedent for such a format, see Custis Atlas Cat. 70.

78 CUSTIS ATLAS

TERRA FIRMA / et / NOVUM REGNUM / GRANATENSE / et / POPOYAN

Jan Jansson, cartographer; engraver unknown

Amsterdam, 1630. Black-and-white line engraving with period outline color. H. 15", W. 18½"

The title cartouche is in the center right. Below is the imprint *Amstelodami/ Joannes Janssonius/ excudit*. A scale of distances is in the lower right corner

One state of the map is known

Reference: van der Krogt, *Koeman's Atlantes Neerlandici*, entry 9810:1

THIS MAP was based on Johannes De Laet's *Terra Firma item Nuevo Reyno De Granada atque Popoyan*, from *Beschrijvinghe van West-Indien*, Amsterdam, 1625.

79 CUSTIS ATLAS
VENEZUELA, / cum parte Australi / NOVÆ ANDALUSIÆ

Jan Jansson (after Henricus Hondius), cartographer; engraver unknown

Amsterdam, 1644 (originally published in 1630). Black-and-white line engraving with period outline color. H. 15″, W. 19¼″

The title cartouche is in the upper center. In the lower right is a scale of distances with the imprint *AMSTELODAMI, Ioannes Ianssonius Excudit* below

Two states of the map are known:
State 1: *Henricus Hondius excudit.* 1630
State 2: (this copy) As described

Reference: van der Krogt, *Koeman's Atlantes Neerlandici*, entry 9830:1.2

THIS MAP was based on Johannes De Laet's *Venezuela, atque Occidentalis Pars Novæ Andalusiæ*, from *Beschrijvinghe van West-Indien*, Amsterdam, 1625.

80 CUSTIS ATLAS
GVIANA / siue / AMAZONVM / REGIO

Jan Jansson (after Henricus Hondius), cartographer; engraver unknown

Amsterdam, 1644 (originally published in 1633). Black-and-white line engraving with period outline color. H. 14½″, W. 19″

A scale of distances is in the lower left center. The title cartouche is in the upper right corner. In the lower right is the imprint *Amstelodami,/ Joannes Janssonius/ excudit*

Two states of the map are known:
State 1: *Henricus Hondius excudit.* 1633
State 2: (this copy) As described

Reference: van der Krogt, *Koeman's Atlantes Neerlandici*, entry 9840:1.2

THIS MAP was based on Johannes De Laet's *Guiana sive Provinciæ intra Rio de los Amazones . . . .*, from *Beschrijvinghe van West-Indien*, Amsterdam, 1625.

81 CUSTIS ATLAS
Nova et Accurata / BRASILIÆ / totius / TABULA

Abraham Wolfgangk, cartographer; Joannis De Broeu, engraver; published in the *Atlas Major* by Joan Blaeu

Amsterdam, 1662. Black-and-white line engraving with period outline color. H. 20″, W. 23½″

The title cartouche in the lower right is followed by *Auctore/ Ioanne Blaev I. F. Abraham Wolfgangk Excudit. Joannis de Broeu, sculpsit* and the scale of distances are below the title cartouche

One state of the map is known

Reference: van der Krogt, *Koeman's Atlantes Neerlandici*, entry 9850:2C

82 CUSTIS ATLAS
PARAGVAY, Ó / PROV. DERIO DE LA PLATA / cum regionibus adiacentibus Tvcvman / et / S.^{TA} CRVZ DE LA SIERRA

Jan Jansson, cartographer; engraver unknown

Amsterdam, 1630. Black-and-white line engraving with period outline color. H. 14¾″, W. 18¾″

The cartouche in the upper right is surmounted by a scale of distances. In the lower right is the imprint *AMSTELODAMI,/ Excudebat Ioannes Ianssonius*

One state of the map is known

Reference: van der Krogt, *Koeman's Atlantes Neerlandici*, entry 9900:1

THIS MAP is based on Johannes de Laet's *Paraguay, O Prov. De Rio De La Plata, . . .* from *Beschrijvinghe van West-Indien*, Amsterdam, 1625.

83 CUSTIS ATLAS
CHILI

Henricus Hondius, cartographer; engraver unknown

Amsterdam, 1644 (originally published in 1630). Black-and-white line engraving with period outline color. H. 15", W. 18¾"

The title cartouche is in the upper left corner of the map. In the lower left is the imprint *AMSTELODAMI,/ Ioannes Ianssonius/ excudit.* A scale of distances is in the upper right

Two states of the map are known:
State 1: *Henricus Hondius excudit.* 1630
State 2: (this copy) As described

Reference: van der Krogt, *Koeman's Atlantes Neerlandici,* entry 9920:1.2

THIS MAP was based on Johannes De Laet's *Chili,* from *Beschrijvinghe van West-Indien,* Amsterdam, 1625.

84 CUSTIS ATLAS
TABULA / MAGELLANICA, / QUA TIERRÆ DEL FUEGO, / Cum / celeberrimis fretis a F. Magellano / et I. Le Maire detectis / Novissima et accuratissima / descriptio exhibetur

Jan Jansson, cartographer; engraver unknown

Amsterdam, 1644. Black-and-white line engraving with period outline color. H. 16¼", W. 20½"

A scale of distances surrounded by figures is in the lower left. A table of explanations is in the upper center. A dedicatory cartouche *Nobilissimo./ Amplissimoque Viro./ D. GVALTHERO de RAET./ I.V.D. Curiæ Hollandiæ, Aee:/ landiæ. West–frisiæque/ Senatori eminentissimo./ D.D.D. Ioannes Iannssonius* in the upper right is surmounted by a coat of arms. The scrollwork title cartouche in the lower right corner is surrounded by native figures. In the lower center is the imprint *Amstelodami,/ Apud Joannem Janssonium*

Two states of the map are known:
State 1: Same title and imprint. The dedicatory cartouche was left blank although the coat of arms was included. Ca. 1644
State 2: (this copy) As described. The dedication was added

Reference: van der Krogt, *Koeman's Atlantes Neerlandici,* entry 9950:1C.2

85 CUSTIS ATLAS
A New MAPP of the / WORLD / According to M.ʳ Edward Wright / Commonly called / Mercator's Projection

John Thornton, cartographer; James Clark, engraver; included in some copies of *Atlas Maritimus* by John Thornton after ca. 1685

London, 1683.[1] Black-and-white line engraving. A complete copy would measure H. 17", W. 26½"

The scrollwork title cartouche in the upper left corner is followed by the imprint *By John Thornton at the signe of/ England Scotland & Ireland in the/ Minories London.* Approximately 4½ inches along the right side of the map have been torn away. In the upper right corner it would have contained a scrollwork dedicatory cartouche surmounted by a heraldic crest *To Sr. James Hayes Knt.*[2] *One of his Maties. Most Honorable Privy-Councell in the Kingdome of Ireland: This Mapp is humbly Dedt. By John Thornton.* In the lower right corner would have been *Ia. Clark Sculp.* The map was trimmed to the outer neat line and mounted on a second sheet when it was bound into the atlas

Four states of the map are known[3]:
State 1: Proof copy lacking the engraver's signature and certain decorative features. Same imprint as above. Before May 1683
State 2: (possibly this copy)[4] As described. Decorative features such as sailing ships and fish were added in the ocean areas. *Tristan Acunha* and *Garliace* islands were relocated to 37° south and marked *I do Tristan Achua* and *I Garlaice.* 1683
State 3: *I Ladrones* was added east of the Philippines
State 4: Tracks of voyages of Dampier and Halley were added. Published in *The English Pilot The Third Book* by John Thornton, 1703

References: Black, ed., *Blathwayt Atlas,* map 1; Shirley, *Mapping of the World,* entry 521

THIS LARGE MAP engraved using Mercator's projection[5] is similar to Morden and Berry's untitled world map ca. 1676.[6] Thornton added data from Sir John Narborough's voyage to South America, 1669–1671. The depiction of Hudson Bay resembles *A Chart of yᵉ North part of America,* Custis Atlas Cat. 87. In 1689 or later, Thornton published a miniature version of this world map as an inset on the title plate used for later copies of his *Atlas Maritimus.*[7]

Because Lea was not the publisher, he did not list this map in his catalogs for 1685, 1687, or ca. 1698. It does not appear in any of the other Lea composite atlases examined.

1. The map was first advertised for sale in May 1683. Arber, ed., *Term Catalogues,* II, p. 217.
2. Sir James Hayes was secretary to Prince Rupert, first governor of the Hudson Bay Company. Hayes, an original investor, served as deputy governor from 1675 to 1685.

3. The states are given according to Black, ed., *Blathwayt Atlas,* entry 1, p. 33. She believed that at the time of its publication, this was the most accurate depiction of the American colonies on a world map. *Ibid.,* p. 32.

4. Due to the absence of the right side of the map where the changes occurred, I was unable to determine whether this is state 2 or state 3.

5. In 1569, Gerard Mercator introduced his new projection on a wall map of the world, *Nova et Aucta Orbis Terrae Descriptio.* Shirley, *Mapping of the World,* entry 119. Mathematician Edward Wright described the principles of Mercator's projection in his *Certaine Errors in Navigation,* 1599, *ibid.,* entry 221.

6. *Ibid.,* entry 472. Thornton's world map also resembles Claes Janszoon Voogt's *Wassende Graade Kaart van alle bekende Zeekusten op den Geheelen Aardbodem,* published in 1682. *Ibid.,* entry 512.

7. Reproduced in Coolie Verner, "Engraved title-plates for the folio atlases of John Seller," in Wallis and Tyacke, eds., *My Head Is a Map,* plate 9, right.

86 CUSTIS ATLAS
A Generall Chart / of the / WEST INDIES

John Thornton, cartographer; engraver unknown; included in some copies of *Atlas Maritimus* by John Thornton and in *The English Pilot The Fourth Book* by William Fisher and John Thornton, 1689, and by John Thornton and Richard Mount, 1698

London, ca. 1685. Black-and-white line engraving. H. 17½", W. 21½"

The title followed by the imprint *By John Thornton at the Signe of/ yᵉ Platt in the Minories. London* is in a scrollwork cartouche that rests on a plinth containing a scale of distances. The map was trimmed to the outer neat line and mounted on a sheet for inclusion in the atlas

One state of the map is known

Reference: Verner, comp., *The English Pilot The Fourth Book,* table 2, map 7

JOHN SELLER'S introduction of *The English Pilot* and *Atlas Maritimus* in the early 1670s marked the beginning of English marine cartography.[1] These ambitious works overextended Seller's resources. In order to continue production, he was forced into a partnership with William Fisher, John Thornton, John Colson, and James Atkinson in 1677. When this consortium was dissolved two years later, most of the assets passed to Fisher and Thornton.

Over the next twenty years, Thornton continued to compile copies of the *Atlas Maritimus.* Initially, he used remaindered charts originally published by Seller or the partnership. Thornton gradually replaced the imprints on these old sheets with his own and added new charts as he completed them. Because Thornton never included a dated title page in *Atlas Maritimus,* it is difficult to assign precedence to the copies or to date the charts they include. However, a copy of *Atlas Maritimus* in the National Maritime Museum, Greenwich, has an inscription on the flyleaf to "Reginald Graham Esqr. Page of honour to King James the Second: his Booke; given to him by King James the Second Anno Domin 1687," establishing that the charts it contains could not have been issued later than 1687.[2] The volume includes several charts also found in the Custis Atlas, including *A Generall Chart of the West Indies.* Traditionally assigned to 1689 when it was added to the first edition of *The English Pilot The Fourth Book,* this chart can be dated earlier based on the 1687 inscription.

1. Verner aptly described the publishing history of these atlases as "a bibliographical monstrosity that is not yet clarified." Verner, "Engraved title-plates," p. 24. This confusion was due to the number of competitors involved in their production, the large quantity of remaindered stock that continued to be used, and the relatively few copies of these rare works available for study. *Atlas Maritimus* was a composite that first appeared in 1675. It continued to be issued with maps bearing the imprints of various members of the consortium until about 1700. *The English Pilot* was a standardized atlas brought out serially from 1671 to 1703, with each part, or "Book," devoted to the navigation of a different part of the world. Seller was responsible for those published before 1677; Fisher and Thornton for most that were introduced afterward. Editions continued to be published until 1794.

2. NMM *Catalogue,* entry 449. The museum assigned a date of ca. 1685 to the atlas, believing that it must have been in existence for some time before it was inscribed to Graham.

87 CUSTIS ATLAS
A Chart of yᵉ North part of / AMERICA. / For Hudsons Bay Comonly called yᵉ / NORTH WEST PASSAGE

John Thornton, cartographer; engraver unknown; included in some copies of *Atlas Maritimus* by John Thornton and in *The English Pilot The Fourth Book* by William Fisher and John Thornton, 1689, and by John Thornton and Richard Mount, 1698

London, ca. 1689 (originally published ca. 1677). Black-and-white line engraving. H. 17½", W. 21"

Because the chart is oriented with north to the right, all of the nomenclature is perpendicular to the title cartouche. The scrollwork title cartouche in the upper right is framed by two figures of Native Americans and is surmounted by a deer, beaver, and fox. The title is followed by the imprint *By Iohn Thornton Hidrographer/ at the Platt in the Minories.* Below the cartouche is a scale of dis-

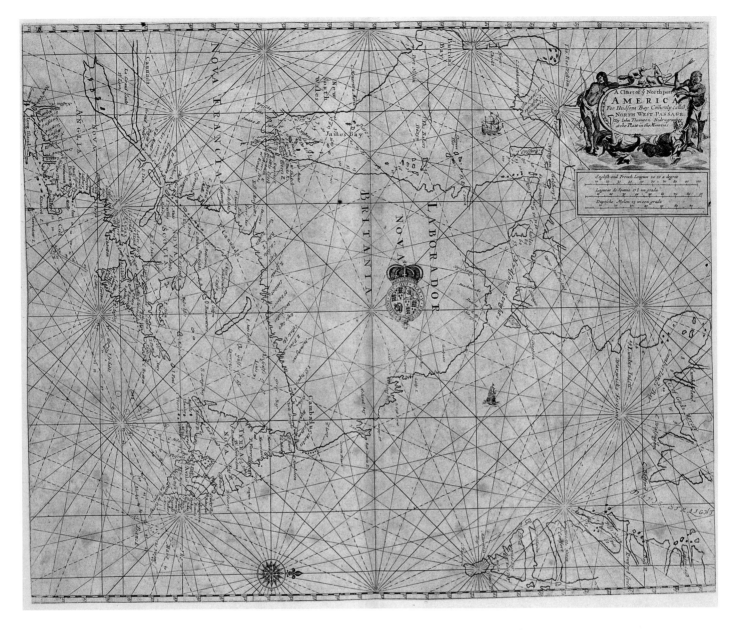

267 *A Chart of yᵉ North part of America. For Hudsons Bay Comonly called yᵉ North West Passage.* (Custis Atlas. Cat. 87)

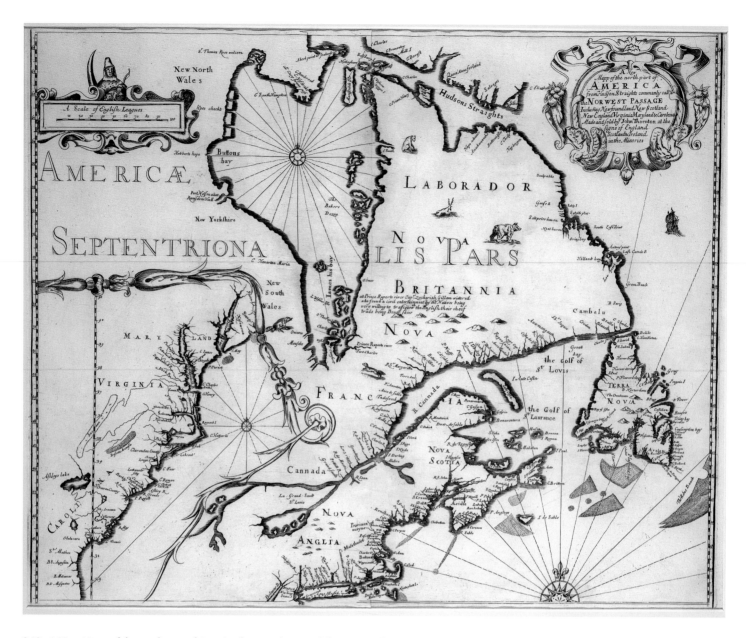

268 *A New Mapp of the north part of America from Hudson Straights commanly call'd the Norwest Passage,*
by John Thornton, London, 1673, black-and-white line engraving. Courtesy, Bridget and Al Ritter.

tances. The map was trimmed to the outer neat line and mounted on a second sheet for inclusion in the atlas. The number "78" appears in ink within the neat line in the upper left corner

Two states of the map are known[1]:

State 1: The imprint is *By John Thornton. John Seller. William Fisher. James Atkinson. John Colson.* Ca. 1677

State 2: (this copy) As described. With Thornton's imprint alone. A native figure in the cartouche was partially erased when the old imprint was removed. A long crack in the plate created the line that runs horizontally from Button Bay into Hudson Bay

References: Black, ed., *Blathwayt Atlas,* map 4, state 1; Kershaw, *Early Printed Maps of Canada,* entry 215, state 2; McCorkle, *New England in Early Printed Maps,* entry 677.5; Phillips, comp., *List of Geographical Atlases,* entry 3455, map 15; Phillips, comp., *List of Maps of America,* p. 563; Verner, comp., *The English Pilot The Fourth Book,* table 2, map 1

IN 1668, a group of English investors sent the ship *Nonsuch,* commanded by Zachariah Gilliam, to Hudson Bay to establish a potentially lucrative trade in furs with the natives in the region. Gilliam was also instructed "to keepe exact Journalls . . . and to be curious in your Soundings that wee may know the depth of the waters in all places where you come and according to the best of your Skill shall provide such mapps as may give us an accompt of the places where you goe."[2] The *Nonsuch* returned with a valuable cargo of furs in 1669 and the Hudson Bay Company was chartered the next year. Gilliam's reports probably provided the basis for John Thornton's 1673 *A New Mapp of the north part of America.*[3] *(fig. 268)*

Thornton engraved Custis Atlas Cat. 87 after the consortium of Thornton, Seller, Fisher, Atkinson, and Colson assumed the publication rights to *Atlas Maritimus* in 1677. In its first state, the chart bore the imprint of all five partners.[4] The geography was more advanced than on Thornton's 1673 map and included data from a second voyage to Hudson Bay. After the partnership was dissolved in 1679, Thornton retained sole ownership of this plate.[5]

Thornton was appointed hydrographer to the Hudson Bay Company in 1680. Many of the manuscript maps he made for the company were, in part, prototypes for the printed charts in *The English Pilot The Fourth Book,* the only volume of the series based largely on original English sources.

1. States are given according to Black, ed., *Blathwayt Atlas,* pp. 46–47.
2. *Ibid.,* p. 50.
3. This may be the first printed map that recorded the activities of the Hudson Bay Company. *Ibid.,* map 5.
4. The 1677 chart was intended to replace John Seller's less advanced

A Chart of the North Part of America, which had been included in copies of *Atlas Maritimus* since 1675. Phillips, comp., *List of Geographical Atlases,* entry 4154, map 37.
5. For information about Thornton's relationship to *Atlas Maritimus* and *The English Pilot,* see Custis Atlas Cat. 86.

88 CUSTIS ATLAS
A New Chart of the Sea Coast of / Newfound Land, new Scotland, / new England, new Jersey, Virginia, / Maryland, Pennsilvania, and / part of Carolina

John Thornton, cartographer; engraver unknown; included in late copies of *Atlas Maritimus* by John Thornton and in *The English Pilot The Fourth Book* by William Fisher and John Thornton, 1689, and by John Thornton and Richard Mount, 1698 and 1706

London, ca. 1689. Black-and-white line engraving. H. 17¼", W. 21¼"

The scrollwork title cartouche in the upper left corner is flanked by two figures of Native Americans and rests on a plinth that contains a scale of distances. The title is followed by the imprint *By Iohn Thornton Hydrographer at/ the Signe of England, Scotland, and/ Ireland, in the Minories/ London.* The chart was trimmed to the outer neat line and mounted on a sheet for inclusion in the atlas. The number "79" appears in ink within the neat line in the upper left corner

One state of the map is known[1]

References: Kershaw, *Printed Maps of Canada,* entry 228; McCorkle, *New England in Early Printed Maps,* entry 689.5; Phillips, comp., *List of Maps of America,* p. 671; Verner, *Carto-Bibliographical Study of the English Pilot The Fourth Book,* pp. 41–43; Verner, comp., *The English Pilot The Fourth Book,* table 2, map 2

A *New Chart of the Sea Coast of Newfound Land* has confusing antecedents. It is a close copy of a similarly named chart published around 1677 by the partnership that briefly brought out *Atlas Maritimus.*[2] Although Thornton's name ranked first in that imprint and he must have been the cartographer, Fisher retained the plate when the partnership was dissolved in 1679.[3]

Thornton engraved this replacement, which differs slightly from its prototype, most notably in the addition of Pennsylvania. The Susquehanna and Delaware Rivers were extended and many place-names including "Philadelphia City" and "Perth" [Perth Amboy] were added. The chart was expanded south and west to include "part of Carolina." Slight variations occurred in the copying of the cartouche. Thornton may not have prepared this plate until he published *The English Pilot The Fourth Book* in 1689.[4]

1. Verner noted that the chart appeared in one state that was discontinued after 1706 and replaced by another plate with a similar title in the 1713 edition. Verner, comp., *The English Pilot The Fourth Book*, p. xix. McCorkle believed that the plate was merely revised. *New England in Early Maps,* entry 689.5.

2. McCorkle, *New England in Early Printed Maps,* entry 676.7.

3. The imprint was then revised to *By William Fisher & Rich'd Mount at ye Postern on Tower-Hill.*

4. The NMM copy of *Atlas Maritimus* includes the old chart with Fisher and Mount's imprint, suggesting that the new engraving with only Thornton's name was not yet in print. For information on the NMM atlas and dating Thornton's charts, see Custis Atlas Cat. 86.

colonies, eliminated Lederer's errors, and added many place-names along the gulf and Florida coasts. While Thornton's new nomenclature was derived from Spanish sources, it was not in complete agreement with de Ruesta's toponomy. It appears that he did not consult the 1654 map directly.

1. This chart was included in the NMM's copy of *Atlas Maritimus,* so it must have been published prior to 1687. See Custis Atlas Cat. 86.

2. Cumming, *Southeast in Early Maps,* entry 75, plate 38. For de Ruesta, see Burden, *Mapping of North America,* entry 310, and Jack Jackson, *Flags along the Coast; Charting the Gulf of Mexico, 1519–1759: A Reappraisal* (Austin, Tex., 1995), p. 108, n. 43, p. 136, n. 160.

89 CUSTIS ATLAS
A General Chart / of the / WEST INDIA

John Thornton, cartographer; engraver unknown; included in some copies of *Atlas Maritimus* by John Thornton and in *The English Pilot The Fourth Book* by William Fisher and John Thornton, 1689, and by John Thornton and Richard Mount, 1698

London, ca. 1685.[1] Black-and-white line engraving with period outline color. H. 17½", W. 21½"

Insets of Jamaica and Barbados are in the upper left corner with a scale of distances below. The scrollwork title cartouche in the lower left corner, surmounted by a scallop shell, is followed by the imprint *By John Thornton Hydrographer:/ At the signe of the Platt in the Mino-/ ries; London.* The map was trimmed to the outer neat line and mounted on a sheet for inclusion in the atlas. The number "80" appears in ink within the neat line in the upper left corner

One state of the map is known

Reference: Verner, comp., *The English Pilot The Fourth Book,* table 2, map 10

A General Chart of the West India differs from *A Generall Chart of the West Indies* (Custis Atlas Cat. 86) in that it extends far enough west to include all of the Gulf of Mexico. This map was loosely based on John Seller's *A Chart of the West Indies,* originally published around 1673, a simplified copy of a Spanish chart of the area made by Sebastian de Ruesta in 1654.[2] Seller added details in the Carolinas from John Lederer's 1672 map. *(fig. 73)*

Thornton preserved much of de Ruesta's information. He improved and updated Seller's depiction of the English

90 CUSTIS ATLAS
A New Chart of the / BAHAMA ISLANDS / And the Windward Passage

John Thornton, cartographer; engraver unknown; included in *The English Pilot The Fourth Book* by John Thornton and Richard Mount, 1698

London, ca. 1698. Black-and-white line engraving. H. 17", W. 21"

A scale of distances is in the lower left corner. The scrollwork title cartouche in the upper right is followed by the imprint *By John Thornton Hydrographer/ At the Signe of England, Scotland, and/ Ireland, in the Minories London.* The map was trimmed to the outer neat line and mounted on a sheet for inclusion in the atlas. The number "81" appears in ink within the neat line in the upper left corner

Reference: Verner, comp., *The English Pilot The Fourth Book,* table 2, map 20

THE EARLIEST recorded appearance of *A New Chart of the Bahama Islands And the Windward Passage* was in the Custis Atlas and in the second edition of *The English Pilot The Fourth Book* in 1698.

91 CUSTIS ATLAS
A Chart of the / CARIBE ILANDS

John Thornton, cartographer; engraver unknown; published in *The English Pilot The Fourth Book* by William Fisher and John Thornton, 1689

London, ca. 1689. Black-and-white line engraving. H. 21¾", W. 17¾"

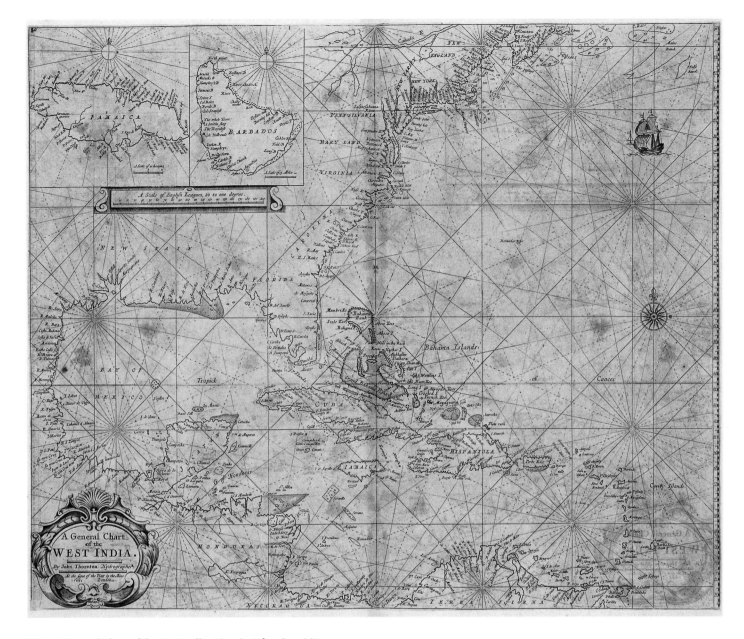

269 *A General Chart of the West India.* (Custis Atlas Cat. 89)

The title in a scrollwork cartouche in the upper center is followed by the imprint *By Iohn Thornton Hydrographer/ at the Signe of England, Scotland/ and Ireland, in the Minories/ London*. A scale of distances is below. The map was trimmed to the outer neat line and mounted on a sheet for inclusion in the atlas

Only one state of the map is known

Reference: Verner, comp., *The English Pilot The Fourth Book,* table 2, map 8

A Chart of the Caribe Ilands probably was engraved just before Fisher and Thornton published the first edition of *The English Pilot The Fourth Book* in 1689. The chart continued in print until 1749. The copy of Thornton's *Atlas Maritimus* in the National Maritime Museum contains what appears to be a different chart with the imprint of Fisher and Mount.[1]

> 1. NMM *Catalogue,* entry 449, no. 50. I have not examined this chart, but, according to the *Catalogue,* the title was spelled "Carribe" instead of "Caribe." See Custis Atlas Cat. 86.

92 CUSTIS ATLAS

To the R.^t Honourable / EDW. RUSSELL Esqr / One of their Maties most Hono.^ble Privy / Council ADMIRAL of their Maties Fleet & / Treasurer of their Maties Navy &c. / This Mapp of the Sea Coast of / EUROPE and ye STRAITS / is Most Humbly Dedicated by R. Morden & P. Lea

Cartographer unidentified; Herman Moll, engraver

London, 1690. Black-and-white line engraving with period outline color. H. 24″, W. 19½″

The dedication and title are in a foliate cartouche capped by a heraldic crest in the upper right. The eastern Mediterranean Sea is shown in an inset in the right center titled *NATOLIA or/ Littel Asia*. A scale of distances is in the lower center. Beneath is the imprint *LONDON, Sold by R: Morden at the Atlas in Cornhill, & by P. Lea at the Atlas and Hercules in Cheapside, and in Westminster Hall*

Two states of the map are known:
State 1: (this copy) As described
State 2: The dedication to *EDW. RUSSELL Esqr* was altered to reflect his new title *Edw. Earl of Orford*. To account for the death of Queen Mary in 1694, the wording of the dedicatory title was changed from *their Maties* to *His Maties*. *By Philip Lea* followed the title and dedication. The imprint is *By Philip Lea at the Atlas and Hercules in Cheapside, and in Westminster Hall*. Ca. 1697

I*N* 1690, the *London Gazette* advertised "Three new maps of the Seat of War, viz. The Sea Coast, the 17 Provinces, part of Germany and France . . . Sold by Philip Lea in Westminster Hall, and by Herman Moll in Yanleys [sic]—Court in Black Friars."[1] This detailed chart of the coast of Europe was probably the first of these—"The Sea Coast"—and was intended as a reference for the naval campaigns of the War of the League of Augsburg.

The advertisement identified Moll as one of the initial distributors. He undoubtedly was the engraver.[2] Since Moll may also have been one of the original publishers, it is likely that an earlier unidentfied state included his name in the imprint.[3] If Morden were a partner from the beginning, it is not clear why his name did not appear in the ad. At any rate, he had an interest in the map by the time Custis Atlas Cat. 92 was published.

Lea listed this map in his ca. 1698 catalog but not in those for 1685 or 1687. State one is in Lea's composite atlas in the Library of Congress. State two is in Lea's composite atlas in the Burden collection. No state appears in the British Library copy.

> 1. Tyacke, *London Map-Sellers,* entry 185.
> 2. The foliate title cartouche is identical to the one Moll used for Custis Atlas Cat. 13.
> 3. For such an example, see Custis Atlas Cat. 22–23.

93 CUSTIS ATLAS

A PLAT / Discovering the Coasts of / Russia Lapland Finmarck / Nova-Zembla / and / GREENLAND

Joseph Moxon (probably after Pieter Goos), cartographer; engraver unknown; published in *A Book of Sea-Plats* by Joseph Moxon

London, ca. 1663 (originally published in 1657). Black-and-white line engraving. H. 17¼″, W. 20¾″

The title contained in a scrollwork cartouche in the upper left is followed by the imprint *Newly Corrected by Joseph Moxon/ Hydrographer to the Kings most/ Excellent Majesty*. The imprint is flanked by dolphins. In the lower right is a scale of distances in a scrollwork frame surmounted by an armillary sphere. The map was trimmed to the outer neat line and mounted on a separate sheet for inclusion in the atlas. The number "84" appears in ink within the neat line in the upper left corner. The mounting sheet was inscribed in blue pencil on the verso "Presented to/ S.A. Green/ By/ Mrs. M. C. Lee/ 1872"

Three states of the map are thought to exist:

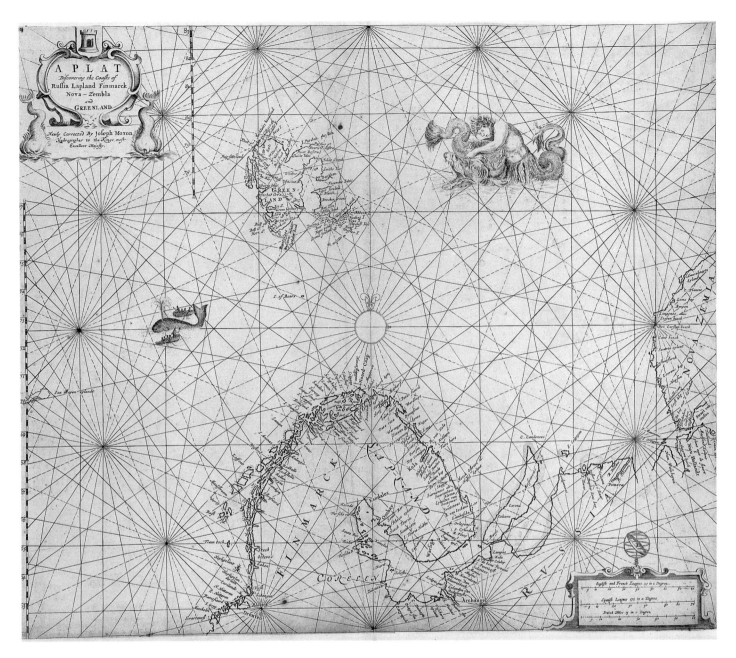

270 *A Plat Discovering the Coasts of Russia Lapland Finmarck Nova-Zembla and Greenland.* (Custis Atlas Cat. 93)

State 1: The title is *A Plat Discovering the Coasts of Russia Lapland Finmarck Nova–Zembla and Spitberg.* The imprint is *Newly corrected by Joseph Moxon and Sold at his Schop in Cornhil at the Sign of Atlas.* 1657
State 2: (this copy) As described
State 3: With Moxon's imprint erased. Ca. 1677[1]

THIS sea chart of the Arctic regions of Europe was one of six included in Moxon's very rare *A Book of Sea-Plats*, published in London in 1657.[2] Although the charts were copied from Dutch originals, they represent the first En-

glish attempt to compete with the Dutch in the field of marine cartography.[3] Helen Wallis noted that the use of "Schop" for Shop in the imprint on the first state suggested that the engraver was Dutch.[4]

1. See Custis Atlas Cat. 94, n. 1.
2. Shirley identified only two complete examples of this small atlas. *Printed Maps of the British Isles,* p. 102. The British Lib. copy is a first edition, 1657. The imprints on the charts in the Bodleian Library copy, Oxford University, were altered to account for Moxon's appointment as hydrographer to Charles II in 1662.

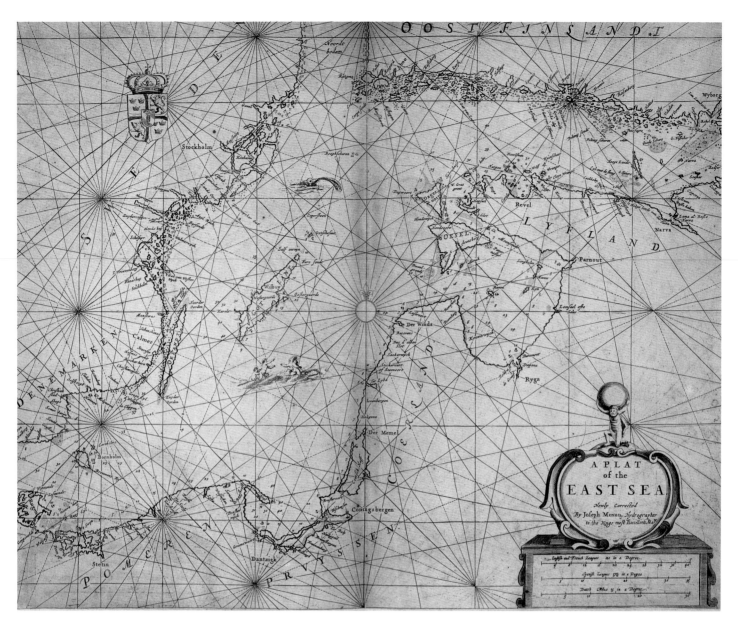

271 *A Plat of the East Sea.* (Custis Atlas Cat. 94)

3. Moxon probably copied plates from Pieter Goos's *Lichtende Columne ofte Zee-Spiegel* (Amsterdam, 1650).

4. Helen M. Wallis, "Geographie is Better than Divinitie: Maps, Globes, and Geography in the Days of Samuel Pepys," in Norman J. Thrower, ed., *The Compleat Plattmaker: Essays on Chart, Map, and Globe Making in England in the Seventeenth and Eighteenth Centuries* (Berkeley, Calif., 1978), p. 9.

94 CUSTIS ATLAS
A PLAT / of the / EAST SEA

Joseph Moxon (probably after Pieter Goos), cartographer; engraver unknown; published in *A Book of Sea-Plats* by Joseph Moxon

London, ca. 1663 (originally published in 1657). Black-and-white line engraving. H. 16¾", W. 21¼"

The scrollwork title cartouche in the lower right corner is surmounted by a figure of Atlas holding a blank globe and rests on a plinth that contains a scale of distances. The title is followed by the imprint *Newly Corrected/ By Joseph Moxon, Hydrographer/ to the Kings most Excellent Ma^ty*. The chart was trimmed to the outer neat line and mounted on a sheet for inclusion in the atlas. The number "85" appears in ink within the neat line in the upper left corner

Three states of the map are thought to exist:

State 1: Same title as above. The imprint is *By Joseph Moxon and Sold at his Shop in Corn-hill at the Sign of Atlas.* 1657

State 2: (this copy) As described

State 3: With Moxon's imprint erased. Ca. 1677[1]

THIS chart of the Baltic Sea was one of six included in Moxon's very rare *A Book of Sea-Plats,* originally published in London in 1657. See Custis Atlas Cat. 93 for further information.

1. An example of this state has recently been discovered in a copy of John Seller's *Atlas Maritimus.* In Feb. 2002, this atlas was in the possession of New York mapsellers Martayan Lan Augustyn.

95 CUSTIS ATLAS
A CHART / of the / NORTH SEA

John Thornton, cartographer; engraver unknown; included in later copies of *Atlas Maritimus* by John Thornton and in *The English Pilot The First Book* by Richard Mount and Thomas Page, 1701

London, ca. 1689. Black-and-white line engraving. H. 17½", W. 21"

The scrollwork title cartouche in the lower left corner rests on a scale of distances. The title is followed by the imprint *By John Thornton Hydrographer/ at the Signe of England, Scotland,/ and Ireland, in the Minories/ London.* The map was trimmed to the outer neat line and mounted on a sheet for inclusion in the atlas. The number "86" appears in ink within the neat line in the upper left corner

One state of the map is known

JOHN SELLER included *A Chart of the North Sea,* engraved by James Clark, in *The English Pilot The First Book* and some copies of *Atlas Maritimus.*[1] A second state of that chart with the imprint "John Seller, John Colson, Willm Fisher, James Atkinson, [and] John Thornton" appeared around 1677.[2] After the dissolution of the consortium in 1679, Thornton published an entirely new chart, *A plat of the North Sea.*[3] By the time the Custis Atlas was assembled in 1698, Thornton had replaced that map with this *Chart of the North Sea.*

1. Rodney W. Shirley, "The maritime maps and atlases of Seller, Thornton, and Mount & Page," *Map Collector,* LXXIII (1995), p. 4.
2. Phillips, comp., *List of Geographical Atlases,* entries 4150, no. 5, and 4151, no. 3. Phillips misdated these copies of *Atlas Maritimus.*
3. NMM *Catalogue,* entry 449, no. 7.

96 CUSTIS ATLAS
A PLAT / of the / CHANNEL / Discovering the Sea Coasts of / England, Scotland, Ireland / and Part of France

Cartographer unknown (after Pieter Goos); Francis Lamb, engraver; included in the second edition of *The English Pilot The First Book* by William Fisher and Richard Mount, ca. 1690

London, ca. 1690 (originally published in 1677). Black-and-white line engraving. H. 17½", W. 21½"

The drapery title cartouche is in the upper left. In the lower left is *F. Lamb sculp.* Beneath is a scale of distances. The imprint in the lower right is *By William Fisher and/ Richard Mount at the/ Postern on Tower hill/ London.* The map was trimmed to the outer neat line and mounted on a sheet for inclusion in the atlas. The number "87" appears in ink within the neat line in the upper left corner

Two states of the map are known:

State 1: With the imprint of William Fisher, John Seller, John Thornton, James Atkinson, and John Colson. 1677

State 2: (this copy) As described

Reference: Shirley, *Early Printed Maps of the British Isles,* Seller 2, state 2

THIS chart originally appeared in the 1677 edition of *The English Pilot The Third Book* with the imprint of the five-member consortium.

97 CUSTIS ATLAS
To the Right Honble my Lord / BERKLEY Admiral / of the Blew / Commander in Chief in the Present Exped. &c. / This Map of the / CHANNEL / is Dedicated by your Lordships / Most Humble Servant with three small maps of *The Harbour of St MALO; The RIVER SEINE from HAVER de GRACE to ROUEN; NIEUPORT, Furnes, DUNKIRK and Places Adjacent*

Philip Lea, cartographer; Herman Moll, engraver

London, 1695. Black-and-white line engraving with period outline color. H. 5½", W. 6¼"; H. 5⅜", W. 6⅜"; H. 5¼", W. 6¼"; H. 12¾", W. 22¾"

Four individually titled maps taken from four plates were printed on one sheet. Along the top from left to right are three small maps of *The Harbour of St MALO; The RIVER SEINE from HAVER de GRACE to ROUEN; NIEUPORT, Furnes, DUNKIRK and Places Adjacent.* The dedication, title, and imprint of the main map, *P. Lea/ at the Atlas & Hercules in/ Cheapside 1695,* are in a foliate cartouche surmounted by a coat of arms in the upper right corner. A scale of distances is in the lower right corner

One state of the map is known

Reference: Weinreb & Douwma, Catalog 17, no. 82

THIS MAP of the English Channel was probably published late in the summer of 1695 to celebrate England's recent victory over the French at Saint Malo. It was dedicated to Lord Berkeley, "Commander in Chief in the Present Exped[ition]" that had bombarded the port.

Although this map was not signed by the engraver, it is stylistically similar to Custis Atlas Cats. 15 and 92, suggesting it was the work of Herman Moll. The insets were printed from separate plates that originally appeared in Thornton, Morden, and Lea's 1694 *Hydrographia Gallia*, a miniature sea atlas of the coasts of France.[1] Copies may have been sold without the insets, but no example has been located. This is one of only two dated maps in the Custis Atlas.[2]

Lea listed the map in his ca. 1698 catalog but not in those for 1685 or 1687. It appears in Lea's composite atlas in the British Library and Library of Congress but not in the Burden collection copy.

1. Tyacke, *London Map-Sellers,* entry 261.
2. See also Custis Atlas Cat. 20.

98 CUSTIS ATLAS
A Chart from / ENGLAND to the / STRAITS

John Thornton, cartographer; engraver unknown; included in some copies of *Atlas Maritimus* by John Thornton and probably in *The English Pilot The Fifth Book* by Richard Mount and Thomas Page, 1701[1]

London, ca. 1689. Black-and-white line engraving. H. 21¼", W. 17"

Because the chart is oriented with north to the right, all of the nomenclature is perpendicular to the title cartouche. The title followed by the imprint *By John Thornton, Hydrographer/ at the England, Scotland, and/ Ireland, in the Minories./ London* is in a scrollwork cartouche surmounted by cherubs and fruit in the upper right center. It rests on a scale of distances. The chart was trimmed to the outer neat line and mounted on a sheet for inclusion in the atlas. The number "89" appears in ink within the neat line in the upper left corner

One state of the map is known

IN JUNE 1689, Thornton advertised "A large Map of the Sea-Coasts of England, Scotland, France, and Ireland . . . the Coasts of Flanders and Holland, Portugal and Spain, and up to the Streights" on six sheets.[2] This one-sheet

Chart from England to the Straits may be a reduction of the larger map.

1. No copy of the first edition of that work has been examined. The chart was included in the 1720 edition. NMM *Catalogue,* entry 428, map 253.
2. Tyacke, *London Map-Sellers,* entry 168. No copy of this wall map is known. Shirley, *Early Printed Maps of the British Isles,* p. 162.

99 CUSTIS ATLAS
A Plat of All the / STRAITS with three small maps of the STRAITES of GIBRALTER; MARSEILLES and TOLON; ISLES of HYERES and TOLON

Philip Lea, cartographer; engraver unknown

London, ca. 1695 (originally published in 1686). Black-and-white line engraving with period outline color. H. 5⅜", W. 6⅛"; H. 5¼", W. 6⅜6"; H. 5⅜", W. 6⅜"; H. 9⅜6", W. 22½"

Four individually titled maps taken from four plates were printed on one sheet. Along the top of the sheet from left to right are three small maps of the *STRAITES of GIBRALTER; MARSEILLES and TOLON; ISLES of HYERES and TOLON.* The scrollwork title cartouche in the upper left corner of the main map is surmounted by Atlas shouldering a blank globe. The title is followed by the imprint *Sold by Philip Lea Globe-/ maker at the Atlas and/ Hercules in Cheape Side:/ London.* The imprint shows signs of an erasure. A scale of distances is in the lower left and a key is in the upper right corner of the main map

Three states of the map are known:
State 1: No copy located. With Lea's Poultry address but lacking the three subsidiary maps. 1686[1]
State 2: With Lea's Cheapside address but lacking the subsidiary maps. Ca. 1693
State 3: (this copy) As described

IN 1693, a large fleet of English merchant ships bound for Smyrna in Turkey was destroyed off Cadiz by the French navy. Lea saw the resulting public interest in the Mediterranean as a business oportunity and republished his 1686 chart of that sea, *A Plat of All the Straits.* To make the chart more topical, Lea added three subsidiary maps to the third state, including two of Toulon, the home port of the French Mediterranean fleet. They were printed from separate plates engraved for Thornton, Morden, and Lea's miniature sea atlas of the coasts of France, *Hydrographia Gallia,* 1694.[2]

Lea listed this map in his 1687 and ca. 1698 catalogs

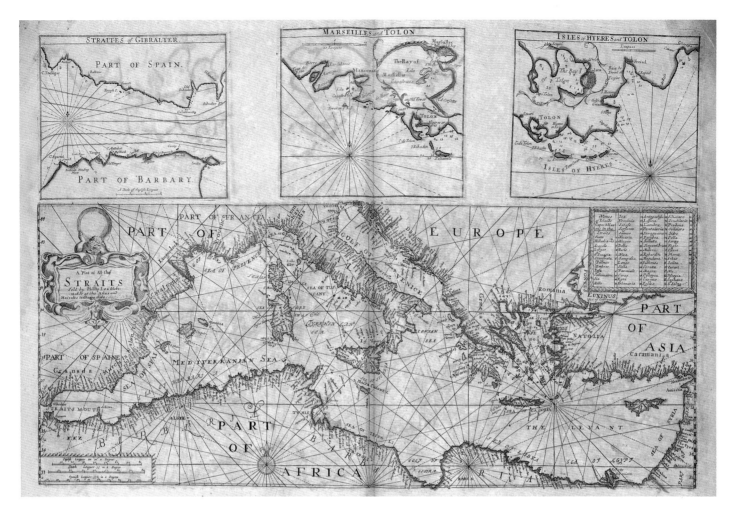

272 *A Plat of All the Straits.* (Custis Atlas Cat. 99)

but not in that for 1685. State two appears in Lea's composite atlas in the Library of Congress. State three is in Lea's composite atlas in the British Library. No state appears in the Burden collection copy.

1. This chart was originally advertised in Dec. 1686 by "P. Lea at the Atlas and Hercules in the Poultry." Arber, ed., *Term Catalogues*, II, p. 190.

2. Tyacke, *London Map-Sellers*, entry 261.

100 CUSTIS ATLAS
A Chart of the Sea coasts of / BARBARY

John Seller, cartographer; James Clark, engraver; included in later copies of *Atlas Maritimus* by John Thornton

London, ca. 1688 (originally published in 1675).[1] Black-and-white line engraving. H. 16¼", W. 21¼"

The scrollwork title cartouche surmounted by a central lion and two other felines is in the upper right. The title is followed by the imprint *John Thornton Hidrographer at the Platt in the Minories*. A crack in the plate runs horizontally through the imprint. A scale of distances is below. In the lower right is *Ja. Clerk Sculp*. The map was trimmed to the outer neat line and mounted on a sheet for inclusion in the atlas. The number "91" appears in ink within the neat line in the upper left corner

Three states of the map are known:
State 1: With the imprint of John Seller. 1675
State 2: With the imprint of Seller, Fisher, Colson, Atkinson, and Thornton. Ca. 1677
State 3: (this copy) As described

THIS chart of northwest Africa, originally engraved for John Seller, was included in his never completed 1675 edition of *The English Pilot The Third Book*.[2] Around 1677, Seller's imprint was replaced with that of the consortium. When the partnership was dissolved in 1679, the plate evidently passed to John Thornton, who altered the imprint after 1687. That state had been discarded by 1703 when Thornton replaced it with a new chart in the first complete edition of *The English Pilot The Third Book*.[3]

1. Because Thornton included a copy of state 2 in *Atlas Maritimus* in the NMM, that state probably was still being issued as late as 1687. See Custis Atlas Cat. 86. The third state with Thornton's imprint alone must date after that year.

2. The NMM has a copy of this rare work with 11 maps and charts, including this example. NMM *Catalogue*, entry 422 C–D, map 55.

3. *Ibid.*, entry 426 H, map 257.

101 CUSTIS ATLAS
A Chart of the / Eastermost part of the / EAST INDIES / and CHINA, From Cape / Comarine to IAPAN, with / all the Adjacent Islands

John Thornton, cartographer; engraver unknown; included in later copies of *Atlas Maritimus* by John Thornton and in *The English Pilot The Third Book* by John Thornton, 1703

London, before 1698. Black-and-white line engraving. H. 17", W. 21"

A scrollwork title cartouche flanked by native figures is in the upper left center. Below the title is the imprint *by John Thornton Hydrographer./ at the England, Scotland, and/ Ireland, in the Minories/ London*. A scale of distances is in the lower left. To the right of the title cartouche is an inset of Japan. The chart was trimmed to the outer neat line and mounted on a sheet for inclusion in the atlas. The number "94" appears in ink in the neat line in the upper left corner

One state of the map is known

FROM about 1675, John Seller included *A Chart of the Eastermost Part of the East Indies with all the Adjacent Islands from Cape Comorin to Japan*, engraved by Francis Lamb, in his *Atlas Maritimus*.[1] Seller's chart was copied from one in Pieter Goos's *Zee Atlas*, 1666. A second state with the imprint "J. Seller, J. Colson, W. Fisher, J. Atkinson, and J. Thornton" was published about 1677.

Thornton engraved this new version with a variant title before 1698. It is clear that he followed a different prototype. While Seller oriented the map with north to the right, Thornton placed it at the top. All traces of Australia (Seller's "Nova Hollandia") were eliminated as well.

1. NMM *Catalogue*, entry 429, map 294.

102 CUSTIS ATLAS
A Chart of the / WESTERN / Part of the / EAST–INDIES. / with all the Adjacent Islands / from Cape Bona Esperanca / to the Island of Zelone

John Thornton, cartographer; engraver unknown; included in later copies of *Atlas Maritimus* by John Thornton and in *The English Pilot The Third Book* by John Thornton, 1703

London, ca. 1682. Black-and-white line engraving. H. 17¼", W. 22"

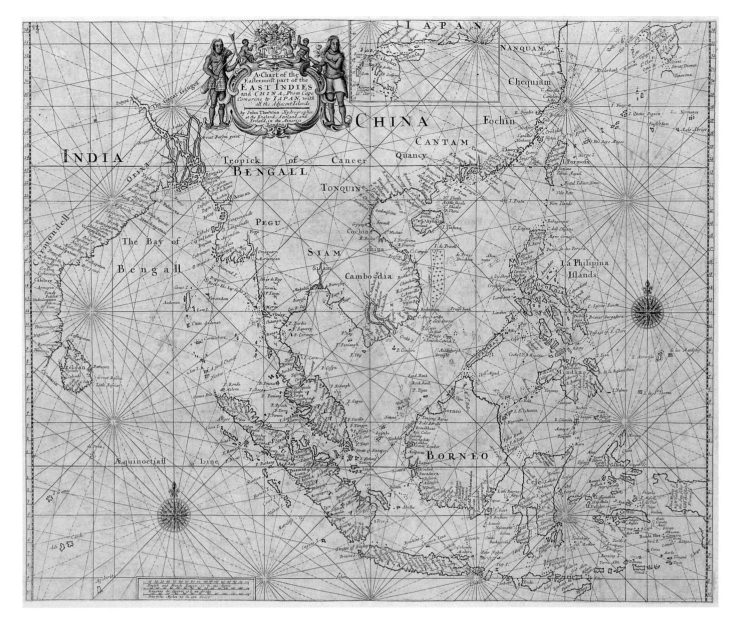

273 *A Chart of the Eastermost part of the East Indies and China.* (Custis Atlas Cat. 101)

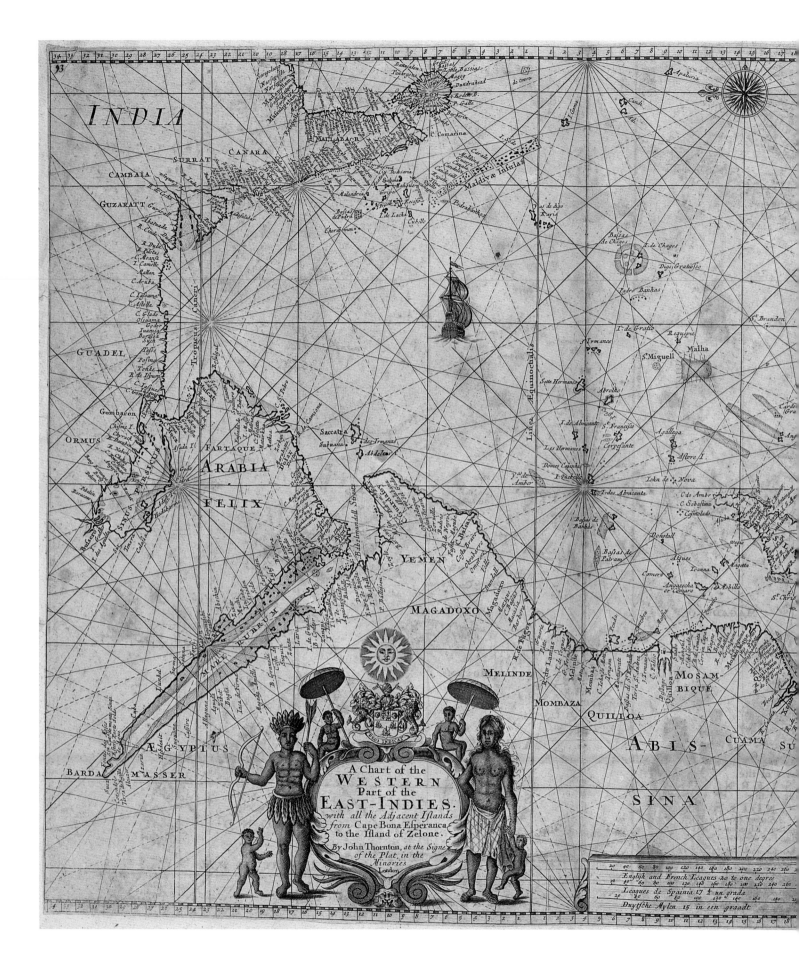

A Chart of the
WESTERN
Part of the
EAST-INDIES.
with all the Adjacent Islands
from Cape Bona Esperanca
to the Island of Zelone.
By John Thornton, at the Signe
of the Plat, in the
Minories
London

The title cartouche in the lower left center is flanked by native figures and pygmies, two of whom hold parasols. Above is a heraldic crest surmounted by a sun. The title is followed by the imprint *By John Thornton, at the Signe/ of the Plat in the/ Minories/ London*. To the right of the cartouche is a scale of distances. The chart was trimmed to the outer neat line and mounted on a sheet for inclusion in the atlas. The number "93" appears in ink within the neat line in the upper left corner

One state of the map is known

From about 1675, John Seller included *A Chart of the Western Part of the East–Indies*, engraved by Francis Lamb, in his *Atlas Maritimus*.[1] Seller's chart was copied from one by Pieter Goos, 1666. A second state with the imprint "J. Seller, J. Colson, W. Fisher, J. Atkinson, and J. Thornton" was published about 1677. An entirely new plate copied from the original was engraved by 1679, also with the imprint of the consortium.[2]

Thornton subsequently engraved this third plate, perhaps in 1682.[3] The geography was extended slightly eastward to include Ceylon, which was absent from the earlier charts. The last words of the title were changed from *to Cape Comorin* to *the Island of Zelone*.

1. NMM *Catalogue*, entry 429, map 293. Seller also included it in his unfinished *The English Pilot The Third Book* in the same year. *Ibid.*, entry 422, C-D, map 59.
2. It had the same title but lacked Lamb's name as engraver. Phillips, comp., *List of Geographical Atlases*, entry 4151, map 11. That Thornton's name was first in the imprint suggests he was the author of this new plate.
3. Roncière mentioned a manuscript chart by Thornton of the "Indian Ocean," 1682, that may have been the prototype for this new printed chart. Monique de La Roncière, "Manuscript charts by John Thornton, hydrographer of the East India Company (1669–1701)," *Imago Mundi*, XIX (1965), p. 46. The original manuscript is in the Bodleian Lib. I have not seen it.

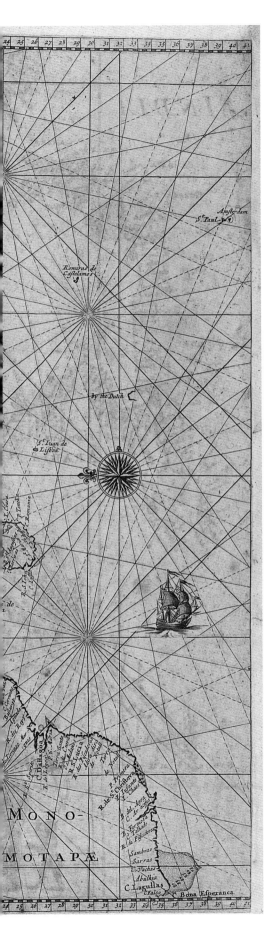

274 *A Chart of the Western Part of the East–Indies.* (Custis Atlas Cat. 102)

103 CUSTIS ATLAS
A Chart of / GUINEA / Describing the Sea Coast from Cape de / Verde to Cape de Bona Espransa

John Thornton, cartographer; engraver unknown; included in some copies of *Atlas Maritimus* by John Thornton

London, ca. 1680. Black-and-white line engraving. H. 17¼", W. 21¼"

The scrollwork title cartouche is in the upper left corner of the map. The title is followed by the imprint *By Iohn Thornton hydrog-*

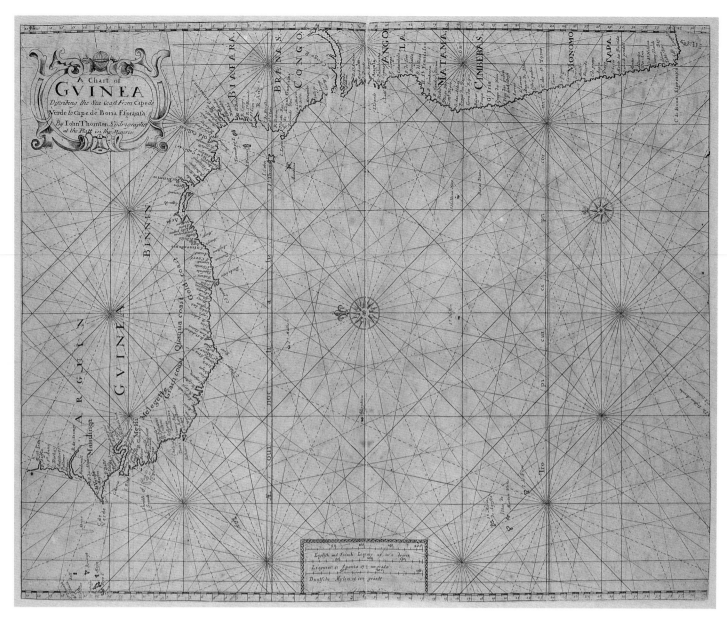

275 *A Chart of Guinea Describing the Sea Coast from Cape de Verde to Cape de Bona Espransa.* (Custis Atlas Cat. 103)

rapher/ at the Platt in the Minories. A scale of distances is in the lower center. The chart was trimmed to the outer neat line and mounted on a sheet for inclusion in the atlas

One state of the map is known

Aғᴛᴇʀ the restoration of Charles II, England increasingly competed with the Netherlands for a share of the lucrative slave trade, establishing a number of successful trading posts along the west coast of Africa. Because the Dutch had dominated the map trade from the beginning of the seventeenth century, English ship captains relied on navigational charts issued by their rivals. England's efforts to claim a larger share of the international market stimulated the development of the map trade in London.

John Seller responded to the growing demand by publishing *A Chart of Guinea* in 1675 in his new maritime publications.[1] Thornton engraved this new chart, a close copy of Seller's. It had been replaced by 1703 when Thornton issued *The English Pilot The Third Book* with an entirely new *Mapp of ye Coast of Guinea.*

1. Seller's chart was based on *Pas-Caart van Guinea en de Custen daer aen gelegen van Cabo verde to Cabo de Bona Esperanca* by Pieter Goos, 1666. It was included in the preliminary edition of *The English Pilot The Third Book*, 1675, and in copies of *Atlas Maritimus.* NMM *Catalogue,* entries 422 C-D, map 58, and 429, map 290.

Philip Lea and the Seventeenth-Century Map Trade

The atlas that Virginian John Custis purchased from London mapseller Philip Lea in 1698 reflects the cultural, political, mercantile, colonial, and scientific advances that were occurring in the English world by the end of the seventeenth century. Selected to suit Custis's interests and intellect, the maps in the composite atlas represented the global perspective shaped by his experiences abroad and his desire to demonstrate he had achieved the learned and sophisticated status aspired to by the colonial gentry.

The Custis Atlas also presents an opportunity to examine the career of Philip Lea, one of the most prolific and successful London mapsellers in the period. The contents represent a significant percentage of the individual sheet maps he published and reveal the scope of the business when Lea was at the pinnacle of his career. The sale of such made-up volumes provided a flexible, economical strategy that allowed Lea to offer clients bound collections with diverse contents while avoiding the substantial publication costs necessary to produce standardized atlases. To reduce expenses further, the individual maps, which were also sold separately, were frequently published in partnership with other London mapsellers. Printing plates were bought and sold regularly, and the changing imprints trace Lea's relationships within the trade and the remarkable growth of his activities. England experienced an economic boom and a scientific revolution under the later Stuarts that increased the demand for maps. Few London publishers benefited more from the expansion in the market than Philip Lea.

For most of the seventeenth century, the Dutch monopolized trade within Europe as well as between Europe and Asia, building a mercantile empire greater than that of all other European nations combined. Cartographers and publishers in the Netherlands dominated the map trade, leaving few opportunities for England and other countries to develop a competitive industry. Amsterdam publishers invested the substantial capital required to employ accomplished geographers, engravers, designers, colorists, printers, papermakers, and binders. The international market was flooded with their maps and atlases. *(fig. 276)*

Map publishing in the Netherlands reached its zenith in the 1650s and 1660s when the great multivolume world atlases of the firms of Joan Blaeu and Jan Jansson appeared in their mature form. These works dominated the world market, even though many of the maps they contained were out of date.[1] In 1664, Philip von Zesen described the House of Blaeu, the largest printing operation in Europe:

On the Bloemgracht, at the third bridge and the third by-lane, stands the world-famous printing house of Mr. Joan Blaeu, councillor and alderman of this city. The establishment is equipped with nine presses for letterpress printing, called after the nine muses, and six presses for printing copper-plates, and also with a type-foundry. The premises on the canal, together with the adjacent residence of the founder, has a breadth of 75 ft and extends 135 ft, or 150 ft if the house adjoining it in the rear is included . . . In front, facing the canal, is a room containing a number of cabinets in which are stored the plates which are used for the atlases, the Dutch and Walloon town atlases, and for the marine and other priceless books, which must certainly have cost a ton of gold. Next-door is the room where the copper-plates are printed; beyond it is the entry where, in the part flanked by the above-mentioned lane, they are wont to wash down the type after printing. Then comes the printing office proper in a long gallery, well provided with windows on both sides. At the far end is a stock-room where the type and other materials used in printing are kept. Before this room is a staircase leading to a room on the next floor where the corrector reads the proofs and revises and marks the errors made by the compositor. Here, too, there is a long ante-chamber or loft where, when the printing of the entire book is completed, the printed sheets are gathered into the order of appearance and also stored. At the very top is a similar loft for the same purpose and at the far end of this, over the previously mentioned proof-reader's room, is the foundry where type for printing in several languages is cast.[2]

276 *Officer and a Laughing Girl,* by Johannes Vermeer, Delft, Holland, ca. 1658, oil on canvas. Courtesy, Frick Collection. The map in the background is Willem Blaeu's map of Holland and West-Friesland, *Nova et accurata totius Hollandiae Westfrisiaeq,* 1621.

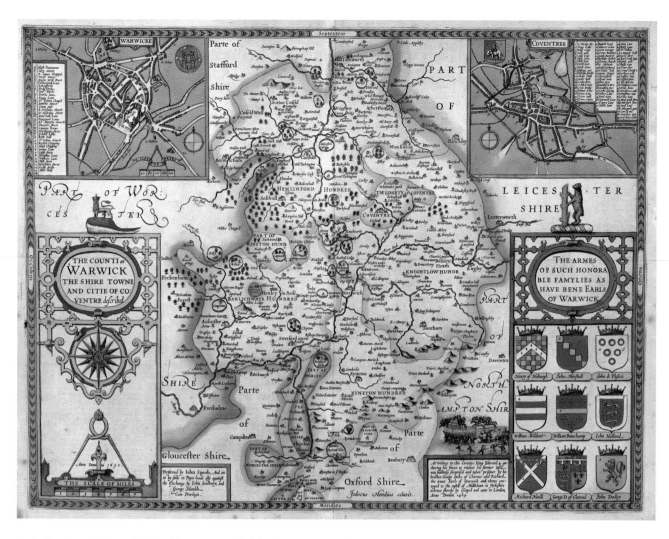

277 *The Counti of Warwick the Shire Towne and Citie of Co:ventre,* London, 1611, black-and-white line engraving with period color. Courtesy, Donald Heald. The maps for John Speed's *The Theatre of the Empire of Great Britain* were based on English surveys engraved in Amsterdam and published in London.

The six rolling presses for printing copperplates and nine letterpresses for printing text enabled the production of complex works such as Blaeu's multivolume *Atlas Major* to be undertaken almost entirely on the premises.[3]

Undercapitalized by comparison to the Dutch, London publishers relied heavily on imported maps and prints from the Netherlands for their stock. For example, William Humble imported "31 bales of globes and 3 packets of maps in 1653."[4] A decade later, mapseller Thomas Jenner stated in his catalog that "you may also have all sorts of Dutch-maps or citties, either on cloth coloured, or on paper in black and white, as also Dutch prints."[5] Surveys and man-uscript maps by English cartographers were frequently sent to Amsterdam for engraving, and the finished plates were returned to London for printing and publishing. *(fig. 277)* Other English surveys were engraved, printed, and pub-

lished entirely in Amsterdam. *(fig. 278)* Even the maps engraved in England were usually the work of immigrants from the Low Countries. English publishers often imported worn and obsolete Dutch plates, which they republished, unaltered except for the addition of their London imprints. Of the maps actually produced in England, most were no more than poor plagiarisms of earlier Netherlandish works.

By the 1660s, France and England had begun to assume larger roles in international commerce. The ambitious Louis XIV took control of France. The king's desire to establish his country as the dominant economic power in Europe was matched by that of his minister of finance, Jean-Baptiste Colbert. Capturing a share of world trade from the Dutch became one of their major goals.

While mapmaking in the Netherlands and England was

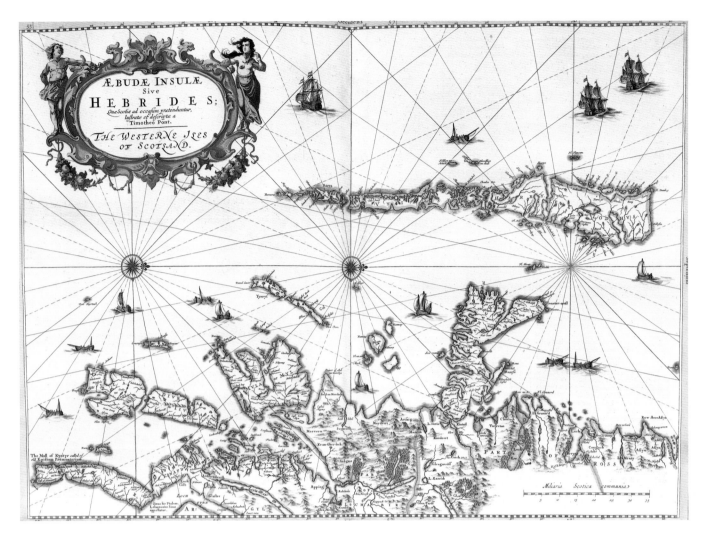

278 *Æbudæ Insulæ Sive Hebrides,* by Timothy Pont, Amsterdam, 1654, black-and-white line engraving with period outline color. Courtesy, Donald Heald. Published in Joan Blaeu's *Atlas Novus,* Pont's surveys of Scotland were sent to Amsterdam for both engraving and publishing.

largely a private undertaking, in France, Louis XIV and his government officially subsidized new surveys. Cartography joined the other arts and sciences as vehicles for the glorification of the monarchy. Colbert founded the *Académie Royale des Sciences* in 1666 for the purpose of the "correction and improvement of maps and nautical charts."[6] *(fig. 279)* The *Académie* authorized a national survey of France based on the technique of triangulation. This approach, which had been used occasionally since the sixteenth century, consisted of tracing and measuring by trigonometry a series of connecting triangles in order to record a territory.

Conditions conducive to the development of a competitive map trade in England began with the Restoration of Charles II in 1660. The king instituted more effective ways to administer the navy through the Board of the Admiralty, while his brother, the Duke of York, was given command of the fleet. Charles's policies of naval and colonial expansion increased the need for accurate charts. Tangier and Bombay were acquired as part of Catherine of Braganza's dowry when she married Charles in 1662. The territory of New Netherland, renamed New York and New Jersey, was added as a result of the second Anglo-Dutch War of 1665–1667. Carolina was chartered in 1663, and English traders were visiting Hudson Bay regularly to obtain furs by 1668. Charles founded two scientific institutions essential to mapmaking. The mathematics school at Christ's Hospital was established in 1673 *(fig. 280)*; the observatory at Greenwich, with John Flamsteed as royal astronomer, two years later. Flamsteed's publications eventually provided the foundation for British astronomical studies.[7]

Charles and his courtiers regarded themselves as patrons of the arts and sciences. The Royal Society, dedicated to the advancement of mathematics, science, and medicine, was chartered in July 1662. Perusing the original charter book, Samuel Pepys noted, "the King hath put his [name] with the word Founder."[8] The diarist John Evelyn visited the king's private library on several occasions. In September 1680, he observed an "Aboundance of Mapps & Sea Chards . . . Pieces relating to the Navy; Some Mathematical Instruments &c."[9] Emulating the monarch and court circles, the gentry and expanding middle classes also began to collect books, prints, maps, and globes to reinforce their educated, worldly status. Cartography was held in such high esteem that Johannes Klenke, an Amsterdam merchant and professor of philosophy, won a baronetcy by his presentation to the king of an atlas of wall maps that some considered the largest in the world. Evelyn saw the atlas in the king's private library at Whitehall, describing it as "a vast book of Mapps in Volume of neere 4 yards large."[10]

The Council for Plantations, established in 1670, was reorganized two years later as the Council for Trade and Plantations with John Locke as secretary. Although the body's primary purpose was to make recommendations to the Privy Council on colonial matters, it was in this office and that of its successor, the Board of Trade, that the structure of British imperial policy was born. Charles II instructed the group "to procure exact Mapps, Platts or Charts of all and Every our said Plantations abroad, together with Mapps and Descriptions of their respective Ports, Harbours, Forts, Bayes, Rivers."[11] The proprietors of Maryland, New Jersey, New York, Carolina, and Pennsylvania also sought current information. These maps, which illustrated vast, unsettled tracts, were used to attract investors with the capital to purchase land and promote settlement.

Maps incorporating information from English surveys began to replace preexisting continental works on which a limited amount of English data had simply been superim-

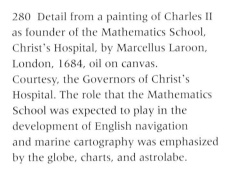

279 Detail from *Colbert Presents the Members of the Royal Academy of the Sciences to Louis XIV,* by Henri Testelin, Paris, 1667, oil on canvas. Courtesy, Réunion des Musées Nationaux/Art Resource, New York.

280 Detail from a painting of Charles II as founder of the Mathematics School, Christ's Hospital, by Marcellus Laroon, London, 1684, oil on canvas. Courtesy, the Governors of Christ's Hospital. The role that the Mathematics School was expected to play in the development of English navigation and marine cartography was emphasized by the globe, charts, and astrolabe.

posed. Once England established settlements in America, London mapsellers gained access to new geographical discoveries unavailable to the Dutch. One of the earliest commercial attempts to portray English holdings from Hudson Bay to Guiana was Robert Morden and William Berry's *A New Map of the English Plantations in America,* 1673 (Cat. 14).

By the 1670s, Dutch control of the worldwide map trade was weakening. The House of Blaeu was destroyed by a fire in 1672 that effectively brought the illustrious firm to an end.[12] Blaeu's surviving plates were sold by auction to other Amsterdam publishers who continued to print and sell impressions, although in greatly reduced numbers, until the eighteenth century. The Dutch monopoly was further challenged as a result of the costly Second Dutch War with France, 1672–1678, which devastated the economy and sharply curtailed cartographic production and distribution.

Once the great Dutch atlases became less available, sev-

eral London publishers announced plans to produce comprehensive works of their own. John Ogilby proposed to issue a multivolume atlas of the world. The first two books, *Africa,* 1671, and *America,* 1672, were merely translations of Dutch geographical texts illustrated with maps previously published in Amsterdam.[13] The third, *Britannia,* 1675, marked a real advance in mapmaking. The one hundred original road maps of England and Wales were the first to give distances in measured miles instead of by estimates.[14] *(fig. 281)* Ogilby died the following year, and his step grandson and associate, William Morgan, eventually abandoned the project.

Nautical instrument maker John Seller also envisioned an ambitious endeavor. Seller acquired a large collection of old Dutch plates to use for his marine atlases, *The Coasting Pilot, Atlas Maritimus,* and *The English Pilot,* the latter projected as a multivolume sea atlas.[15] To these, he added a large number of newly engraved maps, many of which were copied from Dutch prototypes. Seller had become so overextended by 1677 that he was forced into partnership with William Fisher, John Thornton, John Colson, and James Atkinson. The relationship was dissolved after only two years, with Fisher and Thornton retaining most of the assets.

In 1678, Moses Pitt proposed to publish an eleven-volume *English Atlas* of the world. The atlas, modeled on the earlier multivolume works of Blaeu and Jansson, was published in association with Jansson's heirs. With few exceptions, the maps were to be printed from Jansson's old plates brought from Amsterdam and adapted for the project.[16] Pitt intended to print nine hundred pages of text plus six hundred maps and plates. Four volumes appeared between 1680 and 1683 before he was forced to liquidate much of his stock. Work never resumed, and Pitt filed for bankruptcy and was arrested for debt in 1689. In truth, no English publisher had the skill or resources to produce an atlas on the scale of those that regularly appeared on the Amsterdam market. The few volumes that were published, however, rank among the most significant achievements in seventeenth-century English cartography.

By the 1680s, London publishers had largely abandoned multivolume projects, which had proved to be unsuccessful, and concentrated on less expensive, separately issued maps, part of a strategy to husband their limited financial resources. Publishers frequently reduced costs by forming partnerships for a given project and also by acting as retailers. Engravers were poorly paid, and much of the work such as coloring was done by apprentices. Thus, the development of a lucrative map trade in London depended on mapsellers' abilities to channel the talents and resources of several specialists to create new maps.

The remarkably complete publication history of Joel Gascoyne's *A New Map of the Country of Carolina*, 1682, frequently called the Second Lords Proprietors Map, illustrates the various steps in the process of map production.[17] It began when the Lords Proprietors requested new surveys from which a draft suitable for engraving could be prepared. It is likely that *A New Map of the Country of Carolina* was based on several sources.[18] After the material arrived in London, the proprietors commissioned Gascoyne, the cartographer, to synthesize the data and compile a master draft from which an engraving could be made.[19]

An independent engraver was subcontracted to transfer the pattern map to a copperplate for printing. Early in the century, English engravers usually retained ownership of their plates, but by the 1670s, plates were almost always engraved by order of a publisher who financed and supervised all aspects of production, including purchasing the copperplate and paper and hiring the cartographer and engraver.[20] Once the plate was approved, it was delivered to the printer to make the impressions. Samuel Wilson, secretary to the proprietors, recorded the production costs of *A New Map of the Country of Carolina*. He authorized two payments "For a Plate of yᵉ Map of Carolina & printing 2000 £2.3" and "To Pᵈ Mʳ. Gascoyne for the Map of Carolina £11" on May 10, 1673.[21]

The plate bears the imprint *Sold by Joel Gascoyne at the Signe of the Plat nere Wapping old Stayres. And by Robert Greene at the Rose and Crowne in ye middle of Budge Row*, indicating that Gascoyne and Greene were the distributors.[22] Shortly after it was completed, the plate was extensively revised, probably because a written account of a journey to the interior of the colony made by Dr. Henry Woodward, chief Indian agent for the Carolina proprietors, had become available.[23] *(fig. 282)* To summarize, Gascoyne was the cartographer of *A New Map of the Country of Carolina*. The engraver and printer have not been identified, but the payments Wilson approved for engraving and printing the map suggest that the two processes took place on the same premises. Because Gascoyne is known to have engraved some of his own manuscript drafts, it is possible that the plate was his work.[24] The proprietors acted as the publishers and Gascoyne and Robert Greene were the retailers. Often publishers functioned as sellers; occasionally, engravers acted as both publishers and sellers.[25]

The aesthetic quality of English maps did not equal that of those published in the Netherlands. Even the best London engravers lacked the proficiency achieved by their Dutch counterparts and, once printed, the addition of hand color to the black-and-white impressions was less artfully applied. Moreover, the engravers' skills varied greatly, as the maps in the Custis Atlas show. In general, the technical quality of Lea's maps was frequently inferior to those of competitors such as John Thornton and Robert Morden, particularly during his early years when he employed hack engravers such as Sutton Nicholls. Lea's best maps were made in collaboration with Herman Moll, whose work exhibits a polish seldom encountered in that of his contemporaries. Although Lea frequently employed two or more engravers simultaneously, standard practice among London publishers, by 1690 Moll was his engraver of choice.[26]

Decisions concerning decorative details such as costumed figures, cartouches, and coats of arms were usually left to the engravers, who often borrowed design elements

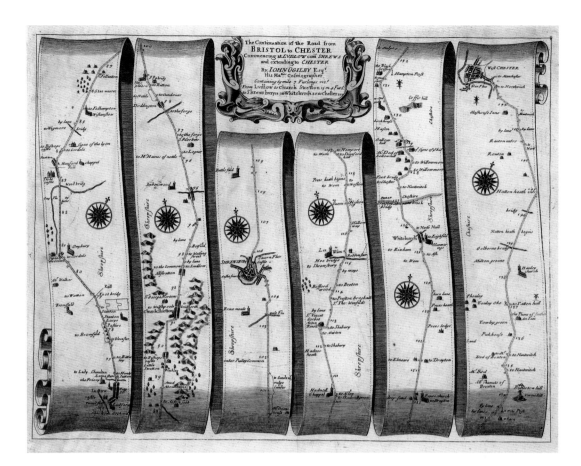

281 *The Continuation of the Road from Bristol to Chester,* by John Ogilby, London, 1675, black-and-white line engraving with modern color. Courtesy, Tessa and Al Louer.

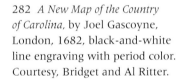

282 *A New Map of the Country of Carolina,* by Joel Gascoyne, London, 1682, black-and-white line engraving with period color. Courtesy, Bridget and Al Ritter.

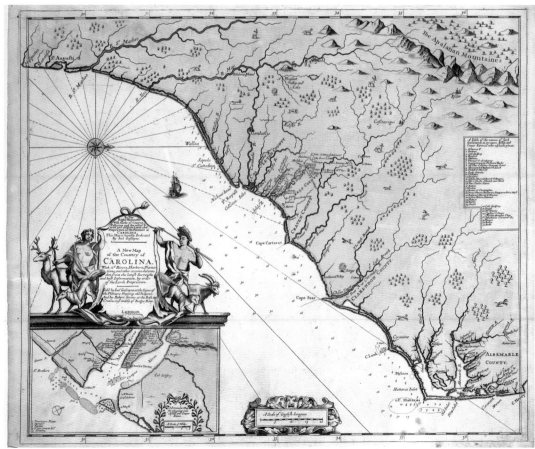

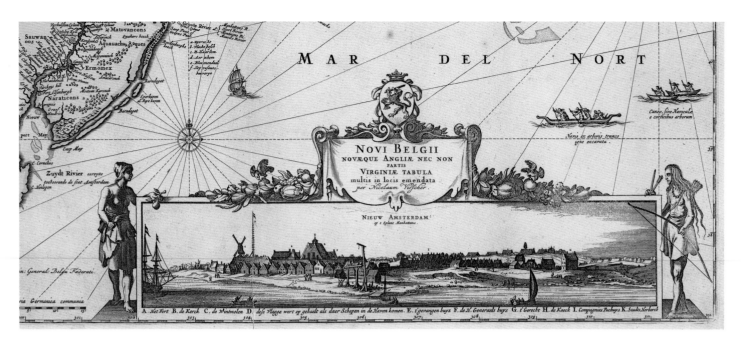

283 Detail of the cartouche from *Novi Belgii Novæque Angliæ Nec Non Partis Virginæ Tabula,* by Nicholas Visscher, Amsterdam, ca. 1684, black-and-white line engraving with period color. 1968-129. (Cat. 11)

from continental maps. For example, the cartouche on Nicholas Visscher's *Novi Belgii Novæque Angliæ (fig. 283)* provided the prototype for two English maps in the Custis Atlas. In each case, Native Americans flank the cartouche. On the left is a female with a pipe while a male on the right holds a bow. *(figs. 284 and 285)*

Color was applied in the publisher's shop. John Garrett included the words "printed, coloured and sold by John Garrett" in the imprint of many of his plates.[27] Virtually all of Lea's maps were sold with outline color only. The Dutch maps in the Custis Atlas are colored identically to those Lea published, suggesting that he imported them from Amsterdam uncolored to be finished in his shop. If the client was important or the item particularly expensive, the publisher probably applied the color himself. Samuel Pepys viewed a pair of globes in Joseph Moxon's dining room, "so painted as I never saw in my life, and nobly done . . . by his own hand."[28] Lea stained and colored maps for Pepys, who had a high regard for his work and judgment.[29]

Lea would have learned the technique of hand coloring during his apprenticeship to Robert Morden, a leading map and globe publisher in London, which began on April 19, 1675. By 1683, Lea was publishing under his own name at the "Atlas and Hercules in the Poultry over against the old Jury [the Old Jewry]." Lea no doubt used "Atlas and Hercules," figures derived from classical mythology, to symbol-

ize his abilities as a globemaker. *(fig. 286)* The shop was ideally situated near the Royal Exchange, the City's stock exchange, and numerous coffeehouses where much of the intellectual and business life of London took place. More than twenty book-, print-, and mapsellers had shops in the neighborhood.[30] *(fig. 287)*

Lea's Poultry address appeared for the first time on two pairs of terrestrial and celestial globes, one ten and the other fifteen inches in diameter.[31] *(fig. 288)* They were advertised in the *Term Catalogues* in June 1683 with the imprint "Sold by R. Morden at the Atlas in *Cornhill;* W. Berry at the Globe near *Charing Cross;* and P. Lea at the Atlas and Hercules in the *Poultrey.*"[32] *(figs. 289 and 290)* Morden, Lea's former master, and William Berry, two of the better known dealers in London, were frequent collaborators. Bringing Lea into the partnership on this project decreased the capital each invested to produce the globes and gave the young mapseller the prestige of being associated with more established members of the trade.

In 1685, Lea published a small sales catalog that shows he continued to sell globes in the early years of his business.[33] The catalog included examples of fifteen, ten, and four inches in diameter. Two years later, he added "A Terrestrial Globe 25 inches in diameter," probably Joseph Moxon's, which the latter sold as a pair with a celestial for twenty pounds.[34] Lea's extensive knowledge of globes was

284 Detail of the cartouche from *A Mapp of Virginia, Maryland, New Jarsey, New York, & New England,* by John Thornton, London, 1679 (originally published ca. 1678), black-and-white line engraving with period outline color. (Custis Atlas Cat. 73)

285 Detail of the cartouche from *A New Chart of the Sea Coast of Newfound land, new Scotland, new England, new Jersey, Virginia, Maryland, Pennsilvania, and part of Carolina,* by John Thornton, London, ca. 1689, black-and-white line engraving. (Custis Atlas Cat. 88)

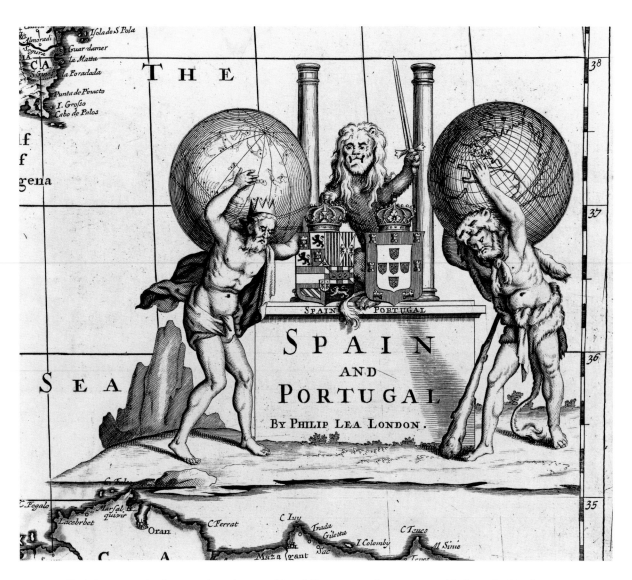

286 Detail of the cartouche from *Spain and Portugal,* by Philip Lea, London, ca. 1690, black-and-white line engraving with period outline color. (Custis Atlas Cat. 40) The design illustrates the name of Lea's shop, with the companion figures of Atlas and Hercules, respectively, supporting celestial and terrestrial globes.

287 *A View of the Royal Exchange London,* by Thomas Bowles, London, 1751, black-and-white line engraving with period color. 1936-723. The name of the commercial thoroughfare known as the Poultry became Cheapside west of the Royal Exchange. Both of Lea's shops were on the left side of this broad street.

acknowledged by Pepys, who noted, "Globes, when and where first invented, and when first here [in England]? Consult Mr. Lee [*sic*] thereon."[35]

Lea also began to publish separate sheet maps. The 1685 catalog listed only eight one-sheet maps that bore his own imprint. By the time he issued a second catalog in 1687, the number of such maps had increased to twenty-three.[36] Many of Lea's maps were collaborations with other publishers. Lea produced a set of four general maps of the continents between 1683 and 1686 in partnership with John Overton. The partners proclaimed that their representation of America (Custis Atlas Cat. 10) was *wholly left out in all Dutch and French Maps.*[37] Lea worked most frequently with the financially troubled Morden. More often than not, Lea ended up as the sole owner of the plates (see Custis Atlas Cats. 12 and 75). He also purchased, revised, and republished the copperplates of other needy or deceased competitors, a common practice in England. As early as 1685, Lea bought some of Ogilby and Morgan's

plates including those for Christopher Saxton's twenty-sheet wall map of England.[38] Morden and Lea apparently purchased an additional quantity of Morgan's stock when he died in 1690.[39]

In May 1685, Morden and Lea, in partnership with John Thornton, announced the publication of a four-sheet *New Map of the English Empire in the Continent of America.*[40] To maximize their profit, one sheet from the set was engraved with its own borders and title so that it could also be sold as a separate map (Custis Atlas Cat. 70). Lea applied the same marketing strategy to a twenty-one-sheet wall map of the world that he acquired from Moxon.[41] Lea continued to sell the map complete, but added borders, individual titles, and his imprint to a number of the sheets and offered them separately. Two examples, *A New Map containing the English Empire* and *A New Map Containing Barbaria,* were bound into the Custis Atlas (Custis Atlas Cats. 62 and 67). The publication history of Moxon's wall map shows why it is difficult to assign precise dates to the states of

289 Printed sheet of uncut globe gores
for the fifteen-inch terrestrial globe,
by Morden, Berry, and Lea, London, 1683,
black-and-white line engraving.
Courtesy, British Library.

288 Detail of a fifteen-inch terrestrial globe, by Morden, Berry, and Lea, London, 1683.
Courtesy, Whipple Museum of the History of Science, Cambridge.

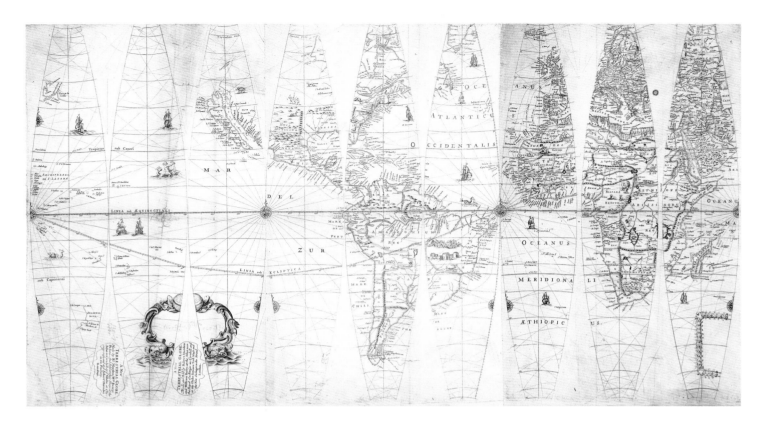

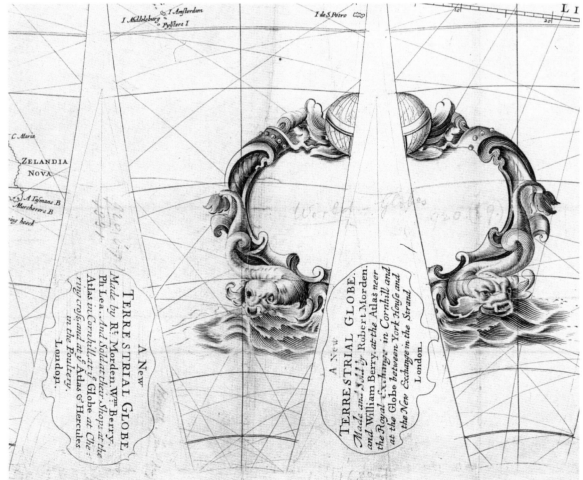

290 Detail from the sheet of uncut globe gores for the fifteen-inch terrestrial globe, by Morden, Berry, and Lea, London, 1683, black-and-white line engraving. Courtesy, British Library. The publisher's imprint, engraved in the void, was designed to be cut and pasted on the assembled globe. This example contains two separate imprints that provided two publishing options. While each was titled *A New Terrestrial Globe*, one was *Made and Sold by Robert Morden. and William Berry*; the other, *Made by R.t Morden. W.m Berry. Ph Lea. And Sold at their Shops.*

many maps. When Moxon sold the plates to Lea, he must have retained an ample supply of sheets because his son, James, was still advertising the twenty-one-sheet map at least five years after Lea acquired the plates.

In 1687, Lea moved his shop to a new location on "Cheapside at the corner of Friday Street," only about three hundred yards west of his old shop on the Poultry. Two years later, he opened a second place of business, a stall in Westminster Hall. In addition to housing the courts of common pleas, king's bench, and chancery, shops and booksellers' stalls were ranged along its walls.[42] *(fig. 291)*

By the late 1680s, the balance of mercantile and political power in Europe had shifted. Louis's military ambitions dramatically enhanced the position of France, and England experienced a widespread economic upturn. In the Glorious Revolution of 1688, a Dutchman ascended the English throne as William III, thereby ending the political if not the economic rivalry between those two countries. No sooner had William assumed power than France declared war on the United Provinces. The onset of the War of the League of Augsburg turned England's attention to the issue that would dominate her foreign policy for the next one hundred and twenty-five years: curbing the power of the French state.

The political threat France posed had a positive effect on the map trade in England. Although Europe was the theater of engagement, the war threatened to become a world conflict and interest in the regions affected forced London publishers to produce a remarkably diverse inventory. The quantity and subject matter of maps advertised in the *London Gazette* and the *Term Catalogues* indicate the enormous increase in demand for maps illustrating the course of the war.[43] Inexpensive separate-sheet maps, miniature atlases, and composite atlases were the order of the day.

This was a period of great activity for Philip Lea.[44] The conflict inspired Lea to publish, by himself or in partnership, a number of single-sheet maps as well as two miniature atlases. The *Hydrographia Gallia,* advertised as "A Pocket Volume of the Sea Coasts of France," was published in partnership with Thornton and Morden in 1694.[45] Shortly thereafter, Lea brought out *Hydrographia Universalis,* a pocket atlas that he described as containing "the sea coasts of the known parts of the world." This work incorporated much of the contents of the *Hydrographia Gallia.*[46] During these years, Lea published new editions of three landmarks of English cartography, Saxton's atlas of England and Wales, Ogilby and Morgan's wall map of Lon-

don, and John Adams's twelve-sheet "distance" map of England and Wales.[47] That Lea was able to acquire the publication rights for such important and lucrative works underscores the flourishing state of his business.

Late in his career, around 1698, Lea published a new sales catalog that ran to twenty-one pages, in which he advertised a wide range of inventory, including many multi- and single-sheet maps, globes, composite and miniature atlases, books on astronomy, mathematics, and geography, prints, playing cards, and mathematical instruments.[48] He offered composite atlases in several formats, such as "The Kingdoms and Countreys in Europe containing 20 Maps," and, more impressively, "The English Atlas, or a Book of Maps of the Empires, Kingdoms and Countreys, in the World, containing 20, 40, 50, or 150 Maps." Some included the printed title page *An Atlas containing ye Best Maps of the severall parts of the World collected by Phil: Lea.*[49] The majority of Lea's sheet maps that have survived exist because they were bound into composite atlases. That Lea apparently did not offer bound collections at the beginning of his career accounts in part for the rarity of early maps with his Poultry imprint.

The most relevant section of Lea's ca. 1698 catalog to the Custis Atlas is the list of one-sheet maps in which approximately seventy-six were itemized geographically by short title. Copies of virtually all of the seventy-six were bound into the Custis Atlas in almost the same order as they were listed in Lea's catalog. The exceptions are the sixteen sea charts at the end of the atlas that Lea did not advertise. Most bear the imprint of John Thornton and were included in the various books of *The English Pilot.* Unlike the other maps in the atlas, they are uncolored.

The Dutch maps Lea imported were invariably of regions such as South America or East Asia where the English had limited commercial or colonial interests. As the increasingly antiquated maps of Blaeu and Jansson disappeared from the market, Lea was forced to patronize a younger generation of Amsterdam mapmakers. Of those, engraver-publisher Frederick de Wit was a particular favorite.[50] From about 1660, de Wit had issued a large number of attractive, if not particularly innovative, single-sheet maps. Probably in the early 1690s, Lea had a London engraver copy some of them. *(fig. 292)* The plagiarisms were practically identical except for English titles and Lea's imprint. *(see fig. 242)* To judge by Lea's ca. 1698 catalog and examined copies of his composite atlases, he does not seem to have traded in the French and Italian maps stocked by other London mapsellers.

In his will, dated February 17, 1700, Lea bequeathed

291 *A Prospect of Westminster Hall,* artist unknown, London, ca. 1690, black-and-white line engraving. Courtesy, British Library. Lea's Westminster stall is in the right foreground.

"one third part of all my Mapps Globes and Copper plates for printing Mapps and Globes" to his wife, Anne, and the remainder in trust for two unmarried daughters and son Philip.[51] His widow continued the business and by 1712 became associated with her son-in-law, Richard Glynne.[52] They relocated to Fleet Street around 1720 and issued new states from Lea's old plates as late as about 1725. Anne Lea was dead by 1730 and a notice of the auction of all her copperplates appeared on August 5 of that year.[53] These plates were later found in the inventories of Thomas Jefferys, Thomas Bowles, and George Willdey. From about 1730, Willdey was selling new states of some of Lea's important maps of America, including *A New Map of New England New York &c., A Map of ye Improved Part of Pensilva-nia,* and *A New Map of Carolina* (Custis Atlas Cats. 70, 71, and 72).

Lea's considerable abilities were as a coordinator and promoter rather than a creator of original maps. Unlike Thornton, who frequently drew and probably engraved some of the maps that bear his imprint, Lea acted almost entirely as a publisher and marketer. He lacked the connections that enabled Thornton to receive commissions to produce quasi-official maps, particularly of America.[54] Despite Lea's success, the quality of his original sheet maps was often low. Nevertheless, his role in the development of the English map trade during the late seventeenth century should not be underestimated. He was perhaps the most financially successful of the London publishers of the

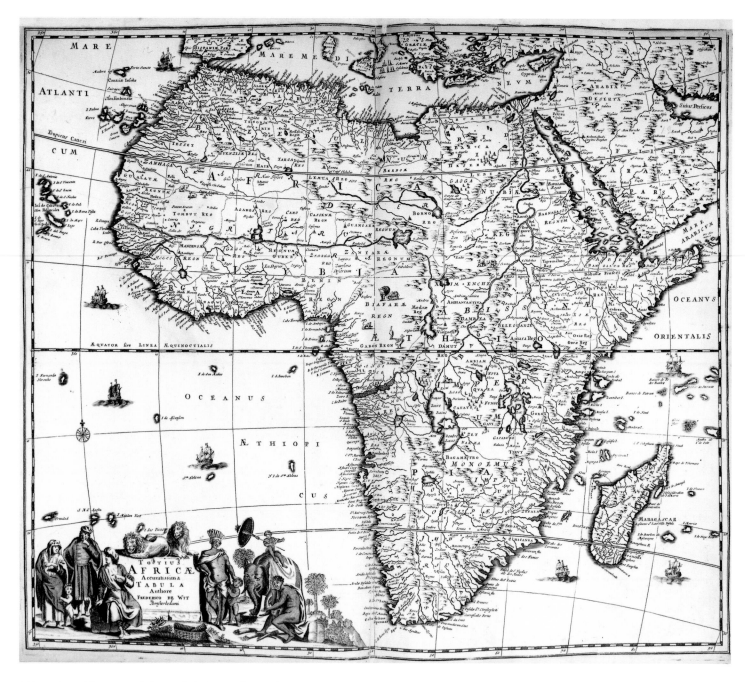

292 *Totius Africæ Accuratissima Tabula,* by Frederick de Wit, Amsterdam, ca. 1680, black-and-white line engraving with period outline color. Courtesy, British Library. This Dutch map was the pattern for Overton and Lea's *A New Mapp of Africa,* 1686. (Custis Atlas Cat. 8)

period, acquiring and preserving many of the old plates of his less successful rivals. Lea was associated with the publication of many fine maps, including a number engraved for him by Herman Moll, whose early career he promoted.

Lea avoided the financial pitfalls experienced by Moses Pitt and John Seller, who had foundered on their ambitious atlas projects. Instead, he devoted himself almost exclusively to the publication of loose sheet maps that could be sold separately or bound. Lea seems to have been one of the few London publishers to offer comprehensive composite atlases. Despite their limitations, they were the most up-to-date world atlases assembled in England in the 1690s. Although his operation paled by comparison to the leading Dutch publishers of the previous generation, Lea must have offered one of the largest selections of English maps found in any shop in London.

NOTES

1. Blaeu's *Atlas Major,* the most ambitious atlas published in the seventeenth century, contained a suite of maps of America that were obsolete by the time the work was introduced in 1662. For instance, the map of Virginia, *Nova Virginia Tabula,* was a derivative of Capt. John Smith's published 50 years earlier. See Cat. 5.

2. Philip von Zesen, *Beschreibung der Stadt Amsterdam,* quoted in Dr. Ir. C. Koeman, *Joan Blaeu and his Grand Atlas* (Amsterdam, 1970), pp. 17–18.

3. Because Dutch mapmakers could have letterpresses on their premises, their maps usually contained explanatory text printed on the reverse, an advantage not available in England where only members of the Stationer's Company were permitted to own presses. If nonmembers wanted to add letterpress text to a map or atlas, they had to pay a stationer. Griffiths, *The Print in Stuart Britain,* pp. 15, 17.

4. Skelton, *County Atlases,* p. 243.

5. Griffiths, *The Print in Stuart Britain,* p. 19.

6. Goss, *Mapmaker's Art,* p. 186. As early as 1663, Colbert had instructed officials in the provinces to "survey the condition of France." Nicholas Sanson, the government's first official cartographer, was to receive all the data. Konvitz, *Cartography in France,* p. 2.

7. Peter Whitefield, *The Mapping of the Heavens* (London, 1995), p. 94.

8. Latham and Matthews, eds., *Diary of Pepys,* X, p. 362.

9. R. A. Skelton, "The Royal Map Collection of England," *Imago Mundi,* XIII (1956), p. 181. A manuscript catalog of the royal map collection compiled shortly after the Restoration is printed *ibid.,* pp. 181–183.

10. Wallis, "Geographie is Better than Divinitie," p. 37.

11. Black, ed., *Blathwayt Atlas,* p. 9.

12. Fire brigade officer Jan van der Heiden stated that "the large printing works with everything in it was damaged to such an extent that even the copper-plates stacked in the far corners melted like lead in the flames and others were completely scorched. A large number of very important plates were lost there." Total damage was estimated at 382,000 guilders. Koeman, *Joan Blaeu,* p. 95.

13. Ogilby's *America* was a translation of Arnoldus Montanus, *De Nieuwe en Onbekende Weereld,* Amsterdam, 1671, containing 54 maps printed from Montanus's plates. Ogilby added accounts of several English colonies. Later issues contained a few original maps such as *A New Description of Carolina by Order of the Lords Proprietors* (Cat. 13) that were based on English surveys.

14. Phillips, comp., *List of Geographical Atlases,* entry 2907; Catherine Delano-Smith and Roger P. Kain, *English Maps: A History* (Toronto, 1999), pp. 168–172.

15. Seller acquired 63 old copperplates that originally had been made for a counterfeit edition of Blaeu's sea atlas, *Het Licht Der Zeevaart,* 1608.

Verner estimated that if Seller had not reused old Dutch copperplates, the cost of preparing from scratch the 25 plates for *The English Pilot Book One,* 1671, would have run to more than £230. He would have had to sell over 400 copies of the book to break even on the cost of the plates alone. Verner, *Carto-Bibliographical Study of The English Pilot The Fourth Book,* p. 70.

16. Phillips, comp., *List of Geographical Atlases,* entry 2831; Skelton, *County Atlases,* p. 249. For a detailed account of the preparation and publication of Pitt's atlas, see Rostenberg, "Moses Pitt," pp. 2–8.

17. Cumming, *Southeast in Early Maps,* entry 92; Black, ed., *Blathwayt Atlas,* map 23. For Gascoyne, see W. Ravenhill, "Joel Gascoyne, a pioneer of large-scale county mapping," *Imago Mundi,* XXVI (1972), pp. 60–69.

18. The depiction of the vicinity of Charleston on both the main map and the inset was based on surveys made by Maurice Mathews, surveyor general of Carolina. An English pilot must have supplied the numerous depth soundings along the coast. Before Gov. Henry Wilkinson was to depart for Carolina, the Lords Proprietors instructed him in 1681 "to send home the mapp of the Country [a]mended by your owne or frds: experience." Cumming, *Southeast in Early Maps,* entry 92. Wilkinson never came to America, but the language in the proprietors' instructions suggests that a map in some form already existed in Carolina. The information was sent to London within the year.

19. Gascoyne had been apprenticed to John Thornton and entered business on his own in 1676. Both were chartmakers of the so-called "Thames School." Black, ed., *Blathwayt Atlas,* pp. 15–22.

20. The capital (about £5) needed to buy a rolling press was considerable, and the investment in copperplates and paper was expensive. Griffiths, *The Print in Stuart Britain,* p. 16. It has been estimated that a publisher would have needed to sell 400 copies of a one-sheet map to cover production costs of about £20 before making a profit.

21. William L. Saunders, coll. and ed., *The Colonial Records of North Carolina,* I, reprint (New York, 1968), p. 344.

22. Black identified three states. The second and third have this imprint. Two lines crudely erased at the end evidently contained the name of a third mapseller. No copies survive of Black's first state with the imprint of all three. *Ibid.,* p. 146.

23. Black, ed., *Blathwayt Atlas,* p. 147.

24. Tyacke, *London Map-Sellers,* p. 145.

25. Tyacke, "Map-sellers and the London map trade," p. 74.

26. Moll engraved at least 9 maps for Lea between 1689 and 1695. Often, Lea as distributor and Moll as engraver published maps jointly. In each case, Lea eventually acquired sole rights to the plates. See Custis Atlas Cat. 22–23.

27. Griffiths, *The Print in Stuart Britain,* p. 29. Griffiths noted that

although maps were colored in the seventeenth century, prints rarely were.

28. Latham and Matthews, eds., *Diaries of Pepys*, IV, p. 302.

29. Wallis, "Geographie is Better than Divinitie," pp. 14–15.

30. Michael Treadwell, "The English Book Trade," in Maccubbin and Hamilton-Phillips, eds., *Age of William III & Mary II*, p. 361.

31. The terrestrial globes were among the earliest, if not the earliest, printed cartographical works on which William Penn's new city of Philadelphia was located. The city had been laid out by Thomas Holme the previous autumn. A copy of Holme's plat map did not arrive in London for printing until Aug. 1683. Irma Corcoran, *Thomas Holme 1624-1695 Surveyor General of Pennsylvania* (Philadelphia, 1992), pp. 113-117, fig. 15.

32. The few surviving globes show that the partners' marketing strategy was more complex. Elly Dekker and Peter van der Krogt, *Globes from the Western World* (London, 1993), plate 30, illustrated a later state of the terrestrial globe with Lea's Cheapside address. They noted that examples are known "with three names, or with combinations of two—Morden and Berry or Morden and Lea." The logical explanation seems to be that these different imprints represent an evolution over time in the partners' relationship. However, the British Lib. has an unassembled partial set of gores for the terrestrial with two cartouches with alternative imprints, one, Morden, Berry, and Lea, and the other, Morden and Berry. The printing plates for the 10- and 15-inch globes were listed in the inventory of Lea's estate: "The two sise of globe plates betweene Wm. Berry and Robt. Mordent valued at £10.0s.0d." Inventory of Lea, p. 319, n. 2.

33. Consisting of four octavo pages, the catalog was appended to Reeve Williams's translation of Claude François Milliet de Chales, *The Elements of Euclid*, published by Lea. Two copies, one in the British Lib. and the other at the College of William and Mary, were examined. Both title pages bear the imprint *London: Printed for Philip Lea, Globemaker, at the Atlas and Hercules in the Poultrey, near Cheapside, 1685*. Both have a frontispiece portrait of Euclid with a second imprint that gives Lea's address as *Cheapside near Friday Street*. Despite the 1685 date on the title page, both copies are a second issue that date no earlier than ca. June 1687. The catalog was continued from the first issue of 1685.

34. In his 1683 *Mechanick Exercises*, Moxon advertised terrestrial and celestial globes of 26, 15, 8, and 6 inches in diameter, plus a 3-inch terrestrial pocket globe. At £20 the pair, the 26-inch globes were priced comparably to the £22 14s 6d that Pepys was quoted for a pair of 26-inch Blaeu globes in Dec. 1687. Stevenson, *Terrestrial and Celestial Globes*, p. 136; Tony Campbell, "A Descriptive Census of Willem Blaeu's Sixty-eight Centimetre Globes," *Imago Mundi*, XXVIII (1976), p. 32.

35. Wallis, "Geographie is Better than Divinitie," pp. 14–15.

36. Lea's 1687 catalog was appended to the end of a one-sheet text titled *Alphabet of America* that was printed to accompany Overton and Lea's *A New Map of America*. See Custis Atlas Cat. Text 9.

37. Custis Atlas Cat. Text 9.

38. Originally published as *Britannia Insularum in Oceano Maximo . . . Anno Dni* 1583, Saxton's map was printed from 20 engraved copperplates. Lea revised the map and published it in several formats. Skelton, *Saxton's Survey of England and Wales*, pp. 13, 20–21.

39. Tyacke, *London Map-Sellers*, p. 124.

40. Although the map was one of the most ambitious published in England in the period and continued on the market until the turn of the century, it survives in just one incomplete copy, in the Bibliothèque Nationale, Paris. For a more detailed description of the map and the individual sheets, see Custis Atlas Cat. 70.

41. Joseph Moxon, the first English specialist in printed sea charts, learned his trade in the Netherlands where his father had worked as a printer. Moxon established himself as a globe and instrument maker and mapseller in London in 1646. Appointed hydrographer to Charles II in 1662, he was elected to the Royal Academy in 1678. One of Moxon's most important accomplishment was as a teacher of the next generation of London mapmakers. His apprentices included his son, James, William Berry, and probably Morden.

42. Lea advertised in the *London Gaz.* using his Westminster Hall address from May 1689 to Jan. 1696. Tyacke, *London Map-Sellers*, entries 165 and 283. A number of loose sheet maps published during those years bear the imprint of both shops. From 1696 until his death in 1700, he operated solely from the Atlas and Hercules.

43. Barber noted that "domestic production reached a peak between 1689 and 1693." "British Cartography," in Maccubbin and Hamilton-Phillips, eds., *Age of William III & Mary II*, p. 99.

44. The Custis Atlas contains a large suite of maps of varying quality relating to the War of the League of Augsburg. Custis Atlas Cats. 21, 22–23, 24, 31, 32, 43, 44, 92, and 97.

45. *Hydrographia Gallia* was advertised in the *London Gaz.* in the early summer of 1694. Tyacke, *London Map-Sellers*, entry 261. It was listed in Lea's ca. 1698 catalog but seems to be quite rare. It is not listed in Phillips, comp., *List of Geographical Atlases*, or the NMM Catalogue.

46. *Hydrographia Universalis* was also in Lea's ca. 1698 catalog. Phillips, comp., *List of Geographical Atlases*, entry 527; NMM Catalogue, entry 382.

47. Saxton's atlas was originally published in 1579. Lea republished it as *All the Shires of England and Wales Described by Christopher Saxton*, ca. 1689, with extensive revisions and new maps. A second edition appeared with the title *The Shires of England and Wales*, ca. 1693. Shirley, *County Atlases*, entries 1, 110, and 112. Ogilby and Morgan's wall map of London, originally published in 1682, was the most significant map of the reconstructed city after the Great Fire. Lea and Morden made extensive alterations to their edition of ca. 1692. The inventory of Lea's estate referred to his interest in "a halfe part of the Greate London with Robt. Morden valued at £15.0s.0d." Howgego, *Printed Maps of London*, entry 33, pp. 14–17. Adams's *Anglia Totius Tabula*, originally published in 1677, was advertised by Lea in the *Term Catalogues*, II, June 1699. Shirley, *Printed Maps of the British Isles*, Adams 1.

48. I wish to thank Ashley Baynton-Williams for supplying the text of this catalog.

49. The ca. 1698 catalog listed the "Title for the English Atlas."

50. Frederick de Wit was an important and prolific publisher. In addition to making maps, de Wit purchased old plates from the defunct firms of Blaeu and Jansson that he published under his own imprint. Koeman, *Atlantes Neerlandici*, III, p. 191.

51. Tyacke, *London Map-Sellers*, p. 120.

52. *Ibid.*, entry 327.

53. *Ibid.*, p. 122.

54. Exceptions are the manuscript maps of Capt. Thomas Phillips published by Lea in 1689 as *A True Survey of the Earl of Donagals Barronie of Enish-owen . . . and Londonderry*. See Custis Atlas Cat. 24.

Glossary

Accuratissima— most accurate

America Meridonalis— South America

America Septentrionalis— North America

Australis— southern

Beschrijving— description

Cartouche— border surrounding printed material such as a title, dedication, imprint, or scale of distances, generally composed of decorative scrollwork, foliate design, cherubs, costumed figures, animals, or scenic elements

Chart— map made specifically to aid in navigation

Compass rose— circular element designed from emanating rhumb lines, generally with a decorative directional arrow indicating north

Composite atlas or atlas factice— bound collection of loose maps compiled to order by the client or mapseller

Delin— drawn

Derivative map— map made by copying the geography from one previously published. A derivative map can vary in size and decoration from its primary source

Edition— some authors have assigned the term "edition" to changes made to a publisher's imprint. They designated geographic or decorative alterations as separate states. We believe that a separate edition should be defined as a direct copy of a map made by cutting a new plate or block. See also "derivative map" and "state"

Excudit— engraved

Gedruckt— printed

Impression— single copy of a map printed from a copperplate

Inset map— smaller separate map contained in its own borders and set within a larger work

Insula or insulæ— island

Issue— all impressions taken from any single state of a copperplate. Subsequent pulls from altered plates (new states) are designated as later issues

Lacus— lake

Margin— uncut paper border surrounding the platemark. Margins were generally trimmed when maps were hung on the walls. Most often, maps removed from atlases still retain their original, uncut margins

Neat line— printed border lines at the outer edge of a map

Nova Belgica— Latin term for the Dutch colonies in America

Norembega— sixteenth-century name for New England and the maritime provinces of Canada

Novus— new

Nunc— now, nowadays

Occidentalis— western

Orientalis— eastern

Outline color— color applied by hand to outline borders or boundaries

Pars— part, for the most part

Paskaert— sea chart

Platemark— depression made in the paper as a result of the pressure created by running the copperplate and dampened paper through a printing press. Platemarks provide a precise dimension for the size of the engraving plate

Prime meridian— meridian from which the longitude of a particular map is measured. In 1884, Greenwich, England, was universally accepted as the point on the globe from which all longitude, both east and west, was measured

Rhumb line— straight lines radiating from the center of compass points that indicate wind direction

Sculpsit— engraved

Separately issued— map published individually and not as part of an atlas or book

Single-sheet map— map printed on one sheet of folio paper

Sinus— bay, gulf

Sive— or

State— any change or alteration made to a copperplate constitutes a separate state. All impressions taken from a plate without alteration belong to a single state. See also "edition"

Tabula— map

Totius— all, entire, total

Zee— sea, ocean

Bibliography

Alexander, Gerald L. "Willdey's enterprising map of North America." *The Magazine Antiques,* LXXXII (1962), pp. 76–77.

Anderson, Fred. *Crucible of War: The Seven Years' War and the Fate of Empire in British North America, 1754–1766.* New York: Alfred A. Knopf, 2000.

Arber, Edward, ed. *Capt. John Smith Works 1608–1631.* London: Archibald Constable & Co., 1895.

——. *Term Catalogues, 1668–1709 A.D.* London: privately printed, 1903–1906.

Babinski, Mark. *Henry Popple's 1733 Map of the British Empire in America.* Garwood, N. J.: Krinder Peak Publications, 1998.

Baldwin, Robert. "Globes as symbols of political and navigational authority." *Map Collector,* LXI (1992).

Barber, Peter. "Necessary and Ornamental: Map Use in England under the Later Stuarts, 1660–1714." *Eighteenth Century Life,* XIV (1990).

Barbour, Philip L. *The Three Worlds of Captain John Smith.* London: Macmillan Co., 1964.

Benes, Peter. *New England Prospect: A Loan Exhibition of Maps at the Currier Gallery of Art, Manchester, New Hampshire.* Boston, Mass.: Boston University Press, 1981.

Black, Jeannette D., ed. *The Blathwayt Atlas.* Providence, R. I.: Brown University Press, 1970.

Blodget, Samuel. *A Prospective-Plan of the Battle near Lake George, on the Eighth Day of September, 1755. With an Explanation thereof; Containing A full, though short, History of that important Affair.* London, 1756.

Bonar Law, Andrew. *The Printed Maps of Ireland 1612-1850.* Dublin: Neptune Gallery, 1997.

Bry, Theodore de. *Grands Voyages.* Part I: *Admiranda Narratio fida tamen, de Commodis et Incolarvm Ritibus Virginiæ.* Frankfurt, 1590.

——. *Grands Voyages.* Part II: *Brevis Narratio Eorum Quæ in Eorum Floridae Americæ Provicia.* Frankfurt, 1591.

——. *Grands Voyages.* Part IV: *Americæ Pars Quarta Insignis & Admiranda Historia.* Frankfurt, 1594.

Burden, Philip D. *The Mapping of North America: A list of printed maps 1511–1670.* Rickmansworth, Eng.: Raleigh Publications, 1996.

Byrd, William. "Report of the Commissioners to Lay Out the Bounds of the Northern Neck." In John Spencer Bassett, ed. *The Writings of "Colonel William Byrd, of Westover in Virginia, Esqr."* New York: Doubleday, Page & Co., 1901.

Campbell. Tony. *Early Maps.* New York: Abbeville Press, 1981.

——. "The Jansson-Visscher Maps of New England." In R. V. Tooley, comp. *The Mapping of America.* London: Holland Press, 1980.

——. "Japan: European printed maps to 1800." *Map Collectors' Circle,* IV (1997).

——. "One Map, two Purposes: Willem Blaeu's second 'West Indische paskaart' of 1630." *Map Collector,* XXX (1985).

——. "The Printed Maps of Barbados." *Map Collectors' Circle,* XXI (1965).

Clayton, Timothy. *The English Print, 1688–1802.* New Haven, Conn.: Yale University Press for the Paul Mellon Centre for Studies in British Art, 1997.

Cohen, Paul E., and Robert T. Augustyn. *Manhattan in Maps, 1527–1995.* New York: Rizzoli, 1997.

Cohn, Ellen R. "Benjamin Franklin, Georges-Louis Le Rouge and the Franklin/Folger Chart of the Gulf Stream." *Imago Mundi,* LII (2000).

Colles, Christopher. *A Survey of the Roads of the United States of America, 1789.* Edited by Walter W. Ristow. Cambridge, Mass.: Belknap Press of Harvard University Press, 1961.

Condon, Thomas J. *New York Beginnings: The Commercial Origins of New Netherland.* New York: New York University Press, 1968.

Corcoran, Irma (Wilma Abigail). *Thomas Holme 1624–1695: Surveyor General of Pennsylvania.* Philadelphia, Pa.: American Philosophical Society, 1992.

Cresswell, Donald H. "Colony to Commonwealth: The Eighteenth Century." In Richard W. Stephenson and Marianne M. McKee, eds. *Virginia in Maps: Four Centuries of Settlement, Growth and Development.* Richmond, Va.: Library of Virginia, 2000.

Cumming, William P. *British Maps of Colonial America.* Chicago: University of Chicago Press, 1974.

——. "Early Maps of the Chesapeake Bay Area: Their Relation to Settlement and Society." In David B. Quinn, ed. *Early Maryland in a Wider World.* Detroit, Mich.: Wayne State University Press, 1982.

——. *Mapping the North Carolina Coast: Sixteenth-Century Cartography and the Roanoke Voyages.* Raleigh, N. C.: Division of Archives and History, North Carolina Department of Cultural Resources, 1988.

——. *The Southeast in Early Maps.* 3rd ed. Revised by Louis De Vorsey, Jr. Chapel Hill, N. C.: University of North Carolina Press, 1998.

Cumming, W. P., S. E. Hellier, D. B. Quinn, and G. Williams. *The Exploration of North America 1630–1776.* New York: G. P. Putnam's Sons, 1974.

Cumming, W. P., R. A. Skelton, and D. B. Quinn. *The Discovery of North America.* New York: American Heritage Press, 1972.

Cumming, William P., and Douglas Marshall. *North America at the Time of the Revolution: A Collection of Eighteenth Century Maps with Introductory Notes.* Part III. Lympne Castle, Kent., Eng.: Harry Margary, 1975.

Cumming, William P., and Helen Wallis. "Popple's Map of the British Empire in North America, 1733." Introduction to Henry Popple, *A Map of the British Empire in America with the French and Spanish Settlements Adjacent Thereto*. Facsimile. Lympne Castle, Kent, Eng.: Harry Margary, 1972.

Deák, Gloria Gilda. *Picturing America, 1497–1899: Prints, Maps, and Drawings Bearing on the New World Discoveries and on the Development of the Territory That Is Now the United States*. Princeton, N. J.: Princeton University Press, 1988.

Delanglez, Jean. "The Sources of the Delisle Map of America, 1703." *Mid-America*, XXV (1943).

Delano-Smith, Catherine, and Roger J. P. Kain. *English Maps: A History*. Toronto: University of Toronto Press, 1999.

De Vorsey, Louis, Jr. "American Indians and the Early Mapping of the Southwest." In William P. Cumming. *The Southeast in Early Maps*. 3rd ed. Revised by Louis De Vorsey, Jr. Chapel Hill, N. C.: University of North Carolina Press, 1998.

——. "Maps in Colonial Promotion: James Edward Oglethorpe's Use of Maps in 'Selling' the Georgia Scheme." *Imago Mundi*, XXXVIII (1986).

——. "Oglethorpe and the Earliest Maps of Georgia." In Phinizy Spalding and Harvey H. Jackson, eds. *Oglethorpe in Perspective: Georgia's Founder after Two Hundred Years*. Tuscaloosa, Ala.: University of Alabama Press, 1989.

Dilke, O. A. W., and Margaret S. Dilke. "Sir Robert Dudley's Contributions to Cartography." *Map Collector*, XIX (1982).

Dunn, Richard S. *Sugar and Slaves: The Rise of the Planter Class in the English West Indies, 1624–1713*. Chapel Hill, N. C.: University of North Carolina Press, 1972.

Elcan, Marcus C., Jr. "Peter Jefferson and Joshua Fry—Mapmakers." *The Iron Worker* (1962).

English Mapping of America, 1675–1715. New York: Mercator Society, New York Public Library, 1986.

Faupel, W. J. "Le Moyne's map of Florida: fantasy and fact." *Map Collector*, MCMXC (1990).

Faupel, W. John. "Appraisal of the Illustrations." Appendix I. In Sarah Lawson. *A Foothold in Florida: The Eye-Witness Account of Four Voyages made by the French to that Region and their attempt at Colonisation, 1562–1568*. East Grinstead, West Sussex, Eng.: Antique Atlas Publications, 1992.

——. "An Appraisal of the Map *Floridae Americae Provinciae*." In Sarah Lawson. *A Foothold in Florida: The Eye-Witness Account of Four Voyages made by the French to that Region and their attempt at Colonisation, 1562–1568*. East Grinstead, West Sussex, Eng.: Antique Atlas Publications, 1992.

Fite, Emerson D., and Archibald Freeman. *A Book of Old Maps Delineating History from the Earliest Days Down to the Close of the Revolutionary War*. 1926. Reprint. New York: Arno Press, 1969.

Foster, James W. "Maps of the First Survey of the Potomac River, 1736–1737." *William and Mary Quarterly*, 2nd Ser., XVIII (1938).

——. "Potomac River Maps of 1737 by Robert Brooke and Others." *William and Mary Quarterly*, 2nd Ser., XVIII (1938).

Fowble, E. McSherry. *Two Centuries of Prints in America, 1680–1880: A Selective Catalogue of the Winterthur Museum Collection*. Charlottesville, Va.: University Press of Virginia, 1987.

French, Josephine, ed. *Tooley's Dictionary of Mapmakers, A–D*. Rev. ed. Tring, Herts, Eng.: Map Collector Publications, 1999.

Fry, Joshua. *The Fry & Jefferson Map of Virginia and Maryland; a facsimile of the first edition in the Tracy W. McGregor Library*. Introduction by Dumas Malone. Princeton, N. J.: published for the Harry Clemons Publication Fund of the University of Virginia, 1950.

Goss, John. *Blaeu's The Grand Atlas of the 17th Century World*. London: Studio Editions, 1990.

Griffiths, Antony. *The Print in Stuart Britain, 1603–1689*. London: British Museum Press, 1998.

Guthorn, Peter J. *American Maps and Map Makers of the Revolution*. Monmouth Beach, N. J.: Philip Freneau Press, 1966.

——. *British Maps of the American Revolution*. Monmouth Beach, N. J.: Philip Freneau Press, 1972.

Harley, J. B. "The bankruptcy of Thomas Jefferys: an episode in the economic history of eighteenth century map-making." *Imago Mundi*, XX (1966).

Hébert, John R. "The Westward Vision: Seventeenth-Century Virginia." In Richard W. Stephenson and Marianne M. McKee, eds. *Virginia in Maps: Four Centuries of Settlement, Growth and Development*. Richmond, Va.: Library of Virginia, 2000.

Harrison, Fairfax. *Landmarks of Old Prince William: A study of origins in Northern Virginia*. Berryville, Va.: Chesapeake Book Co., 1964.

——. "The Virginians on the Ohio and the Mississippi in 1742." *Virginia Magazine of History and Biography*, XXX (1922).

Heidenreich, Conrad E., and Edward H. Dahl. "The French Mapping of North America in the Seventeenth Century." *Map Collector*, XIII (1980).

Henry, John. *The John Henry County Map of Virginia, 1770*. Facsimile. Introduction by Louis B. Wright. Charlottesville, Va.: University Press of Virginia, 1977.

"Henry's Map of Virginia in 1770." *William and Mary Quarterly*, 1st Ser., XIV (1905).

Hicks, Frederick Charles, ed. *Thomas Hutchins, A Topographical Description of Virginia, Pennsylvania, Maryland, and North Carolina, Reprinted from the original edition of 1778*. Cleveland, Ohio: Burrows Brothers Co., 1904.

Howgego, James R. *Printed Maps of London circa 1553–1850*. 2nd ed. Folkestone, Eng.: William Dawson & Sons, 1978.

Howse, Derek, and Billings, Pat, comps. *Handlist of Manuscript Sea Charts and Pilot Books executed before 1700*. London: National Maritime Museum, 1973.

Hughes, Sarah H. *Surveyors and Statesmen: Land Measuring in Colonial Virginia*. Richmond, Va.: Virginia Surveyors Foundation, 1979.

Hulton, Paul. "Images of the New World: Jacques Le Moyne de Morgues and John White." In K. R. Andrews, N. P. Canny, and P. E. H. Hair, eds. *The Westward Enterprise: English activities in Ireland, the Atlantic, and America 1480–1650*. Liverpool, Eng.: Liverpool University Press, 1978.

——. *The Work of Jacques Le Moyne De Morgues: A Huguenot Artist in France, Florida, and England*. London: British Museum Publications, 1977.

Ingram, John. "The English Atlas of John Custis." *Colonial Williamsburg Journal* (1988).

"The John Henry Map of Virginia—1771: John Henry's Letter to Thomas Adams." *Virginia Magazine of History and Biography*, LVIII (1950).

Kahrl, George M. "Captain Robert Stobo." *Virginia Magazine of History and Biography,* XLIX (1941).

Kapp, Capt. Kit S. "The Printed Maps of Jamaica up to 1825." *Map Collectors' Circle,* XLII (1968).

Karrow, Robert W., Jr. *Mapmakers of the Sixteenth Century and Their Maps.* Chicago: Speculum Orbis Press, 1993.

Kemper, Charles E. "Documents Relating to the Boundaries of the Northern Neck from the Originals in the British Public Record Office." *Virginia Magazine of History and Biography,* XXVIII (1920).

Kershaw, Kenneth A. *Early Printed Maps of Canada.* I: *1540–1703.* Ancaster, Ont., Canada: Kershaw Publications, 1993.

Klinefelter, Walter. "Surveyor General Thomas Holme's 'Map of the Improved Part of the Province of Pennsilvania.'" *Winterthur Portfolio,* VI (1970).

Koeman, Dr. Ir. C., comp. and ed. *Atlantes Neerlandici. Bibliography of terrestrial, maritime and celestial atlases and pilot books, published in the Netherlands up to 1880.* Amsterdam: Theatrum Orbis Terrarum, 1967–1985.

——. "Life and Works of Willem Janszoon Blaeu, New Contributions to the Study of Blaeu, Made During the Last Hundred Years." *Imago Mundi,* XXVI (1972).

Krieger, Alex, and David Cobb, eds. *Mapping Boston.* Cambridge, Mass.: MIT Press, 1999.

Krogt, Peter van der, comp. *Koeman's Atlantes Neerlandici.* New ed. Vol. II. 't Goy-Houten, Netherlands: HES & De Graaf Publishers, 2000.

Latham, Robert, and William Matthews, eds. *The Diary of Samuel Pepys: A New and Complete Transcription.* London: Bell & Hyman, 1970–1983.

Lawson, Sarah. *A Foothold in Florida: The Eye-Witness Account of Four Voyages made by the French to that Region and their attempt at Colonisation, 1562–1568.* East Grinstead, West Sussex, Eng.: Antique Atlas Publications, 1992.

LeGear, Clara E., and Walter W. Ristow. "Sixteenth-Century Atlases Presented by Melville Eastham." In Walter W. Ristow, comp. *A La Carte: Selected Papers on Maps and Atlases.* Washington, D. C.: Library of Congress, 1972.

Lindgren, Uta. "Trial and Error in the Mapping of America during the Early Modern Period." In Hans Wolff, ed. *America: Early Maps of the New World.* Munich: Prestel-Verlag, 1992.

Lunny, Robert M. *Early Maps of North America.* Newark, N. J.: New Jersey Historical Society, 1961.

Lynch, James B., Jr. *The Custis Chronicles.* I: *The Years of Migration.* Camden, Me.: Picton Press, 1993.

——. *The Custis Chronicles.* II: *The Virginia Generations.* Camden, Me.: Picton Press, 1997

Maccubbin, Robert B., and Martha Hamilton-Phillips, eds. *The Age of William III & Mary II: Power, Politics, and Patronage, 1688–1702.* Williamsburg, Va.: College of William and Mary, 1989.

McCary, Ben C. *John Smith's Map of Virginia with a Brief Account of its History.* Williamsburg, Va.: Virginia 350th Anniversary Celebration Corporation, 1957.

McCorkle, Barbara B. *America Emergent: An Exhibition of Maps and Atlases in Honor of Alexander O. Vietor.* New Haven, Conn.: Yale University Library, 1985.

——. *New England in Early Printed Maps, 1513 to 1800.* Providence, R. I.: John Carter Brown Library, 2001.

McLaughlin, Glen. *The Mapping of California as an Island: An Illustrated Checklist.* [Saratoga]: California Map Society, 1995.

Malinowski, H. "The Malinowski Collection of Maps of Poland, Part II." *Map Collectors' Circle,* IV (1967).

Martin, Lawrence. "Warner's Map of the Rappahannock and Potomac Rivers." *William and Mary Quarterly,* 2nd Ser., XIX (1939).

Middleton, Arthur Pierce. *Tobacco Coast: A Maritime History of Chesapeake Bay in the Colonial Era.* Newport News, Va.: Mariners' Museum, 1953.

Miller, George J. "The Printing of the Elizabethtown Bill in Chancery." In *Addresses Before the Board of Proprietors of the Eastern Division of New Jersey.* Pamphlet Series No. 1. Perth Amboy, N. J.: n.p., 1942.

Moore, Alexander, ed. *Nairne's Muskhogean Journals: The 1708 Expedition to the Mississippi River.* Jackson, Miss.: University Press of Mississippi, 1988.

Moore, J. N. "'A Map of the Parioch of Tranent': New Aspects of the Cartography of John Adair." *Imago Mundi,* XXXIX (1987).

Moreland, Carl, and David Bannister. *Antique Maps.* London: Phaidon Press, 1983.

Morrison, Russell. "Unidentified Manuscript Map in the Penn-Baltimore Controversy." *The Portolan,* XVIII (1990).

Morrison, Russell, Edward Papenfuse, Nancy Brancucci, and Robert J. J. Janson-La Palme. *On the Map: An Exhibit and Catalogue of Maps Relating to Maryland and the Chesapeake Bay Honoring George Washington at the beginning of the third Century of Washington College at Chestertown, Maryland, February 21–March 6, 1983.* Chestertown, Md.: Washington College, 1983.

Mugridge, Donald H., and Helen F. Conover. *An Album of American Battle Art, 1755–1918.* Washington, D. C.: Government Printing Office, 1947.

Mulkearn, Lois, ed. *A Topographical Description of the Dominions of the United States of America.* Pittsburgh, Pa.: University of Pittsburgh Press, 1949.

National Maritime Museum, Greenwich, Eng. *Catalogue of the Library.* III: *Atlases & Cartography.* London: HMSO, 1971.

Norona, Delf, ed. "Joshua Fry's Report on the Back Settlements of Virginia." *Virginia Magazine of History and Biography,* CVI (1948).

[Ogilby, John]. *The A to Z of Restoration London (The City of London, 1676).* Introductory notes by Ralph Hyde. Lympne Castle, Kent., Eng.: Harry Margary, 1992.

Papenfuse, Edward C., and Joseph M. Coale III. *The Hammond-Harwood House Atlas of Historical Maps of Maryland, 1608–1908.* Baltimore, Md.: Johns Hopkins University Press, 1982.

Pedley, Mary. "Maps, War, and Commerce: Business Correspondence with the London Map Firm of Thomas Jefferys and William Faden." *Imago Mundi,* XLVIII (1976).

——, ed. *The Map trade in the late eighteenth century: Letters to the London map sellers Jefferys and Faden.* Oxford: Voltaire Foundation, 2000.

Pelletier, Monique. "From New France to Louisiana: Politics and Geography." In Steven G. Reinhardt, ed. and trans. *The Sun King: Louis XIV and the New World.* New Orleans, La.: Louisiana Museum Foundation, 1984.

Phillips, Philip Lee. *Virginia Cartography: A Bibliographical Description*. 1896. Reprint. Ann Arbor, Mich.: Arbor Libri Press, 1995.

——, comp. *A List of Geographical Atlases in the Library of Congress*. Vol. I. Washington, D. C.: Government Printing Office, 1909.

——, comp. *A List of Maps of America in the Library of Congress*. Washington, D. C.: Government Printing Office, 1901.

Price, Jacob M. *Perry of London: A Family and a Firm on the Seaborne Frontier, 1615–1744*. Cambridge, Mass.: Harvard University Press, 1972.

Pritchard, Margaret Beck. "Maps as objects of material culture." *The Magazine Antiques*, CLIX (2001).

Ravenhill, W. "Joel Gascoyne, a pioneer of large-scale mapping." *Imago Mundi*, XXVI (1972).

Reinhartz, Dennis. "Herman Moll Geographer: An Early Eighteenth-Century European View of the American Southwest." In Dennis Reinhartz and Charles C. Colley, eds. *The Mapping of the American Southwest*. College Station, Tex.: Texas A & M University Press, 1987.

Reps, John W. *Tidewater Towns: City Planning in Colonial Virginia and Maryland*. Williamsburg, Va.: Colonial Williamsburg Foundation, 1972.

Resende, Maria Teresa. *Cartographia impressa dos sécolos XVI e XVII: imagens de Portugal e ilhas atlânticas*. Porto, Portugal: Comissão Nacional, 1994.

Ristow, Walter W. *American Maps and Mapmakers: Commercial Cartography in the Nineteenth Century*. Detroit, Mich.: Wayne State University Press, 1985.

——. "Captain John Smith's Map of Virginia." In Walter W. Ristow, comp. *A La Carte: Selected Papers on Maps and Atlases*. Washington, D. C.: Library of Congress, 1972.

——. "Early Cartography of Virginia's Northern Neck." *The Portolan*, I (1984).

Rubin, Rehav. *Image and Reality: Jerusalem in Maps and Views*. Jerusalem: Hebrew University Press, 1999.

Sanchez-Saavedra, E. M. *A Description of the Country: Virginia's Cartographers and Their Maps, 1607–1881*. Richmond, Va.: Virginia State Library, 1975.

Schilder, Gunther, and Jan van Bracht. "New light on the mapping of New Netherland." In Joan Vinckeboons, *The Origins of New York*. Zurich: Editions Seefelt, 1988.

Schwartz, Seymour I. *The French and Indian War, 1754–1763: The Imperial Struggle for North America*. New York: Simon & Schuster, 1994.

Schwartz, Seymour I., and Ralph E. Ehrenberg. *The Mapping of America*. New York: Harry N. Abrams, Inc., 1980.

Sellers, John R., and Patricia Molen van Ee, comps. *Maps and Charts of North America and the West Indies, 1750–1789*. Washington, D. C.: Library of Congress, 1981.

Shadwell, Wendy. *American Printmaking: The First 150 Years*. New York: Museum of Graphic Art, 1969.

Shirley, Rodney W. *Early Printed Maps of the British Isles: A Bibliography, 1477–1650*. Rev. ed. London: Holland Press, 1980.

——. *The Mapping of the World: Early Printed World Maps 1472–1700*. London: Holland Press, 1983.

——. "The maritime maps and atlases of Seller, Thornton, and Mount & Page." *Map Collector*, LXXIII (1995).

——. *Printed Maps of the British Isles, 1650–1750*. Tring, Herts, Eng.: Map Collector Publications, 1988.

Simpson, Alan. *The Mysteries of the "Frenchman's Map" of Williamsburg, Virginia*. Williamsburg, Va.: Colonial Williamsburg Foundation, 1984.

Simpson, Allen. "John Adair, cartographer, and Sir Robert Sibbald's Scottish Atlas." *Map Collector*, LXII (1993).

Skelton, R. A. *Saxton's Survey of England and Wales with a facsimile of Saxton's wall-map of 1583*. Amsterdam: N. Israel, 1974.

——, comp. *County Atlases of the British Isles 1579–1793*. London: Carta Press, 1970.

Snyder, John P. *The Mapping of New Jersey: The Men and the Art*. New Brunswick, N. J.: Rutgers University Press, 1973.

Snyder, Martin P. *City of Independence: Views of Philadelphia Before 1800*. New York: Praeger Publishers, 1975.

Stephenson, Richard W., and Marianne M. McKee, eds. *Virginia in Maps: Four Centuries of Settlement, Growth and Development*. Richmond, Va.: Library of Virginia, 2000.

Stevens, Henry, and Roland Tree. "Competitive Cartography." In R. V. Tooley, comp. *The Mapping of America*. London: Holland Press, 1980.

Stokes, I. N. Phelps. *The Iconography of Manhattan Island, 1498–1909. Compiled from Original Sources and Illustrated by Photo-intaglio Reproductions of Important Maps, Plans, Views and Documents in Public and Private Collections*. Vol. I. New York: R. H. Dodd, 1915.

Stokes, I. N. Phelps, and Daniel C. Haskell. *American Historical Prints: Early Views of America Cities, etc. from the Phelps Stokes and Other Collections*. New York: New York Public Library, 1933.

Suárez, Thomas. *Shedding the Veil: Mapping the European Discovery of America and the World*. Singapore: World Scientific Publishing Co., 1992.

Swem, Earl G., comp. *Maps Relating to Virginia in the Virginia State Library and other Departments of the Commonwealth*. Richmond, Va.: Commonwealth of Virginia, 1914.

Tinling, Marion, ed. *The Correspondence of the Three William Byrds of Westover, Virginia, 1684–1776*. Vol. II. Charlottesville, Va.: University Press of Virginia, 1977.

Tooley, R. V. "California as an Island: A Geographical misconception illustrated by 100 examples from 1625 to 1770." In R. V. Tooley, comp. *The Mapping of America*. London: Holland Press, 1980.

——. "Early Maps of Australia, the Dutch period." *Map Collectors' Circle*, XXIII (1965).

——. "Identification of the Maps of America in the various editions of the Theatrum of Ortelius." In R. V. Tooley, comp. *The Mapping of America*. London: Holland Press, 1980.

——. "Maps of Africa, a selection." Parts 1 and 2. *Map Collectors' Circle*, V (1968).

——, comp. *The Mapping of America*. London: Holland Press, 1980.

Tyacke, Sarah. *London Map-Sellers 1660–1720: A collection of advertisements for maps placed in the* London Gazette *1668–1719 with biographical notes on the map-sellers*. Tring, Herts, Eng.: Map Collector Publications, 1978.

——. "Map-sellers and the London map trade, c. 1650–1710." In Helen Wallis and Sarah Tyacke, eds. *My Head Is A Map: Essays*

& Memoirs in honour of R. V. Tooley. London: Francis Edwards and Carta Press, 1973.

Van Eerde, Katherine S. *John Ogilby and the Taste of His Times.* Folkestone, Kent, Eng.: William Dawson & Sons, 1976.

Verner, Coolie. *A Carto-Bibliographical Study of The English Pilot The Fourth Book with Special Reference to the Charts of Virginia.* Charlottesville, Va.: University Press of Virginia, 1960.

——. "Engraved title-plates for the folio atlases of John Seller." In Helen Wallis and Sarah Tyacke, eds. *My Head Is A Map: Essays & Memoirs in honour of R. V. Tooley.* London: Francis Edwards and Carta Press, 1973.

——. "The Fry and Jefferson map." *Imago Mundi,* XXI (1967).

——. *A Further Checklist of the Separate Editions of Jefferson's Notes on the State of Virginia.* Charlottesville, Va.: Bibliographical Society of the University of Virginia, 1950.

——. "John Seller and the Chart Trade in Seventeenth Century England." In Norman J. Thrower, ed. *The Compleat Plattmaker: Essays on Chart, Map, and Globe Making in England in the Seventeenth and Eighteenth Centuries.* Berkeley, Calif.: University of California Press, 1978.

——. "The Maps and Plats Appearing with the Several Editions of Mr. Jefferson's 'Notes on the State of Virginia.'" *Virginia Magazine of History and Biography,* LIX (1951).

——. "Mr. Jefferson's Map." *Imago Mundi,* XIV (1959).

——. "Smith's *Virginia* and its Derivatives: A Carto-Bibliographical Study of the Diffusion of Geographical Knowledge." In R. V. Tooley, comp. *The Mapping of America.* London: Holland Press, 1980.

——, comp. *The English Pilot The Fourth Book.* Amsterdam: Theatrum Orbis Terrarum, 1967.

Vries, Dirk de. "Dutch Cartography." In Robert B. Maccubbin and Martha Hamilton-Phillips, eds. *The Age of William III & Mary II: Power, Politics, and Patronage, 1688–1702.* Williamsburg, Va.: College of William and Mary, 1989.

Wainwright, Nicholas B. "Tale of a Runaway Cape: The Penn-Baltimore Agreement of 1732." *Pennsylvania Magazine of History and Biography,* LXXXVI (1963).

Wallis, Helen. *The American War of Independence, 1775–83: A commemorative exhibition organized by the Map Library and the Department of Manuscripts of the British Library Reference Division.* London: British Museum Publications for the British Library, 1975.

——. "Geographie Is Better than Divinitie: Maps, Globes, and Geography in the Days of Samuel Pepys." In Norman J. Thrower, ed. *The Compleat Plattmaker: Essays on Chart, Map, and Globe Making in England in the Seventeenth and Eighteenth Centuries.* Berkeley, Calif.: University of California Press, 1978.

——. *Raleigh and Roanoke: The First English Colony in America, 1584–1590.* Raleigh, N. C.: North Carolina Department of Cultural Resources, 1985.

Wallis, Helen, and Sarah Tyacke, eds. *My Head Is A Map: Essays & Memoirs in honour of R. V. Tooley.* London: Francis Edwards and Carta Press, 1973.

Walter, Lutz, ed. *Japan: A Cartographic Vision. European Printed Maps from the Early 16th to the 19th Century.* New York: Prestel-Verlag, 1994.

Weinreb & Douwma Ltd. Sale catalogue 17: *The British Isles Part 1.* London: Weinreb & Douwma Ltd., 1977.

Weinreb & Douwma Ltd. Sale catalogue 19: *The British Isles Part 2.* London: Weinreb & Douwma Ltd., 1977.

Wheat, James Clements, and Christian F. Brun. *Maps and Charts Published in America before 1800: A Bibliography.* New Haven, Conn.: Yale University Press, 1969.

Wolff, Hans, ed. *America: Early Maps of the New World.* Munich: Prestel-Verlag, 1992.

The World Encompassed: An Exhibition of the History of Maps Held at the Baltimore Museum of Art, October 7 to November 23, 1952. Baltimore, Md.: Trustees of the Walters Art Gallery, 1952.

Worms, Laurence. "Mapsellers at the Royal Exchange. Part Two: 1666 to 1714." *Map Collector,* XXXV (1986).

——. "Thomas Kitchin's 'Journey of life': Hydrographer to George III, mapmaker and engraver." Part 1. *Map Collector,* LXII (1993).

Zacharakis, Christos G. *A Catalogue of Printed Maps of Greece, 1477–1800.* Nicosia, Cyprus: A. G. Leventis Foundation, 1982.

Index

Bold numbers refer to illustrations.

Delaware Indians. *See* Leni-Lenape Indians

Delisle, Claude, 110

Delisle, Guillaume, 19, 110, 118, 120, 121, 123, 124, 136. See also *Atlas Geographique et Universel; Carte de la Louisiane et du Cours du Mississipi; Carte du Canada ou de la Nouvelle France; Carte du Mexique et de la Floride*

Dell' Arcano del Mare (Dudley), 80

Delmarva Peninsula, 70, 74, 80, 86, 88, 130, 232

De Nieuwe en Onbekende Weereld (Montanus), 411

Denmark, 336, 337

De Ruesta, Sebastian, 380

Des Barres, Joseph Frederick Wallet, 28, 265, 266, 289. See also *Atlantic Neptune; Chart of the Coast of New York, New Jersey, Pensilvania, Maryland, Virginia, North Carolina; Sketch of the Operations Before Charlestown the Capital of South Carolina*

Description of New England, A (Smith), 72

Desnos, Louis Charles, 282, 285

De Soto, Hernando. *See* Soto, Hernando de

Destouches, Charles-René-Dominique Sochet, Chevalier, 276

De Vaugondy, Robert, 159, 260. See also *Carte de la Virginie et du Maryland; Carte des Pays connus sous le nom de Canada; Carte du Canada et des Etats-Unis*

De Wit, Frederick, 324, 325, 336, 337, 338, 351, 408, 412. See also *Accuratissima Galliae Tabula; Accuratissima totius Asiæ Tabula Recens Emendata; Accurratissima Totius Hispaniae Portugalliaeq; Dania Regnum; Nova et prae caeteris aliss Correcta Germaniae Tabula; Nova Persiæ Aermeniæ Natoliæ et Arabiæ; Novissima et accuratissima XVII Provinciarum Germaniæ Inferioris Tabula; Regni Poloniæ et Ducatus Lithuaniæ Volinæ, Podoliæ, Ukraniæ Prussiæ et Curlandiæ; Totius Africæ Accuratissima Tabula*

DeWitt, Simeon, 301, 302

Diamant, Lincoln, 247

Dieskau, Marshal Ludwig August, Baron, 166

Dinwiddie, Lt. Gov. Robert, 24, 152, 157, 160, 171

Dixon, Jeremiah, 10, 132

Dobbs, Gov. Arthur, 52; portrait of, **51**

Dodsley, Robert, 175

Dominions of Empire of ye Grand Signor of the Turkes in Europe in Asia & in Africa, The (Lea), 347

Dongan, Gov. Thomas, 8

Douglass, William, 22, 177, 179; map of New England, 177. See also *Summary, Historical and Political, of the first Planting, progressive Improvement, and present State of the British Settlements in North America*

Dover and the Downes (Lea), 332

"Down Survey" (Petty), 335, 367

Draught of the Cherokee Country, A (Timberlake), 190–193, **191**

Dudley, Sir Robert, 80. See also *Carta particolare della Virginia Vecchia è Nuova; Dell' Arcano del Mare*

Dunk, George Montagu, Earl of Halifax, 21, 156, 160, 170, 198

Dunn, Richard S., 128

Duquesne, Marquis, 24, 152

Durell, Lt. Philip, 143. See also *Plan of the Harbour, Town and Forts of Porto Bello*

Dury, A., 215

Dutch East India Company, 2, 74, 77

Dutch West India Company, 2, 8, 77, 79, 86, 102

East India Company, 237–238

East Part of the River Thames &c., The (Lea), 332

Eliot, J. B., 260, 299. See also *Carte du Théatre de la Guerre Actuel Entre les Anglais et les Treize Colonies Unies de l' Amerique Septentrionale*

Elizabeth I, Queen of England, 61

Elizabethtown, N. J., 9, 150

Elizabethtown Map (Alexander and Evans), **11**, 150, **151**

Elizabeth Town Point, 274, **275**

England: alliances with Native Americans, 14, 18, 21, 26, 116, 123, 152, 166, 190; colonizes North America, 1, 2–3, 14, 59, 61; and conflicts with Native Americans, 190, 193, 230; and forts in Ohio Territory, 21, 24, 26, 152, 157, 160, 164, 166, 190; explorers for, 1, 68, 72, 77, 80; land claims mapped, 21, 98, 136–137, 140, 170–171, 172, 174, 183; land claims mapped by Moll, 19, 114, 123–124; and map trade, 38, 318, 393, 396, 397, 398–400, 408, 409; and map trade with France, 40, 41, 260; and map trade with Netherlands, 337, 343, 354, 383, 393, 396, 400, 408; maps of, 329–333; and Mississippi Valley, 118, 123–124; and Netherlands, 3, 8, 11, 86; and Ohio Territory, 14, 18, 21, 123, 152, 156, 171, 172; and Spain, 98–99, 126, 136, 143, 144; and trade, 2, 8, 11, 13–14, 21, 123, 143, 195, 197. *See also* American Revolution; Boundaries; French and Indian War; War of the League of Augsburg

English Atlas (Pitt), 333, 400

English Pilot, The, 399, 408

English Pilot The Fifth Book, 386

English Pilot The First Book, 385, 411

English Pilot The Fourth Book, The, 102, 105, 195, 376, 379, 380, 382

English Pilot The Third Book, 385, 388, 393

Epitome of Sr William Petty's Large Survey of Ireland, An (Lea), 333, 335

Erskine, Robert, 301, 302

Esnauts and Rapilly, 282. See also *Carte de la Partie de la Virginie ou L' Armée Combinée de France & des États-Unis de L' Amérique a fait prisonniere l' Armée Anglaise*

Essay du cours de l' Oyo avec les Forts François et Anglois (Le Rouge), 160–163, **160–161;** detail of, **163**

Evropam sive Celticam Veterem (Ortelius), 324

Evans, Lewis, 10, 40, 150, 172, 174, 175; and N. J.-N. Y. boundary, 214; maps of, used by others, 230, 231; sources used by, 22, 159, 172, 174. See also *Analysis; General Map of the Middle British Colonies; Geographical, Historical, Political, Philosophical and Mechanical Essays; Map of Pennsylvania, New-Jersey, New-York, and the three Delaware Counties*

Evelyn, John, 398

Exact View of the Late Battle at Charlestown June 17th 1775, An (Romans), **246**

Explanation of the Magnetic Atlas, An (Churchman), 232

Faden, William, 219, 220, 223, 306; in business with Jefferys, 40, 219, 223, 240, 242; as engraver, 215, 220, 250, 252, 262; and maps of battles, 32, 41, 242, 250, 255, 260, 274; as publisher, 32, 215, 240, 242, 255, 256, 274, 290; and trade with France, 41, 260. See also *Atlas of Battles of the American Revolution; North American Atlas; Province of New Jersey*

Fage, Edward, 242, 266, 286, 290, 292. See also *Plan of the Posts of York and Gloucester in the Province of Virginia*

Fairfax, Thomas, Lord, 40, 146, 149, 156

Fairfax, William, 149

Far East: search for passage to, 68, 74, 77, 348

Fauquier, Lt. Gov. Francis, 193

Fenwick, John, 9, 220

Ferne, John, 46

Finland, 2, 8

Fisher, William, 102, 379; and consortium, 376, 379, 385, 388, 391, 400; and Mount, 382; and Thornton, 102, 376, 379, 382, 400

Fitch, Gov. Thomas, 198

Fithian, Philip Vickers, 117

Fitzhugh, William, 46

Five Nations. *See* Iroquois Confederacy

Flamsteed, John, 397

Florida, 1, 26, 38, 93, 108, 245, 248; charts of, 28, 64; expeditions to, 63–64, 65, 124, 125, 273; maps of, 62–65, **62–63, 67, 68–71, 96–97, 98, 121, 125;** Native Americans in, 64, 124; promoted, 248; settlement of, 63–64, 65; under Spain, 61

Floridae Americae Provinciae (Le Moyne), 62–65, **62–63**

Degrees of Latitude: Mapping Colonial America

Designed by Greer Allen

Composed in Meridien and Cochin types

by John J. Moran, North Haven, Connecticut

Color separation by Professional Graphics, Rockford, Illinois

Printed and bound in Singapore by CS Graphics Pte, Ltd.